RANDOM HOUSE
SUNDAY
MEGA
OMNIBUS

VOLUME
2

from
Associated Press
by
Chet Currier

ISBN 0-8129-2908-X

Random House Puzzle Website Address:
http://www.puzzlesatrandom.com/

Text design and typography by Mark Frnka

Manufactured in the United States of America on acid-free paper

9 8 7 6 5 4 3 2 1

First Edition

ACROSS

1 L.A. campus
4 Entertainer Vereen
7 Head start
11 Dervish, e.g.
17 Sis or bro
18 Verse
19 Stettin's river
20 On demand
21 Believe completely
24 Horned beasts
25 Writer Seton
26 Stannite product
27 __ gold (riches)
29 Delphi dragon
32 Fury
34 Musical syllables
38 "__ live and breathe . . ."
40 Farm sound
41 "The __" (1959 western)
43 Multitude
45 Entertain
46 Strictness
47 Rages
48 Biblical pronoun
51 Mil. missions
52 Essence
54 Within: prefix
56 Hiatus
58 Laura __ Giacomo
59 TV series
62 Pittance
65 Beef
66 Mets' home
67 First word in magic
69 Firing-range command
72 Mich. city
74 Egyptian goddess
75 Dialect
76 Bikini event
80 Ralph of fashion
82 Chekhov play
84 Fervor
86 Work unit
87 African fox
88 Smith's "__ Park"
89 Strange
91 Meager
93 Protrude
94 Unit of UAE
97 Fired upon
100 McMurtry tale
105 Placid
106 Flock group
107 Shaft
108 Humorist
109 Literary devices
110 Louver
111 Connect
112 Campus org. of the '60s

DOWN

1 Latin she-bear
2 Stitched
3 Skeet target
4 Manute of basketball
5 Old Tokyo
6 Math man of note
7 __ Greenleaf Whittier
8 Japanese vegetable
9 Harris of TV
10 Amortizes early
11 Singer Reeves
12 Holy Roman emperor
13 Boot by a bird?
14 __ Yutang
15 Rock group initials
16 Real estate abbr.
22 Secular
23 Conspiratorial gesture
28 Will __ wisp
30 Overly
31 Adumbrate
32 Ted Baxter's station
33 Santha Rama __
35 __ Park, N.Y.
36 Elvis __ Presley
37 Soviet segments, for short
38 AKA
39 California missionary
42 Floral arrangement
44 Doctrine
45 Prefix for mate or motive
49 Beatles song
50 "__ Around" (1991 film)
51 Legal matter
53 Ski-lodge style
55 Switch positions
56 Composer-singer Jacques
57 Paper unit
60 Succor
61 Discourse
62 Anti-bird structures
63 Kind of space
64 Exercising
65 Marching gait
68 Columbus initials
69 Actress Gam
70 Old English letters
71 "Sex, __ and Videotape"
73 Furthermore
76 Classic struggle
77 Hawkbills
78 Wapiti
79 Cunning
81 Bar mbr.
83 Chalcedonies
84 Jupiter
85 Gouge
90 Epic ending
92 Sugar source
93 Mock
95 Keen
96 Quinellas, e.g.
97 Fast flyer
98 "Tell __ No" (1965 hit)
99 Iztapa gold
101 Pooh's friend
102 Teachers' org.
103 Zetterling
104 Regard

ACROSS

1 Singular
7 African antelope
13 Humorist Dave
18 Self-contained segment
19 Next day
20 Bring together
21 Cower
22 Reformers of a sort
24 "__ of thousands!"
26 College or Stalin
27 Wallach of baseball
28 Spa
30 Mature
33 D.C. generators
37 Tennis great
38 Purple shade
39 Notified, Twain-style
40 Prefix for bar
41 Purpose
42 Adores conservatives?
44 __ es Salaam
45 Blemish
46 Fashion's Mme. Gres
47 Director Howard
48 Bog growth
50 Place of disfavor
52 White whale
55 Singer Campbell
56 Part of QED
57 Sired
58 Ballet movement
60 Blackbird
62 Arthurian paradise
64 Bids bon voyage
67 March 26 baby
69 Poorly
70 Teen's complaint
71 Supporting
72 Hatch fastener
73 Liberals' treasury?
77 Sample
78 Ski wood
79 Dustups
80 Inspire
81 Rueful words
82 Shooting stars
84 Broadcast
85 Calumny
86 Certain execs
87 Dander
88 More logical
90 Party no-shows?
96 Tycoons
99 G. Bush haunt
100 Toot
101 Mysteries
102 __ as a hornet
103 Takes it easy
104 Did a farm job

DOWN

1 Hesitant sounds
2 Japanese drama
3 Conservative's vow?
4 Custard dish
5 Arm bones
6 Cries of fright
7 Little devil
8 Afr. land
9 Undertaking
10 Inert gas
11 Knowledge
12 Dazzle
13 Daily doings
14 Spirit
15 Thames, e.g.
16 Road map abbr.
17 Agreement
23 Manner
25 Minutiae
28 Oz creator, et al.
29 Brazilian palm
31 Hedge bush
32 Dance step
33 Action
34 Neutral ground
35 River to the Missouri
36 Kierkegaard
38 Nabokov character
39 Food fish
42 Pasternak heroine
43 Synthetic fiber
49 Authority: Var.
51 First name in mysteries
52 La __ Epoque
53 Self
54 __ for your thoughts
57 Ump's calls
59 Onion relative
60 Title of respect
61 Worn down
63 Opinions
64 Parboils
65 Pro __
66 Certain chicken
68 Honed, in a way
70 Competent
74 Eohippus's descendant
75 Supporters
76 Roofing material
81 Punish arbitrarily
83 ". . . not __ mouse"
84 Contest setting
85 Catch
87 Prefix for logical
89 Down with
90 "__ Little Teapot"
91 USN inst.
92 Hazy
93 Burbank initials
94 Asian holiday
95 Grads-to-be
97 Compass pt.
98 Morose

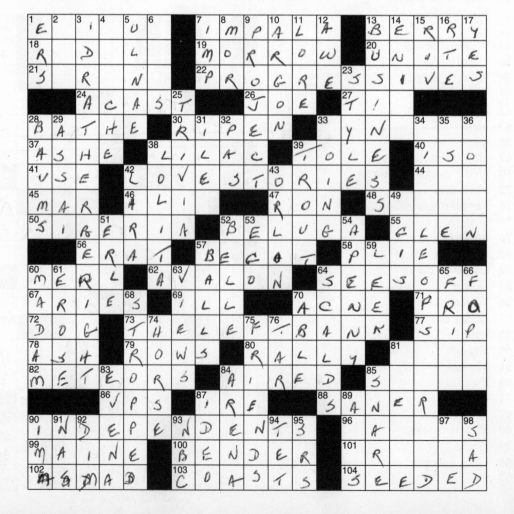

ACROSS

1 Beverages
6 Force in 1588
12 Boatswain's burden
18 Soul
19 Pan-fries
20 On the water
21 Echelon
22 Clancy's "The __"
24 Kite feature
25 Sandwich type
26 Reluctant
27 Reno roller
29 Shroud
31 Standing
32 Porgy
34 Writer Kobo
35 Coquet
36 Progenitor
39 __ pepper (cayenne)
40 Hyphen lookalikes
43 Delude
44 Satisfied sound
45 Cupid
46 Scherzo division
47 Kind of talk or tax
48 Manger
50 Steal
52 Prop
53 Accost
55 Wheat bristle
56 African antelope
57 Train
59 John Lennon song
61 Random
64 Writer Shaw
65 Trudge
66 "Nautilus" captain
68 Tell tale
69 Ember
70 Kind of tax
72 Du Maurier's
    "Jamaica __"
73 Mole
74 Conifer
75 Ensenada aunt
76 Widgeons
78 Mulberry drink
79 Suspend
80 Health club
81 North Pacific island
83 Yours and mine
84 Wild guess
87 Markdown event
91 Excel

92 Ready to go
93 Gold-mining site
94 Rough guys
95 Actress Berenson
96 See 79 Down
97 Lab heaters

DOWN

1 Sea component
2 Draft classification
3 Interstate, e.g.
4 Aviator Earhart
5 __ volatile
6 Beast of burden
7 Santha Rama __
8 Intones unclearly
9 Bikini, for one
10 Adroit
11 Happy-lark link
12 Serving trays
13 Repercussion
14 Tip off
15 Big snakes
16 Swiss river
17 Drops, in
    prescriptions

23 Molise town
28 Austen book
29 Get results
30 __ under one's
    saddle
31 Baylor of
    basketball
32 Bric-a-__
33 Bring up
35 Buckley's "__ Line"
36 Bobby Darin hit,
    1961-62
37 Cartel initials
38 Work together
41 Drive
42 Cargo area
43 Flecks
47 __ Lanka
49 Grill
51 Dorothy of films
52 Liqueur
54 Long time
56 Sometime
57 Calls down (on)
58 Edit photos
59 __ ease (anxious)

60 Jodhpur's land
62 Barnyard sound
63 Hamilton's bills
65 __ blue (morose)
67 Likelihood
70 Porch
71 Draw
74 Xerography
    products
77 Outcome
78 Dolphins' home
79 With 96 Across,
    feminist writer
81 Innoculants
82 Arab VIP
83 Triglyph surface
85 "A Man __
    Woman"
86 Margaret Truman's
    mother
87 Film of 1970
88 Certain records,
    for short
89 Actress Thompson
90 Desert area
91 Elle, in Evanston

ACROSS

1 Dave Clark Five hit, 1964
8 Perform up a storm
13 Fox __ (professionally)
17 Arrogated
18 "Pretty maids" arrangement
19 Bikini parts
20 Thoroughfares
21 Multi-colored instrument?
23 Plus
24 Storehouses
25 Fr. income
26 Barrister's wear
29 "__ Nobis Pacem"
31 Poorly
32 Hazard
33 Bamboozle
36 Animation
37 Draguignan's department
40 Octavian's other things
41 Mich. town
42 __ culpa
43 Hibernia
44 Sumatra creature
46 D.C. title
47 Tar source
48 Fens
49 Ditch
51 Actress Raines
53 "Rhapsody __"
55 W.W. II figure
58 Deprive of an instrument?
61 Doer: suffix
62 "Parade rest" relative
64 West and Murray
65 Liquesce
67 "Winnie __ Pooh"
68 Valid
70 Savvy
72 Spiked
76 Mineo and Maglie
77 Kurosawa film
78 Correctional
80 Cherish
81 Wee small hour
82 Orotund
83 Clawed creature
85 Sports category
87 Sealing-wax source
88 Facility
89 Colony member
90 Blood of the gods
92 Taunted
94 Test site
96 Advertise
98 Corsairs
102 __ uncertain terms
103 Specialized fishermen
104 Carpet bargain
105 Ending for quip or tip
106 Cubic meter
107 Pith

DOWN

1 Multi-circuit conductor
2 Approx.
3 Junkyard dog
4 Zone
5 Overturns
6 Disqualified
7 News execs
8 Involves
9 Christie name
10 Bay window
11 First-rate
12 Meadow mother
13 Monastery VIPs
14 Standout southpaw in baseball
15 Bridge hand
16 Being
18 Ending for novel
22 Faucet problem
24 Quarter-back bird
26 Question starter
27 Kansas town
28 Clutch
30 Creak and squeak
32 Attain
34 Tack
35 Overall
36 Kind of soup or coat
38 Vigilant one
39 Jukebox button
42 Lament
43 Diminish
45 Scepters
47 Fought it out
50 Calif. range, for short
52 Size abbr.
54 Dickens name
55 It's sometimes belted
56 Attorney-__
57 Clear material
59 Arabian gulf
60 African antelope
63 Common diphthongs
66 Soapstone
69 Sup
71 Over
73 Persephone
74 Writer Hunter
75 Balance-sheet item
78 Imagine
79 GWTW's Howard et al.
82 Bastion
83 Better-looking
84 Activates anew
86 Chopper part
87 Stew server
90 Stork relative
91 Dollar part
92 Sugar source
93 Ger. river
95 Poison
97 "__ a Rebel"
98 Prefix for school
99 Ecru
100 Business letter abbr.
101 Genevieve, e.g.

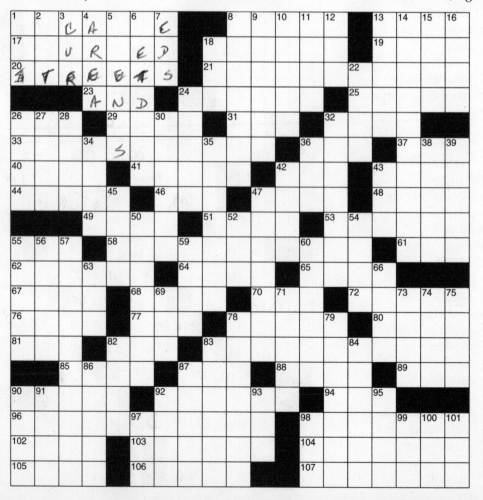

ACROSS

1 Saunter
6 "Julius Caesar" conspirator
11 Erasmus translation
16 Battery terminal
17 AL East player
19 Old-timer
20 Complacent criminal?
22 Repulsion
23 Vetch
24 All together
25 Began
27 USN E-3s
28 M __ Mike
29 Phrygian king
31 Chunk of time
34 MacLaine's "__ A Limb"
36 Last-minute football ploy
39 "Ball Four" author
41 Punished, old-style
42 Distressed
43 Pertinent
44 Wouk subject
45 First letter, phonetically
47 Calls down (on)
48 Dash's double
50 Part of QED
51 Milliner's offering
54 Mortification
55 Slight humidity problems?
57 Bustle
58 Rising times, for short
59 Golfer North
60 Boston airport
61 Cancel
62 Very, at Versailles
63 Existed
64 Disney character
65 Pago Pago's place
68 More sensible
71 Female fowl
72 Spare intellectual?
75 Temple chamber
76 Beast of burden
77 March 26 baby
78 Russian range name
79 Jekyll-Hyde monogram
82 Paper wasp
85 Sound-system part
87 Amo, amas, __
88 Conked

90 Summon the poetic muse?
93 Restaurant of song and film
94 Noisy beasts
95 Spiritual
96 Like some baths
97 Computer key
98 Method

DOWN

1 Marina vista
2 Pope's "An Essay __"
3 Bitter beginnings?
4 "Jagged __" (1985 film)
5 Approval
6 Certain kinsman
7 Inert gas
8 Kind of post or board
9 Ornette of jazz
10 Tavern item
11 Occupy
12 About
13 Watchers in the woods
14 "Skip to my __"
15 Bumble
18 Worn down
19 The Beatles' "__ Woman"
21 Stone worker
26 Buddy
28 Whit
30 Dweller: Suffix
32 __ Dawn Chong
33 Model Carol
35 Western tribe
36 Warning signal
37 Mass. campus
38 Anti-pollution agcy.
39 Iraqi port
40 Reproach
41 Penuche, e.g.
44 Uncivilized country
45 Sectors
46 Greensward
48 "This Nearly Was __"
49 Part of RSVP
50 A Bergen
51 Cause discord?
52 Hogan material
53 Put the __ (cover)
55 Corday's victim

56 Debase
61 Bifold
62 Simple ending
64 Mystery writer Shannon
65 Pigpen
66 Triumphant cry
67 Raisa's husband
68 Informer
69 Throb, old-style
70 Cozy home-maker
71 Choice bit
73 Custody
74 Fury
75 Wrinkle
78 Last Mohican
80 Boutonniere's place
81 Cubic meter
83 For all's companion
84 Actress Donna
86 Foreleg bone
87 "__ That Peculiar?"
88 Nictate
89 Wallach
91 Proponent's vote
92 Fleur-de-__

ACROSS

1 Wavelet
7 Seaweed
11 Modest
16 Initiative
17 Actress Brown
18 Baby item
19 Movie double bill from '73 and '49
22 Shade of gray
23 Gilroy's "The Subject Was __"
24 Turns
25 Spectacle
27 Ambitions
28 Become: suffix
32 Double bill from '81 and '82
38 Subdued
39 Editorializes
40 Eager reader
41 Use a loom
43 French painter
44 Bird-woman of myth
46 Element No. 47
47 Lingerie item
48 Shriver of TV
49 Singer Petula
51 Double bill from '53 and '89
57 December greetings
58 Medley switch
59 Promo relatives
61 Firing range command
64 Broadcast
65 Port __ cheese
67 Collect
68 Embellished, cafe style
70 Seles of tennis
71 __ Madrid, Mo.
72 Double bill from '86 and '69
76 Puff
78 Blue dye
79 Waistcoats
80 Shack
82 Red as __
84 Tex. campus
87 Double bill from '56 and '82
93 "Tarzan the __" (1981)
94 Obstreperous
95 Susurrus
96 Guide
97 Marine eagles
98 Fermenting agents

DOWN

1 "__ Lama Ding Dong"
2 Does a bakery job
3 Egyptian god
4 Brooch
5 __ Alamitos
6 Menu section
7 Swiss artist
8 Diner sign
9 Fleur-de-__
10 Furnish
11 Fly high
12 Capote portrayer
13 Blind ambition
14 Operculum
15 Regulus's constellation
17 Overrun
18 Hallow
20 Writer Jaffe
21 Thighbone
25 Auld Lang __
26 Musician Atkins
27 "Not __ eye in the house"
29 Bohemian
30 Small firth
31 Jug
32 Flop
33 Abstract style
34 Singer Washington
35 "__ Love" ('57 film)
36 Road sign
37 Spin
42 Nev. town
44 Cart
45 Mars
46 Discreet
48 TV equine
49 Immure
50 Blatant
52 Slaughter in the field
53 Ivory or Barbary
54 Spin-chilling
55 In force
56 Distill
60 Sky light
61 Hit the bell
62 Big bird
63 Principia
64 Seed case
65 Copier button
66 Blackbirds
68 Playwright Jean
69 Chrisholm Trail destination
70 PBS series
73 Sanctuary
74 Actor Schreiber
75 Appear
77 Motif
81 Khayyám
82 Tennis call
83 Margaret Truman's mother
84 "The secret __ . . ." (Frost)
85 Soften
86 Functions
87 __ Palmas
88 Decide
89 Flight formation
90 Conjunction
91 McClanahan of TV
92 Org. for Lee

ACROSS

1 State of oblivion
6 Limit
9 Dillon
13 Jemimah's father
16 Strange
17 Prefix for legal
18 Cosmetic ingredient
19 Russian river
20 Movie double bill from '90 and '87
23 Capture
24 Crash cry
25 Coax
26 Interfered
28 Ladd of films
30 Excuse me!
32 Louis XIV, e.g.
33 Double bill from '84 and '64
41 Promissory note
42 Poseur
43 Heredity agent
44 Voice
45 N.C. campus
47 Farina
50 Forster's "Howard's __"
52 Blind as __
53 Attention
56 War: Prefix
58 Singer Petty
60 Keogh relative
61 Double bill from '67 and '56
66 Start of a Hardy title
67 Wallaba
68 Singer Martin, to friends
69 Actress Lenz
70 Singer Billy
72 Mine find
74 Cost
76 Kind of bond or dollar
80 Keats poem
82 __ pickle (troubled)
84 Flag
87 Melee
88 Double bill from '88 and '72
93 D.C. summer time
94 Antitoxins
95 Up to us
96 Comics classic
100 Snakes
102 Full-fledged
106 Absolutely
107 Double bill from '73 and '87
110 Benefit
111 Layer
112 Part of A.D.
113 Dipper
114 Undiligent
115 Juarez wave
116 USN inst.
117 Free's companion

DOWN

1 Jurist's concern
2 Nastase of tennis
3 Factory
4 London asylum
5 "Bird __ Wire" (1990 film)
6 Calvados capital
7 Navarre neighbor
8 Lounge
9 Fairy queen
10 Astringent
11 Manolete, for one
12 Hamstrings
13 Facial feature
14 "Grapes of Wrath" figure
15 Frequency group
17 Apparition
21 "The Mysterious Stranger" author
22 Lukewarm
27 Assertions
29 Guitarist Paul
31 Forty decibels
33 Wish
34 Singer Reed
35 Diving bird
36 Witchcraft
37 Poem part
38 Custom
39 Eared seal
40 Bristle
46 Poetic twilight
48 Parched
49 On the up and up
51 Penalize
54 Turkish VIP
55 "__ Man" (1984 film)
57 Cry of dismay
59 Actress Sara
61 Attacked
62 Essence
63 Calif. county
64 Conductor Georg
65 Check out
66 Père's heir
71 Kind of closet
73 Remnants
75 Italian seaport
77 Amphora
78 Fabled bird
79 Be obliged
81 Total
83 Pay __ price
85 Pitcher Jerry of baseball
86 Get it wrong
89 Realize
90 "The Silver Bears" author
91 The lady, in Spain
92 Star-shaped
96 Gauguin
97 "Born Free" name
98 Writer Haley
99 Expedited
101 Long time
103 Incivil
104 The Bruins' sch.
105 I'll-get-by type
108 Anagram of 53 Across
109 Recuperation aid, for short

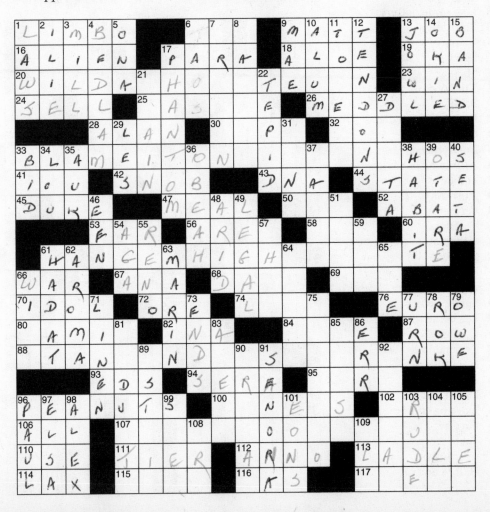

ACROSS

1 Christie's "The __ Murders"
4 Skirt style
8 Compass heading
11 Carefree
17 Old card game
18 Y __ yankee
19 Japanese drama
20 Punishment units of yore
21 J, in a way
24 Scram, in Shakespeare
25 Poised
26 Spill the beans
27 U.K. honor
29 Cheese type
30 Thwart
32 Hurdle
33 Mention
34 Sweetsop
35 Hereditary
37 Disorder
39 Sample
40 N, in a way
43 Mum's __ word
46 Austrian article
47 Hog wallow
48 Like some pottery
50 Pipe down
53 Unsuave sort
55 Bawl
57 Stickler
58 Kind of frost
60 Babble
62 Fruitcake ingredient
64 Gaelic
65 Intertwine
68 Approved behavior
70 Tedious
73 Austrian article
74 Perplexes
76 __ Palmas
78 Catafalque
80 Sky altar
81 V, in a way
87 Hallucinogen
89 Singer Peter
90 Leg bones
91 Quaker pronoun
93 Command to Fido
94 Handle
96 Piscine dish
97 Dirty trick
98 Extreme ending
99 Furrow
100 Table scrap
101 Instrument
103 H, E, A and D

108 Extinguished
109 Consume
110 Total for Canseco
111 Tear
112 Ridges
113 Lament
114 Concerning
115 Express

DOWN

1 Landon
2 Thumbs-down sound
3 "Cousin __" (1975 film)
4 Nokes of baseball
5 Ending for colt or dolt
6 Mythical weeper
7 Excite
8 Cold shoulder
9 Helios
10 "__ Kiss That Girl"? (1942 song)
11 Censure
12 Household god
13 Weather-map line
14 TH, in a way
15 Skater Sonja
16 __ Park, Colo.
22 Empathize

23 Black lacquers
28 "Funny Girl" composer
30 Petty perjury?
31 Bach book
32 Sierra __
33 Gorge
36 Insubstantial
38 Naval amphibs
39 "No __ traffic"
41 Selfsame
42 Spigot
44 "Steppenwolf" author
45 Door sign
49 Uno plus due
50 Ancient Arabian land
51 "Red October" gear
52 LEA, in a way
54 TV's "Major __"
56 Sportcaster Collins
59 Actor Vallone
61 Organized society
63 Pachuca pipe
66 Dolt
67 Gloaming time, poetically
69 Sound's companion

71 Never __ finger (don't try)
72 Son of Jacob
75 Breakaway groups
77 Filament
79 Writer Graves
82 Arrow vane
83 Israeli cape
84 Health-conscious group
85 Daniels of baseball
86 Kiang
88 MCP, for one
91 Bara of Hollywood
92 Probity
93 Horticultural investment
95 Rain checks
99 Shimmying sister of song
100 Thereabouts
102 Born
104 __ de vie
105 River island
106 Creek
107 Deighton's "__ Sinker"

ACROSS

1 Writer Kingsley
5 "Life of Riley" name
9 Tortuous tales
14 Diet concern
17 Singer Tennille
18 Work on galleys
19 Utah city
20 Amiens approval
21 '80s deal
24 Actress Mary
25 Lode burden
26 Ripken of baseball
27 Boston staple
28 Changed the costumes
30 "__ Entertain You"
32 Psychiatrist Alfred
34 Like __ (perhaps)
35 Tributary
37 Tie type
38 Fore relative
39 Singer McEntire
42 Jealousy
45 "That's the way __"
47 Enjoin
48 Pertinent
49 __ generis
50 Invitation inscription
51 Tableland
52 Poorer
53 Catchall abbr.
54 Gleeful cry
55 Smoking et al.
57 "Today __ man . . ."
59 Entangles
60 Smell __
61 Obscene income?
64 Sign of spring
65 Football's Simpson and
   Anderson
68 Fire up
69 See 38 Across
70 Attila's crowd
71 __ anemone
72 Evaluate
73 San Francisco, for one
74 Gasp
75 Computer unit
76 Ten: prefix
77 Spanish hero
78 Fully
79 Churchill title
81 Homeric work
83 __ of wind . . .
85 Garden spots
89 College money manager
91 After-shave application
92 Brawl
94 Era relative
95 Grampus
96 Arctic or tropical
   annoyance?
100 Zero
101 "Games People Play"
   author
102 Roof feature
103 Roman road
104 Enzyme
105 Expression of contempt
106 Kovacs's Nairobi __
107 Clients for vets

DOWN

1 Fugard of the stage
2 Boxer Archie
3 Atlas feature
4 Make a lap
5 Bartok
6 Journalist St. Johns
7 Bridle part
8 Augean mess
9 Kind of mint or fish
10 Schoenberg's "Moses
   und __"
11 Statehouse VIP,
   for short
12 Unwilling
13 Kierkegaard
14 Bad neighborhood?
15 Radiance
16 Bound
22 Cinching score
23 Hang onto
29 Spanish city
31 Kind of fly or flower
33 Intermittent flow
34 Panoply
36 Accident
38 Histories
40 Cream of the crop
41 Entertainer Ed
42 Argot
43 Buff
44 Ordeal in orbit?
46 Power org.
47 Harass
48 Trophies
50 Musician Lewis
51 __ Antoinette
55 Artful
56 Hangouts
58 Criticizes
59 One-celled organism
61 Alumni Day attendee
62 Pink
63 Fanatical
64 Bakery item
66 Protrude
67 Cross-reference word
70 Dutch painter
74 Lead weight
75 Lingerie item
77 Lurch
78 Fever symptom
80 Ft. Dodge's state
82 Poetic feet
83 Do a tailor's job
84 Rome fountain
86 Pan-fry
87 White bird
88 Crystal-glazers
89 __ fide
90 "Mila 18" author
91 Actress Archer
93 Mountain: prefix
97 Exist
98 Face value
99 Ferrule

ACROSS

1 Inaccurate
4 Viva __
8 Susan of TV
13 Drainage place
17 South Seas dish
18 Car-racing org.
19 Oriental
20 Willow
21 From A to Z
24 Clownish
25 Disapproving sound
26 Contented as __
27 Voice a view
29 Baksheesh
31 Made haste
33 Self
34 ". . . what a good boy __?"
37 Birch relative
39 Intraurban transport
43 Singer Estefan
45 Sweet-talk
46 Noted author-illustrator
47 Means
48 Double millenia
50 Do a post-Christmas job
53 Bismarck
54 Writer Rand
55 Cochise, e.g.
57 Nom de guerre
59 '60s campus org.
60 "__ the River" (1966 film)
62 Crudites accompaniment
65 Piscivorous bird
66 Act opener
67 Items for Ovid's omelets
68 "Just You __" (1990 hit)
71 Votes into law
73 Finesse
74 Sickly
75 Harsh
77 Tool's companion
78 Proust's "__ Way"
80 No runs, no hits, no errors
86 Test one's metal
87 Some
88 Prefix for bid or give
89 Tiff
90 Downhill runner
91 N. Dak. city
93 Tan
95 Singer Pinza

98 World Series MVP, 1990
101 Fork over
105 Writer Murdoch
106 Race courses
107 Whirl
108 A Bobbsey twin
109 Jeweler's stock
110 Heals
111 Costly
112 '60s song

DOWN

1 Colorful fish
2 Points of concentration
3 Football stats
4 Stereo meters, for short
5 Greek peak
6 "__ Falling Star"
7 Reminiscent
8 Sci. setting
9 Org. for GIs
10 Ta-ta, in Turin
11 Floor covering
12 Blue shade
13 Dimensions
14 Hagen of films
15 Humanity subgroup
16 Remit
22 Wicker willow
23 Jug
28 Present times
30 Ape, for one
32 Maine native
34 Border on
35 Requirement
36 Happens to be true
37 Turkish bigwigs
38 David __ George
40 Boozehound
41 Dorsey classic
42 Modernists
44 Electrical unit
49 Britisher
50 Uncertain sounds
51 Actress Massey
52 Clenchfists
56 View from Mt. Logan
58 "__ in the beginning . . ."
61 MLs, alternatively
62 Reduction, modern-style
63 A Trump

64 Violet
65 Intense
68 Water buffalo
69 Koestler's "Darkness at __"
70 Impost
72 USN command post
76 Sound system
79 Cockeyed
81 Sarge, e.g.
82 Chamfer
83 Cartel, for short
84 Block's "When the __ Gin Mill Closes"
85 Paced
91 Bryologist's subject
92 Certain fed
94 Cabinet dept.
96 Do __ once!
97 Words with "you don't?"
98 Apparatus
99 Vexation
100 Conrad "Lord"
102 Yore
103 Beast of burden
104 Isr. neighbor

ACROSS

1 Sealing-wax ingredient
4 Seed cover
8 Ways of going
13 Concordes
17 That: Sp.
18 Start of Caesar's report
19 Man-moon link
20 Midwest Indian
21 Ecdysiast Lily St. __
22 Writer Hunter
23 Minor ruler's minions?
25 Sorry about that!
27 French West Indies, e.g.
29 Collar
30 Conjunction
31 Brisbane's state
34 Charbroil
36 Malleus's place
39 Bakery choice
40 Drubbing
42 Muzzle
44 Chisel
47 Fragrance
49 Singer Reeves
50 Writer James
51 Telegraphy unit
54 Clothespins
56 Hurried
57 Mighty
59 Kind of tone
60 Always, to poets
61 __ Harbor, N.Y.
62 Steve McQueen role, 1968
65 Doctrine
68 Con vote
70 Campus building, for short
71 Bespeak
73 O.T. book
75 Davis's "__ Can"
76 Port of Yemen
77 Sports grp.
78 Sully
80 Night music
82 Bluff
83 Specifics
85 Plants
87 Versailles assent
88 Sault __ Marie
89 Radar image
91 Power grab
96 Actress Charlotte
98 Murmur
100 Not masc. or fem.
101 Otherwise
102 "Jazzman" singer

106 Citrus drinks
108 __ es Salaam
109 Stratford's river
110 Chateau payment
111 Pasta type
112 Past
113 Denuded
114 Chekhov
115 Football coach Fielding
116 D.C. title

DOWN

1 "__ d'or"
2 Half a Shakespeare title
3 __ diem
4 Blvd. relative
5 Emend
6 Together
7 Threadlike
8 Hodges of baseball
9 Momentarily
10 "__ a Very Good Year"
11 Ancient Nile city
12 Sunday msg.
13 Promptly
14 "The __" (Ruritanian operetta)
15 Crag
16 Placed
24 "Cheers" employee
26 Functions
28 Hairnet
32 Comedian Louis
33 Bust
35 Intents
37 Yearn
38 Construe
41 Subject
43 Gaelic
44 Maxima
45 __ caliente
46 French Revolution phase
48 Brought up
51 Scrooge's epithet
52 Battery terminal
53 Greatest
55 Gauntlet
58 Barnyard area
59 U.K. award
60 Goal
63 Bernstein's "__ and Barcarolles"
64 Track bet

66 Cicatrix
67 Vile
69 Vast expanse
72 Lure
73 Introduces
74 Converge
75 Shout
76 African dam
79 Defamation
81 Burst
82 Writer Grafton
84 Nauseate
86 Contemptible
87 Double quartets
90 Headland
92 Home-entertainment category
93 __ the hills
94 Procedure
95 Juan or Eva
97 Topflight
99 Aware of
102 Hack
103 Gardner
104 Epoch
105 Pentagon abbr.
107 Command to Fido

ACROSS

1 W.W. II grp.
4 Exec's missive
8 Rim
11 One-horse carriage
17 Guadalupe gold
18 Jewish month
19 401(k) relative
20 Kind of gentry
21 Paper wasp
24 Triple trio
25 Sunrooms
26 Traitor
28 Norse god
29 Sandberg of baseball
30 Hosp. staffers
31 Anaconda
34 Coolidge's VP
36 __ out (plan)
37 Actress Wallace-Stone
38 Cut short
39 Columnist Baker to friends
40 Hushed up
44 S.A. land
45 "Daily Planet" employee
46 Beyond
47 Keep in circulation
48 Zetterling
49 Hoary
50 Relevant
51 Aforementioned
53 Arrangements
55 "Love __ Racket" (1932)
56 Lithography items
60 "Love __ Leave Me" (1955 film)
62 __ de mer
63 Dined
64 Labor org.
65 Meat jelly
68 "Plains of Passage" author
70 Reference line
71 Card game
72 Espionage symbols
75 Comparer's word
76 Heed
77 Ring verdict
78 Free
79 A Ross of note
80 Meadow mother
81 Violinist Bull
82 Check
84 Vandals

85 Kind of school
87 __ Vineyard, Mass.
90 Against the rules
93 Pompous sort
95 Trimming
96 Succor
97 Kind of price or trust
98 Begone relative
99 Surgical dressing
100 Adversary
101 Drat relative
102 Light touch

DOWN

1 Blount and Acuff
2 Martial prefix
3 Emulate, sartorially
4 New Zealanders
5 Moses of track
6 Portrait subject
7 Mouths
8 Equate
9 Worth of comics
10 Hors d'oeuvre staple
11 Detergent, e.g.
12 Custody
13 Will S.'s wife
14 Chem. ending
15 Red or Coral
16 Byrnes of early TV
22 Puts in the hold
23 Vault
27 Welcomes
29 Engrossed
31 German libation
32 Bumbler's word
33 Basilica area
34 Orchestral apparatus
35 Halos
36 Heal
37 Dental degree
38 Ideology
40 Renowned racehorse
41 Swedish city
42 Brazilian port
43 Emulates 68 Across
45 Ruble part
50 Intended
52 In motion
54 Eskimo boat
57 Dress for the dark?
58 Inventor Howe

59 Entertainer Bono
61 Evaluated
63 Eliminated
65 Summit
66 Side dish
67 Opening
69 Japanese salad item
70 Opposed, colloquially
73 On the loose
74 Sorrow
75 Tithing percentage
79 Volleys
81 Gasket type
82 Proportion
83 Musical work
84 "I've __ up to here!"
85 Profit
86 DOD part
87 Epicure's delight
88 Operatic highlight
89 Part of a process
90 Heady times
91 Suede feature
92 To and __
94 Frivolity

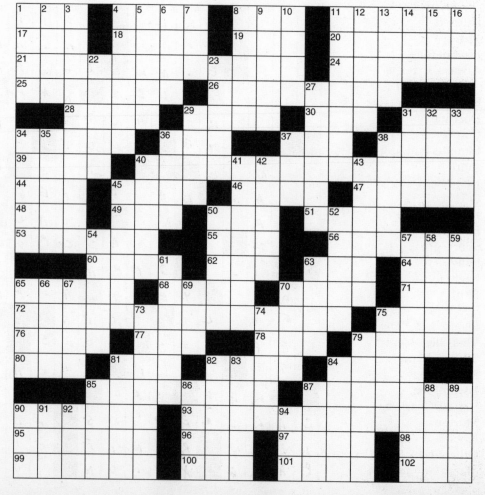

ACROSS

1 __ Cayes, Haiti
4 Exuviate
8 Reclined
12 Strings
17 Uraeus
18 Country bread
19 Sky creature
20 Powerless
21 Pre-season ordeal?
24 Roman date
25 Stigmatized
26 Word with ride or wire
27 Olympian Jesse
29 Refusals
30 Actor Johnson
31 Other things, to 8 Down
32 Employ
35 Daffy
37 Western resort
39 Raised aristocratically?
41 Resource
43 Minor matter
44 Chemical compound
45 Cleave
46 High degree
47 Prince's "Purple __"
49 Not fer
50 Vertiginous
51 To's companion
52 Bluff
53 Impose __ on (forbid)
54 Actress Dawber
55 Dandy
56 Fast-food frauds?
59 Call for help
62 Chary
63 Dobbin's dinner
64 Japanese drama
65 Allotment
66 Sentimental
69 Cptr. terminals
70 Mock
71 Plains Indian
72 Draft classification
73 Mule, e.g.
74 Phrase
75 Disseminate
77 Unafraid?
79 Composer Wilder
81 Concerning
82 Film of 1989
83 Appellation
84 Word with how or way
85 Symbol of gentleness
87 African antelope
89 Greek letter
90 Soprano Peters
93 __ off (minimize)
95 Opts for a different beer?
98 Symbolic object
99 Writer Morrison
100 Rapier
101 River isle
102 __ Solemnis
103 Visionary
104 Meddling
105 Genetic material

DOWN

1 Part of LIFO
2 Como __ usted?
3 Running-gear emporium?
4 Venom
5 Candid
6 Okla. town
7 Lair
8 Roman poet
9 __ of hope
10 Doctrine
11 Puff pastry
12 Direct
13 Presently
14 Chided
15 Before
16 John, Joseph, etc.
22 By __ (barely)
23 Film of 1990
28 Volition
30 Destroy
31 Sun shelter
33 Ship
34 Nelson of films
35 Rockies resort
36 NL West player
38 Santa __
39 Singer Bob et al.
40 Upper edge
42 Low-quality
48 Sore
49 Borders on
50 Lacerations
53 Dies down
54 Support
57 Gloomy
58 Growing out
59 Despise baked goods?
60 Distant
61 Vermont resort
62 Mullet
66 More than more
67 S.A. native
68 Liner's stops
69 Priestley, Pasteur, etc.
70 Hot time
73 Thick piece
74 Frenzy
76 Oven adjunct
78 Puzzle
80 Comes from behind
84 Active
86 The Beatles' "__ Road"
88 Laments
89 Hanker
90 Wall St. deal
91 Bifold
92 Film pet
93 Cleric's degree
94 __ polloi
96 Misery
97 Female lobster

ACROSS

1 Reality
5 Hip boot
10 Catchall category: Abbr.
14 Wane
17 Gumshoe's find
18 Accustom
19 Redolence
20 Seven-faced doctor of film
21 Auto exporters?
23 Lunch stop extremely
25 Bakery line
26 "Understood!"
28 Carpet adjuncts
29 Ragged
31 Actors Robert and Alan
33 Intimation
34 Ululates
35 Journalist Heywood
36 Helps
39 Pointless
40 Writer James F. dined
42 Lackawanna's lake
43 Road sign
44 Fisticuffs
45 Discharge
47 Hail
48 Astronaut Shepard
49 Certain feds
50 Deserved
52 Depress
55 __ deal (much)
57 Stubborn
58 'Midst relative
59 Taj Mahal site
60 Ferrite
61 Blunderer
62 Russian country house
64 Hard hit, in baseball
66 "__ Different Worlds"
69 Vicinity
71 Phony stones
73 Violin holder
74 Touchable
76 King of Phrygia
77 Excel
78 "__ Nobis Pacem"
79 Rabbit fur
80 Lays out
81 Patois
83 Continental prefix
84 Track
85 Beach fellas?
87 Nautilus assignment?
92 Pose
93 Imparted
94 Florida's Tamiami __
95 Inward: Prefix
96 Green light
97 Dominion
98 Growing out
99 Ripened

DOWN

1 TV regulator
2 Miss. neighbor
3 Mongrel appendages?
4 Logical
5 Clever
6 Black cuckoos
7 Pair
8 Ending for east or west
9 Leftovers
10 Ways
11 __ fixe
12 Hellios
13 Second-guesser
14 Decide, declaim?
15 Sailing ship
16 Simon's "The Sunshine __"
22 Certain Wall St. traders
24 Actress Vivian
27 City on the Ligurian Sea
29 Quaff
30 "If I __ Hammer"
31 In __ (consecutively)
32 Cuts
33 Colored
35 Convivial
36 Shock
37 Estuary feeder
38 Unkempt
40 Tribe relative
41 Eliminated
44 Mix
46 Sin's companion
48 Ending for block or stock
49 Tibetan gazelle
51 Sheridan of films
52 Greek colonnades
53 Cognizant
54 Stand up for emmets?
55 Turkish VIP
56 Language study
57 Mine finds
59 Throb
60 Signs, headline-style
63 Movie dog
64 Calif. city
65 "__ just imagine . . ."
66 Slender monarch?
67 Zephyr, e.g.
68 Possessive pronoun
70 For __ (cheaply)
72 Comeback
73 London district
75 "City of __" (Broadway hit)
77 Health clubs
79 Vigorous
80 Country crossing
81 Sailing rope
82 Delicate fabric
83 Lab heater
84 Struck, old-style
86 Innovative
88 Samovar
89 Barn sound
90 Poem of praise
91 Acknowledgment

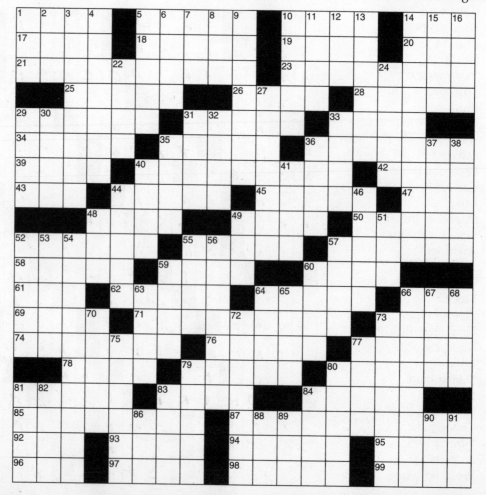

ACROSS

1 Moroccan port
6 Famed name at Notre Dame
10 U.K. network
13 Foremost
16 Battle site, 1836
17 __ about (approximately)
18 Ground
19 Speed
20 Start of a quotation
23 Room-y place
24 Kind of wave
25 Romans' way
26 Hay piles
28 Dining areas
30 Ending for arch or fish
31 Swindle
32 Naval E-7s
35 Quotation author
41 Dog breed, for short
42 Actress Scacchi
43 Bemoans
44 Scale interval
45 Kind of street
47 Egg: Comb. form
49 Colombian cash unit
51 Gilt's home
52 Log of a kind
53 Actor Ryan
55 "Ask __ questions . . ."
57 Quotation, part II
62 "__ Wolf" (1985 film)
63 Bore
64 Advent
66 Firing-range command
69 Mmes., in Madrid
71 Rockies runner
72 Informer
73 Stoles
75 Virginia willow
77 Kiangs
79 Greek letter
80 Quotation, part III
83 Formerly, formerly
84 Crass
85 Stripling
86 Turkish lord
88 Exculpatory story
90 Shinbones
93 Mitigates
96 Delay
97 End of quotation
101 __ Marie Saint
102 Knack
103 Hershiser of baseball
104 Ariz. city
105 Film of 1984
106 James, Jude, etc.
107 Film of 1981
108 Computer key

DOWN

1 Actor Vallone
2 Greatly
3 Italian port
4 Organic compounds
5 Full-fledged
6 Starters' words
7 Actress Swenson
8 Word with deck or out
9 Drive
10 Blessing
11 Overalls feature
12 Ordained person
13 Copses
14 Sound in 51 Across
15 Corrals
18 Postpones bedtime
21 "__ Tomorrow" (1955 film)
22 More desperate
27 Varieties
29 Haggard tale
31 Actress Jacqueline
32 Dolt
33 Financial calamity
34 Witchcraft
36 Make amends
37 Crow relatives
38 Adjudged
39 Reticulated system
40 Cooper's "The __"
42 Singer Crystal et al.
46 Certiorari, for one
48 Kilns
50 "Green __" (1962 hit)
53 Gilded
54 Contemplate
56 Atlanta arena
58 Educe
59 Damp
60 Chemical compound
61 Religious groups
65 "Block __ kick!"
66 Goat's hair garment
67 Particle
68 Medieval song
70 "Twilight Zone" man
72 Rachmaninoff
74 Cold shoulder
76 Addis __
78 "__ of Love" (1989 film)
81 Head and Piaf
82 News VIP
83 __ Island (Rapa Nui)
87 Expedition
88 Actor Baldwin
89 Mauna Loa output
90 Works on hides
91 Piece of land
92 Divest
94 Writer Lathen
95 Exhausts
98 Cloche
99 "Kidnapped" monogram
100 Consult

ACROSS

1 "Julius Caesar" character
6 Sky altar
9 Pacific atoll
14 Unattached: Abbr.
17 Bermuda __
18 Actor Johnson
19 Let loose
20 Kind of pot or party
21 New Year's news flash, part I
25 Itinerary word
26 Grimalkin
27 Greek letters
28 Exhort
29 Insect stage
32 S.A. port, for short
34 Mideast VIP
36 Doubleday
37 News flash, part II
41 Roofing material
42 Compass pt.
43 Service
44 French marshal
45 Boring tool
47 Qty.
49 Kind of cheese
52 Capture
55 Angular measure unit
58 Little leftover
60 Nucleic acid
61 Invalid
62 News flash, part III
66 Comedy-club fare
67 Floor covering
68 Hound sound
69 Kremlin assembly
70 Modern mtge.
71 Nigerian capital
73 L.A. campus
75 Editor Talese
76 Rumpot
77 __, haec, hoc
79 Doer: Suffix
81 Word with whiz
84 News flash, part IV
90 Indentation
91 Ancestry
92 Santha Rama __
93 Dissolve
94 Formal observance
95 See 107 Across
96 Service org.
98 Defective
100 News flash, part V
107 With 95 Across, baseball great

108 Puppy
109 Creek
110 Inventor Howe
111 Argot
112 Peerage
113 Gelid
114 Slavic people

DOWN

1 Deceive
2 Cuckoo
3 Offense
4 Contempary
5 Part of ASW
6 Hail
7 Ill will
8 Sally Kirkland role
9 Kind of buoy
10 Feeble
11 Rally
12 Fernando and Alejandro
13 Numero __
14 Novelist Laurence
15 __ counter (radiation gauge)
16 Modern beam
22 Gets on merit
23 Cash-register list
24 Covered with bumps
29 Actor Hingle
30 "__ Lazy River"
31 Example
33 Fancy
35 __ van der Rohe
36 Entertainer Ed
38 Fakir's faith
39 Eccentric
40 Retracts, in a way
46 Mental facilities
48 Byword
50 Secrecy
51 "Newhart" setting
52 Repurchasing
53 Cosmetic ingredient
54 Oversupply
55 Latvian city
56 Remotely
57 A throwin' Joe
59 Sample
61 Blazing star
63 Fragment
64 Bearnaise, e.g.
65 Silverheels role
71 Football star Ronnie
72 MacNelly strip
74 Raynoso residence
76 "Never __" (1959 film)
78 River to the Arabian Sea
80 Diving acronym
82 Break off
83 Personality part
84 Dress styles
85 Prickly plant
86 Williams of films
87 Handed down, as a story
88 Against expectations
89 Confuse
90 Offense
95 Holy Roman emperor
97 Delhi wear
99 Freshly
101 Fly-by-night creature
102 Good moods
103 Era
104 Grass's "The __ Drum"
105 Clump
106 CIA precursor

ACROSS

1 Netherworld denizens
7 Official in Judea
13 Prefix for structure
18 Take away
19 Valuable
20 Son of Charlemagne
21 Meager
22 Subordinate role
24 Fetor
26 Drake's title
27 Chatter
28 Venus or Vesta
29 Branches
32 Balboa's disc.
34 Kind of room or rose
36 Russian writer, 1880-1934
38 Obdurate
39 Kramden's workplace
41 Foment
43 Jewish month
46 Crew
47 Lashio's land
49 Jackie's second husband
50 '90s fella
51 Bit-by-bit
53 Paris sight
55 Followed, as advice
57 Switch positions
58 Part of ASAP
60 Agassi of tennis
61 Unbalanced
64 Free riding
67 Bow wood
68 "__ Bay" (1985 film)
70 Danish port
71 "__ House" (1970 hit)
73 Executive
75 Word to Lassie
76 Tergiversates
80 Auction action
81 Dined
83 Joyce Carol __
85 Cockpit display
86 "The Proud __" (1956 film)
87 Abrade
89 Dog breed, for short
90 Rubberneck
91 Rawboned
93 Sprite
95 Pluto
97 "Pre-owned"
98 Silkworm
100 Influenced
102 Ballad ending
104 Insubstantial
106 Showy shrub
110 Dickinson's "__ Summer"
114 Magical spirit
115 Offset
116 Taunt
117 Verdant spots
118 "Streetcar" character
119 Calm

DOWN

1 Org. of the '60s
2 Place to shoot from
3 Gardner
4 Knightly exploits
5 Being
6 Pricey
7 Letter-writer's letters
8 Peeves
9 On the up-and-up
10 Atlantic group
11 Word with speed or spot
12 Christian Science founder
13 "__ Dreamin'" ('76 hit)
14 Doze
15 Stuffy person
16 Agitate
17 Out of port
23 Baize or boucle
25 Afghan capital
29 Actress Diana
30 Sandarac tree
31 __ Lisa
33 Junkyard dog
35 __ glance
37 Burdened
40 Blockbusters
42 Abadan native
44 Cherish
45 Freshen
47 Cheap
48 Hall to watch
52 Detach a hatch
54 By the sea
56 Lisbon's estuary
58 Affix
59 Shelley composition
61 Cha-cha's cousin
62 Actor Delon
63 Lawn invaders
65 Heart adjunct
66 Denials
69 Billiards shot
72 Accrued
74 Kind of income
76 Charge
77 Derricks
78 Anecdote
79 Travois
82 Argot
84 Wee bit
88 Covenant
92 Agalloch
94 Wild
96 Leg parts
98 Hence
99 Perlman on TV
101 Hideouts
103 Islamic weight
105 Arrow poison
107 Tool's partner
108 Malines
109 Teacher's org.
111 Actress Lupino
112 Ht.
113 Born

ACROSS

1 Glum
4 Wingding
8 Injects
12 Renaissance poet
17 "Put __ Happy Face"
18 Israeli statesman
19 Place
20 Ala. town
21 Do-or-die times
24 Whatsoever
25 Thousand __, Calif.
26 Hurting
27 O'Neill's "The __ Jones"
29 An FDR VP
31 Ole Miss group
33 Work on quilts
34 Pack
37 Self
39 Benefit
41 Org. in "Roger & Me"
43 Millenium pt.
45 CPA's suggestion
46 Actress Rita
48 Fair-weather friend
51 Displacements
53 '90s hairstyles
54 Bobby of tennis
55 Decision diagram
56 Capek play
58 Jinx relative
59 Doer: Suffix
60 Begley and Begley Jr.
61 Actress Lisa
63 Prod
65 Mass
68 Unrefined
69 Writer Rita __ Brown
71 Understand
72 Minute
73 Snoops
76 Tree snake
78 Diamondlike figure
80 Analyst
82 Supple
83 Endings for dark and damp
84 Helios
85 Bow
86 Japanese salad ingredient
87 Parts of 43 Across
88 Sanity
90 Dance step
92 Holier __ thou
94 Taboo's opposite
96 Takes in stride

99 Miscalculates
101 Part of ABM
104 Philosopher Mortimer
106 Behave consistently
109 C. Robin's creator
110 Colorful fish
111 Data-speed unit
112 Dainty drink
113 Stick
114 Use a beeper
115 "Betsy's Wedding" man
116 Belgian spa

DOWN

1 Middling
2 Pilaster
3 Surprise contenders
4 Progeny
5 Hornbook material
6 Pakistani city
7 Writer Gide
8 Actress MacGraw
9 Louganis feat
10 Adjudges
11 Crime-novel group
12 Hot streak

13 Vehicles
14 Kind of gate
15 __ volatile
16 Bird of prey
22 Double hook
23 Snub
28 Jug
30 Adjust
32 Actress Bernhardt
35 Wash. neighbor
36 History subject
37 Weep and wail
38 Calabash
40 John Irving dog
42 Teutonic deity
44 Harbor
47 Nice time of year
49 Link
50 Minor matter
52 Morning riser
57 Survey again
59 Ancient
61 Footing
62 Fla. bay
64 __ Mar, Calif.
65 Barely triumph
66 Hostility

67 Textile team
68 Minn. lake
70 Film critic Roger
72 President pro __
73 Sound of relief
74 Punjab princess
75 Gives a stable home?
76 A Mrs. in "The Rivals"
77 Toxophilite
79 Israel
81 Manage
86 Fantastic
89 Spoor
91 Buddhist shrine
93 Antilles isle
95 Big bumbler
97 Plains Indian
98 Obstacle
100 Breeding stable
102 Pare
103 Little devils
104 Stereo component, for short
105 Tribe leader?
107 Definite article
108 Harem chamber

ACROSS

1 Prefix for file or fuse
4 Oz creator
8 Entertainer Josephine
13 Wahoo, for one
17 Film of 1967
18 Latin years
19 Well's companion
20 Involved with
21 Blind ambition
22 Coaches' happy events
23 Very gratifying
25 Suspense dramas
28 Boxer Liston
29 Anomalous
30 Singer Stafford et al.
31 Shorten, as a mast
33 Promontory
35 Humble boat
37 Dissipate
40 Run off
44 Georgetown athlete
45 Oceanic abbr.
46 Greek letter
47 Short on courage
48 Means of approach
50 __-ran (non-winner)
52 Actor Franco
53 United
54 Mardi __
57 Musician Jackson
59 Zero
60 Very good mood
62 Claw's place, often
65 Ignites
66 Obscenity
67 Cushion
70 Long-billed bird
72 Lizardfish
73 Put aside
75 Tim's tiptoeing place
77 FDR agcy.
79 Exist
81 Dresden denial
82 Newspaper section
83 Impaled
85 Fleet
86 Migration
88 Historical divisions
89 Ungainly vehicle
90 Soul, to Sartre
93 Unsuitable
96 Bright and bubbly
100 Much happiness
103 Dies __
104 Then's partner
105 Shortly
106 Perfect, e.g.
107 Indian city
108 Dernier __
109 Road sign
110 Void
111 Orderly
112 Consume

DOWN

1 Lot plan
2 Writer Rendell
3 Very happy
4 __ out (reprimands)
5 Blue dye
6 Discompose
7 Interpret wrongly
8 Severe
9 Pub supply
10 Metric mass, for short
11 Manifest
12 Old Roman rules
13 Hale
14 The lowdown
15 Wallboard support
16 Phone button
24 Excitable: Sl.
26 Davenport dweller
27 D.C. title
32 Chemin-de-__
34 Flash
35 Newsman Bernard
36 Baylet
37 Retired
38 A Belafonte
39 Flag ceremony
41 Hot place for 8 Across?
42 Prefix for meter
43 Chemical compound
47 Bruised
49 Cries of disgust
51 Use a natatorium
55 "A guy and __"
56 Contracted
57 Hitters' workouts, for short
58 O.T. book
61 Cubic meter
62 Matches up
63 Border on
64 Cunning
67 Actor Donald
68 Tel __
69 Reject
71 Delta deposit
74 Boredom
76 Jeopardy
78 Mind-boggle
79 Desert of Egypt
80 Come back strong
83 Janet Lynn, for one
84 Before
87 Growing out
89 Barn sound
90 Trojan war hero
91 Actor Paul
92 Sable
94 __ Colada
95 Fling
97 Pasternak heroine
98 Ibsen girl
99 Gibe
101 Ending for end
102 Born

ACROSS

1 Challah ingredient
4 Typographical embellishment
9 Aqua __
13 Lynn of baseball
17 Gainsborough subject
18 Long-running musical
19 Surrounded by
20 Calcium oxide
21 Torricelli's 1643 invention
23 Hunt's 1849 invention
25 Portico
26 Vampiresses
28 Hearts' companions
29 Postpone
31 Where the Damodar flows
33 Bat material
34 Technology item
37 Treasure
39 Confiscate
43 Cry of surprise
44 Inviting letters
46 Empty
48 Ger. river
49 Replica
51 Pizazz
53 Walton's 1860 invention
55 Power source fo Watt
57 Solemn passage
59 Actor Johnson
60 Gentle-lamb link
61 Powder holder
63 Epithets
65 Cap nut
67 Russian river
70 Essence
72 Accumulated, as expenses
74 Market prefix
78 Galileo's 1583 invention
81 Originate
82 Kind of dancer
83 Pro's opponent
84 Avoirdupois
86 Spheres
89 Free
90 Calcareous clay
92 __ lazuli
94 Wail
96 Bush's former org.
98 Broke bread
100 Actor Bogosian
101 Breastbone
105 Signify
107 Sailor's call
110 Buschnel's 1972 invention
112 Oughtred's 1620 invention
114 Marine eagle
115 Caesar's wife
116 Actress Barkin
117 "Wait __ the sun shines . . .''
118 Tidy
119 Barbecue dish
120 Fabric workers
121 Photo abbr.

DOWN

1 Declines
2 Horned beast
3 Foucault's 1852 invention
4 School yr. part
5 Writer Waugh et al.
6 Beatles' meter maid
7 Agenda opener
8 Grain meal
9 Fervor
10 Actress Thurman
11 Jazz phrase
12 Writer St. Johns
13 Auto-engine part
14 Mature
15 Mideast ruler
16 Family rooms
22 Expletive
24 Pitch
27 Pascal's 1642 invention
30 Ventilate
32 Asian sea
34 Soft shoes, for short
35 "There'll be __ time . . ."
36 Knievel
38 Okla. town
40 Notion
41 Olympian bigwig
42 Bombeck
45 Scheme
47 Chem. compound
50 Jabber
52 Sandarac tree
54 Burden
56 Computer list
58 Wine: Prefix
62 Chasm
64 Oriental sport
66 Visceral
67 Gemstone
68 Casino game
69 Pot starter
71 Kind of dog or frog
73 Indiana town
75 Blanchard's 1785 invention
76 Stage direction
77 Theme park attraction
79 Prudent
80 Honey beverage
85 "Arachniphobia" group
87 Kind of valve
88 Prefix for mount or change
91 Chinese, in combinations
93 Intuited
95 Perjurer
97 Bode
99 "Barnaby Rudge" character
101 Cinematographer Nykvist
102 Fatigue
103 Writer Buchanan
104 Skirt style
106 Roofing material
108 Actress Lena
109 Shout
111 Gang
113 USNA grad

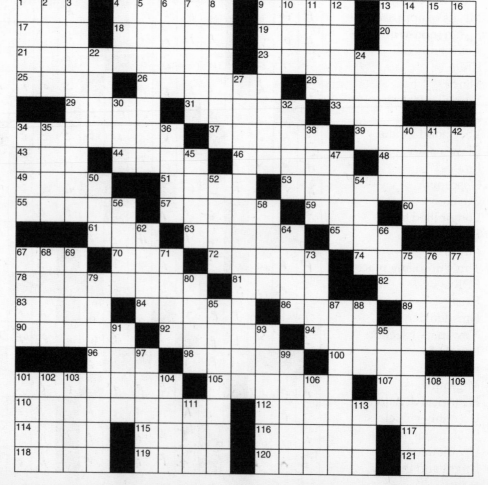

ACROSS

1 Rememberer's word
4 Ballet movement
8 Mil. offense
12 Fresh
17 Business abbr.
18 Bear on high
19 Siamese's descendant
20 Traveler's choice
21 Mitchell character
24 __ Rice Burroughs
25 Permeable
26 Kind of vaccine
27 Floor covering
29 W.W. II area
30 Rafter's problem
31 Roman conquest, 290 B.C.
34 "I've __ thinking . . ."
36 Ready to sleep
38 Nudge
39 L.A. Dodger family
43 Get back
45 Chem. endings
46 Major __
47 On behalf of
50 Intensity
51 Playground equipment
53 Downy coating
54 Shiny surface
56 Advisory
58 Clamp shape
60 Starts a hand over
62 Actor Laurence of TV
63 Rock group: "A Horse with No Name"
67 Pismire
68 Puzzle
71 Kind of computer
72 Pelt
74 Smooth and glossy
76 Tweed's nemesis
78 Card game
79 Ox of puzzledom
81 Catches
82 Hooked
84 Nova Scotia port
86 Big East mbr.
87 P.O. missions
90 Grub
91 Hard work
94 Supermarket section
96 __ fi
98 "__ So Fine" (1962 hit)
100 Exchange premium
101 Actress Annette

103 Rhythm
105 Rock singer
108 More skilled
109 Ski lift
110 Eliot's "__ Bede"
111 Gamin
112 Calif. point
113 Overimbibers
114 Bush alma mater
115 __ Moines

DOWN

1 Tendrils
2 Adriatic port
3 Egyptian amulet
4 Pacific sea
5 Lock
6 Extreme ending
7 "Some Like It Hot" actor
8 Nigh
9 Mighty mammal
10 Gondolier's item
11 Novelist O'Flaherty
12 Grimm character
13 Ingot

14 Nobel Prize winner, 1936
15 French state
16 Son of 82 Down
22 Radio acknowledgment
23 Sky hunter
28 Truckle
32 On __ with (equal to)
33 Seattle player, for short
35 Old times, old-style
37 Waterloos
40 Euripedes tragedy
41 Entertainer Sumac
42 Consolation prize
44 Lamella
45 Troy
47 Chemin de __
48 "Mickey __" (1965 film)
49 Gary Burghoff role
51 Overdramatized
52 Perfumed
55 Will's "__ At Work"
57 Actress Lena et al.
59 Epoch
61 Attack
64 Vizard

65 Murmur
66 Past
69 Kind of shift or shirt
70 Jazz singer
72 Writer Weldon
73 Actress Merkel
75 Mistreat
77 Opponent
80 Physicians' grp.
82 Wife of Augustus
83 Evil spirit
85 Golden Rule word
86 Summoning devices
88 Fall meteor
89 Strauss opera
92 Assaulted
93 Part of LAN
95 Maryland team, for short
96 Longeron
97 Geometric shape
99 Concordes
102 Heavy reading
104 Consult
106 Nigerian native
107 Harem chamber

TERMS OF ENCOURAGEMENT

ACROSS

1 Mills in movies
7 Overalls feature
10 Bottle closer
13 Silence
17 Excite
18 "Mickey __" (1965 film)
19 S.A. land
20 Fierce cetacean
21 Daring deeds
22 Rodeo exhortaion
25 __ Dawn Chong
26 Negligent
27 Make up
28 Mine find
30 Before
32 Suffix for atom or item
33 Pewter ingredient
34 Informal greeting
35 Harvest
37 Allen film
39 Delaney of TV
40 Purfle
41 Baseball exhortation
43 Josh
46 Diving birds
48 Lon__ of Cambodia
49 Lennon's widow
50 Gage book
52 Arrival
54 Less civil
56 Flight prefix
57 Radio fare
59 Shy
61 Actress Valerie
63 Suffix for two or tooth
64 Racing boat
66 Kind of drum
67 "__ Teenage Werewolf"
69 Little devil
70 Make sure
72 Compact
75 Tool for Tennyson
76 Exhortation to Truman
80 Put in storage
81 Narrow margin
82 Actor Jack
83 Steadfast
84 Behave
87 Health-care grp.
88 Ward-heeler
89 Shell contents
91 Good times
92 Cleric
94 San __, Calif.
96 Cousin's pa
98 Football exhortation

100 Nasty
103 Arrow poison
104 Writer Beattie
105 Sine qua __
106 Actress Stritch
107 Actor Bruce
108 Cobb and Detmer
109 Car of '60s song
110 Bleachers

DOWN

1 Owns
2 Blakey of jazz
3 Words to Charlie Brown
4 Allendale's "Eva __"
5 Mrs. Lauder
6 Green light
7 Drilling tool
8 Unfriendly
9 Adorn
10 Signals
11 Tributary
12 Opera great
13 Gordie of hockey
14 Kind of transit
15 Darkness, in combinations
16 Mowed and dried
23 Argot
24 Flowery
26 Take pity
28 Hershiser of baseball
29 Decorator's assignment
31 Inflamed
33 Western lake
36 "__ from Heaven"
38 __ Jima
39 Fop
42 Road trip
43 Cry to long-distance haulers
44 Concerning
45 Fashion house
47 Compass point
51 Dimensionally preeminent
53 Curve shape
54 Medium for Vanilla Ice
55 Greek letter
57 Poet Mandelstam
58 Rob of films
59 Rising star
60 Road-movie man
62 Plus
65 "I, Claudius" character
66 Misrepresents
68 Horrified
70 ". . . __ perish from the earth"
71 Frightful cry
73 Minestrone, for one
74 Lambs' dams
77 "__ I am" (Exodus)
78 Boat's place
79 Meat cut
84 Plant pest
85 Witch
86 Roofing worker
88 Chum
90 Culpability
93 Garden spot
94 Pkgs.
95 Wine: Prefix
97 Sports org.
99 Word with more or time
100 Unseld of the NBA
101 Heel
102 __ Plaines, Ill.

ACROSS

1 Reconcile
6 Nidi
11 Pose, in a way
14 Bark
17 Voracious reader
18 Musical opening
19 Nigerian native
20 Ending for post or peer
21 Took Mozart to court
23 Cheapen
25 Spoken
26 Severe
27 With 38 Down, Ger. economist
28 Submissive
29 Asgard dwellers
31 Bench
33 Train part
34 Belle of the West
37 Original
39 Impudent slave?
43 Darius's realm
45 Warehouse
47 Howard of films
48 Exist
49 Ordinal suffix
51 Shoal
52 Pull
53 Blind ambition
54 Climb
56 Canters
58 "... a poem __ a tree"
60 Sketching prize?
63 Rings
66 Sportscaster Tony
67 Curing agent
71 Actress Hagen
72 From __ Z
73 Explorer Pike, for short
74 Tease
76 Status __
77 "Annunciation" painter
79 Singer Leo
81 "__ Leaves"
83 Munchies holders?
85 Short time, for short
87 Form
88 __ Moines
89 Molokai neighbor
91 European elk
93 Distantly
95 Baby seal
96 "__ Distance" (Midler hit)
98 Revel
102 Protruding
104 Notice officials?
106 Charity initials
107 Dander
108 Brainy group
109 Spaghetti al __
110 Poetic contraction
111 Conducted
112 Agalloch
113 Vilify

DOWN

1 Lhasa __
2 Sullen
3 Zone
4 Itinerant merchants
5 __ la-la
6 B-complex member
7 Lasted
8 Proofreader's word
9 Aligns
10 Mayday
11 Calm
12 Wild goat
13 Mazel __
14 Ivy League race?
15 Fever symptom
16 Quick glance
22 More, in Monterrey
24 Gather
27 Place of commerce
30 Iroquoian
32 __ effort
33 Masticator
34 Trade punches
35 Actress Garr
36 War god
38 See 27 Across
40 European region
41 Actress Tushingham
42 Charges
44 Part of NATO
46 House detective's item
50 "__ you do?"
52 High-rise
55 Tokyo of yore
57 Foot
58 Mideast land: Abbr.
59 Comm. hookups, for short
61 Writer Robert and family
62 Bumpkins
63 Sportscaster Hodges
64 Old school
65 Green food, darn it!
68 Water color
69 Aggregate
70 Pitch
73 Actress Pitts
75 Smooch
78 Sour
79 Bite
80 Anguish
82 Pythagoras's work
84 Diverted
86 Represent
90 Opinion words
92 Blunderer
93 Border on
94 Honshu peak
95 Straight
97 City on 1-80
99 Descartes
100 "__ horse"
101 French river
103 Gas's partner
104 Glaswegian "wee"
105 News execs

ACROSS

1 Hurdy-gurdy feature
6 Greetings
9 African fox
13 Gnome
16 Collared
17 Clockmaker Thomas
18 Julia of films
19 Golfer's concern
20 Southwestern clay
21 Clark's "The __"
24 Energy
25 Moray
27 Flock females
28 Floor covering
29 Globe sector
31 Dustup
33 Corpulent
35 Synagogue
36 London tale
39 Home to 25 Across
41 Gibbon
42 Explosive
43 Great quantity
45 Expand
47 Central courts
50 "The Sheltering __"
(1990 film)
51 Pilcorn
53 Stoked the pot
56 Stutz model
58 Harpo's brother
60 Off track
61 Police msg.
62 Mailer book
66 Cultural collection
67 Actress Andersson
69 Chugalug
70 Writer Calvin
72 Mines' entrances
74 Writer Kaufman
75 Bedazzle
77 "No __" (protest sign)
78 Italian opera
80 Wine type
82 Hallow follower
83 Org. for Jordan
85 Tennyson's
"Locksley __"
87 Vonnegut title
92 Blasphemy
94 Underworld god
96 "__ Faces Have I"
('60s hit)
97 Control
98 Soda-fountain supply
100 Encircle
102 Party in power
104 Ergate
105 Irwin Shaw novel
108 Writer Bret
110 __ judicata
111 Nobelist Wiesel
112 Fiber knots
113 Modify
114 Skill
115 Dispatch
116 Menacing sound
117 Roald and Arlene

DOWN

1 Scarf
2 Salad vegetable
3 Alienation
4 Pen point
5 Patella's place
6 Curse
7 The Beatles' "Let __"
8 Flaunt
9 Breakfast candidate
10 Jose or Jacinto
11 Replace
12 Kazan
13 Robert Standish novel
14 Arrange for
15 Sound shape
17 "Have you sunk __?"
22 Network, tabloid-style
23 Faustus and
Frankenstein
26 Part of QED
30 Up and about
32 Get results
34 Fellow passenger
37 Legislate
38 Ballad
40 D.C. agcy.
44 Road trip
46 Words with dare or
whim
47 Addis __
48 Lukewarm
49 Updike book
50 Folk-song racehorse
52 Stereo component
54 Banks of Chicago
55 Actress Cannon et al.
57 Dental-office replies
58 Semisolid
59 Hockey great
63 Tool's companion
64 Fitzgerald
65 Baseball hall-of-famer
68 Jap. statesman
71 Part of LEM
73 Be still!
75 __ glance
76 Skater Katarina
79 Summary
81 Sports feat
82 Social sci.
83 Cosa __
84 Beach habitue
86 Carried
88 Helvetian
89 Paucity
90 Door beam
91 Joins
93 Word with stack
or rack
95 Sesame plant
99 Complaints
101 Busy person
103 Herring relative
106 "Henry & June"
name
107 Broadcast initials
109 Miss. neighbor

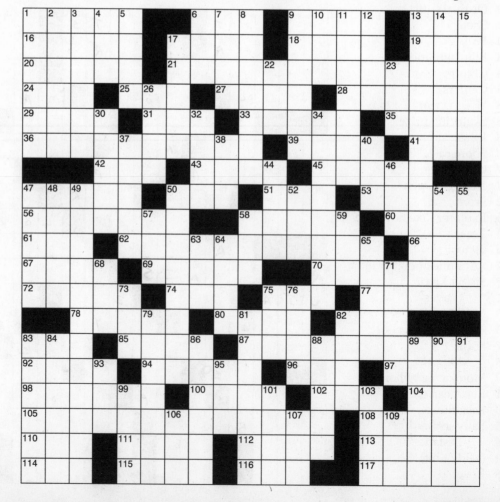

ACROSS

1 Flight-speed word
5 Verdant spot
9 Borneo neighbor
13 Golfer O'Grady
16 Wight, for one
17 Sailing word
18 Perforations
19 Ovid's "I love"
20 Controversies
23 Butter of sorts
24 Pittance
25 Triumphant cry
26 Actor McKellen
27 Papeete's place
29 Tomorrow in Turin
32 Sports org.
35 Orison ender
36 Buffalo team
38 Summer flyer
42 Car-chase maneuver
43 Atty.'s degree
44 Nonconforming
45 "__ Amatoria"
46 Part of MPG
47 Backpackers' places
50 Ross of note
52 Grate
54 __ as a pin
56 Soy dish
59 Italian wine
60 Kind of courtship
64 Presley hit
66 Become: Suffix
68 Wraps
69 Indian city
70 Avid inspector
74 Paean
76 Colin Powell, e.g.
77 Berlin cry
80 Telecast
82 Fanatic
83 To date
85 Mythical creatures
88 Enduring
89 Set course
90 Wizard
91 S. Calif. city
93 Grain blights
96 Dutch uncle
98 North or south ending
99 Everyday article
102 __ glance
103 Much merriment
108 Sunday msg.

109 Dostoyevsky's "The __"
110 Expression
111 Court great
112 Endeavor
113 Domino
114 Lip
115 Melville tale

DOWN

1 Overlook
2 Concerning
3 Gullywashers
4 LBJ pet
5 Turkish bigwigs
6 Crazy as __
7 Ump's cousin
8 Hat for de Gaulle
9 Scribble
10 Brew
11 Confer
12 Movie dog
13 Xylophone
14 Dilettante
15 Arrivals
18 Boss

21 Significance
22 Buzzard
28 Witch
30 Hockey great
31 Big ten team
33 ". . . three men in __"
34 Part of A.M.
36 Above: prefix
37 Comfortable
39 Goof-offs
40 NYC subway
41 Eyrie
43 Tie down
48 Crude
49 Mariners
51 "Star Wars" name
53 Blvd. in L.A.
55 Put __ two together
57 Washington area
58 Dispense, as a hose
61 Mistreatment
62 Neither masc. nor fem.
63 Summer time, for short

65 Oncle's spouse
67 Gosh relative
71 Mendacity
72 Fumbles
73 Singer McEntire
75 Consumption
77 Minimally
78 Written authority
79 Romania neighbor
81 Pandect
84 With 87 Down, Italian port
86 Modernist
87 See 84 Down
88 Rugby formations
92 Approaches
94 Preweekend initials
95 Actress Thompson
97 Lizards
100 Protagonist
101 Hence
104 Ignited
105 Aurora
106 Meadow
107 Cable TV initials

ACROSS

1 Specify
7 Conferred
12 Singer Lee
18 Betel palms
19 Point
20 Kind of lily
21 Potential
22 "I'm no city slicker," he said __
24 List abbr.
25 Conduit
27 Top-notch
28 Cry for attention
30 Gambrinus's concoction
31 Lineage
32 Antony's "frequently"
35 Struck, old-style
37 Devious
38 "No more cotton," she said __
41 Possession
43 Melees
45 Oriental
46 October sportsman
47 Gangling
48 Dive
49 Chart abbr.
50 Drays
52 White House pet
53 TV's "Happy __"
55 "Yes doctor," she said __
58 Helen's mother
62 Raveille counterpart
64 Madrepores
66 __ sequitur
67 Sermon
70 __ craftsy
72 Source
74 Isabella's birthplace
75 Cropped up
76 Compatriot
77 "Who goes there?" he said __
79 Instruct
80 Like French toast
81 Omnium-gatherum
82 Numero __
83 Long time
85 "Agnus __"
86 Meanie
88 Mean
90 Org. for Bird
93 "Ship it fast," she said
97 Poetic fare
99 Herbal tea
100 Black nightshade
101 Goatfish
102 Passing remarks
103 Pot builders
104 Fall __ (suffer from)

DOWN

1 Valley
2 Part of QED
3 "I'll get it," she said __
4 Rapper Vanilla __
5 Young detective Drew
6 O.T. book
7 "__ End" ('70 hit)
8 Danish garment
9 Western
10 Veto
11 Sp. queen
12 "Thy will __"
13 Udometer measurement
14 Being
15 High degree
16 __ Rio, Texas
17 Station ending
23 Certain hardware
26 With skill
29 Rel. of 24 Across
31 "__ bar the door"
32 Actress Lena
33 Ensign
34 Newcastle's river
35 Decorous
36 Brainy bunch
37 Pugnacious
38 Swamp
39 Hairpiece
40 Common
42 Modern
43 Indian princess
44 Midge and mantis
47 Nonsense
48 Missile's burden
51 Road sign
52 Sebring's st.
54 Marsh bird
56 Proboscis
57 Sample
59 "Marry me," he said __
60 Conduct
61 Peeve
63 Jai __
65 Title of respect, in Delhi
67 Riant sound
68 Ellipse
69 Works
70 Woody's son
71 Signer Acuff
73 Got it!
75 DeMille of dance
76 City on the Arno
78 Health-care workers
79 Emerald and aquamarine
83 Stave off
84 Cafe dessert
85 Protest
86 Mouthward
87 Hackman
88 Stratford's river
89 Coarse thread
91 Sugar source
92 Concerning
93 Greek letter
94 Greek letters
95 Greek letter
96 Diddley's "__ Man"
98 Cousin of 30 Across

ACROSS

1 Fight back
7 Fumbling
12 Director's call
18 Pencil adjunct
19 O'Grady of song
20 Made over
21 Nimble accountant?
23 Followed
24 Diamond setting
25 Fake
27 New Deal initials
28 Honor card
31 In reserve
34 Phone abbr.
35 Like __ of bricks
36 Policy
40 "Blue Velvet" filmmaker
42 Exercise
43 Always, poetically
44 Tool's companion
46 Leading
49 Vulnerable
51 Implied
53 Christie's "Murder __"
54 Bellow
56 Sanctify
58 Clamor
59 Heap of trouble
62 Retrieval-system parts
65 African fox
66 Mountaintop meas.
67 Self-contained unit
68 Old school
70 Calculator antecedent
72 Footing
75 Pass up
79 Molybdenum, e.g.
80 Continental abbr.
81 Malay dagger
83 Burn
84 Key
86 Aptitude
89 Lacerate
91 Race part
93 Unfamiliar with
94 Comedian Louis
95 Salamander
96 Singer Nelson
98 Coarse
101 Prompt
103 Quarterly levy
109 Obtain
110 In conflict
111 Stritch or May
112 Kind of parade
113 Consigns
114 Used a rheostat

DOWN

1 Arena arbiter
2 Silkworm
3 __ Harbor, N.Y.
4 "Your time __"
5 Antitoxins
6 Actress Claire
7 Peeve
8 Taboo's opposite
9 High regard
10 Jetty
11 Concise
12 Graceful
13 Actress Kay
14 Personals, e.g.
15 Take attendance
16 Part of a Juarez winter
17 Auto model
22 Good thing to make
26 Wagon part
28 "A Man __ Woman"
29 Brusque
30 Arab VIP
32 "By the Time __ to Phoenix"
33 "__ Mia"
35 Long
37 Ecstasy
38 Columnist Maxwell
39 Minn. town
41 Tweed's skewer
45 Lay __ thick
47 Sale disclaimer
48 Unit of force
50 Prestige
52 Scottish-games pole
53 RPI and MIT
55 Young fella
57 White House nickname
59 Term of respect
60 North Sea feeder
61 "Vital" stuff
63 Terpsichorean wear
64 Attentive
65 Madcap
67 Ponder
69 Fr. river
71 Teller-machine supply
73 Trumpet adjunct
74 Cabbage dish
76 __ impulse (rashly)
77 Foul
78 Prefix for graph
80 And so forth
82 Part of UHF
85 More exclusive
87 Kind of punch
88 Directed
89 Graylags
90 "He wouldn't hurt __"
92 Implore
96 Finish line
97 Analogy phrase
99 Supermarket section
100 Dutch cheese
102 Abridged
104 "__ Woman" (Helen Reddy hit)
105 Mme., in Missouri
106 Raines of baseball
107 Deauville donkey
108 Deleted

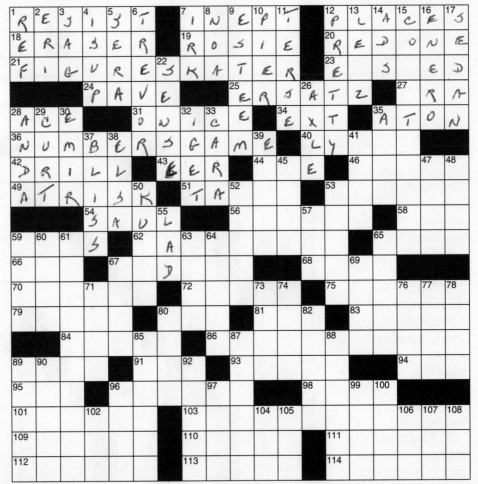

ACROSS

1 Low-tech tool
4 Prepared to glean
10 Corn porridge
14 Existed
17 Spring mo.
18 Vanish without __
19 Legal offering
20 Circle part
21 Flee
24 Wrath
25 March 31 baby
26 Cry of discovery
27 Pre-med subj.
28 Word with dash or stick
29 Pasternak woman
30 Deuce
31 Graphic display
32 Sully
33 Suggestion
35 "__ Love" (1989 film)
37 Cower
38 Vast
41 Tale of suspense
43 Singer Gates
44 Disturbs
46 Heel
47 Mideast ruler
48 Actor Lorenzo
49 Productive
50 Key to Wall St., perhaps
53 Unclose
54 "Petite Suite" composer
55 Singer Simon
56 La-la precursor
57 Then's partner
58 Skip
59 Outworn
60 Nostrum
61 Soft cheese
62 Starboard's state
63 Line dance
64 Operation of 1991
68 Watered down
70 Opening sections
71 Secrecy
73 Salad fish
74 Propeller
75 Sun. msgs.
76 Top dog
78 "The King and I" setting
81 Hop __ (get going)
82 Modern resident of 78 Across
83 __ tizzy
84 Intuit
85 Little devil
86 Mood swings
89 Non-veracity
90 Calvados neighbor
91 Disparage
92 Long time
93 Stripling
94 __ a terre
95 Shut up
96 Lament

DOWN

1 Taj __
2 Famed phantom's hangout
3 Texas college town
4 Actor Vallone et al.
5 W.W. II locale
6 Rotary sign
7 Tear-jerker quality
8 Leander's love
9 Billy __ Williams
10 By-product
11 Words with once or sea
12 Soften
13 Dance step
14 Nursery sound
15 Organize
16 Power symbol
22 Broadcasting boo-boo
23 "Hey, angel, your __ slipping"
28 Canonize
30 Randy's skating partner
31 Blanches
32 Vulgar
34 Drop
36 Acclaim
37 Gum base
38 Music hall
39 S.A. plain
40 Lunatics
42 Played the tease
45 "Since __ You, Baby" (1956 hit)
48 Bounds
49 Outpouring
50 West Virginian
51 Entertainer Victor
52 Word to the helm
54 Appropriate
55 Obstruct
59 "__ Bulba"
60 Guidance
61 Artiste's wear
62 Writer West
63 Actor Gulager
64 Refine
65 Paeans
66 Like a tiger
67 Pinched
69 Follower: Suffix
72 Comedian Bernhardt
75 Classic western
77 Find fault
79 "__ Like It"
80 Intervening, in law
82 Garr of films
83 Arrow poison
84 Travois
86 Burst
87 Media matter
88 Citrus drink

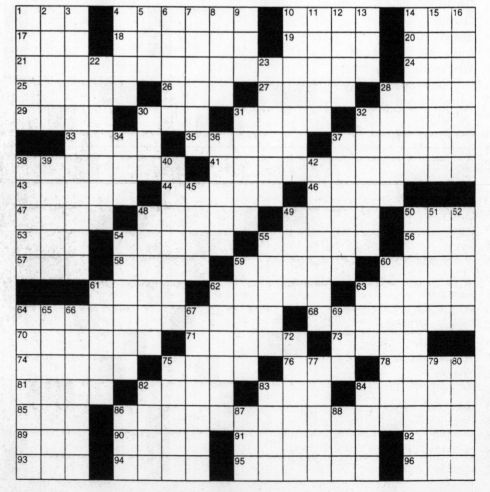

ACROSS

1 Barcelona bank unit
7 Volcanic matter
10 Dwelling place
14 Phenix City's st.
17 Tali
18 Repent
19 Table spread
20 Road sign
21 Abdul and Prentiss
22 Boastful about blood vessels?
25 Dog breed, for short
26 Prefix for version or mission
27 Name in "The Raven"
28 Quite
30 Timetable abbr.
32 Letter opener
35 Clear a counter
36 Mortar tray
37 Spiritual guides
40 Persuade
42 Piscine dish
43 In __ (stuck)
45 Headed for a triceps?
48 Engendered
50 Persian elf
51 Kind of culture
52 Short time, for short
55 Region of India
56 One of a nursery threesome
57 Just so
58 N.Z. parrot
59 Billy __
62 Engineering details, for short
65 Portray
67 Regal pronoun
68 Chum
70 Sty group
72 Sawbuck
73 Word with me or not
74 Okla. town
76 Decibel or dram
77 TV's "The Wonder __"
80 Presentation on cell matter?
83 Distinguish
84 Road rig
87 "Born Free" creature
88 More modern
90 Genetic material
91 Sing joyfully
93 Ending for launder
95 Actress Arden
96 Tricks holder, perhaps
97 Concurs

99 Trenchant
102 Far Eastern truth
104 Inflexible about pith?
107 Roast, e.g.
110 D.D.E.'s command
111 Innocent
112 A Fleming
113 Resolved
114 Part of N.H.
115 Greek letters
116 Stat for Clemens
117 Poker ploys

DOWN

1 Mindless reading
2 Sp. queen
3 Investigations of the head?
4 Actress Raines
5 Pekoe pack
6 Onager
7 Viet Cong opponents, for short
8 Tallow material
9 Descendants
10 Hatch fastener
11 Poorly
12 Sci. branch
13 More acute
14 Loose as __
15 Bay tree
16 Balance-sheet list
23 Sound
24 "You're All __"
26 Break in
28 Gregory Peck role
29 Body of traditions
31 Export from Kingston
33 Singer McEntire
34 Plods
38 Computer customers
39 Funny money
41 Sensational
44 Seized
46 Arranges
47 Fine point
49 Oriental metropolis
52 Emaciated
53 Common Market initials
54 Word with nip or nap
59 Pull
60 Say what?
61 __ d'école
63 Schwarzenegger role

64 Pilfer
66 Quick look
69 Hosiery fabric
71 Like some prunes
75 Levigate
78 Writer Jaffe
79 Booty
80 Roofing worker
81 Consumed
82 Clerical abbr.
84 Flower part
85 Worker ant
86 Following day
89 Eye membrane
92 Sierra __
94 Murphy of the movies
98 Clout
100 Equipment
101 Poet Millay
103 Con
105 Woody's former companion
106 Question marks
107 Heading: Abbr.
108 Chem. ending
109 ACLU issue

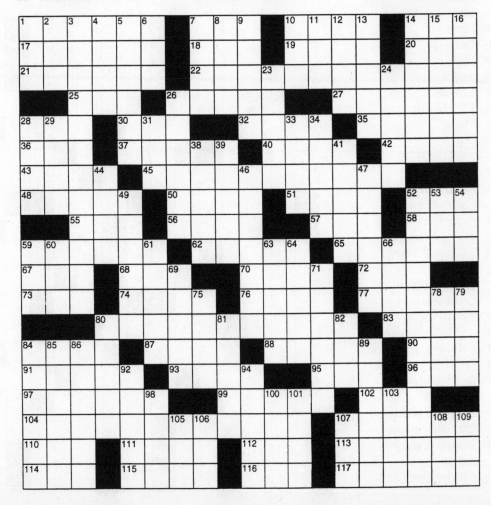

ACROSS

1 Spite
7 Partake
12 Haphazard
18 Weather map line
19 Filmmaker Resnais
20 Comedian Boosler
21 Huff, huff
23 Chuck of baseball
24 Pop
25 Trick
27 Solicitude
28 Inquire
31 Interlock
33 Dried up
34 Phys. Ed. site
35 Cook's collection
37 Use a reagent
39 She, in Chantilly
41 Tape-speed initials
44 Relatives of
 four-flushers?
47 Oriental
48 Food holder
49 Filched
50 Drone
52 Dickensian
 functionary
54 Parts
56 Deficient
59 More accurate
60 Italian wine
63 Crosses
66 TV's Molly
67 Might
69 Bridge
70 "__ Like It"
72 "Big house"
74 Personality parts
76 Encroachment
79 Actor Cariou
80 Mideast land
83 Simon's " The __"
86 Business letter abbr.
87 Energy source
88 Loudness unit
89 Except for
90 "__ Take Romance"
92 Evil-doer, to police
94 Cookout problem
97 Brit. version of
 48 Across
98 Egyptian goddess
100 Mazatlan madame
102 Storied nightclub, for
 short
104 Fundamental

106 London bus, e.g.
111 Syrian city
112 Dais occupant
113 Punctual
114 Even match
115 Textile workers
116 Condition

DOWN

1 Actress Sara
2 Uraeus
3 Mauna __
4 Wading bird
5 Ricochet
6 Wear down
7 Kind of dance
8 "When I was __ . . ."
9 Most reasonable
10 Heading
11 Guarantees
12 Neural network
13 Words with mode
14 Actress Marchand
15 Batman and Robin
16 Singular thing
17 Pool
22 Snaps, for instance

26 Sandwich shop
28 Fitting
29 Axioms
30 Clove hitch
32 LBJ pet
34 Woodwaxen
36 Accounts
38 Library admonition
40 Scientific setting,
 for short
42 Fenced in
43 Bergen's Mortimer
45 Labor grp.
46 Liquefy
47 Cupid
51 Overturn
53 Grueling
55 Exhaust
57 Sp. she-bear
58 Dwelling
60 NYC symbol
61 Kierkegaard
62 Minn. area
64 Conceited
65 Time harmony,
 for short
68 K.C. player

71 Rio de __
73 Seine
75 __ Canals
77 __ on the back
78 Half of MCXII
81 Brood
82 Corrected
84 Genetic
 substance
85 Poetic time
88 Conifer
91 Hobbles
93 Capacious
95 Commotions
96 Frittered away
98 Quarrel
99 A Guthrie
100 Muddy ground
101 But, in Bonn
103 Proceedings
105 Egyptian temple
 site
107 Conductor
 Baxter
108 Little fox
109 Big bird
110 Legal matter

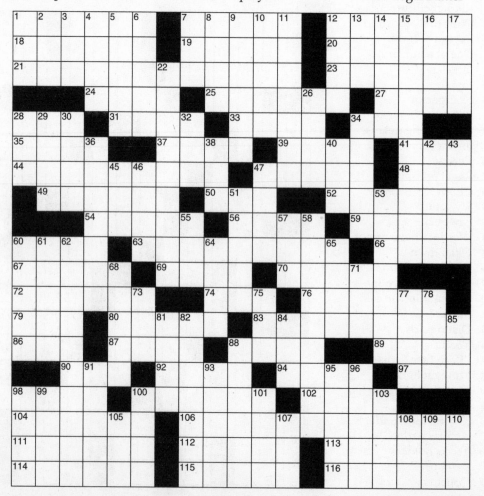

ACROSS

1 Bursa
4 N.C. campus
8 Roman date
12 Aquarius's burden
17 W.W. II agcy.
18 Store sign
19 Alaska cape
20 Endure
21 Sampler sentiment
24 Swain
25 Trattoria seasoning
26 __ avis
27 Canard
28 Yarn
29 Rain checks
31 Set apart
35 Argot
37 Prefix for verse
38 __ plaisir
39 Sandberg subject
40 Enthralled
43 Consecutive
46 Harbor vessel
47 Guillermo's gold
48 Tenebrous
49 Harangue
50 Vets' charges
51 Droll
53 Singer Vikki
55 Trade quips
57 Flat fish
58 Gemlike, in a way
61 Graceful
64 Valley
66 Possessive pronoun
67 Sports-car antecedent
69 Questionable
71 Word on a magnum
73 Which relative
74 Staff
75 Overly
76 Silly goose!
79 Antitoxins
80 Bumble
81 Chem. endings
82 Polish river
83 Fond du __
85 Sportscast fare
87 Michaelmas daisy
89 Hideouts
93 Shell mover
94 __ de vivre
95 Late
97 Reject
99 Author of "The Good
   Soldier"

101 Gate feature
102 Confirmation, e.g.
103 Supermarket
    section
104 Delay
105 Complete
106 Collections
107 Performs
108 Vulpine

DOWN

1 Sections of NYC
  and London
2 Direction at sea
3 Cut gem
4 Thick pieces
5 Suburban expanse
6 Dairy-case group
7 Born
8 Occupy
9 "The __" (1991 film)
10 Writer Lathen
11 Tour
12 Male witch
13 Seething
14 Repeatedly
15 Nigerian city

16 Car of yore
22 White bird
23 Main body
30 Nip's companion
31 Writer Turgenev
32 Religious groups
33 Celebrate
34 __ benedict
36 Israeli statesman
38 ". . . broad side
   of __"
40 Wander
41 "Aeneid" opener
42 Weight-adjusted
44 Jason's craft
45 Florentine iris
48 Dashboard
   display
50 Brace
52 Sojourn
53 Poem part
54 Pub offering
56 Braid
59 Hair styles
60 Cave phenomenon
62 Frozen dew
63 Lab heater

65 Tropical tree
68 Cart
69 Road of Rome
70 Links cry
72 Laments
73 Phoenician
   city
76 Longed
77 Kind of football
   kick
78 "Don't __ get ya
   down"
79 Neckwear
84 __ de Tocqueville
86 Sizeable
87 Heart adjunct
88 Larry Mahan's
   milieu
90 Graven images
91 Part of RFD
92 Like yellow iris
94 Dovetail
96 Field mouse
97 Haggard tale
98 Golfer's target
99 Monk
100 Introduce

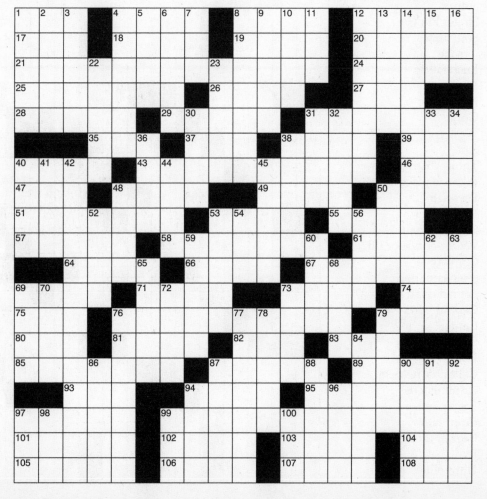

ACROSS

1 Lugosi
5 Paris cop
9 Dusty
13 Bond, for one
17 Hawkeye portrayer
18 Prefix for motive
19 Vintage characteristic
20 Finished
21 Incrementally
24 Unusual
25 Kazan
26 N.Y. city
27 Feasts
28 Cut back
30 "Three Musketeers" man
32 Inn sign
33 Gen. Bradley
34 Part of UAE
35 Horned beasts
37 __ Yutang
38 Disco hit of 1975
41 Brouhaha
44 Singular
45 Brew
46 "Bread and Wine" author
47 Singer Phoebe
48 Soul mates
51 __ sabe
52 Lush fabric
53 Raucous horn
55 Digression
57 Gorge
58 Western
59 San __
60 Thinly distributed
62 Pizzeria place
63 Feverish
65 Floor covering
66 Sawbuck half
69 Writer-educator Jill __ Conway
70 Stein equation
72 Sonnet relative
73 Central parts
74 Canter
75 Stem
76 Edit
79 Captain's helpers
81 Administered
82 Soap plant
83 Complain
85 Baez of music
86 Iwo __
87 Ultra-elite
92 Trebek of TV
93 Winter deposit
94 Keen
95 Where Rhone meets Saône
96 Lamar
97 Scent
98 Demolish
99 Crop starter

DOWN

1 __ Harbour, Fla.
2 Wallach
3 Closer to deadline
4 Buck projection
5 Fido's rider
6 Toss
7 Glacial
8 TV detective et al.
9 The opposition
10 Campus org.
11 "La __ Bonita" (Madonna hit)
12 Actress Ruby
13 Fishing boats
14 Actress Linda
15 Rive Gauche wear
16 Lock
22 Operculum
23 Give-try connection
27 Tax
28 Patrician competition
29 Mixed with
30 Common appliance
31 Former Mideast initials
32 Big blow
34 "Only Yesterday" author
35 Fabled dwarfs
36 Point-return link
38 Partiality
39 Swimwear
40 "__ Three Lives"
41 Old prescription for justice
42 Extinct bird
43 Meany of fiction
47 Phoenix team
49 Bullocks
50 Tartar and tabasco
52 Noncom, informally
53 Flaky person
54 Wash
56 Egyptian goddess
57 Grounds
59 Taunt
61 Backstage collection
63 Heavenly group
64 Docket list
67 Pop's Billy __
68 Salamander
70 Starchy staple
71 Fracas
73 Astronomic group
75 Jewelry items
76 Punjab prince
77 Zola
78 Like many stadia
79 Rising star
80 Actress Charlotte
81 Corpsman
83 Power system
84 San __
85 Nephrite
87 __-Magnon man
88 One of the Gabors
89 Actress Ashley, to friends
90 Curly's compatriot
91 Famous last word

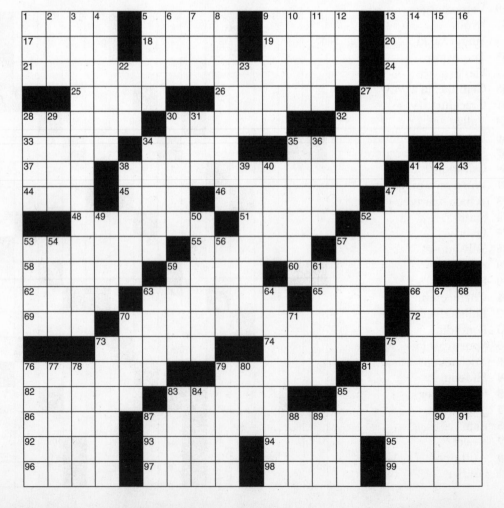

ACROSS

1 Mail-order initials
4 Courier
8 Paris patroller
12 Editorialize
17 Sorrel
18 Pilaster
19 Operatic heroine
20 Welles of films
21 Debussy's "La __"
22 Harvests extra fruit?
25 Writer Binchy
27 Take care of
28 Destroy
29 The Beatles' "__ Love Her"
30 Actress Eilbacher
31 Pluto
32 That: Sp.
36 Antiwar coalition
38 Surfer girl
41 Over
42 Synthetic acrylic
43 Slew of slips
44 River level
45 Plagiarize old stories?
48 Particle
49 L' __ Unis
50 Marner or Lapham
51 Solar disk
53 Fuss
54 Tool for Dickens
55 Model Carol
57 Portico
60 Commedia dell' __
62 Patching material
65 Inspires
66 Invitation
68 Journalist I.F. heeds music?
72 Make sense
74 "Ecclesiastes" word
75 Turner and Cantrell
76 Adolescent
77 Excoriate
78 Philbin of TV
79 Bombay wear
80 Rainbow
81 Freshly
83 Appeals to
86 Examine
88 Dolt
90 Gastropod
91 Cut a leporine allotment?
96 Additionally
97 Medicine: Prefix

98 Carina
99 "__ old cowhand"
100 __ Jima
101 Corset parts
102 Nev. town
103 Camp item
104 Doze

DOWN

1 Caesura
2 Arctic, e.g.
3 Challenged fearsome snake?
4 Trim
5 George's bill
6 Non-movement
7 Videos
8 Loose's companion
9 Fat: Prefix
10 Actress Lupino
11 Primary
12 Fumbler's word
13 Oven instruction
14 "Life __ beach . . ."
15 Conjunction
16 Junior off.
23 Breakwater

24 Relax
26 Lawbreaker
30 Camera attachment
31 Actress Merrill
33 Mar Turner's fancy fabric?
34 Lome's land
35 Forthright
37 Tenn. team
39 Zone
40 Box-score column
42 Bismarck
43 Central
44 Concorde
45 Arranged
46 "The Hollow Men" monogram
47 Sup
52 Finno-Ugric language
54 Caress
55 Bar mbr.
56 Solid caustic
58 Metallurgical study
59 Blockhead
61 Recipe abbr.
62 Alejandro of baseball

63 Molecule, for one
64 Moved __ (saddened)
65 Kind of party
66 Dotty
67 Concept
69 Catch and pass
70 DEA worker
71 Lot
73 Monistic
77 Knock
78 Computer command
82 __ game (pitching feat)
84 Southwestern Indian
85 Sailing vessel
87 Life force
88 Humble
89 Eur. capital
90 Dispatched
91 Family mbr.
92 Derby or trilby
93 Greek letter
94 91 Down, e.g.
95 Fled

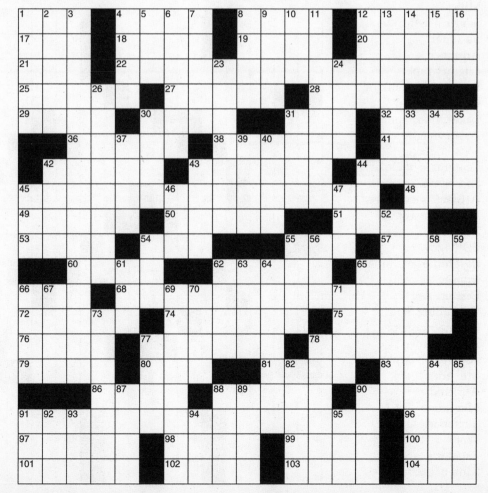

ACROSS

1 Suchlike
5 Essence
9 Bloke
13 Evergreens
17 Cousin's mom
18 ". . . have mercy on such __"
19 Headlong
20 Type type: Abbr.
21 Wavering
23 Quartet member
24 Behold, to Brutus
25 Bank jobs
26 Like Mahler's 10th
28 Day-trade
30 Desert Storm vehicle
32 __ Park, N.Y.
33 San __ Obispo
34 Actress Harper
35 Dissolved matter
39 Amphora
40 Like some laws
45 Of the kidneys
46 Border
47 Jack of "Barney Miller"
48 Surgical instrument
50 Basinger
51 Admits it
53 Literary rabbit
54 Beattie and Reinking
55 Charlotte team
59 Lake Ontario port
61 Asian weight
63 TV's "Green __"
65 Teammate of Duke and Newk
68 Artifact assemblage
69 Pulls from a spool
71 Venom
72 FDR agcy.
73 East Indies mammal
75 Infinite
77 Distress call
78 "__ Falling Star"
80 Geometric shape
81 Protuberance
82 Architect Saarinen
84 Mil. unit
85 Afflicted
86 Like some dictionaries
90 Won
93 Picador's target
94 Kind of opera
95 Steadfast
98 __ mater
99 Kingston, e.g.
100 Wise-owl link
101 Example
102 Hall or Cavett
103 Doers: Suffix
104 Verb for Shelley
105 Spheres

DOWN

1 St. Anthony's cross
2 Vandal
3 Hit for Ray Charles
4 Braces
5 Gentle blows
6 Attends
7 Whirlwind
8 Layer of sorts
9 Kind of case or call
10 King's "The Dark __"
11 Abed no longer
12 Fund-raising tools
13 Italian resort
14 Desire
15 Handicap, for one
16 Travois
22 Padnag
26 Clear, in a way
27 Stravinsky et al.
28 Calumnies
29 Feudal assembly
31 Simulating
34 Jefferson's bill
36 Arlington reposer
37 Mirror backing
38 "Desire Under the __"
40 Former U.N. mbr.
41 Speechwriter Peggy
42 Waste allowance
43 Outward: Prefix
44 __ do-well
49 Amour __
52 Helios
54 Blind ambition
56 Beige
57 Disney film
58 Liquidate
60 Exigency
61 Soapstone
62 Puzzle-roaming ox
64 Cut bread
66 Wear down
67 Mitigated
69 Member of the wedding
70 EPA concern
71 Dweller: Suffix
74 Winter craft
76 Emotional
79 Grain bristle
81 Decorative metal work
83 Scents
84 Wall St. transactions
85 Cuckoo
86 Dixie National Forest site
87 __ contendere
88 Military force
89 Gallop, e.g.
91 Remotely
92 Bombast
95 "Roger & Me" org.
96 Apprehend
97 Mdse.

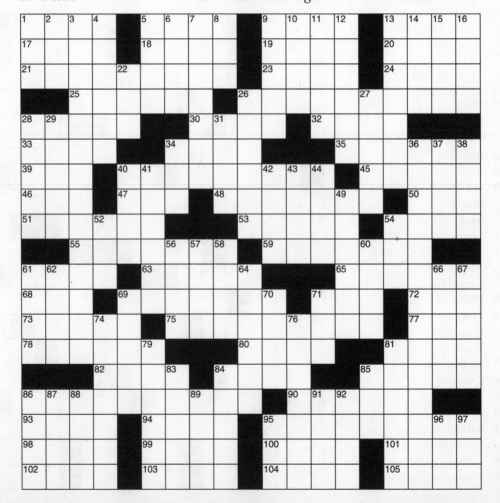

ACROSS

1 Pungency
5 Deplete
10 Like many cheeses
14 Manzanillo Mrs.
17 U.S. border lake
18 Bellini opera
19 El __, Calif.
20 Small degree
21 Military scenario?
23 Interrogate
24 Blvd. relative
25 Boy king
26 Political patronage
27 Royal pronoun
28 Part of a process
29 Service
30 Academe growth
31 Bid's partner
33 Venerated one
34 Household
36 Wounded __ (1890 battle site)
37 Outburst
39 About half a military month?
42 Sausage type
45 Bar
48 Scintilla
49 Street weapon
51 Fast-food item
52 Cajole
53 Sadat
54 Affectation
55 Composer Shulamit
56 Misjudge
57 Hairpin turn
58 Title for Churchill
59 Compass pt.
60 Junkyard dog
61 Salt Lake city team
63 "Ivanhoe" writer
66 Tropical rodent
67 MacGraw in movies
68 Sayers of football
69 Roof overhang
70 Actor Theodore
71 Harass
73 Wearied of military life?
76 Possessed
78 Catafalque
79 Garb
83 Palmer, to fans
85 Wrong
87 Ending for normal or formal
88 Gun, as an engine

89 Truth
90 Crochet
91 Boss of a shield
92 Threshold in time
93 Nabokov title
94 Hoodoo
95 Military courier?
98 Word with top or toe
99 Not aweather
100 "__ Kick Out of You"
101 Hum
102 Aurora
103 Promise
104 Car model
105 __ deucey

DOWN

1 Nasal membrane
2 Provoke
3 Attend
4 Far Eastern holiday
5 Expose
6 Compunctious
7 Actor Estrada
8 "Man in boo"
9 Contrived
10 Ave __ vale
11 Harvest-time arrangement
12 Discordia
13 Gross part: Abbr.
14 Rest period at a military site?
15 Go a-preying
16 Handy
22 Tap
27 Acceptable
28 Computer key
31 Writer Brookner
32 Singer Bob ("Night Movies")
33 Ira Levin novel
35 Sly as __
36 Sense
38 "__ from St. Nicholas"
40 Showy stuff
41 Recipe abbr.
43 Subtlety
44 Temper
45 Polar phenomenon
46 "There's __ against it"
47 Military headwear
50 Entertained, in a way
53 Goggle-eyed

57 Ormandy
62 Extra-dry
63 Tourney round
64 Horn and Hattaras
65 Completed
66 Panthers' coll.
70 "Nobody __" (1972 hit)
72 Heckle
74 Slightly
75 Nutritional hot item
77 Actress Blythe
80 Conciliatory
81 Esteem
82 Rock's __ Brothers
83 "__ worse than death"
84 Milieu for Fred Allen
86 Heterogeneous
87 "__ man who wasn't there . . ."
90 Heavy weight, for short
91 Secondhand
94 Mandible
95 "Encore!"
96 Historical period
97 Hoops group

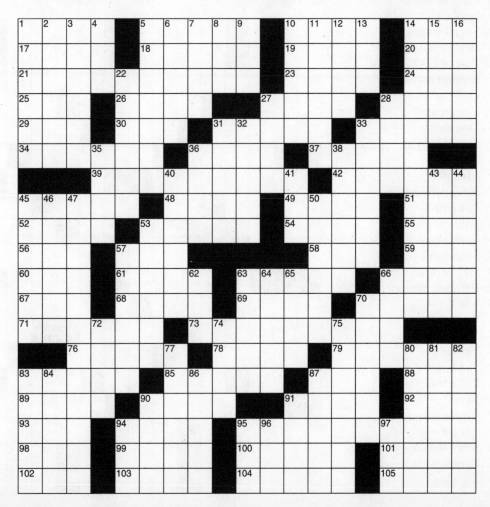

ACROSS

1 Equip
4 __ Carlo Menotti
8 Boone and Benatar
12 Radio acknowledgment
17 Conquistador's prize
18 Quince, e.g.
19 Tennis great
20 Upper crust
21 Like some sapsuckers
24 French painter
25 "A wink __ nod . . ."
26 Actor Ray et al.
27 Cantina appetizer
29 Certain punches
31 Annex
32 Cogency
33 Meadow plaint
36 Aaron's "__ A Hammer"
38 Sharp bend
40 Act of piracy
42 Started over
45 Abundant
47 Actress Reed
48 Assns.
49 Lampoon
52 Endless
54 Sugar ending
55 Actor Richard
56 Part of GATT
57 Kind of insurance
59 Old-timer
61 Competent
65 Doubleday
67 Singer Stubbs
68 Creek
69 Cheapen
72 Slow progress
74 Long time
75 Soul
76 Go it alone
78 Shipboard passage
80 Stalwart fellow
82 Painting category
85 Mark
86 Enzyme
87 Stubby and Danny
89 Fitting
91 Far-fetched
94 Calif. town
95 Benefit
97 Cry of dismay
98 Lessen
101 Smooth talkers
104 Bandage material
105 Big bird
106 Poi source
107 NL East player
108 Outskirts
109 Tennis units
110 Freshly
111 FRB, CAB, etc.

DOWN

1 Shade of blue
2 Castle or Worth
3 Fleming title
4 Mail abbr.
5 Keokuk's state
6 Saunter
7 Taunt
8 Friends
9 Words with recall
10 Day's events
11 Coupe relative
12 Doyle's "The __ League"
13 Table spread
14 Demerit
15 Flight-plan abbr.
16 Matter in law
22 Machine tools
23 Lounge
28 Topeka winter time: Abbr.
30 Cutting tool
32 Gazpacho
33 Mankato's st.
34 Sally Kirkland role
35 "A guy and __"
37 __ Plaines, Ill.
39 Aristocrat
41 "M*A*S*H" setting
42 Corm
43 Gaelic
44 Guare's "Six __ of Separation"
46 Kipper
50 Close
51 Sardonic
53 Little bit
56 "Riki-Tiki __"
58 Titles of respect
59 Wildebeest
60 Cry of fright
62 Horticultural klutziness
63 Wertmuller of films
64 Lenient
66 Bad names
69 Lady of Spain
70 Chem. endings
71 Hollywood Blvd. intersector
72 Asset
73 Neon, for one
74 Holiday drink
77 Former
79 Peeples of TV
81 Butcher's offering
83 Mansard roof feature
84 Athens rival
88 Approvals
90 Behemoth
92 "When __ You" (1977 hit)
93 Expenses
94 Brume
95 Grandfather, to Gaius
96 Traditional info
98 Ripen
99 Young fellow
100 Haul
102 Allow
103 Currently

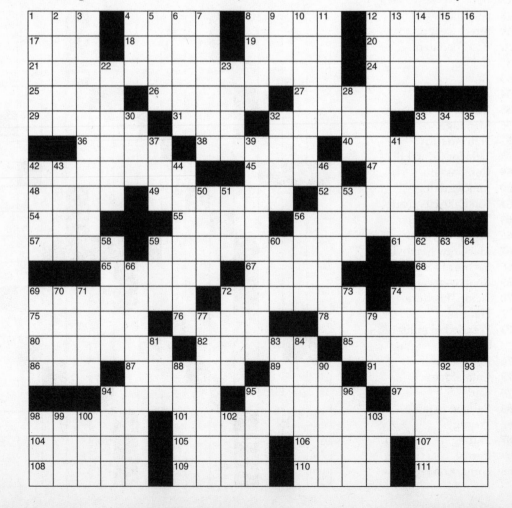

ACROSS

1 One of the Flintstones
6 Villain
12 Rapid
17 Booming
18 Harmonize
19 N. Amer. tree
21 Uses a cassette-player button
23 Posit
24 Exam
25 Actress Patricia et al.
26 Unfashionable accessory
27 Extreme ending
29 Brigand
32 Veer off course
33 Sound systems
37 Chula __, Calif.
39 Baba au __
42 Fish dish
43 Fax-machine button
47 Before
48 Elec. units
50 Branches
51 Actress Young
52 Brooder's perch
53 Alpine area
55 Greek letters
58 Conundrums
60 Mythical fight promoter
62 Hotbeds
64 Clamorous
65 Race ender
68 Etagère feature
70 Merchandise
73 Harvest goddess
74 Attention-getter
76 Profusion
78 Let live's partner
79 Free
80 Calculator button
84 Contend
85 Abstruse
87 Election list
88 Journalist Josephus
90 Encouraged
92 Come forth
95 Lair
96 Soiled
99 Lay off
101 Fan centers
105 Circa
106 VCR button
109 Bamboozled
110 Panama region
111 Sports place
112 Wide-eyed
113 Willing sorts
114 Lingerie item

DOWN

1 Drift
2 "Dies __"
3 Red-ink entry
4 Case
5 Kennel sound
6 Special
7 Fighting
8 Hackneyed
9 Kind of writing
10 Addition word
11 Argonne article
12 Health clubs
13 __ washy
14 Metamorphosing insect
15 Switch in some cars
16 Winter Janowitz
20 Pivotal
22 Barnstorming
26 More pretentious
28 Vast amount
30 Actor Tayback
31 Argots
33 Venetian blinds part
34 "Skip __ loo"
35 Microwave button
36 Attempt
38 Benefit
40 Exhort
41 Ryan and Tilly
44 Foretoken
45 Ceremonies
46 Equip
49 Type
54 Purple shade
56 Residue
57 Cubic meter
59 Paired
61 Comedian Mort et al.
63 Lean
65 Magnate
66 ". . . baked __"
67 Decorticated
69 Gastronome's delight
71 Infamous
72 Gets the picture
75 Title of respect
77 Merchant
81 Road map abbr.
82 Element No. 80
83 Chem. ending
86 Singer Clark
89 Happen genetically
91 Beanery
93 Actress Francis
94 Patron of 91 Down
96 Barrier
97 Eye part
98 Whirlwind
100 D.C. 100
102 Kind of car
103 Deflect
104 Keep
106 St. Louis summer time
107 Trireme implement
108 Stool pigeon

ACROSS

1 Subsidiary propositions
7 Evade
12 Childbirth method
18 Lancelot's lover
19 Bay window
20 Sweet Home's state
21 U.S. general
24 Cellar contents
25 __ mot
26 P.R. concern
27 Legal matter
28 Hershiser of baseball
30 Satisfied sound
33 Genesis name
35 Director of "Breezy"
40 Trifling
44 Sea Biscuit, for one
45 Cancel
46 Diva's showcase
47 Tokyo of old
48 Market
49 "__ the One" (Presley recording)
53 Beast of burden
54 Performance capper
58 Reagan-era name
61 Calls on
64 Homesteader
65 "The Birds Fall Down" author
69 Hush-hush
73 Mouths
74 Game of chance
75 Task force
78 Paddle
79 Frenzied
81 Balkan land of old
83 James or Jackson
85 Western capital
87 "Battle of Blenheim" poet
89 Texas city
91 Ceres
92 Tone down
93 Bat wood
96 Negatives
98 Allow
99 Writer Anne
103 British historian
109 Skier McKinney
110 Yellow stone
111 "... you can do __ better"
112 "The __" (1943 film)
113 Sordid
114 Alluvial deposits

DOWN

1 Ayres and Alcindor
2 Lamb
3 D.C. tourist magnet
4 Berle and Cross
5 Black bird
6 USN builder
7 Discouraged
8 Raw materials
9 Pluto
10 Become
11 O'Neill's "Desire Under the __"
12 Tree-climbing primate
13 Gardens of a sort
14 Torme
15 Gelling agent
16 Sector
17 Far reaches
22 Bicuspids' neighbors
23 Newspaper page: Abbr.
29 Hwy.
30 __ range (nearby)
31 "... that doesn't love __" (Frost)
32 Jan. 1 or Jul. 4
34 Actress Thurman
35 Kitchen toiler
36 N.J. city
37 Obdurate
38 Consult
39 Oil source
41 Sandarac tree
42 Shopping aid
43 Symbol of oppression
50 Unseld of the NBA
51 Humanities
52 Dirk
55 Hail
56 Defeat
57 Become: Suffix
59 Crying
60 Killer whale
62 Golfer Woosnam
63 "It takes __ tango"
65 Fracases
66 Silkworm
67 Good time
68 Throat complaint
70 __ Hashana
71 Mitigate
72 Deuce beater
76 Do something!
77 Noted hypnotist
80 Night deposit
82 Cable TV initials
83 Project
84 Deathless
86 Sacred formula
87 Campus org.
88 Surpass in teasing
90 Songwriter George M.
93 Proceedings
94 Kind of judgment
95 Domicile
97 Tipplers
98 Shiftless
100 "__ She Lovely?"
101 Final section
102 Slaughter
104 Aries
105 Kind of hold
106 Agcy. since 1970
107 Actress Dawber
108 Ed McBain tale

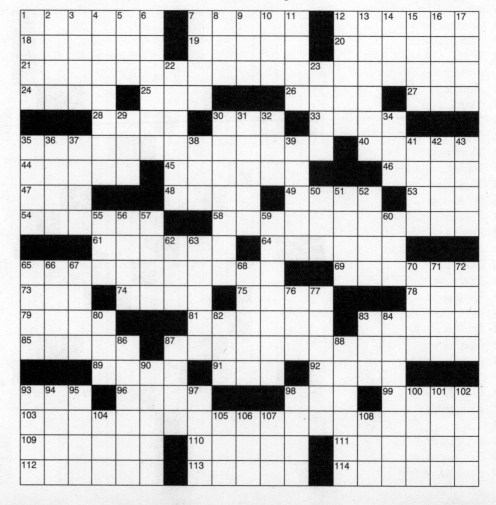

ACROSS

1 "The Outlaw" character
4 "__ above all . . ."
8 Mushroom feature
11 Iroquoian
17 Ordinal suffix
18 Hymenopter
19 Meadow mom
20 Michener book
21 "Song of the Earth" composer
24 Punctilio
25 Oeuvre element
26 Handed down yarns
27 "Hud" director
28 Withered
30 Keogh relative
31 Muscle problem
32 "__ corny as Kansas"
36 Catullus's muse
38 "Extremities" actress
41 Altar stone
42 Hebrew judge
43 Ala. town
44 Modernist
45 Kind of oil or water
47 Lee's "__ Right Thing"
49 Mass
51 Actress Alicia
52 Part of RSVP
53 Mme., in Madrid
54 Misery
55 Haggard tale
57 Bengali bigwig
61 "__ Man Answers"
64 Foot
66 "Exodus" character
67 Pakistani leader
69 Harem room
71 Suit
74 Wilder and Waugh
76 Called balls and strikes
78 Standout
79 Rougish
81 Pairings in this puzzle
83 Viewpoint
84 Film of 1946
87 Intimations
88 Breach
89 D.C.'s Fannie __
90 Epic ending
91 Other things
92 Oates book
94 Hiesman Trophy winner, 1990
96 "It's gonna be __ one"
99 Bryan, e.g.

102 O'Neill play
104 Item for Arbus
105 Sound from 19 Across
106 Actor Richard
107 Words with mode
108 Inflationary pattern
109 Actress Williams
110 Not fooled by
111 "Le Coq __"

DOWN

1 __ Park, N.Y.
2 "Just keep __"
3 Sitcom of early TV
4 Howard Hughes co.
5 __ de Grace, Md.
6 Words after 54 Across
7 Kind of relationship
8 Down-to-earth place
9 Thunderstruck
10 Part of MPG
11 TV news tool
12 Newspaper notice
13 Fervid
14 Exist
15 Steve Allen, e.g.
16 Singer Starr
22 African fly
23 Revolting
27 Weapon
29 Howls
31 Uris book
33 Computer list
34 Up and __
35 Plug
36 Austen novel
37 Cowboy's handhold
38 "Most Happy __"
39 Stars, to Caesar
40 Baylor home
46 Intents
48 "Hamlet" courtier
50 Tahiti wear
54 Vagary
56 Prefix for gram
58 Chemical compound
59 Betel palm
60 Calif. town
62 Keep progressing
63 Journalist St. Johns
65 Etc. relative

68 ". . . fetch __ of water"
70 Citrus drinks
71 Maine town
72 Resound
73 Perceptible quality
74 TV group
75 Deli offering
77 __ summer
80 Digit
82 Pachuca's state
85 Improved
86 Kelley's Sinatra book
91 Notify
93 Israeli dance
94 "__ no choice . . ."
95 Garden spot
97 Eur. capital
98 Despot
99 Mil. training initials
100 M.C. Hammer's metier
101 French friend
102 "Woman in the Dunes" author
103 Car of yore

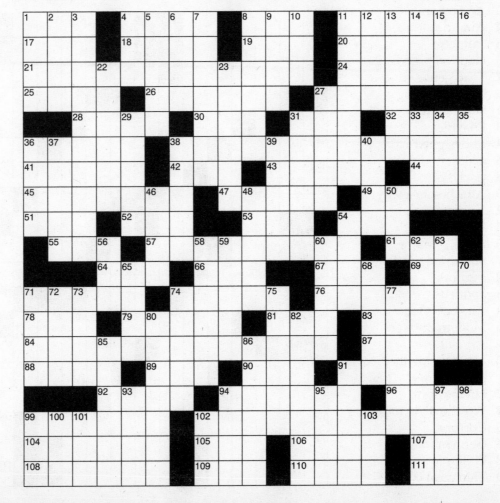

ACROSS

1 Depicts
7 Paris office-worker
12 Feed
17 Discount
18 Biblical prophet
19 Colored
20 Ornament
21 Cornmeal mush
23 Louise's movie cohort
25 Ooze
26 Writer Seton
27 Gazelle of Tibet
29 By the __ one's pants
32 Ticker tape abbr.
33 Lacrimal secretion
34 "__ Dimittis"
36 Bounty
38 Kind of light or stone
40 "__ World Turns"
42 Biscuit-dough concoction
44 Ziegfeld
47 Abjure
49 Rita __ Brown
50 And others
52 Auguries
54 Saltpetre
56 Nautical preposition
57 Toad genus
59 GWTW setting
61 Salamanders
63 Enzymes
64 Ill-designed
66 Chicken __
68 Cache
70 Attaches, in a way
72 Vogue
73 Painful
76 Sault __ Marie
77 Sun-dried snack
82 Purport
83 Spotted
84 Airs one's views
86 Modern Briovera
87 Art cult
90 Plcs. for sidelined players
92 Hit the horn
94 Word with to or do
95 Corrupt
96 German song
98 Philippic
100 Thin meat cuts
104 Sulking
107 Honshu city
108 Okla. city
109 Gawking
110 Familiar phrase for Ryan
111 Canary Islands' nation
112 Bent

DOWN

1 Theater section
2 Turkish title
3 Breakfast choice
4 Snack
5 Grove growth
6 Merchant
7 Half a dance
8 Part of L.A.
9 Extreme endings
10 Calif. point
11 Star in Auriga
12 Pt. of CST
13 Heretofore
14 Cat __ tails
15 Malindi's land
16 Poet Guest
21 Cook up
22 "Couples" author
24 __ oui (but of course)
27 Growl
28 Yorkshire river
30 Triumphant cry
31 Physicist Enrico
35 Soft leather
37 __ Island, N.Y.
39 Prefix for physics
41 Chem. ending
43 Editor Bennett
44 Cooks' fleeting glimpse?
45 Biography
46 Dobbin's dinner
48 Explosive
51 Disconcerts
53 Woebegone
54 Southwestern Amerind
55 UFO riders, perhaps
57 Qualifications
58 Molecule, e.g.
60 Jazz snippet
62 RR stop
65 Existential option
67 Crackerjack
69 Behave
71 Obelisk
74 __ contendere
75 Raise
78 Recruits
79 Del __, Texas
80 Bowlines
81 Bigfoot's cousin?
83 Gazelle hound
85 Successive
87 Rum , for one
88 Dispatch boat
89 Singer Washington
91 Arrangement
93 __ macabre
97 Walter __ Mare
99 Certain info
101 Make lace
102 Words with recall
103 Neb. neighbor
105 Before
106 Actor Danson

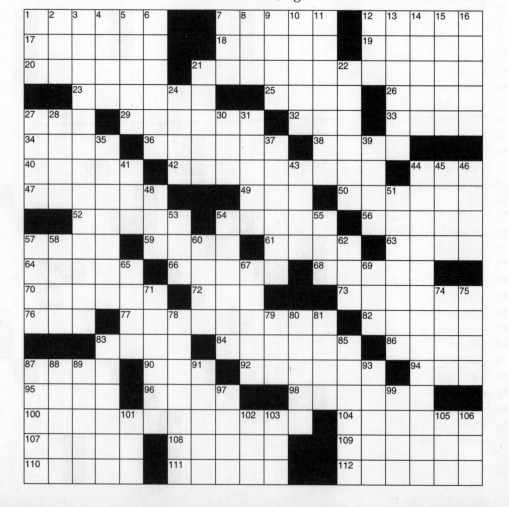

ACROSS

1 Lily unit
4 Third power
8 Erstwhile despot
12 Suspect
17 Granada gold
18 __ for one's money
19 Writer Morrison
20 Baby food
21 Journal
22 With "the", facts of life
25 Collect
27 France's longest river
28 Lacking
29 Carry on
30 Kowtow
31 Biblical verb
32 Melodrama sound
35 Sags
37 Composer Alban
39 Time of day
40 Wide open
42 Günter Grass novel
45 Battery terminal
46 Coarse
48 Turned over
49 DMZ, for one
50 Stir up
51 Count
52 Some
53 Speedy
54 Stir up
56 Contemptuous cry
59 Fish dish
60 Lofty thoughts
62 Staminate
63 Tampa neighbor
66 Liken
67 Adornment
68 Kind of story
70 Refused
71 Formicary group
72 Cain's kin
73 Bob or weave
75 __ judicata
76 Cage components
78 Salamander
79 Gaelic
82 Marinate
83 Hearth
85 African antelope
86 "The __" (Rolling Stones song)
91 Grampus
92 AWS tool
93 Simon
94 Bulrush
95 Compete
96 Painter Edward
97 Major __
98 Auto pioneer
99 Photo abbr.

DOWN

1 Kind of bear
2 Essence
3 Kind of show
4 Urban cruisers
5 Psychic Geller
6 Bag material
7 Equips
8 Navigation aid
9 Whet
10 Plus
11 Slugger's cue
12 Depleted
13 Centers of activity
14 Exist
15 Actress Ruby
16 Green light
23 Offense
24 Holbrook
26 Bit of progress
30 Daze
31 Fay of films
32 Personification
33 English river
34 Engendered
36 Unified
37 Cotton mass
38 Delicate
39 Devout
40 Mideast strip
41 Momentarily
42 Appraisal
43 Bedeck
44 Breakwater
46 Split-up spouses
47 Expert
50 Actress Burstyn
51 Decree
53 Cheese type
55 Pilcorn
56 Military-policy choice
57 Out of the wind
58 Determined
59 Cries of fright
61 Tedious
62 Combined
63 Blemish
64 Pitch
65 Certain stats
66 Wanes
67 Clash
69 "... a __ stormy night"
70 Modicum
73 "From __ Eternity"
74 Wondrous
76 S. Afr. group
77 River to the Rhine
78 High degree
80 Corrosive ester
81 Shine
82 Yankton's st.
83 Take __ view of
84 Manche town
85 Proponents
86 Pipe down
87 Taro dish
88 Ltd. relative
89 Modernist
90 Atty.'s degree

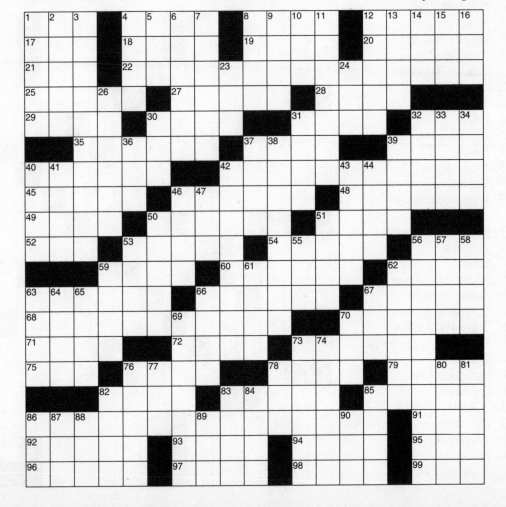

ACROSS

1 Garden pest
6 Iraqi city
11 Soprano
17 Shores
19 Take the lid off
20 Pay out
21 !
23 Rodeo ropes
24 Cow's milk beverage
25 Dickens's "Hard __"
27 __ tizzy
28 Ger. article
30 Talents
33 Joyous
36 Life force
38 Sp. river
39 Plus
40 Build
43 James Bond adversary
45 Potential
47 Rum drink
48 Rubicon, to Caesar
50 __ favor
51 Savvy
52 Stain relative
53 Chem. ending
54 Trig function
55 King mackerel
56 Guy of hockey
59 Persuaded
61 Musical windup
62 Make __ (emphasize)
63 Winglike
64 Frigid
65 Cambodia's Lon
66 Poorly
68 Arena arbiter
69 Explosive
70 Where change takes
  place
75 Certain kitchenware
77 Pathetic
78 Toot
79 Old man, to Ovid
80 Poetic twilight
81 Cheese type
83 Tonsorial subject
84 Costumes, informally
86 Persist in
88 Lbs.' big brothers
89 Guevara
91 "Gloria __"
93 Directions starter
95 Torment
98 Heavy
  cross-examination

103 ". . . blackbirds
  baked __"
104 Finish
105 Father of the Titans
106 Obvious
107 Calif. pt.
108 Bureaucratic abbrs.

DOWN

1 High card
2 Word in old curses
3 Cuts loose
4 Rhodes, for one
5 Cudgel
6 Reservation
7 Cuckoo
8 Glaswegians
9 Indian princess
10 Rendezvous
11 Okla. city
12 Nucleic acid
13 Endings for wait and
  work
14 Irrelevant
15 Trotsky
16 Actress Martinelli
18 Beam

22 Fit for farming
26 Yore, old-style
28 Weather term
29 Buck ending
31 In anger
32 Portly
34 Rend
35 Silkworm
37 Woodworking tool
39 __ Arbor
41 Illinois city
42 On the __ one's
  tongue
44 Miniature
46 Palindromic
  preposition
47 Composite
49 Copal and amber
50 School of seals
54 Plot
55 Moslem official
56 Songbirds
57 Coeur d' __, Idaho
58 Blame
60 Fall mo.
61 Ice cream flavor
65 Compass reading

67 Aspiring LCDRs
69 Theme
70 Particle
71 Go by
72 Addresses
73 Darmstadt denial
74 Suggestions
76 Neckline style
77 Certain military
  student
80 Org. since 1970
82 Formosa Strait
  island
85 Disturbed
86 Youngster: Sl.
87 Aquarium fish
89 Semiconductor
90 Maui town
92 Descartes
94 Vascular
  membranes
96 Emulate
97 Fault
99 Vt. neighbor
100 Happy times
101 Kernel
102 Draft org.

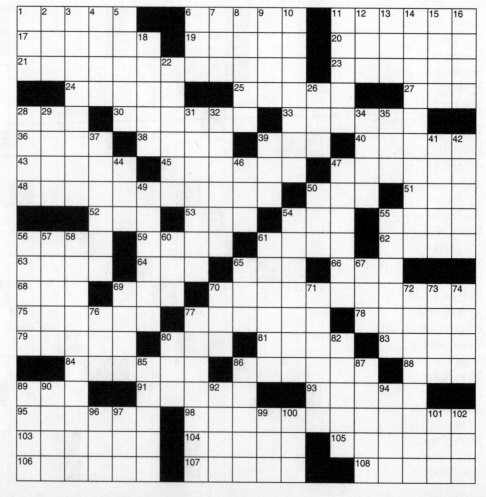

ACROSS

1 Overcrowded
7 Prefix for goat
12 Well nigh
18 Armpit
19 Spectrum element
20 Hate
21 Insurgents
22 Garb for conductors?
24 Chou __
25 Hold back
26 Formed a lap
27 Recipe abbr.
28 Midi time
29 Think
31 Wd. with Cal or Texas
33 Sci. sessions
35 Horace's hope
36 A DiMaggio
38 Safari stops
42 Stone, for one
43 Prevaricated
44 Garb for yellow
   journalists?
46 Ben Jonson play
48 Survive
49 Buncombe
50 Playful
51 June affair
53 Model Carol
54 Swampy places
55 Male swan
57 Circuit
59 Fajardo frau
61 Ariz. city
64 Hallucinogen
66 Word with where or
   when
68 S.C. town
72 Porter's cousin
73 Gardener's art
75 Attribute
77 Wear for candy makers?
79 Cart
80 Actress Joanne
81 Wrap up
82 Cry to Manolete
83 Recondite
84 "Ain't No Woman Like
   the One __"
85 Actress Young
87 Hoods' weapons
89 Dining area
90 Prefix for culture
93 Publicity sketch
95 Discharge
96 Wed on the run

99 Wear for excavating
   engineers?
102 Cromwell
103 Rammed
104 Fr. city
105 Rome's Via __
106 "__ of Honey"
107 Salved
108 Gets up

DOWN

1 Foal's mom
2 Bullocks
3 Wear for a clergy
   member?
4 Barn sounds
5 Songwriter Greenwich
6 Ger. article
7 Abraded
8 Raccoon relatives
9 Unfamiliar
10 Party hack
11 Goes wrong
12 Like bats and birds
13 Israeli town
14 Actor Walter
15 Singer Redding

16 "Old" dog of song
17 Hardy protagonist
23 Hot cereal
25 Nursery rhyme
   name
30 Abridge
32 Toll
33 Aetna output
34 Old struggle
35 Sermon subject
37 Spheroidical
39 Woodman, to Hansel
40 Collar style
41 Fast flyers
43 In __ parentis
44 Harvests wood
45 Beach Red craft
47 Type size
48 Sound with pa-pa
52 Kind of tire
54 Just
56 Alliance
58 Campus growth
60 Suggestive
61 Gender abbr.
62 Jewish month
63 Type of lily

65 "With a silver __
   one's mouth"
67 Least common
69 Wear for
   pediatricians?
70 Sp. river
71 Gender abbr.
73 Larch, e.g.
74 Sweetsop
76 Devitalize
78 Boosts
79 Created
83 Little indentation
84 Big Ten team
86 Tolerate
88 Mends
89 Conger-catcher
90 '70s rock group
91 Oversupply
92 Pro __
94 Leer at
97 Fountain of music
98 Cupid
100 Hanoi holiday
101 OSS successor
102 Items for Ovid's
   omelets

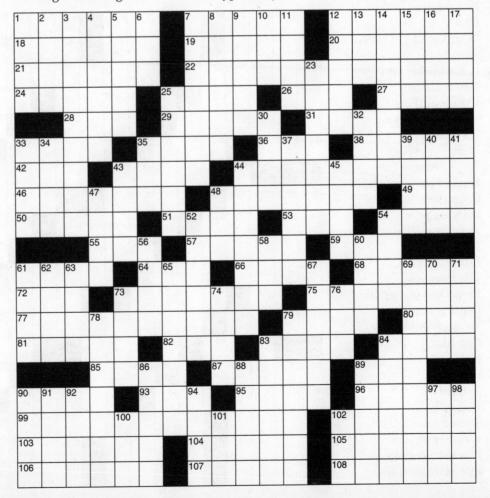

ACROSS

1 Undoing
5 Urchin
9 Trepidity
13 Proceedings
17 Wroth
18 "The Four Seasons" director
19 Classic bad guy
20 Dirk relative
21 A people-loving Gumbel?
24 Inoculation material
25 Touch-y fellow?
26 Cancel
27 Actor Robert's kin
29 Staves off
31 Civilized
33 Product
34 Buntline
35 Writer Levin
37 Blue-chip ratings
39 Gambling initials
40 An agitated Lebowitz?
44 Calls down (on)
47 Fast-food option
50 James's "The Soul Beneath the __"
51 Dial
53 "One Good __" (1991 film)
54 "... a bushel and __"
56 Actress Nancy
59 Cream puff dish
61 Manhattan buyer
63 "See you"
65 "Cat __ Tin Roof"
66 "... __ robins"
68 Kind of train or wheel
70 Corpulent
71 Irish sea god
72 Actor Bogosian
74 Rapier
76 Little leftovers
77 Life force
79 Peron and Gabor, hard to pin down?
83 "__ Lazy River"
85 Constantly
86 Fix
87 Burrow
90 Affront
93 Dodge
96 Setting
98 Weather total
100 Peter Shaffer play
102 Interstate accesses
103 "So that's the thanks __!"
104 A fatherly Boone?
107 Fr. department
108 Suggestion
109 Crude guy
110 __ majeste
111 Lashed
112 Arrangement
113 Concordes
114 "... a wink and __"

DOWN

1 Part of BMOC
2 Get there
3 Requisite
4 Entertainer Bergen
5 Wouk subject
6 Caesar's other things
7 "Since __ Have You" (1959 hit)
8 Creatures
9 Minimal covering
10 Corn unit
11 Long in the tooth
12 Jolly __
13 Fielder's stats
14 Heavenly singer-actress?
15 Alpine area
16 Cry at sea
22 Up and doing
23 Flowering shrub
28 Modernist
30 Monterrey Mmes.
32 Caliginous
36 "Diana" singer
38 Trolled
40 Concentrate
41 Cash drawer
42 Mother-__
43 Parental admonition
45 Talk-show participant
46 Puts down
47 Peppery dish
48 Op-ed writer, often
49 Hackman the charitable?
52 Pro __ publico
55 Predatory bird
57 Flight-plan abbr.
58 Mideast desert
60 Sp. capes
62 Split
64 Kind of trick or tow
67 Heat or Suns
69 __-do-well
73 Spelunker's place
75 Sinister
78 Erupted
80 Quite a few
81 Combatant of 1991
82 Antediluvian shopping center
84 Brew
87 Abate
88 Hit song for Marty Robbins
89 Made a home
90 __ box (the tube)
91 Pola of Hollywood
92 Lukewarm
94 Twin mechanisms
95 Certain bonds, for short
97 Lily type
99 Infamous name
101 Rabbit's tail
105 Kind of ball or party
106 Elevs.

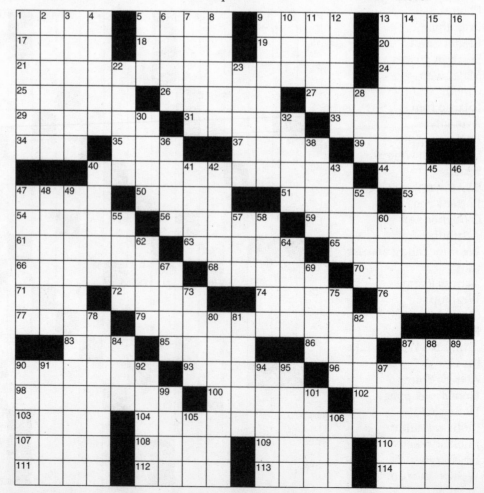

ACROSS

1 Long
5 "Ivanov" character
10 Brook
16 Senses
18 Filter
19 __ l'oeil
20 Tossed around ideas
22 Not so stringent
23 Turf
24 Old violin man
25 Court award
27 Stunted growth
29 Singer Bobby
31 Friend to François
32 Chem. for one
35 Croquette
37 CPA's inference
40 "__ moi le deluge"
41 Beer ingredient
42 Circuit
43 Shirk alternative
44 Portico
45 Grecian growth
46 City map abbrs.
47 Bobby of golf
48 Heavy load
49 Variety
50 Go it alone
52 Kramden's place
53 Chang's brother
54 Diver-philosopher?
57 Brown with a band
60 Farce subject
61 Diogenes's burden
62 Con's vote
63 Epoch
64 Sgt. Friday's quest
67 Gatsby
68 Pittance
69 "Piece of cake"
70 Cosmetic ingredient
71 Acquire
72 Strike breaker
74 A __ stand on
75 Don Adams role
78 Triumphant one
79 Printer's measures
80 Remick
81 Actress Lupino
82 Decimal number
83 Soft sound
86 "__ the Champions"
88 Jokester
91 Fabric patterns
93 Genius's hair application?
96 Evening affair
97 Happened to
98 "Louise" portrayer, 1991
99 Stereo gear
100 Derisive
101 Greek letter

DOWN

1 DOD installations
2 King mackerel
3 Willful
4 Whitney
5 __ free
6 Airport event
7 School yr. part
8 Took note
9 "A Rose __ Baby Ruth"
10 Befog
11 Kind of hero
12 American beauty
13 EPA concern
14 Simian
15 Mal de __
17 Entraps
18 Wild guess
21 Obscenity
26 __ a hatter
28 Durrell book
30 Phone abbr.
33 Heart
34 Inventory for printers
35 Social group
36 Writer Sinclair
37 Child's game
38 Singer John
39 Ark groupings
41 Baseball's Schmidt
45 Show off in the gym
46 Mistake
47 Voir dire selectees
49 Fateful date
50 Sailing brace
51 Resistance unit
52 Actor Bridges
55 Congreve's output
56 Protuberance
57 Like savvy skirt designers?
58 Muse for Marceau
59 Taste
60 Mess hall melange
64 Former TV series
65 Astronaut Shepard
66 Shouter in a shell
67 Dixie drink
68 Deliberated
69 Religious group
71 Consecrates
72 Blue
73 Progressed slowly
74 Hotel supply
76 Omitter of a sort
77 Actress Helen
78 Ralston of films
82 Shadow
84 Rent
85 Wanes
87 Model Macpherson
89 Med. school course
90 Actress Rowlands
91 Seattle hrs.
92 Singer Rawls
94 "__ were you . . ."
95 Bucket

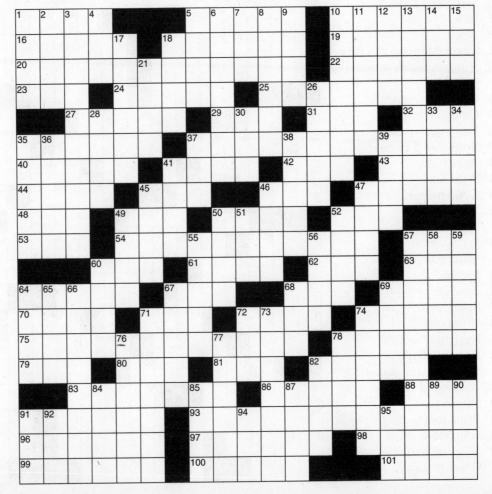

ACROSS

1 Type of house, for short
7 Bucks and bulls
12 Cos __, Conn.
15 Peppard TV role
17 Eaglets' homes
18 Actress Mia
19 Surprise
20 C-food seafood dish
22 Walking distance
23 Prefix for valent
24 Primordial
25 Erstwhile cpl.
28 In reserve
30 Pizza-sauce ingredient
33 C-food seafood dish
37 Exclude
38 Power agcy.
41 Examine
42 New Deal initials
43 Balustrade
45 Strikebreaker
46 Spinless cactus
48 Unsuave sort
50 Skewer
52 Scent
55 Slaughter
57 Jack of films
58 Dry
61 Vegetable soup of a sort
64 Virginia Beach summer hrs.
65 Light or Arden
67 Colonnade
68 Eur. interest rate
70 Brass and bronze
72 Anent
74 Wild ass
78 Constructed
79 Places
81 Doze
84 ". . . __ man who wasn't there"
85 Just so
86 Card game
87 Spun sugar
90 Gives off
93 Designer Geoffrey
94 Sinuous shape
95 California missionary
97 "Silkwood" actress
99 Smear
102 Bagel topping
105 Unreliable
109 "If __ be so bold . . ."
110 Grew anxious
111 Districts
112 Maglie of baseball
113 Pledge
114 Give in

DOWN

1 TV initials
2 Back-stabber
3 Sp. queen
4 Bucolic business
5 Play part
6 Writer Hilaire
7 Mythical sea creatures
8 Certain Semite
9 Above-board
10 Frightful cry
11 Compass pt.
12 Yuppie dessert
13 Spoken
14 Cosset
16 Actor Wynn
17 Gum arabic sources
18 Begone
21 Expensive
25 Bit of bunko
26 Mucilage
27 Young fellows
29 Mideast land: Abbr.
31 Kimono accessory
32 Niger neighbor
34 Insulation material
35 Like pasta
36 Maine campus town
39 Efficacious
40 Red as __
44 ". . . Just __ of cherries"
45 Health club
47 Card game
49 "Merry Widow" composer
51 Inane
53 Minneapolis Mme.
54 Madcap
56 Reagan plan for the DOD
58 Junctures
59 Chou __
60 Boxed breakfast item
62 Shaped like a dunce cap
63 Nigerian native
66 Runner Sebastian
69 "__-Lama-Ding-Dong"
71 Slipped
73 Set to race
75 Drummer Krupa
76 Flight-plan abbrs.
77 Beams
80 Basic integer
82 Blind ambition
83 Mull over
86 Pacific island
88 More portly
89 Approaching
91 CAT scan relative
92 Public display
95 Chem. and biol.
96 Bombeck
98 "__ Rebel" ('60s song)
100 Exhort
101 Wicket bar
103 Dollar pts.
104 Cleave
106 Kind of dance or hold
107 Du Maurier's "Jamaica __"
108 Dallas winter hrs.

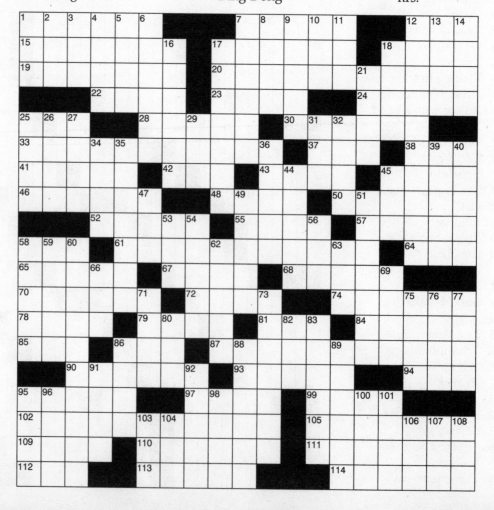

ACROSS

1 Comedy-club sound
5 Domicile
9 Cable-TV initials
12 About
16 Burden
17 Type type: Abbr.
18 Biblical preposition
19 Galley notation
20 No winding road
23 Integument
24 Command to Fido
25 Actress Perlman
26 Inveigh
27 Storied swordsman
28 Float
30 "Mildred Pierce" author
31 "It must have been something __"
32 Deem it proper
34 Rack's companion
35 Double curve
36 Health club
39 Furthermore
40 Skeptical credit analyst?
43 Scurry
44 Unless, in law
45 Forsake
46 Fuzz
47 Destructive carpenter
48 Least tainted
50 Hippocampus
52 Op. __
53 Value system
55 Bill
56 Professed
60 Siouans
62 New Deal initials
65 Site of Koko Head
66 Clinching point
68 Corrida cries
69 Bunch
70 Tweeter problem?
73 Kind of plan or sample
74 Sp. queen
75 Lennon's widow
76 Anthem start
77 Crevice
78 Ice-cream quantity
80 W. Hem. abbr.
81 Vernacular
82 Prickly pears
84 Aleutian isle
85 Senior member
86 S.A. port, for short
89 Will __ wisp
90 Hollywood discard
93 Impend
94 Holly
95 Entertainer Ed
96 __ many words
97 Elec. units
98 Appropriate
99 Slim but strong
100 Writer James

DOWN

1 "Bonanza" character
2 Part of ABM
3 Jilted lover's complaint
4 Contented-cow link
5 Historian Gilbert
6 Different
7 __ Hari
8 Loop lines, for short
9 "__ Crowd" ('65 hit song)
10 Coward
11 Boy king
12 Neckwear
13 Retailing commotion
14 Rend
15 Bismarck
18 __ thought
21 Monte of baseball
22 Characteristic
27 Actress Pitts
29 For the fun __
30 Abstract painter
31 Sets apart
32 Actress Thompson
33 Actor Richard
34 Lawn repairer
35 Singer Brickell
37 Feedlot areas
38 Comedian Johnson
40 Heading: Abbr.
41 Fiendish
42 Mass
44 Vitamin, for one
48 Zadora
49 However, for short
51 Owns
52 Troglodyte's tool
54 Weather map line
56 Be overfond
57 Merit
58 Bargain meat cut?
59 Outward, in combinations
61 Word with whiz
62 Jewelry mixup
63 Menial worker
64 Off target
67 Hotel levy
69 Family
71 Burt's ex-wife
72 Deplete
73 Zurich coin
77 Elegant
79 Shopping cart contents
80 "__ Grows in Brooklyn"
81 Passover rite
82 Soft drink
83 Bit
84 Rights org.
85 Prefix for tasse
87 __ dixit
88 Plains Indian
90 Bream of baseball
91 Cat feature
92 Creek

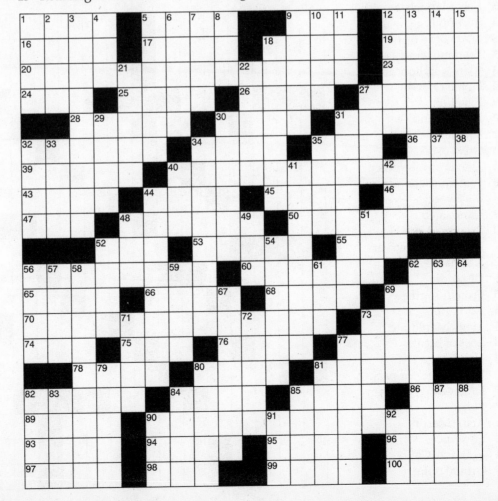

ACROSS

1 Holy Grail seeker
8 Write cryptograms
14 Boring tools
18 Scenery spoiler
19 Close one, in quoits
20 Begone
21 Fitness expert
22 Jodie-Julia team
24 Kind of piece or point
25 Former Mideast initials
26 Little bits
27 Go-between: Abbr.
30 He's mate
32 __ net (bait catcher)
34 Launder ending
35 Billy-Lucille team
38 Tool's companion
39 Fall guy
42 Reckoning
43 Bombeck
44 Kid of films
46 Eye part
47 Gardner
48 Man from Malmo
50 Debt instrument
51 Spread through
53 Poet Mandelstam
54 In conflict
55 Team of two Shelleys
59 Pronouncements
63 Clam's siphon
64 Home remedy
69 Function
70 Accra's land
72 Fall mo.
73 Great expectation
74 __ and out the other
76 Pasternak character
78 Raft wood
79 Dance step
80 Proofread
81 Justice Hugo-writer Norman team
83 Discordia
85 Protein source
86 Corn unit
87 Main, Maple, etc.
88 Loss of breath
90 Hawk cage
91 Kind of pick or pack
93 Singer Al, W.C. team
97 Putrid
101 Actor Martin
102 Introduces
103 __ Beach, Calif.
104 Orbital point
105 Outmigration
106 Kind of shopping

DOWN

1 Turn
2 Firth of Clyde feeder
3 Grassy ground
4 Used-car disclaimer
5 Candor
6 A. Franklin
7 Ger. article
8 Puck, for one
9 Modernist
10 Nonchalant
11 Ready to use
12 Roe, e.g.
13 Fumble
14 "__ in the Dark"
15 Justice Byron-writer C.P. team
16 Ms. Montes
17 Does lawn work
23 Adduced
27 Misbehave
28 Momentous
29 10th president
31 Football team
32 "Casablanca" name
33 In time-honored style
34 Ger. article
36 Eastern European
37 Intimate apparel item
38 Flop
40 Proceedings
41 Equal
44 Clan
45 Ergate
47 Fuss
49 Conspiratorial gesture
52 Ga. neighbor
53 Irving's __ Meany
54 Onager
56 Growl
57 Besmear
58 Nonsense
59 Coffee category
60 N.Y. campus
61 Glenn meets Eliot
62 Royal-straight component
65 Siamese descendant
66 Bakery offerings
67 Dismayed
68 Rick of auto racing
70 Thous
71 JFK's inaugural omission
72 Grampus
75 __ water
77 Blue-chip rating
78 Supermarket marking
81 __ over (stunned)
82 Non-winning racehorse
84 Della of songdom
85 Mind
88 City on the Jumna
89 Bolster
90 Flirtatious one
92 Life force
94 Service charge
95 Actress Joanne
96 Draft initials
97 Conquistador's quest
98 Mich. neighbor
99 Japanese salad vegetable
100 Appeaser

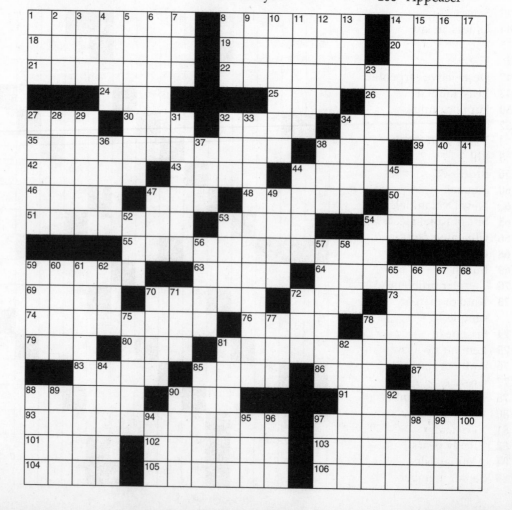

ACROSS

1 Kind of string or tie
4 Coolidge's VP
9 Locking device
13 Hair style
17 Words with recall
18 Seine-side "then"
19 Poet Sexton
20 Empty
21 Buddy-George team
23 Hog relative
24 Auto part
25 Potential
26 Stephen-Carrie writing team
28 Skydiver's aid
30 Refueling area
31 Caesar's words
32 Aggregate
33 Charitable concern
34 Marine killer
36 Bitty bite
39 Realization
40 Wise
42 Whack
43 Portico
44 Trouble in mind?
46 Lush and green
48 Interfaces
49 Poetic preposition
50 Tahiti dish
52 Western Indian
53 Baseball family
54 Actor Ron-poet Robert team
58 Incongruous
61 Screamer's sound
62 Ltd. relative
63 Price bearer
66 Winsome type
67 Cavorting
70 "It's __ thing!"
72 Waste allowance
73 Hershiser of baseball
74 Freshly
76 Fr. articles
77 Needle feature
78 Constantly
79 Quid pro __
80 Rockies trees
82 Soap-opera subject
84 TV room
85 "__ ashes . . ."
86 Rapper M.C.-designer Edith team
90 Any port in __
91 Hibernia
92 Moore of movies
93 Entertainer Dinah-athlete Larry team

96 Film "darling"
97 Writer Murdoch
98 Ed of TV
99 Overmuch
100 Ooh followers
101 Flat bottom boat
102 December greeting
103 Layer

DOWN

1 Nonsense!
2 Sp. bear
3 Columnist George-actor Tyrone team
4 Ohio city
5 Einstein and Brooks
6 Circled
7 Formerly, old-style
8 Quiet!
9 Wont
10 Shortly
11 River hazard
12 Impeccable
13 Nautical cry
14 Actor Michael-writer Evan team
15 Stir up
16 River to the Baltic
22 Missing piece
26 Banter
27 Señor ending
28 Paul Harvey's milieu
29 Self produced
30 Buttress
33 Get on
34 Sports VIP
35 Back-comb
37 Whit
38 Circulate
41 Tel __
42 Cloy
43 Dried up
45 Pinnacle
47 Dark
48 Gathering place
51 Antediluvian
53 Receptacle
54 Please
55 Certain reeler
56 Serious
57 Noxious
58 Entr' __
59 Suppress
60 Writer Danielle-philosopher John Stuart team

63 Broadway's Tommy-Buffalo Bob team
64 Common contraction
65 Painting preparation
67 Prefix for fix
68 Goat-god
69 Numero __
71 Top quality
73 Took to excess
75 Spendthrift
78 Holiday occasion
79 Logician's letters
81 Blacksmiths, at times
83 Amor's conquest
84 Rayed flower
85 Unanimously
86 Gehenna
87 Diva's chance to shine
88 Idol
89 Mideast prince
90 Chan's line
93 __ Luis Obispo
94 Lobster coral
95 Giovanni, e.g.

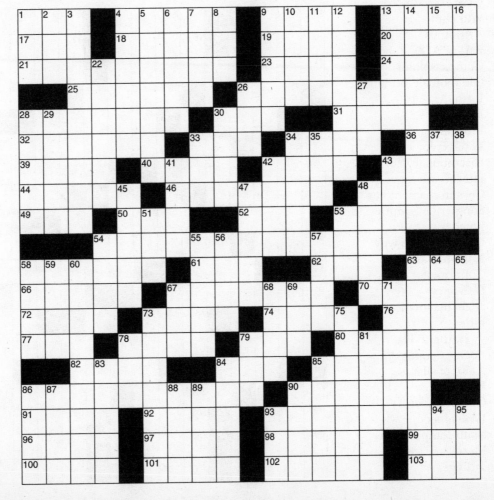

ACROSS

1 Past
4 Apple eater of note
8 Nimble
12 Garbage boat
16 Pumice
18 Terrible
19 Tupelo, e.g.
20 Actress Rogers
21 Sawed-off pyramid
23 Pine
24 Russian sea
25 Gambit
26 Barbecue item
28 Lome's land
30 Shout
31 Music halls
33 Spanish steel
35 "__ Joey"
37 TV creature
39 Sumeria's site
45 Spread
47 "__ for the Misbegotten"
48 Masher
49 Writer Dorfman
50 Taro dish
53 Gym exercises
55 War club
56 Attributes
59 Part of ADC
60 Compass point
61 Old football formation
64 Lush
67 Brother
68 Precisely
69 Water color
70 Discretionary
75 Fuel qty.
76 Certain champagnes
77 Songwriter Sammy
78 Pinch
81 Designate, in a way
83 Korean War area
87 Court matter
88 D.C. agcy.
89 Alabama town
90 Bide __
92 __ Harbour, Fla.
94 Puzzle diagram
97 Naldi of silents
99 Being
101 Old struggle
103 Worshipee
105 Math computations
108 Mariel's place
109 Tidings
110 "Trinity" author
111 Nonsense!
112 Maintain
113 18th Century philosopher
114 Match parts
115 Five-spot

DOWN

1 Elev.
2 Irving character
3 White House part
4 Wood-working tool
5 Vaya con __
6 Take __ (try to hit)
7 Renaissance family
8 NL East monogram
9 Etiquette
10 Truckee town
11 Safecracker
12 Wee, in Glasgow
13 Small __ friends
14 Gen. Bradley
15 Shrewd
17 ". . . two peas in __"
22 A lot to see
27 Tissue layer
29 Ceres
32 Common diphthongs
34 Rock group
36 Pungent
37 Historian Henry
38 San Marino money
40 Comeback
41 Lobster coral
42 Interlock
43 Hazel, for one
44 FB blockers-receivers
46 Honorarium
51 De Gaulle's agreement
52 "__ She Lovely?"
54 Duffer's concern
56 Figure on
57 Self
58 Booty
61 To's partner
62 Greek letter
63 Embassy grp.
64 Prepares to fight
65 Unconventional
66 Assignments
67 The end
69 Tributary
70 Fall mo.
71 Expression of disgust
72 Storied theater
73 Barley bristle
74 Disappoints
76 Ale man
79 Exist
80 Potter's aid
82 In the manner of
84 Tease
85 __ curiae
86 Character
91 Fabulist: Var.
92 Support
93 Fever symptom
95 Lemieux's milieu
96 Notion
98 Slightly
100 Decorative case
102 Suede feature
104 Normandy craft
106 Double curve
107 Bad act

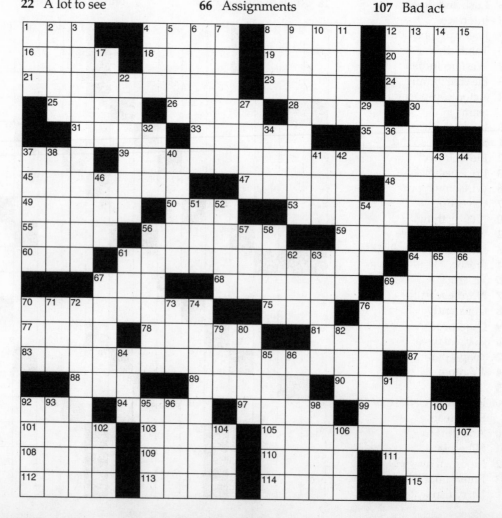

ACROSS

1 Madonna song subject
6 Stillness
10 Winglike
14 Kennel command
17 "Silas Marner" author
18 Singer Paul
19 Differ
20 Employ
21 Abandon
22 Nonalcoholic cocktail
25 Marceau's muse
27 Evil root of note
28 Stud
29 Beer ingredient
32 Business abbr.
34 Prefix for pass or plus
35 Exclude
36 __ streak (clicking)
38 Bursa
40 Spot
42 Barnabas, Ignatius et al.
45 Post-game summary
46 Stringed instruments
48 Pack away again
50 "__ went out from Caesar Augustus . . ."
52 Kind of punch
55 Actress Skye
56 Trevanian's "The Summer of __"
58 Writer Stoker
59 "The Woman __"
60 Lummox
63 Protective assignment
66 Before
67 List for MPs
69 Holy Roman emperor
70 Refuse
72 Punjab wear
73 Imbue with compassion
75 City in 92 Across
79 Actress Claire
81 Customary
83 Type of orange
84 Dry
85 Twist
88 "Nightmare" street
89 Office machine
90 Utterly
92 Nev. neighbor
94 Golden Rule word
96 Enamored of
97 Furthermore
99 Eggs on
101 Grain bane
103 Lunch item
106 Balcony
110 Holbrook
111 Garr of films
112 Pay to play
113 Actor Nolan
114 Chem. ending
115 Word with fine or lively
116 Baseball great
117 NL West player

DOWN

1 Take shape
2 __ de France
3 Creek
4 "The __" (B-52's hit)
5 Gang hanger-on
6 Must
7 Dump a rider
8 Hit the slopes
9 Detriment
10 Means of access
11 Strata
12 Pretentious
13 Sandwich choice
14 Elaborate emporium
15 "La __ Bonita"
16 Abound
23 Part of L.A.
24 Wall St. credential
26 Pretense
29 Israeli dance
30 Unified
31 Clip
33 Buddies
35 S'long
37 Belonging to Winfrey
39 Members' place
41 Be a busybody
43 Supply for 89 Across
44 Bergman, e.g.
46 Old Sri Lanka
47 Concerning
49 Misdeed
51 DDE's command
53 Batty
54 Unscrupled
57 Flight log abbrs.
59 King's "__ Late"
60 Kilns
61 Cognizant
62 Shipboard area
64 Biblical pronoun
65 __ Tafari
68 Ullmann
71 Soap-opera settings
73 Historical time
74 Humdinger
76 Film of 1932
77 "__ the message"
78 Prefix for space
80 Pussycat's shipmate
82 Political pardon
86 Browning
87 Summary
89 Machine part
91 Destiny
93 Ordinal setting
95 Copse components
97 Hurting
98 Part of S&L
99 Ripener
100 Suture
102 Stewpot
104 Day-time link
105 Sp. queen
107 Forget-me-__
108 Scottish river
109 Nuptials phrase

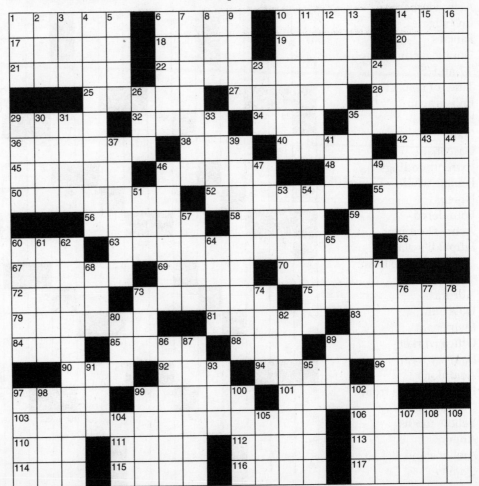

ACROSS

1 Fearless
5 Merchandise
10 Barter
14 Horse color
17 TV's Trebek
18 Motionless
19 "Today __ man . . ."
20 Nucleic acid
21 Double feature from '48 and '86
25 Change of a five
26 Sediment
27 Willie of films
28 Strolling spot in Paris
30 Light linen
33 N.C. St.'s conf.
34 Double feature from '49
41 Convention endings
42 Artistic summation
43 City on the Tiber
44 Cassowary
45 "__ Loves" (1961 film)
46 Certain cats
47 Onion relative
49 Somewhat
50 Actor Herbert
51 Investigate
52 Fancies
53 Double feature from '87 and '57
58 Titles of respect
59 Enlists again
60 Purpose
61 "Jane __"
62 Gasconade
63 Extreme endings
65 Female whale
68 Uraeus
69 Foundered
70 Actress Sommer
71 Fitipaldi's place
72 Double feature from '89 and '41
77 Aurora
78 Dole out
79 Lieutenant
80 Office worker
83 Bombay wear
85 Acidulous
87 Double feature from '72 and '91
94 Yellow moths
95 Angry
96 Atelier stand
97 Quality
98 Narrow passage
99 Far reaches
100 Milquetoast
101 Check

DOWN

1 Ozone, for one
2 Winner in Manila, 1975
3 Encountered
4 Bleeds
5 Riesling, e.g.
6 Updike's Rabbit
7 Tie type
8 Get it wrong
9 T. Williams character
10 Location
11 Means' companions
12 Fr. boyfriend
13 Verve
14 Visor
15 Singer Murray
16 Prattles
22 Kind of worm
23 "__ Angel" (1959 song)
24 Walk
28 Relieved cry
29 Prefix for dynamic
31 Parimutuel factor
32 "__ Happy Man"
33 "Don't look __!"
34 Asian holiday
35 "__ to bury Caesar . . ."
36 African antelope
37 Fresh
38 Iconoclast
39 Eskimo boat
40 Baloney!
46 Excellent
47 Tiptoed
48 Methods
49 Enoch's grandpa
50 Conn. town
51 Asset
52 How sweet __
53 Authority
54 Groucho's brother
55 Maine college town
56 Lynchian twins
57 Proceed in time
58 Farina
62 Scrooge's cries
63 Nev. town
64 Bowling game
65 Milk product
66 Plains Indian
67 Golly relative
69 Actress Kurtz
70 Dining area
71 "__ in the beginning . . ."
73 Newsman Arthur
74 Poi dish
75 Walker and Kramden
76 Cooper
80 Guzzle
81 Hymn pronoun
82 Bridge player
83 Hurtled
84 Puts in
86 Confederate
88 Samovar
89 Bali __
90 CIA forerunner
91 Unconscious
92 Limonite, e.g.
93 Beaver endeavor

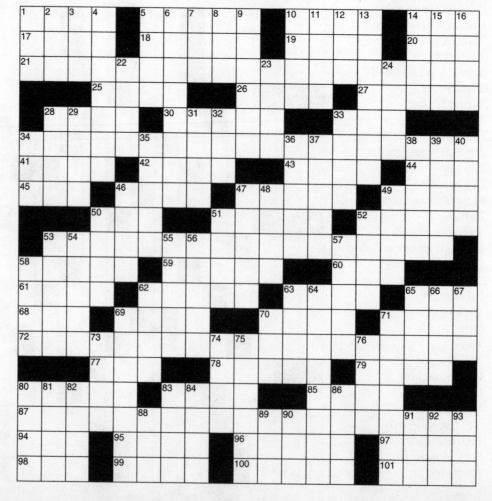

ACROSS

1 Matter
7 Alpine peak
12 Figure of speech
18 Inclines
19 Swain
20 Merchant
21 Frank Capra film
24 Shade tree
25 Sole
26 School grp.
27 __ out (get by)
28 Word with time or style
30 Ocasek of rock
31 Parish official
34 S.A. nation
35 Rose-colored view
41 Zero
42 Sultry
43 Cannes wave
44 Upstart
45 Tropical palm
47 Chalcedonies
49 Cede preceder
51 Neck piece
52 Actor Gulager
54 Evergreen
55 Bovine sound
56 Turn down
57 Legendary rock group
61 Writer McCarthy
63 Tryon's "Salem's __"
64 Pedro or Pablo
65 Superlative ending
66 "__ my brother's keeper?"
67 Top seed's advantage
68 "... many __ twixt the cup ..."
70 Light anchor
74 Shop tool
76 Sped
77 Guadeloupe, for one
79 Scepter
80 Dickensian figure
84 Purpose
85 Screens' counterparts
86 Ref. work
87 Wise and wary
88 Jap. salad ingredient
91 Skater Babilonia
92 Eur. capital
94 Launch site
95 Drifters hit, 1961
102 Kind of band
103 Walking __ (elated)
104 Inspire
105 Like a balalaika
106 Breaches
107 Cartridge

DOWN

1 Small cobra
2 Ziegfeld
3 Countenance capacities
4 Talus
5 Particular
6 Q-U link
7 Tony repast
8 Recline
9 Formosa Strait island
10 Ship-shaped clock
11 Vie
12 Low clouds
13 Writer Levin
14 "Same to you, __!"
15 Vain
16 Garlic relative
17 Gaelic
22 Imposes
23 Craving
28 Allende's "Eva __"
29 Eye part
30 __ Piedras, P.R.
31 Mo.-based church
32 As soon as
33 Hollywood initials
35 Although
36 Go __ (seize the day)
37 Disrobed
38 Plant firmly
39 Light gas
40 Hoary
46 Hurting
48 "... to buy __ pig"
49 Party hack
50 Heckled
53 Ill-natured
55 Actor Paul
56 Palm fruit
57 Vapid
58 Lobster coral
59 Golfer Nick
60 Glacial mound
61 Grain product
62 Canton caregiver
67 Parks of TV
68 Afflicts
69 Rock dove
71 Egregious
72 Summoning device
73 Whirlpool
75 Owns
76 Cigar holder
78 Headed
81 Manual labor
82 Ex-QB Tarkenton
83 Blue funks
87 Actress Lynley
88 G.I.s' places
89 Presley hit
90 Hebrew weight
92 "The wings __ eagle ..."
93 "M*A*S*H" cast member
94 Land on the Pacific
96 Big bird
97 Pittsburg's st.
98 United
99 Light touch
100 Practice
101 Wimbledon cry

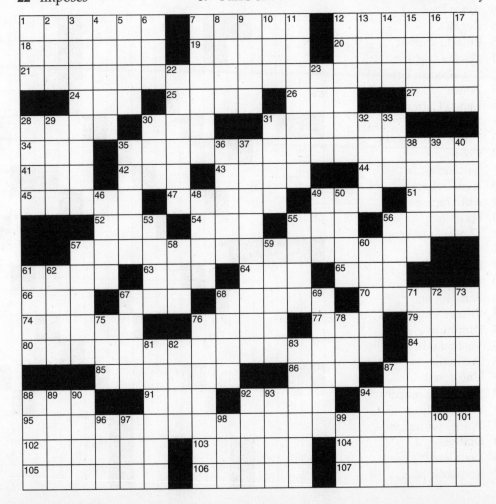

ACROSS

1 Hem's partner
4 Skating spin
9 Kind of drama
13 Existed
16 Job-safety org.
18 Unique
19 Czar, 1547-84
20 Utterly
21 Tornadoes
23 __ mind (don't worry)
25 Work party
26 Singer Clark ("Raindrops")
27 Actress Balin
28 Jug
29 Dining area
30 No gentleman
31 Opponent
32 Rocker Cocker
33 Select group
35 Cry at sea
37 Wouk's "The __"
41 Strutted
43 Kind of fish or bird
44 What vermin do
45 Belgian river
46 Actor Paul
48 Regalia
50 Buffalo's county
51 Piscine group
53 "__ Grecian Urn"
55 Zones
56 Lynda Carter role
59 VP of the '20s
63 Surpass in wagers
64 Chew on
69 Nucleic acids
70 Aves. relatives
71 Auto racing name
73 Feed crop
74 Three __ (full count)
76 __ gratia . . .
77 Leftovers
79 Ineffectual
82 Parliament
83 Printer's measures
84 Diminutive
85 Vast quantity
86 D.C. title
87 Untutored
89 Novelist's concern
91 Señor ending
92 Words with glance
93 Dialect
96 Ventilated
98 Romantic poet
100 Studio area
101 Part of AM
102 Succotash ingredient
103 Claim
104 Library admonition
105 Exploit
106 Fragrance
107 Weir

DOWN

1 "__ ja Like to Love Me?" (1938 song)
2 Court great
3 Coverup of sorts
4 Wooden basket
5 Moslem caliph
6 "Blue" occasion
7 Wound up
8 __ majesty
9 Sycophant
10 Tied
11 Haleakala product
12 Word with track or way
13 "The __" (1973 film and song)
14 Cosmetic ingredient
15 Aspersion
17 Russian sea
22 Purple shade
24 Do a dealer's job
30 Hammurabi's legacy
31 Healthy
32 Bon Jovi
33 U.S.N. addresses
34 Actor Bogosian
36 Greeting
37 Conn. city
38 Command to Fido
39 Vast expanse
40 Road map abbrs.
42 Modernist
43 Midshipman's counterpart
47 __ vivendi
48 Clumps
49 "__ Woman" (Reddy hit)
52 Cries of pain
54 Olympian Jesse
55 Rockport's cape
57 Forget-me-__
58 Match
59 Kind of poker
60 Caesar's years
61 Longfellow name
62 Connoisseur
65 "What __ bid"
66 Sports, ABC-style
67 Astringent
68 On one's __ (alert)
70 Barnyard mother
72 Hibernia
75 Welsh river
76 Gotcha!
78 Chaff
80 Shrewd
81 Firmly fixed
82 Golly
86 Marcus Aurelius, e.g.
88 Upon
89 Circulate
90 Ransom's "Here __ A Lady"
91 Actress Skye
92 Punching tools
93 Stage whisper
94 Willow
95 Bogus
97 Family member
99 Sportscaster Dierdorf

ACROSS

1 Discordia
5 Maxwell and Hudson
9 Ripoff
13 Pen points
17 Inclination
18 Landed
19 Kovacs's "Nairobi __"
20 ". . . to buy __ pig"
21 Noisome patroller?
24 Author of 83 Down
25 Summon
26 NASA vehicles
27 Issue
29 Sausalito's county
31 Go by
33 Writer Rice
34 With 57 Across, extravagant savagery
37 Chekhovian uncle
39 Timetable abbr.
40 Wicker willow
41 A Simpson
42 Kind of dance
45 Holbrook
46 Sierras, e.g.
47 Park in Maine
49 Officeholders
50 Sugar ending
51 Doyle's "__ of Identity"
52 Diving birds
54 Slap
57 See 34 Across
61 Pre-med subj.
62 Wall hanging
64 Rhythm's companion
65 Turn of phrase
67 Stone, for one
68 Danzig's land
70 Tennis term
72 Small stretcher
75 Born
76 Harpoon material
77 Merge
78 Marker
79 Writer Anya
81 TNUPs
84 Photographer Arbus
86 Scholarships
88 Virginia willows
89 Pack with pests
91 __ caliente
92 VIP transportation
94 Signal-giver

95 PAS
100 That: Sp.
101 Exigency
102 Comfort
103 Flank bones
104 "__ of Our Lives"
105 Fountain offering
106 Textile worker
107 Prefix for dynamic

DOWN

1 Nigerian native
2 Court official, for short
3 Devilish
4 Wonder to hear
5 Barrel
6 "I can't tell __"
7 Map abbr.
8 Outstanding
9 Thickset
10 Unrefined
11 Kind of lock or line
12 Status
13 To wit
14 Ego development, football-style
15 Admiral's boat
16 Guide
22 Cpl. and CPO
23 Adjust
28 Intellectual
29 Porridge
30 Pilaster
31 Argots
32 Skirts
35 Organic compound
36 Sermon subject
38 "Exodus" character
41 Inferior
43 One of the Freuds
44 Attention-getter
47 Hurt
48 Food containers
50 "Kind __ Drag" (1966 hit)
51 Son of __
53 Pilcorn
54 Actor James
55 Imperative
56 No-charge protection?
58 Elliptical
59 __ Bator
60 Hit
63 Annoys
66 Former
69 Granada gold
70 Picnic problem
71 NE or SW
72 Bargain-hunter's event
73 N.Y. campus
74 Osculate
77 Free of bandages
80 Monterrey months
81 Buddhist shrine
82 Nickel word
83 Book of 1516
84 Cut in cubes
85 "Made __"
87 Sped
90 British cousin of 48 Down
92 __ majesty
93 Roman road
96 Modernist
97 Ballad
98 Title of 24 Across
99 __ Paulo

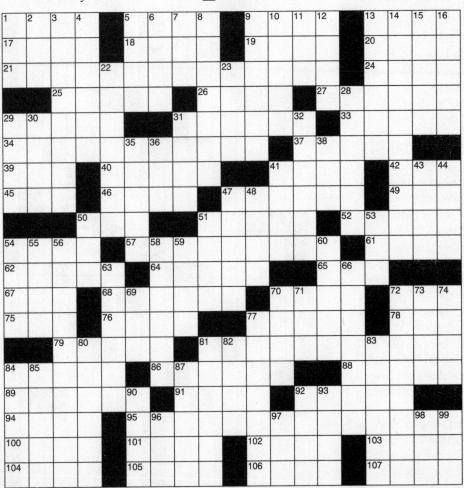

ACROSS

1 Got aboard
7 Strand
12 Skilled in
18 Interstice
19 Big name in the metals game
20 Hazardous
21 Flowering vine
23 Reply to the impatient
24 Virginia willow
25 Pauses
27 __ fixe
28 Lauder of cosmetics
31 Defamation
34 Freight unit
35 Consequently
36 Hesitant sounds
37 Prefix for dollar
39 Corn unit
42 Malleable metal
43 Prolonged bout
46 Make sense
47 From __ Z
48 Beauty-contest wear
51 Language study
53 Guernica girlfriend
54 Footwear
56 Wrigglesome
57 Concede
59 Colossal
61 Alarm
63 Wings
64 Forwarded
65 Tilting
67 Inferior
70 What some toilers burn
75 Lesley __ Warren
76 Part of CPI
78 Concert hall
79 Fannie __
80 Fiber cluster
81 Actress Thompson
82 Dernier __
83 Wild
84 Enzyme
86 Loire city
89 Singer Neville
90 Biblical verb
92 Kind of guard or code
93 Musical foursome
95 Make it
97 Hit song of 1958
103 Truffaut's "__ Kisses"
104 Comedian Ole
105 Battery terminals
106 Bit of grapeshot
107 Moscow demurrers
108 Control boards

DOWN

1 Compulsive performer
2 Rio de __
3 Part of MPH
4 Polo participants
5 Privileged class
6 Jutlander
7 Capture
8 Right-angle joint
9 Squirrel's stash
10 Prepared apples
11 Bumpkin
12 War material
13 Lennon's widow
14 City by the Tiber
15 Wool-gatherer of sorts
16 For __ (professionally)
17 Mal de __ (headache)
22 Energy source
26 Plod
28 Major suffix
29 Street knife
30 Hoofer Tommy
32 Suitcases
33 Martial prefix
34 Storied nightclub, for short
38 Capek play
40 Start of a Dickens title
41 Calhoun of films
43 S. Calif. valley
44 "What's __ for me?"
45 __ on (abet)
46 Shortly
49 Moniker-chooser
50 "__ Did for Love"
52 Signified
55 Substitute
57 Only
58 "The __" (Hawkes film of 1930)
60 "Put your trust __ . . ."
61 Type of lily
62 "High Hopes" songwriter
63 Actor Arkin
64 Hightail it
66 Mendacity
68 Cathedral section
69 New Deal initials
71 "David Copperfield" character
72 Khayyám
73 "Othello" character
74 Spare
77 Former pitcher Steve
82 Red shade
83 Green of the NFL
85 Con-game decoy
87 Humble
88 Droop
89 Sicilian peak
90 Padlock adjunct
91 Comedian Johnson
92 Penny
94 Bloke
96 Triumphant symbol
98 Allow
99 Party in power
100 Chem. ending
101 Actor Gibson
102 Sinuous shape

ACROSS

1 Drove
5 Finds fault
10 Audit group, for short
14 Young lion
17 Reverberate
18 "See what __?"
19 Fr. river
20 Half of dos
21 Ladies' man
22 Coronet
23 Loblolly, e.g.
24 Creek
25 Harsh cry
27 William Perry's sobriquet
30 New Deal org.
32 Japanese salad ingredients
34 Antagonists
35 Fillet
36 Melisma
37 Family room
38 Obloquy
39 Site of Mt. Agung
41 Gambling arrangement
44 PTA members
47 Turkish capital
48 Link with
50 Iowa campus
51 Actuality
54 Skewers
56 Shucks relative
57 __ glance
58 Penance symbol
60 "From __ shining sea"
62 Musical key
64 R.R. stop
65 Slightly
68 Singer Washington
71 Maladies
72 Part of TNT
73 Hawaiian island
75 Fr. embers
77 Trendy desserts
79 Heavy TV user
84 Hustle
85 Name of 12 popes
86 Always, poetically
87 Status __
88 Arise
90 "__ That a Shame?"
91 Grampuses
92 Cry of disgust
93 Politician on the go?
97 Juno
99 "Six __ Riv Vu"
100 Protest
101 Worker's delight
103 Water buffalo
106 Mil. address
107 "Get __ the church . . ."
108 Toilers of yore
109 Hill in Jerusalem
110 Word with hood or kind
111 Citrus drinks
112 "When __ Married" ('61 song)
113 Merit

DOWN

1 LBJ pet
2 "Foucault's Pendulum" author
3 Squabble
4 Activist
5 Newsroom locales
6 Paris pal
7 Brings up
8 Trim
9 Bridle bit
10 Office machine
11 Stuffed shirts
12 Mrs. Shakespeare
13 Oracle
14 Bow
15 Merger
16 Council
26 "The Age of Anxiety" poet
28 Awaken
29 Skilled
30 Thai temple
31 Entertainer Zadora
33 In ready reserve
38 Guitarfish relative
39 Fiber sheet
40 Came up
42 Past due
43 Bristle
44 Pod item
45 All-out
46 Centers
49 Mocking, in a way
51 Declines to dine
52 NL West player
53 Director, e.g.
55 Glum
59 Revenue
61 "__ Andronicus"
63 Symbol of intimidation
66 Immersion
67 Officeholders
69 Son of Jacob
70 Repository for a future bride
74 Bakery application
76 Scandinavian
78 Displace
80 Matured beyond
81 Fishy places
82 Yank
83 Lala precursor
85 Stringed instruments
88 Get lost!
89 Fla. city
90 Diminish
91 Gasket type
94 Actress Samms
95 Like many feet
96 Relaxation
98 Level
102 Comprehend
104 Conjunction
105 Actress Sheridan

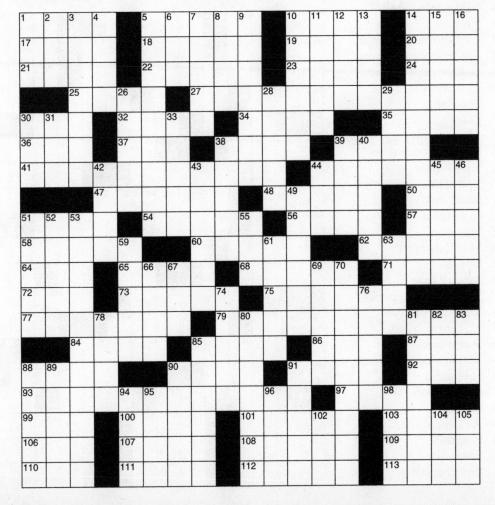

ACROSS

1 Unthreatened
5 Dearth
9 Tight spot
12 Renounce
16 Harness race
17 Antipathy
19 Indignation
20 Golden Rule word
21 Modern fighting force
23 Dais VIPs
24 Bones
25 Pipistrelle
26 Rock group
27 Holiday drink
29 Expedition
31 Converged
33 Perceived to be
36 Chaff
39 Word with stand or start
41 Napoleon, e.g.
44 Natural
48 Mighty
49 Compass heading
50 W.W. II commander
51 Used a lever
54 Banks of baseball
56 Hr. part
57 Prefix for take or trial
58 Gossip-column staple
60 Garden peppergrass
64 Indian city
66 Populace
70 Palo __
71 "The Highwayman" poet
73 Frankenberg's river
74 Shoe width
76 __ de tête
77 Mass. town
80 Cutaneous
82 Intention
83 Mil. endeavors
86 Unstable
88 Kind of base
90 Wash-day assignment
94 Ripening catalyst
95 Haunting
96 Succession
98 Intimate-apparel item
99 Subjoin
102 Conciliation
103 Gewgaw
105 A Cole
108 Promise
110 Pose
112 Bit of banter

115 Impulse
116 Cultural collection
117 Prefix for comic
118 Hibernia
119 Former fawn
120 Actor Tognazzi
121 Cravings
122 Author of "Men of Iron"

DOWN

1 Wild guess
2 Opera part
3 Battle site, 1814
4 Catchall abbr.
5 Raddled
6 "__ Rib" (1949 film)
7 Zero
8 Actress Kathleen
9 Conrad's "Lord __"
10 Roguish
11 Natural terrace
12 News story fodder
13 Dumps
14 Possessive
15 Burns's "__ Louse"
18 Simon's "__ and Only"

22 Cunning
28 Crew
30 Fixed
32 Scratch (out)
34 Salamanders
35 Veil
37 Aspiring grads
38 Watch
39 Actress Nicole
40 Violet blue
42 LBJ pet
43 Cooking vessel
45 Film of 1970
46 Comedian Idle
47 Unless, in law
52 Okla. town
53 Bewildered
55 Block of time
59 Paltry
61 Sinclair Lewis tale
62 Posture
63 Lead-tin alloy
65 Roman bronze
67 __ fugit
68 Do __
69 Oenologist's concern
72 Glossy fabric

75 Sprite
78 Adj. for Abner
79 Org. since 1970
81 Entertainer Martha
83 Canticle
84 Author of "William Wilson"
85 Unfamiliar
87 Chem. endings
89 Paddle
91 Trammel
92 Medicinal application
93 "Believe It Or Not" man
97 Tincture
98 Win __ nose
100 Genesis name
101 Road sign
104 Sp. bears
106 Funicle outgrowth
107 Daly of TV
108 Sign of spring
109 Mine find
111 Chinese truth
113 Before
114 Fiber cluster

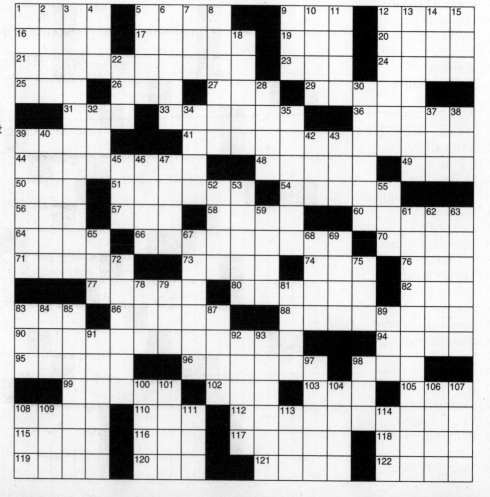

ACROSS

1 Costa __
5 Decides
9 Rotary control
13 Fastener
17 Olfactory stimulus
18 P.D. James's Dalgliesh
19 Menacing
20 Jai __
21 Styptic agent
22 Bushy-tailed creature with tusks?
25 University official
27 Precisely
28 Ground
29 Hurly-burly
30 Certain Eskimo
32 Small cobra
34 Word with be or fly
35 Clash
37 Wine type
39 Sis's daughter
41 Purpose
42 Extinct beast of burden?
45 Chatter
48 Seize
50 Pro __
51 Essentials
52 Merkel of films
53 Patriotic org.
55 Bigfoot relative?
57 Dizzy
59 Thought
62 Valerie Harper role
65 Monotones
66 Added peat moss
68 Writer Leon
70 Time before
71 Right-angle joint
72 Francois's friends
75 USN brass
77 Christie's "Murder is __"
80 Modernist
81 Buzzing, electric creatures?
84 Chart type
85 Bridge strategem
86 The outset
87 Bed-and-breakfast
88 Throttle
91 Foot
92 Actress Laurie
94 Club fighter
96 According to
98 Concerning

99 Posit
102 Horned hawk?
107 Long-running musical
108 Deflect
109 Home to 30 Across, perhaps
110 Actress Skye
111 Within: Prefix
112 "The Proud __" (1956 film)
113 Pole
114 Holiday drinks
115 Dam it!

DOWN

1 Crowd noise
2 Pointless
3 Cat with bony plates?
4 Wanted-poster word
5 Kiln
6 ASAP relative
7 Cross shape
8 Beat
9 Length
10 "__ the message"
11 Still's companion
12 Lixivium

13 Burst of laughter
14 Tocsin
15 __ Fe
16 Cogent
23 Shot
24 Energy
26 Standard
30 Examine
31 Missive
32 Saxophonist Bilk
33 Did a farm job
35 Barb
36 Manner
38 Scull
40 Compass pt.
43 Expletive
44 Fr. river
45 Experimental lizard?
46 Writer Tyler
47 Bellhop's burden
49 French bean
54 Fix up, for short
56 Promissory note
58 Poetry subject
59 Augur
60 Whimper
61 Coy

63 Commonplace
64 __ camp
67 Change for a call
69 Libel
73 Wane
74 Goes quietly
76 Furtive
78 Offense
79 Craving
82 Does a news job
83 Wee quaffs
88 Movie legend
89 Pallid
90 Book back
91 Quid-quo connection
93 Drop by
95 Wedding attendant
97 Far reaches
98 Crafts' companions
99 Proponents
100 Big glove
101 Thanatos's counterpart
103 Motor part
104 Greek letter
105 Kanga's baby
106 U.K. part

ACROSS

1 Involve
7 Did a kitchen job
12 Desperado
18 Actress Henner
19 One of the Brontës
20 Pique
21 Start of a Thanksgiving resolve
24 Cookbook abbr.
25 Sampler word
26 Free
27 Grasp
28 __ now (currently)
30 Cup's companion
33 Like Jaime Sommers
36 Feast
39 Down with
43 Resolve, part II
47 Drop
48 Merchant
49 In the recent past
50 Cobb and Hardin
51 Twice LIII
53 NFL Coach Jim
54 Anatomical canals
55 Yew and wych
57 L.A. athlete
59 Different
61 Crags
65 Stricken
66 Block up
69 Fabric folds
70 Indicate
72 Prefix for graph
73 Resolve, part III
77 Pigeon's home
78 Baldachin
79 Sharply focused
80 Wooden shoes
83 Turkish VIPs
84 "Star Wars" initials
87 Actress Joanne
88 Station
91 Stereo component, for short
94 Resolve, part IV
100 __ regime (pre-1789 system)
101 Guileless
102 Synchronize with
103 Injunction
104 City on the Rhone
105 Was insubordinate

DOWN

1 Release
2 Slangy negatives
3 Junket
4 Afflict
5 Sickly
6 Texas Tech's town
7 Part of N.B.
8 O.T. book
9 The younger set
10 Wallach
11 Stain
12 Alkaline
13 Taken for __
14 Sine qua __
15 Michael Jordan maneuver
16 Uh-huh
17 Gull relative
22 Pixie
23 Ideal for Superman
28 Some kind of __
29 Falstaff's title
30 Singer Leo
31 Star-shaped
32 Roof beam
33 Kind of camp or hill
34 "__ Room" (Beach Boys hit)
35 Singer Redding
36 Feed crop
37 Hard cheese
38 __ Alto
40 Heavyweight champ, 1934
41 Word with fair or well
42 Vulpine
44 Singer Brickell
45 "__ Dreamin'" (1976 song)
46 Full
51 Modern Candia
52 Vice follower
55 Windsor Castle sight
56 "One __ a time"
58 Skating spin
59 Potpourri
60 Motif
62 Feast-preparation places
63 Petrocelli of baseball
64 Beauty parlor sound
66 Kind of bug or berry
67 Solar disk
68 Mr. Sahl
69 Aspiring Spec. 4
71 Islet
72 Myrmecology subject
74 Search
75 Codifies
76 Actress Balin
81 Carpentry tools
82 Small goose
83 Royal-flush component
84 Mop
85 Feast
86 Mosquito's "gift"
88 Singer Collins
89 Astarte's realm
90 Pub choices
91 Son of Hera
92 Speck
93 Trudge
95 Go fast
96 __ shoestring (cheaply)
97 Train unit
98 Atienza aunt
99 Warendorf's river

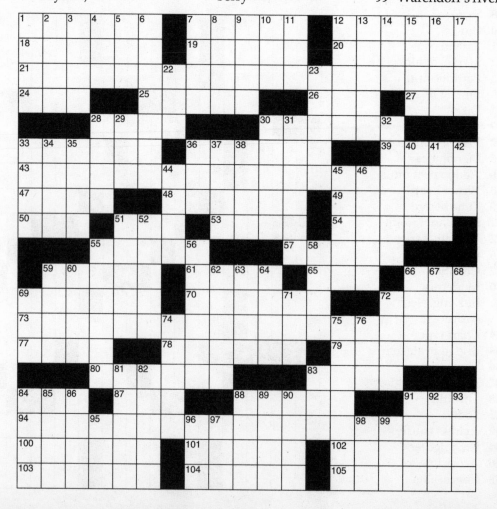

ACROSS

1 Singer Fogelberg
4 Established
9 Mischievous
13 Ivan or Peter
17 Outside: Prefix
18 Asian range
19 Cry to Silver
20 Site of Last Chance Ditch
21 Slogan for drivers
25 Jai __
26 Mountain spur
27 Italian wine city
28 Chem. ending
29 Region, poetically
31 Road-map abbrs.
33 Renters
35 Tympanum's place
36 Tuckered out
40 Poetic contraction
42 Leverage
43 Snooze
46 Poet Alfred
49 Timetable abbr.
51 Like some buckets
52 After
54 Annapolis initials
55 Kowtowed
57 Med check, for short
58 Incline
60 Possessive pronoun
61 Brew
62 "The Outlaw" character
64 HST successor
65 Greek letters
66 Element No. 50
67 "Just You __"
69 Prefix for tract or division
72 Stubborn
74 Pilaster
76 Needlefish
77 Pellucid
79 Smelter input
80 Easy shot
82 Light Brigade complement
85 Migration
87 Consult
88 Garden hopper
89 Ramadan journey
92 Arid
95 Erving in the NBA
97 Affirmed
99 Mideast land: abbr.
100 Thrash

102 Kinshasa's land
106 Gelatin base
107 Film of '71
111 Abound
112 Qualified
113 Character, British-style
114 The Beatles' "__ the Walrus"
115 Handle
116 Concordes
117 Cold War strategem
118 __ out (scrape together)

DOWN

1 Vandalize, in a way
2 Armpit
3 Child's protest
4 Laurel
5 Bravo precursor
6 Ferment
7 Roof projection
8 Regimens
9 Triumphant shout
10 __ Ridge (1972 Derby winner)
11 Bureau
12 Gave a party
13 Part of TNT
14 Phila. player
15 Regarding
16 Reward for 10 Down
22 Raines of baseball
23 Context
24 Flax product
30 Nigerian native
32 Transgress
34 "__ Ben Adhem"
37 Corrosive
38 __ gallop (full tilt)
39 Little kid
41 Card game
43 Summer cooler
44 Minute
45 Travois
47 Whole
48 Fat's companion
49 City in Kansas
50 Numbers with "skidoo"
53 Pyrenees land
55 Ruinous
56 Epoch
59 Aachen article
63 Harem chambers

68 Rainbow goddess
69 Sprightly music
70 Malay dagger
71 Predilection
73 Approving gesture
75 Emanation
78 Fuss
81 Soldier at risk
83 Marked, as a spot
84 News execs
86 Hindu destinies
89 Restrain completely
90 Guyana Indian
91 Composer Kern
92 Nuthatch genus
93 Pale
94 Desensitizes
96 Tel Aviv district
98 Course
101 Region
103 ". . . __ hollers let it go. . ."
104 "Black __" (1991 film)
105 Miscalculates
108 Burns's "little"
109 Bar matter
110 Asian occasion

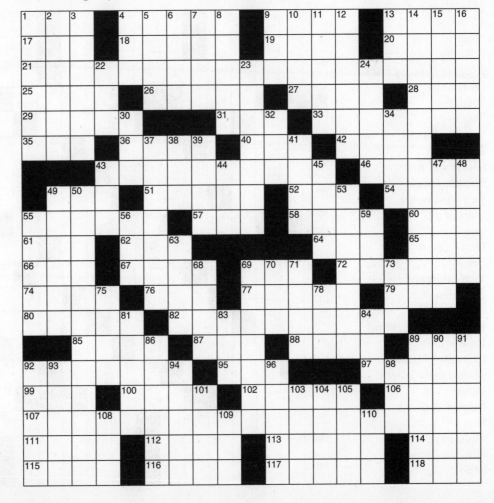

ACROSS

1 Yoga regimen
6 Kind of room or box
11 Gratifies
18 Writer Hoffman
19 Fedrero precursor
20 Sedulous
21 Flower in exalted form?
23 Perturb
24 Catchall abbr.
25 Carrel
27 Lid fastener
28 Petcock
31 __ la-la
33 Farm structure
34 Warbler
36 Heard
38 Delete
40 Head-in-the-clouds types
44 Rumor conduit
46 Keats, e.g.
47 __ culpa
48 Corn mush
49 Compass point
50 Gainsborough's river
51 Meat dish
52 Fled
54 Queue
56 P.R. city
57 Prepares to play back
61 Old car
62 Frenzies
64 Toady
65 School-skipper
68 Long time
69 Merry old monarch
70 Shortcoming
71 Regal pronoun
73 Start of a C. Moore poem
77 Dining area
78 Trice
79 Turned-over flower?
81 Lowlifes
83 __ facto
84 Belgian battleground
85 Enumerate
86 Director Wertmuller
88 Elvis's early label
90 Dine
91 Informed about
93 Bivvy
94 Floor covering
96 Grande dame
99 Map design

106 TV's "__ to Live"
107 Enosis
108 City on the Po
109 Scorsese's "Mean __"
110 Kind of reference
111 Long time

DOWN

1 Cross shape
2 Utterly
3 Match
4 Land unit
5 Mariners' home
6 Garland
7 Numero __
8 "__ Blu Dipinto Blu"
9 Kind of card or check
10 Casino adjunct
11 Maximum
12 Cause-effect interval
13 Silkworm
14 Hymn of praise
15 Reef creature
16 Superlative endings
17 Process element
22 TV companion
26 Torpid

28 License plates
29 Quality
30 Dinghy
32 Center line
33 "Curly __" (1991 film)
34 __ Bend, Wis.
35 Backstabber
37 Inform
39 Cash-register pile
41 Annuli
42 Respond
43 Strongboxes
45 Purvey
46 Artemis's victim
50 Delight
51 Gentle blow
53 Dunkirk donkey
55 For sure
56 "Animal Farm" figure
57 Fast-moving snake
58 Campania town
59 Shy type
60 Where notes are written
63 Guarded
66 Fluster

67 Excellent
70 Sanction
72 GI's hangouts
74 Finish line
75 On the bounding main
76 CBS, e.g.
78 Former sophs
79 "__ Lazy River"
80 TV series
82 Closing section
83 Chant
87 Bring on
89 Hesitant sounds
91 Japanese salad items
92 Seine spanner
93 __ bien
95 Accurate
97 Bestow, à la Burns
98 Newt
100 "Cara __"
101 Engine housing
102 Word with time or day
103 Mouths
104 Title of respect
105 Rookie nav. off.

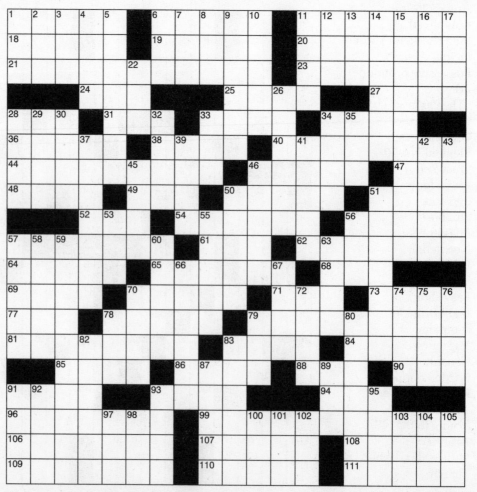

ACROSS

1 __ out (dispense)
5 Swiss hotelier
9 Downhill runner
13 Gudrun's husband
17 Aleutian island
18 Writer James
19 Heavenly wear
20 Greek letters
21 With "The," Levin tale
24 Architect Saarinen
25 Attend
26 Actress Schneider
27 Earp and Ness
29 Cut in cubes
32 Viburnum
33 Capital of 61 Across
34 Kerouac's "On the __"
35 Heyday
37 Toothsome
40 Lincoln's st.
43 Sewing instrument
44 Fr. office worker
46 House mbrs.
47 __ Bend, Ariz.
48 With "the," Joan of Arc
51 Carols
52 Beastly
53 As scheduled
54 Smidgens
55 Youthful pigs
57 Lee's "__ Right Thing"
58 Hydrocarbon prefix
59 Throng
60 Towels, napkins, etc.
61 Mediterranean island
62 Incorporate
63 Hit song of 1970
67 Slay
68 Kind of hound
69 Bette of note
70 Basic integer
71 Baseball stat
72 Formal
74 Bishopric
75 Ballot
76 Affixes
78 Pilcorn
80 Got the gold
81 "__, o ship of state . . ."
83 Testifies
85 Middle European
87 Gumbo
88 A.E. Housman work
94 Cineast's delight
95 Number for two
96 Heroic poetry
97 Legal system
98 Handle
99 Gibb or Griffith
100 Calif. valley
101 Traveling

DOWN

1 Small amount
2 "What am __ do?"
3 Unkempt abode
4 Very quiet
5 __ avis
6 Stravinsky
7 President pro __
8 One of the equidae
9 Counterfeit
10 Sluggish
11 Actor Wallach
12 Check work
13 "__ having fun yet?"
14 Film of 1991
15 Folk wisdom
16 Occupies
22 Central bank, for short
23 Lines
28 Word with one or body
29 Tavern portion
30 Decorah's state
31 Beach Boys hit
32 Munich mister
33 Grove
35 Phonetic openers
36 Sci. branch
38 Scorpion, e.g.
39 Locale
41 "Pomp and Circumstance" composer
42 Liberian native
44 Outer layer
45 Singer Rosemary et al.
47 Florentine painter
49 Muffle
50 Penetrate
51 Tendons
55 Ghost
56 Obeisance
57 Divisions of 12 Down
58 Herschel Bernardi role
60 Household gods
61 Paleolithic hangout
64 Molded
65 Stake
66 Require
68 West Indies isle
72 Twosome
73 Cellist __ Ma
75 Actress Lindfors
77 Camel relative
79 Poplar
80 Deface
81 Couch
82 Related
83 Shake off
84 Dilettantish
85 Mall tenant
86 Singer Stansfield
89 Sky light
90 Hot tub
91 Dejected
92 Nabokov novel
93 Actress Susan

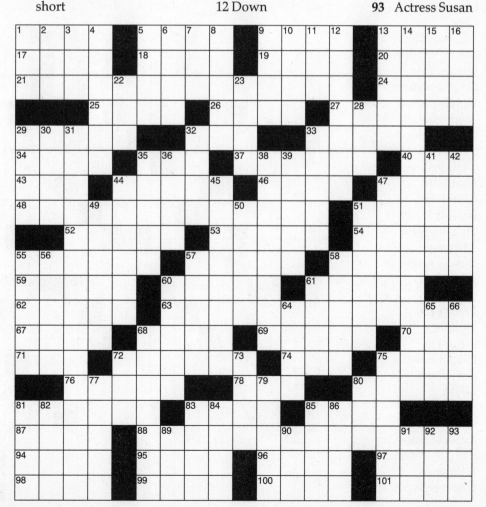

ACROSS

1 Astute
6 Kind of ground or site
10 U.S. diplomat Dean
17 "Pretty __" (Orbison hit)
18 Biting
20 Floor-show performer
21 See 3 Down
23 Chopper's stop
24 Morrison's "__ Baby"
25 Dilutes
26 Dance org.
28 City lines
29 Cord
31 Dry sherry
33 Lingerie item
36 Member of a Catholic order
38 "Coventry Carol" wish
40 Okla. town
41 Rulers of yore
43 "__ the season . . ."
44 Touched down
45 Common viper
47 German river
48 Emotional
49 Commerce
50 Gibe
51 Actress Balin
53 Young antelope
54 Horse color
55 Get the picture
56 Holiday gift of song
60 Marathon's st.
63 Consume
64 Artist Lichtenstein
65 Cuttlefish secretion
66 Nonsense
67 Connives
70 Actress Ryan
71 Sign of spring
73 Disparage
75 Illinois neighbor
76 "__ Woman" (Reddy hit)
77 Student
79 Pot starter
80 Holiday gift of song
83 Actor Don
85 Classifieds
86 Awkward
87 Destroy
88 Sugar ending
89 Shoe widths
90 Tea-leaf reader
91 "48 __" (1982 film)
94 Eminence
98 Gift-wrap combo

101 Forbearing
102 Elitists
103 Aegean region
104 Collects
105 Staunch
106 Hotbeds

DOWN

1 Narrow promontory
2 Maui town
3 With 21 Across, celebrated holiday gift
4 Tie type
5 Abstract
6 Bill of fare
7 Exploits
8 Mal de __
9 Sound system gear
10 Cry in Mainz
11 Feta and gouda
12 Specious
13 Discordia
14 Diminutive draught
15 "Bird __ Wire" (1990 film)
16 Actor Beatty

19 Jazz type
22 Certain kin
27 Attempt
30 Ample
31 Happy sounds
32 "Don't bet __!"
33 Composer Bartók
34 Maraud
35 Comedian Johnson
36 British grasslands
37 Actress McDowell
38 Thigh
39 Tale
42 Learn
46 Gam and Coolidge
48 Stashed
49 Boar features
52 Buff
53 Pivotal
54 Lair
57 Quiver
58 Record
59 Caesar's "I saw"
60 Holiday gift of song
61 Reluctant
62 "__ Grows in Brooklyn"

63 Summary abbr.
67 Typewriter type
68 Power output
69 Fly-by-night creatures
70 Crèche figures
71 Melville's "Billy __"
72 Big moments
74 West and Murray
76 Apprentice: Var.
77 Christmas item
78 Hobbled
81 Op-Ed fodder
82 Brain cavities
84 Limit
87 Intuit
88 Birdsong of basketball
90 Elephant boy
92 Wall St. property package
93 Highlands falls
94 Health club
95 Burns's "__ o'Shanter"
96 One-time link
97 Aliens, to Spielberg
99 "Le Coq __"
100 Caviar

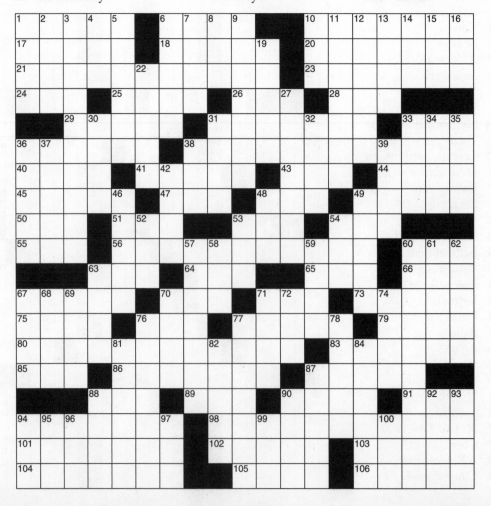

ACROSS

1 Regarding
5 Fruitcake ingredient
11 Sea-ear
18 Songwriter Sammy
19 Secrets
20 Assyrian capital
21 Hawthorne work
23 Copy
24 Platform material
25 __ communes
26 Babette's boyfriend
27 SEC school
28 LBJ pet
29 Noncommital
30 Ricochet
33 Seven-faced doctor of film
35 Gambler's "portfolio"
37 "Network" actor
41 Compulsive sorts
43 Undulating
44 Rodeo rope
45 Make certain
46 Curse
47 Word with hand or type
49 Interpreted
50 Jejune
51 In the course of
52 __ Cruces
53 Bay area landmark
58 Señor ending
61 Nurture
62 Paper quantity
63 Persilicic
67 Part of GATT
69 Stat relative
70 Balkan region
72 Writer Stephen
73 Enthusiastic
74 Fan
75 Perennial presidential candidate
78 Aerobicist's target
79 Bank products, for short
80 Modulate
81 Mountain meas.
82 High degree
84 Possesses
87 Actress Arthur
88 Epoch
89 "I've had it up __!"
92 Item
95 "Pardon my presumption"
97 Restrained
98 Balanced
99 "Little Man __" ('91 film)
100 Grange group
101 Judge
102 __ of worms

DOWN

1 Curtain-raiser
2 Adages
3 PBS show
4 As scheduled
5 Cry of frustration
6 Metier
7 Daedalus's son
8 "The Crucible" setting
9 Chem. endings
10 USN site
11 Elk or echidna
12 Bahamas place
13 Black bird
14 Permit
15 Ellipsoid
16 NBA team
17 Alas, to Livy
22 More macabre
26 Confederate
29 Greek letters
30 Impart
31 Emotionally involved
32 Discharge
33 Sci. settings
34 Busy as __
36 Sylvanite, e.g.
37 Happens by
38 Storm product
39 Heating vessel
40 Platers
42 Cantillated
43 Sidewalk sign
46 Actor Dourif
47 Caprice
48 Laky
50 Long time
51 Bundle
54 Spent
55 Ship-shaped clock
56 Drop
57 Antony's loan request
58 Restless feeling
59 Scarlett's place
60 Sandarac tree
64 Hits a winter hazard
65 Kind of tea
66 Ger. articles
68 MIT, for one
69 State
70 Burns's "__ Mouse"
71 Associate
73 Out of port
74 Sandwich initials
76 Writer Eric
77 Expedites
78 Like crêpes suzettes
81 Jimmy of tennis
83 The "unlucky letter"
84 King's "The Dark __"
85 Zone
86 Luminary
88 Salamanders
89 Sailing chains
90 Church tribunal
91 Mr. Flood
93 Doctrine
94 Guevara
95 Words between roses
96 Endings for form and sign

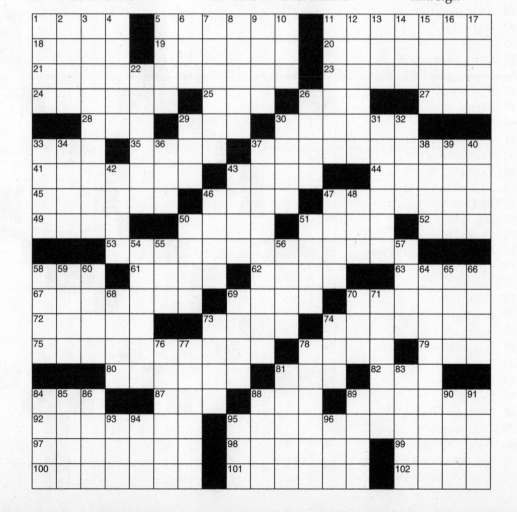

ACROSS

1 Prescribed amounts
8 Writer Kundera
13 Hauls
18 Surround
19 Lombardy love
20 Unconcealed
21 Shipping route
22 New York thoroughfare, winterized
24 Depended
25 W.W. II combatants
26 Pawnbroker, e.g.
27 Winnows
29 Trojan War figure
32 Kind of jump or shot
33 Kennel sounds
34 Dallas dweller
35 Actor Vallone
36 Imposing
40 __ good turn
41 Trade zones, winterized
44 Honshu herb
45 Business abbr.
46 Eccentric
47 Royal pronoun
48 Kind of nature
50 Ugly object
52 Weak
53 Computer button
54 From __ Z
55 Confront
57 Delay
58 Welsh __
61 CSA color
62 Ecological assets
66 Exotic
67 __ Animas, Colo.
68 Strainer
70 Remick
71 Diarist of note
72 Billet-doux, winterized
75 Sp. queen
76 Apparel
78 Wrath
79 Sectors
80 Abound
81 __ up (pay)
83 Sandarac trees
84 Malicious
85 Skillful
88 Verb for Ovid
89 Pogamoggan
90 Illegal commerce
93 "__ see my Pilot face to face . . ." (Tennyson)

96 Ransack
97 Angolan capital
98 Unfold
99 TV award
100 Main, for one
101 Euripedes tragedy

DOWN

1 __ Plaines, Ill.
2 Integrated
3 De Palma film, winterized
4 Measures out
5 Stimuli
6 Slave of yore
7 Comprehend
8 Traveler's aid
9 Lennon song
10 Asian tree-dweller
11 Big boats
12 Teachers' org.
13 Witches' assembly
14 Requite
15 Tear
16 Rightful
17 Ending for song or young
23 Up in the air
27 Ms. Hawkins
28 Unexpected contrast
29 Rodney of football
30 Hatchet man
31 Level
32 Boxer Holmes
34 Cape Cod town
35 Kind of steak or house
37 Wildcat
38 Lupino and Canter
39 Magnolia fruit
41 Basis
42 Effuse
43 Norma of films
49 Imperative
51 Wise
52 Yield
55 Plucky
56 Comfort
57 Thrives on
58 Shop talk
59 Potpourri
60 Band
61 Renown
62 Goat cheeses
63 Safety device, winterized?
64 Article of faith
65 Sordid
68 Antitoxins
69 Road to Rome
73 Door beams
74 Schnitzler play
77 Inconsistent
80 Brown shades
82 Olive product
83 Organic compound
84 Spice tree
85 Skilled
86 Tragic fate
87 Space
88 Japanese gelatin
89 "Silkwood" actress
91 Visceral
92 Channel
93 "__ not choose to run"
94 Water-tester of sorts
95 Harvest goddess

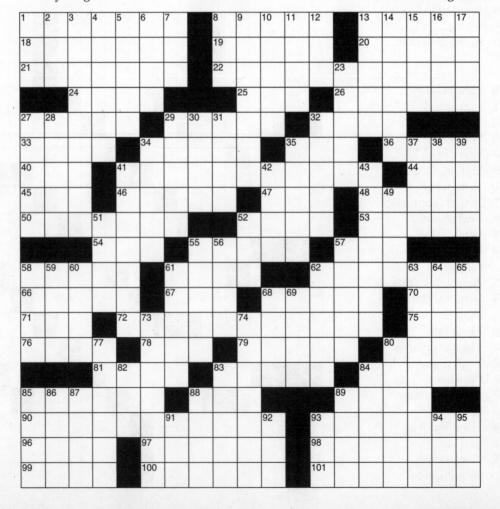

ACROSS

1 Slew
5 Approved
8 Golfer O'Grady
11 Muse
17 Sandarac tree
18 Pod item
19 Pipe joint
20 Fig bird
21 "Can Can" actress
24 Tea biscuits
25 Hitters' stats
26 Zoo worker
27 Kind of gate or light
29 Too good for
30 Animosity
32 Booker T.'s rock band
33 __ favor
35 Writer Hunter
36 Writer Rand
37 Kind of change or chest
38 Greek island
40 Business letter abbr.
41 Duration
43 Net results, informally
46 Kennel sound
47 Matthew Arnold, e.g.
48 Arctic observation
49 Writer Barbara
50 Of a Marianas island
52 Durrell book
53 Nervous as __
57 Sparkling
58 Towel inscription
59 Emissary
61 Vintner's prefix
62 Ring regulars
63 Vocations
64 Imposing
67 Dos halved
68 Philosopher
69 Command to Fido
70 Drugstore-cowboy relative
75 Exhausts
76 Allende's "__ Luna"
77 Dismal
78 Kicks
79 Lowly canine
80 Rumor personified
82 Group effort
83 Summer mo.
84 Socially graceful
87 Robert of films
89 Plagiarizes
91 Sinuous shape
92 M.D.'s org.
93 Actress Charlene
95 Quiet village
98 "That was __ one"
99 Olympics team
100 Mouths
101 Nemesis
102 Gave a hungry look
103 Part of CPM
104 Sunday seat
105 Introduces

DOWN

1 Indian chief
2 Antilles isle
3 Convivial
4 Prefix for pod or cycle
5 Chose
6 Fulfilled
7 Patriotic org.
8 Whimpers
9 Likewise
10 Vivid blue color
11 QB or SS
12 Marine monster
13 Weeper of myth
14 "Catch The Wind" singer
15 Promote
16 Bridles at
22 Uniform
23 Gift __ (verbal talent)
28 Major __
31 Knackebrod
32 Fulfill
34 Disport
37 The Beatles' "__ Leaving Home"
38 Tension
39 Vulpine
41 Item for Will Rogers
42 Heated
43 Chic
44 Contract party
45 Incarnation
47 Norm
51 Surgical instrument
52 Thickset
54 Egg-cheese-anchovy dish
55 Sail position
56 Nesslerizes
59 __ de Maracaibo, Venezuela
60 Before
62 Prepares to smooch
63 French city
65 Possessive pronoun
66 Beetle larva
68 Self-satisfied
70 Disproof
71 Cupidity
72 Cukor film, 1936
73 Composer Wilder
74 Helpful
75 __ generis
79 __ Nostra
81 Thespian
83 Hungry as __
84 Nonsense!
85 Revise
86 Historian's concern
88 Footwear
90 "Casablanca" character
91 "Jane __"
94 Beatty or Buntline
96 Break
97 Exec's degree

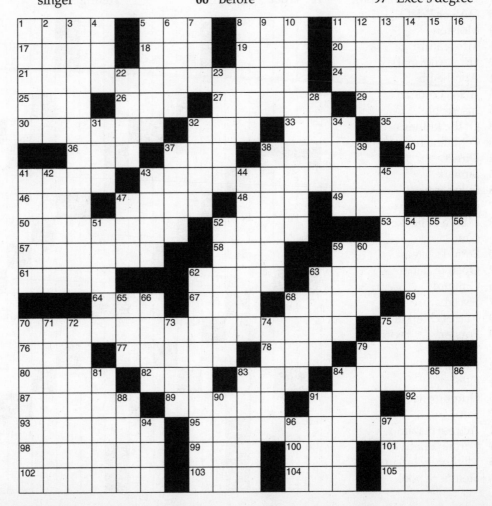

ACROSS

1 Slant
5 Out of practice
10 King of the sea
14 __ T of rap
17 Cuzco valley native
18 "The Cocktail Party" playwright
19 Hotchner subject
20 Brother
21 Long-shot proposition
24 "In extremis" message
25 Door sign
26 Inspires
27 Pull out
29 Get mad
31 Gam and Tushingham
33 Age
34 Road to ruin
37 Hesitant sounds
38 Rancor
41 Actress Joanne
44 Anne Tyler tale
47 Winter Palace figure
48 Gloaming times
50 Regan's father
51 Greasy-spoon offering
53 OAS or WHO
54 Moisten
56 Tire feature
59 Up __ (normal)
61 Apothegm
63 Actor Lorenzo
65 Insensible
68 Of the kidneys
70 Pentateuch
72 Direct
73 Simian
75 Silkworm
77 Chem. endings
79 Mikita of hockey fame
80 Sound system
82 Open to debate
86 Guileful
87 Sea creature
89 Actress Merkel
90 Forster's "__ with a View"
92 Sugar
93 Gloria __
95 Outpourings
99 San __
102 Actress Nazimova
104 Certain relative
105 Mighty, in Japan
106 Steinbeck book
110 Actress Blyth
111 "Mila 18" writer
112 "... not __ mouse"
113 Abhor
114 Joplin work
115 Actress Young
116 Servomotor
117 Part of QED

DOWN

1 Waits
2 __ fell swoop
3 Piercing
4 Dueling gear
5 Court official, for short
6 Malay daggers
7 River-bottom matter
8 "__ with Love" (1967 film)
9 Metallic element
10 EMS procedure
11 Items of interest
12 Tip
13 Exchange
14 Hedgers' options
15 Gator's relative
16 Wood's "__ Lynne"
22 Journeys
23 "Per aspera ad __"
28 Utter defeat
30 Lapidary's instrument
32 "__ sow, so shall ..."
35 Japanese legislature
36 Tangle
38 Board
39 Needlefish
40 Work unit
41 Leverage
42 Back
43 Slippery ground
45 Actor Williams
46 Stick
49 Pigpen: Var.
52 Osteophyte
55 Serf of yore
57 Latin poet's word
58 Faces down
60 Prophet from Judea
62 __ Antoinette
64 December figure
66 Summary abbr.
67 Withhold
69 Historian __ Yutang
71 Descendants
73 Dental-office sounds
74 Apple seed
76 Water color
78 Urban buildup
81 __ many words
83 Remove an opener
84 Previous
85 Water wheel
88 Thinker
91 Crème de __
93 Speakers' stands
94 Translation of 57 Down
96 Rite place
97 Sicily neighbor
98 Dulcet
99 Jewish month
100 Singer Mouskouri
101 Regarding
103 "The Clan of the Cave Bear" author
107 Nimitz's org.
108 Highlands fall
109 Compartment

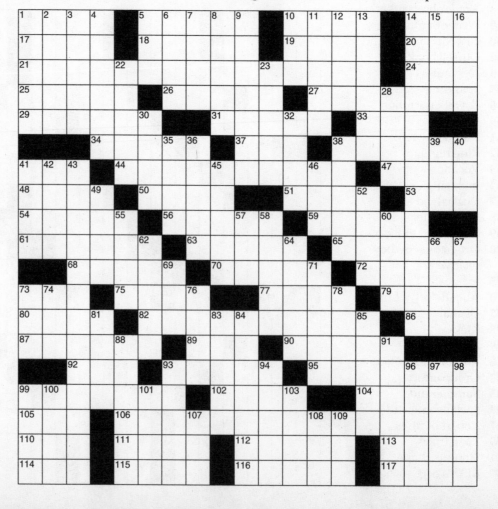

ACROSS

1 Thigh
4 Brutus's bones
8 Essence
11 Repudiate
17 Conquistador's gold
18 Ottoman
19 "Try __ might . . ."
20 Actor Christian
21 Wickerwork problem
24 Durango dish
25 Pledged
26 Haus wife
27 Conducted
28 Sanding sounds
30 Physique
33 Ambition
38 Part of BMOC
40 Standing still
41 Carried
42 Beer relative
43 Head
45 Isolated astronaut?
47 Orator William
49 Behindhand
51 Painter Paul
52 Lamb's dam
53 Word after how or who
54 Tied up
57 Long time
59 Printing stroke
61 Mich. city
63 Sidestep
67 Over-precise
70 Dog breed
73 Hiatus
74 Actor Elliott
77 Transude
79 Bean town?
80 Fr. state
81 Top-quality publicity?
85 Sportscaster Albert
87 __-Magnon man
88 Behaved
89 Tips off
91 Rock growth
93 Stacks' surface
94 "__ Talks" (1984 film)
95 Church council
96 __ Dawn Chong
98 N.Y. campus
100 Packing material
103 Dido's love
107 Mail shade?
110 Pigeon's perch
111 Outward: Prefix
112 Hind's mate
113 Engine part
114 Garden pavilion
115 Writer Rand
116 Daly of TV
117 "48 __" (1982 film)

DOWN

1 __ de combat
2 Lined up
3 Engine gauge?
4 Gets honest
5 Sequel word
6 Goofy-foots, e.g.
7 Remotely
8 Legitimate
9 Olympic delegation
10 Crib
11 Charles dog
12 Mild mixture
13 Squeeze
14 Actress Hagen
15 Unit of reluctance
16 Before
22 Horse-drawn carriage
23 27th president
27 Jobber's transaction
29 Sacred song
31 Pac-10 mbr.
32 Weasel relative
34 Friend of Pooh
35 Marine eagle
36 Once more
37 Paltry
38 Fear and Horn
39 Extant
40 Writer Anya
44 Confucian truth
46 Car of yore
48 Junket
50 Actor Roberts
55 Rock group initials
56 Valley
58 Dover catch
60 Con-man on the loose?
62 Loses weight
64 Channel at The Hague?
65 Hostile look
66 John of music
68 Little demon
69 Illusion
71 "__ little teapot . . ."
72 Primitive
74 Health clubs
75 St. Louis sight
76 Smidgen
78 "Welcome __"
82 Actor Gibson
83 Debussy milieu
84 "In Dreams" singer
86 Classic
90 Spree
92 Vermont sight
95 Pungent
97 Out of port
99 Tweed twitter
101 Verge on
102 Shady grouping
103 Uraeus
104 Itinerary abbr.
105 Hector
106 W.W. II area
107 Soup vegetable
108 Prefix for moron
109 Go for the gold

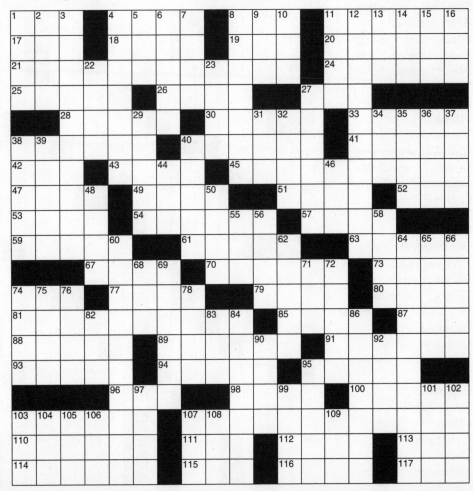

ACROSS

1 "... __ forgive our debtors"
5 Interval
10 Perfecta, for one
13 Barrier
16 Cubic meter
18 Ataturk
19 Silkworm
20 Flurry
21 Actress in "Looking for Mr. Goodbar"
23 Ares's warehouse?
25 Skeptically
26 Covetous look
28 Tangle
29 Coup d' __
30 Flout
32 African antelope
33 Actress Kay
35 Flub
36 Minx
38 Road sign
41 Archaic
42 "The __" (1969 film)
45 "Candid Camera" name
46 Blind-bat connection
47 Actor Maxwell
48 Fitness spot
49 Social stratum
50 Site of Cadillac Square
52 Fleet creatures
54 Rose oil
55 Chunk of history
56 Mentioned
57 Foundation garment
58 Essential ingredient
61 Gourmandizes
62 Plath's "The __"
66 Worth of comics
67 Wine type
68 Conductor Riccardo
69 Yves's agreement
70 Expert advice
71 "The __" (1989 film)
74 Word with game or line
75 Formed a lap
76 Franchise
77 Long-running musical
78 Newts
79 Departure
81 Singer Brooks
83 Girder
85 Writer Henry
87 Cosset
88 More rueful

91 Offense
93 Film of 1977
96 Shirt style
97 Trap
98 Alvin of dance
99 Flirt
100 Russia, formerly
101 Consume
102 Looks over
103 Saffron and carmine

DOWN

1 Movie pet
2 Actor Erwin et al.
3 "__ the Waldorf" (1945 film)
4 Fake
5 Kind of terrier
6 Church seat
7 Simone's soul
8 Postpone
9 Bourtree
10 Stand
11 Wander
12 Prosenchyma
13 Old Burt Reynolds role
14 Jewish month

15 Gangster's escort
17 Poet Millay
22 Don't dither
24 Purpose
27 Savored
30 Corrupt
31 Wyo. neighbor
32 Singer Lang et al.
33 Fill
34 Alternatively
35 Clench
37 Charity
39 Pilaster
40 Ending for poll or pun
42 Loose as __
43 Throe
44 Folklore figures
49 Comedian George
51 Equipage controls
52 Vaisya, for one
53 Blind ambition
56 L.A.'s La __ Blvd.
57 Greek letter
58 Smithereens
59 "Vesti la giubba," e.g.
60 Woody Allen film, 1987

61 Egad relative
62 Mooches
63 Jack Webb role
64 Sarah, to Prince William
65 Frees
68 Allegory
71 Scribble
72 Synthetic fiber
73 Back-comb
76 Countenance
78 Kind of income
80 Deleter
82 Church patriarchs
83 Hawaiian hawks
84 Champagne-bottle word
85 Protrudes
86 Iowa city
87 Predilection
88 "The __ the limit"
89 Affluence
90 Bar choice
92 Actress Scala
94 Tenn. neighbor
95 Millennium pt.

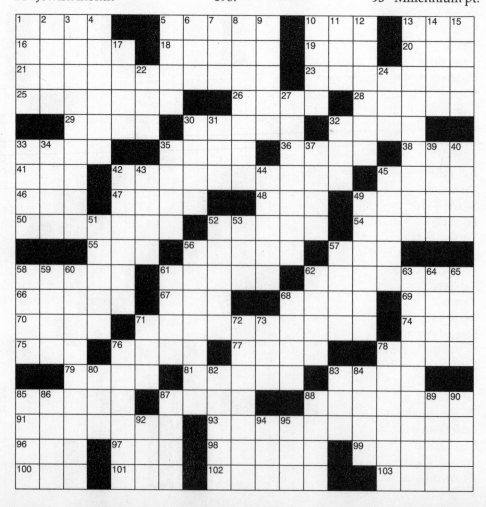

ACROSS

1 Harbor
6 Exhibitions
11 Hero ingredient
17 Whatever
18 Escaped
19 Titania's spouse
20 "Bill and Ted's __" (1991 film)
22 Entered
23 Mayberry denizen
24 Well
25 Write Wyse
27 Vexation
28 Receptacle
29 Actress Claire
30 Valleys
32 Widely
33 More prudent
35 Novelty
38 Claw: Prefix
40 Type of soup
43 Roman poet
46 Perfect
49 Supplement
50 Valentine's Day sentiment
51 Smell __
52 Training-room complaints
54 Pummel
56 Turkish title
57 Kind of pot or spot
58 Dry-bone link
59 Black bird
60 Destiny
61 Born
62 Moistens
64 Demonstrated
67 Actress Nazimova
68 Box-office bomb of '87
70 Antecedent
72 __ pie
74 Belle of the West
75 Costume jewelry
77 Prod
79 Pacify
80 Olympics quest
84 Cryptanalyst's challenge
86 Quick
88 Fleur-de-__
90 Dweller: Suffix
91 Mil. address
92 Newspaper section
93 By
95 Actress Gardner et al.

96 Ransacks
98 Perjury
102 __ terrible
103 Profits
104 Barren place
105 Approvals
106 Stately
107 Zoo favorite

DOWN

1 Bigwigs
2 Ideal spot
3 Violent
4 Veer
5 City lines
6 Clog
7 Give it __
8 Particle
9 Repent
10 Gnomon
11 Porcine, in a way
12 Burrows and Vigoda
13 Actor Cariou
14 Not by nature
15 Shearer of dance
16 Spiritual

18 Retreat
21 Painter Vermeer
26 Tale opener
29 Element in 71 Down
30 Jeers
31 Ronnie of the NFL
32 Styptic
34 Radiate
36 Desolation Canyon's site
37 Crass
39 Resin
41 Quitter
42 __ Gatos, Calif.
44 Luanda's land
45 __ a pin
46 "The __ over and gone . . ." (Song of Solomon)
47 Borgnine
48 Parts of play-action passes
50 Standard
53 Grimalkin
55 Physical principle
58 Honor
63 Fitness center

64 Square root of 3,600
65 Shoshonean
66 Pitcher Hershiser
67 African fox
69 Authentic
71 Ferric oxide
73 Charity
75 Achievement
76 Concedes
78 Phantoms
81 Unload
82 "__ of Honey"
83 Minor
84 Singer Mariah
85 Editorialize
87 To date
89 "__ Could Turn Back Time"
92 Statesman Coty
93 Map mass
94 Persuade
95 Med. school course
97 Sp. article
99 Hail
100 Hang back
101 Ouida's "Under __ Flags"

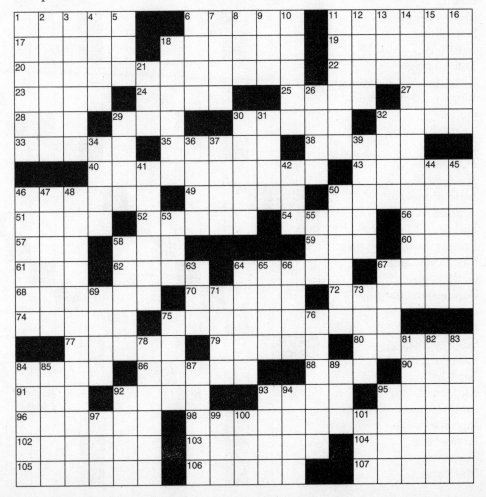

ACROSS

1 Sis or bro
4 Mid-summer babies
8 His and hers
13 __ de tête
16 Meadow mom
17 __ Dame
18 Singer Lena
19 Actress Hagen
20 Momentous
23 Turf rulings, for short
24 Twists
25 "Man's inhumanity __ . . ."
26 Bone of contention
28 Singer James
29 Untangle
31 Heating unit
32 Hwy.
33 "Common Sense" man
35 Rome airport
38 Farmers
41 Holds court
42 Slangy denial
45 Different
46 Scruffs
48 Money premium
49 Loan shark
51 Northers
52 Tracy's target
53 20th Century dictator
54 Word with station or water
55 Visconti's "The __"
56 Insulated
57 Actress Jessica
58 Household
59 Auto pioneer
60 Suppose
61 Paris's __ Marche
62 Feather vane
63 Raspberry stem
64 Gathers gossip
69 Polynesian island group
72 Eccentric
73 Sunday msg.
74 Home flight
76 Bank list
78 Kitchen ending
79 Intermediate
80 Item for Borge
82 Area of Italy
84 Consume
85 Innovates
89 Enzyme
90 Buffalo's milieu
91 Vices
92 Mon. follower
93 Color for 53 Across
94 Rush-hour sight
95 Refuse
96 LBJ dog

DOWN

1 Singer Pete and family
2 "__ be left alone"
3 Chewed out
4 Diminution
5 Ordinal suffix
6 Mouths
7 Colonist
8 Provided with a message
9 Israeli dance
10 __ go bragh
11 Wayside spot
12 Spheres
13 Campaign routine
14 Ave __ vale
15 Beam producer
17 Org. for Penguins and Sharks
21 Musical syllable
22 Mazel __
27 Call down (on)
29 Positioner
30 Uniquity
31 Fragments
33 Stinking
34 Pallid
36 Western resort
37 Contends
39 Athenian councils
40 Hung up
43 __ Semple MacPherson
44 Did a garden job
47 Tonic plant
48 Industrialist Hammer
49 Functional
50 Wrote in stone, in a way
51 Crew
52 Baldachin
53 Dilatory
54 Hip boot
55 Introduction
57 Moon goddess
58 Necessities
60 Benchley book
61 Fever symptom
63 Brains
65 Chanted
66 "Beauty __ . . ." (Keats)
67 Entourage
68 Pathmaker of a sort
70 Ger. article
71 Male ducks
74 Besmirch
75 Flirt
77 Ques. follower
78 Nigerian native
80 Prefix for house
81 Classical villain
82 Threatening
83 Seattle Sra.
86 Santha Rama __
87 Time before
88 Obtain

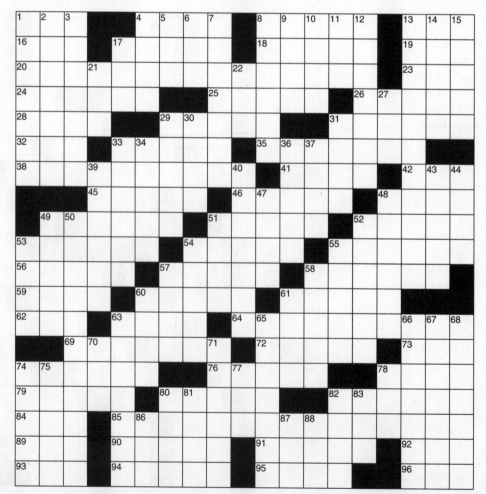

ACROSS

1 Singing foursome
5 Substandard
8 Normandy craft, for short
11 "Time for a change" item
17 Assignment for Te Kanawa
18 Sidekick
19 Wood sorrel
20 Hereditary
21 Dallas team, degenderized
24 Ken Russell's "The __ the White Worm"
25 Muscat native
26 Being
27 Regional conditions
28 Campaigned
29 Certain spot-marker
32 Geologist's subject
34 Litters' littles
37 Keatsian
39 Devotion
41 Obstruct
42 Dance step
45 Scary visions, degenderized
49 Royal pronoun
50 Harm
52 Bizarre
53 Essence
54 Make doughnuts
55 Judicial wear
57 Purple shade
59 Sag
61 Family group
63 Glacial mass
65 Cannily
68 Fantasies
70 Technique
72 __ of thought
73 Abby's sister
75 Words from Caesar
77 Iroquoians
79 Gaelic
80 Interval
81 Fighting vessel, degenderized
84 Aspiring capts.
85 Rainbows
87 Spotted
88 Actress Aumont
89 Day-trade
91 Districts
94 Word
95 Actress Hagen
98 Fortify afresh
100 Capable of
102 "Midnight at the __"
104 Esprit
106 Chaucer character, degenderized
109 Valuable
110 NASA report
111 Devitalize
112 Shivering spell
113 Chargers
114 George's bill
115 Prefix for fit or wit
116 Actress Harper

DOWN

1 Work hard
2 Redolence
3 Couch
4 Spahn's pitching partner
5 Unclose, poetically
6 Writer Weldon
7 Seal's perch
8 __ luck!
9 Sprightly music
10 Ger. article
11 Pickle additive
12 ". . . the bombs bursting __"
13 Hostility
14 Shell layer, degenderized
15 DDE's command
16 NBA figure
22 Author of "Seize the Moment"
23 Capitalize on
27 Went after
30 Singer Brickell
31 Double star in Orion
33 Expression
35 Shift
36 Nimble
38 Wallace of TV
40 Women's magazine
42 Prefix for meter
43 Conn. town
44 Dreiser tale, degenderized
46 Roofing material
47 Listen
48 Ermine
51 Detective's delight
56 Traverse
58 African capital
60 Brute
62 Cloys
64 Actor Montgomery
66 Register
67 Chem. endings
69 Current
71 Singer Huey
73 Regretful word
74 Vice squad mbr.
76 Subject for 74 Down
78 "Mens __ . . ."
82 Ahead of
83 Words with hope
86 Low-life fare
90 Blanched
92 "A pig in __"
93 Erwin of early TV
95 Procedure
96 "__ Andronicus"
97 Ruins
99 World Series winners, 1990
101 __ buco
103 Blind as __
104 U.K. legislators
105 Leftover
106 __ Paulo
107 Été cooler
108 Decide

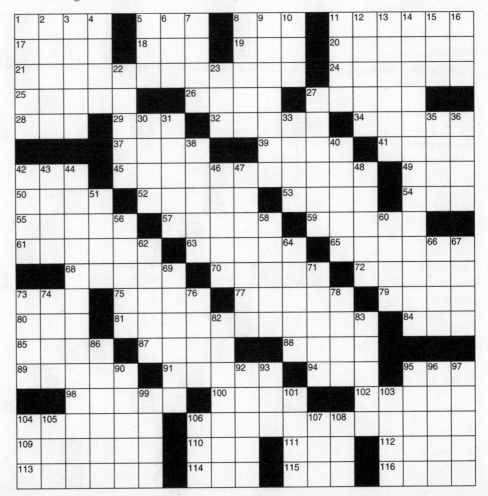

ACROSS

1 Alcott girl
4 Shakespearean sprite
8 Scarce
11 Miscreant
17 Bird: Prefix
18 __ Royale, Mich.
19 Gardner
20 Do computer work
21 Artist Ray's amusement?
24 Arthurian paradise
25 Cherub
26 Mount
27 Pinnacle
28 Demand
31 Sanctified
33 Endures
36 Cellular phone site
38 River to the Rhine
40 Pairs
42 Coalition
43 Reply to "you ain't!"
45 Addresses by Golfer Andy?
49 "I __ Rock"
50 Hangout for Gretzky
51 Pago Pago's place
52 Borscht ingredient
53 Moistened
54 Walking __ (elated)
56 Works on mail
58 Playwright O'Casey
60 Nursery-rhyme name
62 Symbol of obduracy
64 Immobilized
68 NL East park
70 Intimidate
72 Bagpipe sound
73 Pen point
76 Horace's years
78 Characteristic
80 Winged predators
81 Hosp. area
82 Transport for diva Kathleen?
84 Tantrum
85 Lobbying grps.
87 Stead
88 Malayan sword
90 Rds.' relatives
91 Hock
93 Grouses
96 As good __
98 Dispatches
100 Crime scene find
102 Fast-footed
105 Improvise

107 Sounds from singer Neneh?
110 North
111 Salad vegetable
112 Chagall
113 Interval
114 Chablis business
115 Mix in
116 Asian babysitter
117 Kind of light or line

DOWN

1 Peggy Wood TV role
2 Writer Hunter
3 Rest for Rogers?
4 Upstanding sort
5 U.N. member
6 Actor Gulager
7 Hogsheads
8 Crushing
9 NFL QB Jim
10 Conflict
11 Harvest
12 Incus
13 Egyptian talisman
14 Rule for singer Natalie?
15 Commotion

16 Actor Cariou
22 Gender
23 Fireplace shelf
27 Fur pieces
29 Ernie Banks's team
30 Writer Astley et al.
32 Mop
34 Heavy reading
35 Vamoose
36 Locust bean
37 Kind of acid
39 Actor Navarro
41 Clay pigeon
44 "Grapes of Wrath" group
46 W. Hem. defense system
47 Glut
48 Solemn
55 Recovery phase, for short
57 Mackles
59 Pianist Peter et al.
61 Kind of code or colony
63 Nosh
65 How actress Lesly-Anne flies?
66 Dark

67 Nuisances
69 Shenanigans
71 Royal coronet
73 Australasian palm
74 "__ hardly wait"
75 Family of sportscaster Jack?
77 Virginia willow
79 Speaker at Cooperstown
83 Staggered
86 Trick spot
89 Fragment
92 Closing bit
94 Implore
95 Prefix for mount or charge
97 Freudian concern
99 Fishing boat
101 Bombeck
103 Problem with 99 Down
104 Notice
105 Cut
106 Caliph killed in 661
107 P&L specialist
108 Sweet potato
109 Madrid Mme.

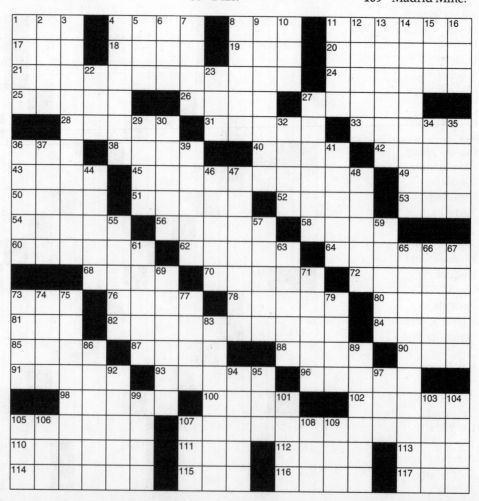

ACROSS

1 Woolly
7 His and hers
12 Produce department item
18 Unprincipled
19 Bisect
20 Washbowl
21 Book by Milton and Hilton?
24 RR stop
25 Flag
26 Sculled
27 Journalist St. Johns
29 Cubic meter
31 Prohibit
34 With "The," Wouk-Tolstoy book?
39 Price component
40 Cut
41 Dilapidated
42 Certain paintings
43 Branches
46 Flounders
48 Mataro Mrs.
49 Stickler
51 Cat __ tails
52 Tennyson-Shakespeare tale?
58 Follett's "__ the Needle"
59 Storehouses
60 Soap ingredient
61 Throwback
64 Actress Martha
65 Farm father
66 Jet black
67 Egyptian goddess
70 A Barrymore
71 Betty Macdonald-Robert Graves book?
77 Pouch
78 Domicile
79 Doubleday
80 Loungeabout
82 Part of QED
83 Agnus __
86 With "The," Ibsen-Swift book?
93 Obtrude
94 Denial words
95 Togetherness
96 Inconsistent
97 Collect
98 S. Calif. city

DOWN

1 Runner's units
2 He loves, to Caesar
3 Mrs. Charles
4 Mouths
5 Down
6 Select groups
7 "A Yank in __" (1941 film)
8 In good shape
9 Rock group, for short
10 Hosp. hookups
11 Born-again tire
12 Shone
13 Special
14 Eager
15 Writer Octavio
16 Nigerian native
17 Sequel word
22 Farm structure
23 Antler
27 Formicary group
28 Dentist's degree
29 Item for Kenny G
30 Uno plus due
31 City on the Kennebec
32 Entr' __
33 Fernando and Alejandro
34 Uncanny
35 Filling
36 Belt's place
37 Fork features
38 Atelier stand
39 "__ fan tutte"
43 Feints
44 Start of a Forster title
45 Anger
46 Wading bird
47 Insert
49 Wining and dining
50 Common article
51 Passable
53 Pier
54 Rule of conduct
55 Mr. Yale
56 Actor Lew
57 Movie part
61 Humanities
62 Weaverbird
63 With, in Val d'Isere
65 Arouse
67 Song of Morpheus?
68 Mix in
69 Business wear
70 Dutch commune
72 Printer's proof
73 Archer's "Kane and __"
74 World Series star, 1956
75 Blind as __
76 Disloyal
80 "Ain't No Woman Like the One __"
81 Sprinkle
82 Bombeck
83 Lucy's costar
84 N.C. campus
85 "Ignorance __ excuse . . ."
86 Family mbr.
87 Roman ruler: Abbr.
88 Mil. address
89 Tenn. player
90 Tanning time in Tours
91 Actress Todd
92 London's Old __ Theater

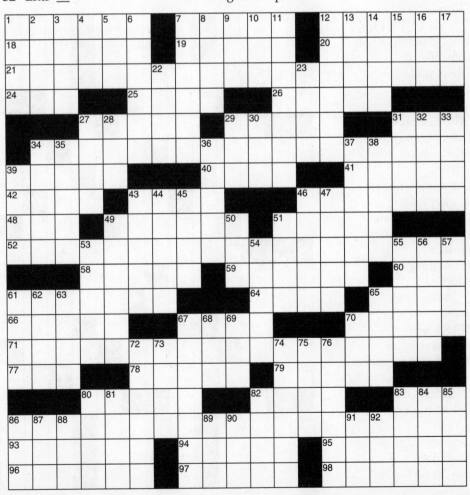

ACROSS

1 Webber musical
5 Philter holder
9 Chunk
13 Indian city
17 __ Rios, Jamaica
18 __ girl!
19 Role model
20 Example
21 Deceptions
23 Energy source
24 Writer Whitney
25 Green light
26 Tenebrific
27 "Bali __"
29 Moby's pursuer
31 NFC team
34 Links outlay
39 Model Tiegs
41 Hobbyist's purchase
43 Gibe
44 Power org.
45 Baseball great Waite
46 Writer Martin
48 Group effort
49 Rat following
50 Follows
52 Calm
54 "__ Man" (1981 film)
57 Unseld of basketball
58 Cezanne
60 Hosp. units
62 Certain payee
63 Great writing
66 White elephant, e.g.
69 Kind of hold
70 Stable shade
71 Bill
74 Odysseus's father
76 Wicker willow
78 Coeur d'__, Idaho
80 Hebrew measure
81 Hostelry
83 Promoting mildew
85 Atop
86 __ Bluffs, Mass.
87 Seep
89 NASA report
90 Washday toiler
92 First Amendment
   subject
95 Daughter of Herodias
97 It was, to Vergil
98 Benefit
100 Sandwich letters
101 Draft org.
104 Hat for de Gaulle

106 Girder
109 Bicoastal crowd
112 Actor Baldwin
113 Journalism
114 Fellini's farewell
115 Juno
116 Ibsen girl
117 Elation
118 Lamarr
119 Oenophile's concern

DOWN

1 Replica
2 Farm unit
3 Hit song of 1969
4 Overimbiber
5 Dessert flavor
6 "Hello, __"
7 Consumed
8 Pelt
9 Moderator
10 Court call
11 Gaudalajara gold
12 Tomorrow in Turin
13 "__ of bread . . ."
14 Recuperate
15 Back-comb

16 Commotion
22 Anxious
28 Go-between: Abbr.
30 FDR's last VP
32 Pretentious
33 Kitchen item
35 Season on the Seine
36 Jug
37 Battle
38 Woodland deity
39 Dog breed
40 Fla. sound
42 Map abbr.
47 Mangle
48 "Stand __"
49 Turkish rulers
51 Exhausted
53 City on the Rhone
55 Steinbeck character
56 Actress Davis
59 Cosmetic ingredient
61 Runs
63 Whirring noise
64 Promptly
65 Undecided
66 Standoffish
67 Mo. town

68 Apiarist
71 Tullahoma's state
72 Part of A.M.
73 "To __ not to
   be . . ."
75 Extent
77 "__ my best"
79 Impend
82 Born
84 Party pooper
87 Sp. she-bear
88 Choosing
89 Hesitant sounds
91 Repetition
93 "All My Children"
   character
94 Anathema
96 Draw __ on (aim at)
99 Imprint
102 Blood fluids
103 Mark of excellence
104 Neb. neighbor
105 Rock group initials
107 Writer Kaufman
108 Mind-boggle
110 Go fast
111 Friends' word

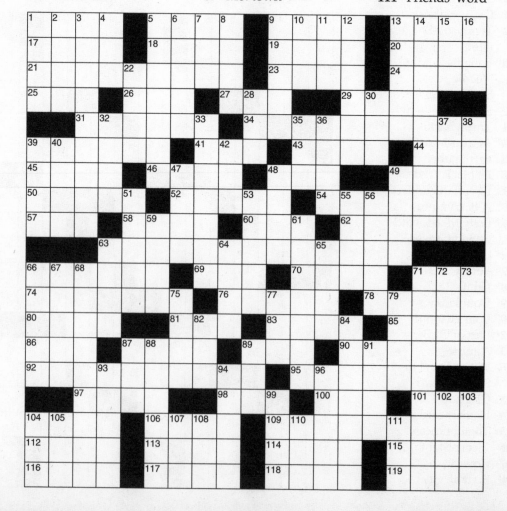

ACROSS

1 Folkestone farewell
5 Site of Fora Beach
8 TV's Bonet
12 Bass grouping
17 "The Thrill __ All"
18 Actress Todd
19 Surmounting
20 Moving force
21 Salad-bar attendants?
24 Nuance
25 Embellished, menu-style
26 Nutty
27 Hazard
29 Tuck's companion
30 Links concern
31 Verity
33 Toll
34 Summer desserts
35 Roush of baseball fame
36 Existed
37 Farm female
38 Regarding
40 How to patronize salad bars?
44 Standard
47 "__ worse than death . . ."
49 Cartouche
50 Home of the Magic
52 "The Harvey __" (1946 film)
53 MacDonald-Eddy effort
54 Migration
55 Prefix for corn or color
56 In __ (bored)
57 Proposal starter
58 Fair
59 Occupy
60 You, to Miou-Miou
61 Marrying time
62 Mock
63 Indian garb
64 Exceed
66 Actor Paul
67 One of the bases
68 Butcher's offering
69 Crouton
72 Tinctures
74 Hold the title
75 Elec. unit
76 Certain records, for short
79 Orchestral group
81 Exchange
83 Czech leader
85 Tell's canton
86 Shoemaker's tool
87 Penury
88 Lieutenant
89 Murphy of films
91 "Mary __": storied ship
93 Salad-preparation spaces?
96 Country
97 Canon
98 Holmes's "__ Hoss Shay"
99 Waste allowance
100 Like __ (probably)
101 Actress Thompson
102 Houston
103 Poet Teasdale

DOWN

1 Chain fastener
2 Pusillanimous
3 In layers
4 Solar disk
5 __ Tafari
6 Pokeweed
7 Words with a time
8 Exercise units
9 Dweller: Suffix
10 Miseries
11 Orbital point
12 Mission
13 Cry of disgust
14 Salad-bar accountants?
15 Actress MacDowell
16 Basketball violation
22 Birdbrains
23 Ordinal ending
28 R.R. stop
32 Clip
33 Distributor part
34 "__ Wonderful Life"
37 Louver
39 Mope
40 Goofy's creator
41 Parade path
42 Times before
43 Bucephalus, e.g.
45 Ingenious
46 Meat cuts
47 Ventilate
48 Salad-bar expanse?
51 Erstwhile auto
52 Cancun cats
53 Aquila star
54 Subject
57 Robitaille of hockey
58 Concrete ingredient
59 Kingfish
61 "The Sun Also Rises" character
62 San __, P.R.
63 Less intricate
65 Remunerates
66 Back street
67 Seethe
70 Convention-hall site
71 Italian city
73 Health club
76 Writer Welty
77 Undercoat
78 Nap
79 Livy's birthplace
80 Athlete Jesse
82 Writer Malraux
83 Towel inscription
84 Granada goodbye
87 Departed
88 Cruising
90 Periods
92 Friend of Pooh
94 Horror-film street
95 Jasper, for one

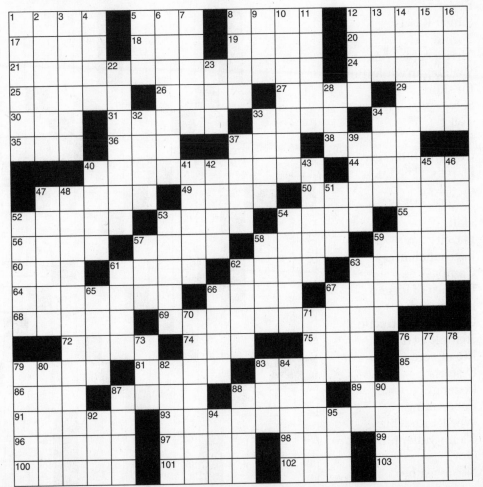

ACROSS

1 Swathe
4 Attention-getter
8 Attention-getters
13 "Just You __"
17 Friend in France
18 Nope relative
19 Corday's victim
20 Bog matter
21 Golfer Crenshaw
22 Infant
23 Sailing vessel
25 Winglike
27 Benton output
29 Shoe width
30 Sparkler
31 Chimney top
33 Stray
34 Moslem teacher
36 "Whiffenpoof Song"
   refrain
38 Placatory gesture
39 Acapulco agreements
42 Rate
43 Pronouncements
45 Once's partner
46 Bloke
48 Singer Rawls
49 Forbid
50 "Irresistable" one
51 Waukegan wintertime,
   for short
54 Selves
56 Twist
58 Purpose
59 Contemptuous cry
60 Harte's "The Luck
   of __"
63 Taunt
64 Hail
65 Fla. city
66 Bacchanalian cry
67 Compass pt.
68 Big bird of legend
69 Hardwood
70 Common contraction
72 Actor Mischa
74 Rio of note
76 Distorts
78 Lozenge
82 Poly ending
83 Word with whiz
84 Glenn Miller hit, 1940
86 Opt
88 Not aweather

89 Isosceles shape
90 Sum, translated
92 S.F. hill
93 Domestic
95 Colloidal dispersions
96 Frightful film of 1980
99 Fibula's terminus
101 __ Tin-Tin
102 Melville tale
103 Embankment
104 Triathlon item
105 Chem. ending
106 Salamander
107 Guide
108 Albertville's river
109 Ger. pronoun

DOWN

1 Rock 'n roll classic
2 Earhart et al.
3 Holiday targets
4 Spot for Andy Capp
5 Hypocrisy
6 Bedroom community
7 Frost's "__ Not Taken"
8 Saunter

9 Lucas of films
10 Miss the mark
11 Concept
12 Harden
13 Pertinent
14 Race-track negativists?
15 Hamlet, for one
16 Particular
24 Music-man Riddle
26 Fiddle relative
28 Help
32 Bacon unit
34 Extinct bird
35 Ventilate
37 Loose __
38 Hurt
40 Actress Massey et al.
41 Environmental
   problem
44 Related by birth
45 Cape Cod town
47 Trespass
49 Spain's Costa __
51 Kind of account
52 Relishes
53 Hot stuff

55 Monterrey Mrs.
57 Crackerjack
61 "__ Ike"
62 Took a hard look
69 Part of ACTH
71 Garbage
73 Towns in N.Y.
   and Ga.
75 Born
76 Clique
77 Slip through
79 Influenced
80 Hard-wired link
81 Lou Grant
   portrayer
83 Gizzard
85 Courier's game
87 Game birds
88 Vexation
90 Lay __ the line
91 Alas
93 Arrow poison
94 NHL feint
97 Torrid
98 "__ had it!"
100 Ballad ending

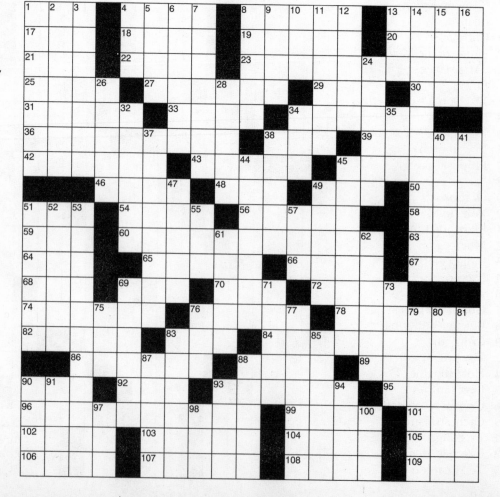

ACROSS

1 Noted slugger
6 Censures
12 Dark red
18 System of belief
19 Pistol: Sl.
20 Sukova of tennis
21 Concerning drum-playing?
23 Captivate
24 Cereal spike
25 Barbecue-chef's wear
26 Autocrat
28 Balance
29 Duck
31 City on the Rhine
33 Eucalyptus product
34 Secant's reciprocal
36 Writer Rand
37 Distilling gear
41 Skating maneuver
42 Concerning pulling power?
46 Self
47 Extend
49 Like some disks
50 Mule's eternal quest
52 Aardwolf's prey
53 Tuckered out
55 Charles pet
57 Bone: Prefix
58 Opera part
59 Jacket style
61 Business: Abbr.
64 Thwart
67 Discussion group
69 Caviar
72 At all
74 Negligent
76 Film critic Roger
78 Lala precursor
79 Concerning examinations?
82 __ on the back
83 Antedate
85 Struggle and strain
86 Flaunt
88 "__ gratia . . ."
89 Like cattails
92 Disney classic
93 No-frills
95 Penurious
96 "It must have been something __"
97 Fix
100 Marked down
102 Concerning sanitation work?
106 Texas town
107 Sponge-cake dessert
108 Hair dye
109 Revolt
110 Weather word
111 One of the Bergens

DOWN

1 Field unit
2 Sector
3 Concerning gift?
4 Paean
5 William the Conqueror, e.g.
6 Savage
7 Forgotten
8 Zebra relative
9 __ fi
10 Tavern-keeper Shor
11 Impression
12 "Mask" actress
13 Actor Cariou
14 Call to battle
15 Concerning club group?
16 Slaughter
17 Bitter
22 Fruit drink
27 Asian range
30 Disgusting
31 "The Corsair" poet
32 Take __ (doze)
33 Actress Rowlands
34 Entertainer Irene
35 Beasts of burden
36 "Edda" king
38 Find
39 "__ Rhythm"
40 Bird shed
43 Musical key
44 IRS watcher
45 Cobb and Hardin
48 Tolstoy subject
51 Howard of films
54 Like some stocks
56 Apprehensive
58 Police msg.
60 Cry to Manolete
61 Poult's place
62 __ about (circa)
63 Concerning specialized cars?
65 Bauxite, for one
66 Chick __
67 Hard to please
68 Court great
69 Concerning male selection?
70 Mouthward
71 Usher ending
73 Peeves
75 "Nickelodeon" star
77 Harpoon feature
80 Withered
81 Outpouring
84 Wrinkle
87 Actor Don
90 Ground
91 Ano opener
92 Textile worker
93 Churl
94 "Just You __"
95 Vault
96 That, to Horace
98 N.Y. campus
99 Watchdog sound
101 Baton Rouge initials
103 Op. __
104 Frequently, in poems
105 Bill's film cohort

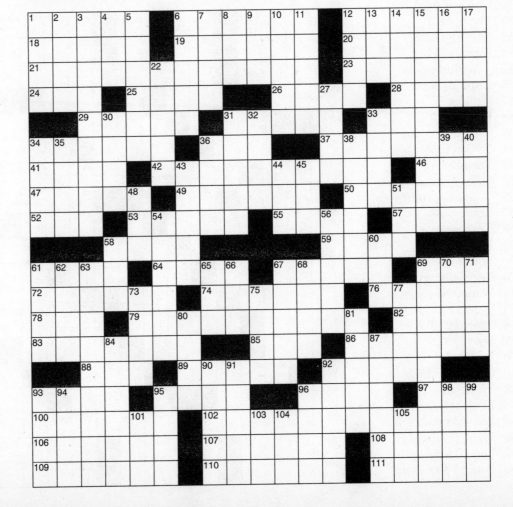

ACROSS

1 Jog
5 Street urchin
9 Singer Marvin
13 Decides
17 Capstone
18 Regarding
19 Hwys.
20 __ accompli
21 Designer Bohan
22 Oscar-winner of 1981
25 Fanciful
27 Birthright-seller of note
28 Freshen up
29 Shoat's hangout
30 Turgenev
31 Squash, e.g.
33 Written words
36 Locale
37 Marionette-maker Tony
38 Common conifer
41 Particle
42 "Easy Rider" items
45 Yours and mine
46 Salientian
48 Brooch
49 Comfortable
50 Mystique
51 Basically
53 Santa __, Calif.
55 __ in the bucket
56 Unpredictable
57 Heckles
58 Expand
59 ". . . Ain't __ fun"
61 Transit tools
62 Trash
65 Pine
66 Cugnot's product
67 Exist
68 Gosh relative
69 The Beatles' "__ Loves You"
70 Legislative grab-bag
74 Pamplona cheer
75 __ favor
76 "Barton __" (1991 film)
77 Shot
78 Spiritual
80 Cline of music
82 Withered
83 River at Balmoral Castle
84 Work on puzzles
86 Eight: Prefix
87 Playoff series
91 Logical way to go?

95 Workshop tool
96 Film of 1987
97 Karma
98 Whistle
99 Writer Maxwell
100 "I've __ there"
101 Walked
102 Nimble
103 Futurist

DOWN

1 Easy mark
2 Hyalite
3 Ecuador neighbor
4 Immoderation
5 Absurd
6 Wan
7 Give-whirl link
8 Always
9 Creak
10 Aleutian isle
11 Green light
12 That: Sp.
13 Proposition
14 Lerner-Loewe musical
15 Flag

16 Cassoulet
23 Father of 27 Across
24 Horror film of 1972
26 Petiole
30 Element No. 26
31 Catsup alternative
32 Victim
33 Sandwich bread
34 Cheer
35 Morally superior
36 "Look __ my way"
37 Battle marks
39 Prefix for dollar
40 Shroud
43 Nashville institution
44 "The Winding Stair" poet
47 Crusoe's creator
50 Yellow clay
52 Nautical direction
53 Mediterranean tree
54 Recline
55 Timetable abbr.
57 Dyed fabric
58 Certain Highlander

59 Hymenopter
60 Resound
61 Jocular
62 Puzzle diagram
63 Tempest
64 Fritzlar's river
66 Writer Martin
67 Busy as __
70 Frequently
71 Employ for
72 Brussels __
73 Place
79 Ganglia
81 Of the birds
82 Plan, for short
83 Eccentric
84 Try
85 Calvados
86 Bismarck
87 Aesir defender
88 Cleo's "highway"
89 Being
90 Simon's "My Favorite __"
92 Not quite e'er
93 Much
94 Org. for G. Bush

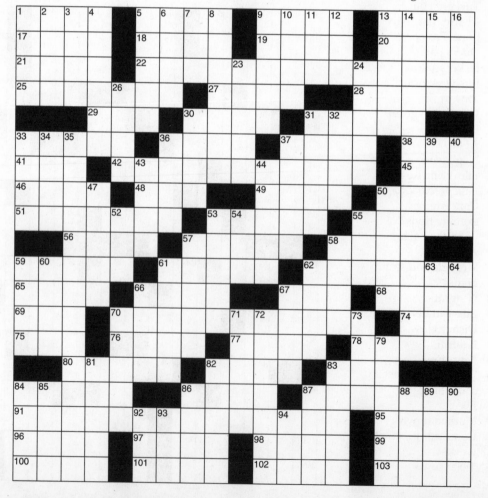

ACROSS

1 Suspires
6 Low-down mutt
9 Fabler septet
13 Power unit
17 Benefit
18 The Beach Boys' "Surfin' __"
19 Baylor's town
20 Impression
21 Byword
22 Florist-shop message?
25 Dry run
27 Concerning
28 "The Power of __" (1992 film)
29 Tableland
30 Check out
31 P.D. James's "The Black __"
35 Burn
37 Ooh followers
39 Cancun coin
42 Gardner
43 Coop female
44 Student error
47 Outfit
48 Apr. 15 fixation
49 "Just keep __"
50 Hawk feature
51 Presque __, Maine
52 Backpack item
54 Steps
55 Vulgar
56 PBS material
57 Modern Cambria
58 Defect
59 "Gather ye rosebuds while __"
61 Scorned
62 Hash-house cook
65 Victim
66 Carnivals
67 Squad
68 Mature
69 Decay
70 Balm for body aches?
72 Breach
73 That: Sp.
74 Kind of rule or trust
75 Dehiscent
76 Possesses
77 Singer Bob ("Still The Same")
79 Pantry lineup
81 GWTW place
83 Altar above

85 Where Lima is
86 Sports stats
89 "Singer Dolly's unlike Hammer"
94 Pentateuch
95 Others, to Horace
96 Nolte
97 Three, in Tivoli
98 "The __" (1960 film)
99 '80s hallmark
100 Fencing sword
101 Spell
102 Went back to the altar

DOWN

1 Hominy dish
2 Composer Novello
3 Security officer's ID?
4 Batsman
5 Black haws
6 Snippy
7 Employ
8 Extremist
9 Avowed
10 Fluency
11 Expert
12 Mediocre
13 Songbird
14 Peculiar
15 CSA VIP
16 Road surface
23 Nucleic acid
24 Victorious
26 Hails
30 Tenuous
32 "Crude Polish Joke!"
33 Iniquity
34 Fads
35 Stylish
36 Juno
38 A play on words
39 Windrows
40 Heroic poetry
41 "Empire of the __" ('87 film)
44 Reverence
45 Most hackneyed
46 Spiked
51 Boxer Barkley
53 Salver
54 "Gloria __"
55 Ascend
57 Belt's place
58 Shows off

59 W.W. I battleground
60 Worn down
61 Mata __
62 Dried up
63 Actor Richard
64 Congress mbrs.
66 Whoopee
67 Recipe abbrs.
70 Pack animal
71 O'Hara's "__ Frederick"
76 AL East player
78 Corrode
79 Panic under pressure
80 River isle
82 "__ Is Born"
84 Singer Murray
85 Erstwhile
86 Fastigium
87 Pliant
88 Loafered
89 Overstate
90 Brew
91 Josh
92 Quick quaff
93 Exist

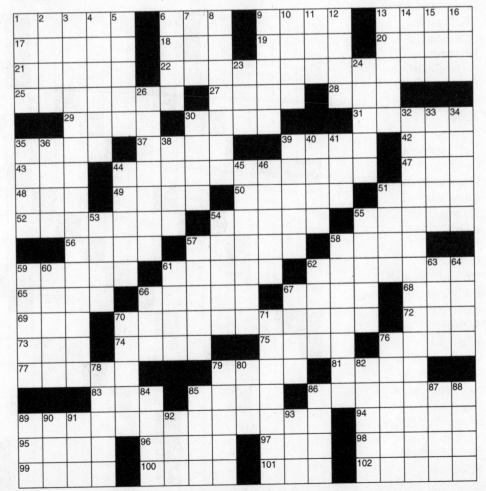

ACROSS

1 Hereto
6 Heggen's "__ Roberts"
12 Envelop
18 Vestige
19 Punctual
20 Toxophilite
21 Steelhead, e.g.
23 Llama relative
24 "On __ Day . . ."
25 __ Tafari
26 "Since __ You Baby"
28 Figs.
29 "__ Three Lives"
30 Workers' equity arr.
32 Genetic material
33 Murray of baseball
35 Koppel
36 Actor Tognazzi
37 Mornay or marinara
39 Legal thing
40 Migratory bird
43 Japanese gelatin
45 Gesture to
48 Painful protest
49 High-impact suggestion
52 Without purpose
53 Crichton's "Jurassic __"
54 Persuade
55 A Gershwin
56 Performing pair
57 "Tono Bungay" author
59 Tarries
60 Boat problem
61 Old French coin
62 Dusseldorf dwelling
63 Juicy fruit
64 "Name of the Rose" monk
65 Avenge
67 Chaff
68 Up and about
70 Radius or carpus
71 Heliotrope
73 Arthur of TV
74 High-risk
76 Office machine
77 Dance step
80 Sawfish feature
82 Reposed
83 Shepard or Paton
85 Vermin
86 Household deity
87 Brioche
89 Writer Burrows
90 Custon, old-style
92 Power-ful name
94 Firefly
97 Delight
98 "The seven hills __"
99 Win by __
100 Bed canopy
101 Matched
102 Check signer

DOWN

1 Dardanelles, e.g.
2 Sage
3 Unsuccessful
4 Pimpled
5 Singer McEntire
6 Cut
7 Opening section
8 Watch adjunct
9 Sp. uncles
10 Cassowary
11 Following
12 Put by
13 Scribe
14 Noun case: Abbr.
15 War film of 1952
16 Matisse and Rousseau
17 Computer key
22 Portland's place
27 Entertainer Davis
31 Plant
32 Sprint
34 Lackluster
36 Numero __
37 Punch
38 Primordial
40 "The Sheltering __" (1990 film)
41 Ends
42 Royal pronoun
44 Guys' counterparts
45 Patient sort
46 Derive
47 Amber-colored fruit
49 Paraphernalia
50 Worn down
51 Boca __, Fla.
53 Advantage
54 Kiosk
57 Question of time
58 Mitigated
59 Egoist's concern
63 Trivial
64 Demeanor
66 Zoo sound
67 Singer Lewis
68 New Zealand town
69 Writer Stout
71 Bivalve mollusk
72 Bergman's "Smiles __ Summer Night"
73 Dickensian figure
75 Poorly
77 Low-tech bowling worker
78 Inculpate
79 Singer Pete
80 Dozed
81 "__ by any other name . . ."
83 Hate
84 Words with see or go
85 __ Carta
88 Uniquity
89 Prefix for culture
91 Cookie type
93 Took a chair
95 "__ Man Answers" (1962 film)
96 Buntline

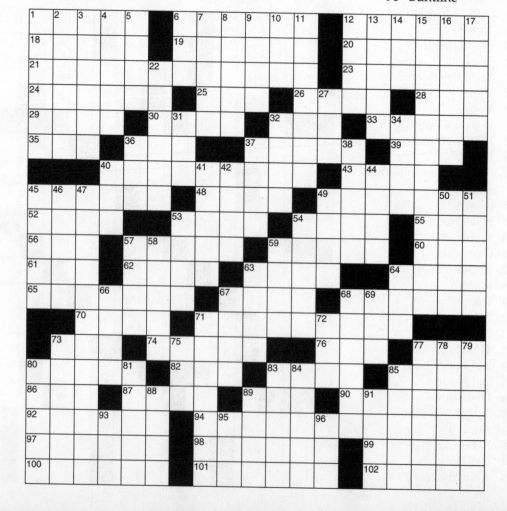

ACROSS

1 Declivity
4 Hard fall
10 Bond rating
13 Doris Dorrie film
16 Common Market Unit
17 Dundee of boxing
18 Drudgery
19 Pongo
20 Va. tourist attraction
22 Aware of
23 Edge
24 Atahualpa, e.g.
25 Black bird
26 NYC suburb
29 Syndicate
31 Plane detectors, for short
32 Pamphlet ending
33 Friend or lover
35 Empowers
37 Wise __ owl
39 Running track
43 Depends
45 Hoot's companion
47 Writer Brookner
48 Susan Lucci role
49 Anatomical tissues
50 Calif. town
52 Tonic plant
53 Sportscaster Rashad
54 Agronomist's concern
55 Day parts, for short
56 Light-and-shadow art
58 Mexican Mrs.
61 PGA or AMA
62 Approaches
63 Domestic
67 Long-running musical
69 Beverly of opera
70 Compendious
71 Eniwetok, e.g.
72 Neighborhood
74 Porthos's friend
75 Reach
76 Indiana town
77 Part of GATT
79 Consult
80 Modernist
82 Sailor's saint
84 Encrusted
86 "Enrico IV" playwright
90 "Cheers" character
91 Prevaricated
94 Actress Lupino
95 U.K. containers
96 Minor fault
99 Demantoid, for one
100 Coarse
101 Lady of 67 Across
102 Delay
103 Exhaust
104 Printer's measures
105 Contribute
106 Switch positions

DOWN

1 Moore of movies
2 Statue
3 Fine point
4 "Bali __"
5 Packages
6 Proxies
7 Supermarket section
8 Right-angle joint
9 Inn units
10 City on the Rhine
11 "Once __" (1985 film)
12 Chap
13 Astronomer's concern
14 Larger-than-life
15 Verne captain
18 Gelatin dish
21 Morrison's "__ Baby"
27 Certain exams
28 Actor Jeremy
30 Eye part
31 Burn, in Barcelona
33 Precinct
34 See 25 Across
36 "__ I Love"
38 British bowers
40 Aqua __
41 Particle
42 Pandect matter
44 Rapper __ T
46 N. Texas town
47 A Guthrie
49 Scottish emblem
51 Pretensions
53 Charlie Chan's remark
54 Mountain-climber
56 Summons
57 Unload on
58 Fraud
59 Pro __
60 Wild
63 __ culpa
64 Sloth relative
65 Mother of Horus
66 Secretary
68 Actress Verdugo
69 Oar
70 "Star __"
73 Ultimatum phrase
74 Obdurate
76 Dais spot
78 Locust tree
81 __ nous
83 Sulked
85 Whitney
86 Barrow and farrow
87 Intimation
88 Freeway adjunct
89 Limits
90 Look over
92 Gusto
93 "The __ of War" (1980 film)
97 Rock group initials
98 Billy __ Williams

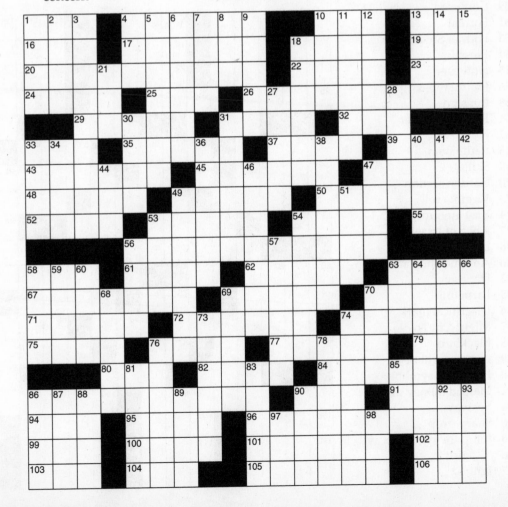

ACROSS

1 Tennis's Bjorn et al.
6 Festive
10 Jeanne or Marie
13 Natterjack
17 Albertville's river
18 Heron relative
19 Moslem pilgrimage
20 Cartoonist Peter
21 Extract
22 Daytime TV fare
23 Before
24 Welles role
25 TV game show
27 Easy chair
29 Hit sign
30 Con
32 Christie's "__ Little Indians"
33 Maize dish
36 Support system
39 "The Story __ Woman" (1969 film)
41 Turkish VIPs
45 Legitimate
46 Dining area
47 Proverbial slow turner
49 Confused
51 Format
53 Former Soviet unit
54 Pressure
55 However
56 Fretful types
59 Inn sign
61 Reliable worker
62 Noria
65 Radio item
68 Skill
70 Garden section
73 Virginia rail
74 Vast amount
77 Abba of Israel
78 Dumbfound
80 Antique-shop attractions
83 Deprive
85 Farm unit
86 Diacritical mark
87 Mighty, in Tokyo
88 Blackbird
89 Libya neighbor
90 Freshness symbol
92 Madrid money unit
94 Sp. wave
96 Sharp drop
100 Jump for joy, in a way
106 "__ girl!"
107 Ignited

108 Melange
109 Knife type
110 Type type: Abbr.
111 Old French coin
112 Easy's partner
113 Cat __ tails
114 Timber
115 Green light
116 Chemical compound
117 Saturn feature

DOWN

1 Heavy-hitter
2 Modern Christiania
3 Bioherm
4 Battleship of 1939
5 Mexican Mr.
6 Core
7 "__ Ben Adhem"
8 Rain-forest vines
9 Rockies resort
10 Marshals
11 Darnel
12 Toss out
13 Assuming control
14 Algerian port
15 Actress Archer

16 Activist
26 Part
28 Meadows
31 Furthermore
33 Command to Fido
34 Comedian Johnson
35 Obligation
37 Lewis's "__ Gantry"
38 Shines
40 Driver Foyt et al.
42 Skedaddles
43 Nervous as __
44 Collector's items
47 U.S. VP, 1877-81
48 Impulses
50 Tennis great
52 Recondite
57 Bodies
58 Deckhand's implement
60 Bear up there
61 Plays the tycoon
63 Cognizant
64 Drift
65 Stage whisper
66 Shoshonean
67 Seed cover

69 __ judicata
70 Sinfonia man
71 Pound
72 Covenant
75 "Howards __" (1992 film)
76 Sixth Century pope
79 Cheese partner
81 Requisite
82 Motorcyclist's stunt
84 Coalition
88 "__ Rouge" (1952 film)
91 Aviator Post
93 Actress Sharon
95 Toil
96 Carpentry item
97 Bismarck
98 Kind of horn or hound
99 Bad habit
101 Baseball's Petrocelli
102 Coward
103 World Series Competitor, 1991
104 W.Va. City
105 Comprehends

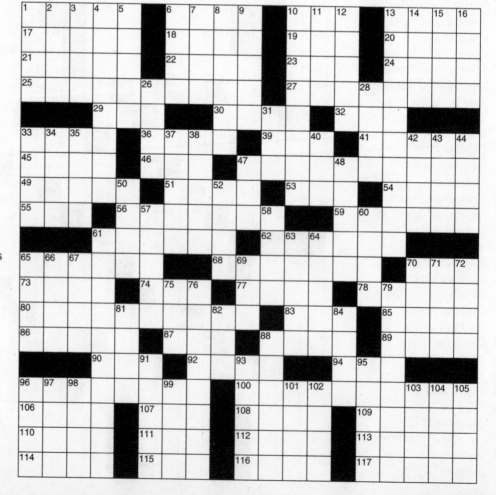

ACROSS

1 Yard goods
6 Arid expanse
12 Roman poet
18 One of the Jameses
19 Boomed
20 L.A.'s __ of the Stars
21 Hard-working beast of burden?
23 Note
24 Actor Christian
25 Rock group
26 Eastern inn
27 Race distance
28 Writer Godwin
30 Embitter
32 __ facto
35 Understand
36 Fish dish
37 Command
38 Thrown for __
39 Opinionated animal?
42 Female rabbit
43 Size up
46 "Time __ Bottle"
47 Manute of the NBA
48 Actor John
50 Range
52 TV room
53 "Berenice" composer
54 Work
55 Incursion
57 Cabbage plant
58 Calif. county
61 Strata
63 Spellbound
64 Frenzy
65 Coast
67 Cooperative effort
68 Actress Alicia
70 Hanoi holiday
71 Skill
72 Timid creature?
75 Clobber
77 Writer Murdoch
78 Eskimo knives
79 Greek letters
82 Computer key
83 "All __" (1984 film)
84 Garden invader
85 Hoodwink
86 __ nous
88 Haggard tale
89 Docket
91 Vinegary
93 Reaction-producing pet?

96 Item for Bourke-White
97 Twelve-step program
98 Cabaret
99 Dodges
100 Film of 1965
101 Species

DOWN

1 Ravines
2 Howard of films
3 Marked down
4 Overused
5 London park
6 Sellout letters
7 Visitors' Bureau concern
8 Studio stand
9 Baby carriage
10 Foot
11 News execs
12 More robust
13 Done
14 Kind of price
15 Contrary creature?
16 Signal
17 Election ending
22 Goad
26 Time-telling device
29 Diatom
30 Cruise
31 Grampus
33 Shortly
34 Newspaper page: Abbr.
36 Abridge
37 Buckinghamshire school
38 Mellowed
40 Sleeping
41 Caen's river
43 Self
44 Kennel sound
45 Bird that irritates?
49 Actress Olin
51 Benefits
52 Pluto
53 Alfalfa
55 Make over
56 Herring relative
57 Boat bottom
59 Chart type
60 Pretense
62 Iniquity
63 Certain law-enforcers

64 Some come with claws
65 Lip
66 Bombeck
67 Soft cheese
68 Rights org.
69 Nutty mixture
73 Tributary
74 Holiday burner
76 Set up camp
79 Indiana city
80 Modernize
81 In a chair
83 Killer whales
84 Journalist Alexander
85 Home furnishings
87 Flag
88 Pentacle
90 Bee Gees family name
91 Standout
92 Film of 1984
93 Motor part
94 MacGraw
95 Chem. ending

ACROSS

1 Goya subject
5 Crispin's product
9 __ Bator
13 Ice mass
17 "How high __?"
18 Catfish
19 Pathway
20 District
21 Flaccid
22 Oscar winner, 1992
25 Maligned
27 El __, Texas
28 Old storyteller
29 Restrain
30 "The More __ You"
32 Dozes
34 Plant pest
36 Scent
37 Floral pattern
38 Stable morsel
41 U.K. dwellers
43 Where FDR died
46 Spirit
47 Scull
49 Ballyhoos
50 Pager sound
51 Phone abbr.
52 "__ Vera" (film of 1979)
53 Call off
54 Martin and marabou
55 "The Lion __ Tonight"
57 All right
60 Drawbacks
63 La-la lead-in
65 Wrigglesome
66 Cuprite color
69 Presence
70 Must
72 Gal of song
73 Role model
74 Fled
77 Cheese dish
79 Danson
80 Swiss river
81 Throngs
83 Solely
84 The Beatles' "__ Love Her"
85 Sp. cigar
86 Humdinger
87 Muscat native
90 Clapton
92 Heat treatments
96 "Hanging paper"
99 Concert halls
100 Suspicion
101 Pilaster
102 Segment
103 NBA team
104 Make a difference
105 Loch of note
106 Didion's "Play __ It Lays"
107 Oaxaca wives

DOWN

1 Uris's "__ 18"
2 Warranty disclaimer
3 Bridge-bidding maneuver
4 Proclivity
5 Twitch
6 Whet
7 Topped
8 Ordinal ending
9 Arm bones
10 Ballads
11 "I am looking for __ man" (Diogenes)
12 Modernist
13 Scorches
14 Discordia
15 Gambling mecca
16 Sound of surprise
23 Drive
24 Monograph
26 Fix up, in a way
31 Plant
33 Elec. units
34 Workmanlike
35 Cannes award
36 Mo. river
37 Begrimes
38 Uniquity
39 Ripened
40 Recipe abbrs.
42 Zilch
44 Writer Jaffe
45 Footnote word
48 Comeback
52 Capp and Kaline
54 Turhan of films
55 Exchange
56 __ speak
58 Brings up
59 First name in jazz
60 Snappy
61 Gospel name
62 Dusty
64 Shopper's query
66 Hoops player, at times
67 Ireland
68 Be overfond
70 Kind of line or light
71 Actress Barbeau
73 Devilish sorts
75 Financial disaster
76 Conjunction
78 Julia of films
82 Bay lynx
84 Yearly record
85 Type units
86 Tilts
87 News item
88 Status
89 Writer Jean
91 Mil. groups
93 Gumbo
94 "__ move on!"
95 Back talk
97 Baker-Finch of golf
98 Prefix for center

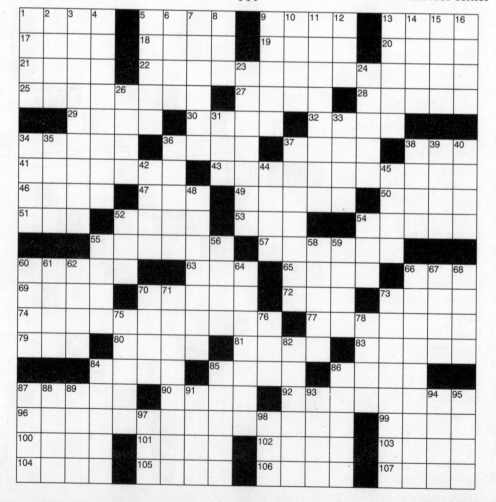

ACROSS

1 Juncture
5 File maker
8 Mo. city, for short
13 Masticate
17 City on the Brazos
18 S.A. port, for short
19 "__ Knows" (1958 hit)
20 Romanian dance
21 Impeachment group
23 Like the car industry?
25 Telethon gear
26 Small amounts
28 Site of Van Gogh's "yellow house"
29 Western Indian
30 Believes
31 Dip
33 Receptacles
35 Comrades
36 Bond
37 Musical syllable
40 Qty.
41 Like a good lawyer?
44 Excuse me!
45 Barn bleat
46 Owns
47 Once more
48 Chancy city
49 Incorporates
52 Telescope part
53 Sandy ridge
54 "It must have been something __"
55 Business
57 English Channel feeder
58 Instructs
60 Actor Dourif
61 Muskogean
65 Leaf angle
66 Fanatical
68 London's Old __
69 Op. __
70 Commiseration
71 Classy quality in mining?
73 Parrot
74 Barnyard spot
75 Mouthful
76 Illusionist's prop
77 Janus and Jove
78 Maintained
79 Divests
81 Ending for east or west
82 Glistened
85 Not __ in the world
86 Bellyaches
89 Forest-products tycoon?
92 Passed
94 Hershiser of baseball
95 Correct
96 __ de siècle
97 Writer Morrison
98 Marquee
99 Revel
100 Tallow
101 Sleipnir's rider

DOWN

1 Quid pro quo
2 Apiece
3 Good banker's need?
4 Intensifies
5 Very, in Versailles
6 Melisma
7 Johnson's companion
8 Slow mover
9 Flacks
10 Scribbles
11 Lennon's widow
12 Common Market initials
13 Phylactery
14 "The __ Baltimore"
15 Pa. city
16 W.W. II group
22 Grasp
24 Vituperate
27 "Demian" author
30 Specious
31 Forecasters
32 Ford
33 "The __" (1992 film)
34 Mosque official
35 Concord
36 Noted rock rollers
37 Criticism of lumber?
38 Coty or Auberjonois
39 Cupid
41 "__ happenin'?"
42 Empty of cargo
43 Kind of tea
44 Torch's offense
50 Marshal
51 Controversy
53 Dispossess
56 Shankar
57 P.D. James's "__ to Murder"
58 Night music
59 Sartre's "No __"
60 Baseball's George
62 Ties up
63 Told tales
64 Greek letters
66 Trickle
67 More recent
72 Absconded
75 "Cheers" offering
77 Cave
78 Genuflected
79 Odor
80 Robust
81 Fumble
82 Descry
83 Tortoise rival
84 Frank
85 Ripening additive
86 Bloke
87 Actress Anderson
88 Corium
90 Spigot
91 "__ Happy Man"
93 Itinerary preposition

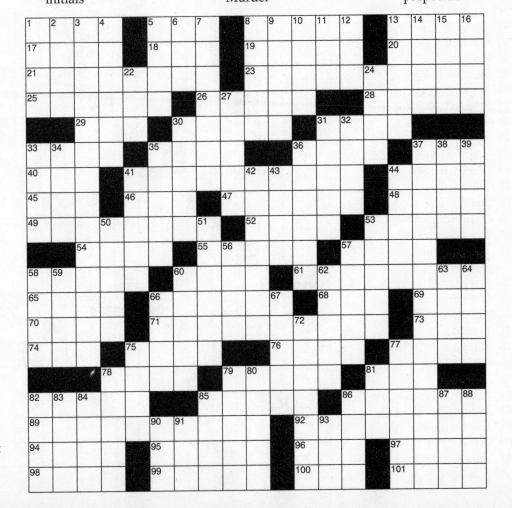

ACROSS

1 Dagger handle
5 Precious ones
10 Tokyo of yore
13 Poverty
17 Polar home: Var.
18 Kind of fool
19 Apple-pie supplier
20 Reference line
21 Smoggy, sooty spot
23 Guileless
25 Virago
26 In progress
27 Command
28 Serfs
30 Supermarket offering
31 Spread out
35 Addison-Steele publication
37 Chose
40 Stow
41 Magazine
43 Actress Sommer
44 Laurels
46 Subject
47 "__ ramblin' wreck . . ."
49 Grazers' goodies
50 That: Sp.
51 Toil
53 Actress Potts
54 Scottish river
55 Rodeo Drive, for one
57 Aspiring grads
60 Assurance
61 Stringed instrument
62 Pump, for one
63 Rummage
65 Invite
66 __ off (depart)
67 Predicament
68 Certain South African
71 Ransacked
73 Formerly
74 Traveler's aid
77 Stubborn
78 Rinds
80 Tony cheese
81 Scrubs
83 "Persuasion" author
85 Writer Calvino
86 Souchong, e.g.
89 Film of 1987
92 Sherwood Forest, perhaps?

94 Advocate
95 Ending for art or chart
96 Architect Jones
97 Subpoena
98 Tourney breaks
99 Grassland
100 Ruhr city
101 Suggestion word

DOWN

1 Sophisticated
2 Indian city
3 Airport, in a way
4 Boy king of note
5 "What a __ Daydream"
6 Fla. tourist spot
7 Melodic
8 Director Martin
9 Crafty
10 Abu Dhabi, e.g.
11 Contribute
12 Atlanta arena
13 Churchill Downs, for example
14 Cleaver
15 Snare

16 Fast flyer, for short
22 Faculty
24 CIA precursor
27 Osculate
29 Actress Verdugo
30 Sportscaster Allen
32 Caper
33 Introduces
34 Last word of "Ulysses"
35 Prerecorded
36 Cropped up
38 Permission
39 Actress Blythe
42 "Cheers" character
45 Linger
48 School subj.
49 Smuggles
51 Deli machine
52 Sibiland sound
53 Martial __
55 James __ Jones
56 Diadem
57 Boutique at the beach
58 Pirate

59 Decrepit
60 Artificial bodies of water
62 Sidetrack
63 Cosecant's repricoal
64 __ homo
66 Distress
67 Burst
68 TV series of the '70s
69 Aesir VIP
70 Dutch uncle
72 Loses enthusiasm for
75 Blunt
76 Vernacular
79 Writer Grafton
82 Insignia
84 Besmirch
85 Particles
87 Blue-pencil.
88 Doers: Suffix
89 Prefix for culture or contract
90 Strain
91 Stone or Space
92 Speed
93 Pooh's friend

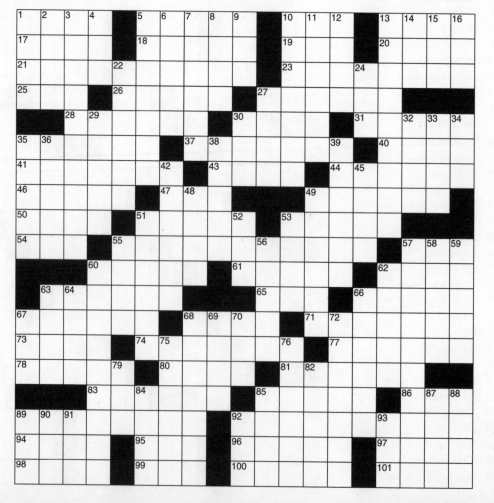

ACROSS

1 Muddles
5 Actor Stoltz
9 Give off
13 Pasternak heroine
17 Attends
18 Indo-Chinese language
19 Bird of yore
20 Geyserite
21 Gossip route
25 Encumbers
26 Calcar
27 Peaceful
28 Inoffensive expletive
29 Piques
30 Standout
31 Sheets, shirts, etc.
33 Modern alliance, for short
34 __ Marie Saint
35 Benchwarmers
39 Due
40 Haw's companion
41 Genealogy
44 Kind of club or cry
45 Scientist Carl
47 Wt. units
48 Golf feat
49 Sinuous shape
50 Guevara
51 A Guthrie
53 Deli line
54 Walt Whitman work
57 __ egg blue
60 Regarding
61 Biblical verb
62 Deficient
65 Cat __ tails
66 Org. for M.D.s
67 Liquescent
69 Parley
70 Culling process
73 Movie ratings
74 Bone: Prefix
75 Writer Paretsky
76 Samovar
77 Loathe
79 Square
80 Mouths
81 Cartoonist Peter
82 Freshly
83 Undertook
87 Beat
88 Fills with mortar
91 Agreement of 1620
94 Actress Skye
95 Zest
96 Advance
97 Eight: Prefix
98 Remorseful one
99 Franchise
100 Cavatina, e.g.
101 Ring verdicts

DOWN

1 Paroxysms
2 Job-safety org.
3 Luther Burbank and friends
4 Overate
5 __ on (abetted)
6 Stadium shouts
7 NYC subway
8 Legion part
9 Outskirts
10 "September __"
11 Actress Lupino
12 Local
13 Singer Darlene
14 Neat as __
15 Indian princess
16 Composer Wilder
22 __ Bator
23 Keats' "The __ St. Agnes"
24 Before
29 "Today __ man . . ."
30 Bird, to Brutus
31 Actor Rob
32 As __ saying
33 Mideast desert
34 Mire in the mud
35 Fairfield U. team
36 Press
37 Chime
38 Notices
40 Riant sounds
42 Dryden's "__ Love"
43 Exuberant
45 Act starter
46 Caribbean port
52 Decay
53 Rural sights
54 Actress Evans
55 Statesman De Valera
56 Gamut
57 Dust-ups
58 Draft classification
59 Catafalque
62 Fight guerrilla-style
63 Piedmont city
64 Profound
66 Taj Mahal site
68 As much as
71 Ballet star
72 Cast
74 Ace or single
78 AL West team
79 Word on a penny
80 Ovid's omelet ingredients
81 "Home __" (1990 film)
82 Word with get or go
83 Ruckus
84 Holier-than-__
85 Descartes
86 Hebrew measure
87 Listless
88 Survey
89 Outward: Prefix
90 RR stops
92 Ziegfeld
93 Friend of Pooh

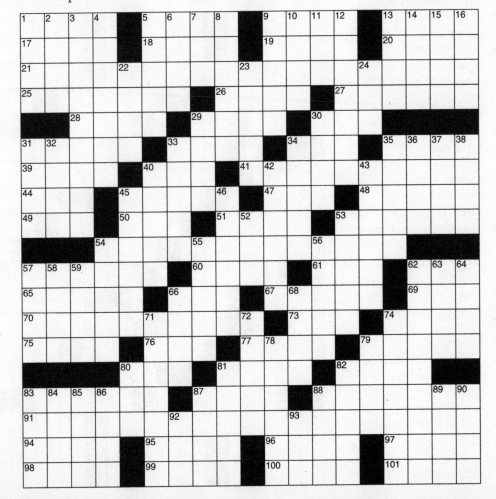

ACROSS

1 Notorious writer
5 Shroud
9 Coin in Cadiz
13 Would-be cpls.
17 Drachma part
18 Where Polo went
19 Surmounting
20 Kirghizian range
21 Old TV series
23 Recommendations
25 Kind of statesman
26 Bohemian
28 Biting
29 Actor Alejandro
30 Baseball great Roush
33 Kind of eng.
35 __ Ferry, N.Y.
38 Martial prefix
40 Quidnunc
43 Actress Garr
44 Business letter abbr.
47 Amazed
50 __ Tin-Tin
51 Clausian sound
53 Seethe
54 Writer Buchanan
55 Sci-fi film of 1954
56 Glory
58 Wild guesses
61 Spicy condiment
63 Genghis Khan, e.g.
65 Whitebait
67 Chartered
70 Bit of info
72 "Middlemarch" author
74 Lute of sorts
75 Pub offering
77 Buffalo's county
79 Sleepy time in Somme
81 __ majesty
82 Supporting
83 Amazes
87 Moisture
88 Formerly, old-style
90 Town of Palestine
91 Mound
92 "__ Little Bit of Luck"
94 Chem. endings
96 __ Lanka
97 Scroogian cry
100 A Gorbachev
103 Zing
105 Diadem
107 Perplexed
110 Film of 1967
113 Jambalaya ingredient
114 Oenologist's concern
115 Venerate
116 Being
117 Invites
118 Overblown
119 Sea bird
120 Fiddlesticks!

DOWN

1 Clean companion
2 Poplar
3 Deep-dish pie
4 Writer Wiesel
5 Logging boot
6 Residue
7 Misinformation
8 Stew server
9 Arriviste
10 Automne precursor
11 Divan
12 Cartel acronym
13 Cockatiel
14 Astonished
15 Film of 1984
16 Shirley, to Warren
22 Stomp
24 Carmine
27 Furthermore
31 Pummel
32 Audition tapes, for short
34 Pitcher David
36 Vivacity
37 Confess, informally
39 Newspaper section
41 Chance word
42 Kind of colony
44 Attention-getter
45 Poison: Prefix
46 Amazed
48 Beloved
49 Valleys
52 Gymnast Korbut
57 Symbol
59 Writer Kaufman
60 Catapult
62 Spencer, for one
64 "Foreign Affairs" author
66 Hard-bitten
68 Comfort
69 Tied
71 Albert Lea's st.
73 Roofing material
75 "... __ good men"
76 Actress Singer
78 Whirlpool
80 Rend
84 Utterly arid
85 Hershiser of baseball
86 Pomeranian
89 Gravesend's river
93 Seek
95 Ermine
97 Raft wood
98 "Give it __!"
99 Underworld
101 Protein source
102 Hachetman
104 Virtual
106 Ending for tranquil
107 Brother
108 Fleur-de __
109 Dine
111 Mayfly
112 Humorist George

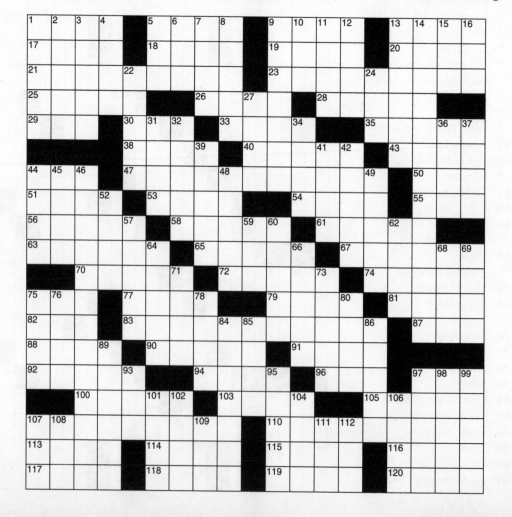

ACROSS

1 Storied elephant
6 Tumble's companion
11 Hag
17 Stubborn as __
18 Involve
20 Beethoven's Third
21 Help-wanted ad quest
24 Witticism
25 Singer Ford of rock
26 Editor's instruction
27 Minuet section
30 Melpomene's sister
34 Entreaty
37 Real-estate offering
41 Memo subscripts
44 Confused
45 Squid's secretion
46 Certain U.K. legislators
47 Murid
48 Kind of suit or blanket
49 Dry gulch
51 Art Spiegelman book
52 Corundum
54 Surrender
55 Report
56 Role model
57 Personals claim
64 "__ Ben Adhem"
65 Sculpture and dance
66 Rabbit's tail
67 Spelunking spots
69 Prefix for dollar
70 Coarse character
71 Underground asset
74 Meteor tail
75 Tissue layers
77 Greek letter
78 Take __ (try)
80 Baseball's Williams
81 Used-car claim
84 Three, in Berlin
85 Violin from Cremona
86 Italia capital
87 Vicinity
90 Precipitate
93 Wee, in Dundee
95 Business-for-sale claim
104 Charlotte __
105 Type in a hurry
106 Desert flower
107 Detected
108 Ped. places
109 "See what __?"

DOWN

1 Offensive
2 Poet Lowell
3 Hamburger holder
4 Dessert order
5 San __
6 Kind of room
7 Switch positions
8 Western Amerind
9 Go fast
10 Sound system
11 Arthur of TV
12 Miss the mark
13 "__ luck!"
14 Nutritionist's concern
15 Piece of property
16 Topgallant, for one
19 Naval amphib
22 Article
23 Malaysian mammals
27 Soften
28 Proportion
29 Part of MIT
31 Brigand
32 Years, to Juvenal
33 For shame!
35 Youth
36 Different
38 Swung off course
39 African antelopes
40 Theater sound
41 Belief system
42 Ricochet
43 Panache
50 Nabokov novel
51 __ man talk
53 Obscure
54 Inspector's delight
55 Fruitless
57 Silent
58 Lessen
59 Waugh's "The __ One"
60 Kapaa's island
61 Obliquely
62 Sgt. or cpl.
63 Persian Gulf port
68 Commotion
69 N.Y. city
70 Zeno's colonnade
71 Pisgah's state
72 Conservatory, for one
73 Lab heater
76 Compass point
77 Radar-jamming gear, etc.
79 Layer
82 Society Islands name
83 Brake part
84 Roald and Arlene
87 Triumphant cries
88 Hoarfrost
89 Actor Richard
91 Place for a B-52
92 Tunisian port
94 Request words
96 Standoff
97 Wine type
98 Trick
99 Haul
100 Mil. school
101 Just ending
102 Sorrel
103 A Bobbsey twin

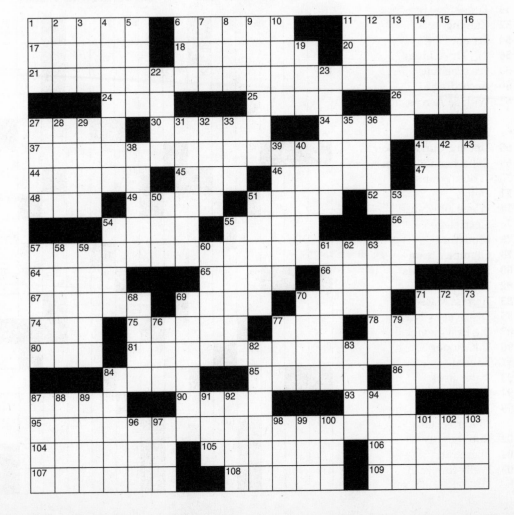

ACROSS

1 With 6 Across, discovery vessel
6 See 1 Across
11 Dipl. title
14 Sort
17 Kind of squash
18 Midwest river
19 Aug. 1 baby
20 "Peggy __" (Holly hit)
21 With 27 Across, hero of this puzzle
23 Delay
24 __ Khan
25 Actress Cattrall
26 Most advisable
27 See 21 Across
29 Modern explorers
31 Jungle printmaker
32 Comprehend
33 Exist
34 Connived
38 Exultant
41 Alarm
44 "Ben __"
45 Latin goddess
47 Golfer's concern
48 Holbrook
49 Tunnel
52 Craving
54 Ermines
56 "__ Three Lives"
58 Fee schedule
60 According to
62 With 64 Across, title for our hero
64 See 62 Across
68 Underground worker
69 Eilbacher and Bonet
70 Writer Whitney
71 Deft
74 Waste allowance
76 Sleep stage
78 Miniature
79 Olympics team
80 Hesitant sounds
82 Sorrel
83 Actress Massey
85 Discovery vessel
87 Big East member
90 U.K. honor
91 Emulate
93 "__ A Rock"
94 Crosses
99 1 and 6 Across, 85 Across, etc.
102 Rub roughly
104 Elec. unit
105 Prefix for cycle
106 Museum fare
107 "Admiral of __" (hero's title)
109 Actor Mantegna
110 "Stagger Lee" roller
111 All together
112 Football feature
113 Switch positions
114 Purpose
115 Ceremonial instruments
116 Pesky group

DOWN

1 Fires
2 __ off the old block
3 Shearer of films
4 Prefix for cycle
5 Solved
6 Thidwick, e.g.
7 Poplars
8 Cries from the crowd
9 "So that's the thanks __!"
10 __ Lingus
11 Permissible
12 Word after oat
13 Fake
14 A sponsor of our hero
15 Berg opera
16 Means of access
22 "__ wounds all heels"
27 Motor part
28 Actress Ryan
30 Train part
31 Fringe benefit, for short
35 Main
36 Rude residences
37 Execrate
39 River isle
40 __ Plaines, Ill.
41 Hood's weapon
42 Colombian city
43 Actor Baldwin
46 Solar disk
50 Press agents?
51 Singer Marvin
53 Contemptuous cries
55 Church calendar
57 Moore of films
59 Suit material, perhaps
61 Scorch
63 Anger
64 Dvorák's First
65 "Break __ Me Gently"
66 Town on the Thames
67 Forage crop
69 Walesa
71 Games's companion
72 Faulkner's "__ Lay Dying"
73 Islands where our hero stopped
75 Lounge, for one
77 Bridge boo-boos
81 Awkward
84 Ferrigno
86 Wallaba
88 Bavarian approvals
89 Puissant
90 Hialeah's county
92 Duck
95 Off to the __
96 "Julius Casesar" character
97 Mideast VIP
98 Burst
99 Stephen King tale
100 Presently
101 The Old Sod
102 Chan's remark
103 Occupy
107 Baseball play
108 Slangy denial

ACROSS

1 Dean's purview
7 Sticker
12 Materialist's goal
18 Excite
19 Cognizant
20 Burns's "To __"
21 Words before front
24 Frau's mate
25 King mackerel
26 __ were
27 Tiff
30 Pear type
33 Bigwig
37 Sapporo salad item
40 Strange
43 Lizardfish
45 __ contendere
46 Words after front
50 Shortly
51 Richard and Eddie
   of films
52 Inferior
53 Distress call
54 Asian capital
56 Disarray
58 Put on
59 Words after side
67 Keogh's cousin
68 Nuclear energy area:
   Abbr.
69 Shropshire, once
70 CPO, for one
73 Laserizes
75 "__ luck!"
78 H.H. Munro
79 Words before
   back
83 Can. province
84 Hibernia
85 Guide
86 Table scrap
87 Audibly
89 Tweed twitter
91 Where Anatolia is
93 Invested bullishly
95 Hazard
98 NYC stadium
102 Words after back
109 Minimal
110 Sound
111 Iroquoian
112 FM feature
113 Locale
114 Living room

DOWN

1 Charge alternative
2 Comedian Johnson
3 Tie up
4 Contented sounds
5 Function
6 Stitch
7 Rendezvous
8 Jug
9 Medit. tree
10 Rainbow
11 Regulus's
   constellation
12 Rages, old-style
13 Filmmaker Resnais
14 State since 1889
15 Campaign material,
   perhaps
16 Columbus initials
17 Fiber cluster
22 Stage craft
23 S. Cal. town
28 Actress Dawber
29 Wings
31 "__ Miss Brooks"
32 Chunk
34 Swamps
35 Toast topping
36 Top dog
37 Property of a
   mountain state
38 Singer Washington
39 Maine college town
41 Dutch cheeses
42 "__ is good news"
44 Pelé's given name
47 Sufficient, poetically
48 Small bone
49 Awaits action
55 Sp. isle
57 Animal tracks
60 Computer
   command
61 Soft knocks
62 Erode
63 "Fuzzy wuzzy __
   bear . . ."
64 Battle site, 1836
65 Joining force
66 Dumped out
70 Sports org.
71 Summon
72 Not fooled by
74 Writer Paretsky
76 __ peek (look)
77 Summer
   refreshers
80 Certain Summer
   Olympian
81 Foot
82 Dernier __
88 Search for water
90 Commerce
92 Son of Jacob
94 Western alliance,
   for short
96 Occupies
97 Brake part
99 Salute
100 Inner: Prefix
101 Jewish month
102 Singer King et al.
103 Dine
104 Exist
105 Maintains
106 Jean __ Godard
107 M-Q link
108 Genetic material

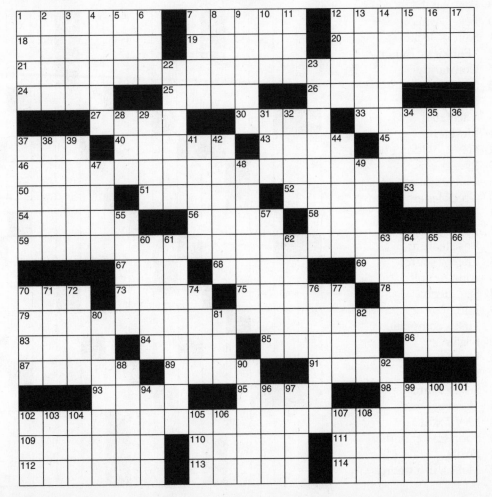

ACROSS

1 Abbr. at the U.N.
5 __ a gun
10 Intention
13 Moist
17 Plains Indian
18 Vestment
19 Neckpiece
20 Fencer's foil
21 Trendy cruise customer?
23 Trendy behavior?
25 Expressed derision
26 Do something
28 Drs.' grp.
29 Bring up
30 Actress Eikenberry
32 Practiced dental hygiene
36 Barbecue dish
38 NBA ''zebra''
39 Service org.
41 Outcast
42 Miscalculate
43 Travels trendily?
47 Actress Mary
48 ''Ululame'' poet
49 Peck's pal
50 Les __ Unis
51 Sailors' lockup
52 ''For kicks'' relative
54 Constantly
55 Struggle
57 Family
58 Vacillated
61 Blunderer
62 Have __! (don't worry)
65 Evergreens
66 Cereal spikes
70 Greek letters
71 ''. . . I say, not __''
73 Pairs
74 Rose feature
75 Energy source
76 Amp or volt
78 Sp. queen
79 Join
81 First's companion
82 Ergate
83 Plant disease
84 Warsaw river
86 Sugar source
88 ''Leave __ me''
90 LXVII x III
91 Sportscaster Barber
92 Posits
95 Makes, in a trendy way?

99 Trendy seasonings?
102 Writer Wiesel
103 Election mo.
104 Wicker willow
105 ''Don't bet __''
106 Coil
107 Maple harvest
108 Thicket
109 I-10, 66, etc.

DOWN

1 Puts on
2 Lay __ the line
3 Trendy business meals
4 Dikes
5 Painter Moses
6 Mouthward
7 Harridan
8 Cry to Manolete
9 Untamed
10 Slightly
11 Particle
12 Taj __
13 Cheapen
14 Prefix for gram
15 See 13 Across

16 Approval
22 Man-mouse tie
24 Soap plant
27 Groups
30 Fool's offering
31 ''__ Ruled the World''
32 Four-time Indy winner
33 Trendy rodeo item?
34 Uncanny
35 Bottom of the barrel
36 ''__ Man'' (1984 film)
37 Obdurate
38 Extend
40 Gawk
43 West African land
44 Roth's ''__ Gang''
45 ''__ Sunday'' (Dassin film)
46 D-Day craft
51 Certain lingerie
53 Shaping tools
54 Prosecutor's concern
56 Raise
59 Blazing
60 Discourage

62 Israeli region
63 Sardinian town
64 Santha Rama __
67 Reine's mate
68 Japanese native
69 Wrangle
72 Miss, in Mazatlan
73 Desert sight
76 Cross: Prefix
77 Make leather
80 Engraved
83 Daze
85 Shaw's ''The Young __''
87 Kind of committee
88 Grenoble's river
89 Recipe abbr.
91 Invitation subscript
92 Simians
93 Pa. city
94 Concordes
95 Scarce
96 MacGraw
97 Theological topic
98 Taboo's opposite
100 Barcelona bear
101 Point

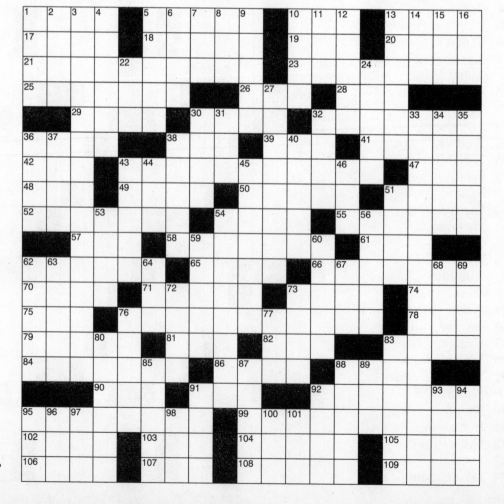

ACROSS

1 George of country music
6 Faux pas
11 Coatepec cloak
17 __ to arms
18 Coral isles
20 Ballparks
21 Oberon of films
22 Confining garb
24 Exclude
25 Jungfrau and Wildspitze
27 Robert Morse role
28 Serf
29 Drowses
31 Dickens's "__ Curiosity Shop"
34 Jutlander
35 Explanations of a sort
36 LPGA member
37 Rathskeller offering
39 Russia, formerly
40 Calif. valley
42 Baseball stratagem
46 Amigo's farewell
48 Part of UHF
49 Cantina snacks
53 Hotbed
54 Kind of gate or wind
56 Highlands fall
58 Khrushchev
59 Epic ending
60 Glyceride, for one
62 Dazzling effect
64 Org. for Bruins and Penguins
65 "Tristram Shandy" author
67 Moisture
69 Get by
70 Murmur
71 Bordeaux wine
72 Slender as __
74 Jerk
76 Uncommunicative
81 Available
82 Slippery __
85 Daughter of Laban
86 Lepidopterist's tool
87 River in 105 Across
89 Ocho __, Jamaica
91 Optical illusion
93 Potpourri
96 Hendricks of baseball
98 Hogshead's little cousin
99 "__ Did" (Dinah Shore hit)
100 Election mo.
101 Restricted room
105 Sudan neighbor
107 Camomile drink
108 Cream and sugar dispensary
109 Run like __
110 Did a farm job
111 Vestibule
112 Fat's companion

DOWN

1 Doorway parts
2 Indian, e.g.
3 Intolerant
4 Cubit
5 Run-down
6 Pants
7 ABA mbrs.
8 On behalf of
9 Ala. neighbor
10 Aristocracy
11 FICA withholding recipient
12 Imprint
13 Inclined
14 Writer St. Johns et al.
15 Mountain-climbing gear
16 Quadragesima concluder
19 Kind of light
23 Plantation libation
26 Ending for ruth or reck
30 Paducah's river
31 Margin for error
32 Gardeners, at times
33 Pa. neighbor
36 Yanked
38 Kiwis, ostriches, etc.
40 Extreme cruelty
41 Use one's head
43 Discontinued
44 Writer Grey
45 Chatter
47 Silk-screen, e.g.
50 Misers
51 Comfortable
52 Taproom
55 Enzyme
57 Buy
58 Carpet feature
61 True
63 Deposit
66 Decay
68 Squeeze
73 Dueling sword
75 Soft drink
77 Sparkler
78 Japanese poetry form
79 Menace
80 Eddy-MacDonald effort
82 Puts up
83 Actress Beatrice
84 Glum
88 Ms. Doolittle et al.
90 Everly Brothers hit, 1960
92 Consent
93 Mildewed
94 Gussets
95 Word with day or where
97 Sandy tract
99 J.C. Harris epithet
102 Logician's letters
103 "The Joy Luck Club" author
104 Extreme ending
106 Okla. town

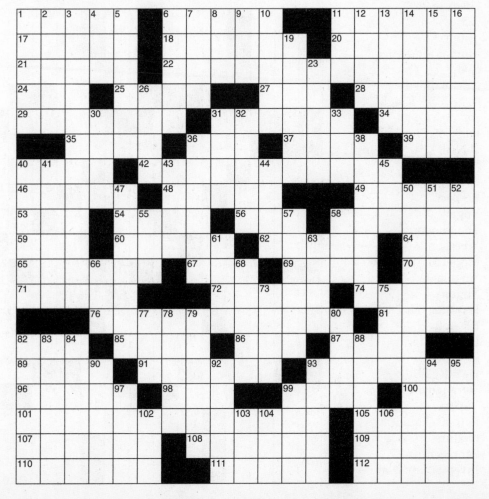

ACROSS

1 Intaglio, e.g.
4 Proscription
9 Inveigh
13 Film dog
17 Hail
18 Folks in debt
19 Renaissance family
20 Mulligan, for one
21 Yeats poem
24 Word with ground or runner
25 Dithers
26 Estuary substance
27 "The __ Still Open"
29 Sea bird
32 Pained expression
35 Tributary
36 With "The," Grisham tale
40 Second person
43 Bounce
46 Vexatious force
47 Ratify
48 __ on the back
49 Composer Charles
51 Entertainer Steve
53 Greek letter
54 Actress Miles
55 __ Inferno
57 Mutual-fund sales charge
59 Not qualified
61 "The Black Knight" composer
62 Bank jobs
64 O'Neill's "__ Millions"
67 Merge
69 Grass genus
70 Respect
71 Vogue
73 Time-honored
75 Precision
77 Model Macpherson
78 Singular
79 Midday
81 Hawaiian bird's things
83 RR stop
84 Prefix for form
85 Easy prey
88 Health club
90 Durango drought
91 Vapors
94 Part of a liquid mixture
97 Far reaches
100 Inventor Lun et al.

102 Gen. Bradley
103 Fool's errand
108 Writer Tyler
109 Director Kazan
110 Sitwell or Head
111 Beerbohm
112 Float
113 Count
114 Dennis of films
115 Guileful

DOWN

1 Fellas' counterparts
2 Ties
3 Health-care provider
4 Kitchen appliance
5 Barley bristle
6 Garden section
7 Table scraps
8 Job-safety org.
9 Plucks anew
10 USN mission
11 Señor ending
12 Impart
13 Regarding
14 Signs of trouble
15 Actress Garr
16 Dazzles
22 Upon
23 N.C. campus
28 Dunderhead
30 Inventor Howe
31 Streamlet
33 Canadian Indian
34 Break
37 Viola's cousin
38 Interstice
39 Flair
41 Regatta implement
42 Actress Hagen
43 Skin
44 Ellipsoid
45 Anatole France novel
48 Fly
50 Posture
52 Bottom
56 Silkworm
58 Amid
60 Certain radio stations, for short
62 Serfs
63 Beeped

65 Modern Gael
66 Augury
68 Writer Morrison
70 Raise
71 Ins. agent's initials
72 Sweetie
74 Be overfond
76 Weight
80 "Have a __"
82 Incomplete
85 Deliberated
86 Da __, Vietnam
87 Window part
89 Soup
92 Titles of respect
93 Twine fiber
94 Fly high
95 Atlanta arena
96 Jug
98 Performs
99 Kind of pop or cracker
101 Lascivious
104 __ de France
105 __ Abner
106 Err, in a way
107 Flight-plan abbr.

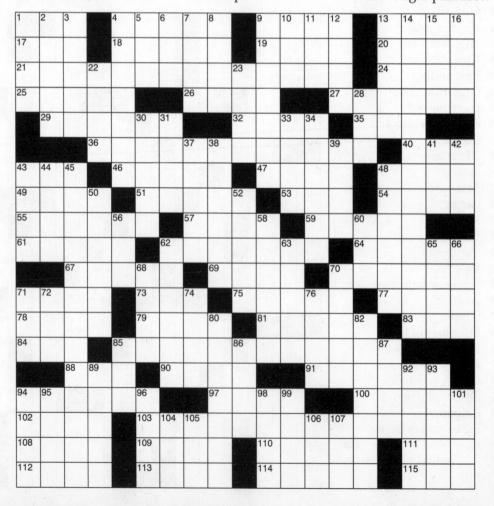

ACROSS

1 Fly-by-night types
5 Main point
9 Garden tool
13 Racer Foyt et al.
16 Airline offering
17 Actress Berger
18 Bumbles
19 Strike
20 Putting in trim
22 Four, in prescriptions
23 Real ending
24 Wall St. market
25 Singer Neville
26 Refuse
27 Scrutiny
28 Damaged
30 Buck's mate
31 All-sudden link
33 Comparisons
35 Catkin-bearer
40 Brooklyn Dodger Sandy
41 Illusionist's word
42 Football Hall-of-Famer Earl
43 Delhi princess
44 Imitate
46 Rural areas
48 Started the pot
50 Sharpen
52 L.A.'s La __ Tar Pits
53 Summer abbr.
54 On the bench: Sl.
58 P&L expert
61 Alaska cape
62 Agglutinins
63 Micawber's problem
67 Retribution
69 Dining areas
71 Norman of TV
72 Salad ingredient
73 Scold
77 Black gum
79 Iowa city
81 Freshly secures
82 U.K. honor
83 __ flash (immediately)
84 Paucity
85 Antarctic floater
88 Medicinal amount
90 Indian pewter
91 Blob
94 Undisciplined
95 Dissolve
96 Sobriquet for the 7th president
98 Hail
99 Pip
100 Mortise mate
101 Ga. town
102 Pallid
103 "Jane __"
104 Object
105 Jewish month

DOWN

1 __ buco
2 Shed a tear
3 NYC suburb
4 Actor Erwin
5 Categories
6 "__ we trust"
7 Confound
8 Gregory Hines film
9 Seek
10 __ for one's money
11 Polish city
12 Extreme ending
13 Met highlight
14 Music type
15 Hook's cohort
17 Cat breed
21 Monte __
26 Chinese idol
27 Casque
29 More frivolous
30 Kind of process
32 Where Oulu is
33 Poet Teasdale
34 "__ old cowhand . . ."
35 Branch
36 ". . . you'll always know __ . . ."
37 Nation
38 Auto pioneer
39 Jerry of the NBA
41 Telecom device
45 Nightmare vision
47 Celebrated architect
49 Meals
51 UFO riders?
52 TV's Milton
55 Cerberus, for one
56 Tilts
57 Fisherman's trap
58 Gator's cousin
59 Soccer great
60 Enthusiastic
64 "__ 4-5789" (1962 hit)
65 Chat
66 Theater signs
68 Get around
70 Fat solid
74 Incident
75 Trellis climber
76 Actress Lupino
78 Augsburg's patron saint
80 Dangerfield
81 Scorching
84 "If I __ care"
85 Defect
86 Aetna product
87 Bullocks
89 River to the Baltic
90 "Sacre __!"
92 "Aeneid" opener
93 Textile worker
95 Purpose
96 Gambling initials

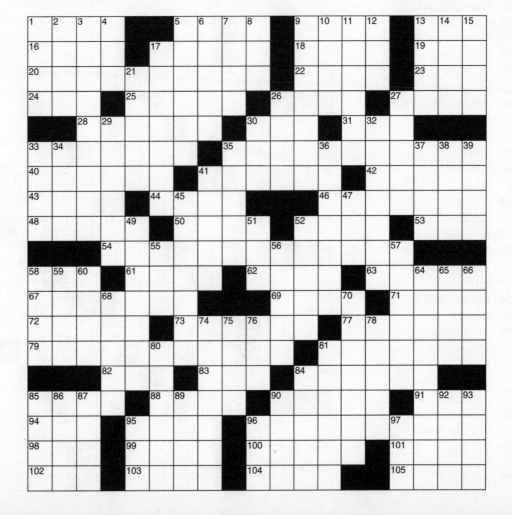

ACROSS

1 Buttons' companion
5 Alias
8 Actress O'Neal
13 Crossing for Hannibal
17 Part of LAN
18 Guided
19 Love, in Roma
20 Passion
21 Eric Clapton hit
24 Horrific
25 Prankster
26 Domain
27 Front ending
29 Walter and Winfield
31 One of the Fondas
32 Bit of auto maintenance
36 Character sketch
37 Accommodate
38 Peak in France
39 Amazement
40 Newspaper page: Abbr.
41 Film of 1987
43 Farrow
44 Hosp. sites
45 Wharf
46 Evergreens
47 Court bench
48 Tough terrier
50 Obscures
52 Consider
53 Harangue
54 Actress Hasso
55 Harrow part
56 Acute
58 Elude
59 Daydream
62 Bash
63 Mood
64 Grub
65 Honorarium
66 NATO, for one
67 "Never Can __" ('70s hit)
70 Carvey or Delaney
71 Benefit
72 __ out (supplements)
73 Playwright David
74 Landscape painter
75 Topography
77 Troubles
78 Farm workers
79 Tourist spot
80 Inkling
81 Underneath
82 Keen

85 Ledbetter-Lomax standard
90 Pterosaur feature
91 Cove
92 Paddock morsel
93 Robert __
94 Charles or Louise
95 Approaches
96 Blind ambition
97 March through mud

DOWN

1 Ebenezer's epithet
2 Precious metal
3 Film of 1947
4 Honored
5 Baseball family
6 Ocean growth
7 Introduce
8 Italy's Gulf of __
9 Chemical compound
10 __ the line (conformed)
11 Amphora
12 "The __ the message" (McLuhan)
13 Sky blue

14 Meat cut
15 Companion
16 Crafty
22 Writer Whitney
23 Thresh
28 Mr. Flood
29 Reporter's delight
30 Blue Grotto site
31 Summer time
32 __ poker
33 Harry Belafonte hit
34 Due
35 Strand
37 Fasten
38 Sure-footed
41 Shuck
42 "__ kettle of fish"
45 Gibe
47 Finery
49 Outcry
50 Part of VCR
51 French toast ingredient
52 Stat for Cy Young
54 Tunes
55 Rendezvous
56 Reconnoiter

57 Kind of play or power
58 Gray eminence
59 Novelist Kellerman
60 Monterrey mister
61 Nobelist in 1923
63 Welcoming
64 Diminishes
67 Penn of films
68 Aligns
69 __ Lama
70 Actress Hart
74 Colombia city
76 Crest
77 Krait
78 Davis of note
80 Kansas town
81 Hindu bard
82 Sewing tool
83 Right-of-way
84 Kind of spot or stand
86 All's companion
87 Gazelle
88 New-fangled
89 Med. check, for short

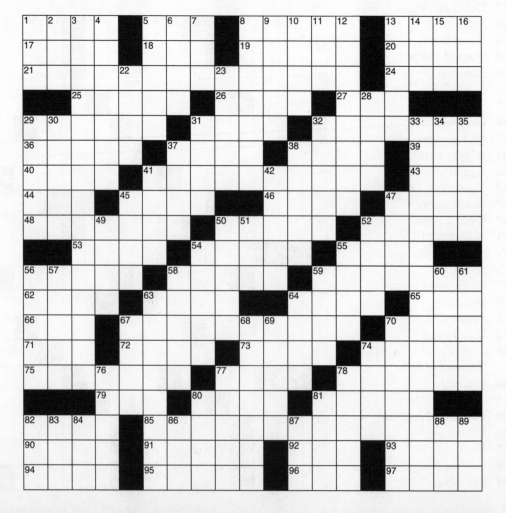

ACROSS

1 Furniture style
5 Business gamble, for short
9 Enthralled
13 Jester
17 Java neighbor
18 Hawaiian city
19 With skill
20 Distinctive
21 One of a Bach group
25 Macabre
26 Western lily
27 Cold cuts
28 Prov. on Hudson Bay
30 Jai __
33 Jibe
37 Dvořák work
44 Collide with
45 Prosperous period
46 Much-puzzled ox
47 Mariner's concern
48 Lieutenant
50 Thornback
53 Bonito relative
55 __ Gatos, Calif.
56 Rudders' rests
58 Pressure
60 Commandment word
62 Liszt work
69 Monterrey Mmes.
70 Whole lot
71 Château-Thierry's river
72 "__ live and breathe . . ."
75 Tennis term
77 Long
80 Partisan group
81 Zilch, in Zacatecas
83 After
85 Head protector
87 Gas: Prefix
88 Film of 1942
93 African antelope
94 Portico
95 Haw's partner
96 Little bit
99 Chamorro's home
102 Capp character
106 Grofe work
112 Profanity
113 Delete
114 Poi material
115 Look over
116 __ du jour
117 Hospitality sites
118 Discard
119 Believed

DOWN

1 Ecclesiastic
2 Be brave
3 Winglike
4 Subordinate
5 "Murder, __ Wrote"
6 Needles' companions
7 Hamburg's river
8 Catamount
9 Taunt
10 One of the networks
11 Go slowly
12 Actress Daly
13 Type of train
14 Paddle
15 Little leftover
16 Tolstoy
22 Alpha Cygni
23 Bakery item
24 Thunder unit
29 Ark groupings
31 Nabokov novel
32 "__ She Lovely?"
34 Stir up
35 Inner: Prefix
36 Viewpoint
37 Destroy, informally
38 Poetic form
39 German city
40 Cooking utensil
41 Woodmen Tower site
42 "Who put __ to this?"
43 Horace and Thomas
49 Seuss's "Green __ and Ham"
51 Sawbucks
52 Primitive
54 Bit
57 Poet Teasdale
59 Quaker pronoun
61 Seraglio spots
63 Element No. 86
64 "Of thee __"
65 Savvy
66 __ Jaya, Indonesia
67 Complete
68 Mystics
72 Chip in, in a way
73 Comedian Mort
74 Notion
76 Sgts., e.g.
78 Versailles VIP
79 Snack
82 As dark __
84 Newt
86 Fido's complaint
89 Scent
90 Forum garb
91 Hangouts
92 Waylay
97 Longtime sitcom
98 Shortly
100 Indian maid
101 Additional
103 Subtle
104 List-shortening abbr.
105 Tear
106 Best
107 Linden of TV
108 Greek letter
109 Horse color
110 Dollar pts.
111 Approval

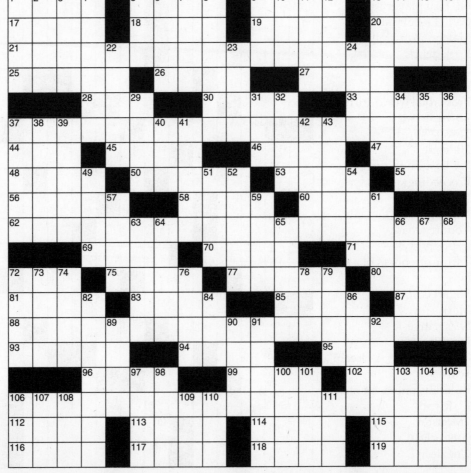

ACROSS

1 Moorea neighbor
7 Implied
13 Drinks
18 Prayer
19 Think
20 Writer's problem
21 Go-getters
22 No-where man's opposite
24 Tennis great
25 Pallid
27 Consume
28 U.K. neighbor
29 Guitarist Paul
30 Weight
31 Brusque
33 Erstwhile
34 Diminish
36 Catchall abbr.
38 Tropes
40 "__ bagatelle . . ."
42 Precursor
45 Portray
47 Serene
48 Ripen
49 Prefix for sent or serve
52 NL East player
53 Camel's-hair fabric
55 Matchmaker Dolly
57 Rock debris
59 Propaganda
60 Bombard
62 Proverbial world-turner
64 Low-pitched
65 Texan "spread"
67 Hideout
69 Far Eastern festival
70 Proceedings
71 Distress call
72 Nigerian native
74 Country road
76 In pretty style
78 Traffic offenders of a sort
81 Jabs
82 Bogart costar
85 Mark
86 N.Z. native
88 Fumbles
89 "Last Night __ A Dream"
91 Sear
92 Ruler distances, for short
95 Fr. friend
96 "Monster __ Box" (1992 film)
97 Guzzles

99 "Grapes of Wrath" figure
100 Preakness winner, 1953
104 Longest-lived
106 Public works official of yore
107 Mission
108 __-well (shiftless)
109 Haberdashery gear
110 Opens
111 Acclimatize

DOWN

1 All-out
2 Come up
3 Party animals
4 Got it!
5 Pinnacle
6 Demented
7 Stock-table category
8 Groundless
9 Discovery of 1898
10 Folder marker
11 Midi saison
12 Prevent
13 Word with free
14 Table scrap

15 Social pursuit
16 Punish
17 Flings
23 PG, e.g.
26 "__ City" (1963 hit)
30 Cartel acronym
31 Calif. town
32 Eskimo knife
33 Shell implement
35 Melodic
36 Age
37 Apprise
39 Encounter
40 Writer St. Johns et al.
41 Town in Mo.
43 Fla. city
44 Ingenuous
46 Light touch
49 Certain NFL participants
50 Soft sound
51 Reflections of a sort
54 "The Enemy __" (1957 film)
56 November figure
58 Legal eliminator
61 Cultivated

63 Catchall abbr.
66 Bond
68 Libertine
73 News story signer
75 Actor Beatty
77 Atop
78 Berlin affirmatives
79 Triumphant cry
80 Self-congratulatory
82 Malefic moundsman
83 Fleet
84 Caviler
87 Felonies of a sort
90 Underworld
91 Hitchcock's "The __"
93 Mess up
94 New Jersey's __ Hall U.
96 Currier's partner
97 Cicatrix
98 Departed
99 Concert halls
101 Sort
102 Skill
103 New Deal agcy.
105 Pinky or Peggy

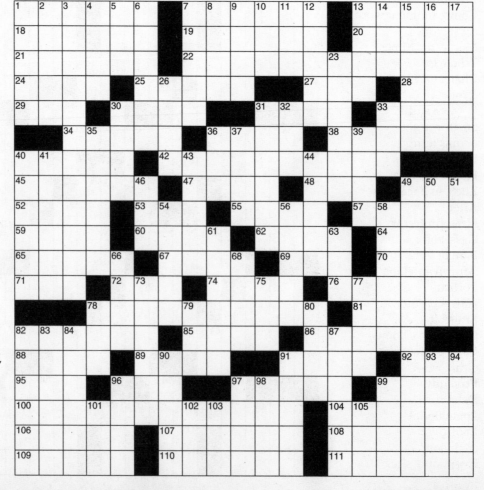

ACROSS

1 Clench
5 Barriers
10 Bedtime music
14 EPA measurement
17 Winterset's state
18 Robert Ruark book
19 Senate VIP
20 Writer Levin
21 Actress Sharon and comedian Jackie
23 Actress Skye
24 Tennis stroke
25 Vouchsafe
26 Clever
28 Item for Casals
30 Governmental
33 Inclination
34 Worrywart
35 March 26 baby
36 Fast's partner
38 Arab ruler
39 Capture
40 Agent James and actor Geoffrey
42 "All That __" (Presley recording)
45 Previous
46 Under restraint
47 Paean
48 Object of dread
49 Copious
50 Vigorous
53 Actress Christine
54 Licentious
57 Camp sight
58 P.O. worker
59 Thin as __
60 Paroxysm
61 Cornelia __ Skinner
62 Presumption
63 Ferrigno of films
64 Played back
66 M.D.s' org.
69 Lamprey
70 Athletes Larry and Catfish
73 Study hard
74 Analyze
76 Standard
77 Take __ (get lost!)
78 Accumulate
80 Petiole
81 Piranha's home
82 Pirate's cry
83 City in 66 Down
84 Insulation
86 Modest
87 Holm oak

89 Actress Karen and singer Kate
94 Before
95 Exclusive
96 Be honest
97 U.S. border lake
98 Leb. neighbor
99 __ off (salute)
100 Circumvent
101 Refuse

DOWN

1 Dogfaces
2 Breakdown
3 __ Jima
4 Complex
5 Squawbush
6 Comparative word
7 Displace
8 Favorably
9 Opah
10 Between
11 Nautical greeting
12 Gudgeon
13 Ghost
14 Philosopher John and writer Richard
15 Working-class sort

16 Eva of TV
22 Discordia
27 Tea-time spread
29 Shoe width
30 __ Alto
31 Orenburg's river
32 Tight spot
33 Day-care client
34 Barrie character
36 Torpid
37 "__ False Move" (1992 film)
38 Dust devil
40 Rock group
41 Oodles
43 Commedia dell __
44 Israeli leader
46 Announce
48 Coxswain's cry
49 Armor item
51 Numero __
52 Breastbone
53 Meat cut
54 Storm
55 Dies __
56 TV's Lucille and golf's Gary
57 Flop sound

58 Luminary
60 Shredded
61 Hershiser of baseball
63 Speech sound
65 Greek letter
66 Nev. neighbor
67 Type of shark
68 TV series
70 Cruel
71 Lowly dwellings
72 Fit to employ
73 Enthralled
75 Loser to DDE
77 City in 17 Across
78 Strides
79 Billiard-ball material
80 Storied battlers
81 Talus
83 Liquefy
84 Pumice or perlite
85 Kind of tea
88 Mauna __
90 Potok's "My Name is Asher __"
91 Spleen
92 Pewter ingredient
93 Cry for attention

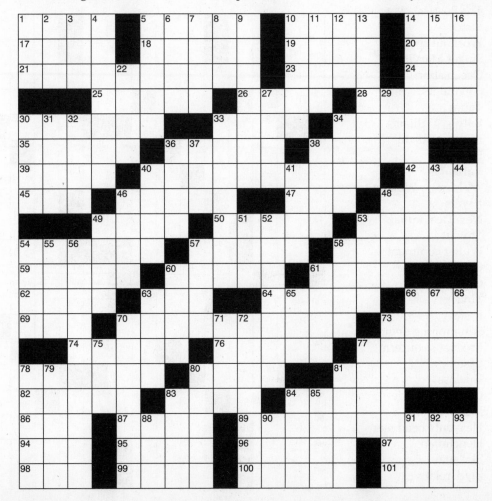

ACROSS

1 Proverbial gain producer
5 Kind of TV
10 Elec. unit
14 Legal VIPs
17 Part of A.D.
18 Ryan of films
19 "I can't tell __"
20 Asian holiday
21 Zaret-North song, 1955
24 Word with one or more
25 Homey deity
26 Prefix for verse
27 Friml's "__ Serenade"
28 Uncertain state
29 Respect
32 Positive pointers
33 Mouths
34 Not alfresco
36 Words with stock or bounds
39 Regal up-and-comer
42 Meat cuts
43 Film of 1992
45 The Beatles' "Let __"
46 Lance
47 Workout spot
48 Singer Marvin
49 Ocean abbr.
50 Squanders
51 Taunt
53 Billy __ Williams
54 Picnic problem
55 Fr. river
56 Variables
59 "A Man __ Woman"
60 Layers
62 New Deal initials
63 Thwart
66 Winter comment
68 Campus group
69 Citrus drinks
70 Tireless
73 Ecstasy
74 Summoning device
75 Breeder's concern
76 Base
77 Unclose
78 Common article
79 Imitative
81 Heavenly headgear
83 Henchman
86 Sky altar
87 Blvd. relatives

90 Past
91 "Man of La Mancha" topic
94 Floor covering
95 Navigational hazard
96 Fla. city
97 Data-base
98 Remunerate
99 Peon relative
100 Three-bean, for one
101 Kind of party

DOWN

1 Volcker or Gauguin
2 Actress Magnani
3 Amazing
4 Japanese drama
5 Wordsmith of sorts
6 Singer Lennox
7 Cooperative effort
8 Actor Alan
9 Sailors' saint
10 Football penalty assessments
11 Agalloch
12 Precise
13 Writer Josephine
14 Swinburne character
15 Knee: prefix
16 Charon's river
22 Traffic units
23 Grant
28 Kind of benefit
30 Loudness unit
31 Impressionist works
33 Mine yield
34 Epic of note
35 Naples night
37 Lizardfish
38 Gobs
39 Lamentations
40 Hue's partner
41 Size up
43 Parvenu
44 Improve
46 Shoal
50 Pallid
52 Arthur of TV
55 Ultimatum
56 Film of 1958
57 Novel

58 Impudent
59 Syrian city
60 Survey
61 Existential alternative
63 Minor mendacity
64 Small bill
65 Set of principles
67 Immediately
69 Jai __
71 Charge
72 Actor Will et al.
73 Spacious
76 Filament
78 Narrow
80 Water arum
81 Dwell (on)
82 __ caliente
83 Barrie pirate
84 Paperwork places: Abbr.
85 Typewriter type
88 Actress Delaney
89 Self-satisfied
91 Ogre on Apr. 15
92 __ Harbor, Fla.
93 "Six __ Riv Vu"

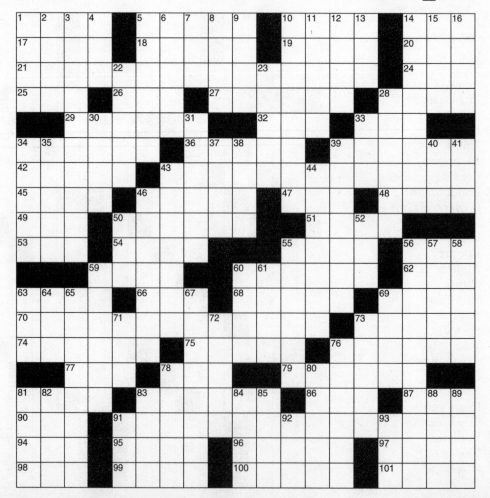

ACROSS

1 Vocation
4 Bad-mouth
9 Verb for P.B. Shelley
13 Polanski film
17 __ Marie Saint
18 Health care: prefix
19 Diva's showcase
20 Choir member
21 Kind of horn or can
22 Concern at the dry cleaners'?
25 "How __ Your Love?" (1977 hit)
27 Crop up
28 Camel relative
29 Semisolid
30 Algerian port
31 Crocodile's home
33 Argument among marathoners?
39 Writer Martin
40 Labor org.
41 Peeves
42 Cut
45 Sleepy's cohort
46 Undulating
48 "Give it __!"
50 Coffee
51 Anonymous John
52 Smelter input
53 "What's __ for me?"
54 Celebrated
55 Concerns at the fire house?
59 Idiosyncrasy
62 Ger. articles
63 Sky altar
64 Logician's letters
67 Arm bone
68 Marquand character
70 Cousin's mom
71 Sapporo salad item
72 Razorbill
73 Estate unit
74 Purpose
75 Billboard
76 Kitchen controversies?
82 West and Murray
83 Hungarian leader
84 Swiss river
85 "The Enemy Below" craft
88 "__ World Turns"
90 Receive
93 Stable worry?
96 Caustic

98 Desperate
99 Word after has or who's
100 Zoo attraction
101 "__ Lazy River"
102 Cries to Manolete
103 Bureaucratic abbr.
104 Hotbeds
105 Converged

DOWN

1 Nozzle
2 Roman poet
3 Curse
4 Straw user
5 Actress Henner
6 St. Tropez saisons
7 "__ gratia artis"
8 Army brown
9 On the decline
10 Work units
11 Curing agents
12 Road surface
13 Coping stone
14 Raines of films
15 Check
16 Psyche opposite

23 Boxer Barkley
24 Stewpots
26 __ benedict
30 Just
32 Relative of "oh, sure"
33 Actress Cheryl
34 Melville tale
35 Pleasant
36 Actor David
37 Regimens
38 Blue-book, e.g.
43 Holiday time
44 Pop
46 "Youngblood Hawke" author
47 Timetable abbr.
48 Indignant
49 Reformer Jacob
50 Munich assents
53 Arrow poison
54 Achievement
55 Lingerie item
56 Couch potato, e.g.
57 Riyadh native
58 Vessel for 50 Across
59 Sine __ non
60 Eskimo food-chopper

61 Printer's stock
64 Leave
65 Nose out
66 Puts on
68 Pinnacle
69 Forbodes
70 One of the Hardys
73 Big name in violins
74 Abetted
75 Unerring
77 Visions
78 Focused
79 Okinawa capital
80 Perfume packet
81 Indiana team
85 Annul
86 Security
87 Bogeyman
89 Joel's "__ Always a Woman"
90 N.T. book
91 Persimmon
92 Sort
94 Org. for 81 Down
95 Blind ambition
97 Sup

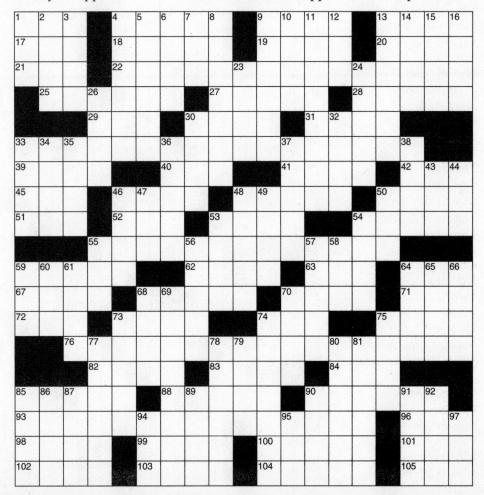

ACROSS

1 Priest's garment
4 Storza Castle site
9 Twine fiber
14 Vexillum
17 Helios
18 On __ (impulsively)
19 "Pagliacci" role
20 Writer Levin
21 Red robins
24 Minutia
25 Subtle
26 Diffident
27 Liliaceous plant
28 Borders
30 Rockne
32 Flight-plan abbr.
33 Cipher
35 Infidel
37 Egyptian goddess
39 Become
40 Well versed in
44 Alienation
46 Hit song of 1959
49 Country mouse
50 "__ live and breathe . . ."
52 Bain substance
53 Reversal of sorts
54 Far reaches
55 Emend
57 Half of MMCII
59 Compass point
60 Stern stuff
61 Guild
63 Curved wedge
66 Inquiring sounds
67 Phase
69 Dipl. figures
73 Standard
75 Just so
76 Large tank
77 Agitate
78 Children's party drink
82 S.C. river
84 Inspire
85 Thole
86 Chagall
88 Balance-sheet item
89 Steam plow inventor
91 Cooper's "The __"
92 Debussy work
94 Creatures
97 Suggestion
99 Property-tax unit
100 Citte of Italia
103 WHO or NFO

104 Annual football all-star game
108 Afflict
109 Ransom's "Here __ Lady"
110 "__ to Be You"
111 Whitney
112 Ballad
113 Bourtree
114 Greek letter
115 Turf

DOWN

1 NBA, e.g.
2 Sites
3 Oil, metaphorically
4 __ de tete
5 In other words
6 Machine tools
7 Dilettantish
8 Teachers' org.
9 Liquid burn
10 Archvillain
11 Reacted allergically
12 Demeanor
13 Downtrodden sort
14 Faction
15 Pa. port
16 Bonkers
22 Calls something else
23 Indigenous group
29 Question
31 Prefix for form
32 Greek letter
34 Sevres summer
35 Overlie
36 Presently
38 Writer Hoffman
39 Horned beast
41 Advantage
42 Yours and mine
43 Hawaiian bird
45 Ground
47 Devour
48 Spoil
51 Gets it
56 Filmmaker Resnais
57 Paragonite
58 Actress Lenya
60 Wall Street order
62 Word of defiance
63 Drink holders
64 __ were
65 Actor Paul
68 Frolic
69 Morning greeters
70 False mallows
71 Take the bait
72 Casino aperture
74 City near Cleveland
75 Sequel word
79 Prefix for center
80 Bumbled in billiards
81 Life part
83 Weir
87 Tired term
90 Synopsis
91 Kind of plum or beet
93 Words with once or sea
94 Farm newcomer
95 Met highlight
96 Vile
98 __ majesty
99 Legend
101 Feed grain
102 Trenchant
105 __ Abner
106 River isle
107 Nabokov novel

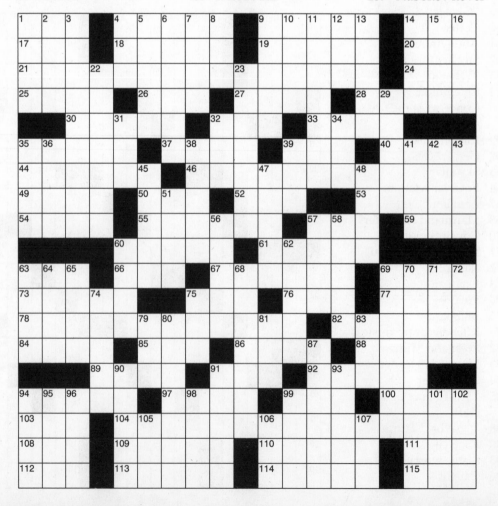

ACROSS

1 Objection
5 Parking-lot sight
9 Bus. consultant
12 Place of confusion
17 Pakistani tongue
18 Words with were or stands
19 Direct
20 Writer Walker
21 Extent for "Spoon River" poet?
24 Kind of wing or whale
25 Casual
26 Con's opponent
27 Deleter
29 Mayday relative
30 Garden shrubs
33 Belgian resort
35 Bouillon
37 Clare Booth Luce's "The __"
38 Subdue
40 Darkroom solution
42 Words with mode
43 A "doctor" of rhyme
45 Personality disorder
48 Poet John Crowe's rough draft?
52 Harvest goddess
53 Quotidian interval
54 Mature
55 Campus VIPs
57 Actress Rowlands
58 The Rolling Stones' "__ Shelter"
61 "__ the Law" (1938 film)
63 Pasture parent
64 Geologist's concern
65 Take __ (doze)
66 Indian province
68 Film critic Roger
70 Chemin de __
71 Sandwich initials
72 Poet Alfred, elated?
77 Hectic
80 Boors
81 Cry to Dominguin
82 Cornwall neighbor
83 Entangled
85 Dray
87 Armor plate
88 Still
89 Obvious
91 __ Harbour, Fla.
93 Words between roses
95 Dispossess
97 Verdant
98 __ off one's mind

100 Fee for poet Robert W.?
106 Work unit
107 Chopper
108 Holding vessel
109 Day divider
110 Church areas
111 Crucible
112 Whirl
113 Couple

DOWN

1 Kind of steer
2 Stat for Bob Tewksbury
3 News execs
4 Unavailing
5 "Cheers" employee
6 Kiangs
7 Free
8 Trek part
9 Glances
10 Bakery item
11 Wall St. place
12 Taverns
13 Clay, later
14 Stephen, the poetic giant?
15 Reverberate
16 Proposal starter

22 Halcyon spot
23 Lubricated
28 Bars, at the bar
30 "__ to end all wars . . ."
31 Author of "The Grog Shop"
32 "__ for All Seasons"
34 Haggard tale
36 Actress Merkel
38 Allotments
39 Fortune 500 co.
41 Mirthful
43 Big D campus
44 Employs
46 "__ not forgotten"
47 Indian maid
49 Hominy cereal
50 Keatsian work
51 Comprehend
56 Appalling
57 Cancun cat
58 Ship's spar
59 "You're All __"
60 Like Andrew's "To His Coy Mistress"?
62 Rk. for a TV dad
64 Ending for east or west

66 Affiliates
67 Russian statesman
69 City lines
71 Trite advice
73 "Irresistible __"
74 Hindu discipline
75 N.C. campus
76 Dispatched
78 One of the Perons
79 Loft contents
84 Polecat
85 Alluvium
86 Close by
89 Mingle
90 Providential
91 Jenkins's "__ Oklahoma"
92 Out of kilter
94 PDQ relative
96 Tang
99 Offering at 12 Down
101 Outward: prefix
102 Roue
103 Singer Orbison
104 Tibetan gazelle
105 Purpose

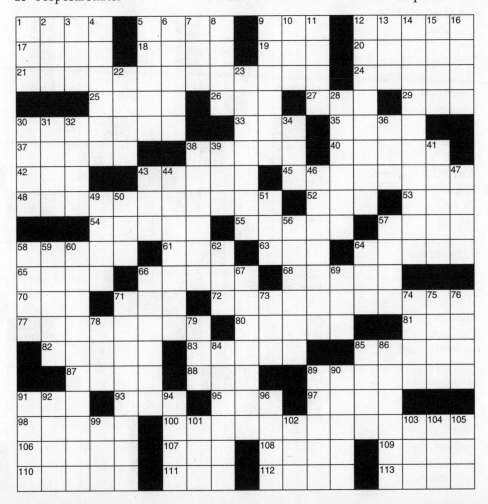

ACROSS

1 Lathan and Lazarus
6 Dairy dish
11 Gerbil relative
18 Soupcon
19 Woodwinds
20 Wild Bill Hickok's town
21 Seafood accompaniment
23 Monomoy and Molokai
24 High-tech banking initials
25 Carl or Rob
26 "John B.," e.g.
27 Increasing
29 Joiner of a sort
31 Prefix for pare or pay
34 __ avis
36 "Meet __ St. Louis"
38 Savage
41 Relish-tray offering
43 Blue-pencils
45 Patois
46 Skeleton
47 Anabaena and volvox
49 Ornamental shelf
50 U.K. part
51 Appetizing
53 Diamond's "I Am __"
55 "I Love Lucy" name
57 Reedbirds
59 Strikebreaker
63 Diorama
65 Consume
67 Wrath
68 Where 20 Across is
71 Torpor
72 Scope
74 Tangled
75 Zooid
77 Bitterness
78 Bat
80 Sonora snack
83 Minute
84 Salonga of Broadway
85 Concocts
87 Geometric unit
89 Footing
91 Junctures
93 Scot's denial
96 Cow and ewe
99 Utes, e.g.
101 Highest peak
102 Garlic sauce
103 __ a limb

104 Moisture
105 "Be __ . . ." (pretty please)
106 Threefold

DOWN

1 Singer James
2 Castle defense
3 Whispers
4 Behave
5 Distinct
6 Trig function
7 __ Shari, Africa
8 Womanizer
9 Condemn
10 Compass pt.
11 Greeters of a sort
12 Incorporate
13 Feed crop
14 Insult
15 Hamilton's bill
16 Forster's "Howards __"
17 Court matter
22 Fr. cathedral city
26 Card game
28 Do road work

30 Drama award
31 Pub order
32 Fury
33 Chem. compound
34 Decked out
35 "__ Together" (1932 song)
37 Rio __, Brazil
39 Jai __
40 Peels
42 Sinuous shape
44 Brief bloomer
47 Stream to the Severn
48 Projection
49 Aggregate
52 Lincoln and Vigoda
53 "Picnic" playwright
54 Farm basket
56 Bone of contention
58 Feckless
60 City on I-75
61 Element no. 18
62 Wallace of films
64 Tranquil
66 Musical syllable
68 Poet Shapiro

69 For __ (professionally)
70 Mrs. Charles
71 Whole lot
73 Pilaster
75 Sticklers
76 Sugars
77 Western competition
79 Preoccupy
81 Grain bristle
82 "__ credit card?"
86 IRS document, for short
88 Susann's "Once __ Enough"
89 Storage place
90 Out of the wind
92 One of the Kennedys
94 Shortly
95 Serf of yore
96 Select group
97 Time before
98 Converged
99 Health club
100 Continental abbr.

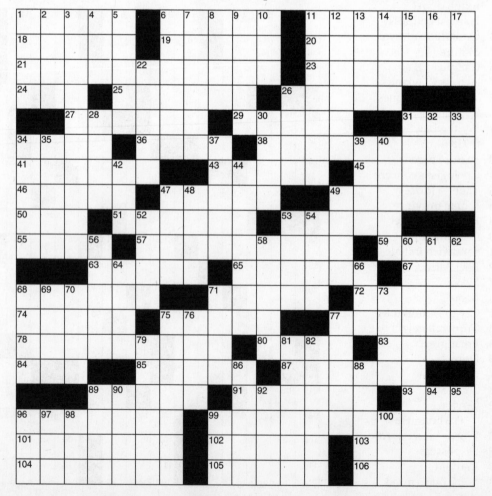

ACROSS

1 Conductor Kurt
6 Morass
12 Subsurface
18 Sentient
19 __ d'hôtel
20 Person who presses on
21 Dog breed
23 Propitious
24 Prefix for thesis
25 Egregious
26 Brave, informally
28 River to the Tyrrhenian
31 Singer Della
33 L.A. campus
36 Skier McKinney
38 Film of 1936
42 Eased off
43 Town maps
44 A touch of the torch
45 Painter Moses
46 Afflict
47 Chestnut clam
49 Bathing spot
50 NHL team
53 Sing like Bing
54 St. Tropez saisons
56 Shaw play
58 Attends
62 Up in the air
64 Grave
66 Words with glance
67 Scathing
70 Pivotal
71 Water buffaloes
73 Perfect
74 Busby Berkeley musical
77 Position
78 Soap opera ending in '93
81 Love apple
82 "Waste Land" monogram
83 Mountain nymph
84 Seattle player, for short
85 Withdraws
87 "__ hardly wait"
89 Flight record
92 Spread
95 Old West route
100 Illusion
101 Permit
102 Family
103 "The __" (1992 film)
104 Iconoclasts
105 Buddy of films

DOWN

1 Corpus
2 Gone
3 Anne Tyler novel
4 Amphora
5 Soak flax
6 Denigrate
7 "That'll __ ya!"
8 Sty sound
9 Actress Hagen
10 Kennel sound
11 Certain futures traders
12 Infected
13 "Trinity" author
14 Actress Schneider
15 Chem. ending
16 Conger
17 Desiccated
22 Manna, e.g.
27 NATO member
29 "... __ the whole thing"
30 Harris characters
31 Nucleic acid
32 Newt
33 The Beatles' "Back in the __"
34 Word with free
35 Pitcher David
36 Finesse
37 Nearby
38 Mettle
39 Ethan or Steve
40 Stoic philosopher
41 Modern Persian
46 Nautical preposition
47 "The Sheik of __"
48 Loudness unit
51 "Unto us __ is given . . ."
52 Aves.' relatives
53 "__ Horseman" (1978 film)
55 Egyptian leader
57 Batman foe
59 Character in "Miracle on 34th Street"
60 "__ ship is a good ship"
61 Renaissance poet
63 Ooh followers
65 Boca __, Fla.
67 Fog
68 Harem rooms
69 Artist Magritte
72 Branches
74 Bureau
75 Arab robe
76 Frenzied
77 Item in lithography
79 Power-plant part
80 Skill
84 Strongboxes
85 Dock
86 Imperative
87 The Beatles' "Let __"
88 Demand
90 Fr. river
91 "Glengarry __ Ross"
92 Ref's cousin
93 Zero
94 Brother
96 Donkey in Dijon
97 Catch
98 Everyday article
99 Deprive

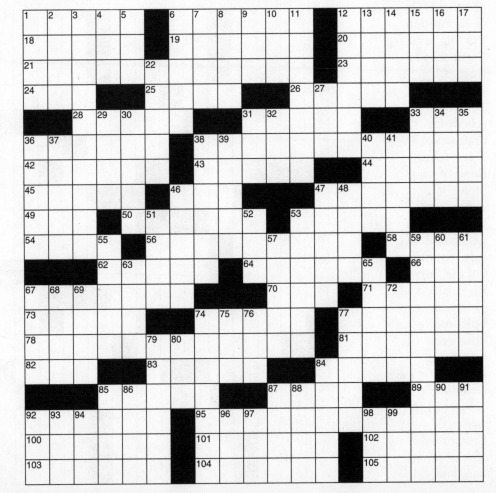

ACROSS

1　Writer Alther
5　Noncommital
9　Boozehound
14　Chill
17　Ingresses: Abbr.
18　Considerably
19　__ bouffe
20　Denain donkey
21　Actor Baldwin
22　Camaguey's land
23　Suit marking
25　Sundry
27　Notwithstanding
29　Jewish month
30　Cat-__ tails
31　__ France Presse
32　Clans
33　Embroidery
35　Attests
38　Immunizing agents
39　Consume
41　Just
43　Varnish ingredient
46　Pessimist's word
47　Name of two
　　presidents
49　Ger. pronoun
51　Praying person
53　Earth-shaped
55　Key
56　Part of VP
57　Tentatively
　　schedules
60　Perlman of TV
61　Tivoli family
62　Rosie of song
63　Stole
64　Actor Erwin
65　On-site art, of a sort
66　Gotcha relative
68　Rds.' counterparts
69　Off the ship
71　River island
74　__ lang syne
76　Epicurean events
78　Resented
83　Summons
85　Figures of speech
87　Dwelling
88　Novel of 1847
89　Arranged
91　Unmanned
　　aircraft
92　Tanglewood

94　Undraped
96　Tweed twitter
97　Wrath
98　More gelid
99　River sport
100　Launder ending
101　Gob
102　Lincoln's in-laws
103　Wrigglesome
104　Action

DOWN

1　Entice
2　Under control
3　Wonder
4　Mounts
5　Ramsgate
　　raincoats
6　Eskimo knife
7　West Indies
　　island
8　Objets d'art
　　display
9　Subject
10　Thinks
11　Corrals

12　Formerly,
　　old-style
13　Informer
14　Cosmetic line
15　Advice, informally
16　Decorticates
24　Teammate of Snider
　　and Gilliam
26　Give in
28　"Puppy Love"
　　singer
31　Traveling
32　Former Soviet units
34　Epoch
36　Stradivari's teacher
37　Land on the Red Sea
40　Count
42　Called, old-style
43　Cherishes
44　Barley bristle
45　Abe Burrows
　　play
48　"__ Kapital"
50　Warms up
52　Born
53　Fla. city

54　Wish
55　Type of vb.
57　Flows
58　Heron
59　New Deal agcy.
63　Flange
65　Extinct birds
66　Grouper
67　Extinguished
70　Serf
72　Footnote word
73　Rout
75　Like a filet
77　Transgressed
79　Contaminated
80　Contribute
81　"__ Fideles"
82　Proven
83　Second feature
84　Soprano Lucine
86　Muntjac and pudu
89　Prefix for motive
90　Fleur-de-lis, e.g.
91　Moist
93　Smack
95　Pa. neighbor

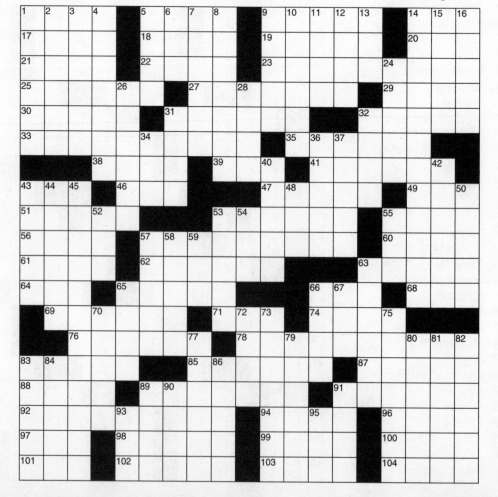

ACROSS

1 Current units
5 Correspondence
9 Chester A. Riley's daughter
13 Strong cotton
17 Folk wisdom
18 Mrs. Shakespeare
19 Stage direction
20 Yemen's capital
21 Mediocre financial institutions?
23 High-quality artwork?
25 Coral Castle's site
26 Cruise
28 Association
29 Division
31 Outlay
32 Thunder unit
33 Decay
34 Region of Germany
37 Word with la la
38 Pound
42 "Court __ session"
44 High-quality gossip?
46 Slave
47 Eighteen-wheeler
48 Conveyance
49 Jukebox button
51 Macrogametes
52 Apply primer
54 Exult
56 Jordanian capital
58 Febrile
59 Thesis
60 Hot tub
61 Penelope or Persephone
64 Dennis of films
65 Manager in 10 World Series
69 Coffee vessel
70 Hearth
72 Olympics runner, '80 and '84
73 Church calendar
74 Grand prince of Kiev
76 Architectural pan?
79 Enlist again
80 Soccer great
81 Leather punch
82 Matriculate
84 Expert
85 Sorgo
87 Highlander
88 Chose
90 Outlet
93 Reversal
94 Showed derision
96 Comedy-club accolade?

98 Most inferior container?
102 Bestowed
103 Deposited
104 Girasole
105 Ox of puzzledom
106 Travois
107 Writer Buchanan
108 Western perennial
109 Contiguous

DOWN

1 Landon
2 Big bird of yore
3 Praise for a racer's effort?
4 Type flourish
5 Title of respect
6 Caesar's years
7 Rorschach raw material
8 Hornbook fare
9 Suit
10 Botanical angle
11 Crib
12 Star-shaped
13 Rampart
14 Jazzman's assent
15 Computer list
16 Part of AM
22 Dotty
24 Kind of nut or fowl
27 "__ sow, so shall ye reap"
29 Friable
30 Schlemiel
31 Appropriates
32 Summit
35 Baseball phrase
36 Erase
37 Pleasure
39 Kind of lens
40 __ Ridge ('72 Derby winner)
41 Actor Ladd
43 Micromarketer's concern
45 Pal
50 Training-room staple
53 An O'Neill
54 Hopeless case
55 Cover
57 Haughty home
59 Unwritten
60 Superman substance
61 Wisecrack
62 Cajole
63 Chemical compound
64 Topsy's creator
65 Mediocre
66 Hamlet, to a reviewer?
67 Excogitate
68 Jogged
71 Medicine container
72 Ringlet
75 Withdrew
77 Mend
78 Boxing combinations
83 Plunder
86 Mountain tree
87 Big Sur town
89 Hickory
90 Ootheca contents
91 Objective
92 Wander
93 Link
94 Crow
95 Site of Frogner Park
97 Furious
99 Spread out, poetically
100 AL sportswear
101 Dine

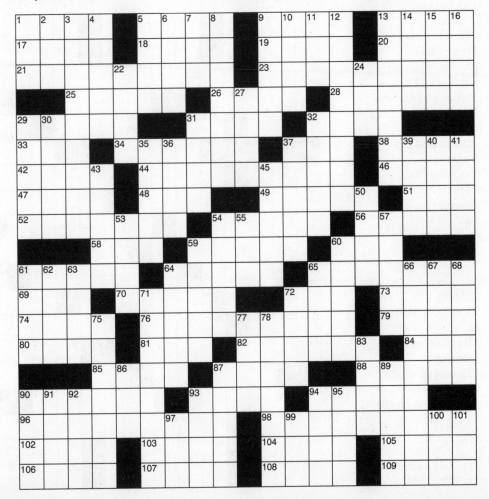

ACROSS

1 "When __ eat?"
5 Gullets
9 Glacial pinnacle
14 Float
17 He loves, to Horace
18 Slightly
19 "Republic" writer
20 Heartache
21 With "The," McMurtry tale
24 Lode yield
25 Languor
26 Quick bread
27 Gasconade
29 Kennel command
30 Hairpin turn
33 Glove material
34 __ in the road
36 Roll
38 Fla. town
41 One of the humanities
44 Modern transaction
47 Purpose
48 Telltale
49 De novo
50 Shine
51 Discern
52 __ of life
54 General makeup
56 Formic acid producer
57 Updike's "Of __"
59 Phibes and Faustus
60 Blue Jays' home
64 Kilmer of films
65 George and T.S.
68 Stair parts
69 Discharge
71 "Thermopylae of America"
72 Skilled
74 Douse
75 Part of UNLV
76 "Saturday Night __" (hit song of '64)
78 Refer to
79 Bachelor's counterpart
81 Sulks
82 Mountain nymph
83 Interval
85 Clairvoyance
87 Greek letters
90 "It's __" (no problem)
92 Heavy weights, for short
94 Proxy
96 Suggestions
97 Pop culture item of the '60s
102 "Where __ the snows . . .?"
103 Map detail
104 Mitigate
105 Continue
106 Rendezvoused
107 Fear and May
108 Tinted
109 Teen's bane

DOWN

1 Evans and Robertson
2 Muscat dweller
3 Question contraction
4 Ides of March words
5 Zetterling
6 TV initials
7 Intelligence
8 Persisted
9 Tax's proverbial companion
10 Other
11 Cry from the crowd
12 From __ Z
13 Rural ringer
14 Film of 1987
15 Possessive pronoun
16 Mangold
22 Bakery offering
23 Reine's mate
28 Lennon's widow
31 Serving of 22 Down
32 Aspect
34 Most fitting
35 Phoenician deity
37 Churl
38 Whilom
39 Gymnastic feat
40 Poet Lowell
41 Nervous as __
42 Film of 1991
43 Innovation of the '30s
44 Outspoken
45 Spot for 43 Down
46 Have a life
51 Slaughter
53 "__ first you don't succeed . . ."
55 "Brother, can you spare __?"
56 March 30 baby
58 Like Welsh rabbit
61 Words with more
62 Cypress, e.g.
63 Bone: prefix
66 Actor Bert
67 Except
69 Loop lines
70 Survey
71 "__ boy!"
73 Sound __ (media snipped)
76 Purifying
77 Against
80 New Deal org.
83 Cores
84 Loser to Holmes, Oct. 2, 1980
86 Prefix to take or boil
87 Bordeaux wine
88 Federation
89 Ligure or logan
90 "__ Bede"
91 Hurting
92 Poleyn's place
93 Kennel command
95 Crazy
98 Nucleic acid
99 Uraeus
100 Verb ending
101 Mars color

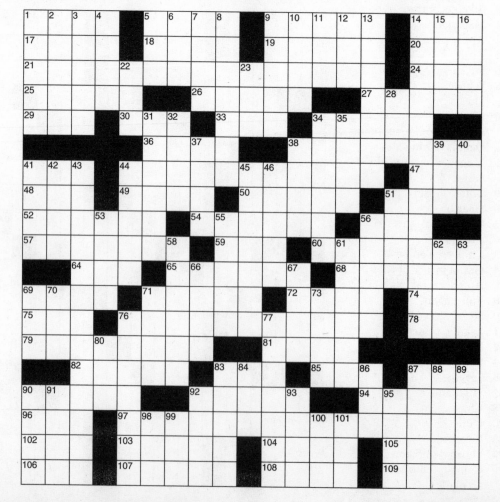

ACROSS

1 Gather
5 Brews
9 Inveigle
13 Actor Harrison
17 "__ Wonderful Life"
18 Seconds
19 "If I __ Hammer"
20 Dies __
21 Pacific isle
22 Fruited-plain topper
25 "A Fool Such __" (Presley hit)
27 European basin
28 For sure
29 Press corps gear
33 Circumscribe
35 U.K. part
36 Benefit
37 Hebrew letter
39 Blacksnakes
41 Space travelers, for short
44 Martin Cruz Smith book
47 Tyndareus's wife
48 Troll relative
49 Actor Robbins
50 Sky altar
52 High-flyer
54 Boxers
57 Doughy dish
59 Clear
60 Wilder's "__ Town"
61 Schwarzwald
64 Opera's Frederica __ Stade
65 Fat solid
67 Cobbler's supply
68 Goriot, e.g.
69 Sports spots
70 Herb or grace
71 Millinery offering
73 "The High and the Mighty" author
74 Author of "La Debacle"
78 Linda Ronstadt hit
83 LTJG-to-be
84 Sequence
86 Nimble
87 Prefix for asian
88 Common article
90 Make a stand
92 Indulge alternative
94 Land
97 Discordia
99 Letter opener
100 Dorothy's destination
104 Indigo
107 All even
108 Goose of 21 Across
109 Kind of bend or bone
110 Fix up
111 Emmets
112 Throws in
113 Propelled
114 "Madam, I'm __"

DOWN

1 Bravo or Lobo
2 Zeta follower
3 Guilt-ridden
4 Caesura
5 Elec. unit
6 __ Diamond Phillips
7 Misjudges
8 Flower part
9 Warm
10 Farm father
11 Assumed
12 Cezanne
13 Conform
14 Sight in Calif. or Fla.
15 Corn crake
16 Reject
23 Hideaway
24 Edinburgh denials
26 Desert Storm combatant
29 Mongrel
30 Enzyme
31 Grad
32 Saline mixture
34 Igloo material
38 Marseilles money
40 Files
42 Actor Howard
43 Untroubled
45 Rds.' relatives
46 Psychologist Eriksen et al.
48 Scull
51 Regarding
53 Elect
54 Prescribed amount
55 Beat via feet
56 Actor Sydney
57 Liberal's state: Abbr.
58 Former footballer E.J.
59 Bronze, to Brutus
61 Lingerie item
62 "Faust" composer
63 Spools
66 __ Arbor
68 School grp.
71 Tarlek of WKRP
72 Bottomless pit
75 Systematic
76 DXX divided by X
77 Part of L.A.
79 "__ Lazy River"
80 Pined
81 Arles assent
82 Amphora
84 Interstice
85 Brace
89 Marks
91 Singer Stevie
93 Royal wear
94 "__ girl!"
95 Facial feature
96 Actress Rowlands
98 Cosecant's reciprocal
101 Plus
102 Hamilton's bill
103 Still
105 Mrs. Cantor
106 Actor Herbert

ACROSS

1 Halfbeaks
5 Nourish
9 Vipers
13 Vespiary denizen
17 Sports org.
18 A Guthrie
19 Rabbit's tail
20 Curtain-raiser
21 Film of 1992
25 Purport
26 Pale green
27 Fish dish
28 Age
29 Exhaust
31 Window dressing
33 Rock's __ Zeppelin
35 Road surface
37 Cloy
39 Express
41 Wanes
45 Closed
47 With "The," Ross Macdonald novel
50 Slangy denials
51 Seraglio space
52 Go-between: Abbr.
53 Arledge of TV
54 Handle
55 The Nutcracker, e.g.
57 Tailored, in a way
58 Built for speed
62 Practices
66 Tracking system
67 Being
71 Mall predecessor
72 Prefix for puncture
75 Switch positions
76 Terror
77 "This Gun for Hire" actress
80 Impassioned
81 Yemen capital
82 Inn
83 Spahn's pitching partner
85 Nev. town
86 Filmmaker Peckinpah
88 Child of Agrippina
90 Inundate
92 Sewing tool
95 Moore of films
97 Apiece
99 Prospect
102 Part of a Byron line
106 "Stagger Lee" items
107 Ananias
108 Pres. Carter's middle name
109 Arctic sea
110 Tip
111 "__ Ever Need Is You"
112 Check
113 Concordes

DOWN

1 Winged pest
2 Land unit
3 Hit song of 1961
4 Relish
5 "__ and Away" (1992 film)
6 Wandering
7 Jewish month
8 Words with disturb
9 Doer: suffix
10 Machinations
11 Absolute
12 Holiday bread
13 Quipster
14 Yearn
15 Recipe word
16 Kind of pocket
22 Scrubs
23 Power device
24 Employ
30 Writer McEwan
32 Hawkeye State
34 Repository
35 Dogtooth, e.g.
36 Shortly
38 Duchin or Fisher
40 Op. __
42 Raw recruit
43 Clavicle, for one
44 Travois
46 Soup vegetable
48 Pro __
49 Network
51 Royal pronoun
55 Matthew, Mark, etc.
56 Belgian resort
57 Chemin-de-__
58 Mikita of hockey
59 Glance
60 Writer Hammond
61 USN inst.
62 "__ Nagela"
63 Senescent
64 Wimble
65 Actor Jeremy
67 Fumble
68 Mariner's milieu
69 Volplane
70 Whirlpool
72 Expert
73 Rio event
74 Lizard fish
76 Afresh
78 "__ rat!"
79 Televised
80 Evergreen
84 Stick
87 Humorist George
89 "Nemesis" author
91 Candle parts
92 Amonasro's daughter
93 Bastinado
94 Guipure or colbertine
96 Hubbub
98 Causerie
100 Piquant
101 Cultural collections
103 Trouble
104 Silkworm
105 Shade tree

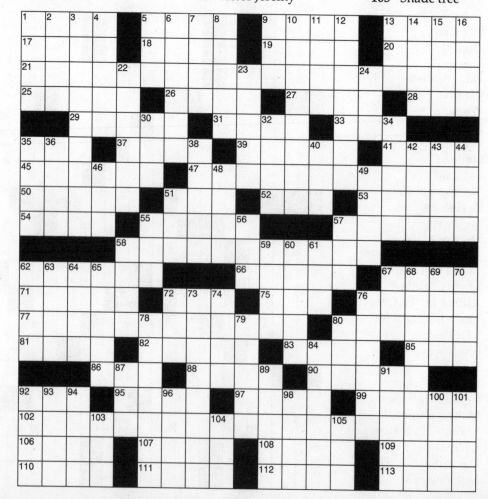

ACROSS

1 Shepherd
6 Buster of films
12 Pivot
18 Photographer Leibovitz
19 Quail groups
20 High-grade
21 Creatures that have SEEN TALK STAR?
23 __ Mirage, Calif.
24 Wrigglesome
25 Fare
26 Topi or toque
27 Age
28 Start of a C. Moore work
30 Live
32 Aperture
33 Morsel for A.P. Indy
34 Sapphira
35 PALE STONE animals?
41 Leading
43 Without __ (benighted)
45 Detached
46 Play casually
47 Force
49 Swindle, informally
51 Coral or Cortes
53 FDR agency
54 Secrecy
55 Golfer's concern
56 Supply for Parton
59 A ULTRA ANT?
62 Variegated
63 Japanese vegetable
64 Pigeon pen
65 Eur. land
66 Prefix for pare or pay
68 Unbridled
70 Decimation amount
72 "You __ Beautiful"
76 Kind of music or metal
77 Calamities
79 Lanky
81 ROOT IS SET for these beasts?
83 Impleads
84 Nev. town
85 Bernadette, e.g.
86 Fangs
88 Capstone
89 End
92 Loop lines
93 PBS series
94 __ Hashana
96 Minos's mother
98 Animal that's the FAULT OF A BREW?
102 Up and about
103 Bespeak
104 San Fran. player, for short
105 Apostatic
106 Fume
107 Paravane

DOWN

1 Billfish
2 Actress Merkel
3 Beast like A TEEN RAT?
4 Accolades, e.g.
5 Hollow
6 Murrow's employer
7 Portray
8 Profit
9 Actor Theodore
10 Borscht ingredient
11 Curve shape
12 Predicament
13 Say again?
14 Particle
15 Corruption
16 Sycophantic sound
17 Trotsky
22 Steve L.'s partner
26 Odious
28 First rate
29 Verruca
31 Cordial
32 Wildebeest
34 Whitewash
35 Model Carol
36 Belay
37 Decide
38 Corsican leader
39 Singer Ford
40 Jouster's mount
42 Disarray
43 Taj Mahal site
44 Passage
48 Regarding
50 "On the double" relative
52 Like __ of bricks
54 Actor William
56 Sausage
57 Moscow's state
58 Pyle of TV fame
60 Certifies
61 "Sixteen __" (hit for 39 Down)
62 Chan Chan's land
64 Roman statesman
67 Poverty
69 Swivet
70 "__ the season . . ."
71 __ monde
73 Beast that gives NEAT HELP?
74 Auction
75 Beast at the ROXY?
78 Neckline type
80 Noted Gandhi follower
82 Nevis or Ibiza
83 Computer command
86 Fields of comedy
87 Occurrence
88 __ as a fiddle
89 Garganey
90 Mystique
91 Golfer's concern
92 Dueling sword
93 Hub
95 Point-return link
97 CIA forerunner
98 Unseld of the NBA
99 Cooperative effort
100 Filmmaker Spike
101 Hockey great

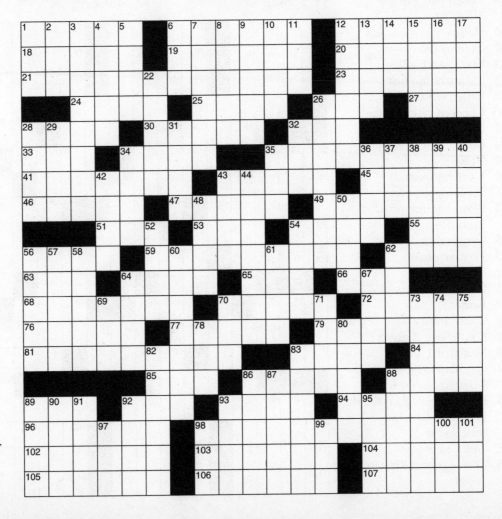

ACROSS

1 Forsake
5 Currying tool
9 Williams College team
13 Kind of price or light
17 Pakistani tongue
18 Environs
19 Greek-letter org.
20 Kingfish
21 "Unto us __ is given . . ."
22 Road sign
23 Public meetings
24 Mouthward
25 Editorial observation of 1897, part I
29 Thus
30 Part of UCSD
31 Attends
32 "__ gratia artis"
35 Sector
38 Caesar's downfall
40 Coaming
44 Observation, part II
47 Common TV fare
48 "__ Like It"
49 Coach Doug of the NBA
50 Hallux and minimus
52 Conveyance
53 Sassafras drinks
55 Moore of movies
58 Down with
60 Checked out, in a way
61 Observation, part III
64 Peck
68 Graf __
70 Moravian, e.g.
71 Sevastopol's place
73 Blind-bat link
76 Mme. Bovary
78 Comprehend
80 Pensive poem
81 Fortune
83 Observation, part IV
87 Faith
88 Calif. county
89 South Seas cloth
90 Modernist
91 "__ Man" (1984 film)
93 Goethite, for one
95 Updike protagonist, 1992
97 Francis P. Church's conclusion
105 Gully
106 Coolidge and Ripken
107 Tease
108 Diagnostic tool
110 Pizzeria need
111 Baseball manager Felipe
112 Drama award
113 Actor Richard
114 Caroled
115 Look
116 Desires
117 Withered

DOWN

1 Sine __ non
2 Lofty bear
3 Object of veneration
4 Skipjacks
5 Thriving business
6 Triglyph surface
7 Feline sound
8 Highlands hares
9 Arab landowner
10 Indonesian boat
11 Actress Julie
12 Remits
13 Child's transport
14 Pizarro's conquest
15 Spoken
16 Actress Ann
26 Assess
27 Inroad
28 Nobelist of 1983
32 Truckle
33 Put another way
34 Manner
36 __ de guerre
37 Wear down
39 Newt
41 Do a sound job
42 __ goat (takin)
43 Tee preceder
45 Bad guys
46 Smirks
47 Lute relative
51 Shell propeller
54 Produce-department leftovers
56 Actor Gibson
57 "__ Spy" (1933 film)
59 Proficiency
62 Haw's partner
63 Happening
65 "See what __?"
66 Transition
67 Authority
69 River of the Carolinas
72 Bring to mind
73 Curvature
74 Title for Anthony Hopkins
75 Honor card
77 Miscellany
79 Greek letter
82 Grown-up britt
84 American marsupial
85 Actress Mia
86 Cochise, Geronimo et al.
88 Cash-register button
92 Typewriter type
94 Bask in
96 Modern messages
97 Braces
98 "__ Nagela"
99 "Close to __" (1992 film)
100 Cosmetic ingredient
101 Existential alternative
102 K __ kilo
103 Exhort
104 Volklingen's river
109 Chem. ending

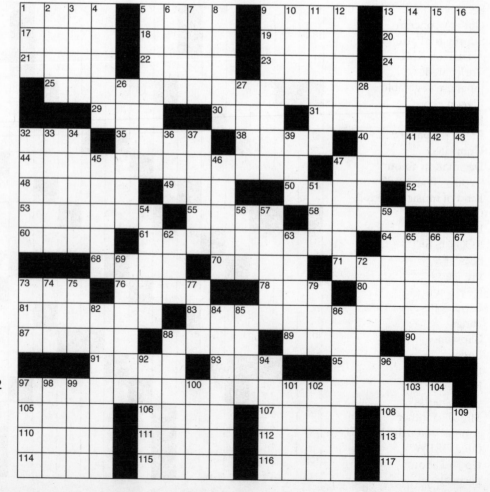

ACROSS

1 Make up, in a way
5 Refrain
11 Virtues
17 Moffo and Magnani
19 Site of the Iron Curtain
20 Road
21 Film of 1979
23 Singer Vic
24 Tyler's "The Accidental __"
25 Chem. endings
27 Film of 1982
28 Festal
29 Assurance
31 Terpsichorean perch
33 Kind of force
35 Pledge
36 Exist
37 Malleable
41 Blandishment
42 NASA places
46 Modernist
47 Nabokov novel
48 Founder
49 Actress Singer
50 Cheap
52 Hags
54 "Western Star" poet
55 Rubble
56 Toad genus
57 Aegean isle
58 Surnai
59 Princess in the news
61 Part of ICBM
62 Provided with personnel
65 Lounge lizard
66 Element no. 10
67 Crosswalk sign
68 Dander
69 Toothpaste type
70 Original stuff
73 Manger
74 Cincture
76 Stapes's place
77 Mass. cape
78 Potiches
79 __ out (supplemented)
81 Modern missile
83 "__ That a Shame"
84 Macho sort
87 Narcissus lover
89 "... pot calling __ black"
92 "Twelfth Night" character
94 12/31 message
97 Constraint
98 Consecrate
99 "Me too" relative
100 In a muddy mess
101 Extents
102 Diamond crew

DOWN

1 Moulage
2 Aware of
3 D.C. social events
4 Do a voice-over
5 Word after per
6 Embrace
7 Mexican gold
8 Picaroon
9 Overturn
10 Withered
11 Irrational
12 Sidestep
13 Delinquent
14 Involved with
15 Diapason
16 Nostradamus
18 Panel frame
22 "Love __ Hurting Thing" (1966 hit)
26 The Dardanelles, e.g.
29 "Caine Mutiny" man
30 Hold the title
32 Ref. work
33 Spill the beans
34 Coarse
35 Camp sights
36 __ ski
38 Not benchwarming
39 Bash
40 Bibelots
42 Star vehicle
43 Benign
44 Obeisance
45 __ mater
48 Expedition
51 __ now (currently)
53 Desert feature
54 __ Rouge
57 Express contempt
58 Amos of baseball
59 Lodgings
60 Hypothesis
61 Overrun
62 Material for 53 Down
63 Buffalo's county
64 American socialist
67 Dryad's milieu
71 Born
72 Hosp. section
73 "__ See" ('77 hit)
75 Flings
78 Op-Ed fare
80 Dumpling relative
81 Writer Alexander
82 The __ the beat
83 Hurt, old-style
84 Mortar troughs
85 Jewish month
86 Spanish artist
88 Singe
89 "Them" menace
90 Rinehart's "The Red __"
91 Discordia
93 Refuge: Abbr.
95 "Animal Farm" figure
96 Relative of 25 Across

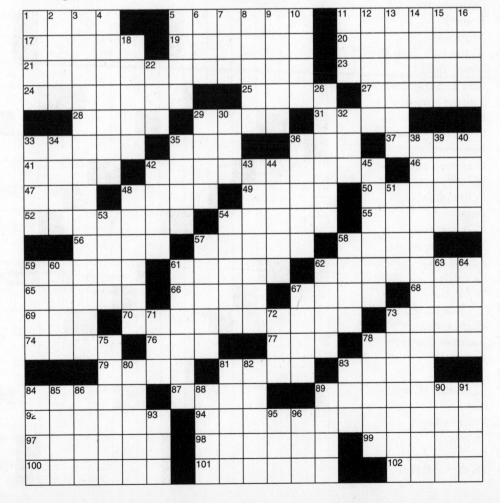

ACROSS

1 "The __ Greenwich Village" (1984 film)
7 Washer cycle
12 Face, to Kramden
18 Like some modern music
19 Shaquille of the NBA
20 Turkish capital
21 Hitchcock film
24 __ speak
25 Obligation
26 Pre-med subject
27 Aspiring execs
30 Cover story
33 Release
37 Sinatra's ambition?
41 '50s get-together
42 Cruising
43 Mariel's land
44 Touch-tone symbol
45 Certain votes
47 Seat of County Clare
50 Comedian Mort
52 Flight-plan abbr.
53 Transplant participant
55 Rook
57 Murmurs
59 At the 11th hour
66 Lowly boat
67 Guy's counterpart
68 Mortise's mate
69 Fairy queen
72 Cornelia __ Skinner
74 Hot news
77 Combustible heap
78 Jai __
80 Polite initials
82 Begone
84 W. Hem. org.
85 Juggles the books
90 Arrow shaft
91 Close by
92 Wild guess
93 "__ just imagine . . ."
95 Highlands wear
97 Summer desserts
101 Fairy tale
108 Stick on
109 "__ Rain" (Clapton hit)
110 Bumbershoot
111 Swamp
112 Betray
113 Ice cream flavor

DOWN

1 Butter units
2 Holy Roman emperor
3 Versifier
4 Bury
5 Scull
6 Ziegfeld
7 Mantle
8 Bearing greenery
9 Chivvy
10 Shop tool
11 Certain Ivy Leaguer
12 Actress Madeline
13 Bisected
14 They're nice on ice
15 Patriotic org.
16 Make mistakes
17 Actor Liotta
22 Hidden
23 Football runner
28 Arthur of TV
29 Church area
31 Bus. regulator
32 Heat amts.
34 Poet Allen
35 Tiny pest
36 Gumbo
37 "Happy birthday" followers
38 Starts
39 Salad dressing type
40 Swiftian creature
41 Pilgrimage to Mecca
46 Barflies
48 Teed off
49 "__ Dracula" (1943 film)
51 Artist's pad
54 Part of P.R.
56 Kind of power
58 Action item
60 __ Dame
61 "__ Shout" (rock classic)
62 Fastener
63 "I Believe __" ('78 hit)
64 Fable's burden
65 Chem. endings
69 Spacy place
70 Significantly
71 John Goodman role
73 Cinematographer Nykvist
75 Calif. peak
76 Singer Axton
79 "My life __ stroll upon the beach" (Thoreau)
81 Opposite of post
83 FDR agcy.
86 Nuts of a sort
87 Revel in
88 African antelopes
89 __ all right
94 Qualifications
96 Suggestion word
98 Leg part
99 Model Macpherson
100 Kind of terrier
101 Teatime topping
102 Mil. address
103 First-aid initials
104 RN's speciality
105 LBJ pet
106 Carson's longtime home
107 Box-office sign

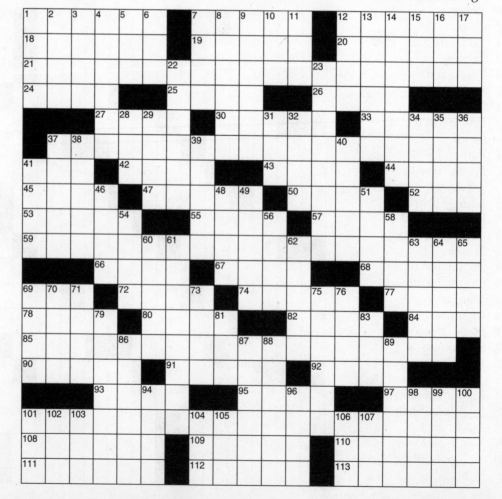

ACROSS

1 Obstinate sort
4 Word with yard or board
8 Lepidomelane
12 Outfights
17 Supermarket container
18 Cushy conditions
19 Particle
20 __ fell swoop
21 Film of 1992
24 Ineligible
25 Vest's lack
26 Give in
28 Salamanders
29 Charlotte and Norma
30 Minute
31 Call to Fido
33 Fischer's field
35 Residue
36 Farm unit
38 Nigerian native
41 Lieutenant
42 Salinger short story
45 Melvillian milieu
46 Inferior
47 Instantaneous
48 York's river
49 Marine mollusks
51 "__ words were never spoken"
53 Alpine transports
54 Prefix for classic or plastic
55 Boor
56 Parson's msg.
57 Grand
60 Distinct
61 Cheese type
65 Cultural lead-in
66 Neat as __
67 Hoot
68 Box-score column
69 Nile flow, perhaps
73 Venerable
74 London's __ Gardens
75 Meander
76 Nev. town
77 Collegiate growths
78 Zero
80 Dirk
81 Wd. rearrangement
82 Cold-shoulder
84 Excessive adulation of a sort
87 Designates
90 __ lazuli
92 Emotional tree?

94 Knock for __
95 Letterman competitor
96 The Beatles' "Abbey __"
97 Time
98 Small sum
99 Immediately
100 Elizabeth I's mother
101 Slump

DOWN

1 Functions
2 Comedian Mort
3 Despised
4 Accommodates
5 The 19th president
6 Goddess for King Tut
7 Scribe's implement
8 Deep purple
9 80 Down's land
10 "__ Go With Me" ('50s hit)
11 The last word
12 N.Y. campus
13 Spiritual
14 Scowl of a caffeine abuser?
15 Conjoin

16 Court units
22 Leave off
23 Cross-examine
27 Leafhopper
30 Echelon
32 Twilight time, poetically
33 Reynosa house
34 Speeds
35 MacNelly strip
36 Old French coin
37 Singe
39 Ignoble
40 Possessive pronoun
42 Gale pet
43 Seize
44 Calabash
46 Victim
50 Madcap
51 Scottish chief
52 Capek play
53 Knowing look
55 Julia in the kitchen
56 "__ Got Everything" (1937 film)
57 Absence
58 Nightmare figure
59 Discourage

60 Interpretation
61 Kingfish
62 Film of 1992
63 Busy as __
64 Purges
66 Revoke, legally
67 "The Sun Also Rises" character
70 Possess
71 Sawbuck
72 Resin
73 Purpose
77 Word with straight or track
79 Stew vegetable
80 Saint Catherine's home
81 Bedouin market
82 Insult
83 Robust
85 Fly-by-night sorts
86 Converge
87 Ancient struggle
88 Mrs. Charles
89 Booty
91 Eavesdrop
93 New Deal org.

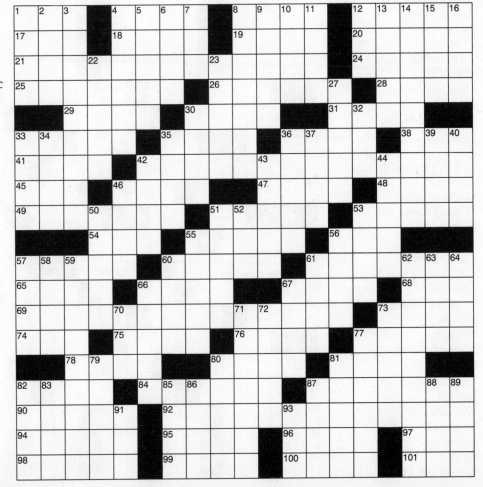

ACROSS

1 Jeune fille
5 Imposture
9 Lined up
13 San __ Obispo
17 Petition
18 "For __ know . . ."
19 Fruit cake
20 To be, in Toulon
21 Olympics souvenirs?
23 Wall St. spot
24 Like __ of bricks
25 Caramel or toffee
26 Pantywaist
28 Paradises
29 Pen
31 Cranny
32 Disinclined
33 Word in a Latin love poem
34 Lycée relative
36 Parlors
38 Literary party-givers?
42 Golfer Massengale
43 Teachers' org.
46 Polite disclaimer
47 USN inst.
48 More than sometimes
50 Grand works
52 Actor Robert
54 Demopolis's st.
55 Refits
56 City north of Lashkar
59 Turf tales?
63 "You're putting __!"
64 Crown
66 Hold the title
67 Nasty
69 Pixies
70 One of Marilyn's husbands
71 Haggard novel
73 Michael Caine role
77 Furtive
78 Much-used article
80 Crew member's complaint?
83 Attributes
86 Storied racehorse of the '60s
87 Trivium
88 Aircraft assembly
90 Nightshade
92 "__ Thesaurus"
95 Pursuit
96 Attacked
97 Gourmandizes
98 Discordia
99 Hubs
100 Belle Boyd, Mata Hari, etc.

104 Hawaiian bird
105 Printer's choice
106 Spoken
107 Banquette, e.g.
108 Proof
109 Optimum
110 Alejandro of baseball
111 Bone: prefix

DOWN

1 Mail abbr.
2 Hardly
3 Org. since 1863
4 Mississippi statesman
5 Paddock worker
6 32 Down, formerly
7 Thoroughly
8 Rockets
9 Faze
10 Famous pharaoh
11 Acquiesce
12 Floor covering
13 Sluggish
14 Out-and-out dowitcher?
15 Actor Jeremy
16 Message
22 Sp. queen
27 Clinching score
28 Stimulated
29 "High Button Shoes" lyricist
30 Melville title
31 Part of N.B.
32 Foreman foe in '74
35 "Julius Caesar" character
37 Costar of Jackie and Audrey
39 Invective
40 Sardonic
41 One way to fly
44 Outer: prefix
45 43 Across, e.g.
49 Rotund
51 Novel of 1740
53 Fortify
54 Writer Bobbie __ Mason
55 "__ live and breathe . . ."
56 Citrus drinks
57 Stream
58 High-flown transports?
60 Bill's partner
61 Pitcher

62 Ties up
65 Fiefdom
68 Race part
70 Ebony
71 Custard apple
72 Drumlin, for one
74 Maneuvers
75 "What's __ for me?"
76 Superlative endings
79 Towel legend
81 Stew ingredient
82 Goodall subject
84 Brown shade
85 Cuffs
88 Whiff
89 Dos Passos's "__ Soldiers"
91 Keats or Shelley
93 Words with whim
94 Plaster of paris
96 Whet
97 Actress Cannon
99 Taradiddle
101 __-game show
102 Chow down
103 Bernadette, e.g.

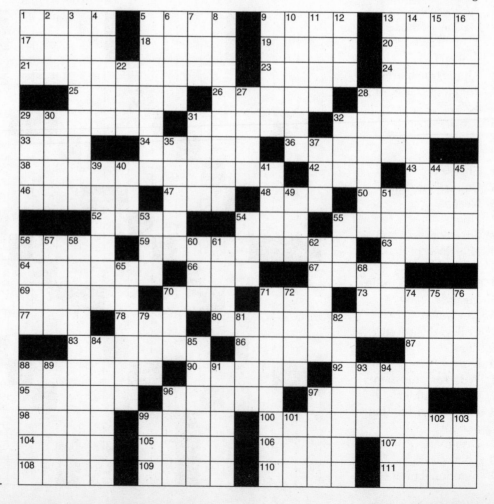

ACROSS

1 Frame timber
4 Drill
9 Tripod part
12 People, informally
17 Tribute
18 Jazz composition
19 Blue-chip rating
20 Muscat native
21 Stiff and formal
24 Bottom
25 Fixes roofs
26 Surreptitious
27 Connoisseur
29 Film of 1992
30 Arrow shaft
32 Party drink
33 Fight-song word
35 Thunder
36 MRI forerunner
38 Suede feature
41 Chang's brother
42 Dangerous curve
45 Personality part
46 __ Wednesday
47 Anastasia's sister
48 Vases
49 Missile of the '90s
50 Coating
52 Pointillist painter
55 Martha's Vineyard's county
56 Levels
58 Dance step
59 Dulcet
61 Federal Reserve's concern
63 Garden tool
66 Flag
69 Rara __
70 Natterjack
71 "__ first you don't succeed . . ."
73 Chem. ending
74 Writer Follett
75 Common apod
78 Crony
79 Joule part
80 Coleridgian effort
81 Due
82 __ out (reprove)
83 Golfer Crenshaw
84 Writer Sontag
86 Circuit
88 Medicinal format
92 Cherished

93 McCullers's "The __ A Lonely Hunter"
96 Peer
97 Lightly capitalized
100 Anathema
101 Buff
102 Mrs. Bunker
103 Extreme suffix
104 Sudden
105 One of the Turners
106 Paretsky and Teasdale
107 Summoning of succor?

DOWN

1 Crowd noise
2 Groundless
3 Austerity
4 For certain
5 Memory exercises
6 Pismires
7 Nuptial reply
8 Continuous
9 Film of 1965
10 Toilet water
11 Stare
12 Margot of dance

13 Council Bluffs neighbor
14 Take aboard
15 Embroider
16 Dam's mate
22 Sci. branch
23 Resin
28 Night sight
30 Virginia rails
31 Surplus
33 Stack
34 Handle
35 Important
37 Litters' littlest
38 Lynchings
39 Fever symptom
40 Schools of whales
42 Darling
43 Director Pakula
44 Type of shark
49 Petitions
51 Burl of films
53 Poetry form
54 Detroit org.
55 Spaghetti al __
57 George Stewart book

60 Indecisive
61 Fabricate
62 Word with look or leaf
64 Service charges
65 Flax product
67 Work like a beaver
68 Dickens character
70 Corrupt
72 Craze
75 "Go west" advisor
76 Floral offering
77 Envelops
82 Hamilton foe
83 Detonation
85 "__ at 'em!"
86 Episperm
87 Expletives
88 Part of MIT
89 Pastel shade
90 Prickly pericarps
91 Lenient
93 Scion
94 __ many words
95 Pepper, York, etc.
98 Glaswegian denial
99 Harem room

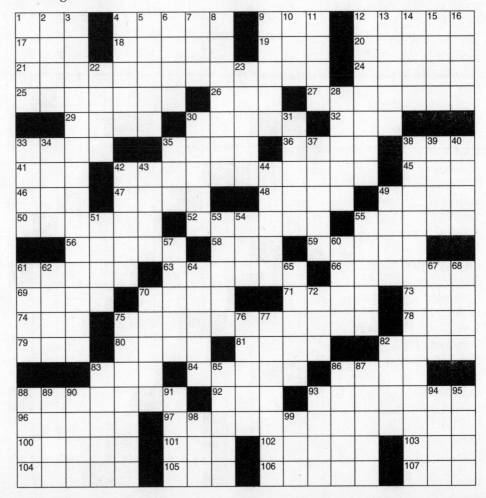

ACROSS

1 Door post
5 Stoker
9 Binge
12 Issue
16 Winglike
17 Hindu trainees
19 "__ of Destruction" ('65 song)
20 Work-bench adjunct
21 What the Groundhog gets on Feb. 2
23 Cassiterite extract
24 Model Macpherson
25 Reddish brown
26 Disturb
28 Stages
30 Telegraph symbols
32 Mucilage ingredient
34 Compete
35 Groundhog's endeavor
43 One of the networks
44 Deprive of sight, in falconry
45 Parrot
46 Faithful
47 Writer Dahl
50 Risky venture, for short
52 Musical syllables
55 Summer refresher
56 Lionize
58 Solothurn's river
60 Flax
62 Groundhog's theme song?
65 Big statuary
68 Fairish
69 "Lawrence of __"
73 "Woman in the Dunes" author
74 Subject
76 Musical Domino
78 Revise
79 Prima donna
81 Alley __
83 Symbol of oppression
85 Relief
86 Risk Groundhog takes
92 Logician's abbr.
93 Gondolier's item
94 Buzz
95 Coordinates
99 Hard's companion
102 Bewildered
106 Lahaina's place
107 Diving bird
109 Groundhog's quest
111 Fishing net part
112 Jamie __ Curtis
113 Japanese verse
114 Mideast gulf
115 Didion's "Play __ It Lays"
116 Messy spot
117 Pedal digits
118 Torn

DOWN

1 Benchley's fish story
2 Jai __
3 Produce
4 One of the Starrs
5 Little-used avenues
6 Big bird of legend
7 Chinese isinglass
8 Kaffir relative
9 Dark mineral
10 Eager
11 Palace of Nations site
12 Town on Puget Sound
13 Odometer interval
14 Man, for one
15 Links supply
18 Roscommon neighbor
22 Entity
27 Hide
29 W.W. II combatants
31 Matches
33 Join
35 Turpentine source
36 Student's concern
37 Fix upholstery
38 Lancets
39 "Cheers" character
40 Dies __
41 Dishabille
42 Turned right
43 Brother
48 Celeb's vehicle
49 Attired, poetically
51 "__ the City" (1948 film)
53 Opera of 1871
54 Dormitory sound
57 Facility
59 Emersonian output
61 Did the crawl
63 Otis of baseball
64 __ the trail of
65 Heels
66 News notice
67 Singer Stubbs
70 Billet-doux writer
71 "What's __ for me?"
72 Introduce
75 Fast-food choice
77 Distort
80 Exonerates
82 Edith of songdom
84 Sea urchin
87 Actor Wahl
88 Exemplars
89 Refuse
90 "The Stand" author
91 Demosthenes, e.g.
95 Prefix for valent
96 High-strung
97 Bonito relative
98 Tallow source
100 Wrangle
101 Peter, Paul and Mary, e.g.
103 Battery order
104 Mideast land
105 Bloke
108 Item on a clavier
110 White House nickname

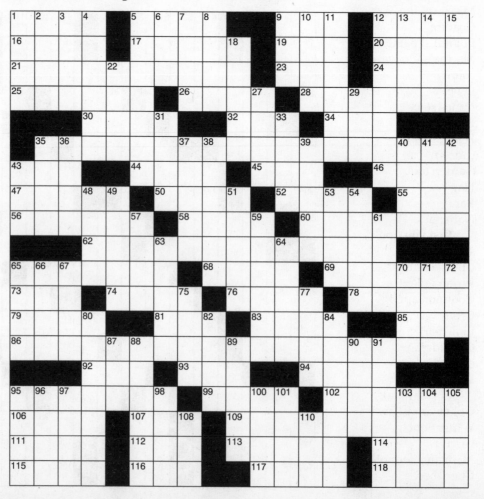

ACROSS

1 Adequate
7 Recipe meas.
10 Londoner's last letter
13 U. of Miami symbol
17 Cicero, for one
18 La la precursor
19 "Shack Out on __" (1955 film)
20 Solitary
21 Attends
22 High-minded affinity
25 News VIPS
26 "...__ right with the world"
28 Aachen article
29 Bid's partner
30 Site of Alki Point
32 AMA mbrs.
33 Chum
35 Dander
36 __ Dawn Chong
37 Remotely
39 Impulse
40 Flight-plan abbr.
41 Sound of surprise
43 Subversive device
46 Guidonian note
47 Lardner
48 Chow
49 Winglike
53 Ozzie and Harriet
55 Link with
57 Sisal, e.g.
58 Glorifies
59 Sic transit gloria __
60 Mountain ridges
61 "Creation" novelist
62 Chastity's dad
63 Semiprecious stone
64 Trade grp.
65 Actor Paul
66 Sires' counterparts
67 Buoy type
68 Dramatic group
72 Penalized, in racing
73 Honest guy
76 Wraps up
77 Work
78 Santha Rama __
79 __ Abner
80 Clamp shape
81 Doused
82 Textile fiber
86 Persona non __
88 Variables
89 Zoning map
90 Butter
91 Diversions for Nike and Nyx?

95 "Ognissanti Madonna" painter
97 Painter Magritte
98 Word with status
99 Mornings
100 Charm
101 Steinbeck's "East of __"
102 Clique
103 Screwball
104 Like some eyes

DOWN

1 Venetian magistrates
2 Wear down
3 Dish from Calpurnia's kitchen
4 Sci-fi beings
5 Write music
6 Scandinavian ogre
7 First rate
8 Helios
9 Hippolytus's lover
10 National park in Utah
11 Long time
12 Half of MIV
13 Misfortunes
14 Wager maker
15 Flip
16 Did a farm job
23 Shakespearean contraction
24 Soothes
27 Discovers
31 Petcock
32 Rk. for Frank Burns
33 Newspaper staple
34 Pretension
38 Navigational hazard
39 "__ Did for Love"
41 OPEC headquarters
42 Tocqueville
43 U.K. food containers
44 Impecunious
45 Game
47 Near Eastern weight
50 Two bits for Tiberius?
51 Pennsylvania, in D.C.
52 Put back in the mail
54 Vernacular
55 Surcoat
56 Bed-and-breakfast
57 Crafts' companions
59 "The Name of the Rose" group
60 Goals

62 Café crème color
63 Determining
65 Writing-on-the-wall word
66 Actress Joanne
69 Summary
70 "A Shropshire Lad" poet
71 Choose
72 Noun case: Abbr.
73 VP in '93
74 Rolled, as a log
75 Comedian Boosler
78 Dye again
81 "Scent __ Woman" (1992 film)
83 Immures
84 Golden Horde member
85 Ga. campus
87 ATF agents
88 "__ You Babe" ('60s hit)
89 Stage whisper
92 Mensa concerns
93 Billiards item
94 Cassowary
96 Seraglio space

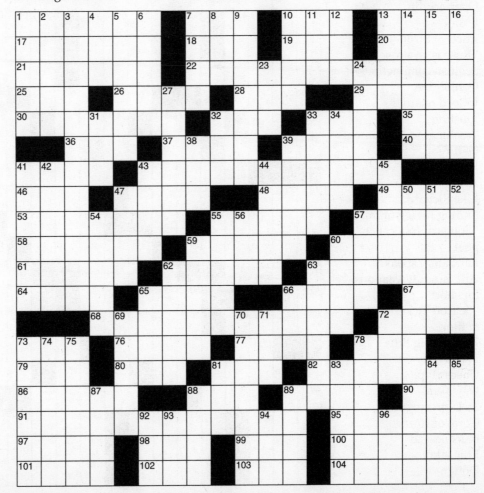

ACROSS

1 Actress Thompson
5 In motion
10 Baldwin of films
14 Flatfish
17 Needle case
18 Valley __, Pa.
19 Service mark
20 Words with mode
21 Baseball pitcher
23 Prizefighters
24 Sportscaster Scully
25 Signed
26 Sonar sounds
28 Beguile
30 Royal flush component
31 Lone: Abbr.
34 Sully
35 Offerings from 67 Across
37 Clytemnestra's mother
39 Cymar
41 Smoke or fog
43 Actor in "Heart Like a Wheel"
46 TV series of the '70s
49 Over-erudite
52 Foster
53 Erich __ Stroheim
54 "Rose is __ a rose"
55 Scottish conjunctions
56 Contention
57 Indeed relative
58 Jousting
60 Washington Monument feature
62 Embellish
63 Alum
64 Like Richard I
65 Ending for leg or fall
66 "Songs of Innocence" poet
67 Laudatory speaker
68 Anti-aircraft weapons, for short
70 "Season Ticket" author
72 Hits the big time
74 Perceived
75 Cheese type
79 Day's end
81 La la precursor
83 Coral or Koro
85 Nucleic acid
86 Epic tale
87 Dough

89 Shower shoes
91 Dance step
92 Stoneboat
95 Actress Karen, baseball's Bobby, etc.
98 W.W. II area
99 Rescind
100 Susan Lucci role
101 Erase
102 Hideout
103 Apiece
104 Kind of board or blade
105 Sp. she-bears

DOWN

1 In sequence
2 Immediately
3 Slammed, Jordan-style
4 Lieutenant
5 Continental abbr.
6 Alchemist's gold
7 Sojourn
8 Match tip, e.g.
9 Royal tenures
10 Eiger and Monch
11 Singer Rawls

12 Nest deposit
13 TV talker Bob
14 Heritage Classic-winning golfer
15 Writer Hoffman
16 Rows
22 Media matter
27 Incremental
29 Donnybrook
32 Free of charge
33 Armstrong or L'Amour
35 Squeeze
36 Peace or polyantha
38 Degraded
40 U.K. beacon
42 Heron
44 Chem. endings
45 Confidant
47 Grieves
48 Game __ (tennis call)
49 Machetes
50 Beethoven's Third
51 Early first lady, modern-style
56 Fashion trend
58 In __ (furious)

59 Enjoys
60 Moon goddess
61 Die's companion
63 Gauntlet
64 Racers at 10 Down
66 Perimeter
67 Compass heading
69 Madrid Mlle.
71 Happy __
73 Permeate
76 Hums
77 Jessica F.'s portrayer
78 The crowd
79 Human, for one
80 Overjoy
82 Wanders
84 Do something
87 Legend
88 Other things, to Octavius
90 Adriatic resort
93 Creek
94 UHF tuning aid
96 Outside: prefix
97 Rob Roy's refusal

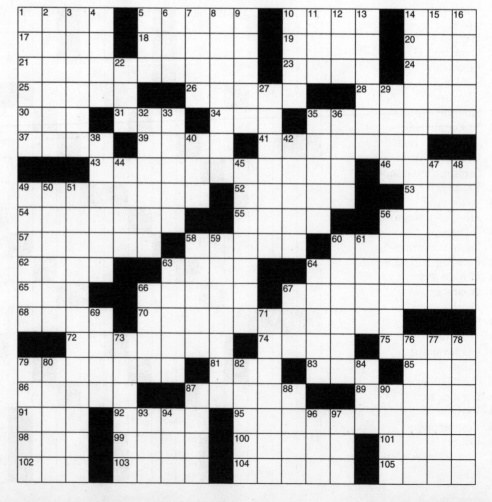

ACROSS

1 Dishearten
7 Under
12 Expedites
18 Charlotte __
19 Originate
20 Big name in astronomy
21 Renounces
22 "Rhythm Nation" singer
24 Tallow
25 Josh
27 "__ the Night" (1985 film)
28 Cut off
30 Sparlings
33 Part of UNLV
36 Uris's "The __"
38 Court judgment
41 Confederate
42 Fountainhead
43 Son of Myrrha
45 Rain-forest climber
47 Michelangelo work
48 Constant
49 Thrilled beyond bounds
52 Wordsworth poem
53 Fix shoelaces
54 Forgiving
55 Genevieve or Jeanne: Abbr.
56 Curvilinear
57 Dull finish
59 Prod
62 Ice formation
63 Storms
64 Dried up
65 Broadway hit of the '90s
70 Tropical fish
71 Yucatan farewell
72 Effloresce
73 Roman emperor
74 Refuse
75 God of the French
77 Mercutio's friend
79 CIA forerunner
80 Culmination
81 Core
83 Corpsman
85 Brews
86 Dutch cheeses
89 Gambol
92 Coach in the '93 Super Bowl
97 Montana capital
99 Mellencamp's "__ Lover"
100 Slender as __
101 Complied
102 Liverpool's river
103 Whipping boy
104 Flings

DOWN

1 Pops
2 Big bird
3 Stephen Dedalus's alter ego
4 Aristocracy
5 Op. __
6 Canopies
7 __ California
8 Chunks of history
9 Actor's assignment
10 Sugar
11 Moisten
12 Hut
13 Treaties
14 Nevada town
15 Old RRs
16 __ volente
17 Thesis starter
23 Actress Eikenberry
26 Deviate
29 Ski town
31 "The __ Love" (Gershwin standard)
32 Gusto
33 Actor Cobb
34 Countertenor
35 Do in
36 Auditoria
37 Tennis term
39 Extract
40 Irresolute
42 Lean
44 What negativists say
46 Pongid
47 Affectation
49 Lapidist's offering
50 "__ while they're hot!"
51 Diet no-no
53 Holds up
56 Acquires
57 Important
58 Crockett's last stand
59 Modern aviators, informally
60 Tapestry
61 Boston dish
62 Satiate
63 Hit song of 1964
64 Sargasso, e.g.
65 Fatigue
66 "Close to __" (1992 film)
67 The Swedish Nightingale
68 Foment
69 Veer
70 Walked
73 Drive
75 Radio employee
76 __ many words
78 Delicious!
81 Drexler of the NBA
82 VCR button
84 British __
85 Iowa college town
87 Performs
88 Actor Garcia
90 Arrow poison
91 Gridiron wear
92 "Father Knows Best" name
93 Chem. ending
94 Debussy setting
95 Gen. Arnold
96 New Deal initials
98 Nigerian native

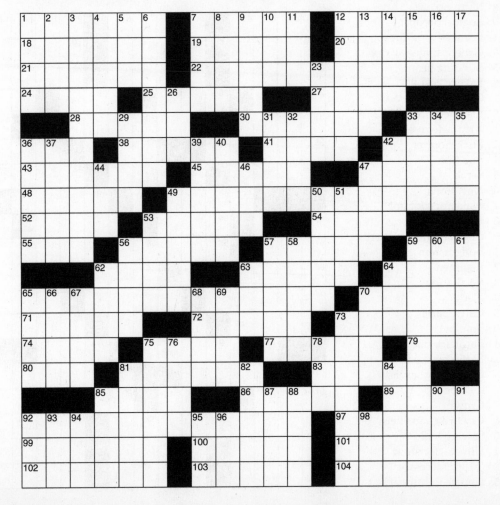

ACROSS

1 Liquid asset
5 Part of R. Adm.
9 Clarsach
13 Hankering
17 Movie dog
18 Vogue competitor
19 Turkish VIP
20 Charcuterie
21 Baba au __
22 Mound
23 Certain French fruit?
25 __ Saud
26 Fiddlesticks!
27 Hatchet
29 __ Paulo
30 Express
31 Certain Montana spread?
34 Beliefs
36 Mountain nymph
37 Like crocetin
38 Injunction
40 Negate
41 Covenant
43 Dunaway of films
44 Squad
47 Theater features
49 More
50 Logical premise
51 Printers' measures
54 Genetic material
55 Building beam
56 Bakery vessel
57 Cut
58 Llanwern lowlands?
61 Atty.'s degree
62 Puck stopper
64 Pub line
65 Serve
66 Nev. town
67 Malay or Mongol
68 Foretoken
69 Common film sequence
71 Budget item
72 Regimen
73 Vacillating
74 Pledges
78 Calyx parts
80 Bon Jovi
81 Perot, for one
82 Battle-marked
84 Down East service member?
87 Crown
88 Cry to a cuadrillero
90 Sewing tool
91 Utmost, for short
92 JFK predecessor
93 Female in Muscat?
96 Ger. river
98 Rank
99 Drama award
100 "Love Potion Number __"
101 Calhoun of films
102 Pound
103 Elvis Presley hit
104 Backbone
105 Pronounces
106 Snuggery

DOWN

1 Reindeer
2 "Hot" town in Georgia?
3 Impaired
4 Butcher's offering
5 Fix-up, for short
6 Mr. Yale
7 Still's companion
8 Familial
9 More robust
10 Machine or Stone
11 Greek letters
12 Flamboyance
13 Chem. ending
14 Arizona house of worship?
15 Confuse
16 How-to fare
24 Mythos
26 Garden section
28 Deleted
32 Western resort
33 Very, to Vouet
35 Mrs. Lauder
38 City in Iraq
39 Needle feature
41 Mother of Perseus
42 And so forth
43 Drawbacks
45 Allen's "Scenes From __"
46 Manilow hit
48 One of the Booths
49 Actor Buddy
50 Inventories
51 "Pomp and Circumstance" composer
52 Thidwick, e.g.
53 Iberian complaint?
55 Key
56 Southern hickory
59 Chair designer
60 Bert of films
63 Subsequent
68 "Lorenzo's __" (1992 film)
69 Wilton's st.
70 Constantly
72 From morn 'til night
73 Industrious types
75 Turn to rust
76 Divagates
77 Despise
79 Stem
80 Mandible
81 Strain
82 Bore
83 Musical group
84 "Olympia" painter
85 Corundum
86 "The Bells of St. __" (1945 film)
89 Abu Dhabi VIP
94 Murdoch's "Under the __"
95 Cuckoo
97 __ number on
98 X

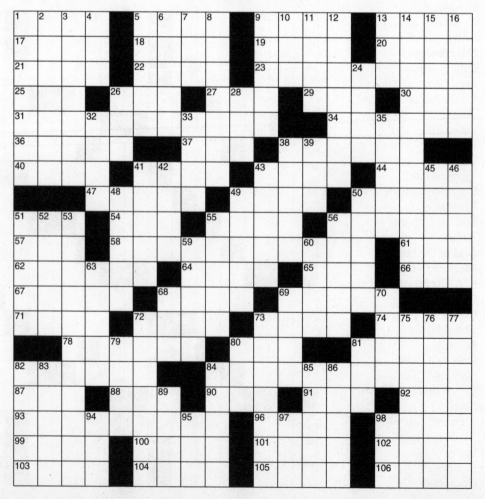

ACROSS

1 Sacred fig
6 Most vile
12 Kearney's river
18 Auricles
19 Fancy
20 Patch up
21 Product of Nashville
23 Morgan le Fay's isle
24 "__ Mame"
25 Moonstone, for one
26 Paste
27 Sault __ Marie
28 "Untouchables" name
31 Gold coin
33 Phone button
36 "__ Song Go . . ."
38 Chaney
39 "Moll Flanders" author
40 Riyadh robe
43 Streetwise sort
46 Power org.
47 Hostile
49 Dry ravine
50 Unctuous
51 Female lobster
52 __ a firecracker
54 Hammerhead parts
56 Health-care professional
58 Tungsten, for one
60 Tartan patterns
62 Unwilling
64 Critical acclaim
66 Fringe benefits
68 Band
70 San Jose Sharks' surface
72 Wd. scramble
74 "Giant" ranch
76 Off the mark
77 Bygone
78 Patriotic feeling
81 Steel's "Message From __"
82 ". . . a man who __ there . . ."
84 Sphere
85 Smart set of sorts
86 Pilaster
87 City on the Arkansas
89 Furore
90 Wall St. abbr.
93 Concede

95 Music medium, for short
97 Baker's tool
99 Contract clause
101 Hit tune of '59
104 Hapsburgs' home
105 Throat lozenge
106 Himalayan habitues
107 Map details
108 Sonnet section
109 Nidi

DOWN

1 Andes animals
2 Slug __ (fight)
3 Trim
4 "__ Nothin' Like the Real Thing"
5 Of Livy's language
6 Gossoon
7 Triceps's place
8 Cozy
9 Mitigated
10 Prods
11 Gumshoe
12 "Towards the Last Spike" poet
13 Matchmaker Dolly
14 Cochise, for one
15 Celebrity
16 Oaxaca uncle
17 Sea bird
22 Use tackle, in a way
26 Dawned
29 Arrangement
30 Designer's concern
32 Chanel
34 Aphrodite's purview
35 Senior member
37 Dormant
39 Wood problem
40 Einbeck exclamation
41 Kind of box or town
42 Film of 1980
44 Light source
45 Jewish month
48 Certain info
53 Scholar
55 Brook
57 Writer Paretsky
59 Actress Olin
61 Musical workout
63 Circle dance
65 Passed up

67 Restrict
69 Opponent of King Charles I
70 Fort Dodge's state
71 House
73 "Georgy __" ('60s song)
75 St. Francis's home
79 Recondite
80 Clark's "Misfits" costar
83 Writer Gordimer
87 Turner and Aumont
88 Cancun farewell
90 Sports-section matter
91 On the up-and-up
92 Attire
94 Blanc, e.g.
96 Schismatic group
98 Abscond
99 Egg: prefix
100 Brooch
101 Gal. pts.
102 Ubiquitous article
103 VFW mbr.

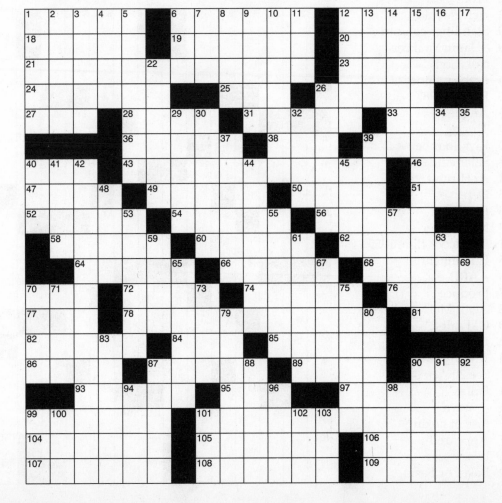

ACROSS

1 Lanza and Cuomo
7 Org. since 1874
11 Busboy's burden
17 Right away
18 Incisive
19 Equestrians
20 With 97 Across, tough-talking maxim
23 Ergate
24 Mortification
25 Lab heater
26 Harpoon
28 Hiatus
31 Anklebones
35 Rule out
38 TV series, 1968-70
41 Expunges
43 Dye chemical
44 Crossword clue: Abbr.
45 Ballads
46 Long story
49 Born
50 Lachrymose
52 From __ Z
53 Actress Julie
55 Standings column
56 "Damn Yankees" assertion
64 In the manner of
65 Film of 1987
66 Anguish
67 Throng
70 Riyadh robe
73 Salamander
74 Al Hirt hit
75 Deprive
76 Ready for
79 More bitter
81 Hitchcock film, 1955
85 Habiliment
86 AARP, e.g.
87 Produce
88 Actor McDowall
90 Old salts
92 Instance
94 Alley __
97 See 20 Across
104 Pallas __
105 __ nova
106 Jose of boxing
107 Appeared
108 Jo's sister
109 Baker or Basin

DOWN

1 Poet Angelou
2 Like __ of bricks
3 Drubbing
4 Ltd. relative
5 Wood sorrel
6 Judgment
7 Loud report
8 Bakery item
9 Three, in Capri
10 "__ Lazy River"
11 Versatile
12 Portray
13 Mann's "__ in Venice"
14 __ Aviv
15 Before
16 Fast flyer
18 Ache
21 Buriram native
22 Highlands creature, informally
26 Cheek
27 Tender lead-in
29 Resembling
30 River in Zaire
32 Verdi work
33 Smirk
34 Questionable
35 Test of patience
36 Ovid's muse
37 Southern slough
39 Implied
40 Irascible
42 Jamaican leader
47 Quid-quo link
48 NYC subway
51 Summer on the Seine
53 Casquetel
54 Bawl
55 Hammers
57 Alternative form: Abbr.
58 Asian capital
59 Exist
60 Old soldiers' org.
61 Sentient
62 Free-lances
63 Rends
67 Miss, in Manzanillo
68 Courts
69 Basics
70 Horrified
71 Swain
72 Humanities
74 Court group
77 Cumulative
78 __ of time
80 Curious
82 Hymn of praise
83 Actress Slezak
84 Centers
89 Body-shop job
91 Top drawer
93 Headlong
94 Monster
95 Cyma recta
96 Stage whisper
97 "Where __ I?"
98 Dweller: Suffix
99 A alternative
100 Middling bond rating
101 Caviar
102 Secured
103 Lapse

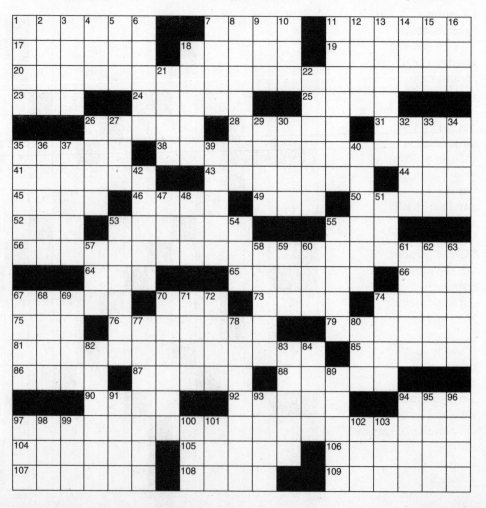

ACROSS

1 Throng
4 Positive factor
8 Buddies
12 Pines
17 Bustle
18 "__ She Sweet"
19 Seed cover
20 Roughly
21 "__ Granger" (1948 film)
22 Kind of base or bank
23 Complicated mess
25 Angelic aura
27 Writer Philip
29 Quietude
30 Numero __
32 Impend
34 Ger. article
35 Adages
39 As good __
41 Reverie
43 Blue
45 Greek letter
46 Oval nuts
48 Road sign
50 Red dye
52 Sporty sort
54 Financial ripoffs
57 __ Dawn Chong
58 Weighty tales
60 Speedily
61 Trial
63 The Beach Boys' "__ Around"
64 Solar disk
65 U.K. honors
69 Indy car
71 Lusters
73 Sigh of relief
74 Shtick
78 Comeback
80 Actress Morris
81 Hoof part
82 Beaned
83 Ruling group
84 Backstabber
87 Presupposed
91 Time of turmoil
92 Suggestion starter
94 Muck
96 Zilch
97 Posed
98 Burns's "To __"
101 MRI forerunner
103 Ski lift
106 Preventatively
110 Zone
112 Past
113 Encore!
114 Certain reps.
115 Pleased
116 Greensward
117 Actor Richard
118 Orderly
119 Brontë name
120 Induced

DOWN

1 Subj. for Fourier
2 Concert halls
3 Kin of square meals?
4 Tablet
5 Dishonest type
6 Countless
7 Dynamo part
8 Lobbying group
9 Sandarac tree
10 Insulated
11 Milieu for Matt Grosjean
12 Statutes
13 Woodwinds
14 Conjunction
15 Candy-counter item
16 Vincent, Vitus, etc.
24 Discussions
26 Shaquille of the NBA
28 Weeding tool
31 Part of O&O
33 Sorcerer
36 Lhasa __
37 Capitol Hill personage
38 Misdeeds
39 Isolated
40 Bristles
42 Film of 1993
44 Lucy's costar
47 Precise
49 Ray
51 Cry of dismay
53 Avid
54 Pipistrelle
55 Kuwait VIP
56 Kind of acid
59 Virtue
62 Harness race
64 Hesitant sounds
66 Naismith's creation
67 Consumed
68 Diffuses
70 Remotely
71 Filament
72 Leopard feature
74 Leaky-boat cry
75 Writer Tyler
76 Essence
77 Machine part
79 __ a time
85 Old struggle
86 Tropical bird
88 Nicholson Baker book
89 Burn up
90 Almost
93 Couture material
95 Missouri feeder
99 Colliery
100 Como __ usted?
102 Vintner's concern
104 Writer James
105 Hope's movie location
106 Poke
107 Actor Tognazzi
108 __ Paulo
109 Superlative suffix
111 "Fables in Slang" humorist

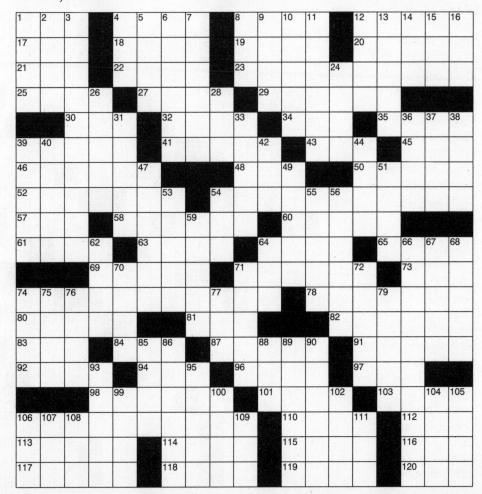

ACROSS

1 Wingding
5 Burn
9 Shocks
13 Pointer and setter
17 Sting
18 Eglatere, e.g.
19 "Mitla Pass" author
20 Sp. river
21 SHIP CAN
24 __ angle (obliquely)
25 Secrecy
26 Tarsus
27 Edentata
28 Christmas hymn opener
30 Prong
31 Dines at home
32 Final sections
33 THAWE
36 Pick out
37 Activity for Judit Polgar
38 Ellipsoids
39 Ger. article
40 Excuse-me sound
41 Details
42 Blend
45 Cajole
47 Singer Sheena
50 __ City, Fla.
51 Psalm verb
54 Thimblerig object
55 Shear
58 Virginia willow
59 High standards
62 Roguish
63 Petrol, in Pittsburgh
64 Appropriate
66 11th President
68 Dutch uncle
71 Slither
72 L.A. arena
74 Deadwood's st.
75 LA PEP
79 Thicket
80 Tycoons
81 Toward shelter
82 Undercover operatives
83 Emanated
84 "__ With Love" (1967 film)
86 Actor Randolph
87 Cookie holders
88 COOL CHEAT
92 Renaissance family
93 Judy's daughter
94 Tennis term
95 And so forth
96 Outfitted with oxfords
97 Software client
98 Early times
99 Godfathers

DOWN

1 Telly initials
2 Manner
3 ENSPUR
4 Gossip
5 Pancake
6 Troughs
7 Nincompoop
8 Mends
9 Discarded
10 Caspian's eastern neighbor
11 Jambalaya ingredient
12 Library admonition
13 Shortages
14 Blunt
15 Ars __ artis
16 Syllabic
22 Doilies
23 Writer Hammond
27 Cries
28 Excelled on
29 Medical measure
30 Motif
31 Leyden relative
33 Elle, in Exmouth
34 Inflict upon
35 Ties up
37 Huntley
40 Ripen
41 Type type: Abbr.
42 TOO PAT
43 Chapel vow
44 Deleting device
46 Nucleic acid
48 Summit
49 Kind of change or chest
50 U.S. honor
51 Fix
52 Actress Hagen
53 Vaisya member
56 Mollify
57 Disgust
60 Range creature
61 Binge
64 Coeur d'__, Idaho
65 Minutiae
67 "__ Mutual Friend"
69 Facade
70 Gains marginally
71 Varnished
72 Leaf
73 Superimpose
74 Placated
75 Dies down
76 La. county
77 Right away
78 Daytona acronym
79 Certain NCOs
82 Tableau
84 Fitzgerald's "__ Side of Paradise"
85 Swamp
86 Inspire
88 Actor Gulager
89 Fuss
90 Where Manhattan is: Abbr.
91 Sp. articles

ACROSS

1 Kind of tea
7 Norton's workplace
12 Shrieks
17 Verdi work
18 In the post
20 Take __ (try)
21 Lynyrd Skynyrd hit
23 Topic
24 Mount
25 Defies
27 Actress Charlotte
28 Fifth tone
31 Machines of chance
34 Musial
35 Dispatch
36 Spectator, e.g.
38 Guileless
40 Orofino's st.
42 Polite greeting
45 Scowled
48 Reversible preposition
49 Jug
51 Afresh
52 Woebegone
57 Sub rosa
60 Spare
61 Ending for fool or bull
62 Montagnard, for one
64 "The Dancing Class" painter
66 Saintonge saison
67 Dip __ in the water
69 Hardship
71 Leaves the aircraft
73 Hosiery thread
75 Russian refusal
77 Dance step
78 Swift or Voltaire
81 Song of 1957
87 Multitude
88 Run like __
89 Sword
90 Encounter
92 Telescope part
94 Grimaces
97 Stereo component
98 Sphere
99 Oust
101 Falling-out
103 "__ Knows" ('58 song)
105 All over the place
111 Ruhr city
112 Jeopardy
113 Form
114 Irritable
115 Unfeeling
116 Trumpet signal

DOWN

1 Word with come or now
2 Number follower
3 Actor Stephen
4 Summer sandwiches
5 Extras
6 Staunch
7 Tex. campus
8 Corn unit
9 Achieves
10 Go by
11 Ease up
12 Dotty
13 Residue
14 "Babes in Arms" song
15 Miller's salesman
16 Knight's mount
19 Point
22 Town on the Penobscot
26 Inward: prefix
28 Greenside admonition
29 Triumphant cry
30 Abject
32 Cross shape
33 Facet
35 Page
37 Garden spot
39 Protestations
41 Barley bristle
43 Killer whale
44 Brewery item
45 Cupidity
46 Gentry
47 Units of force
50 Forster's "Howards __"
52 Christie's "The Seven __ Mystery"
53 Port of Rome
54 TV series
55 Title of respect
56 Stigma
58 Mature
59 Greek letter
63 Vote against
65 Generous portion
68 "Middlemarch" author
70 Salacious
72 "__ sow, so shall . . ."
74 Bumble
76 Oates book
79 Useless
80 Oozed
82 Cry at sea
83 Skirmish
84 FDR agcy.
85 Border
86 Slangy affirmative
88 What 86 Down signifies
90 Impressionist painter
91 Chafed
93 Blazing stars
95 Grand tales
96 __ bleu!
99 Renounce
100 Hence
102 Now's companion
104 Malines
106 Hankering
107 Sardonic
108 Languid
109 Blind ambition
110 Still

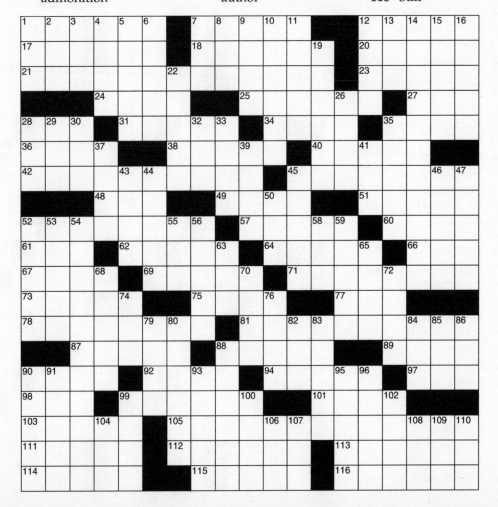

ACROSS

1 Moments, for short
5 Chamorro's home
9 School grps.
13 How awful
17 Lizardfish
18 Part of A.D.
19 Cloak
20 Seized
21 Item for 3 Down
22 Big-eared ballplayers?
25 Treaties
27 Partisans' leader
28 Common contract
29 Scoundrel
31 Welsh __
33 Objective
37 Encouraged
40 Hectors
42 Long-distance rig
43 Gibbon
44 Gets comfortable at the plate?
49 Pinnacle
50 Indigo
52 Blackthorn
53 Cauda
54 __ Savine, France
55 "__ La Mancha"
57 "__ luck!"
60 Crocheted
62 Ambush
64 Requisites
66 Muleta charger
67 Holds together
70 Flower part
72 Mass. campus
75 "A Chorus Line" number
76 Bahrain native
78 Boiling
80 Hibernia
81 Demeanor
82 Benchwarmers' vessel?
86 Actor Stephen
87 Top, rattle, etc.
89 Delhi garment
90 Aide of a sort
92 Glides
95 See 70 Across
98 Gossip
99 Minimum
101 Corrida cries
103 Like ears
106 Near Fenway's Green Monster?
111 Church area
112 Last word
113 Fever symptom
114 Rock's Motley __
115 Genesis name
116 Lot
117 Mete
118 Vernaculars
119 Lairs

DOWN

1 Drainage pit
2 Kazan
3 Salinger on baseball?
4 Loveseat
5 Gas-pump abbr.
6 Component part
7 Playful
8 Slogan
9 Ante relative
10 Flagship beacon
11 Rose lover
12 Attack
13 Unselfish concern
14 Spade's cousin
15 Conjunction
16 Approvals
23 "__ Doone"
24 Dixie grp. of old
26 Churl
30 Sediment
32 Gangster's weapon
34 Makes a start?
35 Ham it up
36 Weary
37 Geoduck
38 Maui town
39 Hollow
41 Marinate
45 Weaver's place
46 Arrange
47 Bugleweed
48 "Silas Marner" author
51 Knowledge
56 Capacitance unit
58 Compass point
59 Garret
61 Legitimate
63 Paddington Bear's homeland
65 Actress Mia
67 Hides
68 Bialy ingredient
69 Droops
71 Actress Olin
73 Linden or limba
74 Barbecue
77 Self-aggrandizing
79 Molly of TV
83 Actress Mary
84 __ the iceberg
85 Nefarious
88 Like the ocean
91 Did a washday job
93 Comprehension
94 Kind of bar or bowl
96 Writer Hoffman
97 Smirks
100 Western lily
102 Veer
104 Writer Hunter
105 __ ex machina
106 Lummox
107 Actress Thurman
108 Hanoi holiday
109 Perpendicular joint
110 __ Moines

ACROSS

1 Opportunity
5 Retiring
8 Urchin
13 Gangplank
17 Verdi work
18 Vinery product
19 Hersey's "A Bell for __"
20 Mystique
21 Mailer's "The __"
23 Staunch
25 Vainglory
26 Desmid
27 Ebony
28 Tracks of a sort
31 Prefix for center
32 Parrotfish relative
35 Marine
38 Nuptial vow
39 __ Tafari
42 Golden Rule word
43 Behave
44 Diminishes
46 Power unit
47 Hwy.
48 Kemo __ (Tonto's friend)
50 Old cars
51 Malory's "Le __ d'Arthur"
52 "All the Way" singer
54 Income source
55 Preparation
56 Stumblebum's cousin
59 Angular
62 Electrical unit
63 Arriviste
67 Merchandise
68 Syrinx
69 Trig, e.g.
70 Seven-faced doctor of film
71 Omnia conqueror
72 Lombok neighbor
73 Standard for Couples
74 One of the Turners
75 Basin
76 Unseld of the NBA
77 Dolt
81 Tonicity
84 Onager
85 Rölvaag's "__ in the Earth"
86 Bridges
88 Apiece
90 Preview word
91 Wild duck
94 Beard
98 Actor Ray
99 "Casablanca" cast member
100 Aurora
101 Cavern sound
102 Meddling
103 Passe
104 President pro __
105 Pairs

DOWN

1 Doleful
2 Fly
3 Canticle
4 Puglia port
5 Meager
6 Towel legend
7 Chatter
8 Trattoria seasoning
9 Work like __
10 Jungle bird
11 Artist's material
12 Conjunction
13 Rum cakes
14 Pitcher's asset
15 Hershiser of baseball
16 Slog
22 Core
24 "What __ rare as a day in June?"
26 In __ (sulking)
28 Aspersions
29 Prefix for gram or grade
30 Consumed
31 Differ ending
33 Barbecue offering
34 Classifieds
36 Moroccan metropolis
37 "__ simple, stupid!"
40 Aleutian isle
41 Gradine
45 Shipboard figure
46 Defeat
48 Nonplusses
49 Stylized
50 Ransack
51 Bog
53 Doubleday
54 Line on a globe
55 Cried
57 Pernicious
58 Security worker
59 Exchange
60 Hindu pleasure
61 Martinets
64 Unfamiliar
65 Assaulted
66 Garden hoppers
68 Beyond
69 Gullets
72 __ canto
73 Luxurious
74 Acknowledged
76 "Fuzzy Wuzzy __ bear . . ."
78 Used a machete
79 Self-centeredness
80 Ocho __, Jamaica
82 Certain diplomat
83 Courage
86 Survey
87 __ Alto, Calif.
89 Farm unit
90 Clog, for one
92 Ticker tape abbr.
93 Neckpiece
94 Hydrous
95 Old French coin
96 Greek letter
97 Distress signal

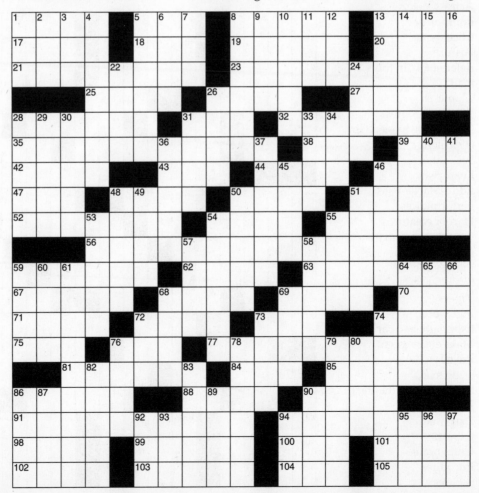

ACROSS

1 Unsettled
5 Achievement
9 Rick
13 Bunked down
17 Vincent Lopez theme
18 Imprudent
19 Piece of land
20 "Dunciad" poet
21 Showcase for bad plays?
23 Horse color
24 Otis Redding hit
25 Certain Sikh
26 Lope
28 Believe
30 Stake
31 Clique
32 DOD part
35 Brooklyn Bridge's river
37 Frothy dessert
39 McBain and McMahon
40 Autocrat
42 Waylay
44 Greek poem that didn't make it?
46 Clockmaker Thomas
49 Actress Velez
52 Pourboire
53 Cheekbone
55 Pasture
56 Relative of "in the mail"
58 Chime
60 Work in progress
62 "__ Old-Fashioned Girl" (1956 song)
63 Sea matter
64 Least risky
65 Eddy-MacDonald performances
66 Harbor creatures
67 "__ what they say . . ."
68 Get it wrong
69 Lihue's isle
71 Sky altar
72 Vipers
73 Ingenious
75 Especially bad car?
79 Make effervescent
81 Relied
82 __ de tête
85 Nonwinner at the tract
87 Deprives
89 Purpose
90 Expert
91 Unfavorable
92 Introduce
94 Secures
96 Romance-language source
98 Northern porgy
100 Spoken
102 Designer's non-sellers?
105 Mitchell setting
106 Protuberance
107 Eye part
108 Pa. city
109 Santa __, Calif
110 Yardarm
111 Bawdy
112 Instants, for short

DOWN

1 Fill
2 Dropped out
3 Parade units
4 Kennel sounds
5 To's companion
6 __ de cologne
7 Bureaucratic abbr.
8 From that source
9 Stags
10 "Foucault's Pendulum" author
11 Hashimite
12 Gray area
13 Wallaba
14 Repositories for rejected shows?
15 Rapiers
16 Spaghetti al __
22 Brahman, e.g.
27 Pledge
29 "Irresistible __"
33 Sonnet part
34 On the move
36 Delicias dish
38 Naval abbr.
41 Hockney's style
43 Cartoonist Lazarus
44 Hautmont headwear
45 Harbingers
47 Prepares to drive
48 Scurries
49 Brimming
50 Problematic
51 Abortive coup?
54 Nucleic acids
57 Carrel
58 Venomous snake
59 Zero
61 " . . . boy with cheek __"
63 Safari member
64 Flower part
66 Please
67 Worth of comics
70 Deserts
71 In the manner of
74 Danson
76 Hamburg's river
77 Placid
78 Incongruously
80 Stephen of films
82 Victor of films
83 Biting
84 Shutterbug's supply
85 Sentimental
86 Americas highway
88 Sidewalk superintendent
93 Discontinue
95 Reclaim
97 Citrus drinks
99 Writer Octavio
101 Nabokov novel
103 Modern
104 Operator without honor

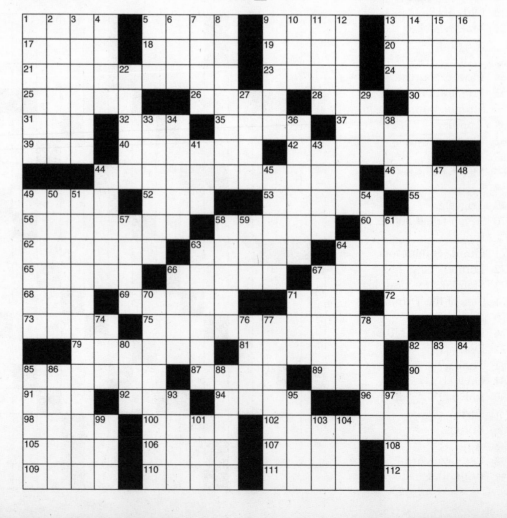

ACROSS

1 Brouhaha
7 Khayyam
11 Piscary habitue
17 Modern version
18 Columbus's birthplace
20 Jimmy Dorsey hit
21 Line from "Cymbeline"
24 Qt. parts
25 Centuries
26 Gibbon
27 Nuisance
28 Compiegne's river
30 Fight
33 On good authority
41 Plutarch's portfolio
42 Ciboule
43 "Leaving __?" ("stay awhile")
45 Playwright Ayckbourn
46 Ishtar's realm
48 George, Giles, etc.
50 Concerning
51 Coagulate
52 Attack
54 "Help wanted" item
57 "Gamesters and race-horses __" (Herbert)
60 Calif. observatory
63 Post __ (prerace ritual)
64 Dead heat
67 "There'll be __ time . . ."
68 Roofing material
71 Miniver
72 Wrongs
73 Appetizer
76 The Last Supper, e.g.
78 Acropolis site
80 Pursue a lost cause
83 Tennyson fare
84 Mountain: prefix
85 Zone
89 Mouths
90 Punjab princess
92 Hullabaloo
95 "What makes horse races" (Twain)
101 Squirrel's stash
102 Greek letter
103 Dog breed
104 Dour
105 Middle Eastern measure
106 Writer Carter

DOWN

1 Finial
2 Absquatulated
3 "__ & Andrew" (1993 film)
4 Vitiate
5 Russian river
6 Nothing new
7 Bugbear
8 Scandal
9 Donges donkey
10 Fracas
11 Hindu retreats
12 Cry of the impatient
13 Handhold
14 County road
15 Work units
16 Breather
19 Syndrome
22 Curved molding
23 Scrutiny
28 Augury
29 Possessive pronoun
30 Dernier __
31 Baza bears
32 Overly
33 Weaken
34 Provoke
35 Racetrack
36 Float
37 Ryan of films
38 Putting into practice
39 Writer Morrison
40 Shofar
44 Not pos.
46 Atitlan output
47 Patent
49 Type of energy
52 Haw's partner
53 Gregory Hines film
55 Rocket compartment
56 Chem. ending
57 Absent from
58 Less risky
59 Cape Cod town
60 Soft shoe
61 Melville mariner
62 Solitary
64 Echelon
65 Lodges
66 Being
69 Oregon peak
70 Stagger
72 Begone
74 South Seas dish
75 Sanction
77 Moviemaker Griffith et al.
78 Battle of Actium commander
79 A alternative
81 Phoenician port
82 Proscription
85 Dramatist de la Halle
86 Part of P.R.
87 __ effort
88 Hair style
90 Surf sound
91 Disney's "__ Off Place"
92 Staff member
93 Runyonesque figure
94 Draft classification
96 New USNA grad
97 Business VIP
98 Shade tree
99 Particle
100 Holiday libation

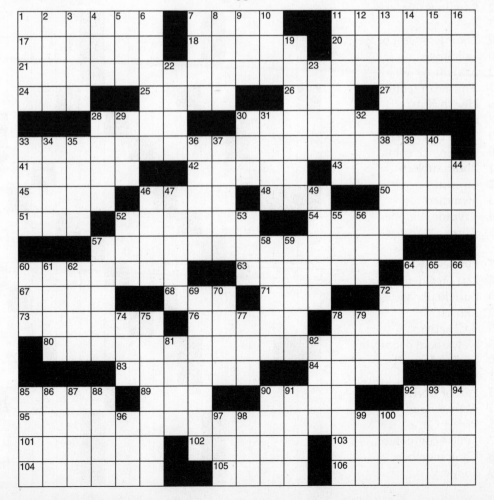

ACROSS

1 Tampa Bay Lightning spot
5 Long
9 __ facto
13 Impertinent
17 Celebes ox
18 Common story starter
19 Sherman __, Calif.
20 Highway part
21 Dotes on
23 Etats __
24 Elec. units
25 Actress Perlman
26 "Three Men __ Little Lady" (1990 film)
28 N.C. campus
30 Save
31 Shade
32 Vein
34 Bamboozle
36 "The Country Girl" playwright
38 Leb. neighbor
39 Three, in Capri
40 Scansion subject
41 Hanoi holiday
42 Rawlings tale
45 Pedagogue
49 Ending for east or west
50 Fall flower
52 Nod off
53 Amritaj of tennis
56 Health clubs
57 Bacchanal
59 "One Day __ Time"
60 Old French coins
61 Rodin subject
62 Overfill
63 Swindled
64 Krypton, for one
65 Agree
66 __ Lang Syne
67 Hoosegow
68 21st President
70 Buffalo player
72 Mexico Mrs.
73 B.C. natives
75 Newsroom neophyte
80 Ending for end
81 Wrong
83 Part of UNLV
84 Actress Balin
85 Writer Gore
87 Time's companion
88 Choir member
89 Slippery __

90 Purpose
91 Quakers' rival
93 Branches
95 Actress Conn
97 Play the diaskeuast
99 Kiln
101 Infatuation
104 Maine tree
105 Mexican Hat's state
106 Being
107 Chem. endings
108 Polymath
109 Wipe out
110 Profound
111 Impression

DOWN

1 Actor Vallone
2 Scrambling
3 The Beatles' "__ Man"
4 Welles role
5 Court
6 Interloper
7 Milieu
8 Flock
9 Marker
10 Boards
11 Frying pan
12 __ buco
13 Melbourne's st.
14 Square dance's British cousin
15 Computer fodder
16 Vermin
22 Fish-processing plant
27 FBI staffers
29 Seal bearer of a sort
31 Strike
33 African port
35 Imperative
37 Art __
40 Travel documents
43 Pro votes
44 Errors
46 Nervous
47 Mrs. Lauder
48 Skillful
51 Painter's tool
53 See 83 Across
54 Tom T. Hall song
55 "I didn't mean it"
56 Sis or bro
58 Switch

61 Opera's Te Kanawa
62 Restrictions
63 Male pig
65 With "The", Sinclair book
66 Addict
67 Metrics
69 Maui town
71 Caustic
72 Tiff
74 Gorge
76 D.C. tourist area
77 __ on (binged)
78 Perk up
79 Thrust
82 Prayer book
85 Certain execs
86 Lucknow's land
88 Divert
92 Ringing
94 Imitated
96 "__ Three Lives"
98 Shirt style
100 Der, in Detroit
102 Vitality
103 Approx. relative

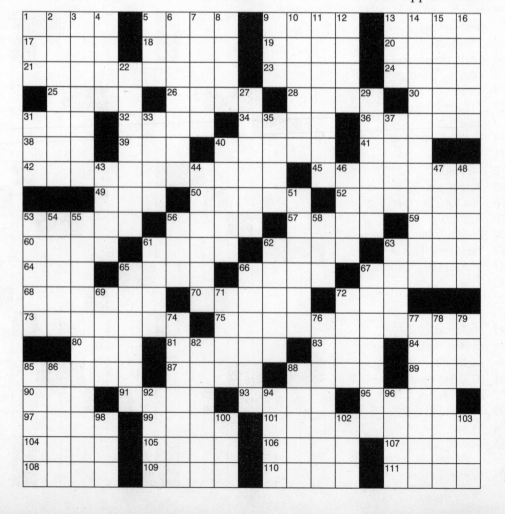

ACROSS

1 Baseball's Blue
5 Lane of the Planet
9 Sect
13 Riches
17 Type type: Abbr.
18 Cousin's progenitor
19 Delano Peak's state
20 Port Maitland's lake
21 Rental in Uruguay?
24 Salinger's "__ Stories"
25 Writer Grey
26 Burden
27 Clobbered
29 Uncanny
31 Pacify
33 Whitney
34 NFO and WHO
35 Shake up
36 Dawdle
38 "Casablanca" character et al.
42 To wit
43 Particle
44 Virginia country tune?
46 Card game
48 Wader
49 Calamity
50 Ergate
51 Hindu water spirits
52 Walrus feature
53 Kind of trail or pole
54 Fajardo fraus
55 Somewhat
57 Taken care of
59 Fledgling equine
62 Cos __, Conn.
63 Kaolin or clunch
64 Storied race
68 Writer Rölvaag
69 Piniella of baseball
70 Break down
71 Lombard of films
72 Patriotic fervor in China?
75 Golly relative
76 Title of respect
77 TV's "__ Buddies"
78 Musician Masekela
79 Blend
80 Eight: prefix
81 Heady times
83 "__ the Life" (1943 film)
85 Noted Chairman
86 Shudder
90 Varsity, for one
91 Take a dip
94 Plunder
95 British hustler of a sort?
98 Competent
99 Like __ not . . .
100 Cozumel and Cuba
101 S.A. port
102 Use
103 Rather and Quayle
104 __ longlegs
105 Ger. article

DOWN

1 Pizazz
2 Japanese statesman
3 Polish evasive maneuver?
4 Acolytes' places
5 Wash
6 Non alternative
7 Out of the weather
8 Office worker
9 Truncate
10 Actress Hagen
11 Exercise units
12 Topic
13 School supplies
14 Psychologist Erikson
15 Goods
16 Farm serving
22 "Howards __"
23 Prospect
28 The same
29 Like twill
30 Writer Jong
31 Part of SFSU
32 Gremlin
35 Actor Mantegna
37 Subdued
39 Skyrocket
40 Dido's sister
41 Certain noncoms
43 "__ long way . . ."
44 Intrusive
45 Meat cut
47 Large number
48 Hyacinth, for one
52 Vessel for 16 Down
53 Cachet
54 Acrid
56 Sacred image
57 Attenuated
58 Warm up
59 Baseball great
60 Toast topping
61 Garlands
63 Retail worker
65 Russian chicken?
66 Touched down
67 Son of Agrippina
69 Hobbles
70 Pugilists
71 Loser to Harding, 1920
73 Knight in action
74 Eliminated
75 Neenah's st.
79 Sensitive plant
80 Expletive
82 Firm
84 Palatable
85 Unkempt
86 Defect
87 Pluvial
88 Kansas town
89 Naldi of silent films
91 Pleased
92 Silkworm
93 Ring verdicts
96 Frederika __ Stade
97 Archaic

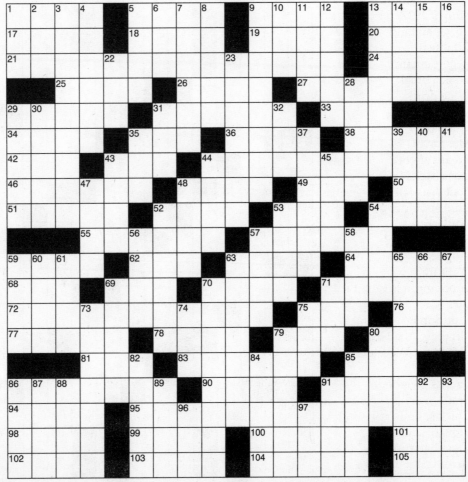

ACROSS

1 Tree trunk
5 Indifferent
9 Discovery of 1898
13 "This Is __ Ask"
17 Truly
18 Close-fitting
19 Outer: prefix
20 Circuit
21 Traps
22 Southern California marmot?
25 With 115 Across, jazz singer
27 Boat bottom
28 Shoe width
29 With reason
32 Merganser
34 Actor Washington
38 Jacobs-Casey musical
40 Lawman Wyatt
42 Definite
43 LBJ pet
45 Pep rallies in Portugal?
49 Creek
50 Actor Jack
52 Musical symbol
53 Film of 1937
55 Phrygian king
57 Establish
60 Legerdemain
61 Took a break
63 Wine drink
65 Lower
68 Spiral bit
70 Mo. town
72 Treaty of yore
73 Goes back over
76 Poet Teasdale
78 Cold shoulder
79 Wallach
80 Saudi stickum?
84 Wagner's "__ Walkure"
85 Drooping, à la rabbit's ears
87 Dam's mate
88 "In the __ the Night"
90 One of the Websters
93 Escapade
95 Czechs' neighbors
98 Brad
100 Chick sound
102 Thread: prefix
103 Canadian property?
109 Actor Calhoun
110 Rapier
111 Level
112 Limuloid
113 Twin
114 Equipment
115 See 25 Across
116 Campion, for one
117 Bone: prefix

DOWN

1 Produced
2 Sheeplike
3 Russian school event?
4 Mark with an asterisk
5 Silence!
6 Yoko __
7 Brood
8 Looks over
9 Metaphor for reform
10 "The Name of the Rose" man
11 Nebraska Indian
12 Marked by protuberances
13 Timon's town
14 Singer Rawls
15 Robitaille of hockey
16 Nettle
23 Aden's place
24 Mediocre mark
26 Genesis name
30 Hideout
31 Wavy shapes
33 Mandamus, e.g.
35 Swiss jet set?
36 Actor Bogosian
37 Rachel's sister
39 Actor Buddy
41 Spring party
43 Keef
44 Kazan
46 Playful creature
47 Writer Hunter
48 Experts
51 Conductor Kurt
54 Exequies
56 Stogie
58 Actor Tognazzi
59 Throb
62 Ten, in combinations
64 Virgule
66 Needle case
67 Mantle
69 Fernando and Alejandro
71 March 26 baby
73 Peruse
74 Actress Joyce
75 Spencer, e.g.
77 Grandfatherly
81 Curtain
82 Toast starter
83 Berkshire school
86 "Old Times" playwright
89 Pig out on
91 Musical talent
92 Deceive
94 Yawl's cousin
96 Jeweler's unit
97 Word with high or life
99 Deposited
101 Trim
103 Actress Ryan
104 Unclose
105 Teachers' org.
106 Pasture
107 Besmirch
108 Wane

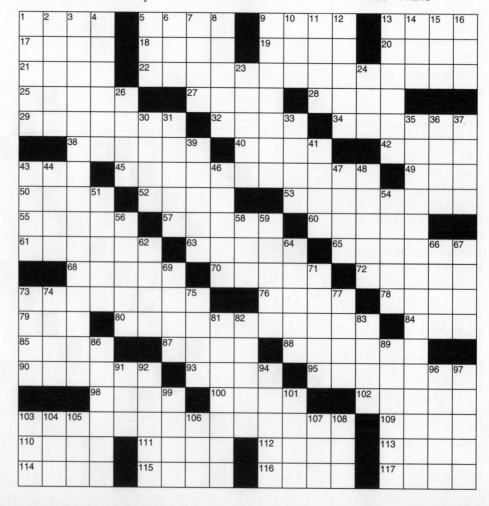

ACROSS

1 Conductor Kurt
6 Attain
11 Spiracles, ostioles, etc.
18 All together
19 Cry of surrender
20 Dissenter
21 NOT mail made of mail
23 Importune
24 Stored
25 Nincompoop
26 Foul
27 Curve shape
28 Noggin
30 Article of faith
32 Cogito ergo __
35 "__ Charlie's Got the Blues"
38 Printer's measures
40 Mustang, e.g.
44 Bagel's companion
45 Actress Alicia
46 NOT necessarily a dirt surface
49 Endings for ideal or equal
51 Hostile look
53 __ generis
54 Gudrun's husband
55 Top performances
57 Mortgages
59 Drumstick alternative
61 Period
63 Emended
65 Belgian resort
66 Training-room complaints
70 Soprano Victoria __ Angeles
72 Vermin
76 Particle
77 Sup
79 Part of LAN
81 Flabbergast
82 NOT circular, fluid bodies
85 Firth
87 Black bird
88 Entertainer Dinah
89 Principle
90 Tyrant
92 Douceur
94 Unwind
97 Control
98 __ Paulo
101 Singer Grant
103 Beethoven's "Fur __"
105 Floribunda, for one
108 Lack
111 NOT broken bits of furniture

113 Aversion
114 Mature
115 Rive Gauche wear
116 Versus
117 Half a '60s singing group
118 Infamous writer, and family

DOWN

1 "__ the Knife"
2 Court great
3 NOT cartons made of cleanser
4 All together
5 Stimpy's sidekick
6 Lamented
7 Lure
8 Thespian
9 Baseball's Boyer
10 LBJ pet
11 Mets' home
12 Inclines
13 Leftover
14 Debussy setting
15 To __ (precisely)
16 Sp. aunts
17 Deeds
22 Insulation
26 Employee's delight
29 Words with glance
31 __ volente
33 TV initials
34 Theriaca
35 Facile
36 Slime
37 Consumers' mecca
39 Slight
41 "Deception" author
42 Flatfish
43 Discordia
46 Rapacity
47 Writer Ruth
48 Frightful
50 Ocean-going ships
52 Broadcast
56 __ Lanka
58 Farm structures
60 Ref's cousin
62 Freshly
64 "__ Hollywood" (1991 film)
66 Adages
67 Egyptian deity
68 Newspaper section
69 Comedian Mort
71 "Elephant Boy" actor
73 NOT a celestial plank
74 Bluefin
75 Dither
78 Lachrymose
80 Potato pancakes
83 Old car
84 Lamb's dam
86 Hither's companion
90 Shoulder
91 Sonora strap
93 Lupine groups
95 "... __ horse to water ..."
96 Florilegium
98 Actress Thompson
99 "__ Hunk O'Love" (Presley hit)
100 Greek peak
102 Convene
104 Cliques
106 Graf __
107 Superlative endings
109 Wallach
110 Diarist Anaïs
111 Highlands headwear
112 A network

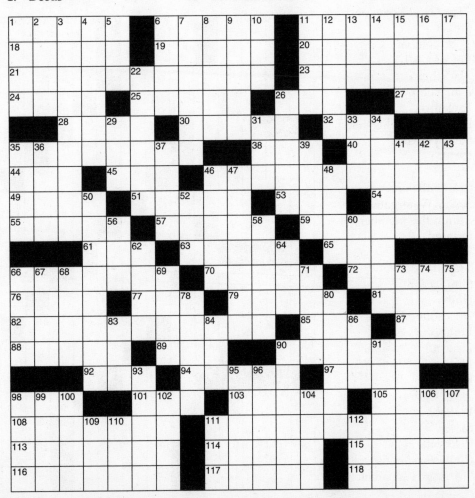

ACROSS

1 Libertine
5 Lordly appellation
8 Suit material
12 Accolade
17 Film of 1988
18 Pithecologist's subject
19 Jug
20 Growing out
21 Fastened, in a way
23 "Designing Women" actress
25 Business letter abbr.
26 Summarize
28 Jump
29 Dawn goddess
30 Flim-flammed
32 On
34 Uproar
35 Word with fore or ever
37 Composer Franck
39 Thus
41 Actress Hagen
44 Adriatic's neighbor
46 Venues
48 Induces
50 Trounce
52 "The Great Pretender" group
54 __ de combat
55 Ref. of a 401(k)
57 Blackthorn
58 Fantastic
59 Exclaim
61 Export from Kingston
63 Steichen work
67 Farina
69 Strain
70 Coulomb parts
74 Senate Watergate Committee member
77 Ignored
79 Tying tally
80 Trap
82 Simulacrum
83 United
84 Do a sound job
86 Philippines bay
88 Dialect
89 Pluto
91 Bay: It.
92 Actor Cariou
93 Wallaba
96 Match
98 Rock pile
100 Civil War initials
103 "M*A*S*H" character

106 Restrain
108 Word with wise or worldly
109 Enamored of
110 City lines
111 Wail
112 Disreputable
113 Privation
114 "Wide Sargasso __" (1993 film)
115 Kind of terrier

DOWN

1 "Hurlyburly" playwright
2 __ for one's money
3 Boer War commander
4 Devour
5 Judicious
6 Tropical creeper
7 Puts a new time-stamp on
8 Bohea, e.g.
9 Controls
10 Words with car
11 Threesomes
12 Retained
13 Numero __
14 Fruit of the palm
15 Writer Whitney
16 Mtg.
22 Trying time
24 Beethoven work
27 Presuppose
31 Seed coatings
33 Ways to go
35 Prefer
36 Clausian utterance
38 Film parts
40 Fix the food
41 Software buyer
42 Actress Garr
43 African fox
45 Sparable
47 Nozzle
49 Western Indian
51 Bit
53 Authorized
56 Zones
59 Stultified
60 Receipts
62 Eliminated
63 Sigh of relief
64 Maneuvered, as a ship

65 Due
66 Khaki
68 Words with pray
70 Chopin work
71 "Harmful Intent" author
72 Wolverine genus
73 Arrest
75 Workhorse
76 Bumpkins
78 Thwarted
81 Small quantities
85 __ Hand, Pa.
87 Lombard of films
90 Romilly's river
93 "__ & Andrew" (1993 film)
94 Appetizer
95 Turkish VIP
96 Ethereal
97 Renaissance family
99 Designer Peretti
101 Dominion
102 One of the Brontës
104 Chatoyant
105 Trough
107 Ger. money

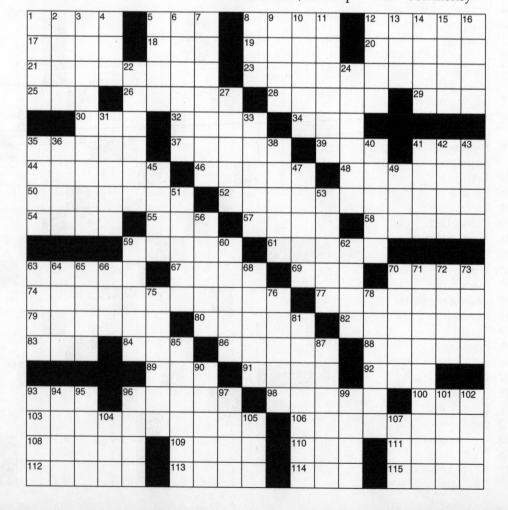

ACROSS

1 Nightclub of song
5 Pagurian
9 Actress Rachel
13 Chafe
16 Lauhalas
17 Heath
18 Here, to José
19 Before
20 Incense items
22 "Kiss of the Spider Woman" author
23 Young guy
24 Implicit
25 Mercenary
27 Enigma
28 Polite denial
29 Outburst
30 Architectural order
31 Opts
35 Beef and vegetables dish
38 Flogs
40 Windlass
42 Interrogate
43 FDR's last VP
44 Elephantine
45 Telecom units
47 Heel
50 Tavern tool
52 Dumas character
54 Gardner
55 N.D. town
56 Main artery
58 Stringed instrument
59 Roguish
60 Patron
61 Malone portrayer
62 Visualize
63 Confront
64 Absorb, in a way
67 Apollo's light
68 Hammer part
69 Calif. missionary
70 Cinema canine
71 Polynesian wear
76 Gawking
78 Ease up
79 Castile, e.g.
81 Papier-__
84 "__ Only Joking" (1977 hit)
85 Magazine
88 Right-hand pages
89 Writer Octavio
90 Herr's mate
91 Formal garment
93 Prefix for caution
94 Mnemonic method
95 "The Hidden Valley" author
96 Zilch
97 Baseball Hall-of-Famer Roush
98 Due
99 Oenophile's concern
100 Possessive pronoun

DOWN

1 Culinary style
2 U. of Maine site
3 Sit in judgment
4 Buffets
5 Dernier __
6 Fecund
7 Musician Bilk
8 Orchestra member
9 Red deer
10 Water color
11 Downfall
12 Archaeology site
13 Adjust instruments
14 Muse for Galileo
15 Festoon
17 Itinerary abbr.
21 Progenitor
26 Plant
27 Jockey Johnny
30 Mother of Horus
32 City on the Rhine
33 Actor Skerritt
34 Bro or sis
36 Calamary
37 Foam
38 Supreme Court Justice
39 Wish
41 Climbed sharply
44 Raven
45 Skirmish
46 "Where __ Going?" (1966 hit)
47 Representative sample
48 Unstinting
49 Durbin of films
51 Japanese drama
53 Baseball's Gant
54 Ger. article
56 Chain sound
57 Ventilate
58 RV of a sort
60 Mediocre marks
61 Fiddlesticks!
63 Outdo
65 Stat for Koufax
66 "__ gratia . . ."
68 Greek letters
69 Provisional
70 Spider: prefix
71 Sick-bay complaint
72 Bounty
73 Thunderstruck
74 Promulgated
75 Lobster coral
77 Iowa city
80 "Gay" place
82 See 87 Down
83 Kefauver
85 Lined up
86 Assess
87 With 82 Down, noted singer
88 Alphabetic trio
90 To's companion
92 Spiritual msg.

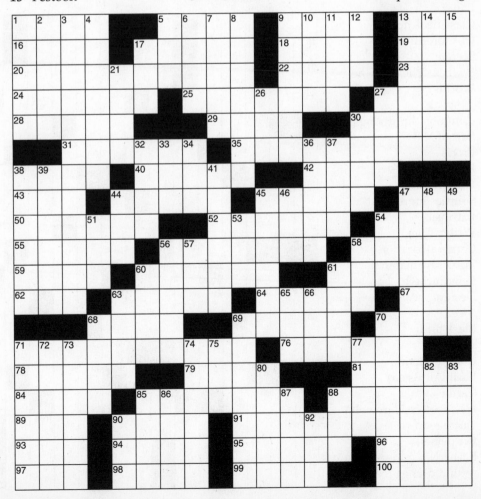

ACROSS

1 Cantina snacks
6 Roof beam
12 Stick together
18 Sprung
19 Sharpened
20 Arctic wear
21 Shakespearean verb
22 Friendly statue's greeting?
24 Auditions
26 Fountain offerings
27 Sweetsop
28 Overimbibe
29 Ripken of baseball
30 Pilot
33 "Today I am __ . . ."
35 Made up
38 Autry's place
42 Nero's noon
43 Got it!
44 Wafers
47 Actor Stephen
48 Intertwined
50 CHEF RN
53 Hosiery thread
54 Expel
56 Palter
57 Classifieds hdg.
58 CIA forerunner
60 Secrete
62 Wells's "The __ of the Worlds"
64 __ speak
67 Common diphthongs
69 Part of N.B.
71 Precis
75 Hit record's reverse
78 Fault-finding
80 Souffle "ingredient"
81 Extrinsic
82 Writer Tyler
83 Carnival location
84 Pizza raw material
86 Handpicked
89 Design
90 Vice __
93 Black bird
94 Tangelo
96 Countertenor
99 Basil, Alexis etc.
101 Caribe
104 Hairdressers' farewell?
108 Outrage
109 Per person
110 Earhart
111 __ und drang
112 Hamstring
113 Interfacing devices
114 Rebel of 1857

DOWN

1 Civility
2 Sandarac tree
3 Ys, in a way
4 Part of ASAP
5 Establish
6 Knocks
7 Stopper on the mound
8 S.C. campus
9 Tex-Mex dish
10 And so forth
11 Splits
12 Pantry container
13 Thunder Bay's prov.
14 Filmmaker Hawks
15 Part of QED
16 Blurb
17 __ out (supplements)
23 Extreme ending
25 Rag
29 Cedar Rapids campus
31 Shun
32 "__ of Elephant Rock" (1976 film)
33 Skating feat
34 Skirt style
36 Shawn and Turner
37 JFK predecessor
39 Plumbing problem
40 For fear that
41 Chow
43 Summer treats
45 Gulf
46 __ fi
49 Remote
50 Fennec, for one
51 Sonorous
52 Merchandise
55 "Steppenwolf" author
59 Bluejacket
61 Female rabbit
63 "Rule, Britannia" composer
64 Immediately, in medicine
65 Where Alliance is
66 Expression
68 Prefix for gram
70 Adolescent's lament
72 Endeavor with hair or a good book
73 Film of 1988
74 Manual laborer
76 Behindhand
77 Rel. of Ltd.
79 Boredom
82 "A Fool Such __" (Presley hit)
85 Professed
87 Dwelt (on)
88 Discounted
89 Jacques of hockey renown
91 Actor Erwin
92 Indian province
95 Zoysia, for one
96 Med. school subj.
97 Jog
98 Bloomington player
100 Prefix for sphere
101 School grps.
102 Paladin
103 Legion
105 Writer Umberto
106 Chess pieces
107 Edge

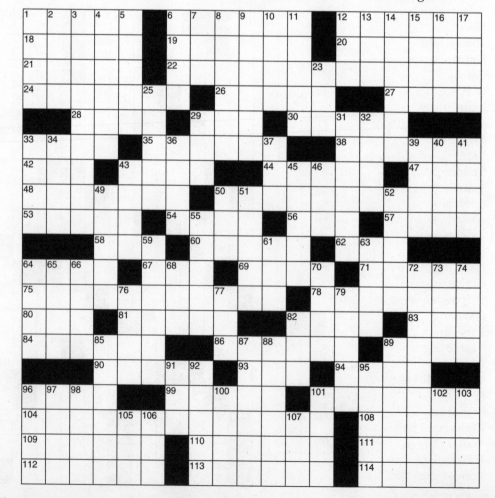

ACROSS

1 Beatty film
5 Amb., e.g.
9 Business letter salutation
13 Scottish pirate
17 Departure
18 __ avis
19 Filmmaker Reitman
20 Pale blue
21 "Guys and Dolls" guy
25 Incense material
26 Ref. work
27 Hokum
28 Merge
29 Bicycle race
32 Bureau section
36 Bit of work
39 Tail of a tale
42 Promoter of harmony
45 Heretofore
46 N.Y. campus
47 By __ (incidentally)
48 Alley __
50 Vermont town
52 Mindanao native
53 Kind of boat or bike
55 Pt. of USNA
57 Preston Sturges film
63 Ultimatum word
64 Greek letters
65 Offering
67 Slow-cook
71 Pickup's cousin
72 Fresco
73 Chan's line
74 Onion relative
78 Turkish inns
80 Upstart
84 Enzyme
85 Wind-borne
86 Filmmaker Riefenstahl
87 Doer: suffix
90 Actor Jacobi
91 Kiang
93 Contradict
95 Up against it
103 Silver Bell's st.
104 Piece of ground
105 Cubbyhole
106 Surety
107 Depend
108 Imperative
109 Purposes
110 Command to Fido

DOWN

1 Extend
2 Ostracize
3 Cut in cubes
4 Emanate
5 Desiccated
6 Actor Hendry
7 A __ (intuitively)
8 Colberteen
9 Part of RSVP
10 Araliad
11 Rule, in Rampur
12 Barracks bane
13 Big name in philosophy
14 Brainpower qtys.
15 Pair
16 Singer Fogelberg
22 Recitation
23 Nelson and Mary Baker
24 Israeli dance
30 Unclose
31 Extirpates
33 Actor Fernando
34 Hail
35 Sodden
36 School since 1440
37 Descartes
38 Taupe
39 The __ New England (Boston)
40 The __ luxury
41 Robust
42 PIN number site
43 Biblical pronoun
44 Scray
49 Will-__-wisp
50 Avails
51 Japanese vegetable
53 Walking distance
54 Buff
55 B.C. neighbor
56 Refractory mineral
58 Common diphthongs
59 Get honest
60 Loan-sharking
61 Singular
62 Louver
66 Sp. articles
67 __ California
68 Greek letters
69 Tennis champion
70 Particle
72 Hollywood stars' hangout
74 Half of D
75 __ polloi
76 Cole Porter's "__ Gigolo"
77 Corrupt
79 Chess pieces
81 Light of the city
82 "Any Which Way __" (1980 film)
83 Dodger manager Walter
87 Dispense
88 Scene of the Palio
89 Chemise
90 Faineant
92 Auld Lang __
94 Wanes
95 Away's companion
96 Wrath
97 Zero
98 Ferber's "__ Palace"
99 Exist
100 Guided
101 Singer Stewart
102 Thumbs-up

ACROSS

1 Bedazzle
5 Miles of movies
9 Carol word
13 Confine
17 Skid Row character
18 Composer Charles
19 Words after whether
20 Director Wertmuller
21 Bates-Ward song, 1895
25 The powers __
26 Purvey
27 Stop on __
28 "Much Ado About Nothing" character
30 Garland
32 Bernadette, e.g.
33 Protrude
36 Irving Berlin song
43 "Pretty please with sugar __"
45 Old times
46 Part of TV
47 Shortly
48 Brace
50 Chibchan
52 Pipe joints
54 Cynical
55 Trickster of a sort
57 Crowd
59 Tenn. neighbor
60 Miscellany
61 "__ and Glory" (1902 song)
65 Subsidiary
68 Pub offering
69 Words with speak
70 Obsess
74 Designer Anna
75 Frustrated cry
77 Bar orders
79 Duffer's "excavation"
80 Woe __!
82 Vegetable dish
84 Where Zanesville is
86 Shade
87 Raye-Jacobs song, 1940
91 Orcein or orpiment
92 Water-tester
93 Trifle
94 Cheese type
96 Western resort
99 Eight: prefix
102 George and T.S.
106 Hit song of 1975
111 Threshold
112 Lil __ (1992 Derby winner)
113 Singer Collins
114 Galba's predecessor
115 Rapier
116 Baton
117 Binghamton campus initials
118 Crooned

DOWN

1 Cuff
2 "The Secret of __" (1982 film)
3 Draft classification
4 Value
5 Provincial governor
6 A Gabor
7 Soaks flax
8 Court great
9 Most lordly
10 Speiss or stope
11 Sp. queen
12 Mrs. Herbert Hoover
13 Baseball pitches
14 Sound system
15 Word on a penny
16 Jeremiad
22 "__ to differ . . ."
23 She, in Chantilly
24 "Little Man __" (1992 film)
29 Fragrance
31 "Got it"
32 "The Sweet __ Success"
33 Banter
34 Commandment word
35 "__ Yellow Ribbon . . ."
37 Actress Sonia
38 City of France
39 Dubai deity
40 State since 1846
41 Product of 40 Down
42 Writer Seton
44 Theme
49 "Cloclo" composer
51 Compound conjunction
53 Toothsome
56 Backslide
58 "I __ Babe" ('60s hit)
62 The Gershwins' "__ Eat Cake"
63 Alpine wind
64 Egress
65 Words with were
66 Limbaugh
67 Actress Rogers
71 Ardent
72 Curtis of films
73 Super ending
76 Declares
78 Location
81 Actress Parsons
83 Achieved a news coup
85 Methodical
88 Scottish isle
89 Pained cry
90 Buckley's alma mater
95 Bearings
96 Church area
97 Bark, for one
98 Windrow
100 Suggestions
101 Pearl City's site
103 Concert halls
104 Vacillating
105 Urban problem
107 Moisture
108 Greek letter
109 Dykstra of baseball
110 Acantha

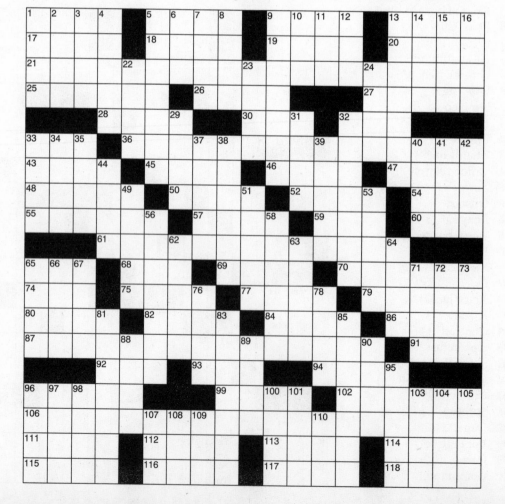

ACROSS

1 Promo relatives
4 Parabola
7 Swig
12 Lunch offering
17 Stake
18 Chart
19 Pierce
20 All together
21 Country music group
23 Shopworn magic gear?
25 Quiets
26 Sailing chain
27 Displace
28 Red River city
29 TV's "__ the Boss?"
32 Cpl.'s job
33 Anthem preposition
34 Pastoral parent
35 Report to Mission Control
36 Daphnid
38 MIT, e.g.
39 Troughs
41 Pariah's lament?
44 U.K. part
45 Superior
46 Cetacean
47 Upper Volta neighbor
51 Completely
52 Shetland bay
53 Ankara natives
54 Carried
55 Called
57 "No __ an island . . ."
58 Bill Haley's backup group
59 Indy 500 winner, 1987
60 Lively airs
61 Tenn. player
62 Metier
63 Vermin
64 __ fixe
65 Edinburgh wear
66 Discern
67 Jhabvala novel
70 Sized up
71 Tempo
74 Puff
75 Greek peak
76 Bank offerings, for short
77 Happy-clam connection
78 Brim
79 Millstone

80 Hold off
83 Shield
85 Crest
87 Poe woman
88 Actress in "The Runner Stumbles"
91 Monstrosity
92 Inuit's neighbor
93 Mindful
94 Burst
95 Doze
96 Feel
97 Meander
98 Word with one or where
99 Grads-to-be

DOWN

1 Faze
2 Greek letter
3 Church material
4 Charlotte __
5 Butts into
6 Numbers cruncher, for short
7 Logician's abbr.
8 Credit hours, e.g.
9 Give it __
10 Bazaar
11 Use a skillet
12 Punjab gear
13 Z __ zebra
14 Fix, as radar
15 Hocks
16 Mojave or Tanami
22 Fisticuffs
24 Wee small hour
29 Actor Rogers
30 Whet
31 Russian river
32 Tablelands
36 Kind of wheel
37 Punishment
38 Dialect
39 Supervise
40 Kind of system
41 Temper
42 Part of RCMP
43 Open, in a way
45 Balky
48 Certain eateries
49 Admission
50 Serene

53 Faculty
56 River of oblivion
57 Phrygian king
58 Fledgling
60 Illuminated
61 Travel papers
65 African antelope
68 Senescent
69 Tumult
70 Illinois expressway
71 Gnocchi and tortellini
72 On __ of one to 10 . . .
73 Bizet protagonist
76 Weird
78 Philippines gulf
79 "Cosi fan tutte," for one
81 Oversight
82 Yorkshire city
84 Cassowaries
85 List
86 Hebrew measure
87 City on the Rhone
89 __ Tafari
90 Barrow's home
91 Org. since 1970

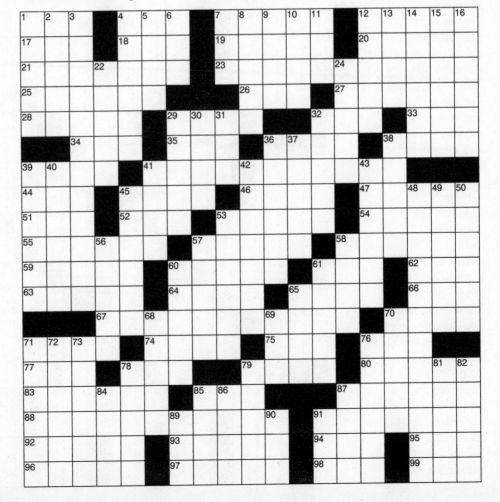

ACROSS

1 License plates
5 Further
9 Touched down
13 Gang
17 Pointless
18 Seed cover
19 Consort
20 Late-night name
21 TV series in '93
24 Scent
25 Recipe instruction
26 Ransack
27 Meat puree
29 Family mbr.
30 Rowan tree
33 The works
34 Gandharva participant
35 Cholla and chichipe
37 Soda-fountain item
38 "The Sheltering __" (1991 film)
41 Beam
44 Type of worker
46 Cobbler, e.g.
47 Smelter material
48 Towel inscription
49 Desquamate
50 Predilection
51 Actor Ralph
53 Fido's complaint
55 Painter Vermeer
56 Hail
57 Viewpoint
58 Marvel
61 Mouths
62 Butcher's offering
63 Bona fide
64 ". . . __ forgive our debtors"
66 Jackdaw
67 Poet Sexton
68 Josh
69 Indian rule
70 With "The," Robin Moore novel
73 Black or Beaufort
74 Consumer protection agcy.
75 Soaks flax
76 Ridge
77 Reprove
79 Schlemiel
80 Bar order
82 P&L reckoner
85 One of the Marshalls
87 Barbershop belt

89 Specie
91 Actress Barbara
92 Carl Perkins hit
96 Riga native
97 Nugget
98 Rumored
99 Pot starter
100 Colleen
101 Selves
102 Hence
103 Fernando and Alejandro

DOWN

1 Poitier role
2 Ike opponent
3 Building material
4 Denomination
5 Millinery item
6 Silkworm
7 Reclines
8 Mollify
9 Appalling
10 Sapphira, e.g.
11 "__ Had a Million" (1932 film)
12 Depot

13 Sully
14 "Why does a fireman wear __?"
15 Grandson of Eve
16 Sported
22 Parrot
23 Vitamin B acid
28 Uniquity
31 Machination
32 Fraught with danger
34 Apertures
36 Dollar pts.
37 Bollard
39 Stock
40 Withal
41 Deprives
42 Precinct
43 Hornets' cousins
44 "__ Fool Believes" (1979 hit)
45 Begins
50 Judge's seat
52 Blandishment
53 Escaped
54 Race unit
55 "Bonhomme Richard" skipper

57 Gillies
58 Hibernal
59 Conneaut's lake
60 Singer McEntire
62 Minos's realm
63 Gibe
64 Kennel sound
65 Dolorous
66 Convincing
67 Mo. neighbor
70 Smirk
71 NFC team
72 Champion
78 How-to material
79 Basketball violation
81 Curve shape
82 Biddy
83 Devotion
84 Church areas
85 Campanile item
86 Suspicion
87 Oriental sport
88 Comice
90 Scorch
93 Haul
94 Investigate
95 Tokyo of yore

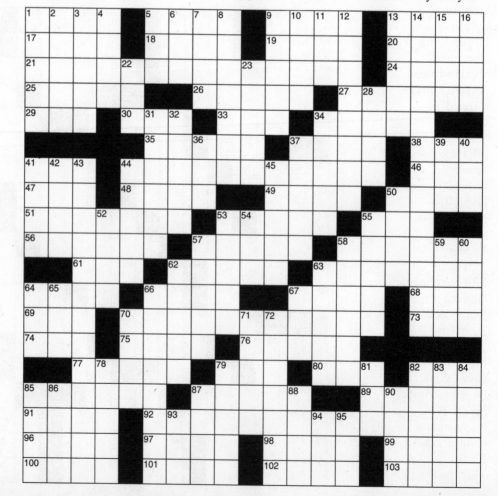

ACROSS

1 Negate
6 Marine habitue
12 Crop pest
17 Excessive
18 Private
19 Belvedere
20 Blend
21 "You Can't __" (1938 film)
23 "How __ love thee? . . ."
24 Highlands hill
25 Frijole
26 Thousand __, Calif.
27 Polyantha
30 Zero
32 Capts.' subordinates
34 Remick
35 "You Can't __" (1939 film)
41 Vermont city
42 Sighs
43 Sailboat plane
47 Unc's niece
48 Cezanne
50 Hemlock relative
51 Part of LEM
52 Medit. land
53 Beat
55 Academic prize
56 Vipers
60 "You Can't __" (1966 hit)
63 Cassoulet
64 Perilous
66 Note
67 Otologist's concern
69 "M*A*S*H" setting
70 Speckle
71 Sole
72 Diffident
75 Castaway
77 Rural sight
79 __ Semple McPherson
81 "You Can't __" (1920 song)
84 Snare
87 Outright
88 Good times
89 Attends
90 __ Bator
92 Strident
94 In shape
96 LBJ pet
99 "You Can't __" (1956 film)
103 Pancake
105 Perron
106 Words with limb
107 Bronco
108 British tube
109 Faulkner family
110 Map detail

DOWN

1 Courtyard
2 Annul
3 Fans
4 __ generis
5 Whammy
6 Angler's alert
7 __ impulse (rashly)
8 Invite
9 Haberdashery item
10 Esculent
11 Neural network
12 Summer sandwich
13 __ Rios, Jamaica
14 Majestic
15 Stimulate
16 Practice conservation, in a way
19 Dylan's "It __ Babe"
22 One of the Scotts
24 Arthur of TV
28 Scull
29 Directions opener
30 Japanese drama
31 Party in power
33 Dusky
35 Radios for the road
36 "Bali __"
37 South Pacific isle
38 Lanier of baseball
39 County abutting Mayo
40 Place names, e.g.
44 Some kind of __
45 Exceptional
46 A Barrymore
49 Pallid
50 Plication
53 Worry
54 Golfer Mark
55 Wigeon relative
56 Rcpts.
57 Whack
58 Smolt-to-be
59 Furtive
61 Sitcom of the '70s
62 Rancor
65 Crete's capital
68 "Von __ Express" ('65 film)
70 Set out
71 Former
72 Stifles
73 Cleave
74 Desire
76 Street and Reese
77 Douceur
78 Hawaiian hawks
80 Actress Lupino
82 "Women in Love" character
83 River island
84 Sausage
85 Extract
86 Insipid
91 Tacket
93 Sci-fi sightings
94 Delicate
95 Senor endings
97 __ dixit
98 Engage
100 Cynical
101 Western Indian
102 Swab
103 Greek letter
104 Filmmaker Howard

ACROSS

1 Toward the fantail
4 Bric-a-__
8 Songbird Edith
12 Pal of Jerry and George
17 "How __ love thee..."
18 Urgent
19 Summit
20 Lodging
21 Math branch
22 Make eyes at
23 Di Lampedusa novel
25 Offends the nose
27 Hamburg's river
29 Elegant
30 Actress Sedgwick
31 Sudan or Siam suffix
32 One of __ days ...
33 Joker
36 New Deal initials
38 Thimblerig prop
39 Lamarr
40 Trig function
41 Stir up
44 Part of ABM
46 Sicilian peak
47 Citing
49 With "The," film of the '60s
53 "Hansel __ Gretel"
54 Game fish
56 French cathedral city
57 African fox
59 Sugar source
60 Femme fatale Montes
61 __ girl!
65 Nick of films
67 Spanish scarf
69 TV's "Hee __"
70 Sobriquet for Richard I
74 Poster color
76 Hannibal's crossing, in Latin
77 Upper hand
79 Disco VIP
80 Purposes
81 Cheese type
84 __ Marie Saint
86 See 36 Across
87 __ es Salaam
88 Video-picture unit
89 Tease
90 Ham's companion
93 Now
95 Being
96 Standard
97 Staked, in a way

100 RPI, for one
102 "Aladdin" prince
103 Tonto's horse
104 Rend
105 Hatreds
106 Rock group
107 They have a house in London
108 Sea eagle
109 TV's Bridges
110 Authority

DOWN

1 "... __ and stormy night"
2 NYC square
3 Star on the tour
4 Family firm abbr.
5 Floor covering
6 Oblivious
7 One of the Clintons
8 Noggin
9 Prum pronoun
10 Actor Don
11 Chopped down
12 Picked
13 Sorry!

14 Accompany
15 Lots of eau
16 Former
24 Unchallenging
26 Ruined
28 Boston container
32 Attenuated
34 Shakespeare's wife
35 Equipment
37 Words with were
40 __ precedent (breaks ground)
41 Water color
42 Scoreboard total
43 Permit
45 "__ Cup" (1996 film)
46 Bête of burden
48 Actress Scacchi
50 Protuberance
51 Take the controls
52 Mind-boggled
55 Squint
58 Female suffixes
60 Business books
62 Jacksonville team
63 Skater Lipinski
64 Get or run follower

66 Questioning comments
67 Gules
68 Harbinger
70 Extol
71 "Casablanca" character
72 Wheeler-dealer
73 Color that's just ducky
75 Shimon of Israel
78 The old runaround
81 Barton __ of film
82 Stir up
83 Wobble
85 Meeting list
88 Westminster Abbey's __ Corner
91 Casque
92 Viscous
94 Hard-landing sound
95 "Jane __"
96 Valley of the Gods site
97 Chart abbr.
98 Cpl., for one
99 Beige
101 Unc's niece, perhaps

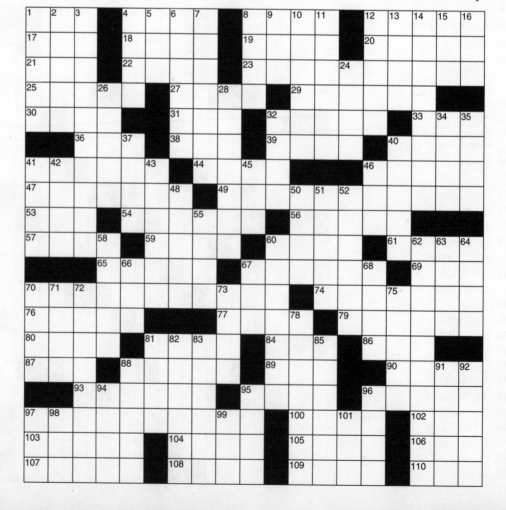

ACROSS

1 Nicks and scratches
7 Cathedral areas
12 Rome invader
18 Tool in school
19 Reach
20 Comfortable
21 Ecologists' grande dame
23 Sourdough
24 Arrow poison
25 Proportionate
26 Generous amount
28 Personal-care product
31 Dispute
32 Modicum
35 "Bali __"
38 Lamb's dam
39 Fervid
40 Distress
42 Watery eminence
46 Rome airport
48 Word with home or bed
49 Disgust
51 Mediterranean sailboat
52 Flip
53 Raccoon's cousin
55 Balms
57 Wilt
58 Burns
60 Louvre group
62 __ Mahal
65 Stash
66 Arid
67 Garden spot
71 Mirabeau, e.g.
73 Mornay or marinara
75 Saturnine
76 American butterfly
78 The man in the street
81 Bid's partner
82 Sad to say
84 Samovar
85 Breed
86 Magazine magnate, to friends
87 Linen
88 Patron
91 Obvolute
94 Fatty foodstuff
95 Bit of jazz
99 Nova __
101 Colonial pony-rider
105 Consequence
106 __ another
107 Region of Italy
108 Obvious
109 Impassioned
110 Sniff out

DOWN

1 Moore in movies
2 Schoenberg's "Moses und __"
3 Partner
4 Ruins
5 Word with whiz
6 Blunder
7 Daughter of Harmonia
8 Actor Coyote
9 Dazzle
10 Site of the incus
11 Plain
12 Kind of parking
13 Solar disk
14 Orderly
15 Locker-holder of note
16 Enzyme
17 Baseball's Dykstra
22 No way!
27 Property
29 Supervisor
30 Anther tip
31 Withered
33 "__ Day" (1964 song)
34 Forcing extra innings
35 Legion
36 Countertenor
37 Fateful date
39 Headwear for de Gaulle
40 Seafaring cry
41 Vamoose
43 Clump
44 Muslim decrees
45 VFW members
47 Back street
50 Relax
53 Saladin's capital
54 Venerable
56 Type of vb.
59 Harmonious sound
60 Considerably
61 Balkan native
62 Actress Feldshuh
63 Spring
64 Cold-weather fellow
66 Pairs
68 "Accommodations of Desire" painter
69 Foul
70 Collet
72 Shirt style
74 Trojan War hero
75 "Fighting Terms" poet
77 Conn. campus
79 Considerably
80 Prefix for side or serve
83 Scott's "The __ the Lake"
87 Scruggs's partner
88 "Gaslight" director
89 Suspicious
90 Weakfish
92 Will-__-wisp
93 Luminary
94 Dagger
96 Lounge
97 Cop in Caen
98 Achievement
99 Dine
100 P&L reckoner
102 Black bird
103 TV's "Major __"
104 Unclose

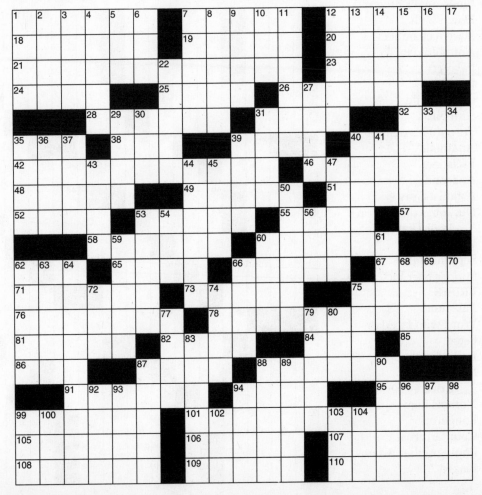

ACROSS

1 Trophy
4 Tiff
8 Furze
13 Pincer
17 Mil. address
18 Bend at the barre
19 As __ (generally)
20 High praise
21 Fracas
22 Infrequent
23 UNION SUITS
25 Kind of street
27 Goatfish
29 Pizzeria needs
30 Boat basins
32 Defile
33 Issue
34 NOW, e.g.
35 K __ kilo
37 "__ Woman" ('70s hit)
38 Gender
39 Inkling
41 SOCKS
45 Hennin, for one
46 Grin
47 Blues singer Brown
48 Down with
52 Harem chamber
53 Antediluvian
54 Palavers
56 Parade
57 Go hog wild
59 Songbirds
60 Turophile's delight
61 Apathetic
62 Indistinct
63 Anaconda
64 Botanist Gray
65 Durante's distinction
66 "__ Well That Ends Well"
67 Sentimental
68 Sportscaster McCarver
69 BRIEFS
73 Pale fluid
74 Word with faced or fisted
77 Immediately
78 Diminish
79 "__ Cried" ('60s hit)
80 Notions item
82 Longeron
84 Counterthrust
88 Photographer Adams
89 Blazed
91 Indiana town
92 SKIRTS
94 Tangelo
96 Chem. ending
97 Part of NIH
98 Actress Papas
99 "The Hustler" endeavor
100 Gypsy man
101 Musical Mama
102 Headquartered
103 Selves
104 Matter-of-fact

DOWN

1 Rebound
2 Once-time link
3 SHORTS
4 Pounced
5 Salt pan
6 Give vent to
7 Abound
8 Courtly
9 Certain tests
10 Bumpkins
11 Niche
12 Command ending
13 Hanker for
14 Coherent light sources
15 Redress
16 Hardy's fictional county
24 Pause signal
26 Cable
28 __ arms (aroused)
31 Three-bean, e.g.
33 Apiece
36 Scrooge portrayer of note
37 Endings for motor or medal
39 Writer Kate
40 White clover
41 Hallstatt native
42 Praying figure
43 Bonkers
44 Foster's "Little Man __"
46 Siege
49 PANTS
50 Canberran
51 Humid
54 Trenchant
55 Female lobster
56 Mojarra
58 Pitcher Hershiser
59 Parapet
60 Hoodwinks
62 Defect
63 Weevil
66 Old struggle
67 Swamp
70 __ Gay
71 Given
72 Cut back
73 "__ on first . . ."
74 Calamitous
75 Actress Ryder
76 Fixate
79 Booty
81 Outdoes
82 Veers
83 Satin finish
85 Inuit dwelling
86 Domingo, for one
87 Opponent
89 Open meetings
90 Fall guy
93 Josh
95 Sci-fi film of 1954

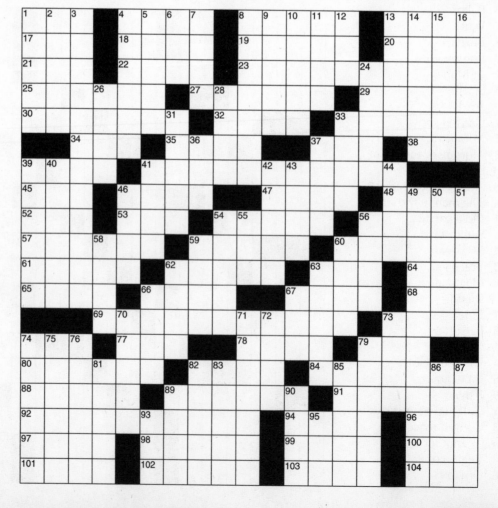

ACROSS

1 Naysayers
6 Sassy
11 Stronghold
18 Unfamiliar with
19 Snow leopard
20 Outlay
21 Film of 1993
23 Tempestuous spots?
24 Almost
25 Yannick of tennis
27 Chem. endings
28 Shoe parts
30 Auguries
32 Faulty
34 Titubate
35 Actress Merkel
36 Barnstorm
38 Keeve
41 Senor suffix
42 Hi-tech gear
44 Wyoming attraction
48 Tex. neighbor
49 Garner
51 Motown's Berry
52 Dossier
53 Roadhouse
55 Singer Grant
57 Pursuing
58 Chart abbr.
59 Paul Simon's "I Am __"
61 Feat for Sampras
62 Actor Jimmy
65 Highly draftable
66 Plunge
70 Writer Ephron
71 Tribe
74 Remark
76 Standard
77 Drifters hit of the '60s
81 Existed
82 Arafat's grp.
83 Mr. Blue
84 Spacious
85 Ring
87 Ringer
88 Polit. group
89 Remnants
91 Strawberry in the field
93 Center of activity
96 Wings
97 Alas
99 Vespertide
102 Overcasts
106 Cortege
107 Kunta __ of "Roots"
108 Edited again
109 Approvals
110 Cloys
111 Signed disapproval

DOWN

1 Mandela's org.
2 "__ Blu Dipinto Di Blu"
3 San Francisco district
4 "How does __?"
5 Heretofore
6 Paddock newcomer
7 "Blue Plate Special" writer
8 Chang's brother
9 Episode
10 Bay bird
11 Mary __ Hurt
12 Chopper
13 Health club
14 Half-hearted
15 Party to
16 Bone: prefix
17 Stack role
22 "48 __" (1982 film)
26 Up and about
28 Mr. Heep
29 Kind of dollar
31 Rash
32 Officious
33 Finesse
35 The Beach Boys "Surfin' __"
37 Primordial
38 Mock
39 Zaire river
40 "Song of the South" appellation
42 Crowd
43 Athrocyte, e.g.
45 Abet
46 Express
47 Propose
50 Tour group, for short
54 Mahler's First
56 Maine college town
57 Discomfort
60 Liberal's st.
61 "__ girl!"
62 Rebuff
63 Brood
64 Siderite extract
67 Stadium area
68 Foray
69 Sing
71 Component of 42 Across
72 Conducted
73 "__ Nice Clambake" ("Carousel" song)
75 Nocturnal predator
78 Brace
79 Hamlet's beloved
80 Charge
86 Cunning
87 Faces down
88 Actress Francis
90 Pillages
91 "__ Hollywood" (1991 film)
92 Cancel
93 Juno
94 Composer Charles
95 Farm medicos
96 Long time
98 Part of Keats's oeuvre
100 Auberge
101 Enthusiast
103 London's prov.
104 Parisian street
105 Part of EST

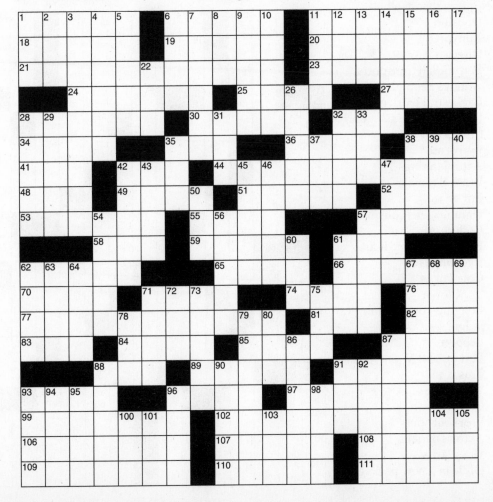

ACROSS

1 Recurring political issue
5 "Dr. Zhivago" star
11 Mandible
18 Meuse river
19 Surface appearance
20 Sticks
21 Obstructs a canal?
23 Tweeds, e.g.
24 Sorrel
25 U.K. machine tools
27 Writer James
28 Timeless
32 Org. since 1970
33 Words with recall
35 Morrison's "__ Baby"
36 Pershing's W.W. I command
37 Ethnic group's efforts?
42 Guaymas gold
43 Ankles
45 Cranny
46 "The Power of __" (1992 film)
47 VIP
49 Purview
51 __ fare-thee-well
52 Division
53 Runyon
55 Direct
57 Bermudian transports
59 Annoys people?
63 Orchestral work of 1928
66 Jean Valentine's "__ and the Poet"
67 Intoxicate
71 Actor Jannings
72 W.W. II female
75 Put on
77 Hamburger's cousin
78 Collection
79 Russian country house
81 Rye fungus
83 Cole Porter's "__ Clown"
84 Logging-competition judge?
87 Gibbon
88 Part of UNLV
89 Plus
90 Train unit
91 Contrite
93 Workout spots
96 Actress Bedelia
98 Hosp. areas
99 Oldie in a new package
102 Excludes loves ones?
107 Minimally
108 Nervous __
109 Swiss painter
110 Celebrations
111 Broadcast
112 Juncture

DOWN

1 Pierce
2 "Lorenzo's __" (1992 film)
3 Custodian's storage space?
4 Rapid-fire, in music
5 USN law enforcers
6 Holbrook
7 Coral isle
8 Costa __
9 More tenebrous
10 Non-removable nail
11 Benchley yarn
12 Fuss
13 Song from "Sunny"
14 L.A. suburb
15 Gold Beach's st.
16 Hawaiian bird
17 Being
22 Jeweler's measure
26 Wont
28 "Have __ You Lately?"
29 "West Side Story" character
30 Lacerate
31 Over again
33 "Ain't That __"
34 Helene or Anne
37 Roofing workers
38 Writer Umberto
39 Skye of films
40 Okla. town
41 Groups
44 Cloy
48 A dynamite guy
50 Buttes
52 Disconcert
54 Neither's companion
56 Slate
58 Spheroid
60 Vis-à-vis
61 "__ she blows!"
62 Bargain
63 Tuckered out
64 Home of the Hawks
65 Actor Neeson
68 Fur markdown?
69 Indian, for one
70 Breakfast selection
73 Function
74 N. Calif. town
76 Of the dawn
79 Hideout
80 Plummer and Cross
82 True's partner
85 Choir members
86 Poet Dowson
91 Order
92 Expeditions
93 __ Spee
94 Himalayan specter
95 Walking distance
96 OTB fare
97 Building beam
100 Perched
101 Dos Passos trilogy
103 Coarse
104 Timetable abbr.
105 Actor Stephen
106 Coll. yr. part

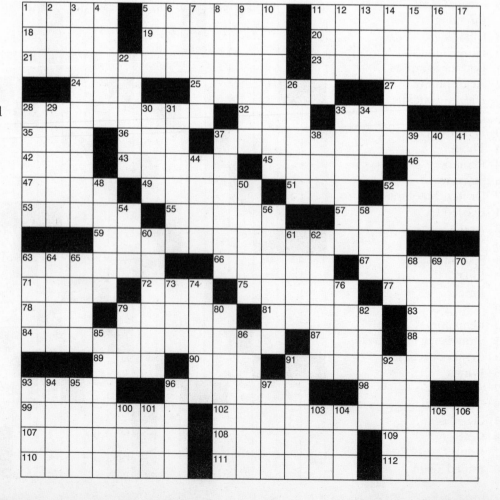

ACROSS

1 Texas river
6 Enthralled
10 Forb
14 Floor covering
17 Occupied
18 Ripening catalyst
19 It passes through Pisa
20 Mine find
21 Bustling
22 Secretary's delight?
25 Pitfall
27 Jughead's pal
28 Ostiary's station
29 Options
32 Actor Erwin
33 Kerouac's "The __ Bums"
35 Shacks
36 Stephen of films
38 Fair
41 Cry of disgust
42 Like overmatched accountants?
45 Music-store selection
48 Saloon selection
50 Japanese native
51 One of the Carsons
52 Cosmetic ingredient
53 Sine __ non
54 Trombone part
56 Jewelry item
58 Parlor
61 Colas, e.g.
63 Swelters
64 Editorialists
66 Upper Volta neighbor
68 Army law enforcers, for short
69 Suggestive
70 Switch
72 A Saarinen
73 Confused
76 Wapiti
77 Like an ambitious trucker?
80 VCR adjuncts
81 Zoroaster's land
82 Rare
83 __ bien
84 Vernaculars
87 Spree
90 Election-night demand
92 Tibia
93 Blind __
96 Chanty
97 Unhappy bellhop's lot?
101 Earthwork
104 Discontinue
105 "Vesti la giubba," e.g.
106 Volvox, for one
107 Antibacterial drug
108 Banda or Baltic
109 Copious
110 Botchery
111 Shark features

DOWN

1 Brain membrane
2 Printer's measures
3 Like an aggrieved manicurist?
4 Egyptian god
5 Glacial ridge
6 Taunt
7 Taj Mahal site
8 Squints
9 Plot
10 Dry gulch
11 Buffalo's lake
12 Business letter abbr.
13 Item in pointillage
14 Efferent
15 "__ With a View"
16 __ cotta
23 Pollex
24 Enoch's grandpa
26 Chile neighbor
29 Lake herring
30 Colossal
31 Bristles
33 Abstemious sort
34 Paul Newman role
37 Amino-benzene derivatives
39 Cry of fright
40 Plumbing problem
42 Siouan
43 League
44 Obscured
45 Teacher's conflict?
46 Hit for Presley
47 Determines
49 Like brie
52 Refit
55 Ready
57 "__ is an island . . ."
58 Knowledge
59 Hyalite
60 Box-score listing
62 Flourish in type
65 Plants
67 Pirate
71 Agnus __
74 Balanced
75 Bureaucratic abbr.
77 Caress
78 Punjab prince
79 Pastoral parents
81 Mallard's hangout
83 Dialect
84 Residue
85 French basin
86 Vidor film of 1946
88 Nautical position
89 Costar for Leigh
91 Littoral
93 Anti, in Dogpatch
94 Sojourn
95 License plates
98 Neil Diamond's "__ I Said"
99 FDR agcy.
100 Ozone or arsine
102 Salamander
103 Encouraging cry

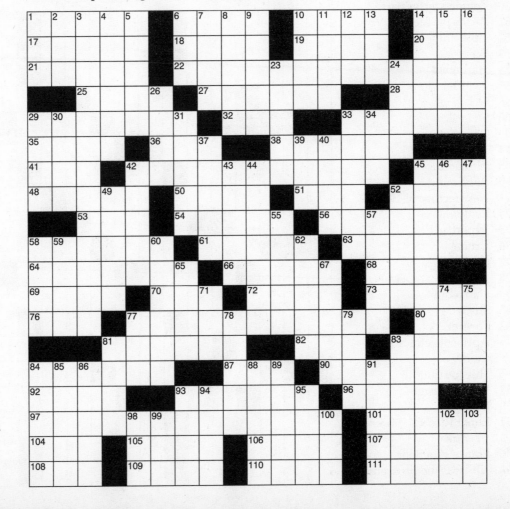

ACROSS

1 Breakfast dish
7 Stallone role
12 Bargain cigar
18 Daybreak
19 N.Y. town
20 Fielding stats
21 Repositories of much change
23 Aerie arrival
24 Caithness fall
25 Name of 11 English kings
26 Drove
28 Orthodontist's degree
29 Departed
30 One of the Hardy Boys
31 Slippery __
33 Quinella or trifecta
36 Pride, e.g.
37 Fools
39 Wall St. group
42 Imitative
44 "On the Beach" author
46 Shredded
48 Gumshoe garb
50 Engine-starter part
51 Peck's partner
52 Up-front fee
53 Whet
54 Hardened
55 Jacinthe
58 O.T. book
60 Swindled
63 Commotions
64 Kind of brand
65 Wiseacres
69 Reprinting
71 New facility of 1914
74 Evaluation
75 Expert
76 Irritate
77 Grampuses
78 Analyze
80 Had a bite
81 Stitch
82 Fortune
84 April collector, for short
85 Hillside dugout
87 Line in design
89 Due
91 Elmer Rice's "__ Scene"
93 __ Lanka
96 France's La Belle __
98 Site near the proscenium
101 Upshot
102 Disarray
103 Matin song
104 Intoxicates
105 Actor Buchholz
106 Less kind

DOWN

1 Claws' places
2 Undoing
3 Sky bear
4 Japanese dance-drama
5 Pa. city
6 Club or sub
7 Mountain ash
8 Vigilant
9 Interfuse
10 __ Harbour, Fla.
11 Domestically
12 Prophet
13 Part of NAFTA
14 Assn.
15 Lucrative discoveries
16 Wroth
17 Approx. numbers
22 Verdon of the stage
27 Cry of fright
30 "West Side Story" gang
32 Desolate
33 March sister
34 Beige
35 Hence
36 Just so
37 Twine source
38 Comedian Arnold
40 Bandore
41 Fleck
43 Aware of
44 Wonder works
45 Animus
47 Cyma reversa
49 Doctrine
50 Telecom device
53 Balzac's "The __ Comedy"
56 Pluviograph measure
57 Chaplin's "__ Life"
58 Pauley of TV
59 Belt
60 Champion
61 Jewish month
62 Waterweed
64 Word with bean or blue
66 Myrmecobius's diet
67 Squall
68 Vast amount
70 A Farrow
71 Gridiron wear
72 Civil War battle
73 Middling mark
75 Writer Iris
79 Coat's companion
80 Bellicose god
83 Young fowl
85 Dumas character
86 Port of France
87 Catnip, for one
88 Rapier
90 Antiprohibitionists
91 Keloid
92 On the mark
93 Bridge
94 Heckle
95 Brain passage
97 Word with status
99 Greek letter
100 Camel's hair fabric

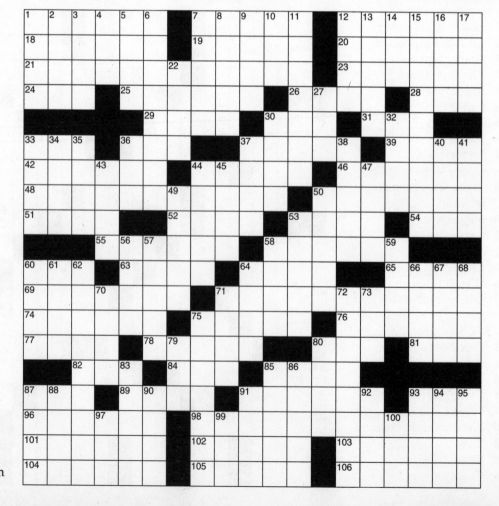

ACROSS

1 Knaves
8 Instructions word
12 Ermine
17 Inspires
18 Floats
19 Buenos __
20 Premium
21 Advantageous spot
23 Dispirited
24 First lady of the '50s
25 Stewpots
26 Impulsive
29 Go campaigning
31 Work on lawns
33 Rose oil
35 Horned viper
36 Bustling
37 Key St.
40 '60s creature
43 Loosen boots
45 Market rumor
46 Channel marker
47 Certain lilies
49 Prefix for mat or mate
50 Factions
51 Repository
52 Clever
53 African antelope
56 Entertainer Fields
57 Ferment
58 Engine-room displays
59 Shed feathers
60 Chasms
61 Piece of land
62 Daniel or Debby
63 Jason's vessel
64 Heat unit, for short
67 __ Ferry, W. Va.
69 Predaceous insects
72 Triumphant cry
73 Op-Ed fare
75 Football's Marino
76 Spurious
77 Bass counterpart
79 Woes
81 Secures
82 Prefix for mentioned
83 Mall tenants
85 Virago
87 Grevillea
89 Lancelot's son

93 Jukebox button
94 Gulls
95 Incensed
96 Take __ at (attempt)
97 Those in favor
98 Calif. community

DOWN

1 Hammer's medium
2 Sky altar
3 Bean-curd source
4 Baksheesh relative
5 Out of port
6 Imparts
7 Jet-set transport
8 Quagmire
9 Blue-footed petrel
10 Campfire leftovers
11 Greek letter
12 Britain's __ Wells Ballet
13 Supermarket division
14 Screw pine

15 Pastures
16 Approx.
18 Trattoria dish
22 Applies colophony
24 Sentimental
26 Slew
27 Gudrun's husband
28 Desist
30 Cantina offering
32 Piano work
34 Insurgents
36 Skillful
38 Fastener
39 A pig in __
41 Actress Lee
42 Golfer Gene
44 Chaucerian fare
48 Indignation
50 Tapioca
51 Goes deep
52 Detonate
53 Gem State
54 O.T. book
55 Wrasse
56 Inordinately

57 Gesture
59 Koblenz river
60 Supine
62 Fixer of a sort
63 Culture media
64 Choler
65 Verify
66 Benefits
68 Mass. peak
70 Tailors
71 Slowpoke
74 Actor Snipes
78 Calgary competition
79 Steers the ship
80 Film of 1953
82 Anthropoids
84 Leporid
86 Wings
87 Mrs., in Mazatlan
88 School grp.
89 Card game
90 Holbrook
91 Stone, for one
92 __ Moines

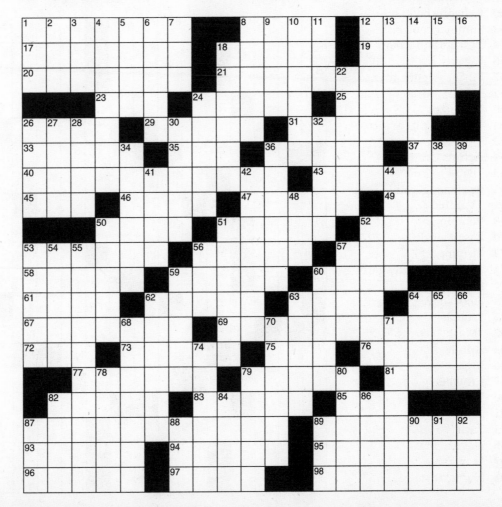

ACROSS

1 Audacious
5 Hurting
9 Boys
13 Bassinet
17 Boatswain's cry
18 Squad
19 Turks' turf
20 Baserunner's goal
21 Except for
22 Supreme Court complement
23 Refreshers
25 Wrath
26 Worn down
28 Item for Azinger
29 Water-testing digit
30 Actor Mitchell
32 Pachacuti, for one
35 Lodger
37 Hence
38 Fly
40 Pt. of VP
41 Curtain-raiser
43 Flowering herb
47 Devastate
49 __ a church mouse
50 Kaneohe hello
53 Summer cooler
54 Resnais and Delon
56 Expert
57 Business letter abbr.
59 Sturm __ drang
60 Mobilize
61 Valletta's place
63 __ tse
64 Actress Grant
65 "Baby __ You"
66 Least dangerous
67 TV initials
68 Bombinate
70 Easter shrub
72 Pismire
74 All-in-the-family garb
77 Fish dish
78 Fiber source
81 Wobble
82 "Mask" actress
84 Admit
86 Jug
87 Crowberry
90 Fall mo.
91 Alley __
93 Tacit
96 Have debts
97 "I'm game"
101 Numskull
102 Barbershop sound
103 Cattle
104 Division word
105 S-curve
106 Poet Millay
107 Travois
108 Basil or Peter
109 Advance
110 Shrewd

DOWN

1 Underlying
2 "Elizabeth Appleton" author
3 Elvis Presley's first film
4 Madder or ruddle
5 Car feature
6 Cibol
7 Peel
8 Lil __ ('92 Derby winner)
9 Race unit
10 Faulkner's "__ Lay Dying"
11 Ordain
12 Purpose
13 Guevara
14 Milling machine
15 Presume
16 Harasses
24 Actress Ryan
26 Coulomb part
27 Sundry
31 Actor Roberts
33 Naldi of silent films
34 Engine parts
36 Doing
38 Travail
39 Legislates
41 Shocking
42 Stuck one's neck out
44 Girasols
45 Muddy
46 Tallow ointment
48 Actress Anna
51 Beach Boys hit
52 Spanish girl's name
55 Hidden
56 Tilting
58 Business worry
61 Seder serving
62 "__ Good Men" (1992 film)
66 Partisans
69 Cry of dismay
70 Diving duck
71 Sampras of tennis
73 Encounter
75 Intensifies
76 Odoriferous
78 Child's toys
79 Shudder
80 Coordinate
83 Cloche, e.g.
85 Werfel's "__ the Murderer"
87 Hunt of TV
88 Patrick of the NBA
89 Compensate
92 Skip
94 Hero
95 Stadium section
98 Blessing of TV
99 Senor ending
100 Neither's companion
102 Short time, for short

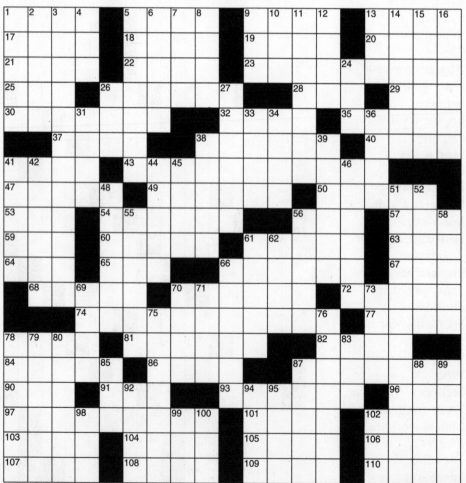

ACROSS

1 Ballpark crew
5 Recoiled
10 Absaroka
14 W. Hem. grp.
17 Stack
18 Minister's home
19 __ Park, N.Y.
20 Keats subject
21 Swap meet
23 Groundless
24 Musical syllable
25 Sp. wave
26 Multitude
27 Washer cycle
29 Bric-a-__
30 Strong
32 Musical movement
33 Grouch
34 Fitting
35 Financier's hangout
38 NASA destination
40 Shipping container
41 Made a sty sound
42 Harbinger
44 Golfer Baker-Finch
45 Economic force
48 Interval
50 Fulfilled
52 N.J. fort
53 Dilatory
57 "Who __ kidding?"
58 Split the difference
62 Senor follower
63 Zola tale
65 Pa. neighbor
66 Actor Vallone
67 Basilisk
69 Convention wear
72 Insolence
74 Tax form, for short
75 Tape repair
78 Writer Walker
80 "__ Beautiful Morning"
81 Film comedy of 1983
84 Heavy wts.
85 Thundered
86 Incensed
87 Native American hut
90 Grandson of Eve
91 Insinuating
92 Touched down
94 Labor grp.
95 "Foucault's Pendulum" author

96 Summon
97 Parley participant
100 Treasury Building's bill
101 Long time
102 Dexter's "Paris __"
103 Yearn
104 Grads-in-waiting
105 Frisky
106 Arenose
107 Triumphant cries

DOWN

1 Nominated as
2 Opera singer Aprile
3 Legal deal
4 Ctenophore's milieu
5 Clever
6 Ill fate
7 Dark
8 Argot
9 Belittle
10 Cower
11 World Series losers, 1986
12 Eye

13 Misery
14 Stand above
15 Settle
16 Noshed
22 Gin pole
28 In a pet
29 Stigmatizes
31 Capsize
32 Borrowed car
33 Facial feature
35 Poli. __
36 Tread on
37 Wheedled
38 "Seapower" writer
39 Soul
43 Jean-__ Godard
46 Structure
47 Prefix for chief
49 Torpid
51 High hill
54 A lamp for a lamp?
55 Plains Indians
56 "A Fish Called __"
59 Actress Ryan
60 Enmity
61 Hosp. figures

64 Stays the course
68 Scoring high
70 Trenchant
71 Kind of bar or bowl
73 Foot
75 McMurtry's "The __ of Laredo"
76 Member of Santa's team
77 Ponds
79 Certain fingerprints
82 Spice rack item
83 Altar figure
84 Sourwood
87 Jocose
88 Lanai goodbye
89 Customs
91 Wise herb?
92 Old struggle
93 Raucous
96 Baby food
98 History-book subject
99 Blue-chip rating

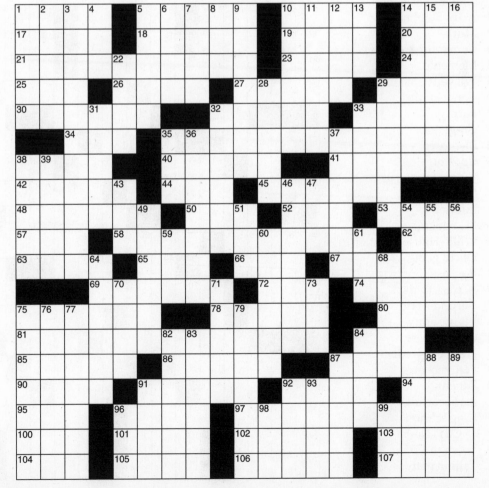

ACROSS

1 Popularity
6 Fundamentals
10 Cover
13 Abaculus
17 Catlike
18 "It's Magic" songwriter
19 Harry Nilsson song
20 Fresh air, in combinations
21 Town in Pa.
23 Town in Ohio
25 Golfer Lee
26 Fad
28 Has a bias
29 Call-day link
30 Highlander
31 Cartoonist Breathed
32 Samms of TV
35 Dowel
36 Cortes conquest
39 Luau wear
40 Provisionally
43 Wine: prefix
44 Circle part
47 Tuna's cousin
49 Singer Lena et fam.
51 Actor Stephen
52 Murk
53 Competitive dance
54 Memento
56 Wicked
58 Town in Mo.
62 Barmy
63 Go-getter
65 Ill-chosen
66 Control
68 __ loss for words
69 Garb
71 Inferior
75 PC hookup
76 White House rejection
77 Uncut gems
79 Purpose
80 Actress Ryder
82 Gerund's tail
83 Recipe amts.
84 Child's wear
86 Frappe ingredient
88 P&L reckoner
90 Benefit
91 Barbecue dish
93 King salmon
97 __ City, Nev.
99 Town in Conn.
101 Tallinn native
102 Capp and Kaline
103 Aleutian isle
104 Run off
105 Toll
106 Wine and dine
107 Counterfeit
108 Singer Della

DOWN

1 Reality
2 Jelly ingredient
3 Gross
4 "Twelfth Night" character
5 Overhaul
6 Height: prefix
7 Outlaw
8 Rock group ("If You Leave Me Now")
9 Entrap
10 Polish city
11 Arrow poison
12 __ Rio, Texas
13 TV's "Fawlty __"
14 Angler Walton
15 Actor Greene
16 Chem. endings
22 "Put __ Happy Face"
24 Bible leaf
27 In the manner of
30 Col.'s superior
31 Part of N.B.
32 "Nightmare" street
33 "Peel __ grape"
34 __ City, Ind.
35 Prefix for side or serve
37 A. Quinn role
38 Mortise companion
40 Tasseled hat
41 Pitcher Hershiser
42 Susurrus
44 __ City, Kan.
45 Spot for a sponge
46 Hypocrisy
48 Cabbage relative
50 Neglect
53 Sapphira
55 States of hatred
56 And so forth
57 Writer Sackville-West
59 Words with lunch
60 League
61 Roguish
64 Trattoria offering
67 Loop lines
70 Va. neighbor
71 NBA crowd-pleaser
72 Souffle ingredient
73 Delicate drink
74 Belgian resort
78 Lubricating process
80 Kitty Hawk name
81 Dipl. title
83 Snarl
84 Packet
85 Service's companion
87 Certain Siouans
88 Greek letter
89 Yearning sort
90 __ plaisir
91 Unplayable volley
92 Lenient
93 Friend
94 Certain Siouan
95 Excuse me!
96 Poleyn's place
98 Siesta
100 R.R. stop

ACROSS

1 Hillside shelter
5 School of seals
8 TV series, 1993
12 Hair style
16 Rawboned
17 Smoothing tool
18 Afflicts
19 Wear in 96 Across
20 Faint praise, in tennis?
24 Hose of a sort
25 Dolomites, e.g.
26 Loss of breath
27 Anguillids
28 Verse header
29 L.A. blvd.
31 Floor covering
33 What tennis aces reach?
40 "__ a Lonely Number" (1957 song)
42 Kramden's workplace
43 My mistake!
44 Nesselrode, for one
45 Solar disk
46 Basketball circle
47 French designer
48 Mineral deposit
50 "Symphonie Fantastique" composer
52 Lenin Peak's range
53 Warplane crew member
54 Tennis confession?
57 Siding material
60 Holiday times
61 Carriage rider's coverup
65 "Un Coeur en __" (1993 film)
66 Constantly
67 __ de plume
68 __ effort
69 Whitney
70 Bread spread
71 Beaver project
72 Episperm
73 Inept tennis player's consolation?
78 Inquiring sounds
79 Kind of beam or glow
80 Actress Thurman
81 High-tech wrkr.
83 Actor Buddy
86 "Days of Grace" author
88 Mass. town
91 Absolutely fair treatments in tennis?
95 Math branch
96 Pearl City's place
97 Dies __
98 Symbol
99 Auld Lang __
100 Sale offerings
101 Strain
102 Safari shelter

DOWN

1 Love lyric
2 Conk
3 Tennis extortionist?
4 Trimming tape
5 Kegler's target
6 Former
7 Pours
8 Pipe tool
9 Coxae
10 Right-angle joint
11 __ was saying
12 Viking's vessel
13 Sherilyn of films
14 Accolade, for one
15 Australian peak
17 Film of 1980
21 Lends a hand
22 Melange
23 Nutmeg spice
28 Quarterback word
29 "Dunciad" poet
30 W-2 form recipient
31 Utah town
32 Part of A.M.
34 Balearic island
35 Incursions
36 "__ I can help it!"
37 Informed about
38 Depend
39 __-do-well
41 "__ Flint" (1967 film)
46 Actor Martin
47 Cohort of Bugs
48 Chugalug
49 Access
51 Roman way
52 Saclike, in combinations
53 Chamorro's home
55 Unwavering
56 Light brown
57 Cartoonist Silverstein
58 Hawaiian city
59 Tel __
62 Useful, in tennis?
63 Joni Mitchell's "__ Sides Now"
64 Divisions of history
66 Pizazz
67 Ryukyus capital
70 Bayamon bear
71 Gig
72 Cares for
74 Issue
75 Actress Skye
76 City of China
77 Site
82 Cry of success
83 Superlative endings
84 Ensconce
85 Joyride
86 Painful
87 Pittances
88 Greek warrior
89 College subj.
90 Tattered
92 Crowd
93 __ de vie
94 La la precursor

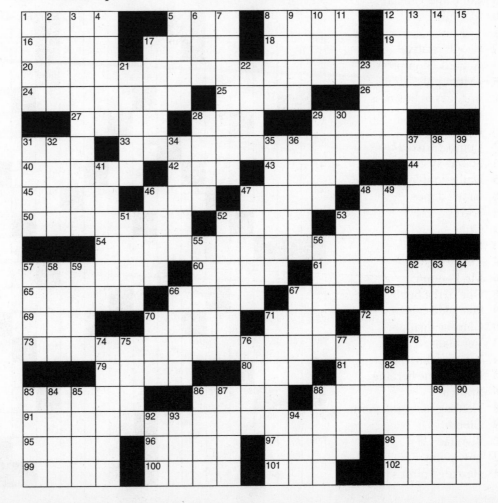

ACROSS

1 Diamond corners
6 Alan of films
10 Soft-drink company
17 Racial prefix
18 Small part
19 Gilded
20 Handsome
22 Imbued
23 Port of Japan
24 Delta material
26 On the __ (fleeing)
27 Approx.
29 Adduce
31 Peruse anew
33 Request
36 "Looking for a Ship" writer
38 Piano style
41 Setting for Sherlock Holmes
42 Conjoin
43 Merchant marine abbr.
44 Health-care worker
45 Son of Seth
46 Jeopardy
48 Cobb and Hardin
50 Makluk
51 __ Aviv
52 Keogh relative
53 Actress Thompson
55 "Monopoly" items
57 Engages in business fraud
60 Harum-__
63 Como __ usted?
64 Sound-system meters
65 Daily double, e.g.
68 Israeli dance
69 Sorrel
71 Gulf
73 Winglike
74 Cold
76 Mr. Landon
78 One of the Bobbseys
79 Scrawled
80 Chinese dish
83 Ventilate
84 West ending
85 Hawthorne heroine
86 Bring in
88 Fielding feats, for short
89 Gibbon
90 Bivouac
92 Low point
94 Hercule Poirot's brother
98 Learning sites
102 Most audible
103 Tuscany city
104 Nebraska natives
105 Got serious
106 O'Neill's "Desire Under the __"
107 Pianist Andre

DOWN

1 Entreat
2 From __ Z
3 Play snooker
4 Far reaches
5 Comforts
6 Africa's __ Bor River
7 Writer Martin
8 "A Bronx Tale" director
9 Golf-course bends
10 __-relief
11 Prohibit
12 Oppress
13 Abound
14 Indy 500 unit
15 Selestat season
16 Gules
18 Reefer or redingote
21 "__ From Muskogee"
25 Aileron adjunct
27 Pismire
28 Quick bread
30 Bochum boar
32 Choice-rhyme starter
33 Jibe
34 Twine fiber
35 Boat bottoms
37 "48 __" (1982 film)
39 Certain poets
40 Displaces
42 Flimsy
46 House ad, e.g.
47 Actress Christine
49 Bawl
52 Marker
54 Durbin of films
56 Approves
57 Roger of baseball
58 Luting
59 Pizzeria need
60 Chagrin
61 Palette choice
62 Element no. 18
65 Turmeric
66 Devour
67 Waste allowances
70 Shrewd
72 Byway
73 Timetable abbr.
75 Sonar effect
77 Subtlety
79 Ridge
81 Threatening words
82 Puzzle solver's tool
83 Russian sea
87 Indonesian ox
89 Lieutenant
91 Oates book
93 Smidgen
94 Sportscasters Michaels and Albert
95 Murmur
96 Polestar
97 Flight-plan abbr.
99 Switch positions
100 Encountered
101 Draft org.

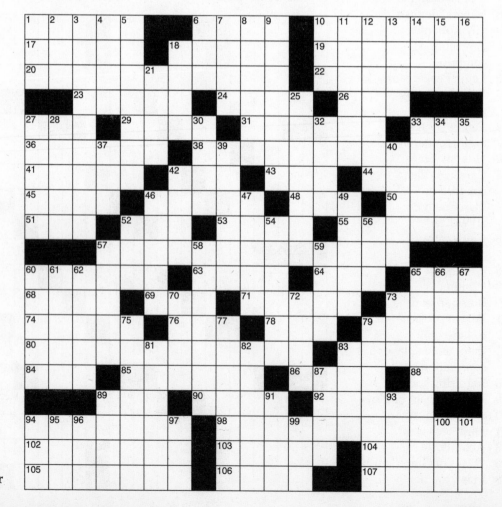

ACROSS

1 Quick-witted
4 Coryphee's garb
8 Foible
12 Zeuglodon
17 Train unit
18 Wyatt of the West
19 Lizardfish
20 Freeway sight
21 "Prince of the City" actor
24 Clinical images
25 Decree
26 Sprawling
27 Frigid
29 Anaconda
30 Lane
31 Hit upon
32 Finish line
34 Partner
35 10,000
37 Expert
38 Souchong and oolong
39 Writer Kobo
41 Pipe joint
42 Bombast
43 Couple
45 Lot
47 Forfeit
48 Slow-cooking vessel
52 Audibly
53 Flee
54 Ethereal
55 Sky altar
56 Truncheon
57 Hockey feats
59 Keep __ (persist)
60 Duroc, for one
61 Moray and murena
62 Buffalo's county
63 Landscape painter
64 Moral
66 Lass
67 De Palma's "Dressed __"
68 Baseball's Carew
69 Brainpower
70 Needlefish
71 Mediocre mark
72 Whey source
75 Luminaries
77 Small antelope
79 Entertainer Ed
80 Advocate
81 Sector
82 Actress Garr
85 Choose
86 Wallaba
87 Cantillated
88 Decorah dweller
89 Subterfuges
91 Having the desired effect
95 Actor Jeremy
96 Beige
97 Farm unit
98 Born
99 Meaning
100 Hart
101 Austen tale
102 Menacing sound

DOWN

1 Misbehave
2 Cold-weather wear
3 Song from "Girl Crazy"
4 Mal de __ (headache)
5 Detroit org.
6 Minor
7 Plateau
8 Resign
9 Gums
10 Dylan's "__ a Lonesome Hobo"
11 Longing
12 Ceraceous
13 "Ben-__"
14 ". . . a patient etherized upon __" (Eliot)
15 Jesuits' founder
16 Montaigne's work
22 Pallid
23 Hallucinogen
28 Hearts
31 Pack
32 Brandish
33 "__ been thinking . . ."
34 Like __ of bricks
36 Clarinet adjunct
37 Abuses
39 Geronimo, e.g.
40 Secret vote
42 Shock
44 Method
46 Baby shark
47 R.E. units
48 Fitness item
49 NBA star
50 Pirol
51 Spill the beans
53 Good time
54 Biting
57 Alert
58 Writer Murdoch
59 NASA report
61 Prefix for logical
63 Lace
65 Exasperates
66 Slop
67 Revenues
69 Humorist
70 Dress fabric
72 N.Z. natives
73 Contaminated
74 Admits
76 Occupations
77 "__ Cruel" (Presley hit)
78 Like-not connection
81 Swiss city
83 Traverse circle
84 Printshop worker
86 African fox
87 Cozy
88 Virginia willow
90 Would-be LTJG
92 Fall mo.
93 Relative of a 401(k)
94 Shade tree

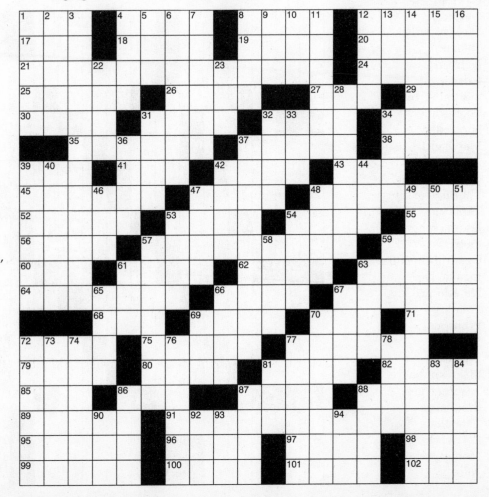

ACROSS

1 Pakistani capital
7 Brooks
12 Kind of shirt
17 Dodged
18 Gagny goodbye
19 Something two can do
20 Diatribe
21 Traffic mishap
24 Actor Mineo
25 Plus
27 Nabokov novel
28 Trust
29 Yang's counterpart
31 Fitzgerald
33 Ernie Banks's team
34 Put down: sl.
37 Timber wolves
39 In-extremis message
40 Search
41 Dillon
42 __ above the rest
43 "Cara __"
44 Weakling
46 Model
48 Eye part
49 Preempt
50 Nasty
51 Du Maurier's "Jamaica __"
52 Network
53 Exist
54 Biblical verb
56 Toothsome
57 Succeeded
61 March girl
62 Actress Judith
63 Okla. neighbor
64 Thurman of films
65 Tara name
68 Ending for gang or mob
69 Cuadrilla member
71 Inevitably
73 Nucleic acid
74 Pointless
75 Whirlpool
76 Iowa city
77 Treadmill
78 Major appliance
79 Teachers' grp.
80 Brouhahas
81 Catafalque
82 Ref. work
83 Money premium
84 Alley __

85 Timetable abbr.
87 Pac-10 mbr.
90 Secrecy
95 Punk
97 Complete reversal
98 Put to additional purpose
99 Interfere
100 Access
101 Emplacements
102 Took advantage

DOWN

1 Proposal opener
2 Et __
3 Uproar
4 Harem room
5 Fortifications
6 Elysium
7 Actor Vallone
8 Exemplars
9 Loma __, Calif.
10 Daughter of Thestius
11 Writer Grafton
12 Gradines
13 Diminish
14 Desuetude
15 Wharton's "The __ of Innocence"
16 Peak
22 Cuban dance
23 Kind of pin
26 Pattern
30 Smidgen
32 Fertile ground
33 Thalia's purview
34 Anathematize
35 "Let __ Me" ('60s hit)
36 Underworld river
37 __ lazuli
38 Town in Fla.
40 Hollow
41 Fr. painter
43 Like costmary
44 Kind of rhyme
45 Con's quest
47 Consternation
52 Convention tools
53 Marketplace
55 Precocious
56 Card-catalog listings

58 Stuffed shirt
59 Soap plant
60 Less common
63 Antipode
65 Irving's __ Meany
66 Lurk
67 Pierce portrayer
68 Desert wind
69 Legitimate
70 Yorkshire flower
72 Bottom
77 Most mature
78 Bedroom window
80 Proxy
81 Fake
83 City of India
84 Cyma recta
86 Freeway entrance
88 Exclusive
89 Signaled
90 Clutch
91 Western Indian
92 Visceral
93 Amphora
94 Legal matter
96 Citrus drink

ACROSS

1 EMS procedure
4 Organic compound
8 Gremlins
12 Supple
17 New Guinea town
18 Mrs. Charles
19 __ contendere
20 Empyrean
21 Patti Page hit
24 Implacable
25 Quiet
26 Stead
27 Social affairs
29 __ polloi
30 Align in advance
32 "Just for the fun __"
34 Polish
36 Network: Abbr.
37 Madrid Mmes.
40 Due topper
41 Study hard
42 Film of 1941
45 License plates
48 __ angle (obliquely)
52 Prefix for medic
   or dox
53 Aspect
55 Pasture
56 Competition for loggers
58 Yardstick
61 Soup vegetable
62 Writer Bobbie __ Mason
63 "Oh __" (1953 hit)
65 Class
67 Tarried
69 Words with recall
70 Emden exclamation
72 Computer lists
74 Drudge
75 Clamor
76 Actor Cobb
78 Detriments
80 "Sing __ Song"
   (1963 hit)
81 Freshly
83 "Springtime in __"
   (1942 film)
87 Virginia rail
89 Zero
90 Take-a-chance venture
91 ABA mbr.
94 Succeed
96 Approvals
98 Bush pet
100 N.E. campus
101 Skater Thomas
103 Fancy transport
106 Actor Buddy
107 Impound
109 Hemingway's "The
    Snows __"
112 Spiritual
113 Control
114 Soapstone
115 Millennium pt.
116 Immures
117 Marine eagle
118 Bilstead or bluejack
119 News execs

DOWN

1 Fasteners
2 Minor
3 Counts
4 Type of saddle
5 Sapporo
  performance
6 Baseball's Hershiser
7 Lawyer Guinier
8 Wearing civilian
  clothes
9 Stable sound
10 Conspirators
11 Loudness unit
12 Inferior
13 Famed conglomerate,
   for short
14 Shangri-La's site
15 Chesapeake bird
16 Writer Pyle
22 Sprite
23 Cry at sea
28 Boardwalk areas
31 Jaunt
33 Wrath
35 Adipose
38 Gelling agent
39 Show of indifference
43 "House of the Seven
   Gables" town
44 Sunder
46 John Calvin's city
47 Smoothed, in a way
48 Fleet
49 Hellman's "__
   the Attic"
50 Olympics sport
51 Teachers' org.
54 Victuals
57 Girasol
59 Chem. ending
60 Magical
64 Textile fiber
66 Broods
68 Miss. neighbor
71 Chuckle
73 Fluff
77 Singer Warnes
79 Appear
82 Misery
84 Panuco or Aragon
85 Conservative
86 Entomology, for one
88 Jockeys
91 Where Strasbourg is
92 In layers
93 Mortises' mates
94 Euterpe's realm
95 Hippodrome
97 Part of RSVP
99 VP in '62
102 Stultify
104 Catcher's item
105 Khayyam
108 Tappan __
110 Relation
111 Brew

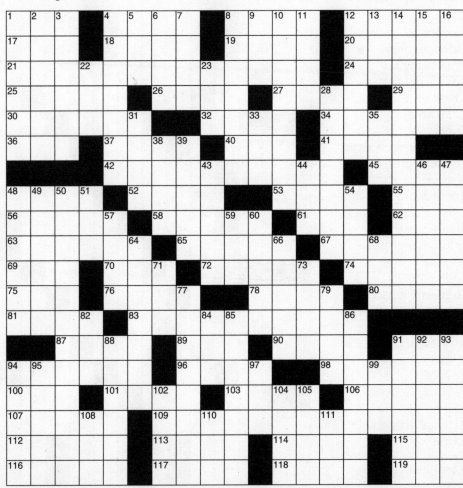

ACROSS

1 Noxious
4 "__ to Order" (1987 film)
8 Eeyore's pal
12 "__ to You" (Rick Nelson hit)
17 Self
18 Jason's vessel
19 Inti worshiper
20 Elevate
21 Suggestion, part I
25 Eternity
26 Flamboyant
27 Thick
28 Watchword
30 Wherefore
31 Rightist
32 Actor Ayres
35 Disarray
38 Acapulco uncle
39 Drubbing
40 Apteryx
41 Kid
42 Suggestion, part II
46 Prefix for form
47 Defiant cry
48 Blvds.
49 Suspicious
50 Calendar abbr.
51 "__ Rheingold"
52 Timbal or taborin
53 Creek
54 Calif. area
56 Phone sounds
57 Poughkeepsie's river
61 Item for Azinger
62 Shades
63 Conrad lord
64 Carry a card balance
65 Planet's path
68 Small change
69 Particle
70 Toll
71 Suggestion, part III
75 Neither Rep. or Dem.
76 Debatable
77 Atty. Gen. of the '90s
78 __-tzu
79 Collect
81 Ostrich relative
82 Chief
83 Artenay article
84 Affright
85 Creak
87 Belittle
89 Mystique
93 Suggestion, part IV
97 Quit
98 Bat's hangout?
99 Plasma and whey
100 Cole Porter's "__ in Love"
101 Well-known
102 Pentacle
103 Paradise
104 Undertake

DOWN

1 Greek letter
2 Wide-eyed
3 Cupola
4 Impair
5 Road sign
6 Stravinsky
7 A bas
8 Devotion
9 Quondam
10 Wood sorrel
11 Freebies
12 Sarcasm
13 Bronzes
14 Second job
15 Service
16 Part of CPM
22 __ buco
23 Sport fish
24 Indian Ocean port
29 Cinders
31 Symbols
33 Jug
34 Lean
35 Shred
36 Asian capital
37 Senescent
38 "Jabberwocky" opener
39 Entertainments
40 Work by hand
43 Midwest airport
44 Red stones
45 Ancient Troy
51 Caused by
52 Golden Rule opening
53 Zoo attraction
55 Tour
56 Famous last words
58 Bulgarian capital
59 Olympian Jesse
60 Requisites
63 Skater Starbuck
65 "All __" (1984 film)
66 Leeway
67 Light carriage
68 Sterilizes
69 Metaphorically
72 Inflict
73 Resin
74 Veer
80 Nasty
82 Whetted
83 Jimmy
84 Writer Malraux
86 Rhapsodize
87 Prima donna
88 Mature
90 Element
91 Back
92 Legion
93 Landon
94 Kind of rose or ring
95 Pistol
96 Singer Janis

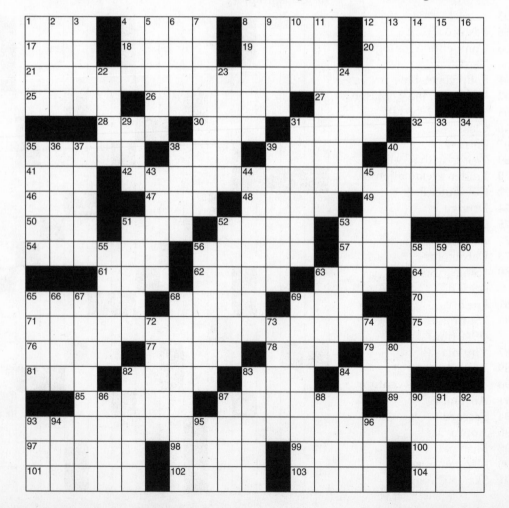

ACROSS

1 Major-leaguer
4 Mongolian expanse
8 Begone
12 Clubs
17 Pinna's place
18 "No man __ island . . ."
19 Shakesperean bad guy
20 Cape Cod town
21 Cooper novel
24 Zoetic
25 Hackman
26 Madison's roommate
27 Bismarck
28 Torrefy
30 Key
31 Ardor
34 Slangy negative
35 Tamil's turf
36 Coastal mammal
38 Cabaret productions
41 Invalid
42 Sailor
45 Lay-thick link
46 __ of pottage
48 Turner of films
49 Tennis Hall of Fame site
53 Goblin
54 All better
55 Noted folk singer
56 Alas
57 Danish king
58 Mr. Marner
59 Reprove
60 Apotheosis
61 Hankering
62 Fight site
63 Absolute
64 Greek letter
65 Blackthorn
66 Seaside attractions
72 Legal proceedings
75 Western Indians
76 Finn MacCool, for one
77 Playwright Behan
79 "__ Hop" ('50s hit)
81 Squalid
82 "Arrivederci, __"
83 Notch
84 Copper
85 Craters of the Moon locale
87 Meddlesome transients

91 Wyoming's Grand __ National Park
92 Long time
93 Speck
94 Kind of tide
95 Party-givers
96 Kind of bug or bird
97 Soft sounds
98 Vote against

DOWN

1 Favorite
2 Cheery sound
3 Wild marjoram
4 Ferber novel
5 Bone: prefix
6 Scrooge's cry
7 Leavening
8 Burn
9 West Point group
10 Ripener
11 Pinnacle
12 Initials on cable
13 Melodic
14 Jitterbugging
15 Catullus's muse

16 Legislator
22 Italian sauce
23 Mother-__
28 W.W. II force
29 Venezuelan export
30 "__ the Sheriff" (1974 hit)
31 Interval
32 "__ Well That Ends Well"
33 Part of RSVP
35 "Per aspera ad __"
37 Antagonist
39 Civil unrest
40 Flatfish
43 __ a customer
44 Aargau town
47 Backyard burrower
48 Type of moth
49 Deferential denial
50 Wharton
51 Hospitable furnishings
52 Egyptian god
53 Profit
54 Cavalier poet
56 Martin of movies

57 Gambling gear
59 Sing like Bing
60 Something from the blender
62 Other things, to Caesar
63 Rueful
65 Pt. of CST
67 Strange
68 Inevitable process
69 Foundry lamp
70 Hogshead
71 Shifty
73 "Cat __ Tin Roof"
74 Blessed
77 B'nai __
78 Calgary competition
80 Stowe character
81 "Ballet Scene" painter
83 Epic
84 Clouseau's valet
86 Switch positions
87 Ripken of baseball
88 Catcall
89 Creek
90 Secret agent

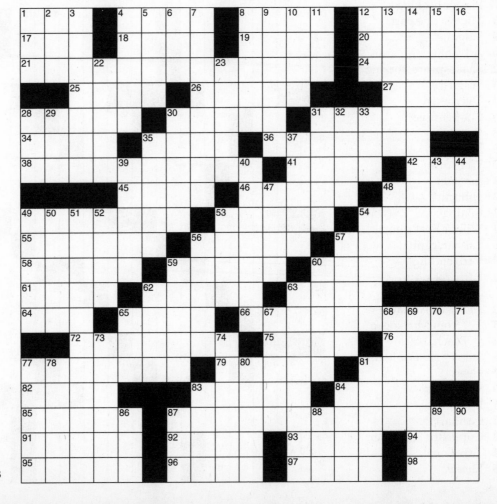

ACROSS

1 Femme __
7 Division
13 World-weary
18 GWTW character
19 Rocker
20 Free-lances
21 Lunch hour
22 Tchaikovsky work
24 Recline
25 Gullet
26 Elliptical
27 Tight spot
29 Wane
32 Semisolid
33 __ out (scrape together)
34 Conjunction
35 Mouths
36 Element no. 16
38 One of the Baldwins
39 Big name in communications
41 Superman series
43 Blockade
46 Where heroes are made
47 Plaster backing
48 Microscope part
49 Singular
50 Advent
52 Shakespeare, for one
53 Disgust
54 Overtaken
56 Cooperative
58 Poignancy
59 Dickinson
60 Wellspring
61 Incubus
62 Hillock
63 Inkling
64 Wilbur Post's horse
66 Latvian capital
69 Verb ending
70 Early rock duo ("Young Lovers")
72 Alexis or Alexander
73 "__ from Muskogee"
74 __ Beach, Fla.
76 Stop __ (intermittent)
77 Heel
80 Scatter hay
81 Interfere
82 Cecilia, e.g.
83 Cupboard container
84 Takes on
86 Ebony
87 Residue
89 "Key Largo" duo
93 Roman officials
96 Abalone
97 Ballet duet
98 Unrestrained
99 Lachrymose
100 Ill. town
101 Writer Anne and family

DOWN

1 Superfluity
2 USN mission
3 Film of 1990
4 "__ Want for Christmas"
5 Quays
6 Scrutinize
7 Hollywood reading: Abbr.
8 __-Magnon man
9 __ tongs (full force)
10 Perfect
11 Leisurely
12 "__ My Shadow"
13 Jazzman Dave
14 Hang about
15 From the birds
16 Take care of
17 Ethyl acetate, e.g.
23 Wild cards
27 Steinbeck name
28 Johnson of TV
30 Cartridge
31 Puff up
32 Spout
33 African antelope
37 Tailor's concern
38 Tip off
40 Effervesce
42 Family
43 Fokine ballet
44 Martian prefix
45 Gibson and Harris
49 Comeback
51 Diffident
52 Memory unit
53 Aries, e.g.
54 King mackerel
55 Actress Suzy
56 Work unit
57 __ only (sole)
58 Stuffy scholar
60 Subject to change
61 One of the Cyclades
63 Maugham's "__ Ale"
64 Painter Cassatt
65 Planter's punch ingredient
67 Excited
68 Elvis's middle name
70 Earthenware
71 River-to-river route
75 Mortal
77 Beacon Hill name
78 Venerate
79 Canon
81 Kind of nut
85 Column
86 Minx
88 Threshold
90 Satchel
91 Ullmann of films
92 Mauna __
93 Consume
94 Continental Abbr.
95 Aves.' relatives

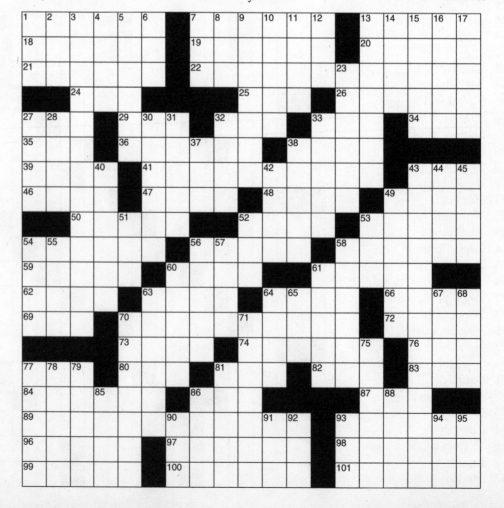

ACROSS

1 Wall St. wheeler-dealers
5 Andes mammal
9 Everyday language
14 Introverted
17 Vincent Lopez theme
18 Literary conflict
19 Refuge
20 Barn sound
21 Movie pairing from 1991 and 1943
24 "A Home of __ Own" (1993 film)
25 Pickled pepper
26 High-tech client
27 Finer points
28 Function
29 Whitney
30 Entertainer Jacques
32 Org. since 1970
34 Attends
36 Double bill from '80 and '88
41 Sioux
44 Auction ending
45 Poetic preposition
46 World Series stat
47 "You __ just whistlin' Dixie"
48 Consummate
51 Chilling
53 Charon's vessel
55 Chem. suffix
56 Tumulus
57 From __ Z
58 Kilmer of films
59 Double bill from '91
66 __ gratia artis
67 Metallica Grammy-winner
68 Yarn
69 Covenant
70 Type of plastic
73 D.C. winter time
74 Sob
75 Work of 1871
76 Fuss
77 Wallaba
79 Orbison
81 Actress Elizabeth
83 Double bill from '87 and '86
88 Bureaucratic abbr.
89 Happy-lark link
90 Top drawer
91 Hill or Houston
94 Dry gulch
96 Pipe joint
98 Symbol of innocence
100 Drew the sleuth
102 Senor ending
103 Double bill from '78 and '58
106 Protein source
107 Search high and low
108 Sine qua non
109 Outland
110 European resort
111 Singer Chrissie
112 Como __ usted?
113 Sweetsop

DOWN

1 Just between you __
2 Majestic
3 Pancake
4 Whined
5 Stipend
6 West Indies rodent
7 Opposite number
8 One of the Brontës
9 Greek letter
10 Tire type
11 Calcar
12 Oregon coastal town
13 Printer's measures
14 More urbane
15 Appointed time
16 City on the Ouse
22 Broke into
23 Loon relative
28 Woden's bailiwick
31 Bracket fungi
33 Innocence
35 Outside
36 Disintegration
37 Word with whiz
38 Actress Myrna
39 Timetable abbr.
40 Hawthorn
41 Hammett's "The __ Curse"
42 Lieutenant
43 Understood
49 Sort
50 Rio Grande branch
52 Spain's __ Brava
54 Wapiti
56 Multiple bets
57 Blind ambition
58 Malefactor
60 Whisky-jack
61 Opening sections
62 Prescript
63 Base
64 Took the jitney
65 Power
70 Family vehicle
71 Affirmation
72 Currently
73 French drink
74 __ nose (barely)
75 Cry of discovery
78 Strength
80 Jack-trades link
82 Tableau
84 Just __ suspected
85 Rabbi's study
86 Eminent
87 Hearty
91 Proboscis
92 Doyle's "__ of Identity"
93 Bulfinch specialty
94 Clever
95 Bit
97 Formidable force
99 Alas relative
101 '70s pop group
103 Box elder
104 100 square meters
105 RR stop

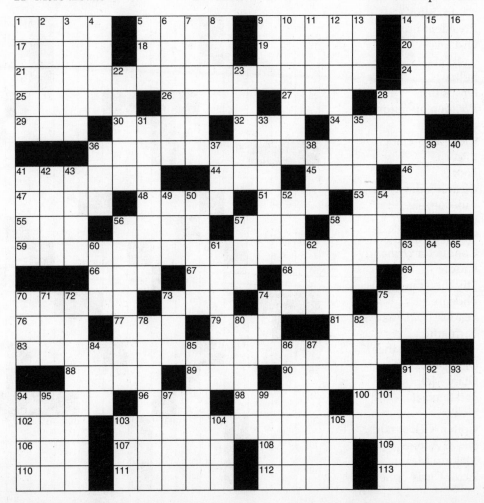

ACROSS

1 Reindeer-country native
5 Polecat
11 Kiang
14 Title of respect
17 Hillside dugout
18 Empower
19 With 35 A, 93 A and 98 A, holiday song
20 Chem. ending
21 Euphorbia plants
23 Painting type
24 Recipe amt.
25 "__ king, always a king"
26 Actor Erwin
28 Italian town
30 Puny
32 Recorded
35 See 19 Across
36 Poetic preposition
37 Bandleader Winding
38 Sorceress
40 Suggestion word
41 Ornamental house plants
47 "__ to differ"
48 President pro __
49 Ordains
50 __ Ark
52 Sultry
55 Drops in
59 Weapon operator: Abbr.
60 Clowder member
62 Pilcorn
63 Foot
64 Cleaning device
65 Yule log, e.g.
67 Bearish
69 Violin maker
71 Conductor Ormandy
73 Paddle
75 "By the Time __ to Phoenix"
76 Feature of 21 Across
80 Farm unit
82 "How __ love thee?"
83 Designer Anna
84 Giant Mel
85 Soil deposit
87 Sickly
89 Golfer Nick et fam.
93 See 19 Across
95 Majorca Mrs.
96 Actor Christopher
97 Prefix for form
98 See 19 Across
100 Close of a holiday song
105 Vamoose!
106 Lobster coral
107 Dynamic
108 Atlanta arena
109 "__ a Rebel" ('60s hit)
110 Actor Wahl
111 Dog type
112 Bridge player

DOWN

1 In the __ luxury
2 Have __ to pick
3 Vincent of films
4 Wreath material
5 Charge
6 Differ ending
7 Bandicoot
8 Stat for Bonds
9 Resilient
10 Seed coating
11 From __ Z
12 Fill-in strip
13 Psalm word
14 Alights
15 Affront
16 Indemnifies
22 Business volume
27 Vindicated
29 At least
31 Part of QED
32 Vermont resort
33 Steel's "Message From __"
34 Nobleman
39 Copse
41 Mild oaths
42 Black
43 Fortify again
44 Riga native
45 Jeremie's land
46 "__ far, far better thing . . ."
51 Search
53 Composer Ned
54 __ Tafari
56 Insect stage
57 Emblem
58 Brochettes
61 Chilly
63 Ring
66 Bidding
67 Loosens
68 "I pass"
70 Phoradendron
72 Fabulist: var.
74 St. Nick's landing spot
76 Movie ender
77 Unfavorably
78 Writer Grafton
79 Belle of the West
80 Have __ on (mock)
81 Actress Sellecca
86 Work alternative
88 Jimmy of tennis
90 Skin layer
91 Bakery equipment
92 Murrow's "__ Now"
94 Bacchanalian cry
99 Honshu cash
101 Bar mbr.
102 Casino area
103 Holiday time
104 Gas: prefix

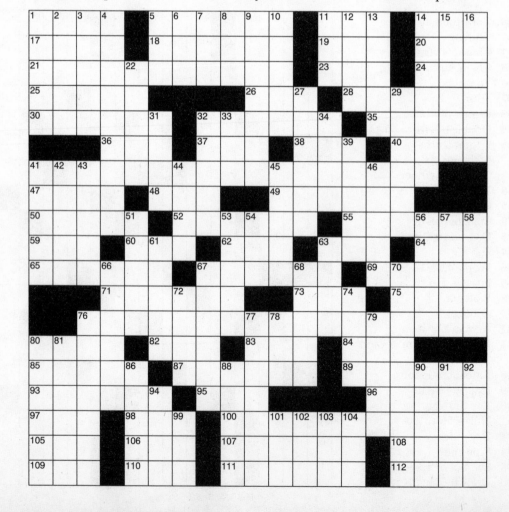

ACROSS

1 Charlotte player
7 Winter wear
12 Occupy
18 Fertile
19 Durant or Dorfman
20 Rumple
21 First part of a writer's vow
24 __ Olivos, Calif.
25 Mortgage
26 Gelatin
27 Turmoil
28 Fragrance
30 Hawaii __
32 Breeze
35 Theme
37 Winter complaint
39 Orpheus's father
43 Vow, part II
48 Playwright Fugard
49 Curly's cohort
50 Increase the RPMs
51 Ointment
52 Hwy.
53 "Seinfeld" character
56 __ Moines
58 Ending for gag or gang
59 Shipboard slammer
60 Gambling initials
62 Big hitter from Baltimore
64 Narcissus's love
67 Namely
69 Bombast
71 Kind of dance
74 Coventry Patmore efforts
76 Teachers' org.
78 Helios
79 Deft
81 Vow, part III
85 Item for Mathew Brady
86 Frequently
87 They just get by
88 Polonius, for one
90 Meadow
92 Being
93 Singer Zadora
96 Jai __
98 "Accommodations of Desire" painter
100 Recaller's word
103 Vow, part IV
109 Amylum
110 "Where __" (1969 film)

111 Like some modern music
112 So far
113 All together
114 Straight

DOWN

1 Drumfire
2 Circa
3 Bowl sounds
4 Org. for 1 Across
5 Dining area
6 Berate
7 Cloy
8 Screwball
9 Melisma
10 Merchant
11 Ensign
12 Ceaseless
13 Forthwith
14 Kind of wire
15 Out of port
16 Delighted
17 Saarinen
22 Knight's appellation
23 USN inst.
28 Holy Roman emperor

29 Phone user
31 Continental abbr.
33 Triops
34 Fertilizer
35 Barbecue accessory
36 Will-__-wisp
38 Recycled
40 Swing
41 Serenade subject
42 Humdinger
43 Wells's "__ of the Worlds"
44 John Lennon song
45 Vive le __
46 "Ask __ questions . . ."
47 Mainly
54 Actress Ullmann
55 Ordinal ending
57 __ generis
59 Failed
61 Autumn pear
63 Pursuer's guide
64 Grand
65 Soft drink
66 Quartermaster's place
68 Cipher

70 Neonate
71 Stratum
72 Unfortunately
73 Part of MPH
75 Blood fluids
77 Besets
80 Jubilation
82 Flamboyance
83 St. Tropez season
84 Davis autobiography
89 Actor Wallach
91 Promo producer
92 Rock group initials
93 History
94 Division word
95 Pilewort fiber
97 "Ritorna, vincitor!," e.g.
99 Der __ (Adenauer)
100 "__ She Sweet?"
101 End
102 Just
104 FDR agcy.
105 Fall mo.
106 Service org.
107 Western Indian
108 Done-turn link

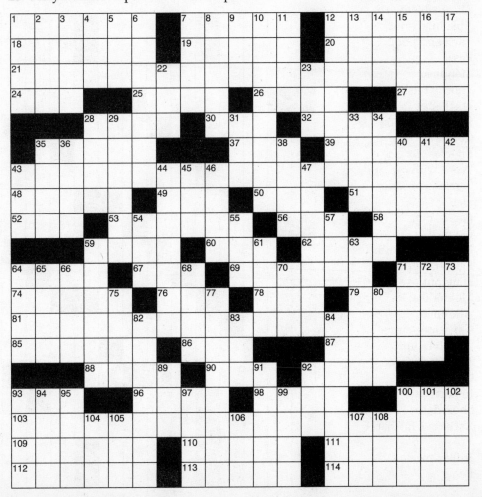

ACROSS

1 Sherman __, Calif.
5 Jetty
9 Wacky
13 Criticize
17 Flagrant
18 Jai __
19 Part of QED
20 Proceedings
21 Circumference of power?
24 Aikman of the NFL
25 Songbirds
26 Odist of old
27 Center of activity
28 Spirit
30 Reject
31 Karpathos neighbor
33 One of the Barrymores
34 Acambaro affirmative
35 Wanted-poster listing
37 Lamented
38 Digressing
40 Needlefish
43 Street in Rome
44 Hero
45 Excited
46 Actress Neuwirth
47 Absolutely not
49 Pitch and pool
51 Passe
52 Mendicant
54 Thorny bush
55 Fusillades
56 Put out of action
57 Coasters
58 Big-eyed lizard
59 Word with cap or deep
60 Farrier's product
61 Flee
62 Pac-10 mbr.
65 Owns
66 Honest transaction
69 Egyptian god
70 Hangout
71 Methodical
72 Allotment
73 Carpaine source
76 Jewish month
77 The Beach Boys' "__ Girl"
78 Inland sea
79 Shored up
82 Racetrack mishap
83 Yokel
84 Irrelevant
88 Being
89 Deposited
90 "Straight-up" occasion
91 Arrow poison
92 Bumppo's quarry
93 Historical periods
94 Pt. of USDA
95 Rep. Gingrich

DOWN

1 Food scrap
2 Satisfied sound
3 Was savvy
4 Got around
5 Silk velvet
6 Oleron and Ushant
7 Crossette
8 Most fertile
9 Currant
10 Strongbox
11 Soapstone component
12 Guidance
13 Sentimentality
14 Bitter
15 Winter warmer
16 Actress Helen
22 "Old Curiosity Shop" character
23 Aegean region
28 Griffin of Hollywood
29 Ornamental case
30 Engine-room display
32 Porkpie, for one
34 Winter fall
35 Rampart
36 Aug. 15 babies
38 Scent
39 Celebrities
40 Misbehaves
41 Foment
42 NL team
44 "If __ a Hammer"
46 Fishing smack
48 Cyma recta
49 Writer Germaine
50 Succor
51 Runway
52 Indian poison
53 Writer Ferber
54 Overstuff
55 Campanologist's concern
57 Disdain
58 Blame-bearer
60 Bicker
61 Stand
63 Cloy
64 Carbonize
66 "__ Anything" (1989 film)
67 Over
68 Unpromising avenue
69 Steal
70 Tack-room item
72 Wisecrack
73 Blanched
74 Sprung
75 Lull
76 LSD and DNA
77 Effete
80 Bring up
81 Where Kampuchea is
82 Hit the mall
85 Fulcrum for Fonteyn
86 Original
87 Hanoi holiday

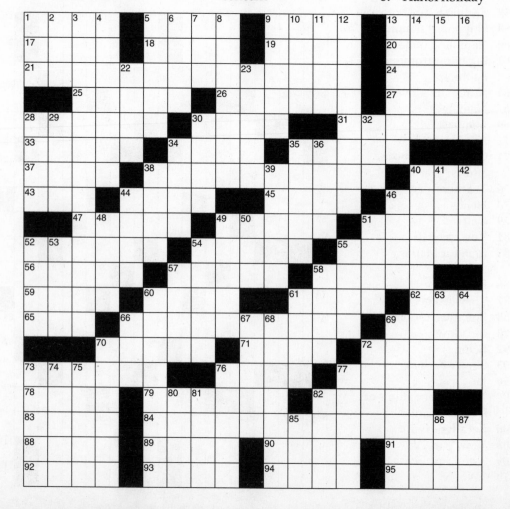

ACROSS

1 Songbird
8 "__ time was had by all"
13 Mean
18 Mean
19 Nouveau __
20 Salk conquest
21 Treatments
22 Pellucid
24 Malicious
25 Cauda
27 "Lorenzo's __" (1992 film)
28 Main lines
29 Committee mtg.
31 Prefix for bar
32 Boobook
34 "__ Face It" (Porter show)
36 Rice dish
38 Tofu material
40 Quaff for Falstaff
43 Sorgues saison
44 Expert
45 Org. since 1970
46 Effective
48 PETA peeve
49 __ deucy
50 Repressive
52 Cold-sufferer's supply
54 Branched
55 Forsake
56 Purpose
57 Poet Conrad
58 Carnival spot
60 Rabble
63 Eyrie arrival
65 Delegate
69 London browns
71 Cobia's meal
72 Conjunction
73 Wind instrument
74 WJM anchorman
75 Biblical pronoun
76 Rightful
77 Tiny
78 Toll
80 Religion
81 Transfer
82 TV band
83 Speed
84 Neighbor of 44 Down
86 "Say __, Somebody" (1983 film)
89 To's partner
92 Uttar Pradesh city
94 "__ Din"
97 Disposal
100 Make like a magpie
102 Rapidly
103 Dive
104 "To Catch a Thief" setting
105 Kentucky Derby quest
106 Ridge
107 Retoucher

DOWN

1 Clumps
2 Northamptonshire stream
3 Rebels
4 June VIPs
5 Kegler's hangout
6 Glair source
7 Balance
8 Crafts worker
9 Clapp's "__ My Dreams"
10 Sorrel
11 Cry of dismay
12 Ricky Ricardo portrayer
13 Health club
14 Kind of victory
15 TV's Trebek
16 Contour
17 Much
23 Tactic
26 Alvin of dance
30 Sci-fi figures
33 Undulate
34 Forsaken
35 Needle case
37 Entertainer Burl
38 Ladle
39 Backstretch repast
40 "I can't tell __"
41 Waterfall
42 Tense
44 Kihei's place
45 Hymenopter
47 Passion
50 __ alive!
51 De Soto
53 Brazilian dance
54 Angry
57 Lace end
59 "Let __ Me" ('60s hit)
60 Lighter
61 Worry
62 Motive
64 Play group
65 Lake at "Clinton's ditch"
66 Resolute
67 Spirit
68 Arbutus, for one
70 Stock-table abbr.
71 Encourage
75 Roy Rogers's horse
79 Switch positions
80 Transmute
81 Confined to quarters
82 Loosen
85 Harmonia's daughter
86 Open a bit
87 E-mail item
88 Greek letters
90 Part
91 Millstone
93 Farm unit
95 Actor Richard
96 Sandarac tree
98 Power group
99 Cuttlefish secretion
101 LBJ pet

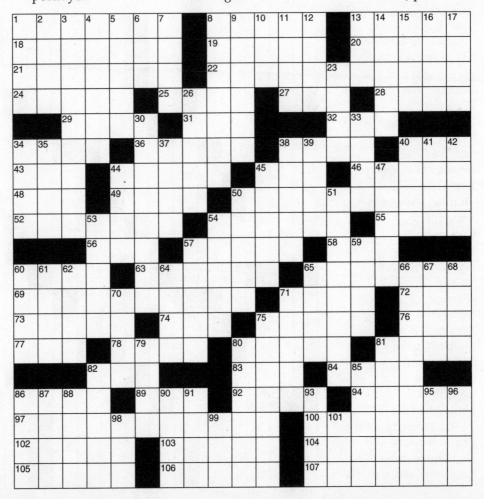

ACROSS

1 Calif. observatory
8 Sweep
13 Big Easy cuisine
18 Kuwait, e.g.
19 Duck
20 __ orange (bowwood)
21 Computer type
22 Truffaut film
24 Trendy
25 Harpsichord relative
27 Wood sorrel
28 Card-catalog entries
31 Farm crop
32 Practical matter
36 Will-__-wisp
37 Dana's "Two Years Before the __"
39 Aspersion
40 Before
41 Misery
42 Berry-bearing weed
45 Give it __ (try)
46 Gardner of films
47 Ulmus genus
48 Quintessence
49 Understood
50 Fantasy
52 Blue dye
53 __ Anne-de-Beaupre
55 "Marriage a la Mode" playwright
56 Broadway deep-pocket
57 Big issue
61 Hope's offering
62 Ocho __, Jamaica
63 Mexican president
64 Product of xerography
67 E-mail transmission
68 "It must have been something __"
69 Concorde
70 Holbrook
71 Easily resolved, to lawyers
74 Divulge
75 Had a bite
76 Roosevelt pet
77 That, to Cicero
78 Dido's sister
79 Bric-a-brac stand
81 Contributed
83 Hidebound
85 Switz., formerly
86 Writer Bernard
88 Guadalupe gold
89 Childrens' social worker
93 Ecstasy
97 Computer command
98 Sprightly
99 Architect
100 Hip boot
101 Poet Marianne
102 Holds back

DOWN

1 Xing user
2 "__ my brother's keeper?"
3 Fighting weight
4 Camden Yards competitor
5 Dull surface
6 Day-time connection
7 Units of reluctance
8 Diffuse
9 __ garde
10 "The Torchbearers" poet
11 Talent
12 Erstwhile Tokyo
13 Group effort
14 Nepalese, e.g.
15 Spree
16 Cry of disgust
17 Snood
23 Miscreant
26 Stations
28 Facing
29 Words with think or talk
30 "__ Faces" ('60s hit)
32 Elyse Keaton's son
33 Actor Jagger
34 Impulse
35 Grimaklin's greeting
38 "Don't look __!"
39 Fop
42 Cleveland suburb
43 Capital of Burma
44 "__ Like Us" (1985 film)
49 Military headwear
51 Skittish
52 Inner being
53 Sculpture
54 Flat sign
56 Game site
58 Fine points
59 Window frame
60 Wrong
63 Comedian Mort
64 Plug
65 Profanity
66 Supplication
67 Fuse
68 Key
71 "The Twelfth __" (1956 song)
72 Pa. town
73 Tammy Wynette hit
78 Heart adjuncts
80 "__ Three" (1936 film)
81 Attain
82 To have: Fr.
84 Dipsomaniac
86 Hockey's Ciccarelli
87 Killer whale
89 Stick
90 Mouths
91 Reckless
92 Actor Neill
94 Timetable abbr.
95 Malarkey
96 Endings for sell and tell

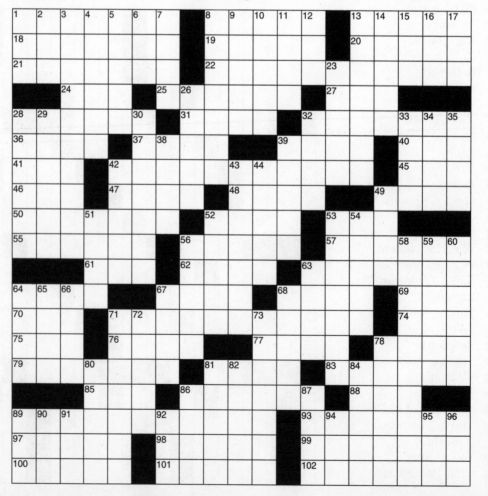

ACROSS

1 Hostile
5 St. Louis sight
9 Campus figure, for short
13 Detriment
17 African port
18 Swerve
19 Tiptop
20 Greek theaters
21 Hugo Winterhalter hit, 1956
24 Trojan War hero
25 Previous
26 Enthralled
27 Ballad
28 Undisciplined
30 Dowitcher
32 Place to use one's PIN
33 Alley __
34 "__ Doubtfire" (1993 film)
37 Get back
39 Powell's exploration
42 Lowers
43 Intimate-apparel item
44 Response to a rodent
45 Bombeck
46 Pius and Caius
47 Galena, for one
48 Norm
49 Musical family
50 Hedge bush
51 "__ Fideles"
53 Ref. work
54 Pluto
55 Past one's prime
58 S&P rating
61 "Cara __" ('65 song)
62 Oxygen-dependent organism
63 Delight
64 Risk
67 Gibson of films
69 Cannon
70 Inspire
71 God of war
72 Ripken
73 Burlesque's Lily St. __
74 Over-adore
75 Hilton tale
78 MCPs, e.g.
79 Approx.
80 Threshold in time
81 Burgoo ingredient
82 Board
83 Ovine parent
84 Part of MOMA
85 Udometer measure
86 Entertainer Sumac
89 Interrogate

92 Site of an 1869 rebellion
96 Former U.N. mbr.
97 Upper-air bear
98 Part of A.M.
99 Composed
100 Worker-protection org.
101 Positive case
102 Cordelia's dad
103 Ark groupings

DOWN

1 Chanel
2 By word of mouth
3 Certain paintings
4 Heredity material
5 Flies
6 Farm machine
7 Change unit
8 "48 __" (1982 film)
9 Straw hat
10 Upbeat
11 Merged
12 Pastern adjunct
13 Elaborate prank
14 Pt. of speech
15 Actor Stephen
16 Utmost: Sl.
22 Instincts

23 Part of UHF
29 Wallaba
31 "__ Please, We're British"
32 Wild
33 River to the Baltic
34 Vidal's Breckinridge
35 Gambol
36 Cinch
37 Hasty
38 Campania town
40 Teachers' org.
41 Unsuave sort
43 "Song of the South" epithet
47 Panegyric
48 Solveig's beloved
49 __ Aviv
51 Carole Maso novel
52 Common article
53 Encouragement to El Cordobes
55 Soybean product
56 Part of MPH
57 __ Saud
58 Securities regulation
59 Intoxicate
60 Has-__ (washed-up types)

61 Dew dropper
63 Arrived
64 Blanch
65 Life force
66 Balance
67 Erstwhile filly
68 Whitney
70 Costa Rica town
72 Felony compounder
73 Raccoon relative
74 Come across
76 Stick
77 Tropical grasses
78 Leonidas's kingdom
83 Pound
84 "Name of the Rose" monk
85 Painter Magritte
87 "Send __ Flowers" (1964 film)
88 Proponents
89 Word with status
90 Navy vessel initials
91 Ese relative
93 Miss the mark
94 Actor Kilmer
95 D-day craft

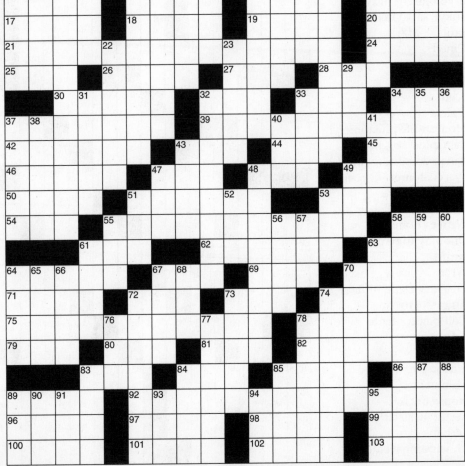

ACROSS

1 Neat's companion
6 Inspiration for Strauss
12 Waterfront area
17 Painter Rousseau
18 Member of the press?
19 Cosmopolitan
20 Investors' neuroses?
22 Hit the __ the head
23 Nesslerize
24 Uno plus due
25 Lives
26 Prize
29 Author Zane
31 Hangout
32 Cheer for Manolete
33 Silkworm
34 Firm
36 Stood the gaff
38 Pearl River spot
41 Fabled bird
42 Roman bronze
43 Frisky
46 Hong Kong investments?
49 Contusion
50 Crowning point
53 Atmospheric gas
55 Bryologist's study
56 Tokyo salad item
57 Sault __ Marie
58 Dined
59 Lummox
61 Tryma
62 Scent
64 Oglers
66 Modern-life phenomena
68 Bicuspids' neighbors
70 Amassed investments?
72 __ a customer
73 Mother of Ceres
74 Broadcast
75 Writer Thomas
79 One way to pay
81 Attire
83 Wrath
84 Treasury Dept. unit
86 Sargasso, for one
87 Golf-bag contents
88 Side
91 Produce
93 Eureka!
94 Kind of sax
95 House finch
96 Result of cash flow, perhaps
102 Concluding elements
103 Virtually
104 Vacation
105 Fools
106 Media maven Myers
107 Sharp

DOWN

1 "Second City," for short
2 Actor Cariou
3 Pulver's rk.
4 Ridge
5 More pleasant
6 Gossip
7 Onassis
8 Cry for Wayne and Garth
9 Part of U.K.
10 Actor Wallace
11 Gaelic
12 Approach
13 Drama award
14 Investments in AT&T or MCI?
15 Mound
16 Prudence
19 Hypnotized
21 Benefits
26 Sleep stage
27 Stat for Smoltz
28 Old theater
29 Old theater
30 Part of P.R.
31 Recommendations
35 Scottish island group
36 "How can you __ cruel?"
37 Penny-back word
39 Foyt et al.
40 Scoreboard entry
42 Wood-shop tool
44 Political subject
45 Bridal belts
47 Jottings
48 False
49 Confront
50 Ex-N.Y. governor
51 Bonus
52 Cooperative ventures for plungers?
54 Attention-payers
58 Beaux __
60 Vendetta
63 Appraise
65 Pick out
66 Weather word
67 Mole
69 Butcher's offerings
71 Pains
73 Oaxaca wave
76 Mendacity
77 Circle part
78 Murdoch's "Under the __"
80 Musical symbols
81 Golly relative
82 Snack-food ingredient
84 Wouldn't hurt __
85 Multiple-birth group
87 Ultima __
89 Outworn
90 Affected
92 Arrow poison
93 USMA, e.g.
94 Pot builder
97 Baculus
98 Siam ending
99 __ Harbor, N.Y.
100 Genesis name
101 Koppel

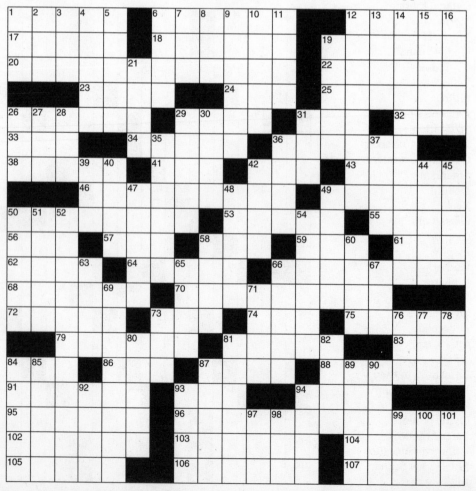

ACROSS

1 Wear and tear
5 Subject to
10 Wilts
14 Twain raft-rider
17 Pause
18 Gallows item
19 Kibitka
20 Flight-plan abbr.
21 Rascals hit, '68-'69
23 Dies __
24 Profit ending
25 Prosecutors, for short
26 Perilous
27 Lampyrids
29 Wont
31 Fragment
32 Gender
33 Bond issuer
35 Allen's "__ From a Mall"
38 Jettison
42 Fan-shaped
43 Exceptional
44 Nickname
46 Walleyed pike
47 Jambalaya ingredient
48 Nigerian native
49 Driven
51 Requires
53 Biotite
55 Energetic
56 Maaing mama
57 Fancy stepper
60 Family mbr.
63 Sarah __ Jewett
64 "The __ the limit"
65 Thompson and Samms
70 Newshound's burden
72 Dutch uncle
73 Mantle
74 Slightly
75 Stake
77 Network
78 Soap plant
79 Modern Lutetia
81 Emend
83 Copied, in a way
84 A alternative
86 Outfit
87 Batters
88 Accurate
92 Quotum
94 Gen. Arnold
97 Snead's starting point
98 Lounge
99 Upper Boston?
101 Sales-slip entry
102 Boost
103 Playwright Fugard
104 Biblical preposition
105 Little leftover
106 Battle site, 1944
107 Clan chief
108 Catty comment

DOWN

1 Joyous
2 Mood
3 Storytelling device
4 Tachina
5 Biased
6 Weak at the plate
7 Ostiary's post
8 Discern
9 Arikara
10 Awkward
11 Prefix for dynamic
12 Chomps
13 Worried
14 Taunt
15 Particular
16 Subject for Asimov
22 Crickets hit of 1957
27 Card game
28 Quicklime, e.g.
30 "__ Grows in Brooklyn"
31 Apiologist's specimen
33 Scurry
34 Kazan
35 Port Arthur's lake
36 Jar
37 Expected
39 Split
40 Party
41 London park
43 Souvenir
45 Drill
50 Writer Lois
52 Suspend
54 Hirt and Hibbler
55 Thwart
58 Swathe
59 They get by
60 Easy pickings
61 Speck
62 Phone button
66 Film of 1983
67 Still stuff
68 Skilled
69 Farmer's investment
71 Piaf
76 Oprah rival
77 Demerit
78 Strange
80 Pasta dish
82 Zing
83 King of music
85 SSBN's ancestor
87 Georgia city
88 936 A.D. German King
89 Stingy
90 Theme
91 Jewish month
92 Clockmaker Thomas
93 Comedy-club sound
95 Palo __, Calif.
96 Furrow
99 Flying fox
100 Audiophile's irritant

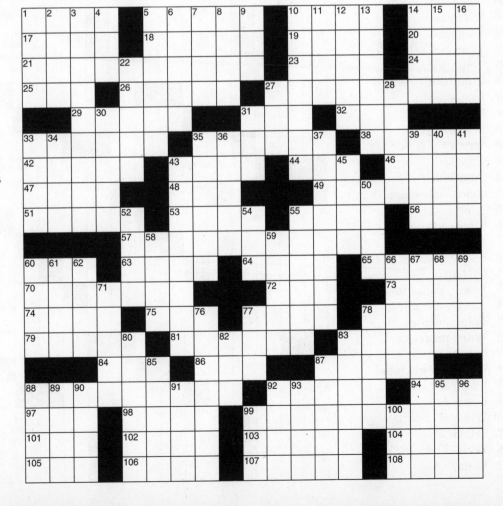

ACROSS

1 Penn or Union: Abbr.
4 Insurgent
9 Room's companion
14 Like an old TV squad
17 Smidgen
18 Minn. town
19 Hedonist's complaint
20 Surface in Lillehammer
21 Long time
24 Study
25 Chuck of "Gong Show" fame
26 Canadian Indians
27 Egyptian amulet
29 Tilting
30 Wild goose
32 Thalassic
33 Anchorman Baxter
34 Standard
36 Like a bump __
38 Bowlful occasion
41 Cartoonist Silverstein
44 Olympics team
46 Forenoons
47 Chemical solvent
49 Power org.
50 Energize
52 Walloped
53 __ on one's shoulder
55 Tonic, soda, etc.
56 Comparative words
57 Iroquoians
58 Hearth
59 Muslim decree
60 "Irma __" (1963 film)
61 Gimcrack
62 Singer Neil
64 Actor Richardson
65 Exist
66 The Beach Boys' "__ Room"
68 See 99 Across
71 Dictate
73 Beauty parlor item
74 Acid-test readings
77 Poipu porches
79 Word-processor output
81 Hatch __ (scheme)
83 Mistreat
84 Concede
86 Witch of Umbria
87 Satisfied
88 With "The," 1993 film
92 Bitter, e.g.
93 Kent portrayer
94 Roman functionary
95 Horned beast
96 Legal matter
97 Sea birds
98 Early Englander
99 Clairvoyance, for short

DOWN

1 "__ Mater"
2 "Hot" item in Huixtla
3 Beloved
4 Entourage
5 Old English letters
6 Celeb's story
7 Pt. of DEA
8 Milan landmark
9 "The Hidden Valley" author
10 Fr. wave
11 Collections
12 Lopez of chess fame
13 Gloomy
14 "In the __" (1965 hit)
15 Antarctic, for one
16 Spaghetti al __
22 FDR agcy.
23 Amphora
28 Life force
30 "... __ some peanuts ..."
31 Charlotte and Norma
32 Poet Angelou
35 Clobbers
36 "The Country Girl" playwright
37 Thurmond of basketball
38 Dubber
39 Moslem month
40 Tea biscuit
42 Demonstrate
43 Recidivate
44 Togetherness
45 Program that debuted Sept. 24, 1968
48 Extol
50 Violin maker of note
51 Bellicose god
52 Marching-band headwear
54 Certain Slav
56 Vestige
57 Depends
59 Feb. 13, for one
60 Singer Frankie
63 Those: Sp.
64 Daughter of Geb
67 Entertainer Sumac et al.
69 Nods
70 Infidel
72 City on the Missouri
74 Telethon response
75 Adobe homes
76 Await 14 Down
77 Mo. town
78 Poplar
79 Wines and dines
80 Actor Silver
82 Ante
84 So be it
85 Wash
86 Manche town
89 Ending for profit or pamphlet
90 Harem chamber
91 Navigator's calculation

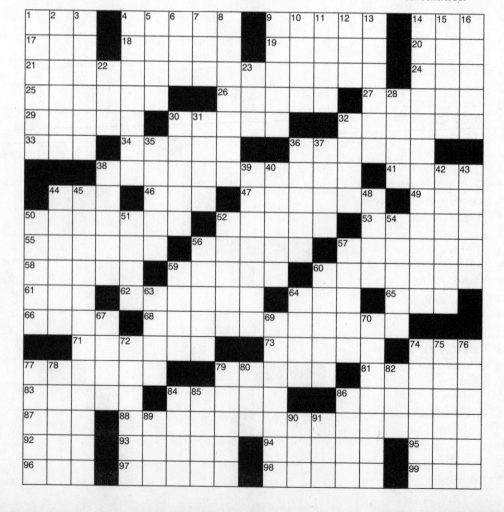

ACROSS

1 Biblical prophet
6 Square off
11 Measly portion
17 Horsy town in Fla.
18 Sentient
19 Summer TV fare
21 Flapper's dernier cri
23 Ensconce
24 Blackfly: Var.
25 Prickly shrub
26 Go __ for
28 Gossoon
29 Bicuspid's neighbor
31 Sincere
33 Writer Janowitz
35 Demoiselle
37 Mission town founded in 1782
41 Gibbon
42 Infatuated
45 Renounce
46 Little drum
47 Ellipsoid
49 Skirt style
51 Freud and Faustus
53 __ Creek, Ill.
54 Pervasive
56 Magnetism unit
59 Immerse
61 Jolson and Jarreau
62 "The __" (Tony-winning musical)
63 Royal flush component
64 NBA coach Doug
66 Operations center
69 Semisolid
71 "__ Sera Sera"
72 Party pooper
76 Type type: Abbr.
78 Latin goddess
80 Billy of music
82 Attenuate
83 __ Verdes, Calif.
85 "Casablanca" character
88 Those in favor
90 Vaccary sight
91 Keen indeed
94 First U.S. VP
96 Patella's place
97 Bring up
98 Grovel
100 Super Bowl initials
102 Shackle
104 Traditional ideal
106 Hindu hero
109 Oceanside
111 Project for Goethals
114 Umbria town
115 Links feat
116 Jimmy Webb's "__ We?"
117 Mother of song
118 Paper unit
119 Does in

DOWN

1 Deride
2 "__ hardly wait"
3 Surfboat
4 Dodger manager of yore
5 Gen. Arnold
6 Significant
7 "__ the One" (Presley)
8 Skier McKinney
9 Age
10 Paraphrase
11 Stall
12 Singer Tebaldi
13 Parvenu
14 Satisfied
15 Whiffenpoof song refrain
16 Modern Briovera
20 Furtive
22 Sky altar
27 Chan portrayer
30 Shank
32 Purpose
34 Wall Streeters' degrees, for short
35 Jam
36 Bloviate
37 Item for Bill C.
38 Polar explorer
39 Brioche
40 Martial __
43 Thunderstruck
44 Guy's date
48 Actor Ayres
50 Turkey neighbor
52 Comparison
55 Set up
57 Old French coin
58 Cobb of films
60 Ward-heeler
65 Sprite
66 Ischia
67 Site of Sevier Lake
68 Crimean War battleground
70 Luau supply
72 Legend
73 Brazilian rosewood
74 "Blue Moon" of baseball
75 Evergreens
77 Deprived
79 Consternation
81 Chaparro
84 Ghost
86 Prairies
87 Motorists' org.
89 Maxim
92 Charge with oxygen
93 Flinch
95 Throw off track
98 Sky streaker
99 Stop-dime connection
100 Sgt., e.g.
101 Horseplayer's concern
103 Liliaceous plant
105 Yarborough of racing
107 Legion
108 Elevs.
110 Just so
112 Satisfied sound
113 Music-store department

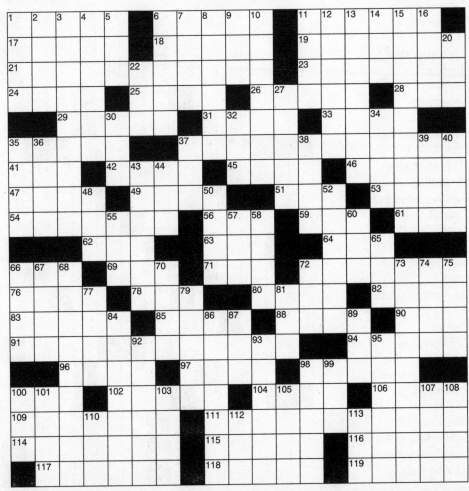

ACROSS

1 Modern mental maladies
7 Swine or equine
12 Casual wear
18 Singer Brewer
19 What amor conquers
20 Balk
21 Demolition workers' fete?
23 Octavia's husband
24 Claims
25 Leb. neighbor
26 Ushered
28 Navigational chart abbr.
29 Descartes
30 "If I __ Hammer"
31 Alpine river
33 Impulse
36 Cross shape
38 World Series time: Abbr.
40 Indigents
42 Youthful otter
45 Alemakers' merrymakings?
49 Jaguar
50 Cassowary
51 Liveliness
52 Chits
53 École attendee
55 Dilettante
57 Dives
59 Zoo group
60 Look lewdly
61 Genealogy entries
62 Kiln
64 Primeval victim
66 Philatelist's study
68 Tough part of golf
71 Curved
73 Cravo
74 Gladys Knight's cohorts
75 Agen agreement
76 Creek
77 Conformists' fete?
80 Zilch
81 Shunned
83 __ Rio, Texas
84 Pilcorn
86 "Able," updated
87 Cries of fright
90 ATF agent
92 Chuckles
96 Conversation, for one
98 Heredity material
99 Nasdaq's realm

100 Conversion
101 __ for sore eyes
104 Gathering of the disabled list?
107 Vocation
108 Gape
109 Disclose
110 Permanently
111 Anchor chain pass-though
112 "Tristram Shandy" man

DOWN

1 Clashing
2 Chutzpah
3 Untried
4 Clandestine
5 Reproving sounds
6 Psych. test initials
7 Gets hung up
8 Accept
9 Miscellany
10 Absurd
11 Irving's "__ of a Traveller"
12 Sp. title

13 Filmmaker Riefenstahl
14 Misbehaves
15 Air-conditioned fete?
16 Lineage
17 Disingenuous
22 Actress Long
27 Oust, in a way
30 Moundsmen
32 Salt-N-Pepa's specialty
34 Ghastly
35 Kefauver
37 Poplar
39 Won
41 Apply
42 __ Xing
43 Thurman of films
44 Press agents' fetes?
46 Something to play by
47 Loudness units
48 Enfolds
54 Concluding
56 Part of N.B.
57 Truman's birthplace
58 Trace
61 Calif. valley
63 Disoriented
64 "Cheers" employee

65 One of the Durants
67 Ballyhooed
68 Brooch
69 Rapa __ (Easter Island)
70 Hodges of baseball
72 U.K. honor
74 Tropical sight
78 N.H. neighbor
79 Bypasses
82 Objective
85 Hemingway's "__ and Have Not"
88 Doughy dish
89 Holiday hero
91 Unbeatable sports feat
93 Personnel official
94 "... with cheek __"
95 Newspaper section
97 TV sitcom
100 Barracuda
101 Pretense
102 __ Paulo
103 Endeavor
105 Argue
106 Hosp. figures

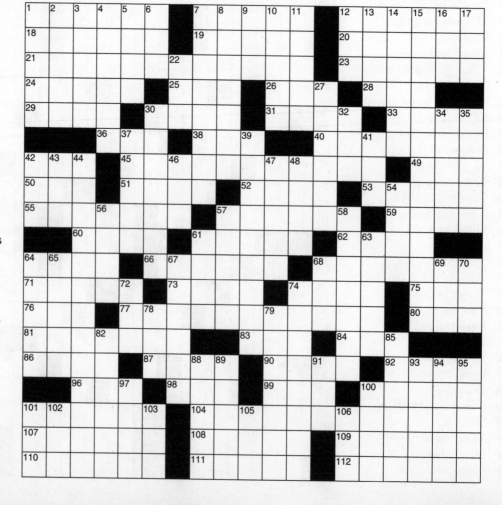

ACROSS

1 Hit the keys
5 Common case
10 Wide's partner
13 "This __ Country"
17 Grand
18 Crawford
19 Singer Lemper
20 "Utopia" author
21 Competitive doorway designers?
23 Grouch
25 Follower's phrase
26 Sugar
27 Abbie Hoffman's cry?
28 CIA forerunner
29 __ Aviv
31 Murmur
32 Hardship
36 Well-designed charitable groups?
41 Falsehood
44 Previous
45 Proverb
46 Actor Alfred
47 Submits
48 Stop for 9 Down
49 Sour
51 Mayday
52 Supremes name
53 Trembles
57 Creek
59 Reveres architects, in a way
65 Mouths
66 School supplies
67 Transfer
68 Donnybrook
71 Alias
73 C: Abbr.
74 Skirmish
75 A Baldwin
77 Head problem
79 Wall St. regulator
80 Bundle
81 Steadfast architect?
85 Unstinting
86 Dipteron
87 Consume
88 Pen point
91 Colloquy
94 Keziah's father
96 Singly
98 Sweaters, scarves, etc.
101 Architectural opiners?
103 Lost species
104 Hail
105 St. Teresa's town
106 Spirit
107 Pond dweller
108 Youth
109 Correctional
110 Harness race

DOWN

1 Don Juan's protestation
2 Flanders city
3 Early Britons
4 Mountain nymph
5 Chem., e.g.
6 Copenhagen's __ Gardens
7 Collections
8 Faineant
9 Shipping cos.
10 Mergers
11 On
12 Enlist again
13 Jeopardize
14 Small sum
15 Doubtfire, e.g.
16 Certainly
22 Turbine parts
24 "Norma Rae" director
27 __ never know
30 Old days, the old way
31 Mass. cape
33 Gambler's "portfolio"
34 Part of A.D.
35 Naval amphibs
36 Attests
37 Serve a sentence
38 Ice-cream choice
39 Pat
40 Oscar, Edgar etc.
41 Business abbr.
42 __ Ben Adhem
43 Hotbed
48 "__ Cried" ('60s hit)
50 Machine tool
53 Follower of Ann Lee
54 Sp. queen
55 Bacon slice
56 Coventry Cathedral architect
58 Per se
60 Musical syllable
61 Common shrew
62 Basin
63 "I can't tell __"
64 Fast time
68 Spellbound
69 Potpourri
70 Ridge
72 Give it __ (try)
74 Wicker
76 Noted guitar man
78 Bid
79 Porker's pen
80 Tour group, for short
82 "There oughta be __"
83 Vulpine
84 Galaxy
88 Formal refusal
89 Lead-in
90 Harassed
92 Bona fide
93 Pumice source
94 Sky deity
95 Actress Lena
97 Ride
98 Singer Lang et al.
99 Demander's time
100 Lupino of films
101 Maximum
102 __ de tête

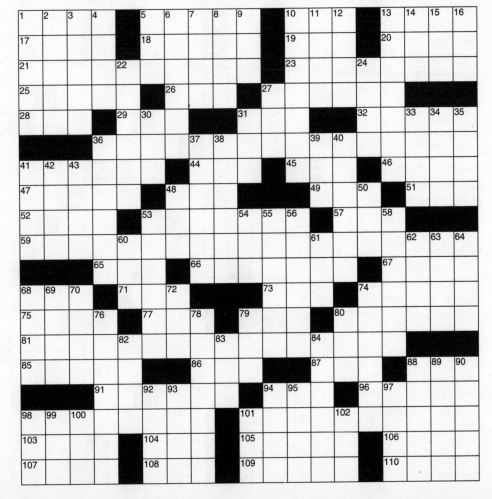

ACROSS

1 Ravine
5 Scarf
8 Stooge
12 Shavian monogram
15 Pretension
16 Euphoric feeling
18 Mishmash
19 Satiate
20 Story of Jim Hawkins
23 Lofty bear
24 Harding et al.
25 Up-front payment
26 Joy
28 Director Besson
29 Guevara
31 Hoops feat
33 Martinque peak
34 Social imperative
36 Reward-seekers of a sort
40 "__ is an island . . ."
42 Schoenberg's "Moses und __"
43 Thompson of films
46 __ Gay
49 Myrmecoids
51 Dance org.
54 Bring boatward
56 Conferences
58 Peanut product
59 __ v. Wade
60 What the smart money has?
64 Ending for tour or terror
65 Buff
66 Relative of 108 Across
67 Departure
68 Fighter at Waterloo
69 Verse collection
71 Fast
73 Bone: prefix
74 Chem. compound
76 Words with shame
78 People with "lifestyles"
85 Absolute
89 Put on __ (ham it up)
90 Pt. of USA
91 Advice to the indecisive
93 Enzyme
94 Country music mecca
97 __ impulse (rashly)
99 Lazy
101 Meager
102 Source of baker's millions?
105 Suggestion word
106 Leave out
107 Flindosa
108 Toiler in many puzzles
109 U.S. Open winner, 1994
110 Singer McEntire
111 Prefix for functional
112 Entertainer Ed

DOWN

1 Turkey feature
2 Freshen
3 Soak to the skin
4 "__, old chap . . ."
5 Encounter
6 Yours and mine
7 On the main
8 Cornmeal dish
9 Corolla petal
10 Elemental force
11 Protuberance
12 Fountain sound
13 Critic
14 Part of USA
17 Sanskrit user
19 Peaceful
21 Vanzetti's codefendant
22 Bewilder
27 TLC provider
30 Abba of Israel
32 Actress Sedgwick
35 Together
37 Kind of switch
38 Observe
39 Premature
41 Pogy
43 Gen. Rommel
44 Reagan cabinet member
45 Substantial
47 Clark's companion
48 Synthetic fiber
50 Dross
51 March 16 baby
52 Leg up
53 Jumpy
55 "Take __ the Limit"
57 Hairstyle
61 Upright
62 "The Wonder __"
63 Dolly Varden, for one
70 Davenport
72 Handle
75 Jake of "Raging Bull"
77 Bent on
78 Mob
79 Zion
80 What hits climb
81 Whets
82 Bashful exclamations
83 Computer list
84 Praying figure
86 Eastern religion
87 Ancient monastic
88 Jimmie and Pee Wee
92 Mess hall workers
95 "I wish" relative
96 Alaska cape
98 Shortage
100 Furniture seller
103 Josh
104 Islet

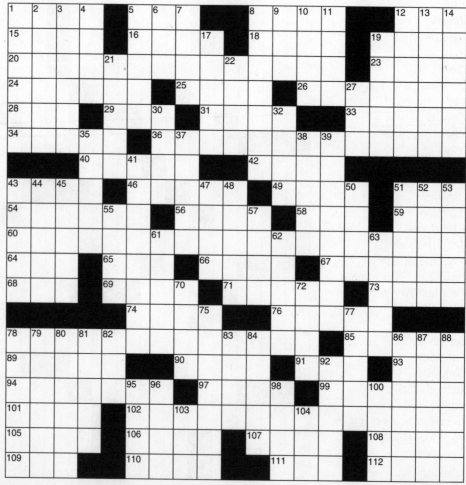

ACROSS

1 Mahogany
8 Poker openers
13 '90s medium
18 Diver's quest
19 Have __ to pick
20 Distribute
21 Pupil
22 Attracted attention
24 __ noire
25 Scarce
26 Busy __
27 Poipu performance
29 Sounds off
33 Hale
34 Old Soviet unit
35 Famed DP middleman
37 Salt-N-Pepa specialty
38 Bar mixture
40 Showed the way
41 Personal-care product
45 Salamanders
49 Kind of value
50 Casino calculation
51 Target chooser
53 One-piece garment
54 Muslim decree
56 Birth announcement words
57 N.J. township
59 Clear as __
60 Kefauver
61 Aggressive
62 At bat's desirable aftermath
63 Chem. endings
64 Good match
65 Untamed
66 Inhibit
68 Movement at the barre
69 Carpet feature
72 Hit the hay
74 Udometer fillers
76 Wildebeest
77 Thrush
79 Daiquiri ingredient
80 Suppress
82 Mil. group
85 Misfortune
86 Items in a reporter's notebook
89 Taboo
90 Mirthful
92 Elvis's early record label
93 Hammer part
95 Nothing to cry over
98 Bad feeling
101 Corolla part
102 Networks
103 Film material
104 Large quantities
105 Irascible
106 Budget concern

DOWN

1 Editor's inventory
2 Telling
3 Hoops blunder
4 Win
5 "Can __ a Witness?"
6 Descartes et al.
7 Doer: suffix
8 High tea item
9 Behind, at sea
10 Diplomatic pouch contents
11 Sensed
12 Vast amount
13 Tape pulley
14 __ zoppa
15 Spills the beans
16 Sheds
17 Anesthetic
23 Spanker
27 Succor
28 Eye part
30 Fall precursor
31 Coxswain's cry
32 Happy moments
33 Dunaway of films
36 Sandbars
38 Muttonfish
39 Stop
42 Confused
43 Design
44 Intensifies
46 D.C. dweller
47 Aikman of football
48 Venality
52 Fix
55 Storybook
56 "So what else __?"
58 Compulsion
59 Indigo source
60 Industrialist Cyrus
62 Pained cries
64 Cyrano's symbol
67 Singer Brickell
68 Sulk
70 Presently
71 Flat-bottomed boat
73 Colin and Dick
75 PBA member
78 Foretoken
81 Brainstorm
82 Pants
83 Drive
84 Piece of music
86 Withdraws
87 Dark
88 Elbow room
91 Cabbage dish
92 Hook henchman
94 Mountain road-sign wd.
96 Navigational syst.
97 Actress Lenz
98 Hardly embellish
99 Actor Erwin
100 Shoe width

ACROSS

1 Decay
4 Disappointed cry
8 Blue shade
12 Merchandise
17 Hail
18 Low-grade
19 Pulmobranchia
20 Fla. town
21 Tradesman's option?
24 Costner
25 Thurible contents
26 Abroad
27 Knockout
28 Org. since 1970
29 Distress signal
31 Hoops coach Doug
33 Guy
36 News execs
38 Merkel of films
39 Grounds
41 Actor Ayres
42 "Hamlet" character
44 Contractor's claim
47 Nation in the news
49 Clairvoyants
50 Ending for Adam or Gotham
51 Urchin
52 Highway sign
54 Require
56 Singer Helen
60 Dutch uncle
61 Innovative
62 Snoop
63 Greek letter
65 Contrition
66 Attack
68 Anthem opening
70 Shofar, e.g.
71 Rel. of a 401(k)
72 "The Outlaw" character
74 Stock
76 Pulque and maguey
78 Menu offerings
83 Film critic Roger
84 Sidekick
85 Carnassial
86 Low
87 Bongo
88 Open a little
90 Fleur-de-__
91 An O'Neal
93 Movie dog
96 Do road work
98 NASA report
99 Applies lavishly

101 Count of note
103 Hospital coffee-shop selections?
106 Rotund
107 Mystique
108 Stopper
109 Enzyme
110 Fishing boot
111 Entertainer Jacques
112 __ dixit
113 Crag

DOWN

1 One of the media
2 Lehrs
3 Doris Day hit
4 Accessible
5 Actor Buchholz
6 Gnat
7 Grampus
8 Baseball family
9 Knock off
10 Cuz's dad
11 Ending for person or parson
12 Came to
13 Tart
14 Pasta dish
15 Wallach
16 __ Salvador
22 Intro
23 "Epodes" poet
27 Actor Joe
30 ". . . __ of robins . . ."
31 Preacher's home
32 De Gaulle's approval
34 Zorro's mark
35 Possess
37 Lab denizen
39 Singer Mariah
40 Alienated
42 Drama awards
43 English Channel feeder
45 Husband of Catherine de Medicis
46 Writer Harper
48 Chopper
53 __ Jima
55 __ volente
57 Command position
58 "Praying Hands" artist
59 Barm
62 Dry out
64 Musical syllable

67 Kennel sound
69 Proofreader's instructions
70 Serf
73 "__ Mio"
75 Mali's capital
77 On the ship
78 Certain spreadsheet user, for short
79 Pilgrimage to Mecca
80 Gone by
81 South Seas dish
82 Glamorizes
89 Cultivate
91 Absolute
92 Satellites
94 Sculptural work
95 Caesar's goose
97 Slew
98 Pitcher Mark of baseball
100 Impulse
101 Bend
102 Camel's hair fabric
103 Flounder
104 Royal pronoun
105 Stat for Bagwell

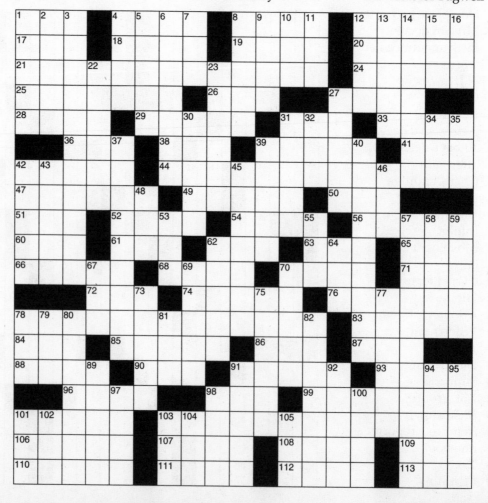

ACROSS

1 Rock's Black __
7 Philatelist's passion
13 Vermin
18 Balzac
19 Big Ten member
20 Kukla's compatriot
21 Michener title
22 Monomania
24 Disheartened
25 Bloodline names
27 Concerning
28 Fork in the road
29 Greek letter
30 Lighter, e.g.
31 __ bitsy
32 Stand
33 Callow
35 Dalai __
37 Young salmon
38 "... are __ thee tonight..."
40 Sooner or later
44 Gaskets
46 Turgenev
47 Identity
51 Equestrian gear
52 Bell-wear for the busy
54 Skater's setting
55 Cambodia's Lon __
56 Sound of disapproval
57 Fellowship
58 Confectioner's commodity
59 Keys on many boards
60 Tommy __ Jones
61 Jetty
62 Tilt
63 Destroyed
64 Art lover
66 Kind of bar or bet
67 Laguna Beach neighbor
69 Jack-of-all-trades relative
72 Sophia of films
73 __ ski
76 Cause for complaint
77 __ the hills
79 Scrammed
80 Strikebreaker
82 Latin-lesson word
83 Catchall abbr.
86 Coating material
87 Twin
88 "Jockey to be named"
90 Like-not link

91 Specialist to a fault
94 Invalidated
96 Disoriented
97 Dwellings
98 Lapwing
99 Cross
100 Records
101 Position

DOWN

1 Reprove
2 High-tech helper
3 Ouster
4 Fatigued
5 Silkworm
6 Period
7 Recreation
8 Air
9 Bellicose god
10 Denver summer time: Abbr.
11 Bluenose
12 Penn and Connery
13 Jab
14 Slippery __
15 Ira Levin novel

16 Musical ineptitude
17 Jewish rites
23 Hue's companion
26 "Othello" character
30 Keg stopper
31 "__ the Mood for Love"
32 Service-department sites
34 Gilt's greeting
35 Jimmy
36 Widely
37 Winter wear
38 Discolor
39 Obliterates
41 Niamey's land
42 Grand tales
43 Represent
45 Elf
48 Whistle stop
49 That's all
50 Lasorda's Dodger predecessor
53 Revoke
54 City on the Seine
57 Starts

58 Concluding passages
62 Conform
63 Portico
65 Did garden work
66 Poseur
68 Law-school degrees, for short
70 "__ the Wild Side"
71 Major __
73 On the water
74 Hockey great Jacques
75 Alcove
78 Easy shots
80 Designer Anna
81 Hide
82 Chasm
84 Invigorating
85 Minos's realm
87 Stoneboat
88 Facial feature
89 Uniquity
90 Suspicion
92 Hanoi holiday
93 Sell option
95 Clear

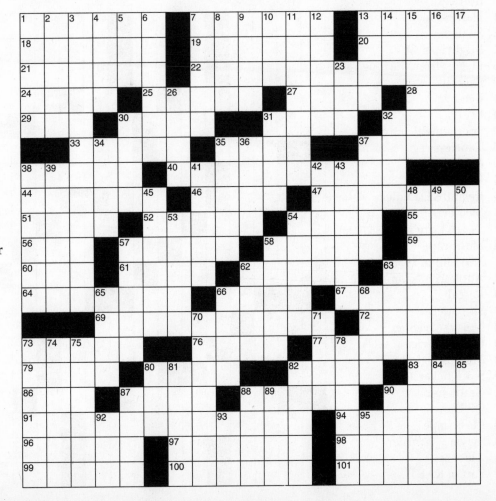

ACROSS

1 Hey, you!
5 Economist Weber
8 La Scala voice
13 Pile in the till
17 Smidgen
18 Project ending
19 Hawke of films
20 Soft cheese
21 Organic compound
22 Hubbub
23 With "The," Vincent Price classic
25 Mexican resort
27 Tribute
29 Polite remark
30 Before
31 Press kit insert
33 Doctrines
35 Tourney round
38 Hard-bitten
40 Comfortable
43 Locksmith Linus
44 Actress Joan
46 Academe
49 Demander's word
50 Borders
51 Harness race
52 Swift
54 Bright star
56 Like __ from the blue
59 Recruits
63 Bye-bye
65 Pry
67 Sports-medicine case
68 Timeless
70 Rejoice
72 Part of UCSB
73 Ireland's De Valera
75 Mediocre marks
77 Devils Lake's st.
78 Mass. cape
81 No. 1 hit of 1963
84 Adolescent's lament
85 Rascal
87 Shredded
88 Noisy scavenger
90 Out of service
92 Madras melody
93 Stock ticker abbr.
94 Grads-to-be
97 QB Dan
100 Mass. cape
102 Sylvia __ Warner
104 Aloof spot
107 Part of RAF
109 "Casablanca" character
110 Polypody
111 Baseball's Boyer
112 Squid's trademark
113 Pricket
114 Spindles
115 Professional
116 Musical syllables
117 Being

DOWN

1 Article
2 ASW gear
3 Rock's __ Pilots
4 Baby powder
5 Shade of blue
6 "Aladdin" prince
7 Foreign prefix
8 Commands
9 From __ Z
10 Interrupts
11 Cincture
12 Draft classification
13 Flat
14 Certain reporter
15 Flight-plan abbr.
16 Clinton trademark
24 Dial settings
26 Jarry's "__ Roi"
28 Phoney sound?
32 "From the Terrace" author
34 Conductance unit
36 Labor org.
37 Darn
39 Domestically
41 Eight furlongs
42 Ties up
44 Action movie staple
45 Serf
47 High shots
48 Painful cries
53 Dweller in Albania's capital
55 Freud and Magnani
57 Bagel's companion
58 Flintlock part
60 Beach projects
61 Colossus
62 Hell's Canyon river
64 Range
66 Supplication
69 Service mark
71 Computer fixers, for short
74 More specific
76 Cavorts
78 Greek letter
79 Ref. work
80 Poet Schwartz
82 Actor Stephen
83 Sweetened
86 Ascertains
89 Harris and Asner
91 Satirical
95 Soeur Thérèse and Betty Prior
96 Gin
98 Tingle
99 __ me tangere
101 Capture
103 Stash
104 "__ Man Answers" (1962 film)
105 Trouble
106 Automne forerunner
108 "Time __ Bottle"

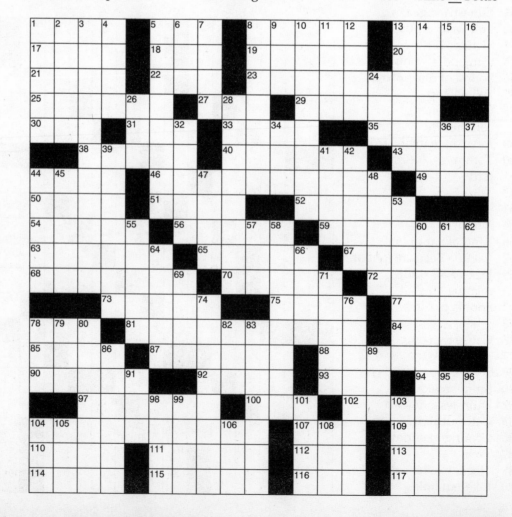

ACROSS

1 Committee leader
6 Exercised
11 Tie
17 Decline
18 Impudent
19 Communicant
20 T.S. Eliot work
22 Vitamin B complex member
23 Uses the internet
24 Pump
26 Clever
27 Ger. river
30 Ship heading
31 Lhasa __
33 Grain bristle
35 Bridles at
37 Scrams
38 Sandwich pockets
41 Mrs. Helmsley
42 Thrust response
43 Rolling Stones hit
44 Parent, eventually
47 Steal
48 Window part
49 Kind of power
51 Dwellers: Suffix
52 Invitation subscript
56 School orgs.
58 Haul
59 Being
60 Rime
61 Martin's erstwhile partner
63 Mountain: Prefix
65 Packages
67 Evolutionist's quest
73 Persiflage
74 Deteriorated
75 Street show
76 Armistice
77 Ms. Reno
78 Ship's company member
80 Debussian milieu
81 Mars
82 W.C. costar
83 Enthralled
84 Standings column: Abbr.
86 Stereo component
87 Delusion
89 Designer Ralph
92 Forgetful
98 Relax
99 Walks
100 Diving gear
101 Uniform
102 With fervor
103 Domingo, e.g.

DOWN

1 Waukegan winter time: Abbr.
2 Defiant cry
3 Salty assent
4 Natural
5 Space
6 Working class type
7 Statutes
8 Doctrine
9 Argot
10 Old TV series
11 Bash
12 Stat for Fielder
13 "__ Mode" (1994 film)
14 Playing fields of old
15 On one's toes
16 Kibitka
18 Rapture
21 Stand up
25 Call for help
27 Architectural fillet
28 Consider
29 Workers' investment program, for short
31 Estate expanse
32 Quetzal
33 Mimic
34 Mays
36 Those opposed
37 Held court
39 Fr. girlfriends
40 Judgment
42 Fiddlesticks!
43 Serving dish
45 Fla. town
46 Kefauver
47 Gloria __
50 Informal
52 Role for Clark
53 Depth-finder
54 Transistor forerunner
55 Gambol
57 Signoret of films
62 Progenitors
64 Troll, e.g.
66 Trick ending
68 Concorde
69 Kan. town
70 "__ la Douce"
71 Kind of tide
72 "King Lear" courtier
74 Rageful road?
77 Fix
78 Wagons
79 Paper unit
82 Mork's TV cohort
84 Benefit
85 Trade jargon
86 Det. Sipowitz
87 Repast
88 Essence
90 Actor Stephen
91 Intent
93 Sis's sibling
94 Coterie
95 Mayfly
96 Nigerian native
97 __ es Salaam

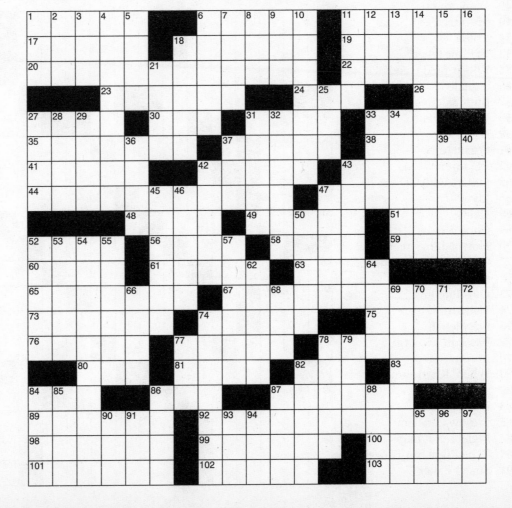

ACROSS

1 Branched
7 Discomfited
13 Prefix for phone
18 Toxophilite
19 Mendacious
20 Mountain nymph
21 An old coffeemaker never dies; it just __
23 Italian wine
24 Expletive
25 TV sitcom planet
26 Wits
27 Demonstrated
30 Greek letters
33 One of the Nixons
34 Singer Reed
35 Exorbitant
37 Iowa city
39 Snug
42 Bouncer's cry
43 An old garbage disposal never dies; it just __
46 Dupin's creator
47 Sierra Madre treasure
48 Govt. agents
49 Dam, for one
50 Sp. queen
51 Trivia
53 Fortune teller
54 Wheat-field weeds
56 Signaled
57 Butte relatives
58 Water buffalo
59 N.Y. river
61 Oscillate
62 PC adjunct
65 Letters with CD
66 Joyous
68 Dalai __
69 Choler
70 Horror-film street
71 Old power plants never die; they just __
73 Out-limb link
74 Fishgarth
76 Needlefish
77 Baseball's George
79 Minutia
80 Where Khartoum is
82 Ananias
83 Disoriented
85 Freshwater clam
87 Piglet's playmate
89 "The Right Stuff" org.
91 Singer Baker

92 Old astronauts never die; they just __
98 Coral isle
99 Folk singer
100 Candy brand
101 "La Grenouillere" painter
102 Hardy setting
103 Aural nostalgia

DOWN

1 Tease
2 Timetable abbr.
3 AT&T competitor
4 "Come, come"
5 Car models
6 Formerly, old-style
7 Word with status
8 Merkel of films
9 Value system
10 Sandarac tree
11 Pet
12 However
13 Koblenz river
14 Mocking
15 Old surgeons never die; they just __
16 Wild party
17 Verse collection
22 Cool cat's clothes
26 Actress Lucci
27 Sailboat
28 Paradisical beauty
29 Old salesmen never die; they just go __
31 Sunoco rival
32 Choose
33 Chrysoprase
36 Suit fabric
37 Blind __
38 St. __, Ohio
40 District
41 Votes in favor
44 Incident
45 Incandescent gas chemical
48 Bent
52 Games' companion
53 Dice rolls
55 Actress Todd
57 Corner joint
58 Medieval headwear
59 Concoct

60 Part
61 Heathen
62 Football coach Joe
63 Golfer Els
64 "Giant" ranch
67 Authorized
68 __ Flynn Boyle
72 Stat reduced by a '94 strike
75 Steal
78 Corn feature
81 Administered
82 Pillages
84 Recorded
85 Title of respect
86 Golden Rule word
87 Uncouth
88 "The Proud __" (1956 Western)
90 Hairstyle
92 Dustup
93 Singer Lemper
94 Strain
95 "As Long __ Have You"
96 Clamp shape
97 Dangerous curve

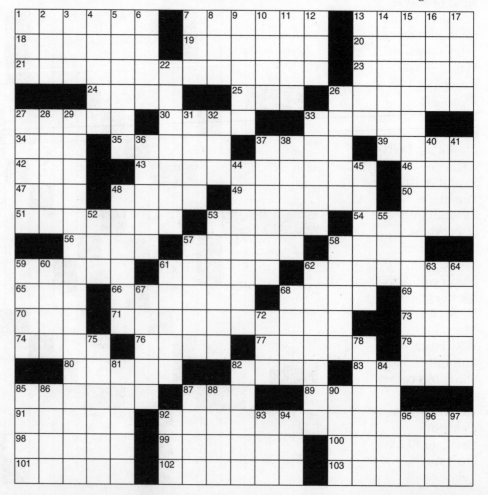

ACROSS

1 Optimal
5 Article
9 Hurried
13 "Candida" playwright
17 Macpherson
18 Costa __, Calif.
19 Strongbox
20 Ms. Montes
21 Related
22 Vaseline
25 Alter
27 USN inst.
28 Concert hall
29 Actor Von Stroheim
30 Kind of case or court
33 Sault __ Marie
34 Swarm through
36 "__ Mode" (1994 film)
37 Football coach Chuck
38 Minimal
39 Xerox
41 Little white lie
44 Ring feats
45 Trouble ending
46 Caress
47 Meadow
49 Rigging
52 Legal matter
53 Put into words
54 Fox of baseball fame
55 Particle
56 City on the Illinois
57 Cayuses
58 Jimmy
59 Jurist O'Connor
60 "Can __ Witness?"
61 Muck
62 Actor John
63 Weighty abbr.
66 Conjunction
67 Velcro
70 "__ Andronicus"
72 Music category
73 Finer points
74 Fade out
75 Shopper's stop, for short
78 Bested in the marketplace
80 Coupon word
81 Robert Ruark book
83 "__ had it!"
84 Generosity
87 Jell-o

91 "La __ de Varennes" (1982 film)
92 Monstrous
93 __ do-well
94 Concerning
95 Dispatched
96 Eglantine, e.g.
97 Retreat
98 Mythical river
99 Being

DOWN

1 Smile
2 Nev. town
3 Zipper
4 Periods in power
5 Collision
6 Shark feature
7 Renaissance family
8 Deface
9 Melange
10 Occupancies
11 Old French coin
12 Barrier
13 Travois
14 Links segments

15 Earmark
16 Fort __, Ind.
23 __ a time
24 Excellent, English-style
26 Enumerate
30 Arctic mass
31 Source
32 Peak
34 Variety
35 Modernist
36 Alas relative
39 Shaft
40 Unconcealed
41 Kleenex
42 Thought
43 Flower arrangement
45 Olympics gear
48 Inits. for NYC commuters
50 Touched down
51 Empties
52 Entertainer Clark
53 Flue
54 Order to abort
55 Implacable
56 Trim

57 Stud
58 Resort hangouts
59 Dines
61 Excess
62 Worker
64 Kramden's workplace
65 Library reminder
68 Word with what-have
69 Mah-Jongg pieces
70 Piquancy
71 Vehement
74 Keystone
75 Forecast
76 On __ (active)
77 Ponders
79 Clear
80 Support
82 Entertainer Martha
84 Imparted
85 Cause for contrition
86 Sermon ending
88 Tavern
89 Born
90 Family mbr.

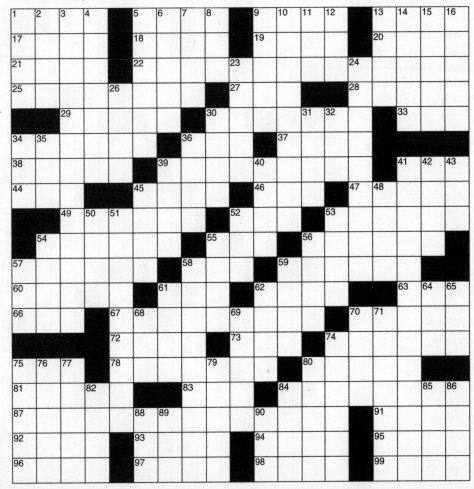

ACROSS

1 "Christmas Song" writer
6 Moosehead Lake's place
11 Cruelty
17 Oriental
18 Bighorn sheep
20 Singer Yearwood
21 Song in "Sun Valley Serenade"
24 Steatite
25 Word with free
26 Fantastic
27 Muddle
29 Apertural
31 Miserable
34 Comedy team
39 Bandung's isle
40 Football coach Tom
41 Red dye
42 Escaped
44 Excessive
45 Telecom need
46 Links org.
48 Agassi of tennis
49 Takeover
50 __ acid (glyceride)
52 Luxuriate
54 Gymnastic maneuver
55 Pew
58 Upper limit
61 Jet sound
62 Gardner et al.
63 Singer Stansfield
64 Alacrity
67 Thimblerig item
70 Ireland's __ Lingus
71 Trademarks
72 Core groups
74 Crystal form
76 Sage
77 Jason's ship
78 Song in "Mary Poppins"
81 King
82 Tom of song
83 Coxswain's cry
84 Jackass
85 Pt. of NFL
87 Hateful states
91 Using a remote control
97 Survive
98 Mollify
99 Gawks at
100 Office skill
101 Skinflint
102 Divagation

DOWN

1 Diplomacy
2 Worker-safety org.
3 Iranian coin
4 Compared
5 Differ ending
6 "Man of La __"
7 Buck follower
8 "__ You Babe"
9 Hayburner
10 High note
11 Warehousing
12 Swirling
13 "Stagger Lee" props
14 Suffix for boy or bear
15 Racetrack wager
16 Noted chairman
19 Bar implement
22 "__, as grave" ("Measure for Measure")
23 Football Hall-of-Famer Mel
28 Estate unit
29 Mil. training place
30 Galleon
31 Actor Alan
32 Across
33 Ford
34 Dimwit
35 Eastern capital
36 Finish
37 More recent
38 Architectural order
39 Scrap
43 Beat
45 Rotund
47 Doubleday
50 Shout of discovery
51 Guevara
53 Summer coolers, for short
55 Cipher
56 Overweening
57 Lacquer resin
58 Belvidere, for one
59 In unison
60 Thick mixture
61 Cipher
63 Romantic ballads
64 Keloid
65 Trim
66 Skittish
68 Postscripts
69 Napoleon's weapon
71 "Cowardly Lion" player
73 Keeping tabs
75 Hostile
76 Milan's La __
79 S.A. cape
80 Marsha Norman's "Night, __"
82 Entrenched
84 __ Brith
85 NBA team
86 Pine
88 Where heroes are made
89 "__ Three Lives"
90 African fox
91 Computer terminal, for short
92 Call for attention
93 Elec. unit
94 Singer Petty
95 __ polloi
96 Free from taboo

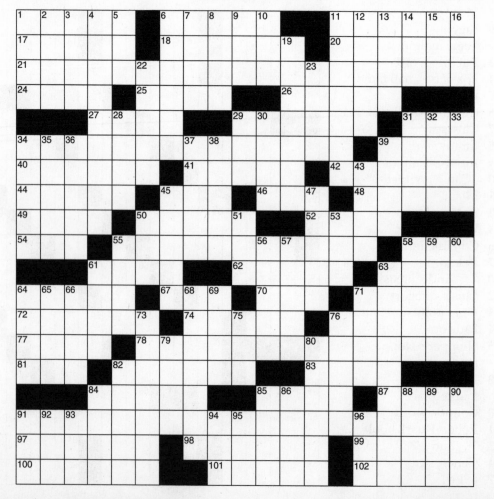

ACROSS

1 Unstinting
6 Double feature component
11 Renew
18 In reserve
19 Maine town
20 Lasted past
21 Henry James work
23 False starts
24 Self-centered sorts
25 Inc.'s British cousin
26 Mer outposts
27 Eeyore's adviser
30 Pyretic
31 Rancid
32 Word with day or way
33 Starbuck's skipper
35 Mil. landing spot
37 Decline
39 Fields et al.
42 Workaholic, e.g.
44 Reassuring word
46 Matter-of-fact
47 Alley __
48 Honest dealer
50 Puccini
52 Sternward
55 Midwest campus
56 Circle
57 Prefix for logical
58 Instruction
60 Outback canine
62 Times itself
64 Rural sight
65 Miniature
67 Yalta's locale
69 Naval E-3s
70 Architect
72 Without favoritism
74 Chem. ending
75 Japanese airline
76 Fortified
77 Taxpayer's worry
81 "You're __" (Buddy Holly hit)
82 Archipelago element
84 Profit follower
86 Wildcat
87 __ de tête
89 AMA mbrs.
90 Prefix for point or way
92 Decide
93 Rush
95 Seek
96 Practices thrift
100 Jumbled

102 "A Nightingale Sang __" (1940 song)
106 Discreet
107 Roman flower
108 Clothes horse's concern
109 Baseball's Howard et al.
110 Gawking
111 Expressionless

DOWN

1 Pull
2 "Swinging __ Star"
3 Contraction for Hamlet
4 Throb
5 Actress Taylor-Young
6 Thinker
7 Table scraps
8 Derisive sound
9 B&Bs
10 Back __ one (starting over)
11 Iowa city
12 Lamented
13 Summary abbr.
14 Romeo
15 Longtime TV show
16 Gardner
17 Celebrated loch
22 Top of the dial
25 Stripling
27 Morsel for Holy Bull
28 Child's query
29 Race unit
31 Combatant in 1900
32 Writer Seton
34 "Be there or __!"
36 Low-quality
37 Film of 1990
38 Inscribed
40 Lure
41 Parodies
43 Vipers
45 Ornamental case
49 Lauren and Jim of films
51 Inc.'s French cousin
52 Cloisters
53 ". . . I will __ evil . . ."
54 Daily diet
56 Evening bash
59 Business letter abbr.
61 Bleak

63 "Last night I __ dream"
66 Lophophores
68 Partied
71 Comet feature
72 Bleacher habitues
73 Settle
78 Pair
79 Demon
80 Make lace
83 Subsidiary
85 Investment concern
88 Concede
91 Showdowns
93 Primed
94 Organic compound
95 P __ papa
96 Dither
97 Ace of Base forerunners
98 Swerve
99 Zoning map
101 Command for DDE
102 "__ All Over Now"
103 Nigerian native
104 Craving
105 Head on

ACROSS

1 Land on the Adriatic
7 Beseech
13 Alexander the Great's consort
18 Behind, nautically
19 Kerry County seat
20 Broom __ of comics
21 "The Lone Ranger" query
24 Act
25 Sports site
26 Opera's Frederica von __
27 Hawk
29 Zetterling
31 Gibbet sights
35 Elvis Presley hit
40 Clan chief
41 Basse-Terre, e.g.
42 TV room
43 London gallery
44 Tipped off
46 Particle
48 Koran chapter
51 Frantic
52 Part of AM
53 Aphrodite's beloved
56 Bit of jazz
58 Family secret
64 Hold back
65 Mock
66 Thespian's quest
67 Joker
70 Take __ view of
72 Deliberated
73 Upshot
75 Long time
77 Teachers' org.
79 Soaker's place
81 Medieval weapons
82 What Cinderella's coach did
87 Tex-Mex item
88 Bounce
89 Artifice
90 Michelangelo work
92 Watering hole
95 Bar mbr.
98 Frankie Laine hit
104 Bone of contention
105 Wise man of myth
106 Singer Sheena
107 Hoops violation
108 Chekhov et al.
109 Lie

DOWN

1 Cry
2 Workplace org.
3 Pack
4 Different's companion
5 Writer Levin
6 Handle-equipped
7 Will __ wisp
8 Cereal material
9 Straw mat
10 Shade tree
11 Beaches
12 Use phenolphthalein
13 Put on __ (preen)
14 Bad guys' lair
15 Ref. work
16 Actress Lupino
17 Part of UCSD
22 Roman fontana
23 Colo. neighbor
27 Doghouses
28 __ fixe
30 Partnership word
32 "Kismet" setting
33 ¿Como __ usted?
34 Carpel contents
35 Blame
36 Writer Bret
37 Troy, to the Greeks
38 Brezhnev
39 Accustomed
40 Poem opener
45 Passé
47 Dressed to the __
49 Kitchen implement
50 Letters with CIO
54 Part of AD
55 Layers
57 Abandon
59 Greek letter
60 Dun
61 Sans __ (carefree)
62 TV's DeGeneres
63 Hanoi holidays
67 Elec. unit
68 __ caliente
69 Bud
71 Pogy
74 HRE rulers
76 Consumes eagerly
78 From __ Z
80 Marble worker's tool
83 Exclusive groups
84 Cervine creature
85 Portugal port
86 Summon up
91 Singer Turner
93 ". . . unto us __ is given"
94 Letter opener
95 Concerning
96 Ring verdicts
97 Actress Daly
98 USO clientele
99 FDR VP
100 Sugar
101 Approx.
102 Possess, to Burns
103 Sixth sense

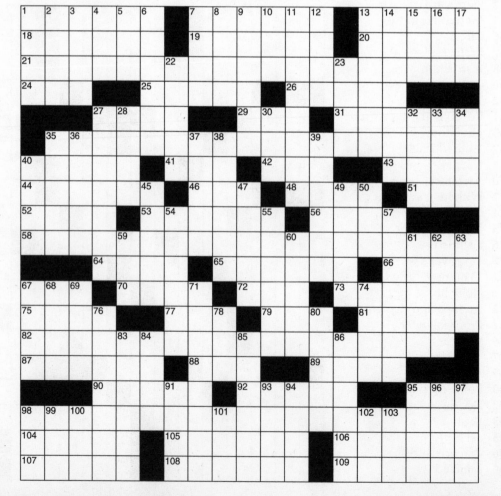

ACROSS

1 Student
6 Stanley Kowalski's cry
12 Invalidate
18 Rocket stage
19 Dillon portrayer of yore
20 Tristan's love
21 Got cold feet
23 State since 1864
24 Mag. publisher, to friends
25 Family transport
26 Pouch
28 "Diary of __ Housewife"
29 Gibbon
32 Sounded off
35 Rift
37 Harassment
40 Services
42 "I think, therefore __"
45 Threw a tantrum
46 Kind of license
48 OR item
50 Conciliatory
52 "The __ Wild" (1994 film)
54 Evidence
55 Central courts
58 Singer McEntire
59 Club payment
60 Spanish hero
63 Frolic
67 Traverse
68 Burden
70 "If __ You" (1928 song)
71 Scratches
73 Virile
75 Loved too well
77 Microscopic sight
81 Print-shop workers
83 Fix shoes
86 Cotton machine
87 Humdrum grade
88 Recluse
90 Repeating
92 Farm-machine name
94 Run down
96 Tokyo of old
97 Introduces
99 Bar order
101 Latin I verb
102 Hayburner
105 Baby's first footwear
107 Store up
113 Furthermore
114 Burrow
115 Atmospheric layer
116 Categories
117 Baleful types
118 Force for Fischer

DOWN

1 Larrigan
2 Cry of disgust
3 Architect I.M.
4 Kind of worm
5 Caspian Sea, e.g.
6 Remo or Rafael
7 Golfer Lee
8 Imperil
9 Sierra __
10 Shreveport campus initials
11 Doers: Suffix
12 Certainties
13 Enzyme
14 Sky lights
15 Refusing to talk
16 Norse epic
17 Example
22 __ effort
27 Masquerade
29 Hillside shelter
30 Carson predecessor
31 Perimeter
33 Dickens protagonist
34 Wheelman
36 Vipers
38 Actress Rowlands
39 Writer Sitwell
41 Kitchen appliance
43 Old French coin
44 Disordered
47 Harangues
49 Suffix for fact
51 __-Magnon man
53 Scram, in Stuttgart
56 Freesia, e.g.
57 On the beach
60 Like opera bouffe
61 Foolish
62 Lowered one's profile
64 Tennyson's "The Lotus __"
65 Free from taboo
66 Disney character
69 Haggard tale
72 Precisely
74 Heraldic borer
76 Brain chemical
78 Writer Wiesel
79 Turn
80 Jason's vessel
82 Reddish-brown horses
84 Peon
85 Derby-winning jockey, 1956
89 Marshal Michel
91 Sandberg of baseball
93 Oleate
95 Obsess
97 Like __ of bones
98 Measure
100 Parnu native
103 Drooping
104 Mideast strip
106 __ de France
108 As
109 "Treasure Island" monogram
110 That's impressive!
111 Actress Sheridan
112 Green light

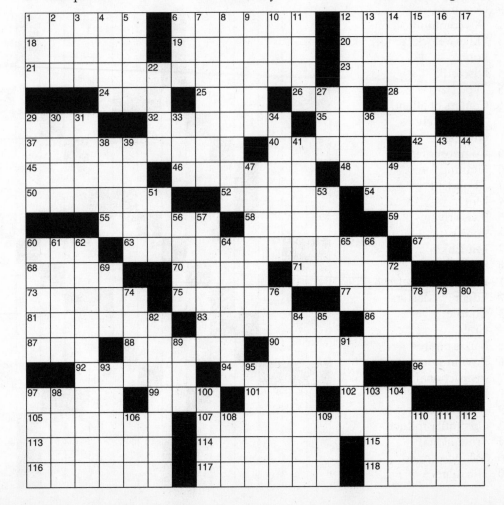

ACROSS

1 Nullify
7 Courtly getup
12 Holder
18 Ms. Earhart
19 Debonair
20 Encrypted
21 Peanut
22 Recurring film role
24 Controls
26 Prefix for China
27 Olympian Jesse
28 Dickens villain
30 "__ Were the Days"
33 Correspondence
35 Words with keep or look
36 Cry of approval
37 Admonish
38 Energy
41 Rose-rose link
42 NFL star
44 Senate complement
45 Upstart
46 Fr. beasts of burden
47 LIVE the wrong way
48 Bond's film debut
49 Occupied
51 '90s communications
53 "Like a Rock" singer Bob
54 Discordia
55 Type sizes
56 Centers of attention
57 "__ a Lonely Number"
59 Composer Harold
60 Fighting force
63 Abundant
64 Much
65 Swiss river
66 Poorly
67 Munchkin
68 Singer Dinah
71 Hot-weather refresher
72 Edgar __ Masters
73 Coddle
74 Grab
75 Barrie pirate
76 Protein source
77 Instructional
78 Removed
79 __ de la Renta
82 Gristmill product
84 Professional
86 "Maude" maid
90 Fluctuate

93 Entertainer Lola
94 Sweet clover
95 __ cloud (suspected)
96 Resilient
97 Whiff
98 Singer Freda et al.

DOWN

1 Hector
2 Ontario town
3 "Summer Days" painter
4 Even though
5 Co-branding deal
6 Bring home
7 __ recall . . .
8 Supervise
9 Federalist Papers writer
10 Sheeplike
11 Interpret
12 Street in Rome
13 Forbid
14 Glower
15 Loudness unit
16 "Exit to __" (1994 film)
17 Belt-tightening regimen
23 "__ a hero to his valet"
25 Screen star
28 Indistinct
29 Confused
31 Butcher-shop offerings
32 Ab __ (from the start)
34 Russian sea
36 Worker's delight
37 Ocean view
38 "Heart of Dixie" actress
39 Skye of films
40 Bog
42 Joplin of music
43 Austin native
48 Ten: Prefix
50 Toledo's lake
51 Squalor
52 Expert
53 Tabitha of TV
55 Verbose
56 Denmark islands

57 Baseball's Hershiser
58 Shade of green
59 Country music group
60 Passover staple
61 Bourtree
62 Nasty weather
64 Schedule word
65 Prefix for prop
69 Set off
70 Untried
73 Tedious
75 Quick
76 Wrap brand
77 Destruction
78 Coliseum
79 Switch positions
80 Insult
81 Ariz. neighbor
83 Aquarium group
85 "Your time __"
87 Life segment
88 Type of buoy
89 Fast flyer
91 Exist
92 Existed

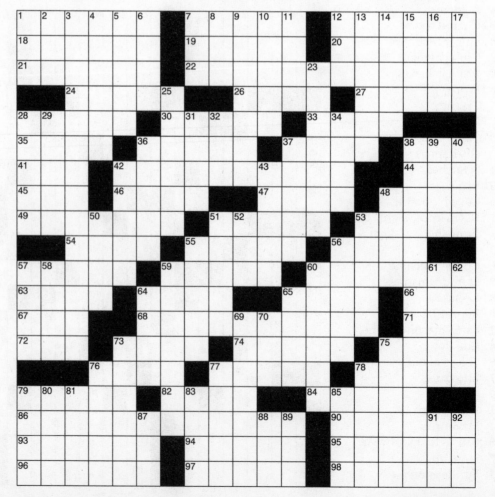

ACROSS

1 Turkey Day invitation, part I
5 Scruff
9 Bulk
13 Writer James
17 Des Moines's northern neighbor
18 Give off
19 Fit to __
20 Wheedle
21 Invitation, part II
25 Joins the party
26 Twine fiber
27 Pasta dish
28 Opponents
30 Op. __
31 Herring
32 Others, to Caesar
34 What a bond represents
36 Accept
37 Health club
40 Invitation, part III
44 Presently
45 Coadunate
46 Commit oneself
47 Allison of jazz
48 Craving
49 Psalm verb
50 Thrill
52 Portion
53 Sardonic
54 Tremble
55 Demijohn
56 Haunted house sound
59 Kama __
60 Reciprocating engine part
61 Brume
64 Vegetable choice
65 Mets' home
66 Smack
67 Film "elephant boy"
68 Invitation, part IV
73 In extremis message
74 Fr. airport
75 Befuddle
76 "ER" image
77 Merkel and O'Connor
78 Kid
79 Shoot
81 Modish
84 Understood
86 "__ of Honey"
90 Invitation, part V
93 Kate's TV cohort
94 Silkworm
95 Zaire river
96 Water's accompanist
97 "__ Daughter" (1970 film)
98 S'long
99 Far reaches
100 Strigine

DOWN

1 Little eatery
2 Portent
3 Brisket, e.g.
4 Ascetic
5 Informative
6 "All Alone __" (Brenda Lee hit)
7 Depressed state
8 Decent
9 Attacks
10 And so forth
11 Swamp
12 Dance pioneer
13 Longed
14 Objective
15 James __ Jones
16 Former spouses
22 Instruct
23 Employing
24 A Belafonte
29 Prejudice
31 Papyrus, for one
32 Top drawer
33 Educator Mary
35 Corrida cry
36 Nightclub
37 Drive away
38 Nuisance
39 Cruising
40 David's rival
41 Rowboat
42 City of Japan
43 Self-satisfied
49 Sacred chest
50 Ala. town
51 Household god
52 Iranian city
53 "Fuzzy Wuzzy __ bear . . ."
54 Ask
55 Taunt
56 Number-crunching force, for short
57 Clinton cabinet member
58 St. Louis bridge-builder
59 Cartoonist Silverstein et al.
60 Desire
61 __ morgana
62 Follow
63 Word with shot or shy
65 Dogies
66 Writer Octavio
67 Atlantic sea
69 Swiss dishes
70 Singer Piaf
71 Denizen
72 End of short freeway trips
77 Loosen, in a way
78 Entertainer O'Donnell
80 Fords
81 __ she blows
82 Count
83 Fitzgerald
84 Cooper of films
85 Ergo
87 Prove
88 Blue shade
89 Pick out
91 Part of www
92 Days of yore

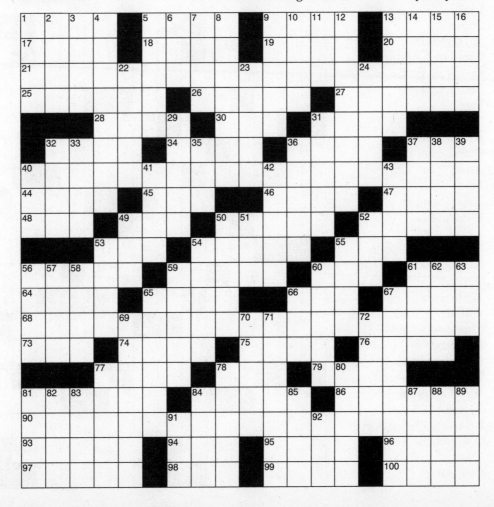

ACROSS

1 Last year's frosh
6 Listing
11 __ nova
16 Up __ (trapped)
17 Calif. peak
18 Quicken
19 Hardy tale of innocence?
22 Aurora
23 Campus VIP
24 Hindu nurses
25 Strain
26 Acapulco agreement
28 Seek
31 Ranked first
34 "The Hope" author
36 Devilish story by Dickens?
42 Books
44 ". . . __ porridge in a pot . . ."
45 Intertwine
46 Argot
47 Punching tool
49 Purpose
52 __ the hills
53 Join
54 Idol
56 Imbue
58 Sp. she-bears
59 James on a mutiny?
62 Outward: Prefix
65 Perimeter
66 Ingress
67 Maxim
70 Actress Christine
72 Damascus's land: Abbr.
73 Tease
74 Singer Lemper
75 Winter falls
77 "__ Like It"
81 Luxury box denizen
83 Hemingway on a radio switch?
87 Writer Rice
88 Wallop
89 Chortling sound
90 Unforced
92 Gambling initials
95 Chem. growth medium
97 Naval amphibs
99 Rested
102 Updike's allergy story?
108 O'Connor's "The Last __"
109 Cavorting
110 Where to see bulldogging
111 One of the Bergens
112 "What's the __ trying?"
113 Rarities

DOWN

1 Cloy
2 Holy Roman emperor
3 Under the gun
4 LBJ pet
5 Oozes
6 Travel agent's info
7 Computer hookup, for short
8 Nigerian native
9 __, bravo, charlie . . .
10 "She's __" (1962 song)
11 Crib
12 Sorrel
13 Little performance
14 Fiji capital
15 Ne plus ultra
17 Brace
18 Mortar's accompanist
20 17 Down plus one
21 Maui town
27 Victor over Adlai
29 "__ little teapot . . ."
30 Greek letters
32 Point-return link
33 Bolster
34 Sigh of relief
35 Fr. river
37 Plateaus
38 Enforcement power
39 Mississippi River engineer
40 Sports org.
41 Stack, in Suffolk
43 Elephant boy of films
48 Goods
50 Exigency
51 Propriety
55 Sluggish
56 James, Jude et al.
57 Malay boat
59 The carrying kind
60 Untamed
61 Therefore
62 "Born Free" lion
63 Leg part
64 Writer Astley
67 Street area, in song
68 Solar disk
69 "__ No Angels" (1989 film)
71 Article
76 Rod
78 Pigpen
79 "Irresistible __"
80 Faller in the fall
82 Existed
84 Imprint
85 Chemist Paul
86 Collections
91 Kind of physics
92 Will __ wisp
93 Lead-balloon sound
94 "Wozzeck" composer
96 Concordes
98 Influence
100 Perfect scorer
101 Ring rulings
103 401(k) relative
104 Roofing material
105 Uncover, in poems
106 Ziegfeld
107 Captured

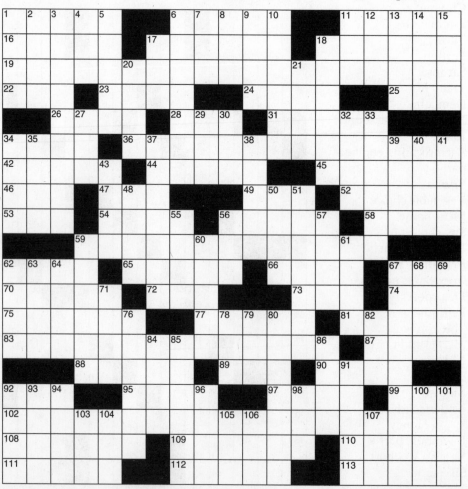

ACROSS

1 Boy
4 Melodrama sounds
8 Spellbound
12 Bumppo's transport
17 Actress Thurman
18 Presence
19 Beige
20 Thrown for __
21 Pork loin product
24 Elementary
25 Actress Morris
26 Avidity
27 Disarray
29 Sky altar
30 NYSE counterpart
31 Cheeky
32 Vulcan's realm
33 Radar image
34 Paris's love
36 Holy order?
39 Brunch's opposite
41 Fury
42 Day-care client
43 Sister of 40 Down
44 Twirled
47 Like most movies
51 Impulsive
52 Thymus and pancreas
54 Good times
56 Actor Tognazzi
57 Type of vb.
58 Don McLean hit, 1971
60 Director Howard
61 Melisma
62 Blue
63 Menace
64 Steinbeck figure
65 Easy shot
67 Fateful date
68 Licorice cousin
69 Rocker Ocasek
71 Actress Dawber
73 Dressers
74 Fast food staple
79 Forward
80 Meniscus
81 Israeli airline
82 Confederate
84 Greek letters
87 N.Y. neighbor
88 Word after get or that
89 District
90 Station
91 Bridle adjunct

93 Indecision in Antwerp?
96 Conform
97 L.A.'s La __ Tar Pits
98 No yacht she
99 Mirth
100 Gibbons of TV
101 North Sea feeder
102 Now's companion
103 Pro vote

DOWN

1 Roman poet
2 Iowa community
3 Coffee-cart offering
4 Actress Thompson
5 Yes from Yves
6 Audacious
7 More cogent
8 Veridical
9 Noun case: Abbr.
10 Covenant
11 Sound system components
12 City sights
13 In the manner of
14 Cash-register button
15 Underworld god
16 Breakout
22 Profoundly
23 Daffy
28 Religious group
31 Part of MPH
32 Evergreen
33 Gamma precursor
35 Actress Melissa
37 Lanai ringer
38 Morgan or garron
39 Consecutive
40 Stargazer's muse
44 Pung
45 Kind of value
46 Module
48 Old-time sweet
49 Fan of the Big I
50 Recipients
52 ABC day-starter
53 Chalcedony
54 Poison tree
55 Racer's stop
58 Jelly
59 Born
64 49 Down's love
66 Samovars
68 Shout of discovery
70 Masticate
71 Devotions
72 Be unwell
73 Hue's partner
74 __ Park, N.Y.
75 Play false
76 Whole
77 Out of shape
78 Delhi wear
79 Parboil
83 Minimum
85 Without __ (benighted)
86 "... like you've __ ghost!"
88 Out of port
89 Chinese isinglass
90 Foil
92 Pince __
94 Protected place
95 Misery

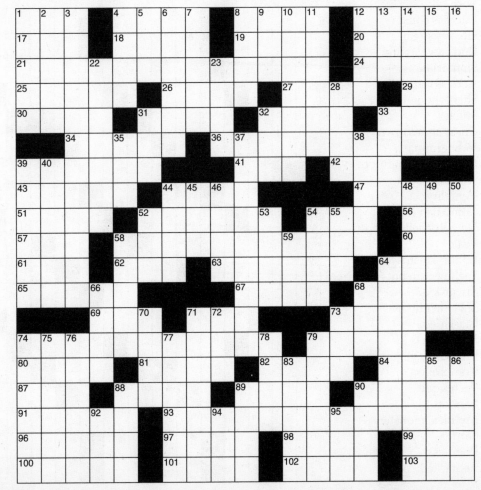

ACROSS

1 Hold in
5 Among others
9 Old town
13 Comedian Rudner
17 Motor sports org.
18 Macrame
19 Breach
20 Chem. endings
21 Normandy town
22 Offhand remarks
25 Jabber
26 M
27 Great Salt Desert site
28 Growing out
29 Minos's daughter
31 Brownie
32 Part of CSA
33 Reason
34 Gal of song
35 Part of Caesar's last line
37 Hosp. areas
38 Fitness spot
39 Unsightly sights
42 Chum
44 Painter Miro
45 Torn
46 Dactyl's cousin
50 Hockey great
51 Rude awakening
52 Stentorian
53 Actress Gabrielle
54 Sharpshooter
56 Stitch
57 Chess showdown
59 Indeterminate
60 Gervaise's daughter
62 Snowflake's st.
63 Veniality
64 Comedian Mort
65 New Rochelle campus
66 Peak
67 Editor's instruction
68 Feeling bad, but not discarded?
71 N.H. neighbor
72 Classifieds
75 Verdi work
76 Musical engagement
77 Commotion
80 Technique
82 Landon
83 Mythical monster
84 Girder
85 Pointless
87 Remarked
88 Yank
89 Feeling bad, and discarded?
92 Pasta dish
93 "The Defiant __" (1958 film)
94 __ Ben Adhem
95 Nerd
96 So be it
97 Queen of Sparta
98 Gingrich
99 Lamarr
100 Balzac's "__ Goriot"

DOWN

1 __ a bee
2 Gawking
3 Obfuscating
4 Writer Umberto
5 Singer John et al.
6 Carson City's lake
7 Height: Prefix
8 Tolstoy
9 Dock
10 Ft. Dodge's state
11 Tribal division
12 Passe-partout
13 Sp. queen
14 Congenital
15 Wobble
16 Judge
23 Writer Cather
24 Surcease
26 Footnote word
30 "__ sow, so shall ye reap"
31 Garner
32 At once, in medicine
34 Begone
35 Alas, to Aeneas
36 Submitted
39 Magnetic coil
40 Stem
41 Chirp
42 Part of M.O.
43 Hippodrome
44 Pride's pal
47 Unproductive effort
48 Bess's successor
49 London borough
51 Spout
52 Yarn measure
53 Trimming tool
55 Bodega relative
56 Breeze
58 Put the kibosh on
61 Handle
62 Take down __ (humble)
65 "__ It My Way"
66 Metaphorical words
67 Spindrift
69 Ruth's mother-in-law
70 Eyed
71 Pound sterling
72 Darkroom chemical
73 Fillet
74 __ prunes
77 Rambunctious
78 Distance racer
79 Transformer
81 Merchant guild
82 Klondike native
83 Rubber-necked
85 "Let __ Me"
86 Arab boat
87 Captain Hook cohort
90 A Bobbsey twin
91 How gross!
92 Fast-forward

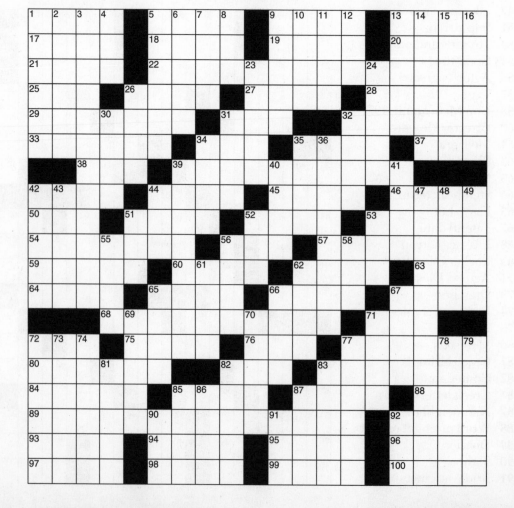

ACROSS

1 Lowlife
4 Go smoothly
8 "Republic" man
13 __ factor
17 "The Box Man" author
18 Where Waterloo is
19 Aye-aye
20 Humor
21 Righthanders
23 Hopi's home?
25 Russian range
26 Parsley unit
28 Defamation
29 Va. town
32 In other words
35 Unkempt
38 Indications
41 War god
43 L.A. judge
44 Exercise-class site
46 Old, old stories?
49 Big moment in W.W. II
50 Traverse the runway
52 Chunk of time
53 Approves
54 __ Park, N.Y.
55 Commences
57 Giraffe relative
59 Chris of baseball
61 Crayon material
63 Words on anthologies
65 Unexciting performance
69 Actress Hagen et al.
71 __ to arms
73 Words after do
74 Depict
77 Once-time connection
79 Alley __
81 Brunch offering
82 __ fixe
83 Brew fit for a king?
86 Word with day or you
87 Peas' place
88 Quondam
89 Still in the treasury
91 Duffer's problem
93 Merchandises
96 N.H. town
99 Perry Square's city
101 "Solstice" writer
104 Amusement park cry
105 Spousal input, of a sort
109 Letter opener
112 Unfortunately
113 Bight
114 Sample effort, for short
115 Actress Long
116 Chump
117 Dens
118 Santa __, Calif.
119 Become

DOWN

1 "MASH" corporal
2 Poplar
3 Issue in Austin
4 Spruce
5 Mauna __
6 Bookish birds
7 Vespid
8 Tartan
9 Berm
10 Latin I word
11 Dairy vessel
12 Metallurgical material
13 Permeate
14 "The __ of Town" (Johnny Rivers hit)
15 Turf
16 Tribute
22 Sourwood
24 Charity
27 Success story
30 Ceres
31 Acknowledge
33 Reynoso room
34 NBA long shots
36 Dateless
37 It has ups and downs
39 Card game
40 Eccentric sort
42 Discourse
44 Occlude
45 Madonna's "__ Don't Preach"
47 Timely
48 Dog breed
49 Nap
51 Harmonious
56 Appoint
58 Turkish city
60 Sound in the shearing shed
62 "The Glass Menagerie" character
64 Writer Wilson
66 After-dark phenomenon?
67 Acerbity
68 Upbeat
70 Barracudas
72 Journals
74 "Sugar __" (1964 hit)
75 Joss, e.g.
76 Pre-Renaissance
78 Double curve
80 Le Pew of cartoons
84 Salacity
85 "Oedipus __"
88 Luau accoutrements
90 Cargo on the info highway
92 Hogback
94 Abase
95 Persists
97 Fantastic
98 Deliberated again
100 Corrupt
102 Dust-devil
103 Perceived
105 Chaw
106 Labor org.
107 Words with word
108 Cantab's rival
110 Fr. soul
111 Actress Russell, to friends

ACROSS

1 Note-able group
7 Biblical landfall
13 Bow passage
18 Dancer Fonteyn
19 Not fixed
20 Poe house
21 Memorable Presley performance
23 Ivan Reitman film
24 Actress Olin
25 News execs
26 Washington, McKinley, etc.
28 Cigar end
29 League
31 Classic bad guy
34 Cabbage
36 Fare for Miss Muffet
39 Teachers' org.
41 Stuff
42 Ibiza or Elba
45 "Six Rms __ Vu"
46 Song from "The Lemon Drop Kid"
49 Medit. land
50 Schooner relative
52 New Haven team
53 Orestes's sister
55 Interstices
56 False conception
57 Basketball's Unseld
58 Mariner's cry
59 Slime
60 Tati's "__ Oncle"
61 Goglet
62 Cry's companion
63 Broad-sided structure
65 Ending for Faust or fust
66 Disavow
67 Xenophon work
70 In compliance
72 Coble or coracle
73 Actress Jackson
74 U.K. honor
75 Words after Rudolph
78 "Days Of __ Lives"
79 S.C. river
81 Ointment: Abbr.
82 Sine qua __
83 Newswoman Ifill
84 Symbol of sadness
85 Burgoo
87 San __
89 Site of 63 Across
91 Aurora
93 Blind ambition
95 "__ Mio" (Funicello hit)
98 Bumbling
100 "Twelve Days" gift
105 Sphere
106 Less biased
107 Critique
108 Mountain curves
109 Smirks
110 Schedules

DOWN

1 D.C. agency
2 Ruling
3 Valid
4 Instrument
5 Outspoken
6 Ordinal ending
7 Betwixt
8 Martini's vermouth partner
9 Bus. letter abbr.
10 Hoops target
11 Fashionable
12 Sounding
13 Sheal or shanty
14 Too
15 Like Saint Nick's beard
16 Dispatched
17 Gaelic
22 Insurgent
27 Mastery
30 Entity
32 "__ Love" (1957 film)
33 Chatters
35 African fox
36 Finish filming
37 Hawaiian city
38 December decor
40 Photographer Richard
43 Singer Laura
44 Cart
46 Indifferent
47 N.C. campus
48 Suspicious
51 Ostentatious flower
54 Reason
56 Personification
57 Perverse
61 Actress Stapleton
62 Conducted
63 Derisive sounds
64 '70s rock group
65 Reside
66 Sidestep
68 Together, in music
69 Tale
71 Virginia willow
72 Propensity
73 Hackman
76 Tchaikovsky, e.g.
77 Actress Louise
80 Synagogue
83 Leofric's wife
86 Riverboat transaction
88 Nightshade
89 Wind instrument
90 Black birds
92 Switch positions
94 Crags
96 "What's __ for me?"
97 Cyma recta
99 NFL highlights
101 Compete
102 Palindromic preposition
103 Clinic VIPs
104 Compass pts.

ACROSS

1 War god
5 NL monogram
8 "__ Dick"
12 Road sign
15 NL Manager of the Year, 1994
16 Flu symptoms
18 Ox of puzzledom
19 Monotonous path
20 Seasonal wish
23 Exist
24 "Put __ Happy Face"
25 __ eyed (angry)
26 Down source
27 Lose it
28 Elec. unit
29 Zero
30 Deviate
31 Old cape of note
32 Start of a Shakespearean observation
37 Proper
40 Mine finds
41 Baroque dance
42 Assume
43 Bandeau
44 '90s rock group
45 Genteel cheer
46 Hindu epic hero
47 Strain
50 Chem. endings
52 Shakespearean line, part II
56 Rock-band gear
57 Dickens's Drood et al.
58 Coward
61 Weave's companion
64 Dental office sounds
65 __ Marie Saint
66 Orleans's river
67 Fly
69 Kind of model
71 Hubbub
72 Shakespearean line, part III
76 Ripkin
77 Interrupts
78 PC hookup
79 Attenuate
82 Spell
84 Irritant
85 Erstwhile
86 Part of TNT
87 "Aladdin" prince
88 End of Shakespearean line
91 Minutia
92 Ever's companion
93 Salamanders
94 Lotion ingredient
95 Decks
96 Actress Diana
97 Onager
98 Certain evergreens

DOWN

1 Important
2 Exclusively
3 Sovereign
4 __ generis
5 Actor Maximilian
6 He, she, et al.
7 Actor Cariou
8 Call for help
9 Jack of hearts, e.g.
10 Hog
11 "Babi __"
12 Magnificence
13 Radiance
14 Gradine
16 Vestibular
17 Simmer
21 Dietetic, in a way
22 Techies' connectors
27 Planted
30 Freakish
31 Where Balaklava is
32 Car unveiled in '58
33 Sophia of films
34 Indemnity
35 Actor Stephen
36 Ordinal ending
37 Much
38 Harem chamber
39 Cavort
43 Ecstasy
44 Isabella, e.g.
47 Naught
48 Comb. of notes
49 "The Rise of Silas Lapham" writer
51 Church councils
53 Explosive
54 Dwelt
55 Besmirch
59 Historian's subject
60 Moon-landing vehicle
61 Noctule
62 Ab __ (from the start)
63 Home-baked fare
66 Simple shelter
68 __ on the back
69 Competition for loggers
70 Escape on foot
71 Fauna
73 Words after walking
74 On the rise
75 Excoriates
79 Pinched
80 Street sign
81 Colo. peak
82 Rivage
83 Hash
84 "__ vidi, vici"
85 Tale of a killer cat?
88 Sully
89 Wide expanse
90 Method

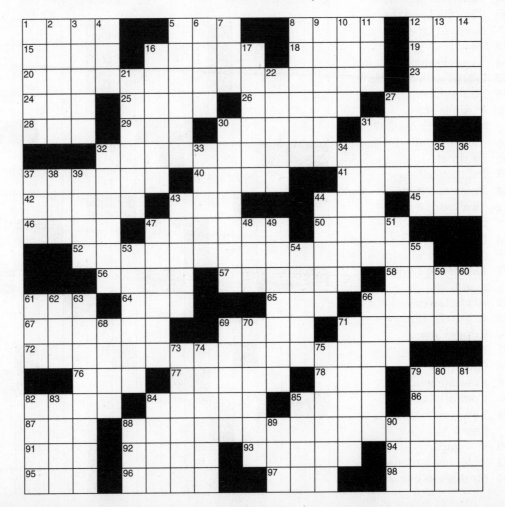

ACROSS

1 H.S. test
5 Dinghy
9 Singer Mitchell
13 Pale turquoise
17 Diatom
18 Humdinger
19 Cosmetics name
20 Haunches
21 Film of 1994
22 Metaphorical phrase
23 Las Vegas commodity
24 One of declarer's opponents
25 Shakespeare play, in matinee
29 Resort near Rome
30 Much
31 Bigwig
35 W.W. II area
37 Méditerranée, e.g.
38 Biblical verb
41 Camel's-hair fabric
42 1969 movie matinee?
47 Ryan of films
48 Pasternak heroine
49 "The Owl and the Pussycat" man
50 Tavern selection
51 Singer Frankie
53 Words with dot or line
56 Midi saison
58 Matinee of a Mercer-Arlen song?
65 Cash-machine, for short
66 Spiritual
67 Jeff Bagwell, e.g.
68 Yours and mine
71 "Rule, Britannia" composer
74 Saab rival
76 Nickname
77 Matinee of an old soap opera?
82 Act follower
83 Cry of the clumsy
84 Copper atoms
85 Kennel sound
86 Gradine
88 Pre-statehood rgn.
90 Comfortable place
94 Thrushes at matinee time?
100 P __ papa
103 __ for one's money
104 Steakhouse order
105 Marquee
106 Cracker type
107 "La Bohème" protagonist
108 Sufficient, to poets
109 Sea eagle
110 Daphnid
111 Free admission
112 Without
113 "The __ the limit"

DOWN

1 Prefix for mime or chrome
2 Vast amounts
3 Lace tag
4 Counted
5 Zoning map
6 Shot of adrenaline
7 Other things, to Antony
8 Auto part
9 One of the Jacksons
10 Galosh
11 Koestlerian dark time
12 __ way (absolutely not)
13 Theater
14 As
15 Sounds of uncertainty
16 Fitting
26 Uncomplaining sort
27 In a quandary
28 Aware of
32 Term of endearment
33 Surnay
34 Botany and Biscayne
36 Son-gun connection
37 Intended
39 Miscellany
40 Rocky debris
42 Farina
43 Klondike home: Var.
44 Disney film
45 N.Y. town
46 Songbirds
47 Auto-license ofc.
52 Common contract
54 Ganef
55 Mature pullet
57 Instruction
59 Insect stage
60 Exploits
61 Honest
62 Conductor Klemperer
63 Mideast gulf
64 Holiday drink
68 Cornelia __ Skinner
69 Here's trouble!
70 Descartes
72 Tie type
73 Elixirs
75 Anhydrous
78 Take off
79 Height: Prefix
80 Controversies
81 Anodynes
87 Mario of music
89 County Clare city
91 Office worker
92 Youngman
93 __ Park, Colo.
95 Pipe tool
96 Silkworm
97 Singer Mouskouri
98 Obdurate
99 Word
100 Yip relative
101 Part of RSVP
102 Mineral suffix

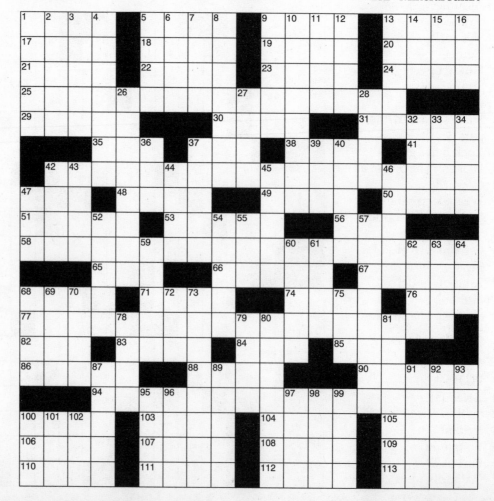

ACROSS

1 Spree
4 Actress Aulen et al.
8 Special
12 Boot adjuncts
17 Hockey great
18 Neithers' companions
19 Authority: Var.
20 Lusitania's end
21 Deteriorates
24 Resentment
25 Judiciously
26 Physic
27 Beatles' meter maid
28 Affray
29 Decree
30 Swindle
31 Cable TV network
34 Film of 1990
38 Beckett's "Waiting for __"
41 Like __ of bricks
42 Baraboo's st.
43 Purposes
44 Footnote word
45 QB Humphries
46 Kind of code
47 Writer Proulx
48 Actor Cariou
49 Inordinately
50 Dance step
51 Zadora
52 Keep dangerous company
60 __ Saud
61 Writer Klima
62 Form 1040 initials
63 Arikara
64 Kind of boat or train
67 Didion's "Play __ It Lays"
68 Horned beast
69 Engels collaborator
70 Skye on the screen
71 Medical corpsman
72 Invite
73 Vertiginous
74 Takes part in a Pamplona rite
79 Remick
80 Mouths
81 Leporide
82 International securities, for short
85 Delete
87 Eliot's "Adam __"
88 Veneers

90 Straighten up
92 Go racing
94 Had a bite
95 Sino-Tibetan tongue
96 Sweetsop
97 Singer Lemper
98 Fringe
99 Aleutian isle
100 Actor Richard
101 Yr. parts

DOWN

1 Lopes
2 "__ with a View"
3 Didapper
4 Plead
5 Like many mittens
6 Contrived
7 Library reminder
8 Edited, architecturally
9 West Indies rodent
10 A British Diana
11 Sinuous shape
12 Actress Ida
13 Slightly
14 French dish
15 Mer material
16 Sault __ Marie
22 Infrequently
23 Big name in power
27 Files
29 White cheese
30 High-tech building block
32 Road rig
33 African fox
35 Historian Bruce
36 Complication
37 Poipu porch
38 Creek
39 Concert halls
40 Disavow
45 Planted
46 Paula of TV
47 Afflicts
49 Shakespeare's Sir __ Belch
50 School grps.
51 Brazil neighbor
53 Unseemly hangouts
54 Necromancer
55 "As The World Turns" character
56 Brahman, for one

57 Mouthward
58 Unsuave sort
59 Lubricious
64 Fille, in Philadelphia
65 Debauchee
66 Expropriation
67 Smidgen
68 Taunt
69 Operated abusively
71 Gossip
72 Artiste's wear
73 Blood sugar
75 Battle "souvenirs"
76 State of __
77 "If I __" (1928 song)
78 Jeté performer
83 Hatred
84 Look after
86 Cyma reversa
87 Thicken
88 Party
89 Compass pts.
90 Humorist George
91 Cover
92 Links org.
93 Virago

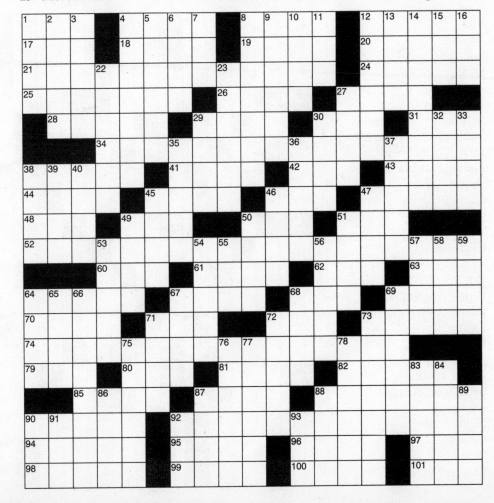

ACROSS

1 Flung
7 Italy neighbor
13 Turkish VIPs
18 "__ Lonely Number"
19 Correct an usher's error
20 Positive thinker of note
21 Sampler phrase
23 Extension
24 Actress Blythe
25 Pluralizing attachment
27 Nervous
28 Ida. neighbor
31 However
32 Fr. river
35 __ passu
37 Toledo's lake
39 Appetizer
41 __-Magnon man
42 Actress Pays
45 Soap plant
47 Cornwell's "All That __"
50 Value system
51 Pay lip service
53 Toughens
55 "Apologia Pro Vita __"
56 Closure
57 Point in favor
58 Dirk
59 Actor Vallone
62 Kind of tower
64 Bergmanesque figure
66 Summer time, for short
67 Like __ out of hell
69 Endings for play or pay
70 Singer Cocker
71 Gurney
73 Computer, e.g.
75 Take action
80 Clientele
81 Tam o' __
83 Couch
84 Writer Anya et al.
86 Euromoney abbr.
87 Entitle
89 Bay of Fundy phenomenon
90 Writer Whitney
91 Bryologist's study
93 Ambition
95 Night deposit
96 Garret
98 Zero
100 Past and future

103 "__ to Pieces" (Patsy Cline hit)
105 Repeatedly
111 Roast host
112 Presently
113 Caldera
114 Essentials
115 Misters in Matanzas
116 Power in films

DOWN

1 Washington Indian
2 Numero __
3 Rock group
4 Paltered
5 Disquisition
6 Came to light
7 Autonomous
8 Take back to court
9 Cinders
10 Modernist
11 Texas town
12 Saisons on the Seine
13 Wallaba
14 Produces
15 Companionably
16 Shake __ (hurry)
17 Risqué
22 Full
26 Health resort
28 Spruce
29 Bombeck
30 Contrabass
33 Burn
34 Psychologist Erikson
36 Compline word
38 The BPOE
40 Singer Roberta
43 Metes
44 Balance-sheet entry
46 Needle case
48 Numerous
49 Poet Teasdale
52 Vineyard __, Mass.
54 Cleft
57 Stole a glimpse
59 Branch
60 Lower
61 Kind of encounter
63 Stopes
64 Chump
65 Did a garden job
68 Garroted

70 God of doorways
72 Mock
74 "__ She Lovely?"
75 Baylor's town
76 Shirker
77 Eager
78 Take on cargo
79 Saw the truth
82 Demarcation in fashion
85 Sequel word
88 Cut in half
92 Newel's place
94 Festive
96 Mortgage
97 "All __"
99 "__ a far, far better thing . . ."
101 Salamanders
102 Principal
104 "__ Misérables"
106 Pope's "Essay on __"
107 Nigerian native
108 Skater Midori
109 Chess pieces
110 Before

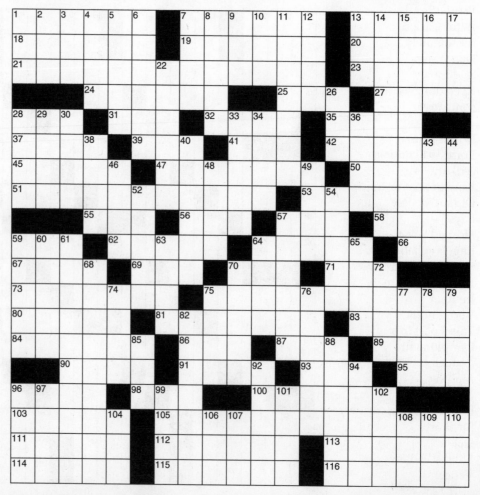

ACROSS

1 Chief Justice, 1921-30
5 Water arum
10 License plates
14 Byword
17 Peek follow-up
18 Nom de guerre
19 Sp. river
20 Gardner
21 Retreated
23 Sale disclaimer
24 Swamp
25 Bid's partner
26 Wrath
27 Like two peas in __
28 Bombast
29 Arikara
30 Sci-fi sighting
32 Relish
34 Construct
35 Lecturer
38 Kind of stove
40 Dog breed
42 Angelus ending
44 Bellow
45 TV's "__ Landing"
46 "__ been thinking"
47 Conceal
50 Pay-mind connection
51 At bay
53 Hawk
55 President pro __
57 Hatch fastener
58 Understaffed
60 Actress Charlotte
61 Dallas campus initials
62 Ivy League mbr.
63 Household case
64 __ Flynn Boyle
65 Nether
67 Threshold in time
68 Singer Bonnie
69 Cries of surprise
71 Pauley of TV
73 Considers
74 Off guard
78 Characteristic specimen
80 Site
81 Kent portrayer
83 Pac-10 mbr.
84 Power org.
87 Burden
88 Phone button
89 __ Aviv
91 Allude
93 Radiation measure
94 Contemptuous sounds
95 __ of the law
97 Porter
98 Dispirited
99 One of the Nevilles
100 Teen's bane
101 Actress Jaime __ Bauer
102 Armory setups
103 Winter falls
104 Title

DOWN

1 Genghis Khan, e.g.
2 Obloquy
3 Tool of deception?
4 Franchot of films
5 Heel
6 England
7 Ananias
8 Strings
9 Consult
10 Social vessel
11 Soaks up
12 Puzzle diagram
13 Call for help
14 Expedition
15 Redress
16 Kind of poster
22 Distills
27 Stratford's river
28 Missouri town
31 Chemin de __
33 Pongid
34 Grooved
36 Football great Graham
37 Taproom
39 Pasch
40 Downward path
41 Inter
43 Intersect
46 Golfer's choice
48 Solemn expression
49 Fireside
51 "The Kids Are Alright" rock group
52 Certain AL players
53 Jacks
54 "And When __" (1967 hit)
56 Supermarket sign
58 Parodies
59 Solar disk
64 Secular
66 Water lily
68 Antiphon
70 Untangle
71 Taunt
72 Pt. of speech
73 Existed
74 Kind of arrangement
75 Isolated
76 Perspicacity
77 Come-ons
79 Luxuriate
82 Hawke of Hollywood
85 Nemo's creator
86 Charged
88 Diva's big moment
90 Architect Saarinen
92 Gosh relative
94 UK broadcaster
95 Tantalum atoms
96 Cricket sides

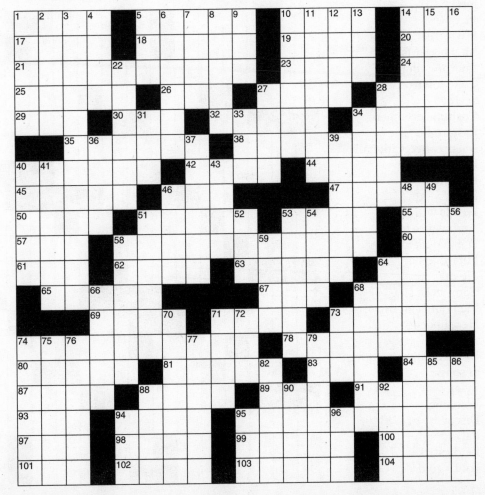

ACROSS

1 Used another's words
7 Stable newcomer
11 Comfortable
17 Helpless
18 God of Islam
20 Ohio town
21 Disneyland refrain
24 Kind of luck
25 "__ Dinka Doo"
26 AFC team
27 Basilica area
29 Chen and nene
30 Newts
34 Film of 1994
39 Pigpen
41 Design
42 Loos and Morris
43 Anapest, e.g.
44 Musical exercise
46 Pay
47 Toward the fantail
48 Midwest Indian
49 Larger-than-life
50 Opossums' hangouts
52 Mississippi River town
54 Pt. of CST
55 Royal Teens hit, 1958
57 Map high pts.
60 Interpretations
61 Calif. town
62 Seethe
63 Costume ornament
66 Pasture
67 Must, conversationally
68 Favorite place
69 Rocketed
71 Plain
72 Words with recall
73 Ambulance letters
76 Don Ho theme
78 Puts together
80 Tip off
82 Gannon U. site
83 Memnon's mom
85 Headliner
87 Act
90 Like a bathing costume of song
96 Relax
97 Weeping
98 Discovery of 1781
99 Pal of Pooh
100 Fiddlesticks!
101 Fool's gold

DOWN

1 Jest
2 Golden Rule word
3 Kiln
4 Not yet set: Abbr.
5 Golfer Ernie
6 Annihilations
7 Columbo portrayer
8 Stewpot
9 Gore and Green
10 Glowing
11 Misguided
12 Hamlet
13 Worn down
14 Murgenthal's river
15 Part of RSVP
16 Purpose
19 Playwright David
22 Freshly
23 Setback
27 Hellman's "Toys in the __"
28 Zoning map
29 Prefix for logical or thermal
31 Deity in the fields
32 Flow
33 Hook henchman
34 Household gods
35 Bumbling
36 Fainthearted
37 Suggestions
38 Anthem
40 Time of life
45 Word with faced or fisted
47 Schoenberg's "Moses und __"
48 Actor Brad
50 Attenuated
51 Calming comment
52 Cable TV staple
53 Zone
55 Rancor
56 Hunt of TV
57 "Psycho" setting
58 Cognomen
59 Does in
60 Daystar
62 Frozen dessert
63 "Misalliance" playwright
64 Simplicity
65 Sovereign
67 Vast wasteland
69 Got off course
70 Abyss
71 Let's go!
74 Pelagic
75 Notch
77 Frijole
79 Authority
81 Former formerly
84 Above, in Austria
85 Antitoxins
86 Experiment
87 Filmmaker Riefenstahl
88 Some kind of __
89 Writer Lois
90 France's __ d'Oleron
91 Étoile's turning point
92 Protein type
93 Road material
94 Sardonic
95 Corn unit

ACROSS

1 Midler and Davis
7 Subsequent
12 Something to bring home
17 Peter of films
18 Almaviva's valet
19 "Why Should __?"
20 Wouk protagonist
23 Soft hit
24 One of the Philippines
25 PC hookup
26 Introduce
27 Long time
29 Draw
32 Improvise
34 Demand
37 Indian title of respect
38 Disney character
42 Interrogate
44 Actress Rowlands
46 Put the kibosh on
47 Chou __
48 Writer Sinclair
50 Scurry
52 Excavate
54 Business letter abbr.
55 Half of ASAP
57 Portico
59 Word after work
   or walk
61 Refer to
62 Figure on a 32-cent stamp
66 Hockey's Robitaille
69 Swindled
70 Teheran coin
71 Let fly
75 Work-safety org.
77 Kennel command
79 Honcho
81 Journalist Pyle
82 Reconfigure
84 Pussycat's co-traveler
86 Running track
88 Pac-10 mbr.
89 "Heartbreak Ridge"
   actress
92 Diarist Anaïs
94 Twilight time
95 Hard work
96 Sonar contact
97 Bustling
99 Wonder
101 Pen point
103 Sp. river
105 Cadence
109 '40s radio personality
114 Tomato disease
115 Neville and Elkins
116 Take a dive
117 Palanquin
118 Exhausted
119 Recognized

DOWN

1 Ill-fated show
2 List-shortening abbr.
3 Corrida critter
4 Beethoven's "Ode __"
5 Weds on the run
6 Sunday msg.
7 Branch
8 Guinea pig relative
9 Pitch
10 West or east follower
11 Muddy
12 Celebrity
13 Summer coolers,
   for short
14 Launchers
15 Mouthward
16 Beavis, e.g.
18 Certain expenses
21 Patti Page hit, 1954
22 Church part
28 S.A. land
30 Roadhouse
31 Okla. town
33 Poet Van Duyn
34 Greenish blue
35 Dines
36 Packaged sets
38 Give-one's-all sort
39 Father of the Centaurs
40 Cloy
41 Ger. pronoun
43 Kind of lens
45 Former org. for Pele
49 Wyle of TV
51 Bracing
53 Mentor
56 Assns. of the '30s
   and '90s
58 Piranha's home
60 Style
63 Vernacular
64 Skater Johann __ Koss
65 Beige
66 Topsoil
67 Cabinet dept.
68 Like a CLU
72 Earlier
73 Provoke
74 Gielgud forerunner
76 Lhasa __
78 Poetic contraction
80 Liberate
83 With "The,"
   Hammett tale
85 SEC mbr.
87 Ignited
90 Other things, to
   Caesar
91 Titania's king
93 Agile
97 Liberal __
98 Play back
99 "My Cup Runneth
   Over" singer
100 Ford
102 Foundation garments
104 Predilection
106 Containers
107 Stringency
108 Pipe
110 Entertainer Sumac
111 Breach
112 Exist
113 Writer Snow et al.

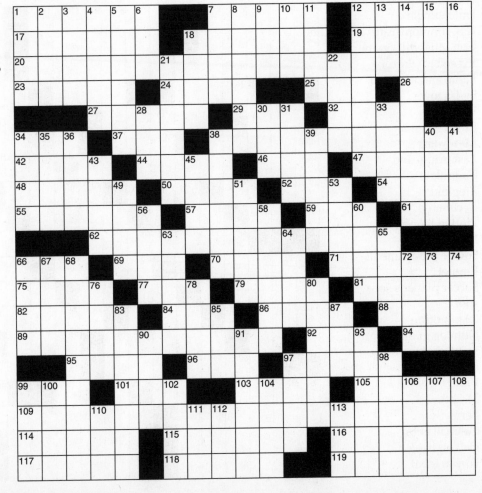

ACROSS

1 Noisy commotion
6 Skiing family
12 Aspects
18 Writer Calvino
19 Eschews
20 Traditional business wear
21 "Cinderella" prop
23 "Seinfeld" character
24 Roman bronze
25 Twilight time
26 Relieved
27 Gotcha!
30 W.W. II command post
33 Form, as a jury
35 Japanese-American
37 Heat qty.
38 Royal court
39 __ di-dah
42 "When I __ to Dream"
45 Kieslowski film
46 Sam's comics cohort
47 Freeway division
48 Merriment
49 Buffalo's county
51 Short time
52 Dutch uncle
53 U.S. conglomerate
54 Col. Mustard's game
55 Exceed in gluttony
56 Lanai and Molokai
59 Swiss town
62 Pelt
63 Protected side
64 Mind stats
67 Last bridge bid
68 Coagulate
69 Ziegfeld
70 __ caliente
71 Linden looper, e.g.
72 Part of TNT
73 Severe punishments
76 Emmet
77 Soccer player's sore spot
79 Commotion
80 Nom de guerre
81 Symbolizing
83 Shipworm
85 Vault
86 Mollify
88 Perfectly
90 Catchall abbr.
92 Deli offering
93 Forum ideal
99 Jointed at the foot
100 Poet Walter de __
101 Actress Edith
102 Medicinal drink
103 Ludicrous
104 Symbolic puzzle

DOWN

1 Important
2 Pt. of NATO
3 Moo counterpoint
4 "Lohengrin" role
5 Flips out
6 Prefix for practice
7 Bird, in combinations
8 Upbeat
9 Full-fledged
10 Paradisiacal
11 Former Soviet unit
12 Like some phone cards
13 Ark. town
14 "Behold __ Horse" (1964 film)
15 Common art work
16 Ger. article
17 Pyxidium contents
22 Concert hall reproach
26 Toot
27 Viewpoint
28 King of Tyre
29 All together
31 "She's __ Mover" ('65 hit)
32 Berkshire school
34 Writer Spark
36 Lamb's dam
40 First letter, phonetically
41 Baseball's Waite
43 __ minds (undecided)
44 Drops from a market
46 Deliberates
50 Urgent
51 N.T. book
53 Holm and Hendrie
54 Via Veneto salutation
55 "Just __ Those Things"
56 Muddle
57 Big 10 team
58 Enthusiastic about
59 Bean town?
60 Atop
61 Global confab
64 Fire, to Flavius
65 Shrill sound
66 Tart-tongued
68 Offense
69 Faithful pet
70 Afflict
72 Come in with __
74 Scene
75 More advanced
77 Flower part
78 Sacred beetle
82 City in 93 Down
84 Common Market initials
86 H.S. test
87 Lawyer Guinier
89 NASA vehicles
91 Spelunking spot
93 Ga. neighbor
94 Misjudge
95 Scratched
96 Arrest
97 Horned beast
98 Tee lead-in

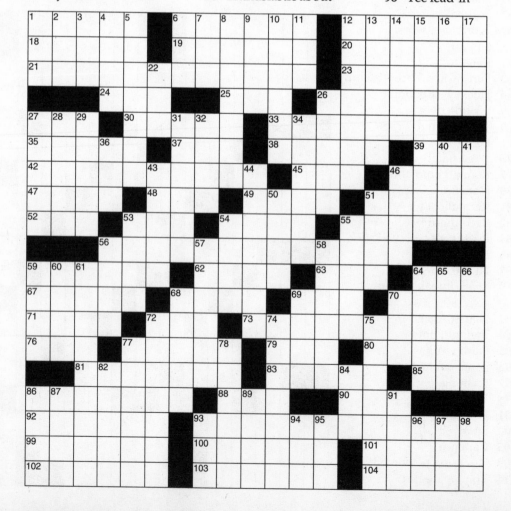

ACROSS

1 Cupboard
6 Rock sunfish
10 Copier problem
13 Ticket-taker's return
17 Heart adjunct
18 Take __ (accept accolades)
19 Actress Dolenz
20 Japan native
21 Procedural point
23 Artificial flavoring
25 Workers' investment program, for short
26 Chow down
27 Mauna __
29 Prophet ending
30 Filigree, e.g.
32 Peak
33 Most enthusiastic
36 Specify
39 Andy Warhol film
41 Goddess, to Calpurnia
42 Toothpaste type
45 How campaigners get dirty?
47 Author Amy
48 Composer Charles
50 Letters with CD
51 Frasier's brother
52 Gulp down
53 Southpaws
55 Opposition
56 Signal
57 Tomfoolery
58 Redolence
60 Even match
63 Serpent tail
64 Spinning-wheel sound
65 Battle refuge
66 Whitman's "__ of Myself"
68 __ the manger
69 Family member
70 Yangs' counterparts
71 Deposit
72 Not high-and-mighty
75 Seven-faced doctor of film
76 Essen exclamation
77 Little hooter
78 Washes
80 "__ of Navarone"
82 Rock group, for short
84 Delta rival
88 Smudges
89 Kingston campus initials

90 Purpose
92 PBS show
93 Jubilant
96 Caught by surprise
99 Clamp
100 Singer Shannon
101 Garrison of tennis
102 Vapid
103 Ballpark figures, for short
104 Town on the Ouse
105 Very, at Versailles
106 Irascible

DOWN

1 Incarcerated
2 Eohippus's descendant
3 Switch attachments
4 Imbecilic
5 Bronze
6 Theda the vamp
7 Border on
8 Phoebus
9 Dandy
10 Borneo neighbor
11 M.D.'s org.
12 Family transports
13 Melange
14 Farmed
15 Prefix for verse
16 Chignon
22 Bridgework of a sort
24 Patisserie application
28 Conjecture
31 Zircon, for one
32 Thoroughly
33 Fr. friends
34 Junior of the NFL
35 Sapidity
37 Bothers
38 Doctrine
40 Lace tag
42 __ monster
43 Smooth
44 Far out-distanced
46 Dante work
49 Rock musician
52 Plush
54 Baiul's milieu
56 Watergate prosecutor
58 Actress Hasso
59 Beast
60 Charles Sherwood Stratton

61 Arm bone
62 Cantina currency
64 Jorums
65 Bastion
66 Falling out
67 Pained expression?
68 Bear's delight
69 Barn sound
72 Uncertainty
73 Nigerian native
74 Female lobster
79 Unattached
81 Outbursts
83 "Tasso" composer
85 Caesar's wardrobe
86 Outcome
87 __ longlegs
89 Foul
90 Green Gables girl
91 Lupino and Kaminska
93 Cain's mother
94 Greek letters
95 "__ Blu Dipinto Di Blu"
97 Balloon filler
98 Dance org.

ACROSS

1 Cartogram
4 School grp.
7 Supple
12 Excellence
17 "All Alone __" (Brenda Lee hit)
18 Hold the title
19 Over
20 Coliseum
21 Choice of words
23 Favorite handiwork?
25 "My Way" songwriter
26 Kiln
28 Prefix for legal
29 Outfit
30 Use a keyboard
33 Boggy meadow
34 Big book
35 Bottle attachment
36 Sported
37 "Bonhomme Richard" skipper
38 Spritz
40 Off track
41 Glib
42 Mr. Roberts
44 Green
46 Be esurient
48 Drive
52 Bedazzles
53 Happen
54 Singer Lewis
56 "__ little teapot . . ."
57 Sound of time
58 Siding material
60 Poseur
61 Irritate
62 Advantage
63 Neat as __
64 Hundred: Prefix
65 Hershey competitor
67 Morrison and Tennille
69 Pool habitue
70 Neighbor follower
72 JFK predecessor
73 Dernier __
74 "48 __" (1982 film)
75 Arrangement
78 Discordia
80 Tropical drink
82 Keen
83 "___ Called Horse" ('70 film)
84 Named
87 USDA, e.g.
88 La Salle of "E.R."
89 Tennis great
90 To be, in Tours

91 When the chips are down
94 Agreement
97 Changdok Palace site
98 Sierra __
99 Pitcher, on baseball scorecards
100 Bravo, for one
101 Tamarind and tung
102 Gremlins
103 Grackle
104 Gender

DOWN

1 __ the world (irascible)
2 Kind of acid
3 Working vehicles
4 Taro dish
5 Catcher, on baseball scorecards
6 In a huff
7 Failure
8 "__ the point"
9 Make lace
10 More au courant
11 Furious
12 __ squinado (spider crab)
13 Before
14 Figure
15 Sooner or later
16 Focus-group subjects
22 Nogales nosh
24 Mouths
27 Credit terms abbr.
31 Camel count
32 Accurate
33 Franchise
34 Lunch-counter order
36 Radio groups
37 Court TV sight
38 Hot off the wire
39 Whole
41 Majesty
43 Newspaper page
45 Artistic medium
46 Part of PCH or ACC
47 Consort of Alexander the Great
49 Substitutes
50 Melodramatic sort
51 Drudgery
53 Actor Gulager
55 Samovar

58 Singer Laine
59 Mayberry character
60 Rigid
62 Dunk
64 Limbe's land
66 Fall follower
68 Gladsheim dweller
69 Oomph
71 Choreographer Agnes
73 Where Sandwich is
75 Cruel sort
76 Tying tally
77 Pussyfoot
79 A Welch
80 Dashboard letters
81 Chem. endings
83 Circle part
84 Grate buildup
85 "Sesame Street" character
86 Poison-control process, for short
88 Aquarium group
89 Teen's lament
92 Cry's companion
93 Mazel __
95 Words with roll
96 Unprecedented

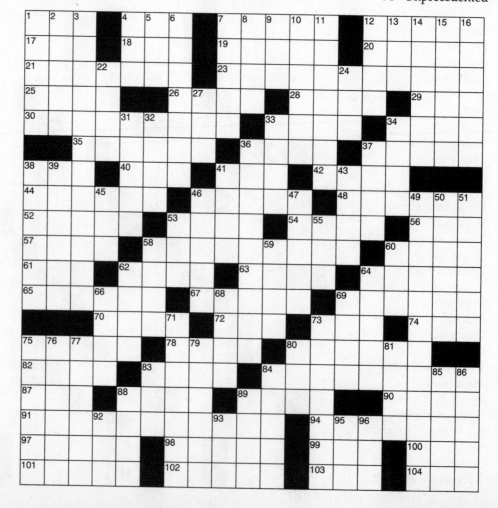

ACROSS

1 Mecca pilgrim
6 Brood
9 Runyon female
13 Shade of blue
17 Peter Shaffer play
18 Newsroom stain
19 Rapier
20 Out of the wind
21 Narrations
25 Polymath
26 Miscellany
27 Poetic time
28 Lordly appellation
29 Cutting
31 Vitiate
32 Use a divining rod
36 Wanigan
39 Bob Dylan song
44 State of Brazil
46 Family member
47 One of the Spellings
48 "Peter Pan" pirate
49 Harem rooms
50 Hoops violation
52 Object
54 Word with pig or play
55 Succeed
57 What Simon does
59 Word with free
61 Cover up's opposite
67 Johnny of films
68 Performs
69 Executor's concern
70 Like a Marvell mistress
73 Flip
75 Medicinal portions
77 Throb
78 Ellipsoid
80 __-do-well
82 Harry's successor
83 Extort
84 Representative of all
88 Insipid
89 Fight site
90 Chagrin
91 Machine parts
93 Variables
95 Kind of code
96 Cry of delight
97 Other
101 Psychological complaint
107 Bring home
108 Water buffalo
109 Amphora
110 Result
111 Sharpen
112 Recaller's word
113 Turf accountant's deal
114 Conduct

DOWN

1 Matched-set half
2 Water color
3 Analytical psychologist
4 Times for dads and grads
5 "__ in Love?" (1932 song)
6 Guide
7 S.A. native
8 Ring verdict
9 Gig
10 Accessible
11 Dawson of football
12 Suggestion starter
13 Strait
14 Fatima's husband
15 Neckline shape
16 Go-ahead
22 Catch
23 Connote
24 Staff member
30 Magic, Heat, etc.
31 Wrote an incorrect check
33 Spineless one
34 Dagger
35 Paradise
36 Nuclear device
37 Navigation aid
38 Uniform color
40 Actress Dianne
41 S.F. hill
42 Syndicate
43 Enlistments
45 "Here am __ me" (Isaiah)
50 __ dime (halt abruptly)
51 Church council
53 Hallux and minimus
56 "There is where __ off . . ."
58 Jejune
60 All-out
62 Distressed
63 Japanese city
64 Led
65 Old anesthetic
66 Hurting
70 Windup
71 Prefix for run or ride
72 Locksmith Linus
74 Consult
76 Retailer
79 Gentle
81 N.J. river
83 Implore
85 Rough treatment
86 Amazon people
87 Continue
92 Rouen's river
94 Thick slice
95 Writer Grey
96 Bugbear
98 __ majesty
99 Kind of poker
100 Peepers
101 Infrequent
102 Bowl cry
103 Before
104 Calif. neighbor
105 Gist
106 Scratched

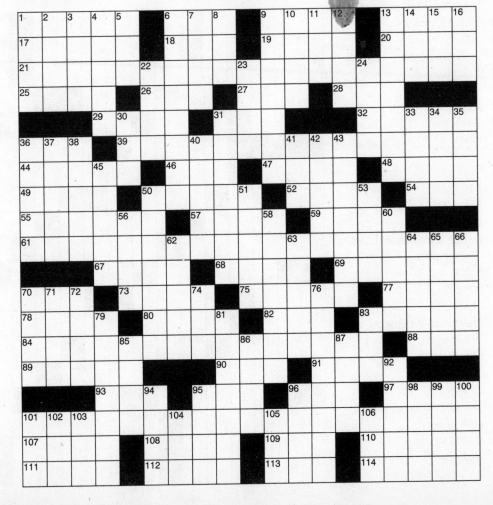

ACROSS

1 Word of mouth
6 Show off
12 Rankle
18 Active ingredient
19 Porthos's pal
20 Machine tools
21 U.S. skier
23 Get one's bearings
24 Pulsating
25 Title of respect
26 Sub's place
27 Motor oil letters
28 Arikara
30 Cranny
33 Playlets
36 Bombeck
38 Seal up
40 Depth-charge launcher
41 Nominal value
44 With "The," 1981 movie
47 Cable TV initials
48 Border on
50 Nests
51 Prefix for communications
52 Entanglement
53 Activists
55 Actress Lotte
58 Party dip
60 Lots
62 Replace the weaponry
64 Bye-bye
67 Harvest goddess
69 Force
71 Subdues
72 Moccasin
74 Stock table abbr.
76 Promontory
78 Labor leader Kirkland
79 "Lorenzo's __" (1993 film)
80 Sobriquet for Namath
84 Doze
85 Historian's subjects
87 Where ghi is spread
88 Davenport
89 Decile
91 Dissever
93 Hornbook threesome
94 Deface
97 Came up
99 Old-time Tokyo
101 Lancelot's lover

103 Comfortable
105 "Cheers" player
108 Stir
109 Coves
110 Sphygmometer measure
111 Candid
112 Polk's' successor
113 Actor Jimmy

DOWN

1 Half a '60s pop group
2 Singer Baker
3 Nouveau __
4 Khayyám
5 Roustabout
6 Faux __
7 Letters' companions
8 Word with to go
9 "West Side Story" song
10 Matrix
11 Approx.
12 Polar mass
13 Gets the money
14 Mucilaginous
15 Alfred Noyes poem
16 Twilight time

17 Q-U connection
22 Fairy king
26 Contravenes
29 '90s communiques
31 Traffic component
32 Impair
34 Subway
35 High-hat
37 Milk snake
39 Tropical trees
41 Football wear
42 Peek follower
43 "Golden Girls" actress
45 Sommelier's offering
46 Subleased
49 Legitimate
54 Cancel
56 China's Sun __-sen
57 Betel-nut tree
59 Aquarium attraction
61 Painter Rousseau
63 "__ Boy Child" (Christmas song)
65 Prefix for 45 Down
66 Preowned

68 Candle bracket
70 Large-scale
72 Ransom or Rimbaud
73 Leeds's river
75 "If I __ Million Dollars" (1934 song)
77 Get released
81 Hdg.
82 Iowa town
83 Old hat features
86 Pitch or putt
90 Realtor's listings
92 '50s new product
94 Prefix for meter
95 "__ of robins . . ."
96 Calif. point
98 Dispatched
100 Conductor Klemperer
102 Astringent
103 Satisfied sound
104 Deuce
105 Little fox
106 Pig-poke link
107 Sub. of Wouk's "The Hope"

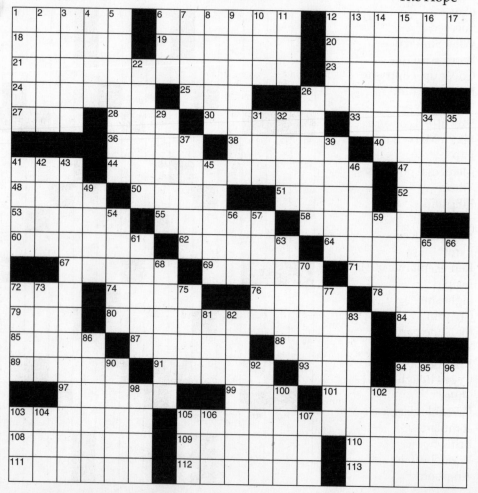

ACROSS

1 Blasé
6 Ready to strike
12 Expedite
18 Existent
19 "__, a leaf, a door" (Wolfe)
20 Wish
21 Summary
22 Duo of song
24 Get the picture
25 __ Dawn Chong
27 Thug
28 Musical symbol
29 Like most academics
32 Glom on to
35 Egoist's listening post?
39 Bestiary
40 Young lion
43 Comedian's muse
44 Worker's delight
46 Ruined
48 "I can't __ lie"
49 Chess pieces
50 Atlas high pts.
52 Macabre
53 Stun
54 "Wind in The Willows" figure
56 Jeopardy
58 Formicary group
59 Excited big-time
62 Lhasa __
65 Dowitcher
66 African fox
67 Actor Tognazzi
70 Trenchant
72 Word processor keys
73 Place for a plane
74 Part of USNA
76 Malodorous
78 Movie ad phrase
80 Wait upon
81 Needle part
82 Caboose, for one
84 Narcissist's fascination
86 Range
88 Informal wear
89 __ buco
92 Escritoire
94 Cable TV initials
95 Health club
98 Lou Christie hit of the '60s
103 Superficial
105 El Greco's town
106 Type of bowling
107 Merge
108 Actress Merle
109 Calculator function
110 Trims

DOWN

1 Cannery row?
2 Sheltered
3 Casino rollers
4 Mrs. Jerome Kern
5 Write down
6 Cry after "lights"
7 Sugar
8 Señor ending
9 Jockey Johnny
10 Inward: Prefix
11 Audition tapes, for short
12 Owns
13 Shade of blond
14 Lean
15 Mariner's concern
16 Cupid
17 Gingrich
23 Santa __, Calif.
26 Turkish VIP
29 Runyonesque character
30 Countersinking
31 Sable
33 Gambling chit
34 Type of defense
35 Singer James
36 Masticate
37 "The Man without a Country" writer
38 Paunch
40 Mawkish material
41 Partnership part
42 Honey bunch
45 '70s pranksters
47 Unheeding
49 Its motto is "dirigo"
51 Milquetoast
55 CIA forerunner
56 "Morella" author
57 Bandleader Baxter
59 Pear type
60 Derby town
61 Vegetarian dish
62 Farm unit
63 Observe complin
64 Trig function
67 Eye part
68 Mob
69 Word for a shoppe
71 Type size
73 Blood factors
75 '90s cash boxes
77 Barrier
79 Words with tired
80 Bedouin, e.g.
83 Low in savior faire
85 Excursion
86 Errand runner
87 Integument
89 Bismarck
90 Deckhand's implement
91 Flatfish
93 Drop off
95 Fuss
96 Sampras or Seeger
97 Mars
99 Fuss
100 Hoodwink
101 Blacksburg campus initials
102 Ger. article
104 Actress O'Connor

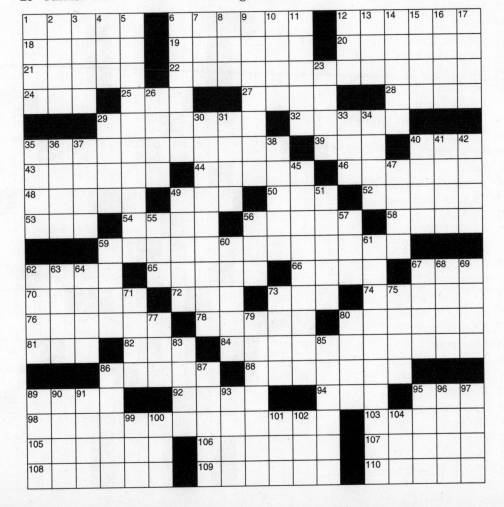

ACROSS

1 RR depot
4 Pen
8 Lump
12 Resign
16 Caparison
18 Child's prop
19 Dynamic lead-in
20 Biblical preposition
21 Select
22 Road sign
23 "Whiffenpoof Song" refrain
25 Where Sophocles shopped?
27 Phoned
29 Dentist's suggestion
30 Dining's companion
32 Self
33 Spumanti town
36 Percipience
37 Taboos
39 Picas
41 Desert region
42 Pigpen
43 In the sack
45 Cries of amazement
49 Soc. studies course
50 Pointless
51 Dutch uncle
52 Tropical fish
56 Dover sight
58 No-frills
62 Consequently
63 "Invisible Man" author
65 Felicitous
66 Ilie of tennis
68 Ledge
69 Antony's word for Brutus
72 Oklahoma player
73 Appears
75 Type of work?
76 Osculate
78 Energy unit
79 Colorado River town
83 RLS alter ego
84 Prefix for amble
87 Kind of steer
88 Ms. Sumac
89 Entertainer Iglesias
91 Dino's nickname?
92 Benefits
94 Info-highway vehicles
96 Honor
99 Upper air
101 Desirable
104 "Sao Bernardo" writer

105 European region
108 __ in a poke
110 NFL team
111 Rural structure
112 Frost's "A __ of Flowers"
113 Annoy
114 "__ Daba Doo!"
115 Chem. endings
116 Atop
117 Old school
118 English hawthorn

DOWN

1 Hat material
2 Prefix for comic
3 "Warm Your Heart" singer
4 TV's Courteney
5 Keen
6 Actress Francis
7 Occupies
8 Proverbial innocent
9 "You can __ horse . . ."
10 Mouths
11 Singer Seger
12 Grade A, e.g.

13 Straightens up
14 Take-comes connection
15 Comfortably warm
17 Spell
24 Put up __ (resist)
26 Pigeon Cove's cape
28 Calif. point
31 Todman's game-show partner
34 Deckhand
35 Musical syllable
38 Helios
40 Contemptuous sounds
43 Entrée
44 Holiday of song
46 "__ a Rebel"
47 Speckle
48 Fray
50 Uncertainties
53 Bump in the road
54 Fix the lawn
55 Strike __ (get a response)
57 Diaphanous
59 Trifling
60 Imitate
61 Certain golf matches

64 Anonymous
67 Distress call
70 Arthur of TV
71 Pugilistic triumph
74 City neighbor
77 DL qualifier
80 Greek letters
81 Mischievous sorts
82 One of the Taylors
83 Poitiers saint
84 Agence France __
85 Keep
86 McMillan's "Waiting to __"
90 Gibbon
93 Prompt
95 Print color
97 Skier Alberto
98 Disquisition
100 Piccadilly Circus statue
102 Reciprocal of "divided by"
103 Pickle flavoring
106 From __ Z
107 Early Elvis label
109 Word with whiz

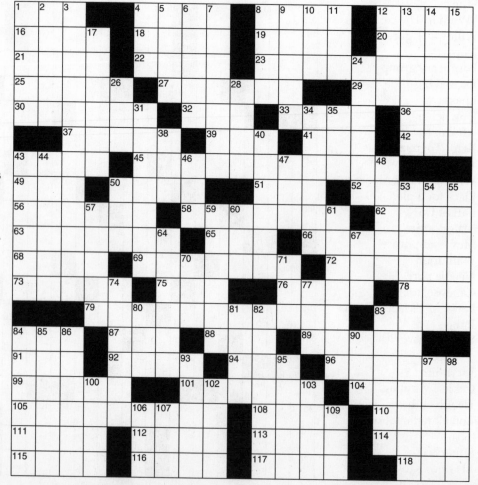

ACROSS

1 Actress Kedrova
5 Hey, you!
9 Mike of football
14 __-la-la
17 Latin lesson word
18 Scipio's state
19 Glacial ridge
20 Haw's companion
21 "An Officer and a Gentlemen" theme
24 The Big I
25 Rock group
26 Shakers founder
27 __ the hills
28 Taxing time
30 "Let's Make __"
32 Son of Priam
34 Storied Plaza dweller
35 Faculties
37 Marsh
38 Kind of price
40 "Stuck __ with You" (1973 hit)
43 Begone
46 Playwright Shepard
49 Detroit org.
50 Mrs. Gorbachev
52 Wine cask
53 No stoic
56 Soda fountain sound
58 Time for Antonioni
60 Space routes
61 Severe
62 Dassin film, 1955
63 Ranch rope
64 Piquant
65 Architectural column
66 Diminish
67 Colossus
69 Alley __
70 Epoch
71 Lifetime
73 Lead singer's spot
78 Abases
80 Visceral
81 Field event
85 Corporal punishment
87 Actress Moorhead
89 Climb
90 Allude
91 Beelzebub
93 Sum, translated
95 Taro dish
96 Dine
97 ELO hit, 1979

101 Capt.'s superior
102 __ Gay
103 Verne skipper
104 __ up (boost)
105 Reddle or rhoadamin
106 Ledger entry
107 Tibetan gazelles
108 Masses

DOWN

1 Dern and Wilder
2 Hinder
3 Earp and Dillon
4 Bat material
5 Straight
6 Sheer
7 Understood
8 Proposition
9 Exploits
10 Madonna's "La __ Bonita"
11 Fight finishes
12 Understanding
13 Big-horned sheep
14 Nighttime, to Ray Charles
15 Daytime TV mainstay
16 Soap plant
22 TV's DeGeneres
23 Little pancake
29 Soprano Lily
31 Words with recall
33 "__ Good Men"
34 With "out," supplements
36 Remainders
38 "... __ and stormy night"
39 Shrug off
41 Alfalfa product
42 London lane
44 Seeking
45 Words with million
46 Hit the mark
47 Over, in Cordoba
48 Early Elvis lament
51 Indigo source
54 Modicum
55 Rat tail
56 Tour of duty
57 Sticky stuff
59 Son-gun connection
61 Bridges
62 Install fresh cushioning
64 Ending for prank or pun
65 Infant
68 Tea choice
69 Bone: Prefix
72 Grievous
74 Actress Samantha
75 In operation
76 Greedy order
77 That: Sp.
79 Expressed
82 Rounded roof
83 Voluntary
84 Smarts
85 Footstep
86 Intoxicating
87 Hitting
88 Greek letter
91 Parvenu
92 Gudrun's husband
94 O.T. book
98 Three Dog Night hit
99 Prefix for plastic or plasmic
100 Grackle

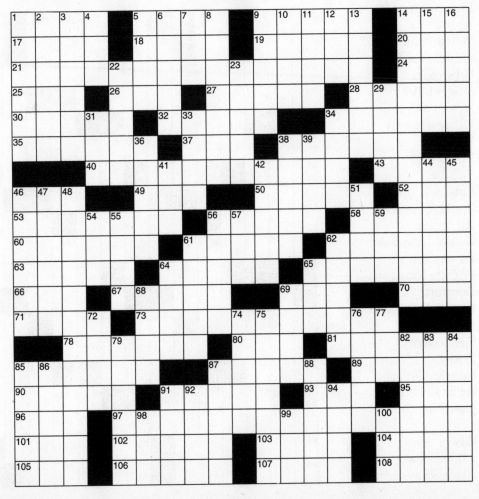

ACROSS

1 Jousting arena
6 Prayerful one
11 Leather worker
17 __ nous
18 Antisocial state
19 Useless
20 Start of an April limerick
23 Bad reviews
24 French heads
25 Vampire
26 Cape Cod town
28 Hold on!
30 Shirt style
33 Limerick, line II
40 Salamander
41 Sugar
42 Throng
43 Pinnacle
44 Porthos's pal
46 Fleet
47 Clever
48 Watered-down
49 Pa. town
51 Demonic
53 Limerick, line III
60 Approvals
61 "Give __ more try"
62 Obsidian source
63 Unspoken
66 Singer Elliott
67 Actor Paul
68 Hidden supply
69 Kind of force
71 Youth org.
73 Tribute
74 Limerick, line IV
78 Prefix for practice
79 Advocate
80 Gambia gamboler
81 Pirates' cries
84 Wichita team
86 Comfort
90 Limerick, last line
95 __ customer
96 S.A. rodent
97 Pricey
98 Intoxicates
99 Actor Robert
100 Irascible

DOWN

1 Athletic feat
2 Actress Swenson
3 Bewilder
4 Assignations
5 Baste
6 __ many (excess)
7 N.Y.'s Copper City
8 "My Cup Runneth Over" singer Ed
9 Minor matter
10 Perfect score
11 Nightshade family member
12 Up and __
13 Nests
14 Don't worry
15 That: Sp.
16 Actor Harrison
18 Reluctant
21 Ornamental cases
22 Writer Walker
27 Greek letters
28 Lean
29 Plus
31 White House room
32 Tel. abbr.
33 Calif. valley
34 Life-party link
35 Belief system
36 Beluga, for one
37 Apprenticeship
38 Year in DDE's presidency
39 Pitcher's stat
45 Lennon's widow
46 Holiday drinks
47 Word with slip or swipe
49 Cabal
50 Recipe word
51 Slaughter
52 Roomy transport
54 Finishing school wear, for short
55 "Victory __"
56 Noirmoutier, e.g.
57 Where Limin Vatheos is
58 Dodge
59 Grade-giver
63 Weaverbird
64 Altar boys
65 Second City, for short
66 Affected
67 Suburban sight
68 Cirque
69 Pop
70 Fix
71 Simon's "__ Blues"
72 Conceal
75 Allotments
76 Take to task
77 Think
82 Aware of
83 Derisive cry
84 Old zither
85 Big birds
87 First-rate
88 Galley instruction
89 Spot
90 Hair style
91 Inzinzac integer
92 Compulsive performer
93 "Where did __ wrong?"
94 Approx.

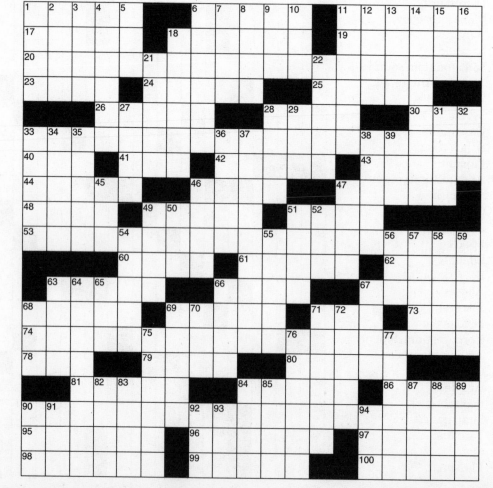

ACROSS

1 Taste
6 Reese and Street
12 Minimal
18 Nearby
19 Compare
20 Classical marketplaces
21 U.S. jurist
23 '90s fashion
24 Inquire
25 March 26 baby
26 Infidel
28 Bribe collector
31 Refuse
32 Moore in movies
36 Charlotte __
38 Words with drink or run
41 Car model
42 "The Tempest" character
44 Humorous
46 Isaacs novel
47 Becomes too much
49 Break
50 Nones word
51 Writer Capek
52 Emotionless
54 Zero
55 Rueful place?
56 Home run king
57 Where Pittsburg is: Abbr.
60 Frequency unit
61 Selfish sort
62 King mackerel
63 Lazy
66 "When I Take My Sugar __"
67 Singer Rivers
68 Sideburns
71 Howells's "__ of Silas Lapham"
73 Markey and Bagnold
74 Saves
76 Made amends
77 Billionth: Prefix
78 Bakery offering
79 Sangfroid
81 Cupidity
83 Word with prima
85 "A Fool Such __"
88 Jeopardy
91 Wide receivers
95 "In __ and out the other"
96 W-2 recipient
97 Stirred up
98 Like a Van Gogh night
99 Fears
100 Latini's student

DOWN

1 "I Thought I __ Pussy Cat"
2 Down with
3 Political patronage
4 Yours and mine
5 Map abbr.
6 Actress Winger
7 Horse
8 Angler's item
9 Delays
10 Blind ambition
11 Basilisk
12 Like 23 Across
13 Taj Mahal site
14 Repetitious song
15 Ending for north or south
16 Droop
17 Half a fly?
22 Called
27 The Beatles' "__ Love Her"
29 Filmmaker Resnais
30 Johnny Mathis hit
31 Splotches
33 Abridge
34 Script lead-in
35 Endings for end
36 Jordanian capital
37 Hollywood neighbor
39 City on the Rhone
40 Cultivate
41 Hoops pickup team
43 Removed
45 Chancel group
48 N.M. neighbor
51 Actress Black
52 Benefit
53 Handle
55 Chiapas change
56 China Sea island
57 "Diner" actor
58 Get up
59 Nipped at the wire
60 Show-off
61 First rate
62 Ricochet
63 Harbinger
64 Dogtooth, e.g.
65 Keep-mind link
66 Trifles
67 "Take __ your leader"
69 Intimation
70 Personally provided
72 More robust
75 Crowded
78 Summer pick
80 Harbor sight
82 Bring up
83 Travel outlay
84 Magnani of films
86 Short performance
87 Key
88 Suggested behavior
89 Aardvark's snack
90 D.C. org. in the news, 1995
92 Gibbon
93 Defective
94 Camel's hair fabric

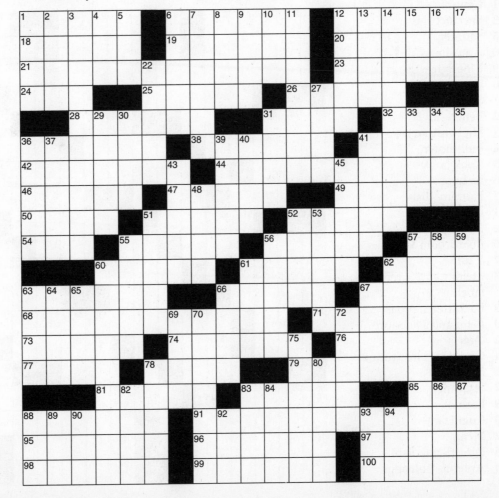

ACROSS

1 Plainsong
6 Recipe instruction
11 Oxonian, for one
17 Endeavor
18 City on I-80
19 Greenery
20 Kind of light
22 Stores fodder
23 Downside
24 Pool
26 Oleum and neroli
27 Impatiens
30 Lion's pride
31 Word with start or suit
33 Violin man
34 Anguish
36 Lett of the NFL
38 Command to Fido
41 Singer Grant
42 Cowardly
45 Actress Thurman
46 Forfeiture
48 Candy unit
49 Forgiving
50 Incision
51 Central
53 Succinct
55 Saunter
56 Amorinos
59 Moor growth
60 Crops up
61 Soap plant
62 Bench sitter
63 Highway sign
64 Full-blown
65 Cook book
66 So long
67 Hominy dish
71 Rubbish
72 Printer parts
76 Boardroom VIP
77 Vault
78 Major Lance's record label
79 Backstretch repast
80 Peter and Theodore
82 Oracle
84 Grand Old institution
86 Barely
87 Stratum
89 Feeble
90 Cognizant
92 Mean
95 Directional display
100 Antenna housings
101 Sportscaster Tony
102 Annulled
103 Comeback
104 Frederica von __
105 Nest noises

DOWN

1 Insurance pro, for short
2 Filmmaker Hartley
3 Dance org.
4 "__ for the weary . . ."
5 Struggle
6 Recipe instruction
7 Judean shepherd
8 Gal of song
9 Gershwin's "__ Love"
10 Consumed
11 Golfer Hogan
12 B&O, Soo, etc.
13 Argot
14 17th Century speculative investments
15 Pitcher Hershiser
16 Noted loch
19 Neckline shape
21 Spirit
25 Liberate
27 Phoenician deity
28 Shells, e.g.
29 Ballads
30 Property-tax unit
31 Baby kangaroo
32 Sturm __ drang
34 Scheme
35 Scottish river
37 Gaelic
39 Writer Zola
40 Singer David
43 Water bird
44 Stanza
47 Beam
50 TV's Jimmy
52 Citrus drink
53 Now
54 Coulomb part
55 Jackie's second spouse
56 Fusses
57 Eskimo boat
58 Bun toppings
59 Sleuth
60 Skating maneuver
62 __ de vivre
63 Viewpoint
65 Pone or scone
66 Trifecta, e.g.
68 Nervous as __
69 Blackbird
70 Affectation
72 Pointer, for one
73 Fitness routine
74 Kind of fever
75 Agitates
81 "Tristram Shandy" man
83 Street sign
85 Compresses
86 __ Plumas, Calif.
87 Actress Fitzgerald
88 Writer Klima
89 Unseld of the NBA
90 Mimicked
91 Aftermath
93 Fr. soul
94 Neth. neighbor
96 Exec's degree
97 Keats work
98 Fraction of a gulp
99 Newsroom VIPs

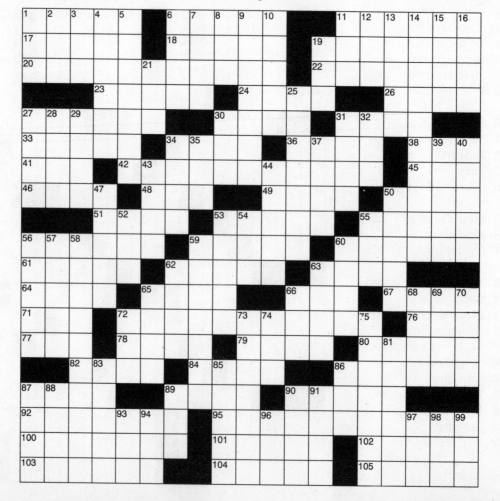

ACROSS

1 Grovels
7 Skilled
11 Showered
17 "It's __ to beat your feet . . ."
18 Extrinsic
19 Admission
20 First course-dessert combo?
23 Delta material
24 Commonly
25 Isle of Man's sea
26 Certain opera singer
29 Actor Burton
31 Wire measure
34 Brunch salad-bar offering?
38 "Our Gang" leader
40 Scopes out
41 Gives the orders
42 Hired group
43 Standard
45 Critics
47 Ky. neighbor
48 Ingenuous
50 St. Catherine's town
51 Dinner dish, informalized?
58 Place for soffit
59 Holds court
60 Pub purchase
61 "We have __!"
64 Possessive pronoun
65 Bone of contention
67 Spokes
68 ". . . the death __ yet"
71 Bogart spouse
72 Fast food-haute cuisine matchup?
77 Rhys's "Wide Sargasso __"
78 Church official
79 Condescending
80 "Gay" spot
82 Pac 10 mbr.
83 Marlinspike relatives
87 Offering at New Orleans teas?
94 Asian capital
95 Actor Lorenzo
96 Cossack leader
97 Shopping area
98 Vintner's concern
99 Mountain ashes

DOWN

1 Baseball wear
2 Maine-to-Fla. hwy.
3 Russian sea
4 Wis. town
5 __ Tse
6 Actor Erwin
7 Touched down
8 Proposal
9 Jamie __ Curtis
10 Escaroles
11 Do an electrician's job
12 Sheridan and Beattie
13 Hankering
14 New Deal org.
15 Cry of fright
16 Sandra of films
18 Concerning
21 Sit
22 Spoken
27 Invites
28 Pigpen
29 Actress Myrna
30 Scottish uncle
31 Symbol of stubbornness
32 Bakery worker
33 Belt-tightener's ration
34 "A Fish Called __"
35 Chutzpah
36 Singer Lopez
37 Rapper Shakur
38 Mobster's knife
39 Window unit
43 Kitchen tool
44 Intentions
45 Partisan camps
46 Information
48 Church area
49 Extreme ending
50 Dither
52 "What Is to Be Done?" writer
53 Hysteria
54 Zodiac ram
55 Attacks
56 Jewish month
57 Close up, in falconry
61 Kennel sounds
62 Merchandise
63 Suggestion
65 Archvillain
66 Repeat rule-breaker
68 Neat
69 Word to a villain
70 Debussian milieu
71 Sis's sibling
73 Disney car
74 Run
75 Durango dwellings
76 Styptic agent
80 "Oh My __" ('50s hit)
81 Thunderstruck
82 Slightly open
84 "Today __ man . . ."
85 Actress Cannon
86 Without
87 Paddington or Penn: Abbr.
88 Roofing material
89 Rocker Ocasek
90 __ Dawn Chong
91 Entertainer Sumac
92 Tennysonian crossing
93 From __ Z

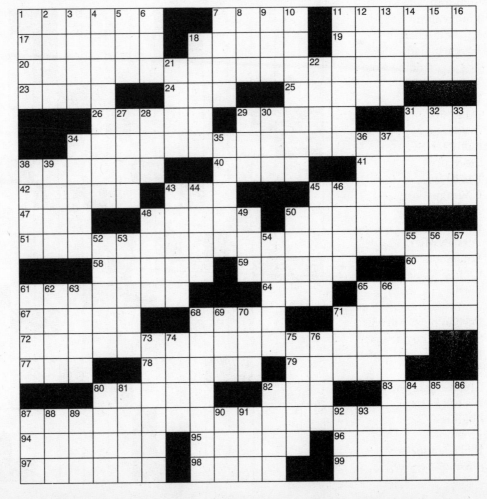

ACROSS

1 Galumph
6 Pagurian
10 Intensify
16 Customary
17 Curaçao neighbor
18 Spot on the Riviera
19 Meteorology instrument
21 Sound system components
22 Slugger Williams
23 Singing foursome of yore
24 "The Planets" composer
25 Diameter halves
27 Sentient
29 Gambling initials
32 Hit song for 23 Across
36 Arachnid
38 Throng
39 "Twelfth Night" heroine
40 Pliable
41 Chapter of history
43 Silenced
45 Standout
46 Identical to
49 "__ you what . . ."
50 Fringe benefit
52 His given name was Milton
54 Drains
58 Build up
60 Border area
62 Golly relative
63 Stack up
66 Doze
67 Courage
69 Baseball family
70 African fox
73 Persian ruler
74 Functionary in a Rolling Stones song
79 Barfly
80 Amortize
81 Psychologist Alfred
82 Sight for the dazzled
84 Pleased
85 Grads-to-be
88 Music man Henry
91 Beatrix Potter libation
95 Line up
96 Rial spender
97 Starts
98 Meager
99 Extension
100 X

DOWN

1 Use your head, in a way
2 Tennis great
3 Bemoaned
4 Needlefish
5 Planer tree relative
6 Kind of card
7 Dirt-road phenomenon
8 Writer Kobo
9 Stripe
10 NYC river
11 Chem. endings
12 Smell __
13 President pro __
14 "Man in boo"
15 Not neg.
17 Speedily
18 Uttered
20 Senior
24 Disservice
25 Heckled
26 Last words
27 Devoured
28 Misery
29 Ancient Greek coin
30 Prefix for communications
31 Actor Pitt
32 Meet-and-greet event
33 Force
34 Foul
35 Factories
36 Exchange
37 Clip
41 Divest
42 Lapidary's offering
43 Deprecate
44 Subject
47 Japanese gelatin
48 Helios
49 "__ Thief" (1934 film)
51 All used up
53 Collier
55 Over
56 Indiana town
57 Plans
59 Gender abbr.
61 Ignominy
63 Corvine sounds
64 Toast topper
65 Highly
68 Part of QED
70 Vipers
71 R.R. stop
72 Cooper's "The __"
73 Comic strip
75 Jacinthe
76 Lofty home
77 Oval
78 Rickenbacker Causeway site
82 Keloid
83 U.K. food packages
84 Fed
85 Peduncle
86 Actress Russo
87 Lip
88 Pas' mates
89 "Ptolemy" sculptor
90 FDR agcy.
91 Intimidate
92 "Who __ to judge?"
93 Kismet
94 Prefix for gram

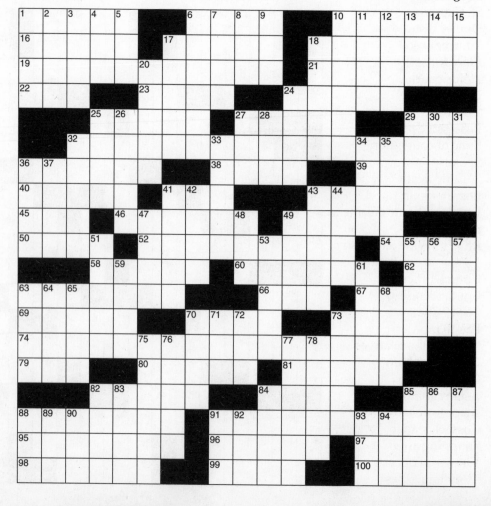

ACROSS

1 Contradict
6 Ornamentation
11 Shock
17 Sandarac trees
18 Imitation gold
19 Famed Wyeth model et al.
20 Never-ending geology?
23 Solicit
24 PDQ relative
25 Molds
26 Neb. neighbor
27 Religious group
30 Pallid
31 Pt. of TGIF
34 Absconded
38 Geological attempts?
41 Nordic
42 Overfills
44 Rock's __ Ant
45 Stir up
46 Songbird
47 Abba hit
48 Dentine
49 Mozart's "__ Giovanni"
50 Desert wind
52 Hail
53 Geologist's weepy song?
61 Greek letters
62 Muscat natives
63 Nucleic acid
64 Golfer Woods
67 Legal matter
70 Raised
71 VP nominee, 1892
72 Scent
73 Stylized scene
75 Positive thinker of note
76 Geological legerdemain?
78 Awful
80 Clique
81 Boss of Mary and Murray
82 José's house
84 Calif. fort
85 Skirmish
87 Baker's unit
89 Mich. neighbor
92 Geologist's expedient motto?
98 Busy __
99 Diehard
100 Pirogue
101 Untruth
102 Humphries and Laurel
103 Flow

DOWN

1 Filmdom's Theda
2 Life force
3 Dearth
4 Annoy
5 Pope's "__ Man"
6 Discontinues
7 Big bird
8 Hoodwink
9 Senior citizens
10 Wife of Boaz
11 Where to head 'em off
12 Neoteric
13 Word with well or fair
14 Actor Tognazzi
15 Windows alternative
16 Importune
18 __ pro nobis
21 By
22 Bow openings
26 Common follower
28 Yuletide libation
29 USN VIP
31 Dog-dish inscription
32 Bring up
33 Wouk's "This __ God"
34 Tuesday, in Toulon
35 "__ with a View"
36 Moribund
37 Nobel winner, 1938
39 "__ to Pieces" ('60s hit)
40 Pitch-black
43 It's elemental in Vegas
46 Intelligence
48 Entertainer Burl
50 Recipe instruction
51 Cable-TV biggie
52 Surrounded by
54 Apply
55 Ingrains
56 Jeanne __
57 "Just what __!"
58 Step
59 Doddering
60 Encumbered
64 Chuck
65 Take it easy
66 Villain
67 Disprove
68 Ordinal ending
69 NASA groupie, perhaps
71 Interpret
73 Mollified
74 Actress Balin
75 Impeccable
77 Sport filament
79 Outcry
83 At __ (perplexed)
85 Rum cake
86 Cuts
88 Dismissed
89 Sack, e.g.
90 Lay-thick link
91 Throw off
92 Fond du __
93 Botanist Gray
94 Family transport
95 Chapter of history
96 Yang's counterpart
97 "Full Metal Jacket" subject

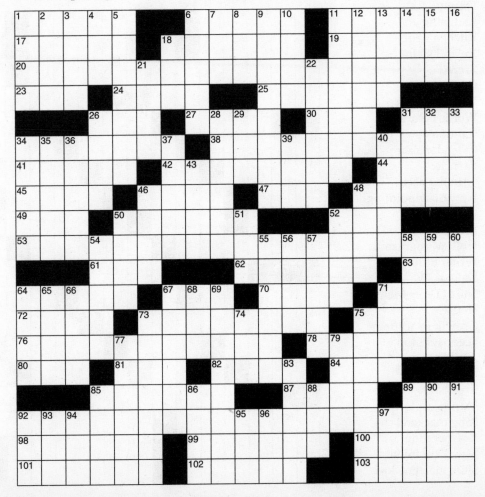

ACROSS

1 Cut to pieces
6 Bleak
12 Nonplusses
18 "__ Will Ever Know"
19 On the beach
20 City on I-25
21 Have debts, talon, dwelling, article
23 Soothes
24 Rose grouping
25 Samovar
26 Sanction
28 "Come Back, Little Sheba" playwright
30 Water buffalo
32 School grp.
33 Possessive pronoun
36 Irritate
38 Stigma
39 Youmans's "__ for Two"
40 Out of the wind
41 Rock's companion
42 Interrogate
43 Sport, vast amount
45 Metallurgist's concern
46 Perfect
47 Disney
48 Laughing
49 Kitchen item
50 Ireland's Lingus
51 Sacred
53 Composed
55 Pitcher's woes
56 Words before time
60 Cautiously
62 Calendar abbr.
63 Particle
64 __ in the neck
67 How disappointing!
68 Chagall
69 ER denizens
70 Hollow, cognizant
72 Writer Blume
73 Daly of TV
74 Site of Perry Memorial House
75 Growth in academe
76 Feedbag fillup
77 Avellaneous
78 Kibosh
79 Expert
80 Marine eagle
81 King mackerel
82 Exasperating
84 New Deal initials
85 Store machine logo

88 Poolhall implement
91 Muslim leader, Fr. river, QB Tittle
95 Ventilate
96 Fiber
97 Strong suit
98 White poplars
99 Medicinal liquid
100 Chuckles

DOWN

1 Elitist
2 Baseball's Steve
3 Caviar, radio control, purpose
4 Business letter abbr.
5 Inundate
6 Four Seasons hit
7 Child ending
8 Tote-board word
9 Importance
10 Field house
11 Big part
12 Austere
13 Terminus of Will Rogers Tpk.
14 Zaire river
15 CEO's degree
16 Thickness
17 Help!
22 Exist
27 Willing to consider
29 Super Bowl insignia
30 "I can't tell __"
31 Role for 65 Down
33 "Casablanca" character
34 Child no more
35 Exchange membership
36 Barley, beans, etc.
37 Goddesses of justice
38 Whetstone
39 Apprises
40 Tangential remark
42 Chess piece
43 Voluble
44 Peaceful
46 Finish
47 Fortress part
51 Writer Bret
52 Bother
54 Sure-footed
55 Tuckered out
57 Ethereal, sector, hesitant sound

58 British weight
59 Photographer Adams
61 "I, Claudius" writer
62 Crazes
64 Mideast gulf
65 Gilpin of "Frasier"
66 Mme. Gres
68 Unspeaking
71 Croquet hoops
72 Deans' musical partner
73 Roofing material
76 Ultimatum
77 Grate
79 Dispute
80 Internet traffic
81 TV's Sharkey or Bilko
82 Elvis, for one
83 Eight: Prefix
84 Roller-coaster cry
86 __ reversa
87 Criticisms
88 Ovine sound
89 Josh
90 Wrath
92 Words between roses
93 Sell option
94 New Deal initials

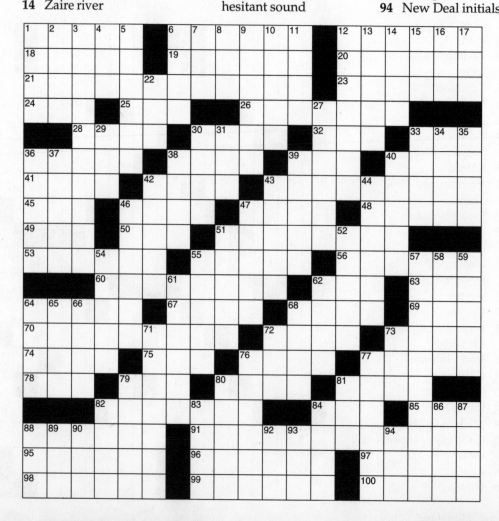

ACROSS

1 Pounds
5 Protective gear
9 Symbol of silence
13 Circumstances
16 Zing
17 Slightly
18 Strong cotton
19 Virginia rail
20 Hearth game?
23 Etats-__
24 Less friendly
25 Pentacle
26 They're on the loose
28 Divisive influence
30 Baseball manager Felipe
32 Verdi work
33 Library reminder
34 Gal of song
36 Approximately
39 Shot
40 Card game photo?
43 Detest
46 Mountain lake
49 Planted
50 Okla. town
52 Compass pt.
53 ". . . and __ grow on"
55 Medulla
57 Type type: Abbr.
59 Words with glance
60 Prometheus, Atlas, et al.
62 Labors
64 Gruesome
66 Actress Dolenz
67 Wood's "__ Lynne"
69 Music-man Puente
71 "You Really __" '60s hit
72 Gibbon
73 Haiku, e.g.
75 Dole
77 Computer client
78 Dozed
81 Sketch a card game?
84 Crag
85 Anent
86 Title of respect
87 "Honest __"
90 Dross
93 Wouk's "The __"
96 Fertile Crescent river
98 Rustic
101 Facial features
103 Mubarak predecessor
104 Pot starter
105 Blackjack's heyday?
108 Acescent
109 Fiber source
110 Actress Aumont
111 Time was his
112 Pill, for short
113 Kennel sounds
114 Famed race site
115 Epochs

DOWN

1 Overhauls
2 Storied restaurant
3 Singer Carey
4 Smirk
5 Sidekick
6 Down with
7 Aphorisms
8 Bargain
9 U.S.N. E-7
10 Resembling
11 Iowa college town
12 Polo
13 Form of solitaire?
14 Bay window
15 "Jerusalem Liberated" poet
19 Excellent
21 Force
22 Confirmation
27 __ girl!
29 Cheery sounds
31 Impulse
35 Picot
37 Baleful
38 "Don't bet __"
40 Tapir
41 Chirps
42 Aware of
44 Punctual
45 School book
46 Box-score line
47 Ethology subject
48 Get serious about a card game?
51 Morse Code symbol
54 Word with day or way
56 Electronic impression
58 Diary
61 Fall guy
63 Branch
65 Womanizer
68 Pop
70 Singer Redding
74 Number-crunching
76 Word-processor mode
79 Skycap
80 PP&M, for one
82 "The Waves" novelist
83 Mill material
87 Zeal, in England
88 Katharina's sister
89 Mrs. Lauder et al.
90 Twitch
91 Pitpan or corial
92 "The Shiek of __"
94 Palace in Florence
95 Trackman Moses
97 Singer Crystal
99 Prefix for culture
100 Entrechat, e.g.
102 Forward
106 Switch settings
107 Skeptic's word

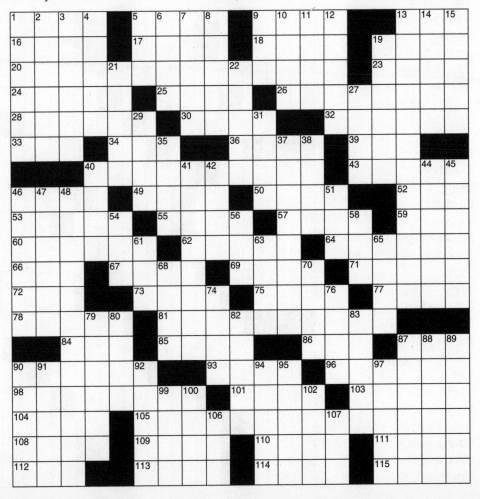

ACROSS

1 Drop
5 Prima donna qualities
9 Giraffe relative
14 Tex. campus
17 Zone
18 Headquarters
19 Sanskrit language
20 Element No. 50
21 Comics kid
24 White robe
25 See 72 Down
26 Swain
27 Painter Max
28 Vivacity
29 Lineage
31 Overfill
32 Kitchen implement
33 Chopper
34 "The Scourge of God"
37 Storage structure
40 Cruelty
42 Weather god
43 "Giant" ranch
45 The i has it
46 Bachelor endings
48 English review, for short
51 Bay window
52 Mil. transports
54 Louis's approval
55 Trendy
56 11th Century ruler
60 Ratify
61 U.K. honor
62 Der __ (Adenauer)
63 General assemblies
64 Extreme ending
65 Harbor sight
67 Leb. neighbor
68 Trance
69 NYSE counterpart
70 "A fine kettle __"
73 Rachmaninoff's "__ of the Dead"
74 Bobby Darin hit
78 Ceres
80 Yearn for
81 Way out: Abbr.
82 It drops flies
86 Singer Jenny
87 Give it __!
89 Charbroil
90 Bitter
91 Geological period
92 16th Century ruler
95 Enzyme
96 Spaghetti al __
97 Molly of TV
98 Quit
99 Quiet greeting
100 Zeal
101 Claims
102 D.C. group

DOWN

1 Effete
2 Entertainer Cara
3 Imparts
4 Ecru
5 Old ascetics
6 Uncover
7 Where Ewa is
8 Sault __ Marie
9 Pay stub entry
10 Doghouse
11 Nabokov heroine et al.
12 Old Roman foe
13 Kind of cream
14 Formality
15 Setting
16 Yet-to-be
22 Wild goat
23 Supermarket sign
28 Catafalque
30 "You never __"
31 Laugh riot
32 Greek letters
34 Foster parent
35 Consultants, at times
36 Sharp's "__ Cult"
37 Look over
38 Penthouses, of a sort
39 Excoriate
41 Eliot work
44 "Aladdin" prince
47 Film of 1982
48 TV's "__ Company"
49 One of the Barrymores
50 Quarrel
53 Kind of chest or change
55 Yo-Yo-Ma, for one
57 Amman followers
58 Palisades
59 Good times
65 Head
66 Minstrel
69 KGB forerunner
71 Estuary
72 With 25 Across, Forster tale
74 Washington suburb
75 Melodic
76 Put up
77 Eager for
79 Young salmon
82 Squalid
83 Bargaining place
84 DeGeneres
85 Swamp growth
87 Declare
88 Writer Ayn
89 Portico
92 Actress Lupino
93 News bigwigs
94 Uncertainties

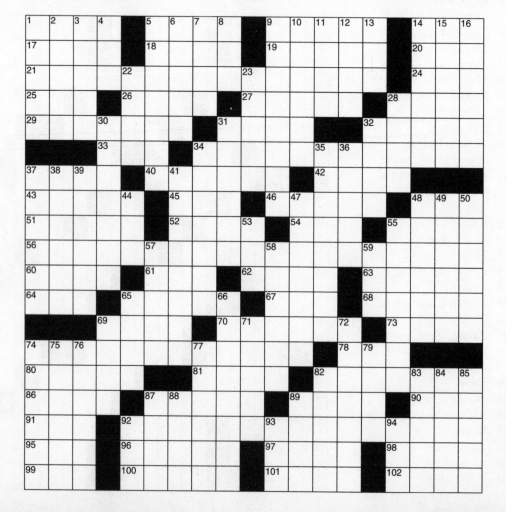

ACROSS

1 Cabrilla
5 Writer Martin
9 Austrian composer
13 Down with
17 Football's Graham
18 "__ moment too soon!"
19 Elvis, e.g.
20 Actress Seymour
21 Musical mecca, 1969
23 Charged
24 "Auld Lang __"
25 Uneventful
26 Dead set
29 Turtosa
30 To a dreadful degree
32 Afflicts
33 Cartoon cry on impact
35 Landon
37 Stat for Cone
38 Quarry
39 Storied tavern
42 Recklessly
44 Assn.
45 Dave Clark Five hit
46 "The Caine Mutiny" character
47 Cassowary
49 Venetian red
51 Innovative
52 Kiang
54 The Beach Boys' "Surfin' __"
56 Reclined
57 Rap's Dr. __
58 Fleck
61 Northern Ireland town
64 Ogler
65 Dropt drops
66 Puffin, for one
67 Aurora
68 Health club
70 Fanatic
71 Garret
73 Possessive pronoun
75 Valuate
79 Investigators
81 Green lights
83 Dutch city
85 Inelegant
86 Pass over
87 Soc. studies course
88 CIA forerunner
89 Wax producer
90 Salinger girl
91 Menace
93 Sine __ non
95 Bullpen denizen
98 East __, England
101 Amphorae
103 Singer Vikki
104 Mo. town
106 Invites
107 Auricular
108 Mayberry character
109 Differ ending
110 Spring
111 __ majesty
112 Fishing village sight
113 Mild cheese

DOWN

1 Buttons' companions
2 Little bit
3 Represented
4 "Me too" relative
5 Stamen parts
6 Jane Smiley novel
7 Restless
8 Benefit
9 Montana City
10 Esculent
11 Wanders
12 Valley
13 Foyt et al.
14 Place known for tides
15 One of the Freuds
16 Attempt
22 Mottles
27 Den
28 Hornbill
31 Not in time
34 All-sudden connection
35 Modern cash source, for short
36 Mauna __
38 PC adjunct
39 Disclaims
40 Eur. river
41 Norton's workplace
43 Trick
45 Tolerate
48 Sic transit gloria __
50 "The Love __" (1973 hit)
53 Longfellow figure
55 Pirate's agreement
58 Perceive
59 Zahn of TV
60 N.C. area
62 Food scraps
63 Damp
64 Facility
66 Tub contents
69 Upstart
72 Okla. town
74 __ as (for instance)
76 Site of Buckhaven
77 Dental office replies
78 Big boats: Abbr.
80 Singer Lemper
82 Chicken __
84 Harangues
86 God of the underworld
90 Overjoy
91 Metaphor
92 Concur
93 Campus area
94 Upper-air bear
96 Environmental subj.
97 Inky
99 Inti worshipper
100 "Up and __!"
102 It's a secret
105 Minutia

ACROSS

1 Derby, e.g.
4 Rock
8 Collapse
12 More, in Madrid
15 Kick-fuss link
16 Pommel alternative
17 Mario of the NBA
18 Pub quantity
19 Full of thrills and chills
22 Gambling game
23 Carreras and Caruso
24 Edison name
25 Wrath
26 Plaster base
27 Misrepresent
29 Easily crumbled
30 Golfer Ernie
31 Designer Ralph
33 Theater district
34 Horrific
36 Cultural lead-in
39 Vocal group
41 "__ far, far better thing . . ."
43 Become
44 Actress Joan
45 Catchall abbr.
47 Responsibility
48 Valletta's land
50 Supervised
52 Sri __
54 Gregarious
55 Played back
56 Prudent
57 Cut
59 Pitch-dark
60 Capital follow-up
61 Frauds
63 Farm group
65 Vassal
67 Humorous
71 Atelier stands
73 Part share
74 U.K. currency
77 Foul weather gear
79 Durations
80 Pastel shade
81 Angular unit
82 Eng. detail
83 Warped
85 "Of Thee __"
86 Tasty
89 Confess
90 Pakistani tongue
91 Grand-scale
92 "__ Blu Dipinto Di Blu"
93 Bit of e-mail
94 Disarray
95 Scrape
96 Sailing chain

DOWN

1 Go get 'em
2 Charisma
3 Stigmatizes
4 Scoff
5 Chooses
6 Luau accoutrement
7 Score half
8 "La Strada" director
9 Kicking's companion
10 Wertmuller
11 Meat cut
12 Awesome
13 Steraph
14 Repository
18 Navidad delight
20 Japanese drama
21 Helmet
22 Leaky-boat cry
25 Goes slowly
27 Volley
28 Blunder
29 Famous last word
31 Gibbon
32 Succored
33 Accolade, for one
34 Nissan rival
35 Deep-six
37 Order on the set
38 Land on the Tyrrhenian
39 Turophile's love
40 Grievous
42 Latin lesson word
44 Comedian Farley
46 Ascends
47 Little integer
49 Top-grade work
51 USNA grad
53 Bureaucratic abbr.
54 Sail extender
56 Protests
58 Sizes up
62 Antigone's uncle
64 Word with where or way
66 Opposite
68 Momentum
69 TV series
70 Family
72 Catch flies
74 Peer
75 Boxer Gene
76 Flock
77 Light-breaker
78 Watering hole
79 Taters
80 Timetable column: Abbr.
82 Touchy
83 Inspire
84 Actor Gregory
86 Noncommittal
87 Network, to tabloids
88 Wallaba

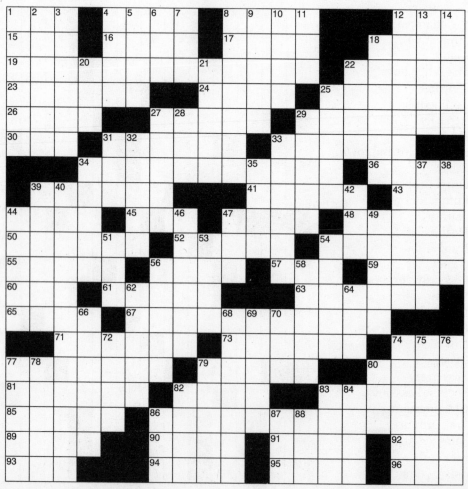

ACROSS

1 Writer Esquivel
6 Strikebreakers
11 Cushiony
17 Little conger
18 City lineup
19 Fatty ester
20 Understands
23 Basswood
24 Kind of belt
25 "Would that" relative
26 Concord
28 Possesses
30 Corrode
32 Pittance
35 Dickens name
38 Tokens hit of the '60s
42 Unfamiliar
43 "A little birdie __"
44 Taken for __
45 Flipper
46 Lawrence's partner
48 Flashed
50 Forum finery
52 Kind of mail or print
54 Nicks
55 Appreciate one's surroundings
58 Without equivocation
59 Casino staple
60 Lofty
64 Singer Lola et al.
66 Packing rings
68 Agnus __
69 Photographer Walker
70 "__ Right" (1976 hit)
73 Pulque
75 Enjoy life
78 Dumas character
79 Wapiti
80 Perimeter
81 California's __ Woods
82 Resembling
84 Unspoken
87 Rooftop structure
91 Arrangements
94 Part of a phone-company suggestion
97 Fly
98 Fast
99 Actress Gabrielle
100 Frankness
101 Appetizing
102 Mulberry relative

DOWN

1 Belt-tightener's ration
2 Out of the wind
3 Eye part
4 Fix up
5 Illustrations
6 Cassoulets
7 City on the Cauca
8 Main line
9 Conceit, informally
10 Suggestion in the stacks
11 Civil
12 Came down
13 Disavow
14 Sire
15 Saison on the Seine
16 Burrow
21 Intimate
22 Mozart's "Cosi fan __"
27 Ixnay relative
29 Faction
31 Tributary
32 Apertures
33 Like many shoppes
34 Habituated
35 Bonkers
36 Melange
37 Call up
38 Platitude
39 Decide
40 Billiards surface
41 Poet Dowson
43 Sings lustily
47 __ Culp Hobby
48 Cave
49 Filmmaker Hallstrom
51 On the bias
53 Inquiring sounds
54 Complain
56 Parson's home
57 DeGeneres
58 Lab vessel
61 He started it
62 Singer Stubbs
63 "True __" (1994 film)
64 Fancy party
65 Grandparently
67 Delhi water
70 Aboveboard
71 Have debts
72 Polish river
74 Flora's realm
76 Come-on
77 CEOs
78 Motive lead-in
81 Sentimental
82 Type space
83 Able to handle
85 Top-drawer
86 Jazzman Baker
88 Decorah's state
89 Hitch
90 Call to Fido
91 Pouch
92 Stowe character
93 Malaysian export
95 Not quite e'er
96 Chairman of note

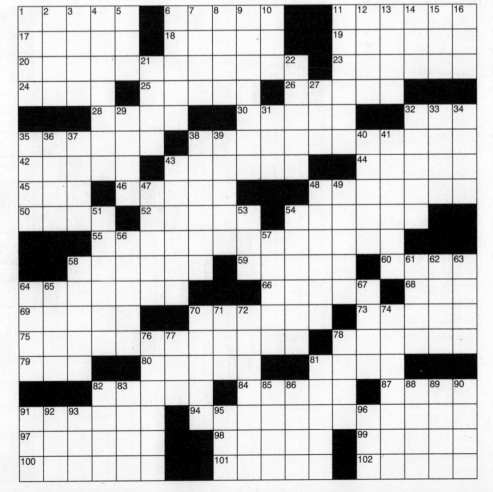

ACROSS

1 Doesn't wear out
6 Israeli port
11 Regarding
16 Countenances
18 Actor Quinn
19 European standout
20 Colonial notes?
22 Roadside sights
23 River in 19 Across
24 Austrian river
26 Dickens name
27 Chafe
30 Whey
33 Farm-machine name
35 Appeal
36 Elliptical fish
38 Computer key
40 Prefix for comic
42 Flowing Handel work?
45 State of mind
48 Rapid transition
49 Recurring theme
51 He played Grant
52 Wet blanket
55 Crumple into a ball
57 __ time (never)
58 Silkworm
59 Poet Hunt
63 Contradict
65 Free
66 Vanished
68 __ mail (post)
70 Neil Diamond hit
72 Stubborn as __
74 Film of 1994
76 Main, for one
77 Soak
79 Uncomplicated tunes?
84 Skip over
85 Auxiliary proposition
86 Traveling
87 Former gilt
89 Military color
91 Do the job
94 Purpose
95 Part of UAE
97 "Absolutely Fabulous" character
99 Assignment
101 Writer Henry
103 New kind of tunes?
109 Slow-witted
110 Perseus's mother
111 Straw mat
112 Applies sealer
113 "George Washington __ Here"
114 Abominable snowmen

DOWN

1 Tour of the track
2 Utterly
3 Furtive
4 Big book
5 Ointment applicators
6 Oh, sure!
7 Kind of force or fare
8 Nuptial vows
9 False front
10 Pastern's joint
11 Outback denizen
12 Clockmaker Thomas
13 Tunes at no charge?
14 Supply ship
15 Hoarse
17 Bound
19 Turkish hostelry
21 Shredded
25 Ebullient
27 Donnybrook
28 "__ Lazy River"
29 Flutter
31 Indecisive sounds
32 Disfigure
34 See 58 Across
37 Computer command
39 Garbage vessel
41 Birth announcement words
43 Totter
44 Erstwhile fillies
45 Lieutenant
46 Everyday fabric
47 Wear down
50 Check
52 "Young Dancer" sculptor
53 Essence
54 Once around the dial?
56 Big fig
60 Substitution word
61 Stare
62 Go fast
64 Writer Wiesel
67 Jewish month
69 __ majesty
71 __, bravo, charlie . . .
73 Norwegian explorer
75 Uses a rheostat
76 Capital of Laconia
78 Stick
80 Mrs., in Montmartre
81 Be obliged
82 PC hookup
83 "Spanish Tragedy" playwright
85 Hereditary
87 Aegean island
88 Veldt antelope
90 Varieties
92 Enormous
93 Disquisition
96 Melancholy
98 First rate
100 Franklin's flyer
102 Double curve
104 Upper limit
105 Court call
106 Grimalkin
107 Actress Dolenz
108 Fleur-de__

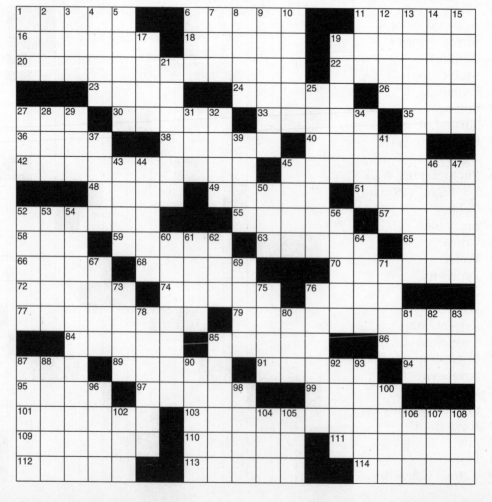

ACROSS

1 Equivocations
5 Furies
10 Recycled sound?
14 Fishing device
17 Much
18 Friendship
19 Secular
20 High-toned poem
21 Extra-special sunshade?
23 Prefer
24 Sum total
25 "Effi __" (Fassbinder film)
26 Extra-special queues?
28 Bandeau
30 Neural network, for short
31 Go it alone
33 Fishing device
34 Dickensian setting
36 Summer ermine
37 Position
41 Culture medium
42 Tries
45 Occasion
46 Dawn
48 Otto's realm: Abbr.
49 Attracts and holds
52 Chai
53 High standards
56 Baseball manager Felipe
57 Floor covering
58 Extra-special application?
60 A Murphy invention
63 __ vera
64 Singer Julius
65 Hopper painting
68 Picturesque
70 PC hookup
71 Freight
73 Tommie of the '69 Mets
74 Roald Dahl book
79 Bring up
80 Method
83 Haste
84 Seek out
86 __ Marie Saint
87 Requisite
88 __ Plaines, Ill.
89 Half a score
90 Extra-special velocity?
94 Kind of election
96 Kind of lift or line
97 Royal highness
98 Extra-special insults?
102 Rockets' org.
103 Stock table abbr.
104 Time being
105 Mishmash
106 Atty.'s abbr.
107 Affectation
108 Out-and-out
109 90-degree joints

DOWN

1 __ relief
2 Director Grosbard
3 Extra special fruit?
4 Trick attachment
5 City in Italy
6 Wrong
7 Essence
8 W.W. II command
9 Mideast ld.
10 Actress Maxine
11 "Double Indemnity" writer
12 Outdoorsy sorts
13 Spotted cat
14 Painter Miro
15 Thoughtless
16 Toothpaste types
22 Puerto __
26 Uproar
27 Where Moscow is
28 Wild party
29 Scoundrel
31 Contemporary of Addison
32 Dutch uncle
35 Actress Joanne
36 Machine-gun
38 Something to conform to
39 Hemingway hangout
40 Former "formerly"
43 Wolfe's "The Web and __"
44 Bars
47 Indian fig
50 Actress Diana
51 Cashew family member
54 Lunch stop
55 Minimum wage: Abbr.
56 Timorous
59 Conversed
60 Prejudice
61 Uptight
62 Cudbear and gallein
65 Extra-special hair extender
66 Taw
67 Tabitha of TV
69 "__ have it!"
72 Bow
75 "__ Lovely?" (Wonder hit)
76 Graf __
77 Get the picture
78 Lean
81 Balance
82 Football's Dan
85 Belize bears
88 Nitwit
90 Sheet of stamps
91 Barbecue offering
92 Baghdad's land
93 Fundamentals
94 Harangue
95 Arctic sight
98 Wildebeest
99 Decay
100 Property-tax unit
101 Call for help

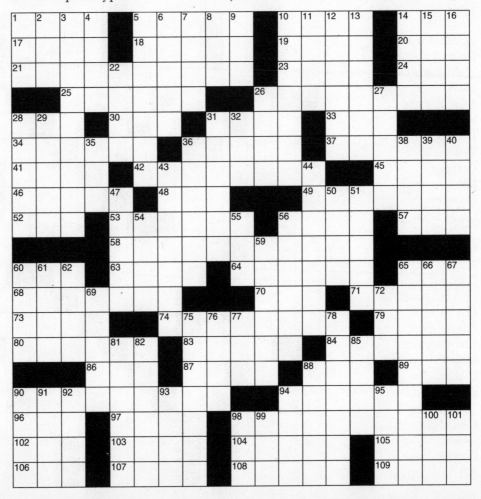

ACROSS

1 Naval amphibs
5 Writer Octavio
8 Gentle sort
12 Vaults
17 Where Red Oak is
18 Verse lead-in
19 Cosmetic ingredient
20 Niles or Frasier
21 Jack
24 Rush
25 For fear that
26 Antigone's uncle
27 Tie
28 Murena
30 Writer Barbara
32 Landon
33 Compulsive performer
34 Form-ful agcy.
35 Check
37 Begrudge
39 "From __ Eternity"
41 Chuck
44 Manute of the NBA
45 Salad dressing type
48 Comeback
49 Cosecant's reciprocal
50 Extra
51 Dominion
54 Ryder of films
56 Genesis name
57 __ Abner
58 Mark
62 Aug. 10 baby
63 Pleased
65 Dressed-up dessert
66 Optimally
68 Particle
70 Machine tools
71 Flower part
73 Oscar de la __
74 "The Good __" (1993 film)
75 Nick
79 Lecture
81 Fringe benefit
82 Emolument
83 Engine-power meas.
85 Campaigned
86 Moist
87 Uris's "The __"
90 Smoked salmon
91 __ to handle
93 Umbrage
95 Gossip
97 Crooked
98 Art

102 Plagiarize
103 VIP transport
104 Pilcorn
105 Burden
106 Convenient
107 Example
108 Comedian Louis
109 Fishing gear

DOWN

1 Duffer's concern
2 Helios
3 Resident
4 Feat for Brodeur
5 Malleable material
6 Cuckoo
7 Sphalerite extraction
8 In recent times
9 Haughty
10 Look longingly
11 __ canto
12 Devious group
13 Smell __
14 Tony
15 Join
16 Mystics
22 Uraeus
23 Kind of boat or train
27 Sailor
28 Approx.
29 Ordinal ending
31 Whimper
33 City on I-15
36 Memento __
38 Thumbs down
39 Obeisance
40 Spanish hors d'oeuvre
42 Crusades
43 Baldwin and Wilder
44 Toot
46 Algonquians
47 Serf
49 Mr. Marner
51 "Pomp and Circumstance" composer
52 Pooh's creator
53 Frank
54 Midweek deity
55 Modernize
59 Poughkeepsie's river
60 Bialy ingredient

61 And so forth
64 Be overfond
67 Exploded
69 Just a little
71 Title of respect
72 Engrave
75 Words with pray
76 Doughy dish
77 Actor Tognazzi
78 __ Mex
80 Doily
81 Starbuck's vessel
83 Hide
84 Plantain lily
86 One of the Flintstones
88 Diminish
89 Protrude
92 Good thing to use
93 Ballet bend
94 Old school
96 Utah national park
98 Madonna's "__ Remember"
99 Beam
100 Fanatic
101 Draft org.

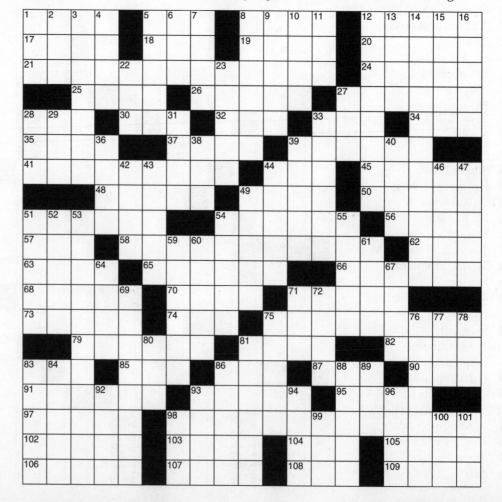

ACROSS

1 Flashy
7 Japanese city
12 Not so messy
18 Gehazi's master
19 Harsh
20 On __ of one to 10 . . .
21 Pool
22 Wolfe book, in the mirror
24 Silencer in the stacks
25 Clump
27 Gas's companion
28 "True __" (1994 film)
29 Uno plus due
31 Sable
33 Singer Celine
34 Stable mom
37 Gallic pursuit
39 Staff
40 Token
41 "Rule, Britannia" composer
42 Speleology spot
43 West Indies swimmer
45 __ garde
46 __ of Worms
48 Baseball Hall-of-Famer, in the mirror
50 Hockey great
51 "__ is it!"
53 Common article
54 Amphora
55 Matter for lawyers
56 Desert growth
58 Metaphor
60 USN VIP
63 Helios
64 Printer's measures
66 Building manager, for short
67 Meadow
68 Manifesto, in the mirror
73 Batman foe
75 Standard
76 Defector
78 __ mater
79 Spare
80 Perpetually
81 Personality part
82 In other words
83 "__ a Rebel" ('60s hit)
84 Surrounded by
85 Irrupt
86 Ship-shaped ornament
87 Discordia
88 "Foucault's Pendulum" author
89 Hayburner

91 Acapulco uncle
94 Artsy part of Paris, in the mirror
99 Draw support from
101 Less solemn
102 Herschel Bernardi role
103 Has ended
104 Entertain
105 Eccentric
106 Put away

DOWN

1 Certain shaving products
2 Too bad
3 Post-holiday snacks, in the mirror
4 Prefix for bar
5 Cloudburst
6 Maui town
7 Nosh for Nihilator
8 Goblet
9 "Oysters __ season"
10 Veto
11 Block attachment
12 Land
13 German city
14 Takes steps
15 Cross shape
16 Gremlin
17 Ump's cousin
23 Getaway
26 Everyday
30 Lamented
32 Enjoin
33 Gossips
34 Swig
35 Writer Tyler
36 City on the Moselle
37 Thespian
38 Skiing family name
40 Vision
41 Stratford's river
43 Interest
44 In good shape
45 Consensual
47 Words with play
49 Modern bourgeois
52 Indoctrinated
57 Facing
59 Wilder work
60 Hit song of 1970, in the mirror
61 Considers

62 Corday's victim
63 Belt
65 Aves.' counterparts
68 Hinterland
69 Rachmaninoff's "__ of the Dead"
70 Filmmaker Buñuel
71 Profuse
72 Hurry
74 Broward County neighbor
77 Historical period
80 Exile
82 Consume
84 "The Tempest" character
85 Meager
87 Silkworm
88 Spanish river
90 MacGraw and Baba
92 Skye of films
93 Merged
94 Roofing material
95 Hurry
96 Work unit
97 Smidgen
98 Pivotal
100 Fuss

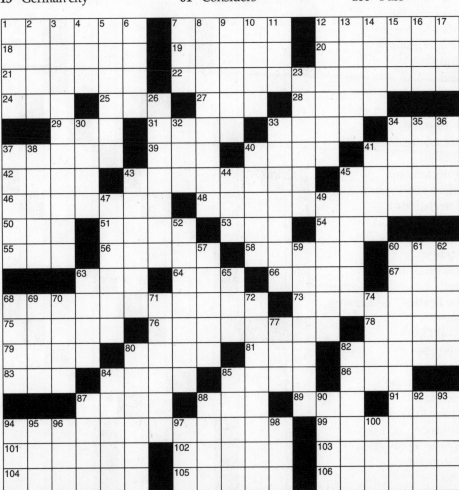

ACROSS

1 Saturnine
5 Embed
10 Working team
14 Duke's conf.
17 Actress Russo
18 Ventilated
19 Andesite
20 Strip
21 Solving
23 Okla. town
24 Writer Grafton
25 Paucity of people
26 Flying formations
28 River to the Rio Grande
30 Robert Morse role
31 Looks
34 Succor
36 Epochs
37 Nasdaq regulator
38 Skating maneuver
39 James's "An __ Job for a Woman"
42 Despised
44 Enamored of
45 Singer Fogelberg
46 Hammett hero
48 War material
49 Salad-bar staple
53 Airport queue
54 Muddled
56 Base
57 Acknowledgment
58 Lion's share, actually
59 By mistake
61 Blacksburg campus initials
62 Protected area
63 Before you know it
64 Materialistic
65 Post
66 Phalangers
68 Scourge
69 Loudness units
70 Prefix for cycle or section
71 The Beatles' "__ Leaving Home"
72 "__ d'Or"
74 Guiltless
78 Bread type
79 Naval initials
82 Appear
83 Davis Cup squad
84 Fantasy
85 Give-try connection
86 Disconcerted
89 Loyal
91 Sat
93 Astronaut Grissom
94 Advocate
96 Like many symphonies
99 Rock group, for short
100 Mortgage
101 Locale
102 Baseball's Aaron
103 Part of UCSD
104 Qualifications
105 __ jerky
106 Silesian river

DOWN

1 Sty sounds
2 Poe woman
3 Ness and associates
4 Nasty
5 Delay
6 "Lorenzo's __" (1993 film)
7 Claptrap
8 They're all in the family
9 Picot
10 Corrida cry
11 Coleridge setting
12 Wretched
13 Nothing, to Juan
14 Take in
15 Determinative
16 Wrinkle
22 Offset
27 __ Domingo
29 Intended
32 Chopper
33 Londoner's last letter
35 Late lead-in
39 Unique
40 Paradigms
41 Cheap
43 Media revenue source
44 "Today __ the Boy I'm Gonna Marry"
46 Day-trade
47 Ancient: Prefix
48 G __ golf
49 Hypotenuse neighbors
50 Faulkner's "The __"
51 Grove
52 Works on copy
54 Alienation
55 Pairs
56 Easy assignment
59 Seize
60 Olympian messenger
65 Jane Smiley book
67 Florist's cuttings
68 Staple crop
69 Seafood dish
71 James, Jude, et al.
72 Prevaricate
73 Itinerary abbr.
74 Lexicographer's concerns
75 Galaxy
76 Think
77 Prodded
78 Like
80 Addison contemporary
81 __ but wiser
84 Fool
87 Poipu performance
88 The Old Sod
90 Limbaugh
92 __ buco
95 NROTC product
97 Press coverage
98 French marshal

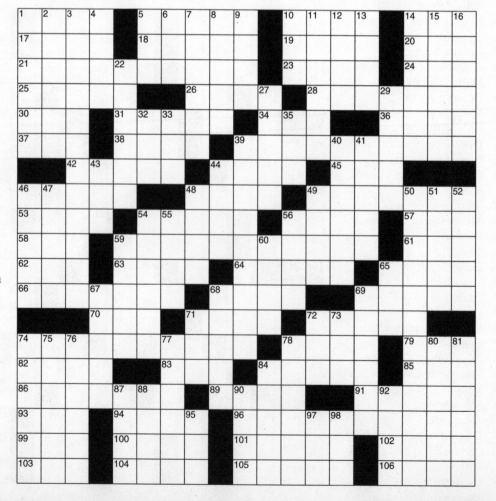

ACROSS

1 "The Life of Riley" character
5 Street sign
9 Ford
13 Sea shade
17 Colorful fish
18 Actress Lena
19 Slightly
20 Complain
21 Cry at a county fair
23 Fair creatures
25 Eternal
26 Frivolous
28 Profit follower
29 Blob
30 Berkshire village
31 Impressed
34 Wool-gather
35 Deplete
36 Uncertain sounds
37 Writer Rita __ Brown
38 Bombast
39 Dither
40 Exec's degree
41 "This __ Country"
42 Catchall abbr.
43 Purges
44 Stereo components
47 Signal
48 Choler
49 Shoplift
50 Aquarium attractions
54 Dep. follower
55 Fair sight
58 All-sudden link
59 Flower part
61 Diminishes
62 Prefix for practice
63 Bronze component
64 Shields
66 King mackerel
67 Turner
68 Low
71 Press coverage
72 Dribbles
73 __ poly
74 "Am __ brother's keeper?"
75 Consume
76 Bureau
78 Contort
79 Ruler
81 Successes
82 Campus org.
83 Seek
84 Guanaco
85 Cries of elation
88 Fair fare
91 Fair sites
93 Think it over
94 Summer condition
95 Flag
96 Together, in music
97 Comply
98 Hospitality chain
99 __ Beach, Calif.
100 Endings for Brook and Ros

DOWN

1 Boxer Riddick
2 Neat as __
3 Fair event
4 Green onion
5 __ case scenario
6 Baba and MacGraw
7 Actress-model Hurley
8 Israeli parliament
9 Smack
10 Leaning
11 Jones of the sea
12 Dutch commune
13 Pursuing
14 Representative majorities
15 L.A. campus
16 Consult
22 Lowly toiler
24 Back-lot installations
27 Hosp. area
30 Sale tag
31 Spurious
32 Engine part
33 Pitch
34 Seasoned
35 Experienced
36 Reduction
38 Summary
39 Dam's partner
40 Fit together
41 Leb. neighbor
43 Pillage
44 Masquerades
45 Files
46 Arroz con __
49 Fix
51 Fair treat
52 Straying
53 Arenose
56 Absolute
57 "I'm all __"
60 Cannon ending
65 Proclamation
66 Imprecate
68 Order
69 "Congo" character
70 Nervous-system point
72 Meals
73 Hung-jury aftermath
75 Salinger girl
76 Sails along
77 PA system problem
78 Yokel
80 Alvin of dance
81 Unblemished
82 Spur part
84 Mortgage
85 Circle dance
86 Depth-charge weapon
87 Compass pts.
88 Verb for Vergil
89 Alehouse
90 Greek letter
92 Go fast

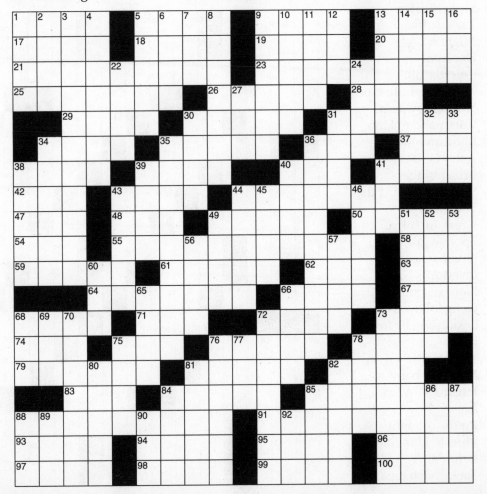

ACROSS

1 Shape
5 Discussion sites
9 Surly
14 Stage initials
17 Virginia willow
18 Secular
19 According to
20 Clodhopper width
21 Governor's address
24 Gibbon
25 "Stagger Lee" roll
26 Sermon takeoff point
27 Paternal relative
29 Exist
30 Traditional
33 Challenged
36 Avenal
37 Malice
40 Prospector's claim?
42 Brook
44 Clinching score
46 Singer Francis
47 Revoke
49 Due
51 Family mbr.
52 Strikebreaker
56 Tar's duffle
58 Mighty
60 Deprive
62 Celestial altar
63 "Pag" coproduction
64 Hot bakery item?
67 Command to Fido
68 Blind ambition
69 Actor Gulager
70 British singer
71 Steinbeck's "__ Eden"
73 For fear that
75 Great, in Tokyo
77 Spotted grouper
79 Opera voice
80 Overturns
83 Nonexistent
85 Gang follower
86 Disillusion by fowl fuzz?
90 Terre Haute's river
92 March 26 baby
93 Fugard's "A Lesson from __"
95 Prefix for night
96 Threshold in time
99 James's "A __ Murder"
101 Backstretch repast
103 Quipu keepers
105 Post a price for
106 How to get averages?
111 __ great extent
112 Epicure's problem
113 Letters
114 Old serf
115 Blind River's prov.
116 "__ Knows" ('50s hit)
117 Quarry
118 Ollie's partner

DOWN

1 "__ Solemnis"
2 Lutra member
3 What autumn does?
4 Tryst
5 Ziegfeld
6 Lummox
7 "Hud" director
8 Hurt
9 Digestive
10 Alphabetic trio
11 Kick-fuss link
12 Cheese type
13 Baseball manager Jim
14 Italian desserts
15 Defeated
16 Calm
22 Organic compound
23 Student's concern
28 Roster
31 Waikiki wear
32 Art __
34 Cabell of baseball
35 Actor Robert
38 Commoner
39 Banister post
41 Shoe part
42 Blackguard
43 Brainstorm
45 Wall St. transactions
48 Chagall
50 Actress Manoff
53 Throws out actors?
54 Melodic
55 Go to __ (support)
57 California's self-descriptive
59 Spanish port
61 Spill the beans
65 Angola city
66 Freshen up
72 Lip
74 Set the dial
76 Hero
78 Grogshop offering
81 USPS workers
82 Actress Kurtz
84 Sapporo sash
86 N.Y. senator
87 Prayer
88 Overlook, in a way
89 Orderly
91 Take __ view of
94 Unsubtle dance
97 White of TV
98 German city
100 Vintner's prefix
102 Asterisk
104 Wedding-announcement words
107 Yucatan year
108 Type of buoy
109 Speed
110 Nev. town

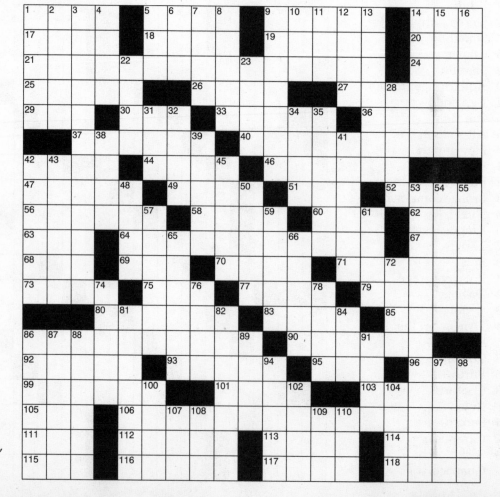

ACROSS

1 Poke
4 Florentine's farewell
8 Night music
12 Midwest tribe
16 Miscalculate
17 Keen
18 Melville tale
19 Well-trained
20 God of war
22 Folding perch
25 First name in Congress
26 Actress Susan
27 Clarsach
28 Customize
29 Hormone material
31 Gibson of films
32 Former
34 Sp. queen
35 St. Louis team
36 PC operating system
37 Chart type
38 Capital following
39 Indistinct
41 Minimum amount
44 Writer Seton
45 Tussaud's raw material
46 Site of Gravel Pit Park
47 Phantasm
51 Sault __ Marie
52 Filmmaker Wenders
53 Poke
54 Bust
55 "Apologia Pro Vita __"
56 Perfect
58 Break
60 Tout's offering
61 Shoe part
63 Unadorned
65 Museum material
66 Terpsichorean turning
    point
67 Malodorous
68 Rose lover
69 TV initials
70 Tableland
71 Means of estimation
74 Mushroom
75 Don't look __!
78 Diamond feats, for short
79 Pond floater
80 Pops
81 Agnus __
82 Tokyo drama
83 "The __ Up There"
    (1994 film)
84 Modern artery

87 Ms. Dinsmore
89 Kiln
91 Ending for diction or
    discretion
92 Baccarat item
93 Suction cup on a stick
96 Expression
97 One of the Farrows
98 Gate receipts
99 Concerning
100 Saison on the Saône
101 British gun
102 NBA, e.g.
103 Pillar's counterpart
104 PC hookup

DOWN

1 Casual wear
2 Sovereign decree
3 Vitamin-B source
4 Crewel
5 Like some campus
    halls
6 Ethereal
7 Tribute of a sort
8 Absolute
9 Latin love

10 Bottle-nosed dolphin
11 Call for help
12 Comedian Mort
13 Reduces
14 Grisham's "The __"
15 Rugged ranges
21 Layers
23 Store employee
24 Heartbreaker
30 "Peg __ Heart"
31 Philosophy subject
33 Directed
36 Amalgamate
37 Hubris
38 Moslem holy man
39 Alpine block
40 Pitched properly
41 Innocuous
42 Worn down
43 Forestall
45 Far's companion
48 18th Century invention
49 Pointless
50 Abrogate
52 "Ballad of Reading
    Gaol" poet
53 Obvious

54 Actress Laura
57 Certain bishops
59 Rooftop sight
62 River to the Seine
64 Break
68 Two-handled jugs
69 Charisse
70 Unassuming
72 Big deal
73 Malleus's place
74 West
75 Experts
76 "Go __ on the
    Mountain"
77 Ill treatment
80 Decay of a sort
82 Mo. neighbor
83 Pale
84 Guitar ridges
85 Arterial trunk
86 Sana's land
88 Actress-model
90 Invites
91 Lhasa __
94 Flight-plan entry,
    for short
95 Race part

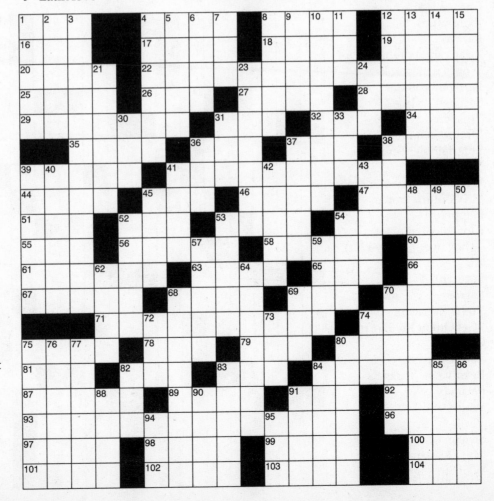

ACROSS

1 Like some teeth
7 "East of Eden" character
11 Infant's playthings
17 Drug
18 Zones
19 Secret
20 Radio transmission
21 Fast-food offering
23 Historical period
24 Mubarak of Egypt
26 Wroth
27 "Hamlet" courtier
30 Roma fontana
33 Believe
36 À votre __!
38 Marx Brothers film
43 Mrs. Lauder
44 Ghost-chance link
45 "Baby, __ You"
46 Scope
47 Girl in a Beach Boys song
49 Goes through
51 Dairy product
52 Flying formation
53 Construction strip
55 Garden tool
56 Extremities
58 Rare as __
61 Briard and borzoi
65 Words with smoke
67 Barn newcomers
69 Seat belt's place
70 Prospered mightily
73 Mountain home
75 Entertainment enterprise
77 Rose oil
78 Word with guard or gold
79 "In Country" force
81 Happen
82 Kid's menu morsel
85 "The Love __" (1973 hit)
86 Ad __
87 Substantial
88 Parrot
90 Prefix for valent
92 "Get Out of My Dreams, Get into __"
95 Tarbush, e.g.
98 Relative of "the cat's pajamas"
103 Watch out!
106 Verily
107 Sicilian peak
108 Muse of astronomy
109 Wall Street group
110 Storied loch
111 Beach wear

DOWN

1 __ Nostra
2 Buy __ in a poke
3 Walking awkwardly
4 Basin
5 Greek letter
6 Indian city
7 __ for one's money
8 Suits
9 Actor Vallone
10 Happy-clam connection
11 Smelter refuse
12 Sewing-machine inventor
13 Eager
14 Coop
15 Coulomb part
16 Map abbrs.
18 Body-builder's concern, for short
22 Plutarch's specialty
25 __ Rios, Jamaica
28 British gun
29 Rushes
31 Property fund
32 Salamanders
33 Refracted
34 Spur
35 Romans's river
36 Provide for
37 Pallid
39 "The wages __ is death"
40 Monsoon
41 Micronesia group
42 Distinctly unpopular
48 Garden invader
50 Stench
51 Thai coins
54 Actor Cariou
55 Map line: Abbr.
57 Poisonous plant
59 Patrick of the NBA
60 École attender
62 Rio Grander of song
63 __ Julius Caesar
64 Squash, for one
66 Coffeemaker type
68 Marcus Aurelius, e.g.
70 Baroque composer
71 Roman emperor (69 A.D.)
72 Auricular
73 __ bravo, charlie
74 Computer mode
76 Pac-10 school
78 "__ a Lonely Number"
80 "Aeneid" opener
83 Fire aftermath
84 NL club
89 Photographer Diane
90 Busy as __
91 Soybean product
93 Cravings
94 Civil War monogram
96 "Vesti la giubba," e.g.
97 Greenish blue
98 Poetic contraction
99 An FDR VP
100 Farm mom
101 Mo. neighbor
102 Born
104 Stat for Nomo
105 Pale

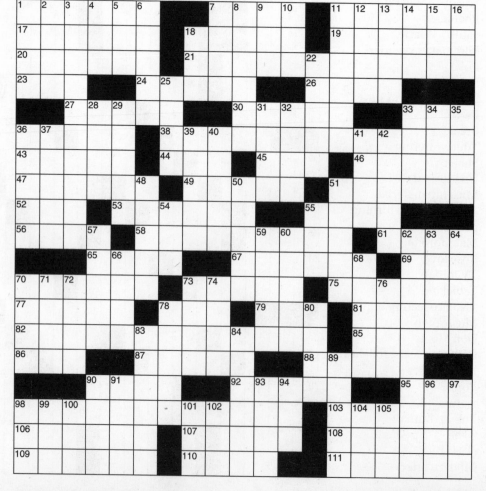

ACROSS

1 ''What __ bid?''
4 Resounded
8 ''High'' stuff in the '90s
12 Former Soviet units
16 Blackbird
18 NL manager
19 Kailua's isle
20 Systematic
21 Church area
22 Subject of a TV mystery
25 Ripken's club
27 Butterfly type
28 Manner of speaking
29 Leather worker
30 Chan's remark
31 Align
32 Thousand bucks
33 Polar sight
34 An O'Neill
36 Certain sports cars
37 Deprive
39 ''Cry Me a River'' singer
42 Concert halls
44 ''The __'' (1995 film)
45 Diagonal
46 Elec. units
50 ''Splash'' creature
52 Mortgages
54 Clever
55 Diagonally
56 Ad hoc group
57 Credit-card user
58 ''Of Thee __''
59 Nori and nostoc
60 Give a new name to
61 Supermarket sight
62 __ Brith
63 P.D. James's ''Original __''
64 Quaker addressee
65 ''The Dinner Party'' artist
69 Superlative suffix
70 Music store stock
73 Kazan
74 Burden
75 Revamped
77 Bring to mind
79 Cautious strategy choice
80 Flower stalks
83 Allen's ''Scenes from __''
84 The March King
86 Nobility
87 ''The Dick Van Dyke Show'' cast member

90 Duffer's downer
91 Brain passage
92 Philippines sea
93 Sandwich shop
94 Suggestion
95 Hangout
96 Road sign
97 Grasps
98 Conscription org.

DOWN

1 ''I __ a crook . . .''
2 Actress Anne
3 ''Blue Skies'' composer
4 Athlete of a kind
5 Regrettably
6 Conjunction
7 Detective
8 Scout's rider
9 Unhurried
10 Barbecue
11 Fifth Century marauder
12 Insinuating
13 Prelude to belief
14 Melange
15 Unsubtle dances

17 ''Spaghetti western'' filmmaker
23 Support for an artist?
24 Chicken __
26 Actor Cobb
30 Landed
31 Slaughter on the field
33 Ran
34 Cat __ tails
35 Harem rooms
37 Greek vernacular
38 Texas city
40 Kind of pricing
41 Portly-plus
43 ''__ home is his castle . . .''
46 Scope
47 ''Chronica Majora'' author
48 Working-class types
49 Gritty place
51 S.W. Afr. neighbor
52 Computer circuits
53 Words between roses
54 Situated
56 Desert basin
57 __ Xiaoping

59 The Beatles' ''__ Love Her''
60 Creeks
62 Durham player
63 Rabbit's tail
65 Preserves relative
66 Kind of wine or work
67 Works
68 Story starter
70 Pack
71 Bust
72 Panics
76 Kind of mother or mover
78 On guard
79 Construct
80 Tourney round
81 Actors Richard and Eddie
82 Clans
84 Obscenity
85 Modern Christiania
86 Protected area
88 Kiang
89 Grampian Mountains river

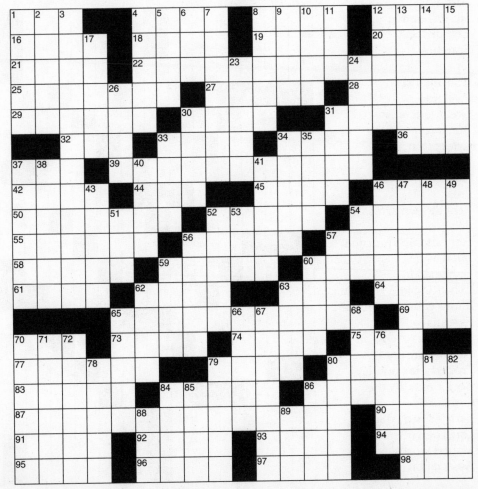

ACROSS

1 Learn about
7 Oar pin
12 Aspects
18 Fleet
19 Macho types
20 Work on roads
21 Ill-fated sandwiches?
23 Brunch selection
24 Home-entertainment item
25 Director Grosbard
27 Japanese airline
28 Linkage piece
31 Bluefins
32 Held safe
35 Vizquel of baseball
37 Onassis
38 Took to court
39 Excessive
42 Workshops for sandwich makers?
45 Fly
46 Teheran native
47 Hip-hop artist
50 Actress Cannon
51 False report
53 Airfoil
54 Heron relative
56 Circumspect
57 Searches
59 Open
61 USN mainstay
64 Wallaroo
65 Greek letters
66 Bunkroom sounds
70 Cries of surprise
72 Lament
74 Skirt
75 Frost
77 Item thrown across the deli?
81 San Antonio attraction
82 Blind as __
84 Conjunction
85 "The King and I" setting
86 Phone company workers
88 Essential oil
90 Hosp. sites
91 Health-care org.
93 Property-tax unit
94 Rock classic by the Cadillacs
95 Paris's spurned love
98 Cruel deli offering?
104 Mahler works
105 Association
106 Theater district
107 Pretty soon
108 Pot starters
109 Made a smooth transition

DOWN

1 Petasus or porkpie
2 Fumble
3 Grp. of MDs
4 Scandal sheet
5 Pindar, for one
6 Accurate
7 "Walking in __" ('60s hit)
8 Emcee's introductory word
9 Melville tale
10 Entertainer Pinky of yore
11 Guarantee
12 Lofty
13 Haw's companion
14 Simian
15 Prime time in the deli?
16 Not erratic
17 Bristle
22 Matisse
26 Boy
28 Laughable
29 Soprano Lucine
30 Yucatec
32 Turning point
33 Film of 1969
34 Okla. town
36 Jaffe and Barrett
38 Look over
40 Sugarville's state
41 Choice rhyme opener
43 Classical sorceress
44 Writer Murdoch
45 Seed covers
48 Name of 12 popes
49 Diminish
52 Confidence spoiler
53 Memo line
55 Tendon
58 Advent follower
59 Insignificant
60 Inlets
61 Joey of baseball
62 Mutual fund, e.g.
63 Deli skeptic's cry
65 Brewery need
67 One of the media
68 Poet Guest
69 Appears
71 Eighteen-wheeler
73 In the blink __ eye
76 Baseball's Gant
78 Means
79 Famous
80 Earth-moving equipment
82 Fr. friend
83 White whale
87 Sandpaper ingredient
88 Make __ (get rich)
89 Entertainer O'Donnell
91 Granada greeting
92 "Meet __ St. Louis"
94 Little drama
96 Flaky
97 Teachers' org.
99 "Sister Act" figure
100 Child's game
101 Actor Gulager
102 All-purpose vehicle
103 Dusseldorf demise

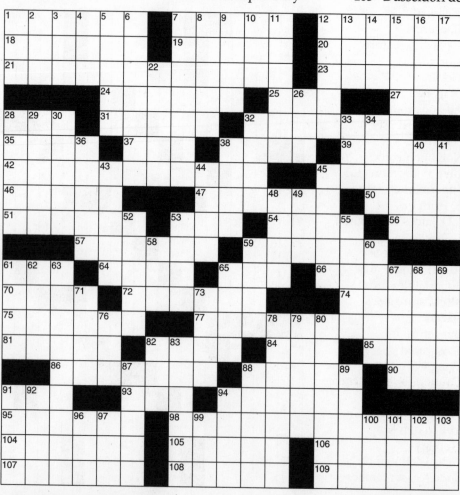

ACROSS

1 Burst
7 Pursuit
12 Titania's husband
18 Infuriate
19 Recurring film role
20 Oddsmaker's copout
21 Rock-star matchup
24 __ of tea
25 PP&M, for one
26 Exist
27 Ready to blossom
30 TV's Kudrow
33 TV's LeBlanc
36 Matchup of two singers
43 Columbus initials
44 Opposite of ne'er
45 Othello's ensign
46 Exhausts
48 Valentine sentiment
50 Nucleic acid
52 Glaswegian, for one
53 Ice pinnacle
56 Peewee and Della
59 Cambridgeshire town
60 Soul-pop matchup
63 West ending
65 Wool fabric
66 Harpoon
67 Lancaster
69 Arid: Prefix
70 Kind of street
74 Smock
77 Phone button
80 Rearward
81 Bitter
82 Matchup of veteran rockers
86 Dissolve
87 "Court TV" figure
88 "Tell It Like __"
89 Wall St. staple
92 Merkel and O'Connor
95 Practice
98 Rolling Stone joins Beatle (real name)
106 Access
107 Goddesses of the seasons
108 Loose as __
109 Available
110 Irish poet
111 Grooves

DOWN

1 Dowel
2 Sole
3 Paid performer
4 Flaunt
5 Breakfast order
6 Mysterious
7 Appraiser
8 Ad __
9 Emden exclamation
10 Three-handed card game
11 Scrutinizer
12 Part of the crew
13 Stadium sound
14 Right-angle joint
15 Hayworth
16 __ about (circa)
17 Hawaiian flyer
22 Bicuspid's backup
23 Branch
27 "Get __" ('50s hit)
28 Vile
29 Quarter-back word
31 Snowboard alternative
32 Botanist Gray
34 Crag
35 Poetic contraction
37 Beliefs
38 Deride
39 Bogeymen
40 Enneads
41 More pleasant
42 Organic compound
47 Pigpen
49 Capital ending
51 PDQ
54 Greek hero
55 __ close (just missed)
56 Stimpy's friend
57 In the __ storm
58 Perspectives
60 Sign up
61 Gaiety
62 Assay subject
63 Fade
64 Call the shots
68 S. Afr. bishop
71 Time before seating
72 Jai __
73 Cravings
75 "The Good __" (1993 film)
76 Lasted
78 Museum material
79 Q-U link
80 Gulf
83 Singer Mitchell
84 Chopin output
85 Metal brace
89 Stone shed
90 Mo. neighbor
91 Friends and neighbors
93 Hurting
94 Forge product
96 Slightly
97 Wide-eyed
99 __ la-la
100 She's no chick
101 Sky altar
102 Stool pigeon
103 Chinese statesman
104 Argot
105 Go-ahead

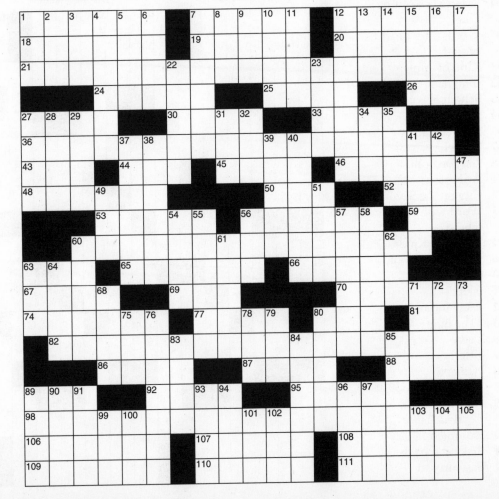

ACROSS

1 MacLaine's "Out on __"
6 Intensify
12 Old-style discipline
18 Shipboard scanner
19 Fundraiser phrase
20 Mrs. Sargent Shriver
21 Words after head
24 W.W. II area
25 Erich __ Stroheim
26 Occupies
27 Disposition
28 Rockies resort
30 Act follower
32 Ending for awe or irk
35 Words after head
43 Dilapidated
44 Jr.'s heir
45 Writer Joyce Carol
46 Float
47 Understand
48 Dais figures, for short
49 Radials, e.g.
50 Mountain endings
51 Colorful fish
53 Nuisance
54 "There Is Nothing Like __"
55 Words after head or foot
61 Kind of apple
62 Intaglios
63 Schedule word
64 Maladies
65 Seed covers
67 Hostelry
68 Aragon aunt
71 Arikara
72 City on the Seyhan
73 Word with way or where
74 Hockey's Kindrachuk
76 Words after foot
80 Clinton AG
81 Islet
82 A la Pindar
83 "The Egg __"
86 Drive
89 Utterly
90 Wallaba
93 Words after foot
99 Peggy Parish's "__ Bedelia"
100 Hummed
101 Pick up the tab
102 Ease up
103 Frays
104 Milquetoast

DOWN

1 Tennis legend
2 Churl
3 Be creative
4 Doorway item
5 Conciseness
6 Realization
7 Org. since 1970
8 Whitney
9 Finish
10 Summers on the Seine
11 Actor Franco
12 Sawbuck
13 Paul Newman film
14 Glaze
15 Baseball's Brogna
16 __ Rios, Jamaica
17 Exploit
22 Part
23 Handle-equipped
29 Carney
30 Nature goddess
31 Sapporo sash
33 Cash-drawer pile
34 ER habitues
35 Gal. parts
36 Mideast initials
37 Nouveau __
38 Babel
39 Pub game
40 Girder
41 Bellini opera
42 Actor Buddy
48 Gullet
49 Agreement
50 Swirl
51 Resistance units
52 Small naval craft
53 Coll. program
54 Actress Alicia
55 Highlands property-holder
56 Couch potato
57 Helmet
58 Senescent
59 Singer Tucker
60 Grass bristle
65 Tennis term
66 Expired
67 Pitch-black
68 Madeleines
69 Nautical chart abbr.
70 Pt. of NATO
72 Historical period
73 Sky altar
74 Small deals on Wall Street
75 Stat for Salmon
77 Car part
78 Colorful cat
79 Football coach Chuck
83 Distantly
84 Celebrity
85 Go one-on-one
87 Staffs
88 Quayle's successor
89 Introduces
91 Vegetable dish
92 Pretentious
94 Bronze ingredient
95 Deliberated
96 Pismire
97 Modernist
98 Dernier __

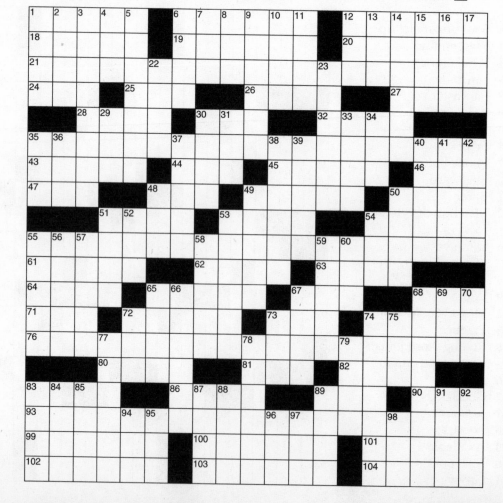

across

1 Value system
6 Bill
11 Advisor to Eeyore
14 Melancholy
17 Won't
18 Opening section
19 Charge
20 Conceit
21 Metalious burg
23 Issues
25 Brood
26 Cultural collection
27 Sportscaster Allen
28 Good enough
29 Bunker
31 Plunder
33 Singer Reeves
35 Wallace's "Ben __"
36 Learn
37 Trollope town
41 Capital-city Turk
43 Loquacious
44 Central courts
45 Impoverished
46 "Hamlet" hangup
47 Difficult
48 Film pet
49 Ferber novel
51 Tit for __
52 Word with culpa
53 Faulkner county
58 Soft shoe
61 What sleeping dogs do
62 Aegean region
63 Recipe abbrs.
67 In Morpheus's realm
69 Trident parts
71 Uninspiring
72 Artemis
73 Made a mistake
74 Aperitif brand
76 Christie village
78 Sapporo sport
79 Cyberphile's hangout
80 See ya
81 Gumbo ingredient
82 Long time
83 Botanical angle
86 More, in Madrid
87 __ fi
88 Man of the haus
90 Endlessly
92 Baum vision
96 Diving bird
97 U.K. part
98 Derring-do
99 Café dessert
100 Hwys.
101 Acapulco uncle
102 Jumpy
103 Dutch cheeses

DOWN

1 Sixth sense
2 With 8 Down, Stephen King tale
3 Square in Harris's "The Bomb"
4 Victorious
5 Obstruct
6 Swell, for short
7 Like a mosaic
8 See 2 Down
9 Killer whale
10 Caviar
11 "The quality __ is not strained . . ."
12 Prosperity
13 Allow
14 Half a fortnight
15 Taj Mahal site
16 Meddling
22 Oleanders
24 Nice and warm
27 Student's concern
29 ". . . sharper __ serpent's tooth . . ."
30 Mystical musings
32 Writer Beattie
33 Panama cape
34 Brazier
36 Saute
37 Haggled
38 Decorate
39 Ger. article
40 Hindu music
42 Per diem
43 Journey
46 Camel's hair fabric
47 Mulberry bark
49 Pass by
50 Only's partner
51 Prefix for light or night
54 Noted Chicago cow-owner
55 __ the line (conformed)
56 Ques. follower
57 On
58 Football gear
59 Words with were
60 Pelecypod
64 James Hilton hideaway
65 Blender output
66 Actor Jimmy
68 Permit
69 Low cards
70 Dies __
71 Medical org.
73 Ban
74 Mongrel
75 Menotti protagonist
77 Sana native
78 Outlying area
81 Vast amount
82 Traversed the sky
83 Remotely
84 Scratch
85 Peeves
87 Barrie pirate
89 Margin
91 Stable healer
92 Newt
93 Enzyme
94 President pro __
95 Approval

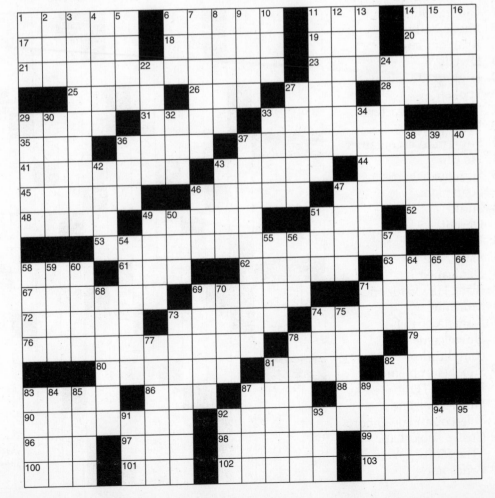

ACROSS

1 Prefix for plane or marine
5 Spiders' nests
9 Kid
12 Comet feature
16 Calls for payment
17 Sale tag
18 "I could __ horse!"
19 Church calendar
20 Spiteful sort
23 Joust
24 Singer Lemper
25 Alas, to Aeneas
26 Emanate
27 Disconcerts
28 Face value
29 Service-station abbr.
30 Kennel command
31 Utterly
32 Mayhem-maker
39 '50s hit by Skip and Flip
42 Application entry
43 Baseball wear?
44 Prefix for verse
45 Spanish conquest, 1509
46 Old-gasoline brand
48 Phone button
50 Ryan of films
51 Dwells
53 High-grade cotton
55 Spoken
57 "Congo" character
58 Risky purchase
61 Supermarket container
64 Ho Chi __
65 Starchy dish
66 Soap plant
68 Stark
71 Darn it!
73 Eurasian deer
75 Flair
76 Demeanor
77 Black Hawk, for one
78 Murmurs
80 Nagana carrier
82 Unwelcome complication
86 Snooker implement
87 Pt. of NATO
88 Japanese airline
89 Telescopium neighbor
92 Gossip subject, for short
95 "The More __ You"
96 Gruesome
97 Pale
98 Semite
99 Actual asset
102 Sonora snack
103 Gibson and Tormé
104 Rent
105 Exhort
106 River of Hades
107 Messy spot
108 Is obliged
109 Apiarist's concern

DOWN

1 Make sense
2 Sales target
3 Madison's roommate
4 Do-say link
5 Actress Baye
6 "War __" (Sherman)
7 Gallic god
8 Social follower
9 Storms, biblically
10 Detail
11 Candy unit
12 Box score line
13 N. Mex. neighbor
14 Baseless
15 Much
18 Lures
21 Wine-and-lemon drink
22 Indian state
27 Linseed oil source
31 Parka
32 Deadly poison
33 Perception
34 One of the Judds
35 Part of a Stein line
36 Speaker problem
37 TV's "Murder __"
38 "Animal Farm" figure
39 Kansas town
40 Molding, e.g.
41 Undulating
47 Vegetable dish
49 Highest
52 Houston
54 One or more
56 Actress Thompson
59 Freebooter
60 A Neville
61 Shock
62 Unfortunately
63 Actress Russo
67 Come together
68 Battle of Britain force, for short
69 Trouble
70 Sardonic
72 Coots
74 Reeks
77 Cold shoulder
79 Lubricated
81 Moccasin, for one
83 Fridge
84 Without travail
85 __ d'hôtel
89 Cognizant
90 Gamut
91 Guanaco's milieu
92 Broadway hit
93 Part of QED
94 Gossamer
95 "Oh, sure" relative
96 Gallico's "The __ Goose"
99 Forenoons
100 Judge Lance
101 Center

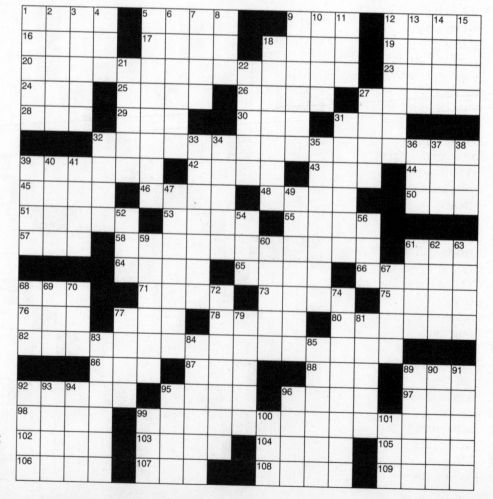

ACROSS

1 Spotted
4 Sill
9 Singer Collins
13 "If I __ Hammer"
17 Piolet, for one
18 Whatever
19 A Kennedy
20 Theater award
21 Fleur de __
22 Shaper of the London skyline
25 Elec. unit
27 Beak
28 U.K. honor
29 Turn
30 "Self-Reliance" man
32 Variation
34 "I __ Parade"
35 Case of jitters
36 Waste allowance
37 Benefit
39 Mag managers
40 Descry
41 "All I Wanna Do" singer
44 Mother of Louis XIV
45 Other things, to Caesar
46 Approves
47 Salamanders
51 __ fi
52 Court figure
55 Sausalito's county
56 Ladder peak
58 Once around
59 Slaughter
61 Intellectual's love
62 Hunting dogs
64 Overwhelming amount
65 Quiescence
66 Nucleic acid
68 "Three Men __ Baby"
69 Knife
70 "Reality Bites" actor
74 Bakery line
75 Keogh relative
78 Took first
79 Confederate
80 Wrench
81 Oleanders
83 Harbor sight
85 Choir's place
88 Flowering shrub
90 __-Magnon man
91 Supporting

92 Hence
93 Sprite also known as "Puck"
97 Football's Parseghian
98 Post
99 Sp. river
100 Sierra __
101 Clear
102 Kennel command
103 Roars
104 Got along
105 Ordinal ending

DOWN

1 Emollient
2 Truism
3 "Major League" player
4 Resinous material
5 Group character
6 "Splish Splash" singer
7 Smooth-talking
8 Golfer Ernie
9 Virtue
10 Optimism
11 Freak ending

12 Lascivious look
13 Instructional phrase
14 "__ man dies only once"
15 Counted calories
16 Achates's friend
23 Bulwark
24 Loggers' competition
26 Worthless stuff
31 Belle Boyd, for one
32 Golden syrup
33 Nip's partner
36 Attenuated
38 Grads-to-be
40 Put in cypher
41 Decline
42 __ Gatos, Calif.
43 Make independent
44 Up and doing
45 Exist
48 "I'm listening" character
49 AL team
50 Pussyfoot
52 Qt. subdivisions
53 Attention
54 Extends

55 "__ Doubtfire"
57 Cloy
59 Relinquish
60 Sky altar
62 Ecru
63 Cimmerian
66 Greek letter
67 Bobbsey and others
69 A Keaton
71 Sawyer's creator
72 Coiffures
73 __ a sudden
74 Soup vegetable
75 Ready to fight
76 Apply fresh paint
77 Lawrence's milieu
80 Sovereignty
82 Without warmth
84 Oak for the 2000s
85 Hue
86 Heron relative
87 Unwilling
89 Hoary
91 Pet's pest
94 Kimono adjunct
95 Sprite
96 Marry

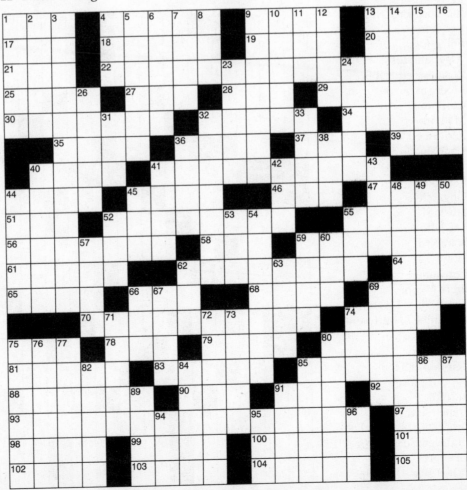

ACROSS

1 Indecisive sounds
4 Ovine observation
7 Freight repository
11 Faux pas
16 Taboo's opposite
17 Yours and mine
18 Scruff
19 Staggering
20 Gump metaphor for life
23 Actor Christopher
24 Take __ (relax)
25 Fans' claim
26 Deleted
28 Actor Baldwin
29 Part of TNT
30 Appellation
32 Mannerism
34 NYC subway
35 Prefix for logical
36 Actress Sara
37 Indian title of respect
39 Bear it's companion
41 Mule team
43 Gloucester's cape
45 WHO, e.g.
46 Get in rebounding position
47 Just-suspected link
50 Larynxes
54 Fill in for
56 Algerian port
57 Business letter abbr.
58 Moore in movies
59 Corn unit
60 Mail drop
64 Performed
65 Charismatic quality
67 "Bali __"
68 Passion
69 Oligarchy
71 Huskies
73 Lab leftover
74 Songbird
75 Howl
76 Consume
78 Bit of humor
79 "Hungry __" ('80s hit)
81 Beginning of nutrition?
83 Weave's partner
84 U.S. honor
87 Belt-maker's tool
89 Type of sauce
91 Indeed
93 French soldier
95 Uris's "__ 18"
97 Undergraduate degrees, for short
99 "The Lady __ Tramp"

100 Pamper
101 Suspect's "out"
103 Grounded to the pitcher
106 Novelist Wilson
107 Troll, for one
108 Marx
109 Holiday moment
110 Place to play
111 Burden
112 Hedge bushes
113 Carmine

DOWN

1 Removing from storage
2 Lead singer of the '90s
3 __ say (presumed)
4 Support
5 Bow
6 Tone-deafness
7 Flat-headed fasteners
8 Jaguarundi
9 Summit
10 Pinball button
11 Needlefish
12 Sector
13 Claustrophobic
14 Mania
15 Choose
17 Relative of "too, too"
21 Traffic unit
22 Circumstances
27 Volleyball maneuver
30 Malaysian export
31 Period
33 Gator's cousin
36 Floor covering
38 Protest
40 Enraged
41 Helios
42 Kind of fiction
44 Time being
46 Uprising in 1900
47 Craftsman
48 __ Paulo
49 Prefix for structure
51 Olympic surface
52 Transude
53 Word with step or walk
54 Coral and Red
55 Cezanne
56 River to the Missouri
61 Triumphant cry

62 Do re mi followers
63 Underwear type
66 Per diem
70 Court cry
72 Chay and cudbear
74 Internet part
77 Boy king of old
78 Bliss
80 Blubber
82 Phyles
83 Flight recorder
84 Gossip maven
85 Bushing
86 Defeated in the ring
87 Accumulate
88 Writer Cather
90 Brute
92 Cable TV network
93 River City trouble
94 Certain med. practitioner
96 Have __ hair day
98 Index
100 Players in the middle: Abbr.
102 Memo drop
104 Robert Morse role
105 Scottish jackdaw

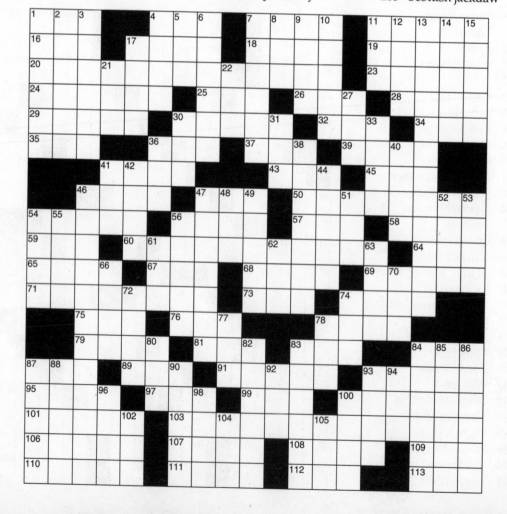

ACROSS

1 Pretense
5 Film of 1995
9 City on I-90
14 Embryo
17 Insipid
18 Client
19 Writer Ephron et al.
20 Little "Locomotion" singer
21 Disgusting
24 Stitch
25 Part of E.T.
26 Scent
27 Kind of horse
29 Inside post
32 Cassowaries
34 Furious
35 Coddle
38 Rural sight
40 Shirt type
42 Opt
45 Expert
46 Previously
50 Gudrun's husband
51 One of the Barrymores
53 Chow-hall gear
54 Headlight setting
56 TV's "__ Haw"
57 Stanley Falls locale
58 Anticipatory occasion
59 Stupid
61 Actress Long
62 Any guy
64 Dine
65 "Father Knows Best" family name
68 Gant of baseball
69 Indolence
72 Decay
73 Hither's companion
74 Hampton __, Va.
76 Mr. Yale
77 Will __ wisp
79 Inside the ship
82 Born
83 Laments
85 Pittance
86 Appropriate
87 Postpone
88 Music man Puente
90 Dipteron
93 Roy Orbison hit
95 Subterfuge
98 Coffee grind
100 Lacquer ingredient
104 Letters with CD
105 Place to read
109 Mimic
110 Rose oil
111 Western resort
112 Field mouse
113 Unseld of basketball
114 City of France
115 The Beatles' "__ Leaving Home"
116 __ vera

DOWN

1 French cleric
2 Hedge bush
3 Vituperate
4 Amontillado
5 Protrude
6 Volcanic product
7 Art __
8 Diminish
9 Deceptions
10 Hallux, for one
11 "__ la Douce"
12 Italian isle
13 Gawking
14 Irrelevant
15 Eye part
16 Realization
22 Blue-chip rating
23 __ de guerre
28 Composer Bartók
30 Pleistocene age
31 Arty abode
33 __ biscuit (hardtack)
35 Singer Joan
36 Proceedings
37 Antiquated
39 Passed
41 Give
43 Durrell tale
44 Linked
46 Ill-defined
47 Partner of 3 Down
48 Cosmetician's detail
49 Clamor
52 Gannon University site
55 Scandals
59 Glued
60 Hockey great Bobby
62 O'Neill's "The Emperor __"
63 Cargo
65 Lined up
66 Remark
67 Cry
70 Writer Astley
71 Rocker Lewis
74 Baseball antecedent
75 Pond surface
78 Grand-scale
80 Record
81 Parrot
84 Take a __ (try)
87 Mucin-containing mixture
89 ". . . and __ grow on"
91 Hectare part
92 Shades
94 Gibson of films
95 Gullet
96 Aspire
97 Famous last words
99 Egyptian deity
101 Organic compound
102 Kind of drama
103 Hmmm relative
106 Conflict
107 Garden tool
108 Double bend

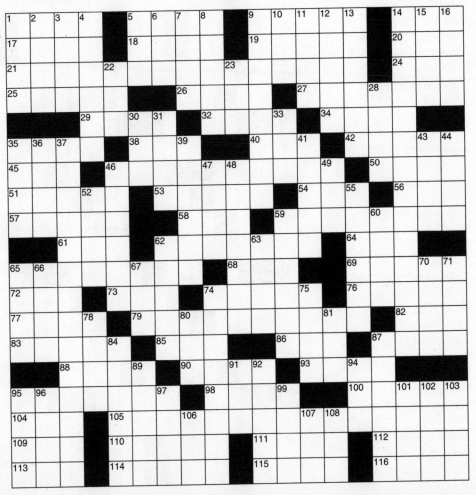

ACROSS

1 Oxford features
6 Mt. Parnassus town
12 Hopeless
18 In reserve
19 Spore filament
20 Sailor tying up
21 Start of a seasonal verse
24 Crucial
25 Bigwigs
26 Town in 40 Down
27 Sandwich's cape
28 M.D. grp.
30 Writer Fleming
31 Actress Delaney
34 Verse, part II
41 Out of port
42 Measure
43 Golfer Trevino
44 Word-processor mode
45 Belinda of baseball
46 Prix __
47 Promos
48 Radiate
49 Hosp. locales
50 Make a note
51 Be obliged
52 Kaz Dagi
53 Verse, part III
61 Dimercaprol
62 USN inst.
63 Kind of box or line
64 Mrs., in Madrid
65 G-5 member
68 '90s pop group
69 Calls down (on)
71 Landed
72 Chinese gelatin
73 Before
74 Prefix for mate or motive
75 Rhythmical flow
76 Verse, part IV
81 Consult
82 Public works project
83 Acknowledgment
84 Actor Tognazzi
85 PBS threesome
87 Cathedral area
89 Machine tool
92 End of verse
98 Rough
99 Jimmy Carter's town
100 Nifty
101 Determinative
102 Attacks
103 Painter Anna Mary

DOWN

1 Glance
2 "Three Musketeer's" queen
3 Burg
4 Common Market currency
5 Power controls
6 Profound
7 Culbertons et al.
8 Stripling
9 School org.
10 Prime
11 Dies __
12 Aunt-niece relationship
13 Italian type designer
14 Connect
15 West ending
16 So-so mark
17 Prefix for cycle
22 Film of 1995
23 Woodstock relatives
27 Actor James
28 African fox
29 Mrs., in Montmartre
31 Antelope
32 "__ It My Way"
33 Apportion
34 Jar type
35 Kind of physics
36 Ferment
37 One of the Bunkers
38 Fenway garb?
39 Turney wood
40 "Giant" setting
46 Turkey, e.g.
47 Amazement
48 Circular current
50 Actress Collins
51 Ceres
52 Printer's inventory
54 Ski lifts
55 Cove
56 PC operating system
57 Scarf
58 L.I. town
59 Cross-examine
60 "The Lonesome Death of __ Carroll"
65 Pokes
66 Fever symptom
67 Noggin
68 Quiver
69 Took to court
70 Where __ at
71 Mighty Dog competitor
73 Early Ga. governor
74 Latin I word
77 Town in 40 Down
78 Shoe part
79 Displace
80 Form of discrimination
85 Old salts
86 Sales workers, for short
87 Water buffalo
88 History
89 Club money
90 Unaccountable
91 Fish dish
92 Noun case: Abbr.
93 Extinct bird
94 Seine material
95 Corpulent
96 USO habitues
97 Cube root of eight

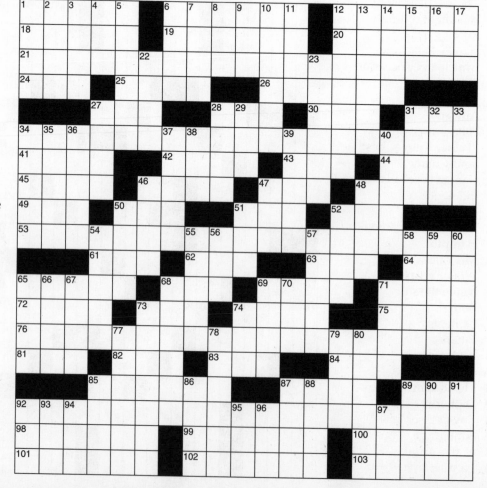

ACROSS

1 "A Christmas Carol" cry
4 Askew
7 Oxidizes, in a way
12 Less debatable
17 Lennon's widow
18 Exist
19 Info highway traffic
20 West Point fledgling
21 Grate item
23 Olio
25 Evidence
26 "Second City," for short
28 Loft
29 Certain moths
30 Adolescent
31 Littoral
33 Perceived
35 Bit of Chihuahua change
37 "__ My Life"
38 Performed
40 Prevaricated
43 Snicker
46 Big bird
48 Entertainer Williams
50 Swindled
51 Fighting
53 Olios
55 Octogenarians' time
57 Actor Voight
58 Telcom abbr.
59 Autonomous
60 Fountainheads
63 Vizquel of baseball
67 Toss
70 Diminish
71 Candy-store staple
74 Olio
78 Biological building blocks
79 Haggard yarn
80 Homogeneous
81 Ballston __, N.Y.
83 Shut, in a way
85 Knee: Prefix
86 Fashion monogram
88 Coulomb part
90 Paper unit
91 Gumbotil or galt
93 "Baseball __ of inches"
96 Luxuriate
99 Fitting
101 Hubbub
103 Unclose
104 Word with Rica or Brava
105 Olio
108 Cabretta, e.g.
110 Soup
111 Logic
112 OAS, e.g.
113 Holiday time
114 Libel
115 Take __ (get comfortable)
116 What pessimists say
117 D.C. title

DOWN

1 Gasconade
2 Singer Lennox
3 Olio
4 Coxswain's cry
5 To's partner
6 Undecided's perch
7 Put on record
8 Actress Thurman
9 Edible olio
10 Leaning
11 Aperture
12 Keyboard key
13 Director Grosbard
14 Work on furniture
15 Sp. river
16 Fernando and Alejandro
22 Private
24 Make a checking error
27 "Bali __"
31 Conductor Georg
32 Material ending
34 Presidential voter
36 Right away, to RNs
39 Hosp. hookups
41 Vernacular
42 Prosecutors, for short
43 Brasserie bigwig
44 Friseur's concern
45 Lambs' dams
47 Informed about
49 Put the kibosh on
52 According to
54 Subtlety
56 Advantageous
57 Foresail
61 Ruthian collection
62 Ledge
64 Olios
65 Pine
66 Pipe
68 Perfect game totals
69 "We will __" (Khrushchev)
72 Galway neighbor
73 Bone: Prefix
74 "The Winds of War" protagonist
75 TV's "Murder __"
76 Medicinal solution
77 "Six __ Riv Vu"
78 Seaport sight
82 Kind of fowl or jacket
84 15th Century explorer
87 Cotton fibers
89 Caesura
92 Wrath
94 Rouen's river
95 Brunch offering
97 Martin of the movies
98 One of the Carpenters
99 Vipers
100 Guerdon
102 "Casablanca" character
104 Shrewd
106 __ culpa
107 Sp. she-bear
109 Slice of history

ACROSS

1 Besides
5 Golfer Norman
9 Little bit
13 Unvarnished
17 Enter
18 "Green Mansions" girl
19 Kind of oak or act
20 "Close Encounters" craft
21 Loser to Johnson
23 Tavern item
25 Item to save
26 Happy sound
27 Concur
28 Get cleaner
30 Horrible
32 Split
34 Like-not link
35 Shoe part
36 Deputy
37 Health club
40 Without precision
43 Foot medicament
46 What -30- means
47 Mortgage
49 Early chief justice
50 Wharf
51 Istomin's instrument
52 Sault __ Marie
53 Bear in the air
54 Nucleus
57 Actor Vallone et al.
59 Mid-term, for one
62 Angelus ender
63 Hypothesis
64 Purpose
66 Veldt beast
68 Bronzes
69 Comedian Poundstone
71 __ out (dispense)
72 Pub pour
75 Gauze
78 Limp
80 Popular
81 Court matter
82 Stag
84 Stash
85 Clinton AG
86 "La Bohème" role
87 Attached
89 Ms. Dinsmore
92 Favorable factor
94 Amusing
96 Abrasive
98 Marcia Brown tale for kids
101 Ballet bend
102 Carrel
103 NL team
104 Beige
105 Barks
106 Precious
107 Hmmm relative
108 Pelt

DOWN

1 Custard ingredient
2 Card game
3 Nichols film of 1983
4 Charms
5 Calculator display
6 Hierurgy
7 Arise
8 Needlefish
9 Scrapbook
10 Stratum
11 Bursting
12 Debussy milieu
13 Swell
14 Distantly
15 Eglatere
16 Being
22 Filmmaker Craven
24 __ hoot (cared)
26 Steers
28 Agitate
29 School since 1440
31 Kind of room or hall
33 Without foundation
35 Noisy scavenger
36 Took over
37 __ und drang
38 Kind of porridge
39 Nordic
41 Actor Wallach
42 Ananias
44 Speed
45 Team
48 Kind of insurance
51 Aspect
54 Business presentation
55 Craters of the Moon site
56 Article of faith
58 Sam's comics cohort
60 Flying
61 Updated agora
65 Singer Johnny
67 Teachers org.
69 Menial
70 In disarray
72 Modern music form
73 Adriatic island
74 Rice's "Exit to __"
76 Declivitous
77 Son of Noah
79 Leyden and Livarot
83 Grimace
85 Fair diversions
86 Unclear
87 Uptight
88 "Now __ seen everything . . ."
89 Spot
90 __ Land (Southern California)
91 Tonsorial sound
93 For fear that
95 Brain part
97 Okla. town
98 Poli. __
99 Yankee Conference mbr.
100 Equivoque

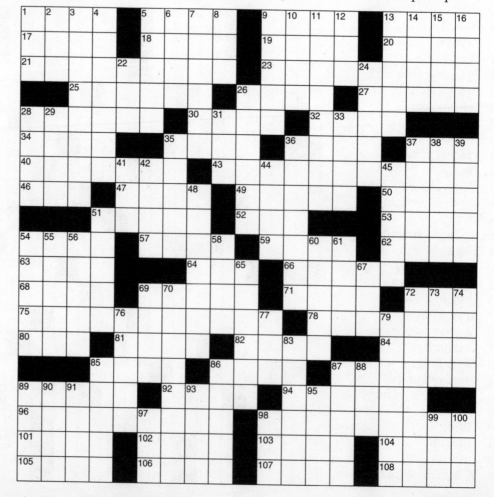

ACROSS

1 Mercenary
6 Attacks
11 Cranky sorts
18 Maltreatment
19 "__ Name" (Jim Croce hit)
20 Rescue site, 1976
21 Have trouble sleeping
23 Biting
24 Nabokov novel
25 Flimsy
27 Actor Stephen
28 Cigar case
32 Casa room
33 Kind of shoe or elbow
36 Campus growth
37 Skip
39 ¿Como __ usted?
41 Advantage
42 President pro __
43 Good-natured exchange
47 Merrymaking
48 "I __ Little Prayer"
50 Model Macpherson
51 Pitcher Hershiser
52 Part of UNLV
53 Reliable sort
56 Greensward
58 Sugar
59 Only's partner
60 Wholesalers
64 Labor org.
65 In the old days
67 S.A. land
68 Contemptuous retort
69 Okinawan capital
71 Squelch
72 Faint
73 Up and __!
75 Model
77 Dupe
81 Political initials
82 Move about the ring
86 Unclose
87 High spirit
89 Exceptional
90 Watch part
91 Schwyz neighbor
92 Men of Mazatlan
94 Cottage cheese morsel
97 Forever young
99 Forest female
100 Baker's "__ Is Depravity"
102 Miscellany
103 Ropes
106 It began in the '50s
111 Big stone
112 Pot starters
113 Heron relative
114 Hotel name
115 Detectives' raw material
116 "The Dancing Class" painter

DOWN

1 Barrel
2 Nigerian native
3 Greek letters
4 Very, in music
5 Head of a sled team
6 Stashed
7 Certain reps.
8 Missionary's concern
9 Heart chambers
10 Complex
11 Achievement
12 Mom's sib
13 Cubic meter
14 Unruffled
15 Tidal action
16 Box-score column
17 Dry
22 One of the Judds
26 Must
28 Box-score column
29 Eye part
30 Tut-tut relative
31 Split
33 Observes
34 Tropical herbivore
35 Intuits
38 Inform
40 Fortune-teller's card
44 Actor Delon
45 With "The," old TV series
46 Resin
49 PD msg.
54 Road-to-recovery spot
55 Smooth talkers
57 Nothing doing, informally
60 O.T. book
61 Ripken, for one
62 Football defender's tactic
63 Ancient Mideast land
66 Phone abbr.
70 War god
74 Polo
76 Ms. Hari
78 Primordial mire
79 Work
80 Staying power: Sl.
83 Dispassionate
84 Meat and dairy shunner
85 Revised
88 Pasta item
93 Interprets
95 River to the Mediterranean
96 Pronouncements
98 Voluminous
100 Blood components
101 Tax form, for short
103 One of the networks
104 Perfect-game totals
105 Become
107 Onager
108 Assn.
109 Thompson of TV
110 Aspiring capts.

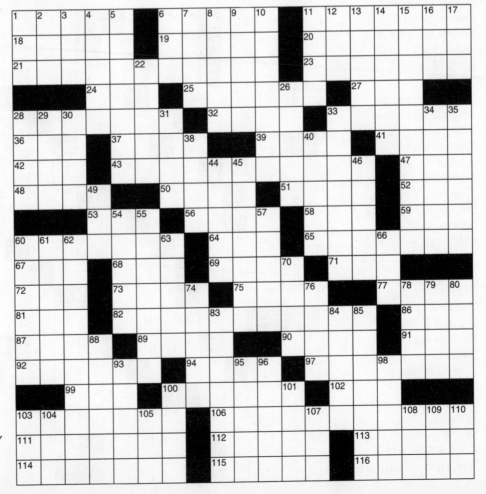

ACROSS

1 Cook wear
5 Gotcha!
8 Commingled with
12 Stimulus
16 Figure of fright
17 Hurly-burly
19 Nonexistent
20 Stock in trade
21 Brace
22 Pirates' delights
25 Himalayan high point
27 "__ Not Dressing" (1934 film)
28 On high
29 Coupe alternative
30 Italian wine
32 Philosophical question
34 Perfect score
35 First-rate
37 Chart type
38 Dernier __
39 Question opener
40 Cogent
42 They run in a bed
46 Animal assmblge.
47 Wheel's partner
48 Decomposition
49 Words with know or bag
53 Biblical verb
54 Fury
55 Drastically reduce
57 Rive Gauche wear
58 Entertainer Ethel
60 Yaws
61 Bovine
62 Standard
63 Peer
64 Undergrads' degrees
65 Initials on the el
66 Cubic meter
67 Haul
68 Financial loss
69 Understanding
70 "The Whiskey Ain't Workin'" singer
74 Knowledge
75 Follow
78 Question opener
79 LBJ pet
80 Sommelier's concern
82 Hideout
83 Media matter
84 Ganesh follower
86 "(I Can't __) Satisfaction"

89 Corrode
91 N.Y. campus
92 Boston drive
94 Decked the halls, in a way
98 Gull's cousin
99 Hatcher of TV
100 Sakhalin native
101 Pretension
102 Facility
103 Mars
104 Space
105 Kiang
106 Gang hanger-on

DOWN

1 Pouts
2 "__ at the office"
3 Old reliable
4 Patio
5 Humanities
6 Impairs
7 Enzyme
8 Sky-blue
9 Trifling
10 Wrath
11 Exact moment

12 No fashion plate
13 Swivels
14 Hit-or-miss
15 Bridle at
18 Michener tale
23 Film of 1995
24 Actor Liotta
26 Compass pt.
31 Iridescent stone
32 Fury
33 __, haec, hoc
36 Severe
38 Grumpy
39 "So what else __?"
40 Detective
41 Check
43 Scottish explorer
44 Fish, in a way
45 Damper
47 Phone feature
50 October ultimatum
51 Role for Demi in '95
52 Natural gas
55 Garden pests
56 Meadow
59 Award-winning film of the '50s

60 Calamary
61 Spiteful
63 U.S. king
64 Pipistrelle
68 Swift, e.g.
71 Introduce
72 "To __ own self be true"
73 Singer Tebaldi
74 "Hamlet" character
75 Folk singer
76 Kind of bond
77 Whole
81 Self
83 '90s cash dispenser
84 Run-of-the-mill
85 Clientele
87 Vikings
88 Skybox occupant
90 "Lucky Jim" author
91 Pay __ mind
93 Hardy heroine
95 Musical aptitude
96 "O __ Mio"
97 Creek

ACROSS

1 Refluxes
5 __ Cynwyd, Pa.
9 Draconian
14 Student's stat
17 Greek chorus accompaniment
18 In the rack
19 Pressing
20 OECD, e.g.
21 Nephew Fred's words to Scrooge
24 What to do with gay apparel
25 Stiller partner
26 Writer Rand
27 Pricker
29 Dulling influence
32 "The Maid of the Mist" sight
35 Tavern selection
36 Mont. neighbor
38 Buddy
39 Food-processor button
40 Connection
41 With 81 Across, song of 1934
44 Deliver
47 "Love me, love __"
48 Farm father
49 Dissipate like steam
51 Sales specialist, for short
53 No hit
55 Sort
56 Actress Hagen
57 Unctuous
60 Supremes alumna
62 Bell sound
64 Occupies
65 Actor Tognazzi
66 Alley __
67 Actress Fitzgerald
69 Craving
71 Setbacks
74 Football owner Wellington
76 Wordless depictors
80 Reliable
81 See 41 Across
84 Past
85 Didn't stop
86 Popular
87 Teachers' org.
88 Teen's lament
90 Incubus
91 Ranch rope
93 It may be a master
95 Maui valley
97 Egg-shaped
100 Muslin pilgrimage
101 St. Nick's parting words
106 Sp. bear
107 Lucknow's land
108 Notice
109 Trim
110 "The Bridge at San Luis __"
111 Disreputable
112 Collector's delights
113 Movie dog

DOWN

1 Actor Jack
2 "Stand __"
3 Words with butter or water
4 Calif. missionary
5 Horse color
6 Easy as __
7 "Merry Widow" composer
8 Not __ eye in the house
9 Owns
10 Advice to the indecisive
11 Street fight
12 Sky sight
13 "__ Rebel" ('60s hit)
14 Cratchit sentiment
15 Low-ranking sort
16 Choreographer DeMille
22 Run wild
23 Animates
28 Site of Moosehead Lake
30 D.C. money-raising grp.
31 Right-angle joints
33 Onassis
34 Word with majesty
36 Saying, for short
37 Calendar unit
39 Stickler
40 Reservoir
42 Conservative
43 Purposes
44 Comeback
45 Eight, in combinations
46 Signify
50 Street in Rome
52 Humdrum
54 Source of pain
57 Yours and mine
58 "By the Time __ to Phoenix"
59 Wassail wish
61 Unclose
63 Make money
64 "What's __ for me?"
66 Church calendar
68 Cleaning substance
70 Sentiment
72 Keen
73 Ripoff
75 Turkish VIP
77 Composites
78 Ram's consort
79 Highlands fall
82 Lennon's widow
83 Rocky pinnacle
85 Overhauled
88 Loathe
89 Quit
90 "Lorna __"
91 Free
92 Sp. province
94 Singer Redding
96 Long time
98 Which
99 Sicilian peak
102 Cover
103 Ballad
104 Elect
105 Functional lead-in

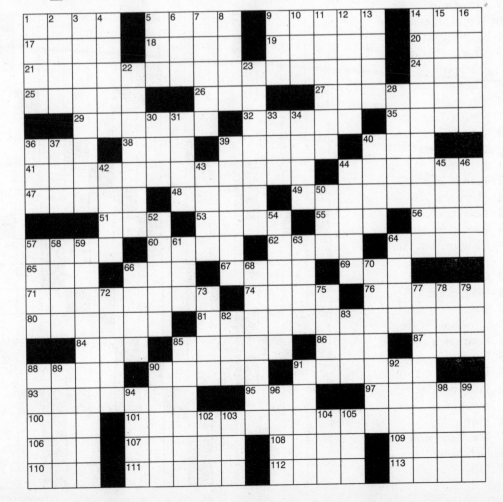

ACROSS

1 Penny part
4 Boxscore listing
7 Court star
12 Perfect
17 Lifetime
18 Shanty
19 Playground item
20 Time being
21 Treasury
23 Going-nowhere track
25 Club
26 Clamp shape
27 Swerved
28 Nincompoop
30 Reach
34 Top rating
35 CIA forerunner
36 Borders on
38 Stag
39 Grain bristles
40 Situation
41 Skillful
43 Tan
44 Sunday msg.
47 Luau wear
48 Nintendo rival
49 Constrain
50 Wood-shaping tool
51 __um (gnat)
53 Chingachgook's transport
54 Charge
55 Template
57 __-Tin-Tin
58 Certain interstate
60 Garden pest
61 Manner
63 Pair
64 Happens
65 Basketball violation
66 Beer ingredient
67 "Diggin' On You" group
70 Catchall abbr.
71 "Windows 95" button
72 Beat
73 __ polloi
74 Sasquatch's cousin?
75 Gunny
76 Used up
78 Body builder's pride, for short
81 Born
82 Most winsome
84 Debauch
85 Lift

87 __ Harbour, Fla.
88 Hindu festival
90 Film sequel of '95
93 Bounce back
96 Gold braid
97 Nearby
98 MDs' org.
99 Silkworm
100 À votre __
101 Imporous
102 It's good!
103 Plow into

DOWN

1 Windows competitor
2 "__ to Pieces"
3 Abandoned
4 Actress Perlman
5 Myanmar
6 Common contraction
7 Librarian's reminder
8 Fetch
9 Napery
10 Sharpness
11 IRA variant
12 Vehement
13 Be overfond
14 First page of a Catalan calendar
15 Large area
16 Imparts
22 Fedora material
24 Redress
28 Dumpty's experience
29 Surnay
31 California
32 South Seas cloth
33 Skill
34 Hawthorne book
37 Mouthed off to
39 Prefix for space
42 Caribou or chital
43 __ foi (good faith)
44 Betrayed
45 Pound
46 Jerry of the Red Sox
49 Disappoints
50 Gudrun's husband
52 Cornelia __ Skinner
53 Vault
54 Nominee groups

55 Beep
56 ". . . pease porridge in __ . . ."
59 Rice team
62 Actress Hatcher
65 Unflinching
66 Horn adjunct
68 Protracted
69 Burg
71 Nervous system juncture
72 Sell option
75 One of the Caesars
77 Tony sport
78 Greek city-state
79 Diamond Yogi
80 Reject
82 Holy writ
83 __ park
86 Discharge
87 Actress Neuwirth
89 Sorrels
91 Antic
92 Israel follower
93 Beam
94 Historical division
95 Hoops target

ACROSS

1 Substance
5 Vatican vestment
8 Counter
13 Facial feature
17 Throb
18 Semblance
19 Thespian
20 Music man Schifrin
21 Try to see
22 "Aladdin" prince
23 Miami team
25 Kind of corn or culture
27 Uraeus
29 Transgress
30 Flushed
31 Liquid meas.
33 Figure
36 Noted diarist
38 Gets on a soapbox
40 Robert __
42 "Ptolemy" sculptor
43 Social Hill architect
46 Synopsis
47 Royal headwear
49 The rest
51 Habituate
52 Intensive training
54 Flocks in flight
56 __ Moines
57 Important
58 Snack
59 Halfhearted
61 Audition tapes
63 Slick
67 Chaney
68 Grown-up gilt
69 Dietetic
74 Night-game need
77 Bête __
78 Charm
79 Baker's purchase
81 Guitarist Segovia
82 Teachers' grp.
83 Coulomb part
85 Fan sound
86 Fix an ushering error
87 Map detail
89 Ogle
91 Tachina
92 Bit of Bern "bread"
95 Santa Fe, Southern, et al.
97 __ Dawn Chong
98 Part of RSVP
100 Film of 1974
103 Bench-warmer

105 Snapper or sucker
108 Level
109 Dissolved
110 Sugar
111 Party
112 Too
113 Practiced
114 With "The," 1995 film
115 European river

DOWN

1 Mush
2 Polar formation
3 Camus novel
4 Sandwich type
5 Top credit rating
6 Blueblossom
7 Meat cut
8 Cheerful cry
9 Common Market currency
10 Anchor position
11 Eye part
12 Part of TNT
13 Noel name
14 Assistance
15 "__ Three Lives"
16 Meddling
24 Kind of clearance
26 One of the tenses
28 Guarded
31 Portends
32 Edge
34 Approx.
35 Closes in on
37 Canis Minor star
39 Actress Garr
41 Historical period
43 Gilpin of TV
44 Formerly, old-style
45 Uh-huh relative
48 Out of whack
50 Center
53 Haw's partner
55 Actor Peter
56 Squalid
60 South Seas dish
61 File
62 Shakespearean output
63 In the blink __ eye . . .
64 Latin "that"
65 Femme fatale Montes

66 Rita Coolidge hit
68 Lesley of TV news
70 Dozes
71 Summer's-eve sights
72 "__ Nice Clambake" ("Carousel")
73 Cross
75 Soak
76 Stick
80 Perfidy
81 Sky altar
84 "Ing" word
87 Opening section
88 Commerce
90 Put to extra purpose
92 Greek cheese
93 Inveigh
94 Mars
96 Cavort
99 Questionable
101 Sine __ non
102 D.C. summer time
104 Trifecta, e.g.
106 Sault __ Marie
107 "Tell __ No" ('60s hit)

ACROSS

1 "Walk Like __" ('60s hit)
5 Treasure hunt aid
8 Considerably
12 As
15 "First of all, __ harm . . ."
16 Pt. of UAE
18 Repository
19 Samovar
20 They're known by their bark
23 Boston ending
24 Acquaint
25 Blackthorn
26 Fit for drinking
28 Born
29 Guadeloupe, e.g.
31 Influence
33 Diminish
34 They have trunks
40 Impressionist
43 Kind of change or chanty
44 Mariposa lily
45 Clothing-catalog blue
46 Dog breed
48 Dutch cheese
51 Cries from the crowd
53 Kind of bean
54 Shipyard sight
56 Great lake
58 Aram's grandfather
60 They have roots
64 Fabric ridge
65 "The Wayward Wind" singer Grant
66 Dodged
69 Defective
72 Abominable snowman
74 Canonical hour
76 Melpomene's sister
77 Actor Baldwin
79 Skirt style
81 Thurman of films
83 Ring verdicts
84 They have leaves
89 Sawbuck
90 Insult
91 Ida. neighbor
92 Past
95 Bewilder
99 ". . . __ saw Elba"
101 Equivocate
103 Go wrong
104 They have branches

107 Mature
108 Check
109 Unheeding
110 Inflection
111 Billy __ Williams
112 Halcyon spot
113 Pirate's reply
114 Trumpeter, e.g.

DOWN

1 Expand
2 Writer Susanna
3 Actress Dickinson
4 Proboscis
5 Cloaks
6 Tank attachment
7 Goalie wear
8 From __ Z
9 Closed circuit
10 Church calendar
11 Not just presumed
12 Finds fault
13 Russian river
14 Boleyn
17 __ Knolls, Calif.
18 Workout wear, for short
21 Indigo source

22 Surgeon's wear
27 Egg on
30 Saber relative
32 Eur. river
34 Heretofore
35 Pluto
36 Guam capital
37 "Is there __?"
38 Prominent chairman
39 Cunning
40 Home of "NYPD Blue"
41 __ favor
42 Student's big moment
47 Remote-control device
49 ". . . __ and a bone . . ." (Kipling)
50 King of Crete
52 Balm
55 Mass. and Ore. towns
57 Picot
59 Card game
61 Plexuses
62 Comedy staple
63 Lead's st.
67 Command for DDE

68 Suggested actions
69 Cudgel
70 In the manner of
71 Clean, as a balance sheet
73 Lodging chain
75 Certain feds
78 Staff sign
80 Least productive
82 Menhaden
85 Make possible
86 Mitchell manse
87 Overturn
88 Word after hand or hang
92 Put on __ (ham it up)
93 Actress Davis
94 Kent and Lane coworker
95 Drop
96 Spur
97 Deposited
98 "This one's __"
100 Concept
102 They make a play
105 Relatives
106 Wail

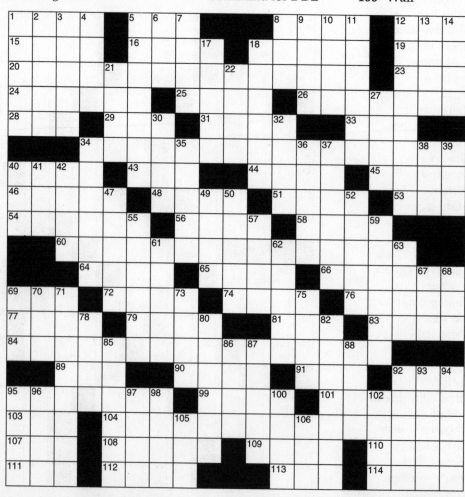

ACROSS

1 Solon's city
7 Ancient Arabian land
12 Unpretentious
18 Bakery offering
19 Consumed
20 "Got __ Livin' to Do"
21 Determined
22 Fast-food sauce
24 Roman goddess
25 Concordes
27 Squirm
28 Malines
31 Dregs
33 Slime
34 Fella's date
37 Takes refuge
40 Gush
42 In __ (fuming)
44 Glory
45 Constantly
47 Blacksmiths, at times
48 Tenor Carreras
49 Shoots for
50 Related
51 It agitates sailors
52 Greek isle
54 Chicago airport letters
55 "Tyger, Tyger" poet
57 Venin, e.g.
58 FDR's successor
61 Delight
62 Comply
63 Hayrick
64 Adduced
67 Top flight
68 Skimpy
70 Life experiences
73 Additionally
74 __ you so
75 Calcar
76 Think
77 Actions to take
78 Inspect
79 Peer
81 Transgress
82 CD owners
85 Singing four-some of yore
87 Loose end
90 All kinds of conditions
94 Bari's region
97 Hold
98 "The Man __"
99 Tourist hangout
100 Proust's "__ Way"
101 Is overfond
102 Nap

DOWN

1 Kind of rock
2 Telecom choice
3 Inconsistent
4 __ out (get by)
5 "Henry and June" friend
6 Scene sites
7 Group of seven
8 Anchor opening
9 Automne precursor
10 Complaint
11 West Indies island
12 Sweet pepper
13 Word for a shoppe
14 Biblical verb
15 DDE's command
16 Actor Erwin
17 Feather's companion
23 Embellish
26 Poor place
29 Caught congers
30 Despot
32 Twitch
34 Wag's collection
35 Turkish title
36 Riga native
37 Must
38 Gods' blood
39 Aptitude-test initials
41 "__ of little faith . . ."
42 Charged particle
43 Tire mounts
45 Mete
46 "Accommodation of Desire" painter
48 "The Sun Also Rises" protagonist
51 Grimalkin
52 Medicinal portion
53 Outer: Prefix
55 Coffee type
56 Actress Cheryl
57 A lot
58 Everywhere
59 Winter fall
60 __ Haute, Ind.
61 Catchall abbr.
62 "Extasie" poet
63 Singer Page
64 Pound sterling
65 Doing
66 Barcelona bears
67 Bedazzle
68 Make faces
69 Discordia
71 Grande dame
72 Took to excess
73 Go out of business
76 Herons
78 Actress Edith
80 Extant
82 Look over
83 Related
84 Manche town
86 Chalcedony
88 Lofty demeanor
89 Postern
90 NFL feats
91 Cleave
92 Señor ending
93 Stolen
95 Pt. of MPG
96 G.I. hangout

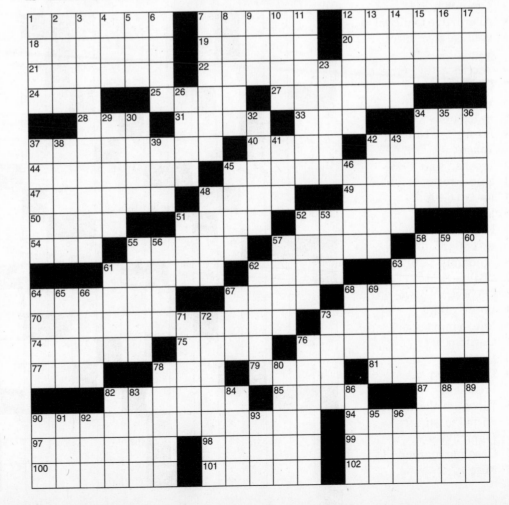

ACROSS

1 Figures
5 Wing supports
11 Loses one's cool
17 Fragrance
18 You-alone link
19 Refrigerator drawer
20 Hat size?
22 Insurgents
23 Flaxen fiber
24 Clever
25 Brants
26 Fuss
28 God of conflict
30 Lombardy's capital
32 Remote
35 Tease with bait
36 "M*A*S*H" setting
38 Hydropower problem?
41 UK part
43 Frail
45 Icy
46 Embroidery
47 Conniving
50 "__ idea!"
51 Doctor's orders
53 Top-notch
54 Alternative to digital
55 Political tremors of a sort
59 "Ecclesiastes" subject
62 Catalan cat
63 Western lake
68 Indigenous
69 Frost's "__ Not Taken"
72 Brosnan role, 1995
73 Upper caste
74 Part of GPA
75 Joyous
77 Friends without exception?
79 Ignominy
82 "Bali __"
83 Orchestra's place
84 Imprecations
86 Idle in movies
87 Corrida cheer
88 Dotes
90 Paris haven
92 Frequently
94 Ice cream alternative
97 Forbid feasting?
101 Filmmakers
102 Gasoline compound
103 Mire
104 Receives
105 Part of SWAK
106 Spot

DOWN

1 Sleepy's cohort
2 Okla. town
3 Favorite subjects?
4 Exxon competitor
5 Bludgeon
6 Lost-shipment inquiry
7 Disqualify
8 Kind of trust or price
9 Symbol
10 Pigpen
11 Comrade
12 Ocho __, Jamaica
13 Renaissance family
14 Gibbon
15 Writer Jill __ Conway
16 Aspiring alums
19 Peanut butter choice
21 Sentient
25 Iris relatives, for short
26 Grown
27 Perseus's mother
29 Scepters
31 __ fixe
32 Golfer Nick
33 Unstoppable process
34 Overhaul
37 Theater
39 Horrified
40 Soybean product
42 Asian holiday
44 Came out
48 Writer Joyce
49 Explanatory word
50 Ending for end
52 Turn
54 Ox of puzzledom
56 Blind ambition
57 Nostrils
58 Judge in the news, 1995
59 Singer Frankie
60 Leaning
61 Naldi of silent films
64 Camel's hair robe
65 Popular resorts?
66 Olajuwon's rival
67 Murphy of films
68 Kind of tide
69 Waste allowances
70 Eatery offering
71 Moore in movies
74 NL or NFL team
76 "__ d'Or"
78 Reduces
80 Kind of tea
81 Inscrutable
85 Stars' locale
88 Autonomous
89 Border on
91 Pilaster
93 Melt
94 Droop
95 "Ben __"
96 Midi saison
97 Jackson and Diddley
98 Actor Beatty
99 Outdo
100 Eavesdrop

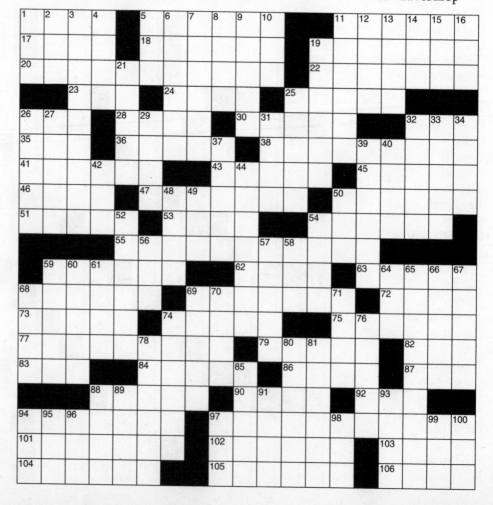

ACROSS

1 One of the Kramdens
6 Cormorant
10 Iranian city
13 Taj Mahal site
17 Word of mouth
18 Cougar
19 Parisian integer
20 Adverse judgment
21 Bureaucratic raw material
23 Short story
25 Lacking
26 Traffic unit
27 Go blithely
28 Gender
29 Utter
31 '50s horror flick
32 Argot
34 Temporary "wheels"
37 Stick together
39 "The Way We __"
42 Parking lot quests
44 Like fire-sale goods
47 "Lenny" director
48 Off course
50 Used a sonar
51 Besides
52 Cash in
54 Coxswain's cry
56 Artful
57 Brusque
58 "Les Misérables" man
59 Tasseled hat
62 Custard dessert
63 T. Williams title-starter
65 Scrooge portrayer in '52
68 Ideological program
70 Caulking compound
72 __ Dame
74 Rodeo ropes
76 Invalid
78 Presently
79 Equivocate
81 Mountain nymphs
82 Hawaiian hawks
84 Tivoli's Villa d'__
85 Boxer Max
86 Rockport's cape
88 Mountain ridge
90 Actress Joan
92 Pro __
96 Govern
98 Astronomical phenomena
100 Actuate
101 Milieu for Cousteau
102 Gross
103 Dote on
104 Offspring
105 Party in power
106 Traveling
107 Davis of films

DOWN

1 Police msgs.
2 Ooh follower
3 Boxer Barkley
4 Agrees
5 Wapiti
6 Declaim
7 Actor William
8 Shells, e.g.
9 Road sign
10 Friend
11 Anonymous
12 Assemble
13 Interject
14 Goslings' humble beginnings?
15 Memorizer's method
16 Nasdaq rival
22 Exhibitions
24 Mediocre mark
27 "__ Lady" ('60s hit)
30 McBain cop
31 Heat unit
33 Mature cygnet
34 Abandoned
35 Melville tale
36 Lhasa __
37 Garrison-town barracks
38 Double quartet
40 Rod's companion
41 Dust-devil
43 Livy's birthplace
45 Airport area
46 Prefix for take
49 "Now __ me!"
53 Applause
55 Marketplace
58 Actress Berry
59 FDR pet
60 Actor Richard
61 Focusing
62 Rx regulator
63 Motive
64 Music-man Previn
65 Classical promenade
66 Garden bloomer
67 Rx matter
69 El __ (Pacific current)
71 Growing out
73 Superseded
75 Sugar-coat
77 Conn. town
80 Fragrant compounds
83 __ volatile
85 "Vanity Fair" protagonist
86 Letter's companions
87 Pianist Peter
89 Branches
90 Crab feature
91 Maui town
93 Cosmetic additive
94 Gull relative
95 Out of port
97 Good times
98 Intimate apparel item
99 Wicked witch

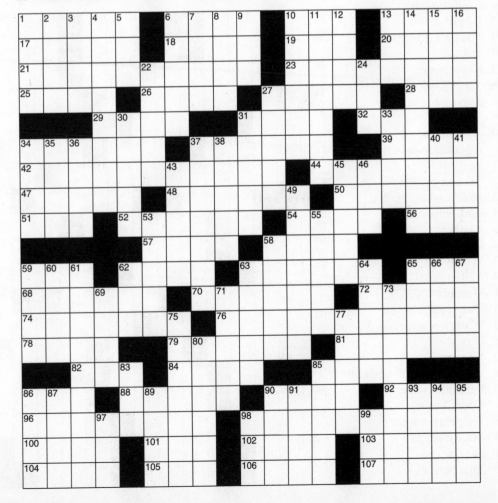

ACROSS

1 In-box pile
6 Math for Mickey Mantle
9 Gymnasium pile
13 Associate
16 Violin celeb
17 Conducted
18 Longing
19 __ a-la Crosse, Canada
20 Alliance for No. 41
22 Wallace Stevens's "The Emperor of __"
24 20th Century conflict
25 Derive
26 "__ la Douce"
27 Caroline's portrayer
29 __ es Salaam
30 Water buffalo
31 Glaswegian
32 Bizarre
35 Personnel cards, for short
37 On the other hand
38 Compete
39 What No. 18 wanted
42 Calumny
46 Conjunction
47 Cupid
49 Jessica's portrayer
50 Sulk
53 Grate sight
56 Amber color
58 Purpose
59 __ effort
60 Afternoon entertainment
61 Restraint
62 Cruiser mover
63 Hole-making tool
64 Eminence
65 Analyze
66 Doers: Suffix
67 Words with dressed
69 Italian port
71 Humble horse
73 Dulse, e.g.
75 Waterways for No. 38
81 Grackle
82 Nonsense
84 "__ Baby Baby" ('60s hit)
85 Berkshire village
86 Conn. town
88 Turpentine source
89 Tidal current
91 Bashful
92 Riga native

93 Completed
94 Huge
97 Engraving
99 Fruit for No. 6
102 Writer Grafton
103 Japanese native
104 Singer Bennett
105 Prank
106 Coach Marchibroda
107 Certain NCO
108 Model Carol
109 Follow

DOWN

1 Fairy queen
2 Cassowary
3 Cosmetics staple
4 1st Century Roman emperor
5 Ledge
6 Signoff word
7 Smudge
8 Chem. ending
9 __ d'hôtel
10 Stresses
11 Dissertation subject
12 Short time, for short

13 Intimates of No. 14
14 Hertz competitor
15 Actor Paul
17 Michener tale
21 Baseball Hall-of-Famer Roush
23 Ascendant
25 Testimony
27 Journey part
28 Convention trailer
33 Secret
34 W.W. II area
36 Natural followers
38 Feather part
40 Seek a pin
41 Go wrong
43 Flickering
44 Prufrock chronicler
45 Interstate adjuncts
48 Aspersion
50 Supermarket sign
51 Tale __ (lament)
52 No. 11's vowel with an umlaut
54 Extinct bird
55 Feather part
57 Form-ful org.

61 Al Qahirah
62 Script installment
64 A lot
65 Quid-quo link
68 "__ girl just like . . ."
70 À la
72 Sky altar
74 Like some rains
76 Inactive
77 Sister Kate's dance
78 Tolerates
79 Jane Smiley book
80 Pigpen
83 Baseball situation
86 Sought-after party guests
87 Site
88 City-state
90 Foot
94 Hero
95 Scruff
96 Revolved
98 Road sign
99 Words with glance
100 Singer Rawls
101 Compass pt.

ACROSS

1 Sophistication
5 Menacing
8 Very unpopular
13 Nimble
17 Expletive
18 Be obliged
19 Dean Martin subject
20 Actress Raines
21 "Born Free" lion
22 Actor Vallone
23 Service organization
25 Moore in movies
26 Hot spot
28 Ameliorates
29 Decade pts.
31 Highfalutin group
32 Cavort
34 Recurring film role
37 W.W. II area
38 Barbecue
39 Harem room
42 Marine
44 PR work
47 Scald
48 Tennis surface
50 Thousand __, Calif.
51 Murk
52 Yang's counterpart
53 Close
54 Hannibal's crossing
55 Solstice occasions
56 Fetter
57 Summarize
59 Reticule
60 Cursed car
63 Inventory
64 N.C. campus
66 Battle of Britain force, for short
69 Adamant
70 Infatuated
71 Grand __ (auto race)
72 "Here __ again!"
73 Party circuit
76 Come through
78 Seek
79 Diamond sacrifice
80 Big bruiser
82 Expedient
83 Clogs
84 Naps
86 Pt. of NATO
87 Cretin
90 Herbal beverages
92 Constantly

95 Chubby Checker's suggestion
98 Novel
99 Badger
100 Actress Lena
101 Singer Gill
102 Letter for Plato
103 Actress Swenson
104 Belt-tightener's ration
105 Famed fur trader
106 Myrna of films
107 Ripened

DOWN

1 Like many schools
2 Robust
3 Green arrow's meaning, to a motorist?
4 Top executive
5 Tennis champ of yore
6 Savvy
7 Gorge
8 Car type
9 Soap plant
10 Lug
11 Historian's subject
12 Ger. article
13 Ruin
14 Dining areas
15 Boiler pipe
16 Watch
24 Long
27 Bubble-headed
30 Posed
32 Bushel parts
33 Where Luang Prabang is
34 Coddle
35 Here, in the Yucatan
36 Cranny
38 Sport fish
39 North African port
40 Catch a few Zs
41 Tavern selection
43 Insurance agent's initials
45 Kansas town
46 Goon
49 Dexter
53 Sermon subject
54 Charade
55 Painter Vermeer
56 Writer Morrison
58 Actor Morales
59 Shorts type

60 Mona __
61 Life force
62 Faux
63 Suburban expanses
65 Top
66 Kind of door
67 Field of Rome
68 Presidio
70 Morose
71 Carrefour
72 Plantation growth
74 Subside
75 Chanticleer
77 TV's Thompson
81 Carrot relative
83 Artist Jasper
84 Pop music category
85 Take care of
87 Joss, for one
88 Apportion
89 "Tell It Like __"
90 Shade
91 Influence
93 Nose out
94 Study
96 Power initials
97 Ill. neighbor

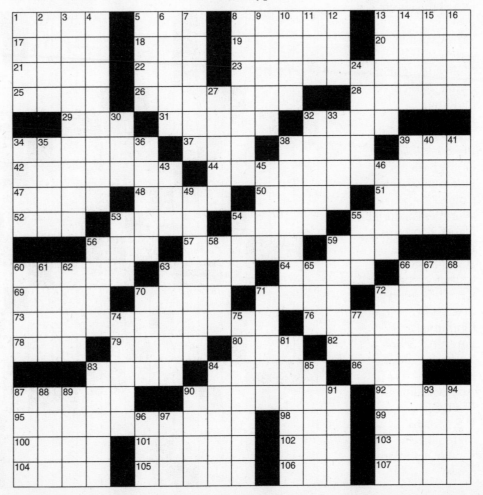

ACROSS

1 Good conductor
6 Elaborate
12 Traitor
17 Egg-shaped
18 Reddened
19 Jonquil appendage
20 Nacogdoches native
21 OG
23 Bumble
24 Genetic material
26 Farewell
27 Tolkein creatures
28 True nature
32 Breathing passages
34 Beer choice
36 __ Hand, Pa.
39 Kind of iron or weed
40 Cistern
43 Standard
45 __ wait? (be patient)
47 Far and away
49 Eye part
51 KOOL
53 B&B relative
54 Farm deposit
56 Clip
57 Out of the wind
58 Fear
60 "The Crucible" setting
63 Molokai neighbor
66 Cyma __ (S-curve molding)
70 Place for lunch
71 Brother
74 PU
78 Gravy base
80 Florentine painter
81 Coined
83 Worthless material
84 Negative prefixes
85 Explosive
87 ASAP's middle
89 Collected poems
90 Grandma in art
92 Fresh start, figuratively
94 Forever-day link
97 Turkic language
100 Anaconda
101 Actress Ullmann
104 ELBUOD
108 U.S. "island"
110 Materialize
111 Kind of equation
112 Souse
113 Film parts
114 Extras
115 Sibilant

DOWN

1 Speck
2 Always
3 XAT
4 Words with loss
5 Imparts
6 Living
7 Friend of Pooh
8 Shell contents
9 Turkish title
10 __ up (ready to drive)
11 Poet __ Arlington Robinson
12 Actor Voight
13 Impulses
14 Kind of payment
15 Med. school course
16 Claims
19 Runner
22 Harvest
25 Wyo. neighbor
29 Actress Young
30 Limulus
31 Ferber and Millay
33 Yikes relative
34 Daughter of Lady Bird
35 "The Race __"
37 Hankering
38 Adidas rival
40 String-section instrument
41 Skin-cream ingredient
42 Curtain-climber
44 Villainous visage
46 Tale header
48 Criticize
50 Historical period
52 Kuwaiti, e.g.
55 Attire
58 Kind of bag or bike
59 Consider
61 Record
62 Theater sign
63 Calif. point
64 Neat as __
65 Sci-fi sightings
67 Greek letters
68 Martinez of baseball
69 Writer Myrer
71 Writer "SPOLF"
72 Two-part transaction
73 Sweetsop
75 Bismark
76 Scary creature
77 Sand hill
79 L.A.'s La __ Blvd.
82 Actress Pam and family
86 Spree
88 Road sign
90 Singer Mercer
91 Pillar
93 Venus neighbor
94 Jewish month
95 Informal refusal
96 Stooge
98 Keen
99 Split
102 Fateful date
103 Selfsame
105 Part of UNLV
106 Early car
107 Part of UCSD
109 __ polloi

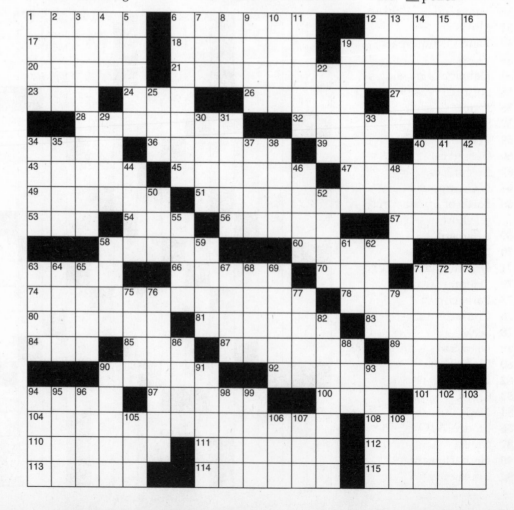

ACROSS

1 Davis of note
6 Humble
11 Blessed
18 Gods' blood
19 Scuttlebutt
20 Servitude
21 Hit from the Who
23 Dakar's land
24 "A __ be born . . ."
25 Supply ship
27 Out-of-date
28 Idyllic spot
29 Noticed
31 Singer Sheena
33 Nucleic acid
34 Sites
35 Intents
37 Para's opposite
40 With 26 Down, Ligurian port
41 Roadside eateries
44 Hibernia
45 Greek letter
46 "Old MacDonald" refrain
47 Prefix for gram or graph
49 Pismire
50 Fundamentals
53 Contract agreement
56 Offensive offspring
57 __ Amin
58 Connives
60 Pile
61 Idle chatter
62 Per __ (yearly)
64 "__ my word!"
65 Nervous
67 Sectors
69 African fox
70 Movie of 1967
71 Broadcast
72 Pipkin
73 Technique
75 Vernaculars
77 "Miracle in the Rain" actor
81 Yarmulke
84 Turkish inn
86 Part of a three-piece suit
87 N.C. campus
88 South Seas assembly
89 Hollywood symbol
91 N.M. resort
92 Wide-eyed

93 "__ Something Good" (1964 song)
95 Career enlistee
98 Son of Daedalus
100 Interest-paying group
102 Diorama worker
104 Dahl and Francis
105 Man from Muscat
106 Act up a storm
107 Farm implements
108 Telemetry calculation
109 Irrigate

DOWN

1 Gin accompaniment
2 Australian mammal
3 Average value
4 ". . . good will __"
5 Part of QED
6 Onassis
7 Pastoral
8 Bounds
9 Embodiment
10 Gaelic
11 Double records of the '50s
12 Requisites

13 Inflicted on
14 Just-chance connection
15 Old West sights
16 Inoffensive oath
17 Erase
22 "Carpe diem" relative
26 See 40 Across
30 Eurocurrency, for short
32 Malign
34 Would-be capts.
35 Used-car disclaimer
36 Judge in the news, 1995
38 Varna members
39 Punctual
42 Shawn of the NBA
43 Health club
45 Seattle winter time
48 Señor ending
50 Fruit-stand offering
51 Smock
52 Kind of bond
54 Etch
55 Beam
56 Proscribe

59 Thalassographer's subject
61 Barbarian
63 Skeptic's viewpoint
66 Mil. unit
67 Saxophonist Sims
68 Kurtz of "Sisters"
72 Bedtime wear, for short
74 Writer Beattie
76 Virtuous
78 Dickens girl
79 Close to
80 Road sign
81 Quadriga, e.g.
82 Sculptor Rodin
83 Piece of eight
85 Chant
90 More painful
91 LBJ was one
92 Kind of globulin
93 Lupino and Cantor
94 Insignificant
96 Like-not link
97 19 Across, personified
99 Off-camera workers
101 Draft org.
103 Casino roller

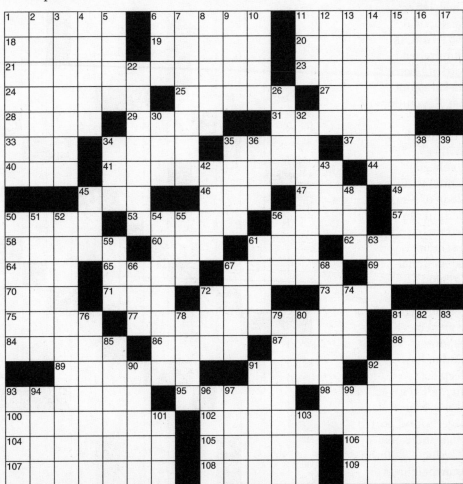

ACROSS

1 Hotel-shop offering
6 ''The King and I'' venue
10 Undisguised
14 Command to Fido
17 Tally
18 Jai __
19 __ about (approximately)
20 Frank or freak follower
21 Show contempt
22 Karl Marx theme
25 Simple Simon's encounter
27 Cut in cubes
28 Cuckoos
29 Sweetsop
30 Implore
34 Duckling's dad
35 The word for Oedipus
36 Vegetable oil
37 Phenomenon of 1964
39 Sharkey of TV fame
41 Like a maxiskirt
44 Soft leather
46 Personification
47 Greek letter
50 Car-lot deal
51 I-95 terminus
53 Comprehends
54 Lord of poetry
55 Tuckered out
56 Am. Revolutionary general
58 Like French toast
59 Soothes
60 Go-aheads
61 Canton ending
62 Glenn of films
64 Medical center group
65 Veterinarian's job possibility
68 Cell material
69 Agitated
72 Mideast VIPs
74 Common contraction
77 Revival meeting responses
78 Kind of hawk
80 Deep-six
81 Hightailed it
82 Look askance
84 Puget Sound port
86 Lanai and Kauai
91 ''__ Much'' ('50s hit)
92 Tenn. neighbor
93 Greatly
94 Talk up
95 PC command
96 Kind of dream or care
97 NBA team
98 Skittish
99 Shoe parts

DOWN

1 Adventurer de Portola
2 Touch off
3 Give and take
4 Crawls
5 Blood factors
6 Blackhawk, for one
7 Poorly
8 Blue-chip rating
9 Bridge problem
10 Dutch painter
11 Up-front payment
12 Baron
13 Actress Joanne
14 Transmission
15 ''Life __ a box of chocolates . . .''
16 Propositions
23 Thus
24 Singer Brooks
26 Org. for the Heat
31 In a word
32 Small change
33 90-degree bend
34 Stag's lack
36 __ cropper (collapse)
37 __ Brith
38 Albumin source
40 Rice field
42 Kind of poker
43 TV award
44 Cliffs
45 Oleum
47 Grantville, Pa., race track
48 Puts on the burner
49 Philosophies
50 Murmast, for one
51 Brawl
52 ''__ Woman'' (Reddy hit)
53 Commissioner of 26 Down
55 Mud dauber
56 Eureka winter time, for short
57 Computer clientele
59 Pen
60 Wrath
62 North Atlantic fishes
63 __ Diamond Phillips
64 Arrow poison
65 ''The Prisoner of __'' (1937 film)
66 Infant
67 Urchin
69 Sportscaster Ahmad
70 African antelope
71 Tolerance
73 Alphabetic trio
75 Private
76 Olympic pair
78 Manager's concern
79 Night predator
80 Incision
82 Chessboard row
83 Outbreak
85 Freshly
87 Actor McKellen
88 Acknowledgment
89 Burrowed
90 Pigpen

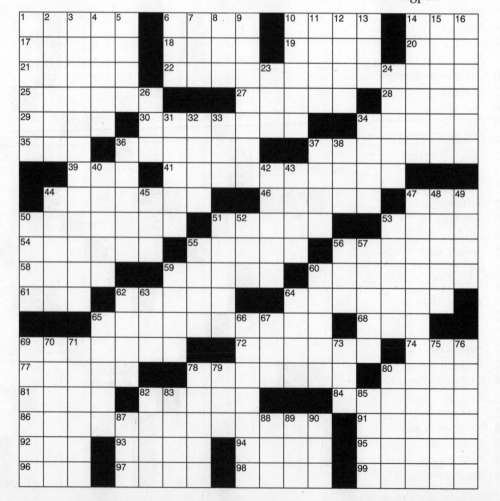

ACROSS

1 Steffi's rival
7 Flinch
13 Committee head
18 The Beatles' "She's __"
19 Pekoe hue
20 Therefore
21 Council
22 "The orchestra strike left me __"
24 Recipe abbr.
25 Cloy
27 Shack
28 Goethite or galena
29 Writer Esquivel
31 Top type
32 PC flashers
36 __ in one's throat
38 Gangplank
40 Singer __ J. Blige
41 Enthusiast
42 Kind of berry?
43 Speed
44 N.Y. campus
45 Japanese aborigine
46 Hosp. VIPs
47 Zones
48 "On the becalmed boat, we were __"
50 Exaggerated
52 Augury
53 Speed-trap device
54 Fla. horse town
56 Savage
60 No newcomers
63 Pastiche
65 "When the power failed, we were __"
68 Coppice
70 June honoree
71 Spoil
72 Descartes
73 Knowledge
74 Crossword pioneer Will
75 Mouths
76 Entertainer Mabley
77 Marching-band standout
78 Analyze
79 Highfalutin
81 Iranian city
82 __ und drang
84 Coulomb part
85 Calculator product
86 Tyrant
87 Judge of the '90s
90 "The depth-finder malfunction was __"
95 Movers' big problems

97 California explorer
98 Thwarted
99 Glacial ridges
100 Play for time
101 Shoelace tags
102 Ballparks

DOWN

1 Marina sight
2 Carries a credit-card balance
3 "Broken calculator? I'm __"
4 "__ Man" (Bo Diddley song)
5 Common condiment
6 Close by
7 Depended
8 Silkworm
9 Kind of nut
10 As planned
11 "__ Rhythm"
12 Actor Cariou
13 D.C. bloomer
14 Toast word
15 Ergate
16 Ed McBain tale

17 Carmine
23 Pluck
26 On the back burner
30 Elec. unit
31 First-rate
32 Shakespearean verb
33 "Pretty please with sugar __"
34 Enigma
35 Card game
36 Enthusiasm
37 Chrysalis-to-be
39 Creek
40 One of the Shearers
43 Dernier __
44 Hero
45 Caesar's stars
47 "Kind of __" ('67 hit)
49 Cry of surrender
51 Arrested
52 Dance step
54 Calcars
55 Yield
57 "The ore shortage left us __"
58 Actors Richard and Eddie
59 Shelf

61 Washed up
62 Particulars
63 Swamp
64 Night before
65 Discontinue
66 Continental prefix
67 Actor Neeson
68 Morose
69 Hold up
74 Conflict
76 Not-God
77 Collapse
78 Stickler
80 Writer Buck
81 Bobwhite
83 Surveillance material
85 Environmental problem
86 Danson and Shawn
88 Singer Amos
89 Greek mountain
90 Naval abbr.
91 "The __" (1995 film)
92 Brother
93 All-sudden link
94 Ending for cut or out
96 Alias

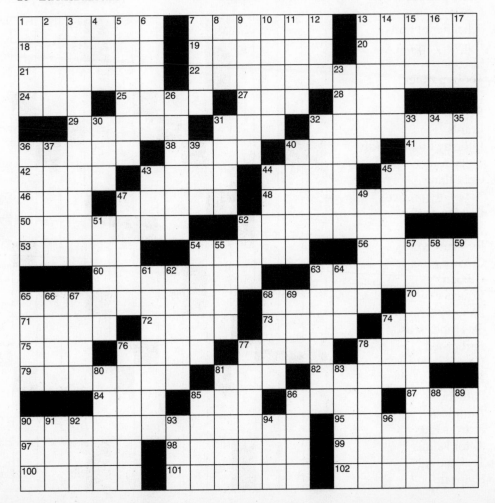

ACROSS

1 Chris of baseball
5 Northern nomad
9 Wanders
14 Cruise in films
17 Make __ for it
18 State
19 The blahs
20 Mimic
21 Blackbird
22 Fall spectacularly
25 Blessing
27 Adriatic Isle
28 Brochures
29 Sets straight
30 Towel inscription
31 Zero
33 Fast-food carrier
34 Teachers' org.
35 Drums' accompaniment
37 Pastures
39 Uru. neighbor
41 Stravinsky work
44 Scram!
47 Salinas airport letters
48 Schaeffer of films
49 Itinerary word
50 Singularly
52 Tool's partner
53 Barley bristle
54 Repair
55 Brants
56 Little by little, liquidly
58 Elytron
60 Gets along
61 "The City of Trees"
62 Dryden, for one
63 __ Tzu
64 Russian river
65 Circe, e.g.
66 Gibbon
67 Voucher
69 Identify
70 St. Tropez season
71 Barbecued
75 Wrath
76 Pier
77 Pathetic
78 Amphora
80 Actress Pitts
83 Actor Kilmer
85 Text ending
86 Helps up
89 Whole
91 Roman years
93 "Please Mr. __" ('60s hit)
94 Mel Brooks film
97 Picador's target
98 Decay
99 Saxophonist Randolph
100 I blew it!
101 One who just gets by
102 Expert
103 Conceal
104 Cheerful
105 Aggregation

DOWN

1 Rio dance
2 Staggering
3 Keen wish
4 Computerized
5 Nigerian port
6 Stratford river
7 Foot, in combinations
8 Fecund
9 Tear
10 Cibol
11 Actress Sheridan
12 Car part
13 Ledge
14 Circus star
15 "Idomeneo," for one
16 Unkempt
23 Older companion, sometimes
24 River islands
26 Headquarters
30 Sound system
32 Epic of old
35 Bracken
36 Cut
38 Acrobatic dance
39 Not silent
40 Fan's letdown
42 Cleaves
43 Tight spot
44 Vanishes, in a way
45 "The horse's mouth"
46 Adolescent
51 Court call
53 Insight
54 Floor covering
57 Real ending, in London
58 Fly high
59 Mullen and squill
60 Karma
62 Desert basin
63 Scarlet anemone
67 Hall
68 Charter
72 Deprived sort
73 Meat cut
74 Performing pairs
76 Interrogate
79 Nasty
80 African equid
81 Vietnam town
82 Condition
84 Hangs in there
86 Controlling
87 Undesirable growth
88 Stable sound
90 Barbecue dish
92 Packard contemporary
93 __ up (stimulates)
95 Tibetan gazelle
96 Card game

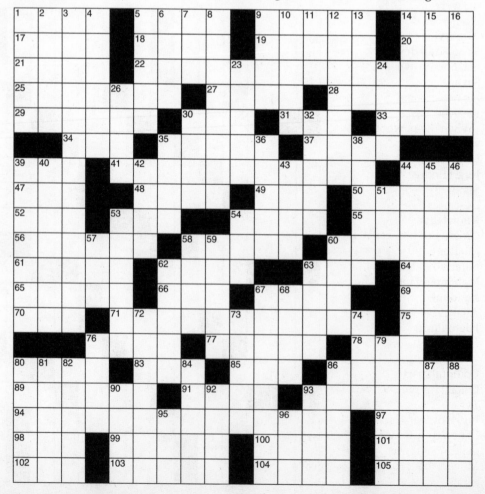

ACROSS

1 Sitcom audience cry
4 Bishop of Rome
8 Actuate
12 Cartoon impact
17 Gardner
18 Hedge bush
19 Whet
20 Verdi's "__ Miller"
21 Next-in-line types
24 Out-and-out
25 Disassemble
26 Apples
27 __ shanter
29 Health club
30 Ariz. city
31 Workout spot
32 Western alliance, for short
36 Clausian greeting
39 False
41 Plant part
43 Y __ yankee
44 Rotter
46 Señor follower
48 Seek hastily
49 Title of respect
50 Animator's sheet
51 Advice to the indecisive
53 Town near Adelaide
55 Hanoi holiday
56 "__ the Chief"
58 Inspires
59 Hosp. settings
60 Heavenly groups
62 "Le Coq __"
65 Hurl
66 Checkmate
67 Harem chamber
68 Each
70 TV series
71 Part of many?
72 Casino's take
73 Like a couch potato
74 Genetic material
76 Work unit
77 Cozy
78 Ukraine port
80 Countersink
83 "__ Ex" (punk-rock hit)
85 Cellar contents
86 Floor covering
88 "Mr. Holland's __" (1995 film)
90 NYC transit line
91 Skittles' companion
93 "All My Children" character
94 Chafe
97 Cedar Rapids native
100 Child's game
103 Resembling
104 Actor Richard
105 Clothing-catalog blue
106 Kind of tide
107 Allied
108 Mr. Roberts, to fellow officers
109 TV award
110 Vegan's choice

DOWN

1 Site of Hanauma Bay
2 Where pizza comes from
3 Penance symbols
4 Iowa town
5 Sp. wave
6 Energetic
7 Comment
8 Menace
9 Forest females
10 Danube feeder
11 Minor
12 Lower oneself
13 Act high and mighty
14 Ignited
15 Enzyme
16 Roofing material
22 Wis. campus
23 Shells, e.g.
28 Mornings
31 Obtained
33 Matins ender
34 Mal de __
35 Lennon's widow
36 Must
37 Willow
38 Maritime
40 Deliberate
42 Parched
45 Properly positioned
47 Kind of protest
50 Alpine hideaways
51 Pt. of NATO
52 Winter warmer
54 Broadcasts
57 Meat cut
58 Barfly
61 Stick close to
62 Servants' country
63 Hatred
64 Long-limbed
65 Early stage of progress
68 "A Rose __ Baby Ruth"
69 Rind
70 Bind
73 Saturniid moths
75 Refusal
76 Teach
77 Sawfish
79 Amazement
81 Dull
82 Mighty
84 To the extreme
87 Wanted-poster word
89 Ore. city
92 Okla. town
93 Jacob's twin
95 Half a sextet
96 Notice
97 Mind stats
98 Yes from Yves
99 Clump
101 Actor Tognazzi
102 Engine part

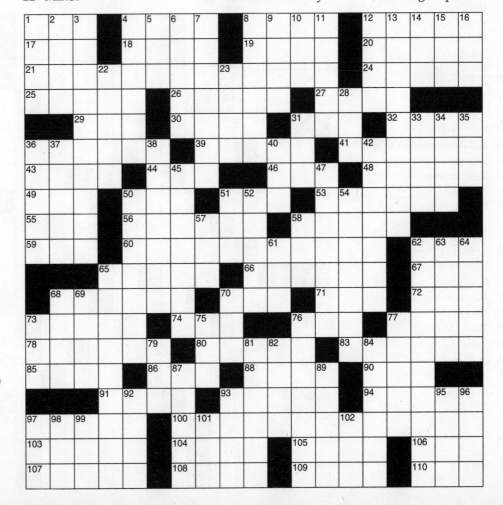

ACROSS

1 Crown
7 Improved
13 Uninspiring
18 Whole
19 Goddess of wisdom
20 Lower
21 Quarreling
23 Bogged down
24 Kind of fight or court
25 Noxon alternative
26 Rocketed
27 More recent
30 Wedding announcement word
31 Common article
32 Misery
35 Demijohn
37 Involved with
39 Poised
42 Hearten
44 Shipboard direction
46 Stammel
47 Eastern Indian
48 Lean
49 Kingston Trio song subject
50 "Exit, pursued __ bear"
51 Drift
52 Word with drive or market
53 Anubis
55 Oh so much
57 Contrivance
58 Now
60 Blond shade
63 Stage whisper
64 Do an electrician's job
65 Roman emperor (69 A.D.)
66 Resentment
69 News execs
71 Negative beginnings
72 Playwright Brendan
73 Essence
74 Advent follower
75 Pongid
76 Controversy
77 Whatever it takes
80 Brochette
82 Prefix for night
83 Ecru
84 Sprite
85 Missile type: Abbr.
87 Tolerate
89 Entertainer Carvey
91 Congenital
93 "__ the One" (Presley song)
96 Insipid

98 Super-polite sentiment
101 Carried
102 Close one, in horseshoes
103 Placate
104 Stratum
105 Accounting category
106 Leash

DOWN

1 Like Gallaudet students
2 Enamored of
3 Finally
4 Rectifier
5 Coulomb part
6 Ryan of films
7 A Roseanne surname
8 Actor Hawke
9 At __ of power
10 China grouping
11 Inner: Prefix
12 __ Tafarian
13 Disrupt
14 Drama award
15 Nuts, bolts, etc.
16 Purpose

17 Kind of school, for short
22 Spanish river
26 Jettison
28 Consort
29 Differ ending
31 Movie chain
33 Gladsheim occupant
34 Looked over
35 "__ Gigolo"
36 Stimulant
38 "You bet"
40 Rugby score
41 Convention endings
43 NYC subway
45 Shams
49 Words with fact
50 Antonioni film
51 Explosive
53 Baseball's Snow et al.
54 Soul, in Paris
56 "__ Sweet Day" (1996 hit)
58 Enzyme
59 Haggard's "King Solomon's __"
60 Comfortable around
61 Entertainer Lewis

62 Keen
63 Influence
65 Anthem preposition
66 H.S. exam
67 Small amount
68 Perplexing situation
70 __ Plaines, Ill.
72 "__ Do" (1960 hit)
74 NCAA basketball champs, 1995
75 Dry __
76 Little stretcher
78 Bank, e.g.
79 Singer Tucker et al.
81 Football wear
86 Vinegar bottle
88 Fairway piece
90 Writer Tyler
91 Dwellers: Suffix
92 Goes astray
94 Throb
95 Mystic
96 Oil qty.
97 Mauna __
98 In the manner of
99 Extreme ending
100 Brooklyn Preacher of yore

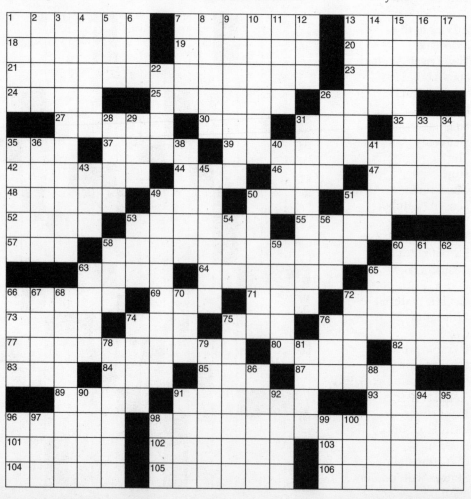

ACROSS

1 Realty unit
4 Fundamental
9 Auto-sticker letters
12 Lofty
16 Gardner
17 "Do as I say, not __"
18 Garb
19 Ovid's others
20 Oscar-winner Gibson
21 Author of "Lady Chatterley's Burglar?"
24 One of the Fondas
26 Sales charge
27 Duffy's Tavern manager
28 Litigate
29 Receptacles
30 School grp.
31 Words with glance
32 Author of "Ulysses' Trees?"
38 Word-of-mouth
39 "When __ My Sugar to Tea"
40 Welsh river
41 Composer Wilder
45 Craving
46 Turgenev
47 Gusto
48 Dude's usual milieu
49 Garden toiler
50 Busy spot
52 Where many want to get
53 Author of "Portrait of Eternity?"
57 Manner
59 __ Bator
60 And so forth
61 Kind of line or dream
62 Dissolve
64 Ocean-hoppers
65 Frenzied
68 Angelus ender
69 Babe, e.g.
70 Charter
72 Trim
73 Author of "The Purple Moviegoer?"
77 Zetterling
80 TV's "Murder __"
81 Arouse
82 Atty.'s abbr.
83 Greece
85 Writer Morrison
86 Casuals hit of '58
90 Author of "Garp and the Ecstasy?"
93 Whitney
94 __ impulse

95 Chinese dynasty
96 Law partner
97 Elvis's early label
98 NL team
99 Mole
100 Verges on
101 Clique

DOWN

1 Shish kebab ingredient
2 Finished
3 Charm
4 Convention accoutrements
5 Wimbledon winner, 1975
6 Delta deposit
7 Nev. neighbor
8 Unruly tuft
9 Repair
10 Lobbying grp.
11 Emersonian subject
12 Toiletry ingredient
13 Hilo hello
14 Aboveboard
15 "__ Rolling Stone"

18 "__ your cooperation..."
22 Actress Blakley
23 Hillside
25 Showdown
29 __ eyelash (just barely)
30 Appeal
32 Delight
33 Exist
34 Smooth talker
35 Eared seal
36 Kills time
37 Writer Carson
42 Propaganda
43 Greek letter
44 Charisse of films
46 Actress Skye
47 Balanced
49 City on I-15
50 Seraph's "lid"
51 "__ Believer"
52 Cultural collections
53 Buildup
54 Reckon
55 One of the Jameses
56 Frolicsome mammal

57 Buxton, for one
58 Allen of TV
62 Angry
63 Subtle
64 Benefit
65 Earl's superior
66 Circle part
67 Actress Susan
70 Scottish explorer
71 "Invisible Man" author
72 Bit of Manzanillo money
74 Sites
75 Abuse
76 Singer Roberta
77 Significant
78 Expiate
79 "__ to Be You"
84 Lodging chain
85 Minute
86 Pop
87 Humdinger
88 Model-builder's supply
89 Suggestion
91 Limo rider, often
92 Uno plus due

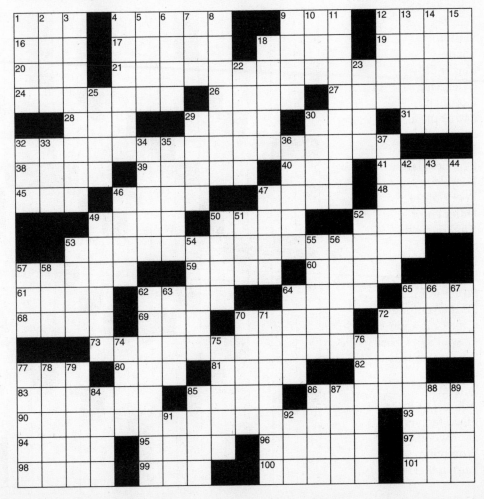

ACROSS

1 Home-entertainment hookup
6 Not candid
11 Common garnish
18 TV's "Green __"
19 Mission lead-in
20 Zinc-bearing mineral
21 N.J. town
23 Stop for the night
24 Understand
25 Powder
26 Word with knows or cares
28 Sault __ Marie
29 Actor Byrnes
30 Chart type
31 Colloquialisms
34 Bombeck
37 Cafe au __
39 N.C. inlet
41 South Seas dish
42 Promote
44 Like a sturgeon
45 Not alfresco
47 Jai __
48 Linkage parts
49 Recipe abbr.
52 Win by __
53 Skillful
54 Shade
55 Singer Billy __
56 Offenbach's "__ of Hoffman"
57 Maine place
60 Substantial
64 Fluff
65 Begone relative
66 Recycled
70 Poet Guest
71 Differ ending
72 Kind of cherry
73 Staff
74 Intaglio seal
76 Angler's effort
77 Foster in films
78 Ordinal ending
79 Cape Cod town
83 Hawaii's __ Coast
84 "__ was no lady . . ."
86 Caparison
87 Smidgen
88 Adjunct to 1 Across
91 Blood factors
93 Hardwood tree
94 Promotion
96 Farm father
97 Judge
100 Calif. community
103 Later Tertiary
104 Salome's props
105 Tone alternative
106 Crimson
107 County Clare town
108 Waste allowances

DOWN

1 Store
2 Hurt
3 Vt. mountain
4 Lascivious look
5 Lion ending
6 Vexation
7 Burden
8 Radio choices
9 Cry of fright
10 Enticed
11 A Picasso
12 Okla. town
13 "Silhouettes" rock group
14 Clobbered
15 English city
16 Vacation time in Valence
17 "__ dern tootin'!"
22 Redact
27 Ad __ (improvised)
30 Orchestra's place
32 Stridulous
33 Street runner
35 Cervid
36 Buenos __
38 Words with were
39 Finishes
40 Growing out
42 Defective
43 Corrida cry
44 Trinket
46 Heredity material
48 Comedian Margaret
49 Peak
50 Greedy
51 Protest
55 Printer device
57 Harps
58 Explosive
59 Hogshead
60 Harassed
61 Piaf
62 Wis. town
63 Summer cooler
66 Informed about
67 Ore. town
68 Yalie
69 Billy __ Williams
72 "English"
75 Marker
76 Naval space, for short
77 Scribble
80 Approached
81 Dentist's degree
82 "Yes, __ No Bananas"
83 Chicken __
85 Viscous
87 Consecrate
89 Mentadent rival
90 Calif. point
92 Young follower
95 "You're __ Need"
96 Obloquy
97 Plus
98 Actor Stephen
99 Chem. ending
101 Coop
102 Fitting

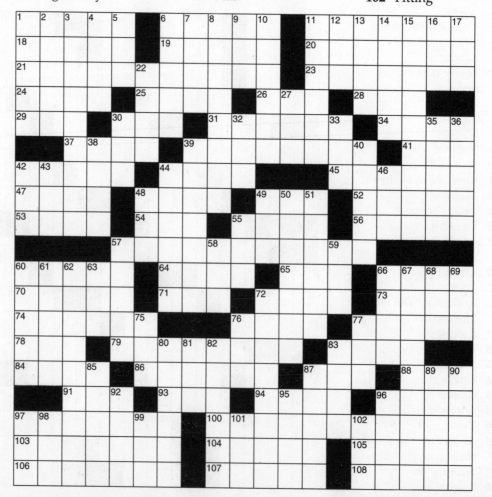

ACROSS

1 New Deal initials
4 Communications lead-in
8 Lairs
12 Mustard name
17 Oh, sure!
18 "I'll get __ right away"
19 Much
20 Extract
21 Handy folk classic?
24 Winner of 30 Grammies
25 Bit of Chihuahua change
26 Russian range
27 Paklay's land
29 Hither's partner
30 Jug
32 __ do-well
34 Excuse
36 Expunges
39 Speedy vessel
44 Ouster
45 Court great
47 Resentful
48 "Sharper __ serpent's tooth . . ."
49 Russian spacecraft
50 Unclose
52 Paean
54 Revel
55 UFO riders?
56 Roman statesman
60 Fluctuates
62 Emotional experience
65 Below
68 Helixes
69 Fox rival
72 Diva's showcase
73 Dam of a lamb
76 Insolence
77 Sine __ non
78 Road sign
80 Like a bump on __
83 Pitcher Jose
86 Potter's project
87 Citrus cocktail
90 Widespread
92 Thailand of old
93 __ impulse (recklessly)
95 Computer balloon
96 Colloquial ending
99 No from Nikolai
101 Headband
103 "Casablanca" character
106 "In Love with Daylight" writer
108 Handy NCO?
111 Bit of wisdom, figuratively
112 Zaire river
113 Russian range
114 Buoy type
115 Certain Ivy Leaguer
116 Equal
117 Boston suburb
118 Star quality, often

DOWN

1 Shoulder burden, perhaps
2 Boite relative
3 Self-dealing sorts
4 Burned __ crisp
5 Lasts
6 Ananias
7 Zenobia Frome's husband
8 Lasses
9 Slippery __
10 Coward
11 Having cash-flow problems
12 Just reward
13 Labor agcy.
14 Hot time
15 Bismarck
16 Refusal from 15 Down
22 Sewing-machine inventor
23 One of the Baldwins
28 Violinist Bull
31 Greek letter
33 "The Outlaw" character
35 On the beach
36 "South Pacific" song subject
37 Depart
38 Cut
40 Money player
41 Mata __
42 "Come Back Little Sheba" man
43 Brings results
46 Grand-scale
51 Williams College team
53 Nasty
56 Exist
57 Actor Richard
58 Domino dot
59 Indigo source
61 Mornings
62 Cetaceans
63 Sinister
64 Candle
65 Those opposed
66 Writer Ambler
67 Level
69 Water-skis alternative
70 Use up
71 Pessimist's word
74 Got ready to play
75 Whitney
79 Shrink
81 Ab __ (from the start)
82 Less violent
84 Arid
85 Fr. soul
88 Life part
89 Inside post
91 Ballet bend
94 Whiny
96 '60s TV series
97 Home of the Mets
98 Corn product
100 Copse component
102 Count
104 Cozy
105 __ time (never)
107 Silkworm
109 Basse-Terre, e.g.
110 Trap

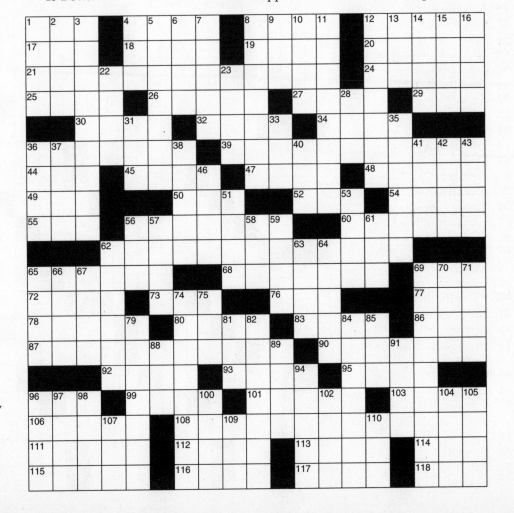

ACROSS

1 NFL VIPs
4 __ buco
8 Roman emperor
13 Computer instructions
17 First word of "Wooly Bully"
18 Mexican Hat's state
19 Police chief under 8 Across
20 __ in a poke
21 Dickens follower
22 I
25 Repudiates
27 Singer Buck
28 Like bugleweed
29 Apparatus
30 Hall-of-Fame umpire
31 Forecaster's concern
33 A
37 Woo-pitcher
38 Turtosa
41 Granada goodbye
42 Kind of nitrate
43 WHO, e.g.
44 Windbag
45 Promised land
46 Lingerie item
47 Ger. article
48 Great
49 D.C. summertime
50 Skier Tommy
51 "Just the Two __"
53 Rector
54 L
57 Wrongful
60 Pornography
61 Sardonic
62 Tour grp.
65 Brutish sorts
66 Emolument
67 Horticultural tool
68 Singer Celine
69 Warfare
70 TV series
71 Internet exchange
73 "__ to the animal fair . . ."
74 Suede feature
75 Arrived
76 R
78 Campaign
80 Guaranteed
81 Thoroughly
82 Word with shave or shock
84 Minimal
86 Crocheted
90 P
93 Method

94 Poet
95 Loosen
96 "I can't tell __"
97 Loose-goose link
98 Pretentious
99 Founded
100 Helen's mom
101 Thesis starter

DOWN

1 Pounds
2 __ Brith
3 Certain offspring
4 Bamboozles
5 "Sophie's Choice" character
6 Fall guys
7 Triumphant cry
8 Kind of card
9 Abou Ben __
10 Mortgage
11 Hiker's lament
12 NRC forerunner
13 Stateroom
14 What Ds can do
15 Racing surface
16 Like French toast
23 Whimsical structure

24 Big bird
26 Welles
30 __ Sutra
32 Cleaning implement
33 Rattle
34 "__ It My Way"
35 Outburst
36 Got along
37 Claim
39 Jason's craft
40 Avid
44 Unadorned
46 Punt, for one
47 Paired performance
48 Cagney's partner
50 Disarray
51 "Heart __ Heart" ('50s hit)
52 Common affliction
53 Straight
54 Shanties
55 Ozarks river
56 "It Takes __ Tango"
57 __ Bator
58 Mrs. Nick Charles
59 J

62 Pinto
63 Audible signal
64 Part of A.M.
66 Hemingway setting
67 Mist
68 Lived
70 Predicament
71 Very sad
72 Poker Flat's creator
73 "Life __ box of chocolates . . ."
75 Medicament
77 Offensive
79 Chemise
80 "Trois Gymnopedies" composer
82 __ Longa
83 Film of 1996
85 Salamanders
86 Cabbage
87 First word of "Jabberwocky"
88 Lenient
89 Actress Cannon
91 Chafe
92 Chum

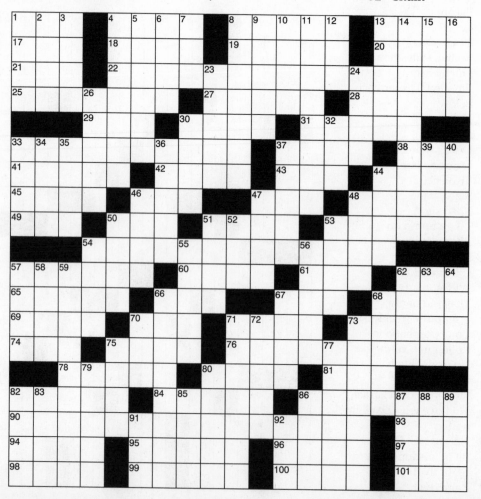

ACROSS

1 __ Raton, Fla.
5 Yawn
9 Singer Joan
13 Listless
17 Sci-fi sightings
18 Silkworm
19 Key
20 Pro __
21 Vacillations
23 Milk glass
24 Footnote word
25 Mock
26 NL, MVP, 1954 and 1965
28 Hawaiian city
30 Sweet potato
31 Automne precursor
32 Butcher's offering
34 Old school
36 Impudent
38 Irritation symptom
40 Horticultural wear?
42 Check attachment
43 Hit song of 1957
44 Feudal prince
45 Kremlin info source
48 Ornamental case
50 Bulgar
52 Level
55 Stalks
57 Health problems
59 Setback of sorts
61 W.W. II area
62 Feckless footwear?
66 School org.
67 Shrank
69 Sleipnir's rider
70 Coat fabric
72 66 Across, e.g.
73 Telescope part
76 Mosul's land
78 Sins
79 Melange
81 Active
83 Actress Hagen
85 "Laugh-In" line
87 Fun-house staples
91 Roman rhymester
92 Aleutian isle
93 Judy's daughter
94 Go fast
95 Buckingham palace initials
96 Racer's concern
98 British gun
100 Ethiopia neighbor
102 Entertainer Sandler
104 Nimble
106 Almodovar film
108 Stable father
109 Penury
110 Tangelo relative
111 Tardy
112 Genesis locale
113 Probability calculation
114 Throw off
115 Cupid

DOWN

1 Cushion
2 Recently
3 Ready to spring
4 Vipers
5 Toiletry format
6 Scents
7 Sacred fig
8 Comfortable
9 Publicity sketch
10 Lily
11 Cohort of Jerry and George
12 Old-time announcer Harry Von __
13 Pt. of TGIF
14 Garden balsam
15 Comfortable
16 Debbie Reynolds hit
22 Heated condition
27 Formalize
29 Job-safety org.
33 Being
35 __ chic!
37 Concern for a cardiologist
39 Hotbed
40 Interrogate
41 Defiant reply
43 Stubborn footwear?
45 Sheath
46 Parking-lot aggregation
47 Common lapin
49 N superscription
51 Sports spot
53 Acetate, for one
54 Peruses
56 Title of respect
58 __ Canals
60 D-Day craft
63 Varna Masjid's place
64 Take __ (fall)
65 N.Y. island
68 Legislate
71 Apparel
74 Babbled
75 Casino repository
77 Interrogate
80 Card game
82 Radio celebrity
84 Shlock
85 Grubby
86 Packed down
87 Socialize
88 My, my!
89 Theater district
90 Reason
91 State
93 A Gable costar
97 "Ignorance __ excuse . . ."
99 Hence
101 Zaire river
103 Kingsley's "__ in White"
105 RB's stats
107 Sequestered

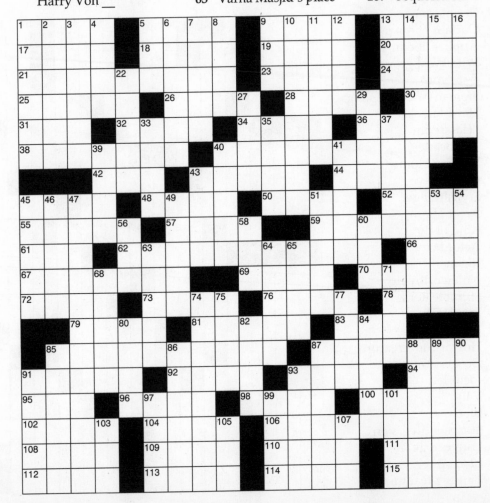

ACROSS

1 Leg part
5 Ermine
10 Kneecap
17 Agalloch
19 Savvy
20 Shelley elegy
21 Robert Redford role
23 Queen singer Freddy
24 Actress Dolenz
25 Cuts into kernels
26 In other words
28 Scottish explorer
29 Ga. city
30 Hoodwink
31 Wash. agcy.
33 "Carmina" poet
36 Kikuyu rebel
38 Wild
41 Rapidly
42 Burns's "To __"
44 Christmas in Cremona
46 "Frasier" character
48 Helping hand
50 Countertenor
51 Curtain-climber
53 Applies liberally
54 Wild West group
55 __ to you!
57 Sigman-Maxwell song
61 Hard-knocks "classroom"
63 The Beatles' "__ Leaving Home"
67 Close shave
69 Stylish singer
71 Actor Hugh
72 Kind of fly
74 Actor Peter
75 Rigan
76 Noteworthy rio
78 Humble horse
79 Prepared
81 Det. Sipowicz
82 Horror-film creature
84 Do something
86 Included
88 Valid
89 Blue
92 Summer diversion
94 Louvre exhibit
97 Line up
98 Tinker's teammate
99 Gross part
100 Dog breed
101 Thin and pliable
102 Painter Benjamin

DOWN

1 Reynoso residence
2 Styptic agent
3 Actress Anderson
4 Nourished
5 Vanzetti's codefendant
6 'Midst relative
7 Forest stalwarts
8 Jackie's mate
9 Tiresome
10 Richardson novel
11 Citrus drinks
12 Legal specialty
13 Business letter abbr.
14 "Eyes of __" (1978 film)
15 Milan money unit
16 "__ sow, so shall ye reap"
18 Arab
22 Word of praise
27 Vaults
29 Virile
30 Beasts
32 Ulan __
33 "We __ ball!"
34 Girasol
35 Spellbound
36 Roger and Marianne
37 Ill-mannered
39 Bread spread
40 "Smoke Gets in Your Eyes" man
42 Entertains
43 Cabin material
45 "We'll drink __ of kindness . . ."
47 On the wane
49 Discombobulates
52 Harangue
54 Kind of cotton
56 Actress Hatcher
57 Organic compound
58 Neuwirth of TV
59 QB in Super Bowl I
60 Hackneyed
62 Chemise
63 À votre santé relative
64 Al of New Orleans
65 To be, in Toulouse
66 Gang follower
68 Mere
70 Referred
73 Mass. town
77 Park patroller
78 Frog's milieu
80 Singer Lopez
82 Pepo
83 Mischievous girl
84 Blind as __
85 Main memory
87 Sens seraph
88 Dirk
89 Tailor's concern
90 Brews
91 Proscription
93 Roofing material
95 First mate
96 Cut

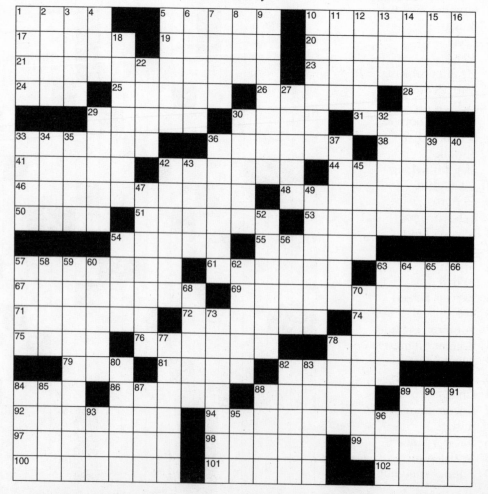

ACROSS

1 Seaside shelter
7 Of a dowry
12 Sugar source
17 Lawrence's place
18 Élève's milieu
19 Extent
20 Blank space
21 Dance arrangement
23 Annoys
24 Consecrate
25 Cuzco dwellers
26 Medieval knight
29 Portico
30 Musical aptitude
33 Fuss
35 __ spumante
36 Moving about
38 Handle
39 Sapporo performance
41 Beveled joint
43 Restless
44 Most idiotic
46 Agree
49 Fast-food offering
50 Computer symbol
52 Consumed
53 Consult
54 Singer Carly
56 Upper air
57 Busy sound
60 Where Toledo is
61 Too
62 Track division
63 In close competition
67 Insults
70 Tuckered out
71 Abalone
73 Wears down
74 Tennyson poem
75 Rampage
77 Kitchen add-on
79 Rugby score
80 Within, in combinations
81 Heat amt.
82 Lord Nelson
84 Bollard
86 One of the five Ws
88 Fraudulent
91 Compete directly
94 One of a bunch
96 Boulevard
97 Permission
98 Halcyon
99 Foundation
100 Discourage
101 Takes one's time

DOWN

1 Colombian city
2 Sandarac tree
3 Consecutive
4 Mistreatment
5 Writer Anaïs
6 Top credit rating
7 Orate
8 Yellow color
9 On one's __ (alert)
10 Brews
11 Mating ground
12 Fugard's "The Road to __"
13 Turkish title
14 Poise
15 Jamie __ Curtis
16 Cry of fright
19 Eleemosynary sort
22 Leatherwood
24 Sandwich initials
27 Brand
28 Greek letters
29 City scene
31 Pale
32 Entertainer Martha
33 Dog breed
34 Carvey and Andrews
36 Solar disk
37 Bishopric
38 Like __ of bricks
40 Start of a Catalan count
42 Occupies
43 Passage
45 Indecisive
47 Brute
48 St. Tropez saison
51 Jimmy of tennis
54 Cross
55 Actor McKellen
56 Sommer of films
57 Kind of combat
58 Reporting to
59 Unkempt
60 Spinout relative
61 Peak
62 Melissa of "Homicide"
63 Identify
64 Flair
65 Grasp
66 Before
68 Type of cheese
69 Worry
72 Sign of a satisfied customer
75 Frederica von __
76 Green challenge
78 Three, in Tivoli
81 Dandies
82 Fling
83 "So what else __?"
85 Filmmaker Riefenstahl
86 Roller coaster cry
87 Pressure
89 Indigo
90 Middle Ages weapon
91 Chat
92 Eggs
93 Former
94 Garden part
95 Okla. town

ACROSS

1 Dampens
5 Distort
9 Chop
13 Purvey
17 Composer Satie
18 Bread type
19 Piece of property
20 Keillor's "__ the Wolf Boy"
21 Clarence Day book
24 Road sign word
25 Take down a peg
26 Set loose
27 Toot
28 Argot
29 Louver
30 Logical lead-in
32 Mass. campus
35 Mass. music source
40 Aristocratic game
41 Side dish
42 Trendy
43 Eye part
44 Perplexing situation
46 False witness
48 Nod off
49 Actor Fernando
50 Spielbergian creatures
51 Job
52 Leers
53 Film of 1970
56 Flying fish?
60 Contrived
61 Resin
62 With "The," rock group
65 Assuage
66 Sports spots
67 Bridle buyer's place
69 "The doctor __"
70 Bill's companion
71 Vanished
72 Cant
73 Crane fly
77 Clothes choices
78 "__ be surprised!"
79 Wine: Prefix
80 Caress
81 Responds quickly
84 Sierra __
86 Seers
90 Toast topper
91 Ancestral group
93 Child's play
94 Adolescent woe

95 Thicke of TV
96 Computer function
97 Terai and tarbush
98 IRS form, for short
99 Connection
100 Minus

DOWN

1 Fuse, in a way
2 Buffalo's county
3 Spat
4 Kind of crew
5 Malice
6 Park flyer
7 Ordinal ending
8 Dithers
9 "... how I __ get up ..."
10 Yearn
11 Bankruptcy-filing party
12 Writer Jill __ Conway
13 Overall sentiment
14 Mideast VIP
15 Zilch
16 Venetian official
22 Cycle in the kitchen

23 Saracen
27 D.C. title
29 Chaise
31 Internet punctuation
32 Initials in old Rome
33 Grimace
34 Faulkner's "As __ Dying"
35 Succinct
36 Military headwear
37 Finished
38 Glance
39 Drains
41 Bikes' places
45 Loser in '48
46 Hangs in there
47 Cosby-Culp series
48 Clobber
51 Expression
52 Room
54 Synthetic fiber
55 Architect's output
56 Professional
57 "Casablanca" character
58 Declined
59 Sweet treats

62 Expert
63 Good place for an ace
64 Decides
66 Cheerful sentiment
67 Deli order
68 Laughter, figuratively
70 Insurance agent's initials
71 Widespread
74 Informal greetings
75 Slipped up
76 Letterman rival
77 Base
80 Stunt
81 Tease
82 Arm bone
83 Vegan's no-no
85 Sea eagle
86 The blink __ eye
87 Helen's mother
88 Hibernia
89 Ocean-hoppers, for short
91 W. Hem. grp.
92 Whitney

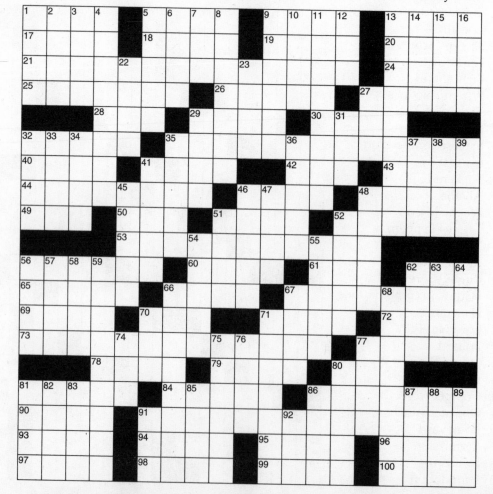

ACROSS

1 Contributes
5 Writer Chopin
9 Civil War initials
12 Attires
17 Auger
18 Egyptian goddess
19 Prefix for bug or drum
20 Dickensian first name
21 Haydn work
24 Singer Helen
25 Seventh positions
26 Blockhead
27 Southwest Indian
28 Soggy
29 Suspension
31 Eight, in combinations
34 Enthusiasm
38 Song based on Ecclesiastes
40 Execrates
41 Grant in films
42 Mauna __
43 Shelter
44 Singer Diana
45 Angular
46 Old French coin
48 Frock
50 Whitney
51 Like a bump on __
52 Wing
53 Go fast
54 With "The," "Thomas Crown Affair" theme
61 Doze
62 Mouse-spotter's report
63 Work units
64 Aug. 15 baby
65 Manganese, e.g.
68 Alphabetic trio
69 Kind of worm
70 Earth
71 Olympic surface
72 Begone relative
74 Arm bone
75 Polished
76 Wagner works
80 Deposit document
81 Dorothy's dog
82 Lunch-counter lineup
83 Put on
84 Prefix for dollar
86 Russian river
87 Studio boards
92 Nightingale, for one
94 Hit song of 1969
96 Staggering

97 Corral
98 Story starter
99 Woody G.'s son
100 Frivolous
101 S.A. land
102 Brocket
103 Tendril

DOWN

1 Hornbook material
2 Apportion
3 Discontinue
4 Schismatic group
5 Fate
6 Hereto
7 Allen and Burton
8 Second sight
9 Anointed
10 Twilight time
11 Golfer Alcott
12 Spiritual guide
13 "You __ alone"
14 Deride
15 Tainted
16 Demur
22 New Zealanders
23 Torment

27 Nonexistent
29 Wrath
30 Natal native
32 Very, at Versailles
33 Change for a five
34 Mole relative
35 Pa. town
36 "__ the bag!"
37 Legal matter
38 Complexities
39 Low points
41 Laid back
45 Radar image
46 Sprite
47 Kind of pepper
49 '90s rock group
51 Italian coastal town
52 NASA report
53 Grant in films
55 Genetic material
56 Prepared
57 Killer whale
58 Old story
59 Chutzpah
60 Fond one
65 Wear for Frank Thomas

66 Narcissus lover
67 Wobbled
68 Mil. unit
69 Infirmities
70 Horse color
73 __ many words
74 Bruin from Westwood
75 Might
77 Awakened
78 Barrel-maker
79 Joining
80 Ray of "The Wizard of Oz"
83 Pavane, e.g.
85 Count
87 Yearn
88 Winter warmup
89 Actress Hatcher
90 Aquarium group
91 Swill
92 Hector
93 Kingston campus initials
94 Health club
95 Approving gesture

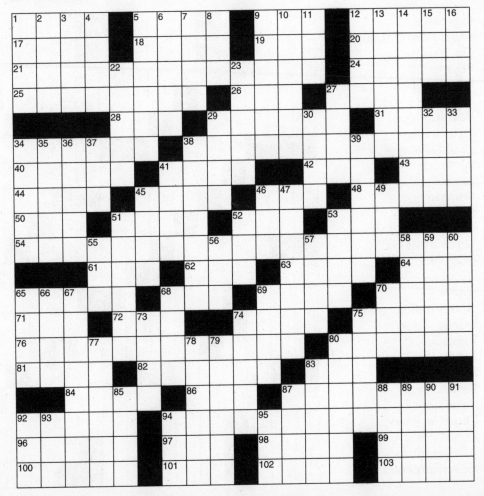

ACROSS

1 Exhausts
5 Ecdysiast's accessory
8 To the side, nautically
13 PC operating system
16 Waste allowance
17 Wild West name
19 Calgary competition
20 Outside: Prefix
21 AL old-timers?
24 Gratuity
25 Laughing
26 Visual reference point
27 Edict
29 Decimation remainders
31 Wall St. transaction
32 Meager
33 Location
35 Outdo
38 Hideo of the NL
41 Train unit
44 NL transgression?
48 Tease
49 Much
51 Howler
52 "Ask __ questions . . ."
53 Player for pay
54 Hoops "gimme"
56 Expensive
59 Cable TV's "__ Diaries"
61 On __ with
63 Bright
65 Japanese sport
66 Like some paper
69 Besmirch
71 "If You Knew __"
74 Pt. of NSW
75 "__ first you don't succeed . . ."
77 Muntjac
79 Singer Vince
80 "__ been thinking . . ."
81 NL newsperson?
85 "Guys and Dolls" character
86 Notify
88 Authorization
89 Ooze
91 Brassica
93 Bandleader Puente
96 Kurosawa film
100 Kind of finish
102 Vacillates
105 Court judgment
106 Cuba Libre ingredient
107 AL inventiveness?
110 Historical period

111 Revoke
112 Proposal word
113 "Kiss from a Rose" singer
114 Green light
115 Yorkshire city
116 Summer time, for short
117 Macpherson

DOWN

1 Race part
2 '70s TV series
3 Georgia product
4 Tours of duty
5 "Leaving Las Vegas" protagonist
6 Imprecation
7 Protection
8 "Raising __" (1987 film)
9 Rep. from Palm Springs
10 Garden spot
11 __ Lingus
12 City on the Tigris
13 NL trans-mogrification?
14 Plant stem
15 Manage
18 Trim

22 Work, for one
23 Wis. town
28 Relations
30 Ace
32 Bristles
34 Discordia
36 Horror-film street
37 Client
39 Catalan surrealist
40 Hautboy
41 Ripken
42 In the manner of
43 AL greetings?
45 Something to connect
46 List components
47 Complication
50 Amazon Valley native
55 Lose one's cool
57 Dine
58 Mambo man Perez
60 Self-satisfied
62 Garbage
64 Level
66 Entity
67 "The Craft" actress Campbell

68 "Yaba __ Doo!"
70 Captures
72 Variety
73 Nev. town
76 Test
78 Rush
82 Admires
83 Graceful state
84 Played back
87 Auction offering
90 Read
92 True
94 Dog feature
95 Held
97 "The Tempest" character
98 Molybdenum, e.g.
99 Newspaper section
100 Advice to the desperate
101 Mammoth
102 Dirk
103 __ out (supplemented)
104 Certain NCOs
108 Humorist George
109 Approx.

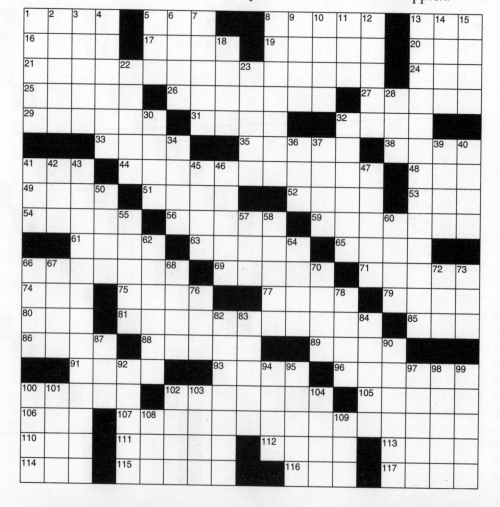

ACROSS

1 Skewer
7 Turkish VIPs
12 Frighten
17 Fan fin
18 Moslem decrees
20 Non-native Hawaiian
21 Dessert delicacy
22 Elaborate effort
24 Expecting
26 Born
27 Chaw
28 Ger. article
29 Laughingstock
31 Overhaul
33 Studio-tour sights
35 Roman date
36 Italian port
38 Kansas town
40 Chosen democratically
42 Marie, e.g.
43 Sewing-machine attachment
46 In effect
50 Paris school
52 Infuse with oxygen
54 Nabokov novel
55 Awaits action
56 __ rat (sense trouble)
57 Tranquil tag
58 Rachmaninoff
60 Actor Wallace
61 Wide-spreading tree
63 "Redemption" author
64 Militaristic cry
66 Young love
67 Rocker Phair
68 Highway divider
69 Calif. town
72 N.H. town
74 Opera legend
76 Actress Caldwell
77 Type size
79 Modern law-enforcer
80 Newspaper section
82 Soil
85 Soprano Ponselle
87 Abound
89 "__ hardly wait!"
90 Put-show link
91 Alphabetic trio
92 Grimalkin
94 Beer type
96 Golf champ
100 "__ Butterfly"

103 Big name in Vienna
104 "__ My Sunshine"
105 Doolittle et al.
106 Gorse
107 Net
108 Singer Tucker et al.

DOWN

1 Mer outpost
2 Soft shoe, for short
3 Artistic honor
4 Firenze "forward!"
5 Ericson
6 Official scorer's verdict
7 Broadcast
8 Modern snack
9 Smog
10 Wood-shaping tools
11 Choice abbr.
12 Menhaden
13 La __, Bolivia
14 Seeped
15 Stan's partner
16 Wails
19 Of a zone
23 Sprinkle
25 Holds sway
29 Choir member
30 Golden Rule word
32 Nap
34 Phil or Don of early rock
35 Actress Lupino
37 Atmospheric substance
39 Trojan War leader
41 Cain's mother
44 Compose
45 Actor Will et al.
47 Like summer days of song
48 Concept
49 Inoffensive oath
51 Adjures
53 Iranian city
56 Hostelry
57 __ many words
58 Mope
59 Lorain's lake
60 Casino surfaces
62 Force fields of a sort
65 Beethoven work
66 Offset
68 Ryan of films
69 Passion
70 Tropical nut
71 Perceived
73 Major league: Abbr.
75 Model
78 Nev. neighbor
81 Linked
82 Removes
83 Accustom
84 Levelled
86 Without __ (benighted)
88 "The Cryptogram" playwright
91 London park
93 Jai __
95 Festival
97 Swiss town
98 Aurora
99 Arikara
101 Barn bleat
102 Chucklehead

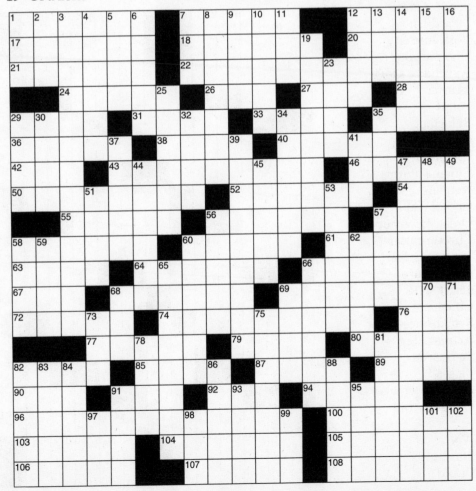

ACROSS

1 Bridge signal
6 Leopard feature
11 Old TV series
17 Booming
18 Joins together
19 Girl of the Plaza
20 Cinema blurb
24 Fast flyer
25 Snide
26 "The King and I" milieu
27 Macabre
29 Remotely
31 Lunchtime initials
34 With 51 Across, cinema blurb
41 Covered carriage
42 The opposition
43 Oven-cook
44 Lawn-care tool
45 Kind of case or ball
47 Dried-fruit dish
48 Muck
49 End of a river
50 Smudge
51 See 34 Across
59 Lizardfish
60 Yorkshire city
61 Uno plus due
62 Aphrodite's love
65 Marina __, Calif.
67 Pallid
69 Reluctant
70 Caesar's sleep
71 "Seinfeld" character
72 Cinema blurb
76 Neonate
77 God of war
78 Orchestra group
79 Curtain-raiser
81 Type of Greek architecture
83 Chart style
86 Cinema blurb
93 Betake oneself
94 Actress Rigg
95 Standards
96 Biases
97 French lawmakers
98 Old gold coin

DOWN

1 Sunshine
2 Cupid
3 Match
4 "When __ with You"
5 Actress Joanne
6 Order
7 Rhymester
8 __ dokey
9 Asian holiday
10 Theater admonition
11 Yearning
12 Mich. town
13 Impend
14 Ullmann or Tyler
15 Just __ suspected!
16 Bishopric
21 Theater drop
22 Follow
23 Writer Dinesen et al.
27 Being
28 __ effort
29 Der __ (Adenauer)
30 Dart
31 __ eyelash (barely)
32 Shed
33 Disapproving sounds
34 On __ (moving)
35 Sported
36 Silver bar
37 Squander
38 Scrivener's well
39 Misplay
40 Sulks
45 Presage
46 Summer mo.
47 Point in favor
49 "Take __ I am"
50 Viscosity
52 Searches
53 Mr. Yale
54 Iron: Prefix
55 Affirmative vote
56 Group of values
57 Game setting
58 Aver et __
62 Landed
63 Inflict on
64 Kiln
65 Be overfond
66 Grand-scale work
67 Cosmetic ingredient
68 Backtalk
70 Type flourish
71 Light of jazz
73 Film classifiers
74 Milk type
75 Slightly
79 __ angle (obliquely)
80 Voucher
81 Noted model
82 A Chaplin
83 Fringe benefit
84 "Today __ man"
85 Former, formerly
86 Form 1040 recip.
87 __ Aviv
88 Health club
89 Wallet cards, for short
90 Recline
91 Purpose
92 Generic pronoun

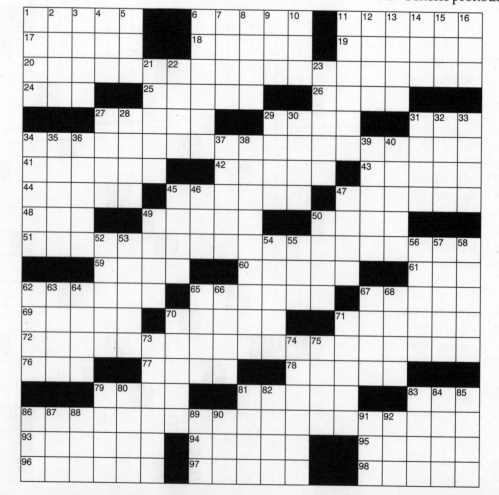

ACROSS

1 Use a rheostat
4 Sam on "Cheers"
10 Past
13 Jostle
17 Gardner
18 Winter wear
19 Pittance
20 Chem. compound
21 "Can I Get a Witness?" singer
23 Favorite
24 Roust
25 Part of ASW
26 "__ Pat" (1994 film)
27 Brake type
28 Shade
29 Greeley
32 Go wrong
33 Viking deity
35 Medicos
37 "Gong Show" regular
41 Collar
42 Writer's quest
43 Informal greeting
44 "The Island of the Day Before" author
45 Raging
46 Withdrawn
47 Sierra Madre treasure
49 Burdened
51 Trinket
52 Jacques of films
54 Candle brackets
56 Peeved
58 "The Secret Life of Walter Mitty" player
60 Domino features
64 Versatile
66 Stage, e.g.
68 Vast amount
69 Kind of car?
72 Doctrine
73 Foot
74 Gelatins
76 Sky altar
77 Sgt., e.g.
79 Wow relative
81 Ermines
82 "Network" actress
85 Ill-defined
86 Testifies
87 Capture
88 Recoil
89 Triumphant cries
91 Western resort
93 Anaconda
94 Mist
97 Polite inquiry
98 Plus
99 Golf great
102 Hershiser of baseball
103 NYC suburb
104 Infuriates
105 Silkworm
106 Quick on one's feet
107 "__ Rheingold"
108 Squinted
109 Call for help

DOWN

1 Lady of Spain
2 Turgenev
3 "The Farmer's Daughter" actress
4 Zetterling
5 Writer Beattie
6 Computer elements
7 Speechify
8 The opposition
9 __ out (supplement)
10 Have a dream
11 Proceeds
12 Result
13 Get moving
14 Demented
15 Daydream
16 Intrigue
22 Mauve
27 Shipyard site
30 Lanes button
31 Biblical verb
32 Musical aptitude
34 Watson's creator
35 Part of Hispaniola
36 Miscue
37 Delight
38 __ a three-dollar bill
39 Expert
40 Sine qua __
42 Snivels
46 Assign
48 Wandered
50 Uraeus
53 Fuss
54 Thesis lead-in
55 Animator's sheet
57 DOD, e.g.
59 "I asked him what his __ . . ."
61 "Shaft" singer
62 Swan River metropolis
63 Impudent
65 Baseball pitcher Johnson
67 Consumed
69 Actor Vallone
70 Slice of history
71 Pessimist of a sort
73 Remuneration
75 Touché relative
78 Papaw
80 Bit of humor
81 Slope runner
83 Far and away
84 Dwellings
85 Assassin
88 Make
89 Singer Tori
90 Clarsach
92 Writer Seton
93 Undoing
95 Cipher
96 Discordia
99 Division
100 Text header
101 Hallucinogen

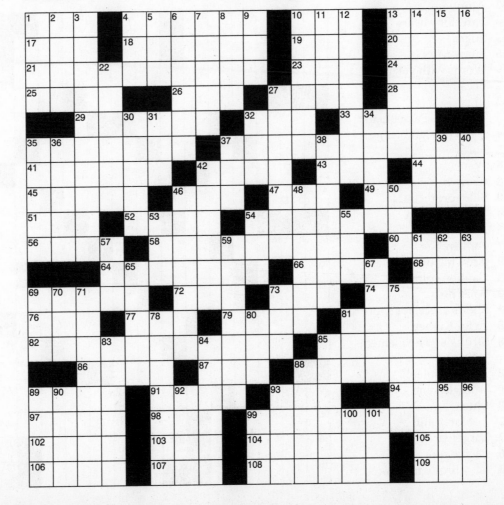

ACROSS

1 School-skipper
7 Encourages
12 Converse
17 Sadat predecessor
18 Fictional
20 Foolish
21 Hit film of '92
23 Reason
24 Fatty
25 Floor covering
27 Trudge
28 Meat cut
31 Malines
32 Pop song of '58
34 Free
35 Stereo mechanism, for short
36 Frankenberg's river
38 Kind of dozen
41 Bay window
43 Negative
46 Fray
47 ". . . __ for ice cream"
49 Hail
51 Conducted
52 __ nose (barely)
53 Amphora
54 Barcelona bears
55 Sugar
56 Film of 1995
59 Words with valentine
61 Became
62 Jug
63 Football's Parseghian
64 __ up (invigorates)
65 Fortify
66 Wane
68 Crowd
69 Silkworm
70 Vocal partisan
75 Actor Peter
77 Fantasy
79 Growing out
80 Caution colors
82 Solar disk
83 Sports execs, for short
85 Actor Kilmer
86 Strunk's "The Elements __"
88 Actress Dolenz
89 Wrigglesome
90 Much
92 __ Mar, Calif.
93 Targeted
96 Pacific spot
98 Isley Brothers classic

103 Outdo
104 Thompson et al.
105 Actor Ray
106 Strong point
107 TV's "The Wonder __"
108 Affix with an asterisk

DOWN

1 Explosive
2 Sound from 70 Across
3 Employ
4 Songwriters' org.
5 Cyberphile
6 Difficult
7 Reply to a name-caller
8 Luggage
9 Advantage
10 Social affair
11 Hot times
12 Umpire Voltaggio
13 A pig __
14 "More Die of Heartbreak" author
15 __ many words
16 Got ready to drive
19 Bog material

22 Expectorant drug
26 Bill
28 Boast
29 Rent out
30 Hateful states
32 Kernel
33 Adam Dalgleish's creator
35 Supporter
36 Word with day or one
37 Senior member
39 Singer Della
40 Passover rite
42 North Sea feeder
44 Timpani
45 Comfort
48 Symbol of military power
50 I, for one
54 Abalone
56 "La __" (Valens hit)
57 "__ with a View"
58 Child of the '50s
60 Mighty
61 Inexperienced
62 Abba of Israel
64 Coequals

65 Regretful words
67 Apiary group
70 Mention
71 Apparel makers: Sl.
72 Columnist Barry
73 And so forth
74 Depend
76 Omitted
78 Corridor
81 Pt. of CST
84 Center
87 Relatives of ifs and buts
88 Collect
89 Beliefs
90 __ now (presently)
91 Wool, in combinations
93 Big part of the world
94 Passage
95 U __ uniform
97 Mimic
99 Chem. ending
100 Mel of the Giants
101 Actress Hagen
102 Road surface

ACROSS

1 "Days of Grace" author
5 Tree snake
10 Baltimore specialty
14 Sights object: Abbr.
17 France of yore
18 Lots of liquid
19 Zeus's sister
20 Hockey's Bobby
21 Uproar
23 Thunderstruck
24 Pittance
25 Baseball Hall-of-Famer Joss
26 Sort
27 Mardi __
28 Heat amt.
29 Froth
31 Energy type
33 Praying figure
34 Implore
36 Actors Fernando and Alejandro
38 Stuffed shirt
40 Southern constellation
42 Social position
44 Granada goodbye
45 Spicy seasoning
46 Liberal's st.
47 Shirts' opponents
48 "We __ ball!"
49 Orthodontia gear
51 Salad-bar offering
52 Crafty
53 Heart of the matter
55 Existed
58 Par plus one
59 Now
60 Presley hit
61 Scored with wheel marks
62 Favorite
63 "Lorna __"
64 Large size
65 Cut
68 Dog breed
69 Insipid character
71 Grime
73 Reply in westerns
74 Sp. province
75 No conformist
77 Health-care regimen
79 Hackman
80 Foundation garments
81 Unclose
83 Oranjestad's place
86 Carte lead-in
87 Hangout
88 Spontaneously
90 Noted diarist
91 Dwell
92 Computer command
93 Aspersion
94 Mich. neighbor
95 Extorted
96 "John Brown's Body" man
97 "Jane __"

DOWN

1 Turkish title
2 Ibn __
3 Barrel organ
4 Songwriter Greenwich
5 Throng
6 Sharpness
7 Blackbird
8 Hesitates
9 Word with way or how
10 Pretense
11 Reinforce
12 God of war
13 Offensive
14 Mexican dish
15 Basis
16 Reliable
22 Annual
27 Inventory problem
28 Trojans' L.A. rivals
30 See 18 Across
32 Possessive prepositions
33 Quirk
34 Musical family
35 Peer
37 Meager
39 "__ Yak" (Coasters hit)
41 Keogh relative
43 Det. Sipowicz
46 Actress Sagal
47 Assail
49 Circus tent
50 Bilko's rk.
51 Patient types
53 "__ long shot!"
54 Cord
55 Novelty song of the '60s
56 Singer Lennox
57 Precipitous
58 Act ineptly
60 Four qtrs.
61 Meditative
63 Ala. town
64 Field event
65 Libeled
66 Diminishes
67 Hardy's Eustacia __
68 Runner Sebastian
69 Honshu city
70 Get there
72 Ultimatum
76 Bay of Biscay feeder
78 Get up
80 Cry in a leaky boat
82 Scheme
84 Smudge
85 Queensland town
87 Law deg.
88 Internal part
89 However

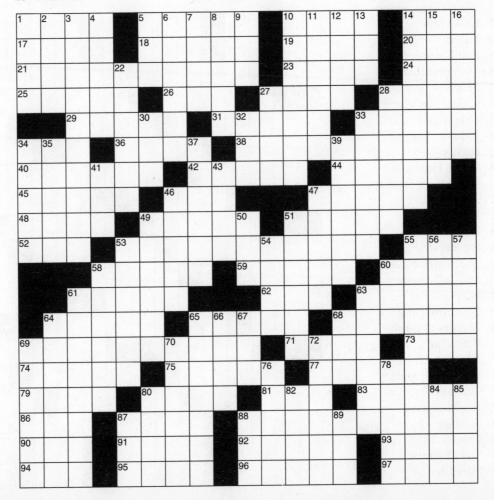

ACROSS

1 Street in N.Y.'s Chinatown
5 H.S. test
9 You love, to Catullus
13 Intemperate
17 European region
18 Actress Lenska
19 Do the job
20 Singer James
21 Bertolucci film
24 Crossword part
25 Sibilant
26 Minn. attraction
27 Indistinct
28 Hardware-store department
30 Pigeon pens
31 Termagant
32 "Picnic" playwright
33 One Ivy Leaguer
35 E-mail command
36 Skier Phil
38 Stevenson tale
41 Roofing material
44 USN mission
45 Journey
47 Dear's companion
48 Links unit
49 Pallid
51 Fall libation
53 "We do what __"
54 Prime
56 Chat show group
57 Misguided
58 Paine's "The Rights __"
59 White House pet
60 Illusory illustrations
61 Take a bath
62 Worn out
63 Dither
64 Fig. expert
67 South attachment
68 Minnelli musical
71 Boring
73 Pound sterling
74 "Henry and June" character
76 Hindu hero
77 Round-trip part
80 Orotund
82 Poolside wear
84 Strange
85 Palmer, to his fans
86 Son of Amittai
87 Shredded
88 Peckinpah film
92 Unrestricted
93 Hmmm relative
94 Abba of Israel
95 Farmer's investment
96 Beatty and Buntline
97 Cayuse
98 Offspring
99 Salamanders

DOWN

1 Doubtfire, for one
2 Word with line or look
3 Noyes poem
4 Backstretch boss
5 Squeamish
6 Binghamton campus initials
7 Math branch
8 Newspaper type
9 Sentient
10 Grimaces
11 Crafts' companions
12 Vault
13 Esteem
14 Central halls
15 Deception
16 "It __ Be You"
22 D-Day lander
23 Devoured
27 Unearth
28 Cotton variety
29 Cultural collections
30 Rate
31 Swerve
34 Consanguineous
35 Exchange blows
37 Hawke of films
39 S.A. range
40 Decorticate
41 Hitchcock film
42 Hawkeye's portrayer
43 Tony-winning musical
46 Marina del __, Calif.
48 Munich mister
50 I-90 crossing
51 Chichpies
52 Calamary's defense
53 Fury
54 Garden item
55 __ effort
56 Info
57 Prefix for log or gram
59 Outbuilding
60 "Dedicated to the __ Love"
62 Leg part
63 Command to Fido
65 Cougar
66 "__ for All Seasons"
68 Become
69 Spokes
70 Part of L.A.
72 True __
73 Part of NYC
75 Derides
77 Tell tales about
78 Run off
79 Weary
80 Gloat
81 Stop transmitting
83 Deauville donkey
85 Chan's remark
86 Sibelius
88 Suggestion
89 '80s transaction
90 Hanoi holiday
91 News execs

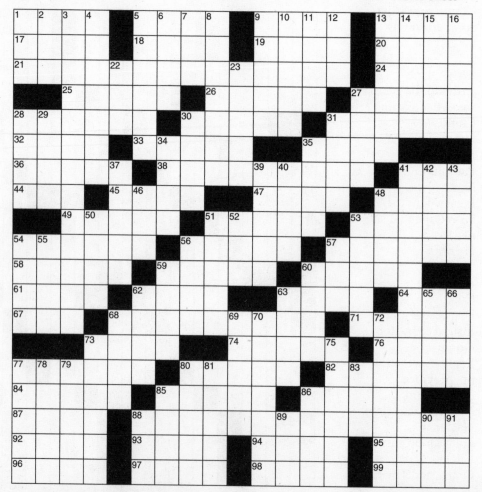

ACROSS

1 Have __ (converse)
6 Politician Alexander
11 "Gymnopédies" composer
16 Candy brand
18 Furious
19 Skating figures
20 Don't go steady
22 Actress Leachman
23 Correct an ushering error
24 Scurry
26 Sugar ending
27 Many times
29 __ girl!
31 Paddington Bear's homeland
32 Kind of song or dive
33 Calendar contents
36 Blemish
37 Hill dweller
38 School org.
39 Mess up
42 Ignore the alarm
46 Where Dingle is: Abbr.
47 Tree trunk
49 Permeate
50 Ordinal ending
53 Slap
56 Kilmer of films
58 Provocateur
59 Snappy
61 Blind ambition
62 Stashed
63 "I Can't __ Satisfaction"
64 Beer name
65 Ala. neighbor
66 Dossier container
68 Fancy boats: Abbr.
69 Handle-equipped
71 Poet Crane
73 Floating leaf
75 Giggles
77 Have good fortune
83 Spell
84 Hyson, for one
86 S.A. land
87 "If You Knew __"
88 Scored high on
90 Fourth canonical hour
91 Male raccoon
93 Sample
94 Ingot
95 River to The Wash
96 __ time (singly)
99 Nearby

101 Seeking business
107 Schedules
108 Soprano Leontyne
109 Brawls
110 Hot spot?
111 Circus star
112 Bowler's button

DOWN

1 Abstract artist
2 Film animator's work
3 __ heart (earnest)
4 "__ sow, so shall ye reap"
5 Hanoi holidays
6 Soda-can fixture
7 Jackie's second husband
8 West of Hollywood
9 Oceanic abbr.
10 Blush
11 Delta buildup
12 Past
13 Entertain
14 "__ far, far better thing . . ."
15 Ger. city

17 Home of the Mets
19 Beige
21 Cake inscription
25 Humanities
27 Illogical
28 Remote
30 Fit for farming
31 Satiate
32 Wonder of music
34 Prefix for gram or center
35 Honky-tonk area
38 Confine
40 Female fowl
41 Auction unit
43 __ Abner
44 Dog tag, e.g.
45 Roman line
48 Nefarious
50 Celebrity
51 Singer Lopez
52 Departs
54 __ volatile
55 Glen Canyon's state
57 Tack on
60 In a chair
62 Spa

63 Seizes
65 Chemin de __
66 Brother
67 MPG rater
70 A memorable Ritter
72 Nervous as __
74 Actress Joanne
76 Marie, Jeanne, et al.
78 Pop singer
79 China's __ He River
80 Trusts' companion
81 Manner
82 Pivotal
85 Immune
88 Daunt
89 "Cheers" worker
90 Washday workup
92 Paper unit
95 Cash register pile
97 Impressionist
98 Abacula
100 Singer Lemper
102 Heavenly altar
103 Kipling tale
104 Frost's "Fire and __"
105 So-so grade
106 FDR's last VP

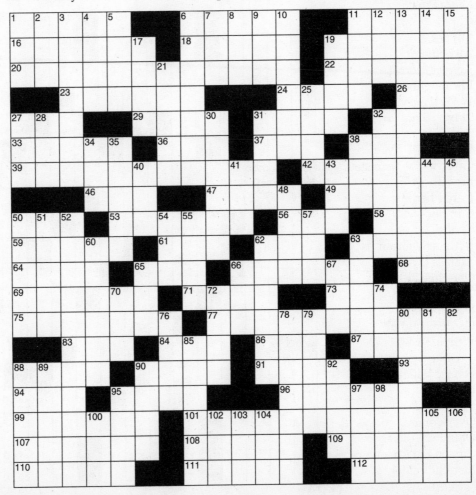

ACROSS

1 Jetty
5 Milliner's output
9 Mil. miscreant
13 Ends' partners
17 Latin years
18 Speck
19 Virginia rail
20 Udometer measure
21 Flowers that make you cry?
24 Latvian capital
25 Driver's spot
26 Supplements
27 __ do (dance call)
29 Prefix for plus
30 Finally
32 Wane
34 Old photo
36 Grimace
37 World Series mo.
40 Historical period
42 Clapton
43 Woody green?
47 Legislate
50 Reciprocal
53 Corn unit
54 Night music
56 Cupid
57 LBJ pet
58 All better
61 Actress Merrill
63 Ida. neighbor
64 W.W. II agcy.
65 "My __ True Love"
66 Bout enders, for short
68 Road sign
69 Carey of the Teamsters
70 Brooch
71 Hardy heroine
73 Cliff lines
75 Goal
76 Actress Swenson
78 Actress Lenska
80 One-time link
81 Think piece
83 Demanding
85 Garden combo?
88 Vituperate
90 __ canto
91 Happy Valley campus initials
92 Mine finds
96 Overworked
99 Old times, old style
101 City on the Rhone
103 Erstwhile chick
104 Recipe instruction
106 Get smart
109 Kilmer of films
110 Computer command
112 Proteinaceous evergreen?
115 Fever symptom
116 Singer Anita
117 Border
118 In a temper
119 Jerry of baseball
120 Hawaiian bird
121 Trade jabs
122 NL team

DOWN

1 "Pensées" philosopher
2 Natural
3 Facilitate
4 Sunder
5 Car model
6 Slightly
7 Clothing
8 Clobbered, old-style
9 Words with recall
10 Turpentine source
11 Like it __
12 Early TV series
13 Hockey great
14 Flower-tree combos?
15 Unearth
16 Catch
22 "__ Rheingold"
23 Poker pass
28 Anent
31 Military force
33 Wine word
35 Actress Aumont
38 Sanitizes
39 Turquoise
41 Sch. of a sort
44 __ in the dark
45 Long journey
46 Bon mots
48 Wreath
49 Fashionable
50 Mazurka man
51 Fret
52 Fruity flower?
55 Easy assignment
59 Jug
60 Recommended behavior
62 Helpful quality
67 Ella F.'s specialty
72 Disheveled sort
74 On
77 One of the Arkins
79 To __ (precisely)
82 Promise word
84 Case of nerves
86 "For __ Know"
87 Portentous type
89 Admits
93 Esteem
94 Ducked
95 Menu section
96 Cut
97 Simple tool
98 Rectifier
100 Engine-room displays
102 Biol. branch
105 Clancy protagonist
107 Barbershop sound
108 Millay
111 Writer Josephine
113 So long
114 Russian spacecraft

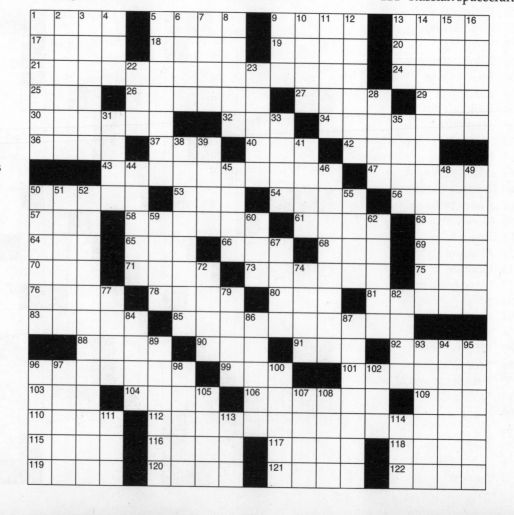

ACROSS

1 Snack
5 Jonathan Butler hit
10 Variables
13 Hyde Park pet
17 Kitchen attachment
18 Segment
19 Cheerful cry
20 Trebek of TV
21 Actress Natalie, writer Raymond
23 Distribute
25 Mazatlan mister
26 "__ Tu" (1974 hit)
28 Solitary
29 Puzzles
32 Rapidly
34 Quinella, for one
37 Actress Rogers
39 Conger
40 Justice Hugo, economist Adam
42 Built up
44 Out of practice
45 Goddesses of the seasons
46 Succulent
47 Psalm word
48 Grand
49 Personality part
50 Kind David's anointer
53 Infants
54 "__ Nobis Pacen"
56 Actress Sally, Judge Learned
59 Epochs
63 Persuade
65 Expulsion
67 Have a debt
68 Clapton specialty
71 Boutique choice
73 Host
75 Concerning
76 Pauley and Powell
77 More streamlined
79 Entertainer Minnie, Fitzgerald character Dick
81 Brother
82 Demands
83 C'__ la vie
84 Furthest
85 Barbary state
87 Look over
88 Actress Hatcher
90 Lab heaters
93 Furrowed
97 Philosopher John Stuart, writer Richard
100 Japanese native
101 Caustic soda
102 Dust-up
103 Western sight
104 Bell
105 Fashion monogram
106 Balance-sheet item
107 Life force

DOWN

1 Media staple
2 Plains Indian
3 Actress Sharon, comedian Jackie
4 Pleasure-seeker
5 Hot tub
6 Soufflé ingredient?
7 Disclose
8 Classroom whizzes
9 Call to Fido
10 Keogh relative
11 Misconception
12 Low-quality stuff: Var.
13 Confront
14 In the manner of
15 Court call
16 Chopper
22 Dernier __
24 Stand-alone
27 Pop-music form
30 Mild exclamation
31 Kind of school or fly
33 Trail
34 Ouzel, for one
35 And so forth
36 Bridge team
37 Bested in chess
38 Insect stage
40 Construction machine
41 Code type
43 Pt. of CBS
44 Stagger
47 Writer Grafton
48 Abundant store
51 Remotely
52 Blend
53 Cable network
55 Stage presence
57 Shades
58 Beast of burden
60 Entertainer Chris, writer Isaac
61 The Beatles' "Eight Days __"
62 Oracles
64 Dingy fixture
66 Arikara
68 Yawn
69 Benefits
70 "__ first you don't succeed. . ."
71 Except for
72 Sedentary
74 Gourmand's big moment
76 Buses
77 __ Lanka
78 Race unit
80 In two ways
81 Extras
85 Samples
86 Poetic preposition
87 Like spandex
89 Film of 1996
91 Chan's comment
92 RR stops
93 Humorist
94 Grande, for one
95 B&B relative
96 __ Mar, Calif.
98 Sheltered side
99 Saturated

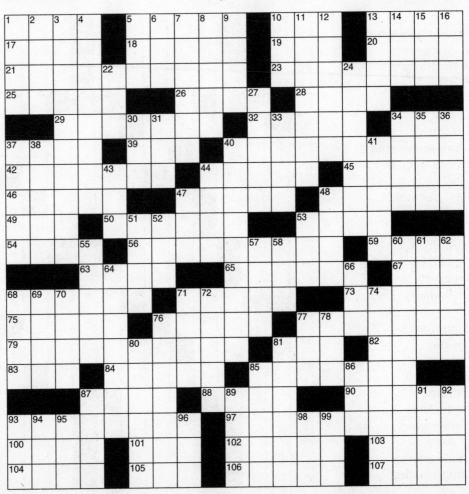

ACROSS

1 Speck
4 In confinement
9 Slow train
14 Panasonic competitor
17 Cry of surprise
18 Too good for
19 Growing out
20 Inquiring sounds
21 Enraptured
23 Politician Cuomo
24 Prefix for guided or giving
25 Baseball's Chris
26 __-Tin-Tin
27 Calculation
28 Cast
29 Laughing
31 Deemphasized
35 Full force
37 "Hamlet" character
39 Sardonic salute
40 Music-man Lanin
42 Stock-page listing
43 "Citizen Kane" man
44 Tennis great
45 Go by
47 Triumphant shouts
48 Caprice
49 Actor Richard
50 Fanatical
52 Lobster trap
55 Sprite
56 Cougar
57 Third-quarter mos.
58 Only's companion
59 OED entry
60 At __ for words
62 Wallabas
63 __ Longa
64 Ness, for one
65 City on I-5
67 Predilection
68 Custodian of sorts
71 Fray
72 Aquarium fish
74 Spoken
75 Height
77 Poe house
78 Over the hill
80 Hades river
82 Adolescent
83 __ Aviv
84 Circle graph representation
85 Writer Ferber
88 Olympics chant
89 Buckets
91 Set straight
93 Actor Cariou
94 Put to rest
95 Central theme
96 Rx regulator
97 Kiang
98 Study
99 Positive force
100 Marsh

DOWN

1 Honcho
2 Where Oskaloosa is
3 Cold shoulder
4 Kind of bird or boat
5 ". . . the broad side of __"
6 Accompany
7 Writer Hunter
8 Actress Susan
9 Moon vehicle
10 Shipping tycoon
11 Legendary singer
12 "__ to Kill" (1996 film)
13 Singer Sayer
14 Transfer
15 Mandarin
16 Declares
22 Sharp
28 Equipment
30 Devoured
31 Bellyache
32 Delays
33 Miscellaneous category
34 Fears
35 Pointed fingers
36 Fix shoes
38 Scarlett and John
41 Standard
43 Doubly afflict
46 Dud
47 Nautical direction
51 __ as a church mouse
52 Consumed
53 Ready to be driven home
54 Come-on
56 __ Anderson Lee
61 Lieu
62 Misbehave
63 Intimidated
64 Mature
66 Aleutian isle
68 Kitchen implement
69 Writer Gay and family
70 Cape Cod town
71 Outstanding
73 Repetitive place
75 Singer __ E.
76 George and T.S.
79 Hackneyed
81 Choice word
84 Points in favor
86 Unadorned
87 __ angle (obliquely)
89 Chum
90 Tax lead-in
91 "__ Believer"
92 Salamander

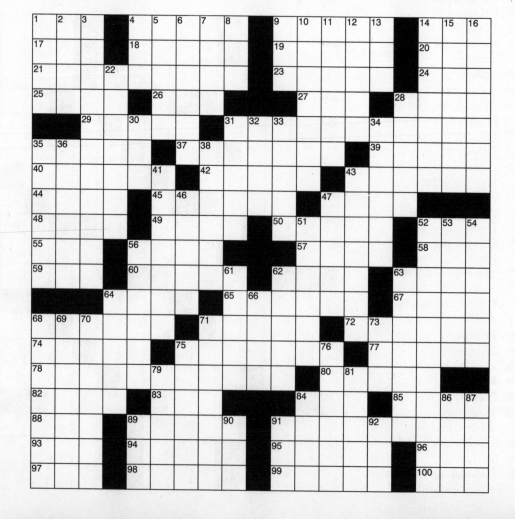

ACROSS

1 Communications device
6 Current
12 Sacred beetle
18 An __ the ground
19 N.J. town
20 Heretofore
21 Insubstantial ratiocination?
23 Blacksmiths' blocks
24 Mount of Israel
25 Immerses
27 Get __ the beginning
28 Morass
30 Heal
32 __ Paulo
33 Crepes' cousins
34 Haunting
37 Heat amt.
39 Writer Morrison
41 Greek letter
42 Forest creature
44 Desperate football flip?
47 Humble
48 Allegory
49 Sunday seat
50 Triumphant cry
52 Off course
54 Bridge player
57 Tourney round
61 Big rodent
63 "__ Me" ('60s hit)
65 Impulse
67 Tilt-a-wheel, e.g.
68 Tape-player button
70 Keen
72 Merkel and O'Connor
74 PC hookup
75 "__ Love" (1995 film)
77 Sea substance
79 Care
81 Timid artistic approach?
86 Antenna housings
89 "__ had it!"
90 Perception
91 "Battle Hymn" composer
93 Banishment
94 Kind of poker
96 Cash dispenser, for short
98 Long story
100 Turned on
101 Fill the hold
102 Porgy
104 Pouted
107 Comfortable
109 Unconvincing soft soap?
113 Singer Lightfoot
114 Hun of note
115 Fighting
116 Imitation
117 Sadat predecessor
118 Certain sculptures

DOWN

1 Favorite
2 That's better!
3 Unhappy, unhappy look?
4 Lab heater
5 Goes to pot
6 Elapse, in a way
7 Lessee
8 "MASH" extra
9 Okla. town
10 Japanese natives
11 Tycoon
12 RR stops
13 Hoodwink
14 Tylenol competitor
15 Cascades peak
16 Sports site in '96
17 Brutish
22 Compulsive performer
26 Rock's __ and the Gang
28 Implore
29 Poetic preposition
31 As appropriate
33 Mosquitoes' specialty
35 Idol ending
36 Pound
38 Cloy
40 Afternoon refresher
43 Vulgar
45 Warm up
46 Jug
48 Asian starling
50 Simian
51 Pilgrimage to Mecca
53 Unrefined
55 Slammed
56 "__ Cup" (1996 film)
58 Gentle fungi?
59 Actress Lupino
60 D.C. title
62 Peak
64 Essence
66 Roy Orbison hit
69 Recordings
71 Plaster accompanist
73 Entrée adjunct
76 Time unit
78 Aug. 15 babies
80 Nero's night
81 Ransack
82 High-flyer of sorts
83 Top dogs
84 Goneril's father
85 Singer Gloria
86 Typical
87 Actor Wallach
88 Clique
92 Flipflop
95 __ book (study)
97 Where Valletta is
99 Hard-rock connection
102 Mercedes __
103 Wilander of tennis
105 Attempt
106 Caesar's famous cry
108 Boozehound
110 Christmas carol word
111 Turncoat
112 Cen. parts

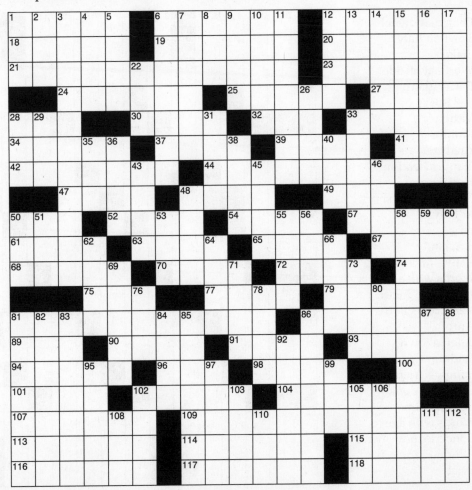

ACROSS

1 Rice dish
6 Encomium
12 Corday's victim
17 "I want __ just like . . ."
18 Singer Sheena
19 Bacterium
20 Words with age
23 __ glance
24 Poet cummings et al.
25 Hail
26 Heat amt.
27 Wood sorrel
28 Fr. soul
29 ". . . __ you old man!"
30 Stat for Pettitte
33 Words with ate
39 Significantly
40 Free
41 Laments
42 Tiny bit
43 Cambridge initials
44 Jejune
46 License plates
47 Reno or Jackson
48 Kitty
49 Dumfries denial
50 Town in Italy
51 Stake
52 Words with ade
59 Porter alternative
60 S.F. tower
61 Variety
62 Mouths
63 Analyze
66 Nautical lead-in
67 However
68 Periodical, for short
69 Mighty
70 Jai __
71 S.A. land
72 Cathedral area
73 Words with ate
78 Tommy __ Jones
79 Verse collection
80 Aurora
81 Belgian town
82 Stadium sign
83 Stimpy's friend
84 Deauville donkey
85 Coral, for one
88 Words with age
94 Concerto movements
95 Whirled
96 Evict

97 "__ a Grecian Urn"
98 Steps up
99 Loss of oxygen

DOWN

1 Family man
2 "So that's the thanks __!"
3 Milanese money
4 Curve
5 Hoodwink
6 Hotel no-no, at times
7 __ Tafari
8 Rueful
9 "Think __" (Buddy Holly hit)
10 Hurting
11 Differ ending
12 Jellyfish
13 Industrial __
14 Caviar
15 "Woman in the Dunes" writer
16 Perfect score
19 Funny business
21 Approach
22 Dwellings
27 Choose
28 Keen
29 ". . . nestled all __ their beds . . ."
30 Sable
31 Memory method
32 Med. school course
33 Packs down
34 Prufrock's creator
35 Watchword
36 Bay window
37 Noah's landfall
38 Rodeo rope
44 Talus
45 Playwright David
46 Texas town
47 Spasmodic
50 Smelter refuse
51 Cotton pod
53 "Julius Caesar" character
54 Vast amounts
55 Outback dog
56 Wanderer
57 Solemn

58 Keen
63 Ring
64 See 72 Across
65 Hillock
66 Former San Francisco mayor
67 Sea monsters
70 Jellies
71 Shelley poem
72 Turn down
74 Church worker
75 __-well (slacker)
76 Prefix for second
77 __ Leone
82 Inward: Prefix
83 Make over
84 Introduces
85 Avoid
86 Comfort
87 Pilaster
88 To's partner
89 Singer Stewart
90 "She's the __" (1996 film)
91 Food ctgry.
92 Born
93 Burst

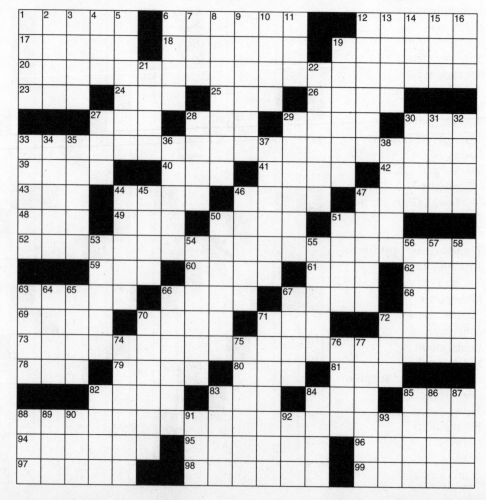

ACROSS

1 Door part
5 Wedding festival
11 Thimblerig prop
14 Half a mistake
17 Mishmash
18 Isolated
19 Phone abbr.
20 Sphere
21 Don Ho's theme
23 Love story
25 Hmmm relative
26 Holiday time
27 Pretense
28 Upbeat
29 Onager
31 Residence
33 Philosopher Pascal
35 Shore wear
37 Trivial matters
42 Okla. town
43 Stephen of films
45 Rose fancier
46 Savvy
47 Stipulated
49 Unseen character on "Mary Tyler Moore"
51 Explosive
52 Bismuth, e.g.
53 Neat
54 Thoroughly
56 Evergreens
57 Smokey Robinson hit
61 Honey drink
65 Architect I.M.
66 Chinese port
67 ". . . wouldn't hurt __"
72 Finally
74 Permissible
75 Romeos
76 Grudge
77 Cosecant's reciprocal
79 Kennel command
81 Discontinue
82 Early in the morning
85 Kingdome site
87 Coves
88 Rice dish
90 Household god
91 Steady
94 Words with carte
95 Frederica __ Stade
96 Lake
98 Embark
100 Alcott tale
104 Test header
105 "__ Fine Day"
106 An often-wet Williams
107 Kingfish
108 Hither's companion
109 Pivotal
110 Writer Dorothy
111 Sensed

DOWN

1 Scribble
2 Olympic torch-lighter, 1996
3 Innovation of the '60s
4 Backroom group
5 Robin relative
6 Deprive
7 Slumbering
8 Investigates
9 Out of the wind
10 Adverbial endings
11 Sheet fabric
12 Strange
13 Cash dispenser, for short
14 Pro __ publico
15 Sea monsters
16 Follow
22 Coffee unit
24 Basement access
27 "You're __ Need"
29 Alongside, nautically
30 Burn
32 Sugar
33 Eleanor, to FDR
34 Bogus
36 Glimmer
38 __ Eddy
39 Newton of the NFL
40 Expand
41 Fish dish
44 Cover story
48 Rock grp.
50 Nabokov novel
51 White vestment
53 Everyday article
54 Frost's "__ Will"
55 Reclined
58 Choose
59 Ms. Sumac
60 Veer off course
61 Harbor sight
62 Engrave
63 __ vera
64 Evolution theorist et al.
68 Staunch
69 Alcott tale
70 __ Gay
71 According to
73 Observed
74 Burden
75 Clambake offering
77 Romantic poet
78 Speck
80 Chart abbr.
83 Cohort of Cosmo
84 Intermittent
86 "__ Good Men"
89 Ace-hole connection
91 Notice
92 Fla. beach
93 Old school
95 Mastercard rival
97 Type of music
99 NASA report
100 Orchestra leader Baxter
101 Babylonian god
102 Before
103 City of the impatient

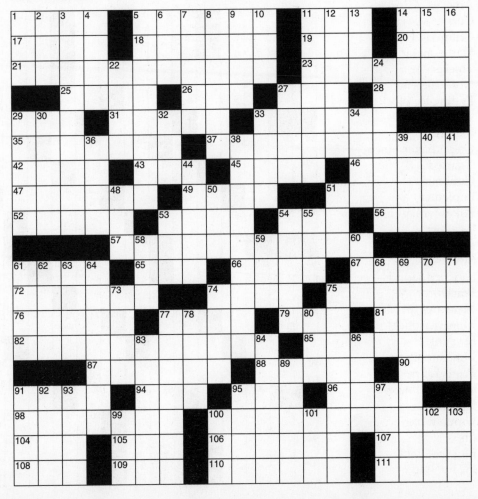

ACROSS

1 British blackjack
5 Mooch
10 Hail
13 Ski lift
17 Look over
18 Spring time
19 Tex __
20 Supporter
21 Jerry Lee Lewis hit
23 Close
25 Straight routes
26 "__ That Peculiar?"
28 Purpose
29 Scrivener's tool
30 Enzyme
32 Certainly
36 Fla. beach
39 Hence
41 Parisian passage
42 Tommy __ Jones
43 "Pretty Little Angel __"
   (early rock hit)
44 Pianist Claudio
46 Vital
47 Repair
48 "__ gratia artis"
49 Amazes
50 Currier's partner
52 Outmoded
53 Home-making
55 Thicke
56 Not so serene
57 Ending for block or
   stock
58 Refine
59 Golfer Baker-Finch
60 Charted
63 Gondolier's
   implement
64 Rakes with gunfire
68 Agalloch
69 Benefit
70 Sweetsop
71 Satisfied sound
72 Blackbirds
73 Measures for Mensa
74 More reasonable
76 Straight
77 Blind ambition
78 Prefix for perfect
79 Words with were
80 Means
82 Unremitting
85 Fix
87 Mel the Giant
88 PC hookup

89 Lamb's pen name
91 Like sand
95 Invigorate
98 Unfounded
100 Title
101 Carmine
102 Term of endearment
103 Attends
104 Lump
105 Double curve
106 Journalist St. Johns
107 Vipers

DOWN

1 Type of salad
2 Bogeyman
3 Tossing and turning
4 Medicos
5 "September of My
   Years" lyricist
6 Cop __ (admit guilt)
7 Bureaus
8 W.W. II grp.
9 Actress Martinelli
10 Kind of acid
11 Endeavors
12 Phone abbr.
13 Dravidian language
14 Innocent
15 Model Carol
16 Crop for Salinger?
22 Singer Turner
24 "It must have been
   something __"
27 Nuptial reply
31 Period
33 Accept
34 Use your intuition
35 The Last Supper, for
   one
36 Dizzy of baseball
37 "Jane __"
38 Acted bored
40 Naive
45 __ U.S. Pat. Off.
46 Painter Rockwell
47 Spiritual nourishment
49 Staff members
51 Singer Jerry
52 Greengrocer's offering
54 Music-store line
55 Wild
56 Solution strengths
58 Health clubs

60 Title of respect
61 Winged
62 Short on authority
64 Sault __ Marie
65 Perfect
66 Noble fellow
67 "__ the One" (1996
   movie)
69 Embraces
70 Oedipus's daughter
73 Poorly
75 Ventilate
76 Film of 1968
78 Sonar sound
79 Do-say connection
81 Lily's home
83 Golf-course sight
84 Coasters
86 Twistian fare
90 Turkish title
92 Writer Seton
93 PDQ relative
94 Alphabetic trios
95 Shade tree
96 Actress Long
97 Wrath
99 Scepter

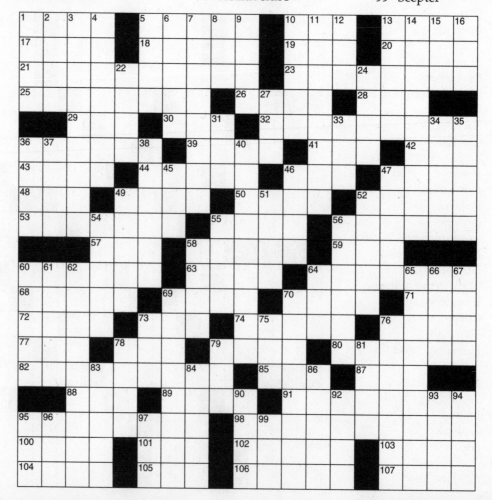

ACROSS

1 Andalusian port
7 Summaries
13 Cartoonist Jimmy
18 Social groups
19 Incongruous
20 Blood of the gods
21 With "The," comedy of 1955
23 Funny-man Martin
24 Waste allowance
25 NBA team
27 Arthur of TV
28 Inquire
31 Actor Hawke
34 Japanese salad vegetable
35 Puffin, e.g.
36 N.Y. campus
38 Polar phenomenon
41 Ruffian
43 Film of 1983
46 Easy victory
49 Town near Binghamton, N.Y.
50 Informal
52 Dodge
53 The Beatles' "__ Be"
56 Eddy-MacDonald repertoire
58 Silkworm
59 Article in Arles
62 Lily relative
64 Evil spirit
66 WJM's Baxter
67 Fragrance
69 Essences
71 Brawl
73 Weary
75 Western Indian
77 Tuscany wasp
80 Directions starter
82 Delighted
86 Back road
87 Country singer West
88 Sasquatch relative
89 Sate
91 Historical period
93 Gaiters
96 Free
97 Hawaiian hawks
98 The soaps, e.g.
101 H.S. juniors' test
103 Actress Scacchi
105 Apply extra pressure
111 Road sign
112 Rococo
113 Ultimatum words
114 Takes five
115 Farm machine
116 Sign up

DOWN

1 Map abbr.
2 "Where __ they now?"
3 Actress Tyler
4 Egg on
5 Category
6 So far
7 Creek
8 Slip up
9 Distributor adjunct
10 Theater org.
11 Kind of truck
12 Tax form, for short
13 Feline sound
14 Behave
15 Nickname for baseball's Thomas
16 Devotee
17 Mountain nymph
22 Value system
26 Church calendar
28 River isle
29 NYC neighborhood
30 Understood
32 Bavarian exclamation
33 Simon of note
35 Mint plant
37 Genesis name
39 Oaf
40 Audibly
42 Shade
44 "__ the point!"
45 Arose
46 "Don't __ Be Lonely"
47 Singer Brickell
48 Go by the book?
51 Appear
54 "__ Ike" (campaign button)
55 Leatherwood
57 Do math problems
59 Much
60 Word-processor mode
61 Grudge-holders
63 Kind of finish
65 Requisite
68 Amortize
70 Houlihan portrayer
72 Spot
74 Put on
76 N.T. book
78 Breakwater
79 Prefix for social or septic
81 Approach
83 Runner Kimeli
84 Minimal
85 Banter
87 Coy
89 Champion racehorse
90 Actor Peter
92 Fla. player
94 Stateline's lake
95 Harsh
98 Blackbirds
99 Water buffalo
100 Break
102 Author Silverstein
104 Nursery denizen
106 Singer Lemper
107 Part of MPG
108 Certain Ivy Leaguer
109 Kiang
110 Hanoi holiday

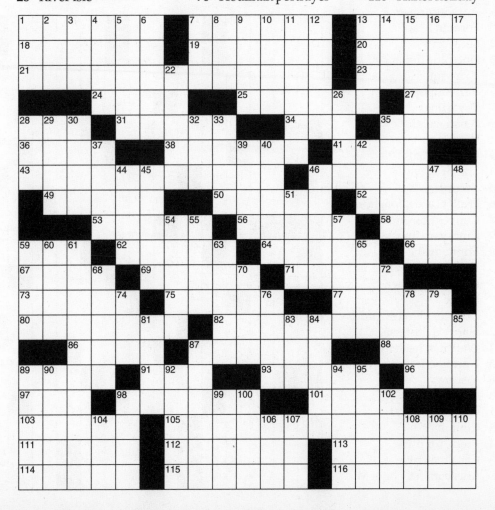

ACROSS

1 Wroth
5 Small amount
8 Manifest
12 Actress Guard
17 Idée __
18 Pi follower
19 Calif. valley
20 Words with these days
21 Tropical getups
24 "This __ I Ask"
25 Agony
26 Do a supermarket job
27 Possessive pronoun
29 ". . . beauty is __ forever"
30 Fell hard
32 "The Bartered Bride" composer
34 Zetterling
36 Fustic product
37 Anaconda
38 Entertainer Don
41 Treatise
43 Baltimore district
47 Adam of "Chicago Hope"
48 Agricultural area
50 Formed a lap
52 Silkworm
53 Uno plus due
54 __ masque
55 Very unpopular
57 Ray trilogy
59 Asian weight
61 Vivacious
62 Naval initials
63 The right way
65 Record
66 Wallet cards, for short
68 Convention ending
69 Cutesy ending
70 Euphemistic
75 Talus
77 Garden bloomer
79 Merge
80 Double-edged sword
82 Hardy's Eustacia
83 Wall St. wheeler-dealer
85 Unrefined
86 Viscera
88 "Gigi" author
91 Out of the wind
93 Container
94 Prefix for plus
95 Carolinas river
98 Music man George M.
100 Semiformal garment
103 Personification
104 Amazon native
105 Teachers' org.
106 "Ignorance __ excuse . . ."
107 Passé
108 __ angle (obliquely)
109 Attempt
110 Tread

DOWN

1 "__ please the court . . ."
2 Abounding
3 Health suggestion
4 Appointments
5 Formal
6 Cry of discovery
7 Frozen dessert
8 Comfortable
9 Bali __
10 Best
11 Squander
12 Taro dish
13 Less rational
14 Sailors' wear
15 Tony sport
16 __ in the ointment
22 "__ not, here I come"
23 Blue
28 RR stop
31 Cleaved
32 Computer command
33 Tropical tree
34 Greeted
35 Blond shade
37 Phone symbol
39 Puts on the payroll
40 Okla. town
42 Misbehave
44 Road for the Beatles
45 Butcher's offering
46 Eur. river
49 Evocative of the past
51 Greek
55 Artist Edgar
56 Brooke S. role
57 Sports spot
58 '40s headgear
60 Much
61 Kelly strip
63 Oval fruit
64 Relatives of 80 Across
65 Angler's item
67 Not believed
70 Avers
71 Inflation-adjusted
72 Most weary
73 Itinerary abbr.
74 Moisture
76 Ancestry
78 Balance
81 Tease
84 TV sports staple
87 Instructions
88 Director's order
89 Praying figure
90 Garr and Hatcher
91 Biting
92 __ Linda, Calif.
94 Pelt
96 Slave of yore
97 Famed fabulist: Var.
99 Composer Rorem
101 Number-cruncher, for short
102 Front follower

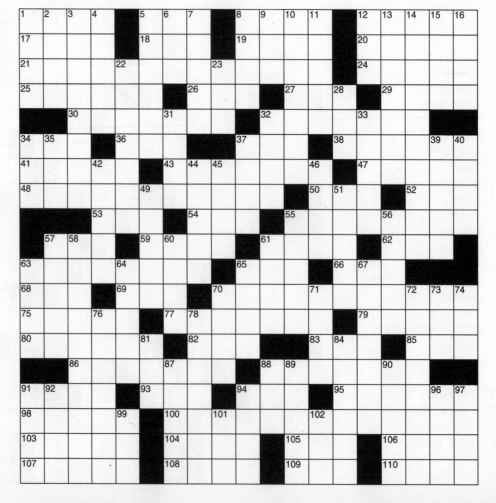

ACROSS

1 Precipice
6 First-rate
12 __ curiae
18 Superficial
19 Doyle protagonist
20 Poe poem
21 Halloween strategy?
23 Toyota rival of yore
24 Sixpence
25 Popular
26 Prescription words
27 Plus
28 Demand payment
30 Condition
33 Cold shoulders
36 Melville tale
38 Stoltz and Braden
40 Utter
41 Ecclesiastical wear
44 Halloween patch material?
47 Stat for Smoltz
48 Child follower
50 Virtual
51 Baseball's Vizquel
52 Unemotional
53 Yellow
55 Fungus structure
58 Supply-demand matcher
60 Receptacle
62 Foolish
64 Grammer
67 "I __ am not in my perfect mind" (King Lear)
69 Picayune
71 Occupy
72 Dog in a '71 hit
74 Orbison song
76 Golf-bag bunch
78 Taj Mahal site
79 "Days of __ Lives"
80 In a proper Halloween mood
84 USN inst.
85 Right away!
87 Mahler's first
88 Differ ending
89 Not so hot
91 18th Century movement
93 Alias
94 Sound investments, perhaps
97 First-rate
99 Dance step
101 And so forth
103 Citte in Italia
105 Oct. 31 ultimatum
108 Ridges
109 Mighty
110 Tropical vine
111 High-tech beams
112 Corrects
113 Consumed

DOWN

1 __ Rica
2 Roman poet
3 "Try __ see"
4 Polypody
5 Liberty
6 Half a dance
7 Highlands sight
8 Choir group
9 Infatuated
10 Mutual fund regulator, for short
11 Kiang
12 Actor Ray
13 Wherewithal
14 Chant
15 Halloween award category?
16 S.A. land
17 D.C. VIP
22 Man from Independence
26 Pull up stakes
29 Snoots
31 S.A. land
32 Bandleader Puente
34 Brogue
35 Command to Fido
37 Giraffe relative
39 Incite
41 Starbuck's skipper
42 Calif. point
43 Plays a Halloween game
45 Actor Jeremy
46 Iroquoians
49 Feint
54 Domain
56 PC capacity measure
57 Growing out
59 Durrell book
61 Quality
63 École attendee
65 Pound
66 Affirmative votes
68 Confidential
70 Hotelier Helmsley
72 Punt or packet
73 Sussex river
75 Entr' __
77 Chump
81 "Bali __"
82 Motivate
83 City on Lake Washington
86 Corsair
90 Film of 1982
92 Ga. city
94 Bollard
95 Keaton of films
96 Beelzebub
98 Gametophyte
100 Sideslip
102 Operatic highlight
103 Prefix for practice
104 Keogh's cousin
105 A alternative
106 Rock group
107 Mil. training course

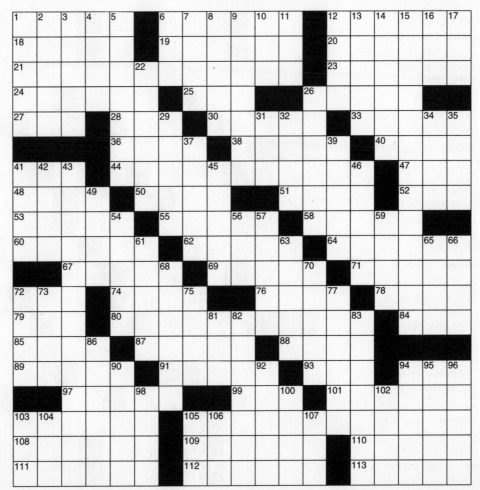

ACROSS

1 Tolstoy subject
4 Belt
9 Hard cheese
13 Actor Alan
17 Mrs. Cantor
18 One of the Nevilles
19 Subtle
20 Latin for 1 Down
21 High Plains husband-seeker's lament?
24 Cordial
25 Slope
26 W.W. II area
27 Biblical verb
29 Jamaican dance
30 Antitoxins
31 Succor
33 __ the line
35 Like some buckets
37 Governed irrationally by the Chesapeake?
42 Dernier __
45 Three, in Italy
46 Camel's hair fabric
47 Computer unit
48 Do a blacksmith's job
50 __ Abner
51 Tibetan gazelle
52 Utility building
56 Down East, for sure!
58 Allende's "Eva __"
60 Bilbao bear
61 Compulsive
62 Permission word
63 Clowder member
64 Chaff
66 Match
67 Balance
69 Austin inflow
71 Easy assignment
73 Carte heading
74 Labor grp.
75 Glaring
76 Hoops matchup
78 Exist
79 D.C. money pool
80 __ volente
81 Sunbathe along the Missouri?
87 Sharon of Israel
88 Purpose
89 Shade tree
90 Clammy
94 Uproar
95 Pro voters
98 OAS, e.g.
100 Basketball player
101 Debt instrument
103 Snowbird's winter hat?
107 Out of port
108 Throw a tantrum
109 "__ to please"
110 PC hookup
111 Student's hangout
112 Mudville group
113 "Funny Girl" composer
114 Wapiti

DOWN

1 TV series
2 Revere
3 Early TV's "__ of the Jungle"
4 Compos mentis
5 Barn bleat
6 Skill
7 Thalia's realm
8 Clove hitch, e.g.
9 Salamander
10 Crown
11 Part of A.D.
12 Vegan's no-no
13 Code part
14 Baked __
15 Opacate
16 Exact
22 One of the Arkins
23 Conspicuous
28 Entertainer Axton
31 Relevant
32 Martinique, for one
34 Man-mission link
36 Pub choice
38 Immediately
39 Weather word
40 "She's __ Mover" ('60s hit)
41 Actor Robert
42 Inhibits
43 Stay
44 "__ Letter to My Love"
49 "'Bali __"
50 Tropical vine
51 __ Wellcome (pharmaceutical giant)
53 Conned
54 Old ascetic
55 Inflicts on
57 Earhart
59 Cunningham's decision at Taranto
63 Gossip subject, for short
65 Ingest
68 Weathercock
69 Done with, and then some
70 Pang
72 Muskellunge
77 Sole
78 Gloucester's cape
79 Sidekick
81 "__ Leroy Brown"
82 Melodic
83 Miscreant
84 Quit
85 Sorrow
86 Jewish month
91 Resourceful
92 Decoration
93 Dido
96 Merit
97 Jai __
99 Files
100 Advance
102 Weir
104 Solway Firth feeder
105 Wray
106 Writer __ Yutang

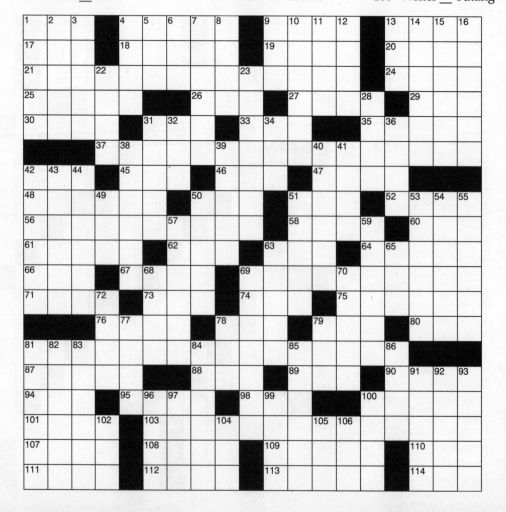

ACROSS

1 Perdition
6 Dance
12 Mind boggles
18 Spry
19 Oakmoss
20 Modern
21 Lives well
24 Strongbox
25 Watch over
26 __ deucey
27 N.C. campus
28 Cocoa's st.
29 Sea eagle
31 Herring relative
34 Zola
37 Midge
38 Bestiaries
39 DOD branch
42 Athena
44 Unreal promise
47 Hedge bush
48 Apr. 15 collector
50 Forerunners of CDs
51 Mainz refusal
52 Intersection type
53 Ganges delta native
56 Roguish
58 Don't fight the odds
61 Hones
64 Typically
65 Bounce
68 Pequod's skipper
69 Road radios, for short
71 Caress
72 Knight apprentice
73 With "The," Dr. Seuss classic
78 "The Little Drummer Girl" author
80 Singer Oslin et al.
81 Part of QED
82 Dregs
84 Insurance-policy attachment
85 Shower
86 Fear of the superstitious
87 Deplorable
88 Algonquian
91 Jog
93 Lean
95 Conciliatory gesture
98 Couldn't sit still
103 Parish's "__ Bedelia"
104 Kind of wire
105 Points of departure
106 Baum character
107 Hotel supply
108 Storage place

DOWN

1 Comedy club sound
2 Gelatin ingredient
3 Info container
4 Whitney
5 Colonist
6 Family
7 Recondite
8 Ventura
9 Italian wine
10 Therefore
11 Down payment
12 Exist
13 __ amis
14 Hurt
15 Passion
16 Inward: Prefix
17 British gun
22 "Cry __ River"
23 Certain teas
28 Bend
30 Hip-hop relative
32 Sultry
33 Hardwood
34 Give off
35 Eight furlongs
36 Arrow poison
37 Menu word
38 Kind of code
39 Computer owner
40 Short performance
41 Where to find B'way
43 Opinions
45 Yale
46 Sufficient, poetically
49 Bilko, e.g.
53 Conk
54 Make __ of (bungle)
55 Junior offs.
56 Schedule
57 Ward-heeler
58 Arid expanse
59 Sixth sense
60 Contributes to
61 Pillage
62 This's companion
63 Cry of frustration
65 Arduous
66 Figure of fear
67 Squint
69 Gregorian __
70 Chemin de fer transaction
72 Professional
74 Teachers' org.
75 Cycle starter
76 Slightly
77 Top rating
79 Overcrowded
83 Degree
85 Dominion
86 Amittai's son
87 Lordly appellation
88 Internet room activity
89 Branches
90 Halcyon place
92 Barbecue dish
94 Fixes
95 Shears sound
96 Bismarck
97 Hey, you!
99 Actress Long
100 Beige
101 Speed
102 Hatchet

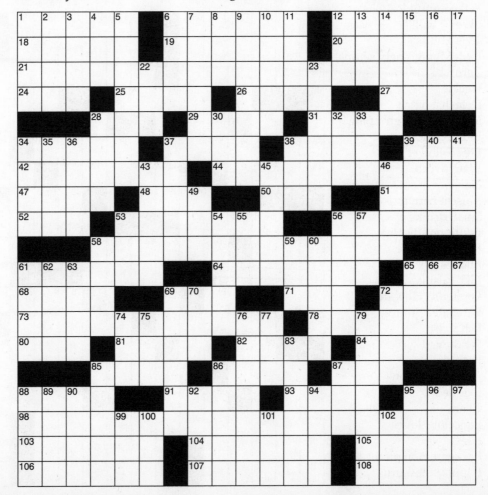

ACROSS

1 "That's the __ could do . . ."
7 Bordeaux wine
13 __ Saxon
18 Chemulpo
19 Interstice
20 Farm machine
21 Informal wear
22 St. Louis Cardinals of yore
24 Skoal relative
26 Dagger
27 Timetable abbr.
28 Wallaba
31 List-shortening abbr.
32 Kind of mint or head
34 Newswoman Ifill
35 Upsets you
39 Lizardfish
41 Profanity
42 Toast
43 Came out
46 Marty Robbins hit
49 Pt. of speech
51 Christie's "There Is __"
52 Disconcert
55 '90s communications
57 "We __ ball!"
58 TV's Melissa
59 L.M. Montgomery setting
64 Zero
65 Heckle
67 Detach a hatch
68 Mathematical grouping
70 Library choice
72 Free follower
73 Watchword
76 Naive
78 Muscat native
80 Small drinks
84 Boutique adjective
85 Horrific drama
88 Buenos __!
90 Like raisins
92 Forster's "Howards __"
93 Baseball's Jimmy
94 U.K. part
95 Wild-eyed
96 Proust
99 __ (Lord) Byron
103 Extolled
107 Claim
108 Lancelot's lover
109 Dress
110 Backgammon piece
111 Popular thesaurus
112 Intensify

DOWN

1 Ignited
2 New USNA grad
3 Black Forest cry
4 Companion attachment
5 __ Pines, Calif.
6 All together
7 Crèche trio
8 Sum, es, __
9 __ Moines
10 Sound of surprise
11 Skeletons' hangout?
12 Hot spot
13 Busy as __
14 Plater
15 Many Scots
16 Magnifying glass, in Madrid
17 Heart, for one
23 Whey
25 Diver's rig
28 Past
29 Shell-game prop
30 Business letter abbr.
32 Foment
33 Straw hat
34 Singer Brooks
36 Author Silverstein
37 B&O, C&O, etc.
38 Slime
40 Caroline portrayer
43 Offensive
44 Van Halen
45 Administered
47 Haul
48 Indiana town
50 Ointment amount
52 Part of UHF
53 More recent
54 Miracles hit, 1965
55 Nest item
56 For fear that
60 Termini
61 Tokyo, once
62 That's all!
63 Prefix for charge
66 Makes the difference
69 Report
71 United
73 "The Glimmer __" (1996 film)
74 Addition word
75 Bamako's river
77 Marsh plant
79 Impetuous
81 Sign, in headlines
82 "William Wilson" author
83 Crafty
85 Bimbo counterpart
86 Nude
87 Reflect
88 "Landscape with Smokestacks" painter
89 Motionless
91 Moore of films
95 Writer James
96 Blanc, for one
97 Chem. endings
98 Guitar relative
100 Manage
101 Tease
102 Tool's partner
104 "Thank-you-ma'am"
105 Before
106 Family room

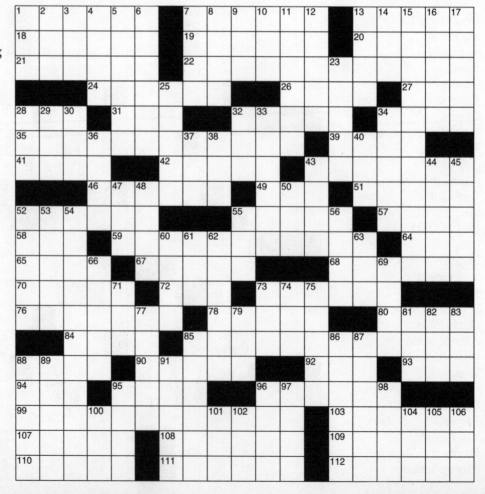

ACROSS

1 Stage group
7 Farm bundles
12 Verge
18 Glass-making material
19 Mall forerunner
20 Chemical ester
21 Thanksgiving thought, part I
24 Dry
25 Bat. avgs., for one
26 __ Marie Saint
27 N.Y. neighbor
28 Caterpillar competitor
30 Approvals
34 Wood-shaping tools
37 Actor Robert
39 Perseus's mother
42 Thanksgiving thought, Part II
47 Rutabaga
48 Greeting
49 California missionary
50 Yo te __
51 __ a witch
54 Circle part
56 Cheer
57 Changed course
58 Bacon units
60 Baja's opposite
63 Spitz, for one
64 "Last Chants" writer Lia
65 Poorly
68 Western hero Lash
70 Prize
72 Skulls
74 Thanksgiving thought, Part III
78 Untrue
79 Watchword
80 Barnyard sounds
81 Summon
84 __ out (inconsistent)
86 Introduce
89 Wrath
90 Understood
91 Cry of discovery
94 Thanksgiving thought, Part IV
101 Windup
102 Hag
103 Jimmy Dorsey hit
104 Kind of throw
105 Deference
106 Card game

DOWN

1 Business grp.
2 Footwear
3 Auricular
4 Actor Vallone
5 Benefit
6 Form
7 Energy source
8 Intermediaries: Abbr.
9 Mrs. Herbert Hoover
10 Stumble
11 Purposes
12 "A __ girl . . ."
13 Former
14 Actor Stephen
15 "Banana Boat Song" refrain
16 Old school
17 Broadway award-winner
22 Cancel
23 Holiday time
28 Cain of TV
29 Success d'__
30 Pains' companions
31 Author Silverstein
32 Makes lace
33 Scoffs
34 __ girl!
35 Ear part
36 Aught
38 "__ to Be You"
40 Continental prefix
41 Continental prefix
43 Hasten
44 National park in Okla.
45 Actor Peter
46 Map abbr.
52 Essence
53 Israeli desert
55 About
57 Storage areas
58 Port __ cheese
59 Rector
60 "Aladdin" prince
61 Greensward
62 PP&M, for one
64 Important
65 "I knew __ instant . . ."
66 Computer connection
67 Ballads
69 Other
71 Audition tape
73 Surrounded by
75 Whetstone applications
76 Scorpion feature
77 Copier supply
82 Freud, Frankenstein, et al.
83 Retrieve
85 Under water
86 War god
87 Impression
88 Woodworking groove
90 Gambling game
91 Distantly
92 Actor William
93 Tavern choices
95 Biblical subject
96 Little integer
97 Grenada gold
98 __ mot
99 Kind of hold
100 Epoch

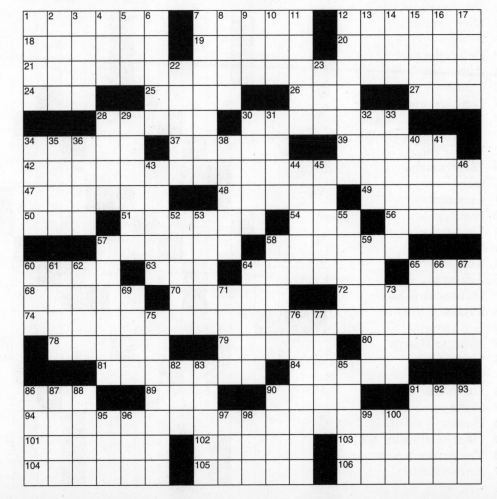

ACROSS

1 Varnish material
4 "__ silly question . . ."
8 Actor Lorenzo
13 Sayings
17 Lennon's widow
18 That's companion
19 Fla. city
20 Portico
21 Words with whim
22 Eatery offering
23 Sacred through-and-through
25 Fun-house installations
27 Tense lead-in
28 Razorback call
29 Form for Keats
30 Noted TV street
31 Honeymooner
33 Prodding type
35 First mate
36 Historical units
37 Plater
39 Convention endings
40 "__ in Royal David's City"
42 Didn't loosen up
45 Vientiane's land
46 Blind ambition
47 Intent
48 Dr. Westheimer
51 Cassowary
52 __ mater
53 Long and lean
55 __ on one's shoulder
57 __ up (dressed garishly)
59 Martin Van __
60 "Tristram Shandy" man
61 Confused
62 Family group
63 Prevaricate
64 Dutch town
65 Attend to
66 Actress Joanne
67 Dickens' persona
68 Mad as __ hen
69 Legal request?
73 To be, to Thierry
74 Mediocre
77 Qty.
78 The BPOE
79 Stacks reproof
80 Deciles
82 What Zarathustra did
84 Newspaper department
87 Actress Alicia

88 Oceanic abbr.
90 Numero __
91 "No trespassing"
92 Directors needing direction?
95 Interlaced
96 Japanese salad item
97 Singer Paul
98 Jibe
99 Slumbering
100 D.C. party
101 Examine
102 Oxen-master, at times
103 Disavow
104 "48 __" (1982 film)

DOWN

1 Impends
2 Writer E. __ Proulx
3 Unkempt golf venue
4 Comfortable
5 Partake
6 Osculate
7 Blond shade
8 No skyscraper
9 Hurt
10 Chairman of note
11 Shakespeare title starter
12 Entertainer Lea
13 Fool trailer
14 Straight man
15 Decay
16 Gale of football fame
24 "Irresistible" one
26 Thumbs-up reviews
27 Ask for help
31 Highlands hillside
32 Flag
34 Figure out
36 Singer James
38 "__ Front Door" (1955 hit)
40 Singer Adams
41 Actor-athlete Joe
42 Uttered
43 Actress Claire
44 Wroth
49 Bypassed the cutoff man
50 Impede
52 Steinbeck's "The __"
53 Accumulate
54 Blakey of jazz
56 Golfer Clavin

58 Tempest site, perhaps
59 Explodes
60 Dimensions
62 Sandler of TV
63 Setback
67 Oven setting
68 "The Grasshopper and the Ants" man
70 Oakland, Calif., vicinity
71 Hero's lover
72 Nev. town
74 Take a __ (try)
75 Paris's wife
76 Lewis Carroll creatures
79 Rapid
81 Possessed
83 Blender output
84 Film of 1995
85 Architectural style
86 Organ pipes
89 Commercial symbol
91 Japanese city
93 Nibble on
94 Mo. neighbor
95 Clump

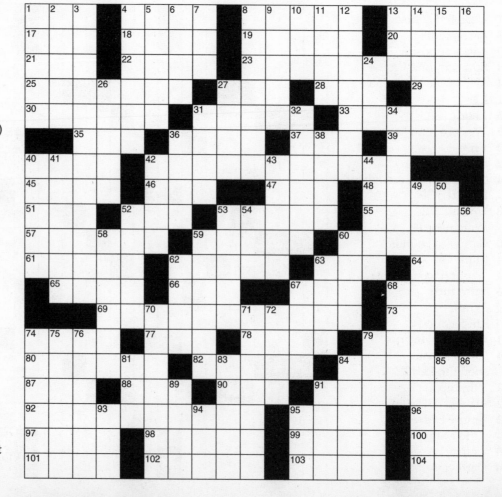

ACROSS

1 Apple acid
6 Stadium cover-ups
11 Do away with
18 "Image of __" (1960 hit)
19 Toughen
20 Overrule
21 Look
23 Beach spread
24 Threshold in time
25 Internet part
26 Training room application
27 Stewpot
28 NL team
30 Modern music form
32 Opening section
34 Health club
37 "We're in trouble"
42 Rolling wreck
45 Weizman of Israel, et al.
46 Merge
47 Borders on
48 Navy code expert, for short
49 Synthetic fibers
52 Salacious
53 Unctuous
55 Mideast sultanate
56 Pigpen
57 Gets cold feet
60 U.N. VIP
63 Lunule
64 Aspirations
65 Graf __
66 Take __ (like)
70 Personalities parts
71 Demon
72 Entertainer Peter
73 Pola the vamp
76 Nerve center
77 Temporizes
81 Noah's craft
82 Syndicated program
83 Gibson
84 Wild
88 Lingerie line
90 Amazement
92 Holiday drink
94 Actor Vigoda
95 Finish enacting
98 Negotiates
101 Franc subdivision
102 Stan's costar
103 Biggest deer
104 Baseball-bat application
105 Peruses
106 Not candid

DOWN

1 Alma __
2 Pulque
3 Popular
4 Fury
5 Talon
6 It's often in hot water
7 Gloucester's cape
8 Designer Gernreich
9 Meticulous
10 Less rattled
11 Bowers
12 Writer Hilaire
13 Ellipsoid
14 Horne
15 Peeve
16 Compass heading
17 __ up (agitated)
22 Mulligan of jazz
29 Begrimed
31 Kind of license
33 One of the Farrows
34 Short performance
35 Sampras of tennis
36 Citrus drinks
38 Happy times
39 "Fame and Folly" writer
40 Put __ (annoyed with)
41 Words with even keel
42 Shakes up
43 Blind as __
44 Kay Scarpetta's niece
48 Eastwood
50 Loses enthusiasm
51 Big birds
53 Crispin's product
54 Barrico
57 Highway markers
58 Bête __
59 Cruelty
60 Tip
61 Computer list
62 Hospital count
63 Musteline carnivore
65 Palio site
66 Man-woman link
67 Acerbic
68 Pawn
69 Uniquity
71 Ziegfeld
74 Global line
75 Oarlock position
76 TV tryout
78 Shock to the system
79 Ms. Prynne
80 Present and perfect
85 Certain sharks
86 Extra-weighty
87 __ up (agitated)
88 Computer unit
89 L.A. lawyer Natasha
91 Fitzgerald
93 Hanks role
95 Psychedelic drug
96 Luau wear
97 Actress Sheridan
99 Boxer's nickname
100 Piglet's cohort

ACROSS

1 Tzara's cult
5 Welles role
9 Busy as __
13 __ Rios, Jamaica
17 Flair
18 Obdurate
19 Adjoining
20 For example
21 Hellman play
24 Butcher's offerings
25 Goes to
26 Optimal
27 Pace
28 Words with you so
29 Barry Manilow hit
31 Gardener's purchase
32 A Bobbsey twin
33 "Now __ down to sleep"
36 Stone marten
37 Marx Brothers movie
40 Sea monsters
43 Yarborough of auto racing
46 Point
47 Astonish
49 Witticism
50 Environmental study
52 Initiated
54 Divert
56 Country gentleman
57 Swains
58 __ Pointe, Mich.
59 Parents' sisters
60 Midler
61 Like some consommé
62 Apparatus
63 "__ Mio"
65 Scram!
66 Biblical book
67 Gang follower
69 Sports standout
73 Crowbar
75 Temporary "wheels"
76 Sounds of uncertainty
79 Dwelt
80 Burdened
82 Chekhov uncle
84 "Djamileh" composer
85 Fury
86 Party animal
88 Vizquel of baseball
89 Flight-crew member
92 Merchandise
93 City on the Oka
94 Masher
95 Sandarac tree
96 Naval amphibs
97 Locksmith Linus
98 Thelonius of jazz
99 On the __ (exactly)

DOWN

1 Confine
2 "Got __ Livin' to Do"
3 Ohio city
4 Photographer Adams
5 Variety
6 Humanities
7 Tokyo drama
8 Compass heading
9 Fed the kitty
10 Golfer King
11 Egress
12 List-shortening abbr.
13 Olivier role in '65
14 String quartet fare
15 Camel features
16 __ buco
22 Calif. desert town
23 Doubleday
27 Rubber duck's home?
29 Popular video game
30 Fr. soul
31 Singer Joan
34 Stick
35 Xiamen, formerly
36 Look over
37 Fired up again
38 Indistinct
39 Radio name
41 Pamper
42 Chargers
43 Actor Romero et al.
44 Exonerate
45 Social parasite
48 Noble
51 Circa
52 Asian palm
53 Sup
55 Back tooth
57 Type of pepper
58 "Hello sweetheart, __ a rewrite!"
60 Male raccoon
61 Baseball's Gonzalez
64 Throw off
65 In the blink __ eye
68 Esteems
70 Like days of yore
71 Opponent
72 Senator Sam
74 Zoo consultant
76 Designer Emanuel
77 Noisy scavengers
78 "Nausea" writer
79 Certain beans
80 Tag
81 Fast on one's feet
83 A beginning __ end
84 New Year's Day event
85 __ avis
86 Shock
87 Half a fortnight
89 Like a Marvell mistress
90 Fortify
91 Furthermore

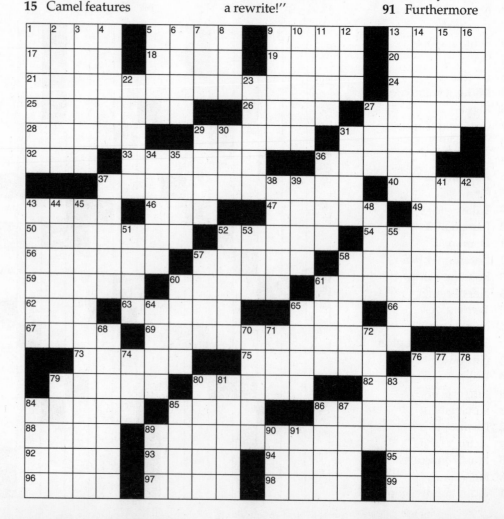

ACROSS

1 A Broadway Joe
5 Fitzgerald
9 Bight of Benin port
14 Sandwich type
17 Familiar noise
18 Task force
19 Undisguised
20 Meadow
21 Light show of a sort
24 Unction
25 Notorious Romans
26 Dry-cook
27 Small change, in Sussex
29 Supplies
31 Storied hill-climber
32 River to the Dead Sea
33 Sahara sectors
34 Centers of attention
35 Least reasonable
37 Ecdysiast Lily St. __
38 Film of 1994
41 Updike's "Rabbit __"
43 Steed
44 Mouse accessory
47 Book publisher's mark
49 Corset feature
51 Alas
52 Bored reactions
53 Ultra-conservative
54 Certain road work
56 "I cannot tell __"
57 Spoken
58 Delay
59 Yr.-ender
60 Big family
62 Famed jockey
63 Aversions to light
66 Sandwich type
69 Worn out
72 Sorrels
73 Lome's land
74 Green
75 Certain E-3s
76 Bed type
78 Economist Alan
79 Little songbird
81 One of the Churchills
82 Musical syllable
83 Acid test material
88 Shrieking sound
89 Let up
90 Above, in Bavaria
91 Bombeck
92 __ judicata
93 Ceremonies
94 More than a few
95 Spot

DOWN

1 Palindromic energy
2 Black Forest cry
3 Kind of record
4 Conundrums
5 Group characteristics
6 July 31 babies
7 Choreographer Lubovitch
8 Howe subject
9 Kind of news
10 Birds, to Brutus
11 Bloke
12 Grampus
13 Hurry!
14 Pop music's Concrete __
15 Nikon alternatives
16 Gift
22 Caution lead-in
23 Dependable
28 Silkworm
29 Dry
30 Endeavor
31 Shock
32 Singer Sebastian
34 Symbol of intimidation
35 Andrew __ Webber
36 Composition
38 Formal
39 Barnyard group
40 Telecom fare
42 Dependable
44 Deep thinkers
45 Paquin of films
46 Rap's Snoop Doggy __
47 "If __ my druthers . . ."
48 Spy
49 Throat complaint
50 Confucian truth
51 Finished
53 Wooden shoe
54 Type of type
55 Amo, __ . . .
57 Guam city
58 Speaker of baseball
60 Film of 1994
61 Line
62 Down with
63 Stuffed shirt
64 Shack
65 Paper nautilus relative
67 Cry of disgust
68 Word after oh
69 Car coat
70 Main course
71 Anuran sounds
73 Kerry County seat
75 Jabs
76 Skier Phil
77 City planning org.
79 Waistcoat
80 Arrow poison
81 Prow
84 "Bali __"
85 Cable TV initials
86 Little devil
87 Anti's vote

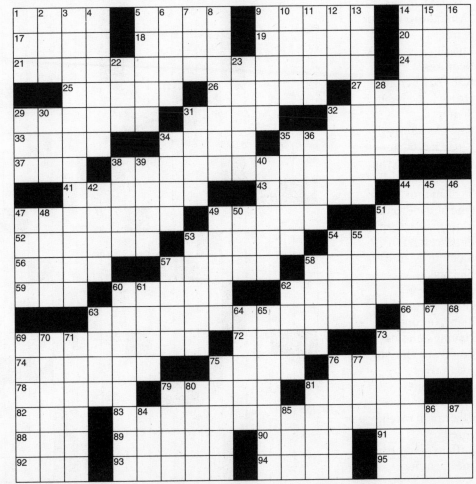

ACROSS

1 Certain NFL pass-rushers
4 Wisecrack
8 Wired, in a way
14 Folder marker
17 Abstract sculptor
18 Golden Rule word
19 Actress Dahl
20 Tribute
21 Vote in favor
22 Work like __
23 Tropical mulberry
25 Sulky
27 Writer Cousins
29 Play hard __
30 Out of alignment
32 "Xerxes" composer
35 Actress Elisabeth
36 Kept moving
40 Purple shade
42 Chem. ending
43 Carson successor
44 PC command
46 Lummox
49 Actor Wood et al.
52 __ even keel
53 Tokyo sash
54 "Minotauro-machie" painter
57 Lhasa __
59 Requires
61 Nabokov heroine et al.
62 Drury Lane habitue
66 Swing
67 Reeboks alternative
69 Kitchen attachment
70 Informal gatherings
72 Actress Caldwell
73 "__ Rhythm"
76 One of the Fromes
78 Mornings, informally
79 Plutarchian fare
81 Metallurgy study
82 Blockhead
85 All together
87 Grand promise
91 Blanc, for one
93 Having handles
95 Rowdy of "Rawhide"
96 Asian river
98 "__ of Honey"
101 Waste allowance
102 Champion racehorse of yore
105 Buffalo's county
108 Social ending

109 Texas's __ Ross State Univ.
110 Rock-band staple
111 Street sign word
112 Clinton, e.g.
113 Simian
114 Well
115 Pungent flavor
116 Hosp. areas

DOWN

1 Kind of center
2 Capital crime
3 Effervesce
4 As
5 Sturm __ drang
6 "Let's Get __" (Gaye hit)
7 Kelly strip
8 Certain hack
9 Set up
10 Mixture
11 Caroline portrayer
12 Purpose
13 Skillful
14 Gritty competitor
15 Flanders farewell

16 Davis of films
24 Santa __, Calif.
26 __ Aviv
28 Greek letter
31 "The Time Machine" author
33 Pizazz
34 Actress Eilbacher
37 System of morality
38 Loire Valley region
39 Mauna __
41 Imparted
45 Space
47 Poplar
48 Brawler's display
49 Readiness
50 Tool handle
51 Dog breed
54 Quixote's pal Sancho
55 Dialect
56 Maugham work
58 Dagger
60 First letter, phonetically
63 Party
64 Squirrel's prize
65 "I pass"
68 Sam's comics cohort

71 Suspicious
74 Johnny Mathis hit
75 Pizzeria need
77 Chart-topper, for short
80 Like squares and circles
82 Standing over
83 "End of the World" singer Davis
84 Computer field
86 Ticket-taker's return
88 Give __ (take a shot)
89 Shoe widths
90 Consume
91 __ Solemnis
92 Outdo
94 Pan-fry
97 Autograph
99 Sermon starting point
100 Silkworm
103 Designer Anna
104 Warship compartment, for short
106 B&B relative
107 Farm deposit

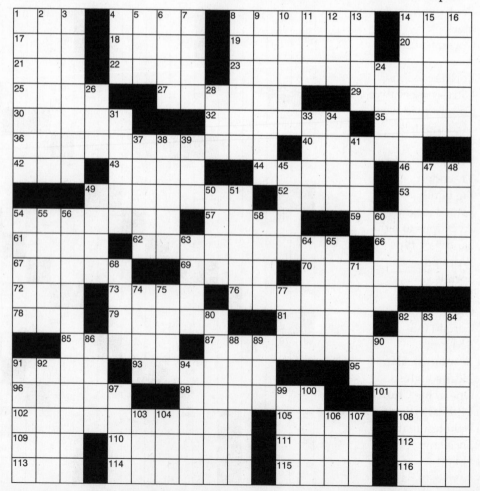

ACROSS

1 Outcropping
5 Singer Collins
9 Philosophical subject
13 __ buco
17 Cry of dismay
18 Round dance
19 Rack's companion
20 Roy Orbison hit
21 New Year's resolution
24 Faithfully
25 "__ fits all"
26 Put into words
27 Large amounts
28 Unwind
29 Fogs
30 Excuse me!
31 Film of 1953
33 Chemical variant
36 Basketball's Longley
39 New Year's resolution
42 Backstabber
43 From __ Z
44 James portrait subject
45 Citrus drinks
46 Letterman rival
47 Small fowls
49 Instances
51 Sana's land
52 Actor Randall
53 Ruling group
54 Erstwhile bird
55 Weary
57 Singer Springfield
58 School-skippers
61 Biarritz bears
62 Trunk fastener
63 Trumpeter, for one
64 Meadow mom
65 Absolutely
66 New Year's resolution
69 Hither's companion
70 Roundabout ways
72 Gasket of a sort
73 Chem. compound
74 "__ This Be Magic?"
76 Soprano Lucine
81 Ready to fight
83 Soft cloth
84 Extra wager
86 Native Egyptian
87 New Year's resolution
89 Over again
90 Church calendar
91 U.N. veto
92 Eight: Prefix
93 Poi source
94 Road sign
95 Embroiders
96 West Indies dances

DOWN

1 Shade
2 Avignon's river
3 Adams with a camera
4 "A little __ long way"
5 Facial expression, old-style
6 Stopped, nautically
7 Wrath
8 Plover
9 Kind of cake or cup
10 Cousins' mothers
11 Current
12 NROTC grad
13 Brunch offering
14 New Year's resolution
15 Diving duck
16 Coxswain's cry
22 Navigator's calculation
23 On land __
27 Booted
29 Writer McCarthy
30 Enzymes
31 Squalid
32 Mortar troughs
33 Endings for equal or idol
34 Stamp booklet
35 Old school
36 Campus spot
37 Actress Hagen
38 New Year's resolution
39 Insipid
40 Troublesome
41 Concept
46 Spartan queen
48 The alert are on them
49 Horns of the moon
50 Pismire
51 Offspring
53 Equitable
54 Sturm und __
55 "Wind in the Willows" figure
56 Rachmaninoff's "__ of the Dead"
57 Rostrum
58 Minn. player
59 Couple
60 D.C. VIP
62 Fling
63 Sliding wedge
66 Part of QED
67 Put on a pedestal
68 Cape Cod town
71 Kind of punch
74 "Guys and Dolls" refrain
75 Victorious
76 Fuss
77 Office flow
78 Spend __ ('85 Derby winner)
79 Cyma __
80 Greek peak
81 Nervous as __
82 Writer Jaffe
83 Computer connection
84 Distort
85 Ideal endings
87 Suggested actions
88 Soap ingredient

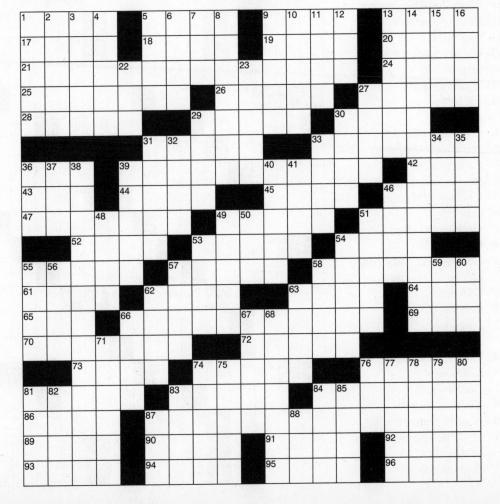

ACROSS

1 Lily-livered sort
5 Angel feature
9 Solicitude
13 "Picnic" playwright
17 Eight: Prefix
18 Czar of 1550
19 Pitcher Hershiser
20 Part of a process
21 "My Fair Lady" song
24 Auld Lang __
25 Diner offering
26 River to the Rhone
27 Contrapuntal piece
28 Distantly
30 Inspire
31 Diaphanous
33 Tunisian port
34 Hindu ascetic
36 Occupies
37 Child's game
40 Japanese drama
41 Certain newspaper
43 Entertainer Sumac
44 Cry of surprise
45 Yielding metallurgical matter
46 Anthology, for one
47 Pindaric oeuvre
48 Flourish
50 Close on screen
52 Sharp
53 Hammer part
54 Middle
55 Barbecue
56 Limpid
58 Burgundy grape
59 Criticized
62 Recuperate
63 Underworld chieftain
64 Trolled
65 High-jump obstacle
66 B&B relative
67 Convention gathering places
70 Gardner
71 Bolster
72 Likewise
73 Sicilian peak
74 Understood
75 Kind of oil
77 Doctrines
78 Auction routine
79 Waters of music
81 "__ little something for a rainy day"
83 Russian sea

85 Cereal material
86 Campus rite
91 Quetzal, e.g.
92 Litigant
93 Actor Pitt
94 Reverberate
95 Protein sources
96 Postponement
97 Comfort
98 Million laughs

DOWN

1 Awesome!
2 Mainz pronoun
3 Kingston Trio hit
4 Long-handled weapon
5 Feel the heat
6 Composer Charles
7 Apprehend
8 Spiritually aware
9 Blush or flush
10 __ for one's money
11 Hard times
12 Wapiti
13 Bone of contention
14 "Long Hard Road" performers

15 Knee: Prefix
16 Fencing event
22 Roofing material
23 Imaginary creature
27 Actress Sherilynn
28 "__ and his money . . ."
29 Celebrated virtues
30 Tax form, for short
32 Basketball shot
33 Social climber
34 Singer Young
35 Up's companion
36 "Since __ Have You"
38 Iowa town
39 Pant
41 Doormat
42 Siskel's partner
47 Word-of-mouth
49 "Kiss from a Rose" singer
50 Salami center
51 __ Tzu
52 Guzzles
54 Zoo attraction
55 Crete's capital
56 Semi-conductor

57 Actress Olin
58 Faints
59 Satyr
60 Gutters' place
61 Standoff
63 Unfriendly
64 Concordes
67 Carry
68 High-tech beam
69 ". . . be with ye wherever __"
74 Good working condition
76 Tears
77 Dove rival
78 Pasture plaint
79 Dies down
80 Jazz grouping
82 Precinct
83 Miscellanies
84 Astronaut Sally
86 Conscription org.
87 Keogh's cousin
88 Perfume brand
89 Triumphant shout
90 Succinct denial

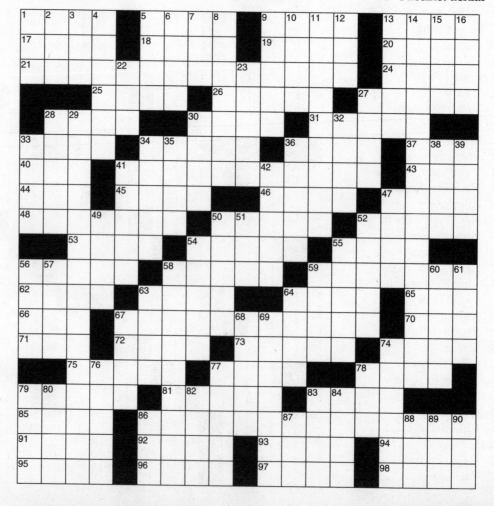

TIMES BOOKS CROSSWORD ORDER FORM

VOL	ISBN	QUANTITY	PRICE	TOTAL PRICE

Random House Masterpiece Crosswords
Elegant, all-new crosswords plus profiles of famous puzzlemakers in a hardcover-spiral format.

1	96373-3	____	$16.00	____
2	92619-6	____	$16.00	____

Boston Globe Sunday Crosswords
Clever puzzles by Hook, Cox, and Rathvon.

1	92540-8	____	$8.50	____
2	92539-4	____	$8.50	____
3	92612-9	____	$8.50	____
4	92613-7	____	$8.50	____
5	92746-X	____	$8.50	____

Los Angeles Times Sunday Crosswords
Witty, contemporary puzzles.

10	92228-X	____	$8.50	____
11	92229-8	____	$8.50	____
12	92230-1	____	$8.50	____
13	92231-X	____	$8.50	____
14	92232-8	____	$8.50	____
15	92788-5	____	$8.50	____

The Washington Post Sunday Crosswords
N.Y. Times-quality puzzles from the nation's capital.

1	91933-5	____	$8.50	____
2	91934-3	____	$8.50	____
3	92109-7	____	$8.00	____
4	92396-0	____	$8.50	____
5	92648-X	____	$8.50	____

Random House Sunday Crosswords
Intelligent, witty puzzles, a few notches less difficult than the New York Times.

1	92554-8	____	$8.50	____
2	92766-4	____	$8.50	____

The New York Times Daily Crosswords
America's favorite mental exercise!

35	92270-0	____	$8.00	____
36	92340-5	____	$8.50	____
37	92358-8	____	$8.50	____
38	92450-9	____	$8.50	____
39	92481-9	____	$8.50	____
40	92538-6	____	$8.50	____
41	92617-X	____	$8.50	____
42	92706-0	____	$8.50	____
43	92760-5	____	$8.50	____
44	92801-6	____	$8.50	____

The New York Times Sunday Crosswords
The standard by which other crosswords have been judged for more than 50 years.

15	91781-2	____	$8.50	____
16	91839-8	____	$8.00	____
17	91878-9	____	$8.00	____
18	92268-9	____	$8.50	____
19	92083-X	____	$8.50	____
20	92451-7	____	$8.00	____
21	92615-3	____	$8.50	____

Random House Club Crosswords
120 Sunday-size puzzles from America's exclusive clubs.

1	92638-2	____	$12.50	____

The Puzzlemaster Presents
200 word games from Will Shortz's popular Sunday morning radio show.

96386-5	____	$12.00	____

Very Tough Puzzles
The toughest puzzles ever published in book form!
Random House UltraHard Crosswords

1	96372-5	____	$8.50	____
2	92482-7	____	$8.50	____
3	92701-X	____	$8.50	____

The New York Times Toughest Crosswords

1	91694-8	____	$9.00	____
2	91828-2	____	$9.00	____
3	91912-2	____	$9.00	____
4	92178-X	____	$9.00	____
5	92618-8	____	$9.00	____

Random House Sunday MegaOmnibus
America's biggest crossword book! 300 Sunday puzzles, edited by Will Weng.

1	92708-7	____	$12.50	____

Crossword Omnibus Volumes
Each with 200 crosswords, at a great price!
Los Angeles Times Sunday Crossword Omnibus

1	92758-3	____	$12.00	____

Will Weng Sunday Crossword Omnibus

1	91300-0	____	$11.00	____
2	91645-X	____	$11.00	____
3	91935-1	____	$11.00	____

The New York Times Daily Crossword Omnibus

1	91094-X	____	$10.00	____
2	91018-4	____	$11.00	____
3	91066-4	____	$10.00	____
4	91117-2	____	$11.00	____
5	91708-1	____	$11.00	____
6	92124-0	____	$11.00	____
7	92541-6	____	$11.00	____
8	92759-1	____	$11.00	____

The New York Times Sunday Crossword Omnibus

1	91139-3	____	$11.00	____
2	91791-X	____	$11.00	____
3	91936-X	____	$11.00	____
4	92480-0	____	$11.00	____

The Crossword Answer Book
The most comprehensive crossword reference, guaranteed to have more of the answers you're looking for!

92729-X	____	$27.50	____

The New York Times Crossword Dictionary
The revised edition of the classic reference book for crossword fans.

92373-1	____	$27.50	____

Parent and Child Puzzles
The only books specially designed for parents and children (ages 8 to 13) to do together.

1	92543-2	____	$12.00	____
2	92703-6	____	$12.00	____

Acrostic Puzzles
Change-of-pace puzzles with a literary flavor that reveal interesting quotations when completed.
Random House Crostics (All new puzzles!)

1	92768-0	____	$8.50	____

The New York Times Acrostics

5	92537-8	____	$8.50	____
6	92620-X	____	$8.50	____

GAMES Magazine Crosswords & Word Games
Lively, solver-friendly puzzles from America's most fascinating puzzle magazine.
World's Most Ornery Crosswords

92081-3	____	$14.00	____

The Giant Book of Games

1	91951-3	____	$15.00	____
2	92614-1	____	$14.00	____

Will Shortz's Best Brain Busters

91952-1	____	$12.00	____

Games' Best Pencil Puzzles

1	92080-5	____	$12.00	____
2	92553-X	____	$12.00	____

Brain Twisters from the World Puzzle Championships

1	92146-1	____	$11.00	____
2	92616-1	____	$12.00	____

More Puzzles For Kids
Start your favorite youngster on a lifetime of brainbuilding fun! (ages 7 to 14)
GAMES Magazine Kids' Giant Book of Games

92199-2	____	$12.00	____

GAMES Magazine Riddlers for Kids

92385-5	____	$11.00	____

Cryptic Crosswords
Sophisticated puzzles in the British style, using American English.
Henry Hook's Cryptic Crosswords

1	92767-2	____	$11.00	____

Random House Guide to Cryptic Crosswords

92621-8	____	$14.00	____

Random House Cryptic Crosswords

1	96371-7	____	$11.00	____
2	92562-9	____	$10.00	____
3	92770-2	____	$11.00	____

GAMES Magazine Cryptic Crosswords

91999-8	____	$8.00	____

N.Y. Times Best Diagramless Crosswords
The only series of diagramless crosswords!

1	92608-0	____	$8.50	____
2	92707-9	____	$8.50	____

Additional Times Books crossword puzzle books are available through your local bookstore, or fill out this coupon and return to:

RANDOM HOUSE, INC., 400 HAHN ROAD, WESTMINSTER, MD 21157. ATTN: ORDER PROCESSING

TO ORDER CALL TOLL-FREE
1-800-793-2665

☐ Enclosed is my check or money order payable to Times Books

☐ Charge my account with: ☐ American Express ☐ Visa ☐ MasterCard

EXP DATE (MO/YR) _____

Please send me copies of the crossword books I have checked off, in the amounts indicated.

POSTAGE & HANDLING

TOTAL DOLLARS	ADD
0-$14.99	$3.00
$15.00-$29.99	$4.00
$30.00-$49.99	$6.00
$50.00-$99.99	$10.00

Total Books _____

Total Dollars $ _____

Sales Tax $ _____
(Where applicable)

Postage and
Handling $ _____
See chart at left

Total Enclosed $ _____

Name (please print) _____ Signature _____

Address _____ City _____ State _____ Zip _____

Price applies to U.S. and territories only. In Canada write Random House of Canada, 5390 Ambler Drive, Mississauga, Ontario. (Prices subject to change.)

ANSWERS

TIMES BOOKS CROSSWORD ORDER FORM

VOL	ISBN	QUANTITY	PRICE	TOTAL PRICE

Random House Masterpiece Crosswords
Elegant, all-new crosswords plus profiles of famous puzzlemakers in a hardcover-spiral format.

VOL	ISBN	QUANTITY	PRICE	TOTAL PRICE
1	96373-3		$16.00	
2	92619-6		$16.00	

Boston Globe Sunday Crosswords
Clever puzzles by Hook, Cox, and Rathvon.

1	92540-8		$8.50	
2	92539-4		$8.50	
3	92612-9		$8.50	
4	92613-7		$8.50	
5	92746-X		$8.50	

Los Angeles Times Sunday Crosswords
Witty, contemporary puzzles.

10	92228-X		$8.50	
11	92229-8		$8.50	
12	92230-1		$8.50	
13	92231-X		$8.50	
14	92232-8		$8.50	
15	92788-5		$8.50	

The Washington Post Sunday Crosswords
N.Y. Times-quality puzzles from the nation's capital.

1	91933-5		$8.50	
2	91934-3		$8.50	
3	92109-7		$8.00	
4	92396-0		$8.50	
5	92648-X		$8.50	

Random House Sunday Crosswords
Intelligent, witty puzzles, a few notches less difficult than the New York Times.

1	92554-8		$8.50	
2	92766-4		$8.50	

The New York Times Daily Crosswords
America's favorite mental exercise!

35	92270-0		$8.00	
36	92340-5		$8.50	
37	92358-8		$8.50	
38	92450-9		$8.50	
39	92481-9		$8.50	
40	92538-6		$8.50	
41	92617-X		$8.50	
42	92706-0		$8.50	
43	92760-5		$8.50	
44	92801-6		$8.50	

The New York Times Sunday Crosswords
The standard by which other crosswords have been judged for more than 50 years.

15	91781-2		$8.50	
16	91839-8		$8.00	
17	91878-9		$8.00	
18	92268-9		$8.50	
19	92083-X		$8.50	
20	92451-7		$8.00	
21	92615-3		$8.50	

Random House Club Crosswords
120 Sunday-size puzzles from America's exclusive clubs.

1	92638-2		$12.50	

The Puzzlemaster Presents
200 word games from Will Shortz's popular Sunday morning radio show.

	96386-5		$12.00	

Very Tough Puzzles
The toughest puzzles ever published in book form!
Random House UltraHard Crosswords

1	96372-5		$8.50	
2	92482-7		$8.50	
3	92701-X		$8.50	

The New York Times Toughest Crosswords

1	91694-8		$9.00	
2	91828-2		$9.00	
3	91912-2		$9.00	
4	92178-X		$9.00	
5	92618-8		$9.00	

Random House Sunday MegaOmnibus
America's biggest crossword book! 300 Sunday puzzles, edited by Will Weng.

1	92708-7		$12.50	

Crossword Omnibus Volumes
Each with 200 crosswords, at a great price!
Los Angeles Times Sunday Crossword Omnibus

1	92758-3		$12.00	

Will Weng Sunday Crossword Omnibus

1	91300-0		$11.00	
2	91645-X		$11.00	
3	91935-1		$11.00	

The New York Times Daily Crossword Omnibus

1	91094-X		$10.00	
2	91018-4		$11.00	
3	91066-4		$10.00	
4	91117-2		$11.00	
5	91708-1		$11.00	
6	92124-0		$11.00	
7	92541-6		$11.00	
8	92759-1		$11.00	

The New York Times Sunday Crossword Omnibus

1	91139-3		$11.00	
2	91791-X		$11.00	
3	91936-X		$11.00	
4	92480-0		$11.00	

The Crossword Answer Book
The most comprehensive crossword reference, guaranteed to have more of the answers you're looking for!

	92729-X		$27.50	

The New York Times Crossword Dictionary
The revised edition of the classic reference book for crossword fans.

	92373-1		$27.50	

Parent and Child Puzzles
The only books specially designed for parents and children (ages 8 to 13) to do together.

1	92543-2		$12.00	
2	92703-6		$12.00	

Acrostic Puzzles
Change-of-pace puzzles with a literary flavor that reveal interesting quotations when completed.
Random House Crostics (All new puzzles!)

1	92768-0		$8.50	

The New York Times Acrostics

5	92537-8		$8.50	
6	92620-X		$8.50	

GAMES Magazine Crosswords & Word Games
Lively, solver-friendly puzzles from America's most fascinating puzzle magazine.
World's Most Ornery Crosswords

	92081-3		$14.00	

The Giant Book of Games

1	91951-3		$15.00	
2	92614-1		$14.00	

Will Shortz's Best Brain Busters

	91952-1		$12.00	

Games' Best Pencil Puzzles

1	92080-5		$12.00	
2	92553-X		$12.00	

Brain Twisters from the World Puzzle Championships

1	92146-1		$11.00	
2	92616-1		$12.00	

More Puzzles For Kids
Start your favorite youngster on a lifetime of brainbuilding fun! (ages 7 to 14)
GAMES Magazine Kids' Giant Book of Games

	92199-2		$12.00	

GAMES Magazine Riddlers for Kids

	92385-5		$11.00	

Cryptic Crosswords
Sophisticated puzzles in the British style, using American English.
Henry Hook's Cryptic Crosswords

1	92767-2		$11.00	

Random House Guide to Cryptic Crosswords

	92621-8		$14.00	

Random House Cryptic Crosswords

1	96371-7		$11.00	
2	92562-9		$10.00	
3	92770-2		$11.00	

GAMES Magazine Cryptic Crosswords

	91999-8		$8.00	

N.Y. Times Best Diagramless Crosswords
The only series of diagramless crosswords!

1	92608-0		$8.50	
2	92707-9		$8.50	

Additional Times Books crossword puzzle books are available through your local bookstore, or fill out this coupon and return to:
RANDOM HOUSE, INC., 400 HAHN ROAD, WESTMINSTER, MD 21157. ATTN: ORDER PROCESSING

TO ORDER CALL TOLL-FREE
1-800-793-2665

☐ Enclosed is my check or money order payable to Times Books

☐ Charge my account with: ☐ American Express ☐ Visa ☐ MasterCard

EXP DATE (MO/YR)

Please send me copies of the crossword books I have checked off, in the amounts indicated.

Name (please print) _____

Signature _____

Address _____ City _____ State _____ Zip _____

Price applies to U.S. and territories only. In Canada write Random House of Canada, 5390 Ambler Drive, Mississauga, Ontario. (Prices subject to change.)

POSTAGE & HANDLING

TOTAL DOLLARS	ADD
0-$14.99	$3.00
$15.00-$29.99	$4.00
$30.00-$49.99	$6.00
$50.00-$99.99	$10.00

Total Books _____

Total Dollars $_____

Sales Tax $_____
(Where applicable)

Postage and
Handling $_____
See chart at left

Total Enclosed $_____

ANSWERS

1

```
USC  BEN  JUMP  MOSLEM
REL  ODE  ODER  ATWILL
SWALLOWWHOLE   RHINOS
ANYA    TIN    POTOF
    PYTHON  WRATH  TRAS
ASI  OINK  JAYHAWKERS
LEGION   AMUSE   RIGOR
IRES  THOU     RECONS
AROMA  ENTO  BREAK
SAN  FALCONCREST  SOU
    GRIPE  SHEA  HOCUS
RELOAD     ALMA  SATI
IDIOM  ATEST   LAUREN
THESEAGULL  ZEST  ERG
ASSE  GORKY  EXOTIC
    SCANT   JUT   ARAB
SHOTAT  LONESOMEDOVE
SERENE  EWES  RAY  WIT
TROPES  SLAT  TIE  SDS
```

2

```
UNIQUE   IMPALA   BARRY
MODULE   MORROW   UNITE
SHRINK  PROGRESSIVES
   ACAST    JOE    TIM
BATHS  RIPEN  DYNAMOS
ASHE  LILAC  TOLE  ISO
USE  LOVESTORIES  DAR
MAR  ALIX  RON  SEDGE
SIBERIA  BELUGA  GLEN
   ERAT  BEGOT  PLIE
MERL  AVALON  SEESOFF
ARIES  ILL  ACNE  FOR
DOG  THELEFTBANK  TRY
ASH  ROWS  RALLY  AHME
METEORS  AIRED  SMEAR
   VPS  IRE   SANER
INDEPENDENTS  BARONS
MAINE  BENDER  ARCANA
ASMAD  COASTS  SEEDED
```

3

```
SODAS   ARMADA   SEABAG
ANIMA   SAUTES   AFLOAT
LEVEL  SUMOFALLFEARS
TAIL     BLT    AVERSE
   DIE  PALL  ERECT
BREAM  ABE  FLIRT  MOM
RED  MINUSSIGNS  DUPE
AAH  AMOR  TRIO  SALES
CRIB  PURLOIN  CRUTCH
   GREET  AWN  ORIBI
SCHOOL  IMAGINE  SPOT
IRWIN  SLOG  NEMO  LIE
COAL  VALUEADDED  INN
SPY  CEDAR  TIA  DUCKS
   MORAT  STAY  SPA
   SAIPAN  OUR   STAB
REMAINDERSALE  SHINE
PRIMED  PLACER  HOODS
MARISA  SONTAG  ETNAS
```

4

```
BECAUSE   EMOTE   AFEE
USURPED   INAROW  BRAS
STREETS  STRIPEDBASS
   AND  ETAPES  RENTE
WIG  DONA  ILL  RISK
HORNSWOGGLE  PEP  VAR
ALIA  NILES  MEA  EIRE
TAPIR  SEN  COAL  BOGS
   LOSE  ELLA  INBLUE
WAC  DISORGANIZE  AST
ATEASE  MAES  MELT
ILLE  REAL  HEP  LACED
SALS  RAN  PENAL  LOVE
TWO  FAT  FIDDLERCRAB
   PROS  LAC  EASE  ANT
ICHOR  BAITED  LAB
BEATTHEDRUM  PIRATES
INNO  EELERS  REMNANT
STER  STERE  ESSENCE
```

5

```
MOSEY   CASCA    BIBLE
ANODE   ORIOLE   SENIOR
SMUGSMUGGLER  HORROR
TARE  ASONE  OPENED
SNS  ASIN  MIDAS  ERA
   OUTON  LATELATERAL
BOUTON  CANED  UPSET
ADREM  WAR   ALFA
SICS  MINUS  ERAT  HAT
RUE  MILDMILDEWS  ADO
AMS  ANDY  LOGAN  DROP
   TRES   WAS  DUMBO
SAMOA  SANER  PEAHEN
THINTHINKER  CELLA
YAK  ARIES  URAL  RLS
   HORNET  TUNER  AMAT
BEANED  CALLCALLIOPE
ALICES  HYENAS  INNER
TILED   ERASE  STYLE
```

6

```
RIPPLE  KELP  SMALL
ACTION BLAIR BOOTIE
MEANSTREETSOFLAREDO
ASH  ROSES  VEERS
   SCENE  AIMS  ESCE
BODYHEATANDDUST  LOW
OPINES  PORER  WEAVE
MANET  HARPY  SILVER
BRA  MARIA  CLARK
  THECRUELSEAOFLOVE
   NOELS  SEGUE  ADS
RELOAD  AIRED  SALUT
AMASS  GARNI  MONICA
NEW  THEBIGEASYRIDER
GUST  ANIL  VESTS
   HOVEL  ABEET  SMU
LOVEMETENDERMERCIES
APEMAN  NOISY  RUSTLE
STEER  ERNS  YEASTS
```

7

```
LIMBO  CAP  MATT  JOB
ALIEN PARA ALOE  OKA
WILDATHEARTBURN  WIN
SELL  WANGLE  MEDDLED
   ALAN  OOPS  ROI
BLAMEITONRIOCONCHOS
IOU  SNOB  DNA  STATE
DUKE  MEAL  END  ABAT
EAR  AREO  TOM  IRA
  HANGEMHIGHSOCIETY
FAR  APA  DINO  KAY
IDOL  ORE  TOLL  EURO
LAMIA  INA  TIRE  ROW
STANDANDDELIVERANCE
   EDT  SERA  OURS
PEANUTS  ADDERS  TRUE
ALL  PAPERMOONSTRUCK
USE  TIER  ANNO  LADLE
LAX  ONDA  NAS  CLEAR
```

8

```
ABC  MINI  SSW  BLITHE
LOO  ASIN  NOH  LASHES
FOURTHOFJULY  AROINT
   SET  BLAB  DSM  BRIE
FOIL  LEAP  CITE  ATES
INNATE  MALADY  TRY
BEETHOVENSNINTH  THE
   EINE  STY  EARTHEN
SSH  NERD  SOB  PURIST
HOAR  YAP  NUT  ERSE
ENLACE  DOS  DULL  DER
BAFFLES  LAS  BIER
ARA  ONEFIFTHOFVODKA
   LSD  CETERA  TIBIAS
THEE  STAY  ANSA  EELS
HOAX  EST  KNIT  ORT
ENGINE  HEADQUARTERS
DOUSED  EAT  RBIS  RIP
ARETES  RUE  ASTO  SAY
```

9

```
AMIS  BABS  SAGAS  FAT
TONI  EDIT  PROVO  OUI
HOSTILETAKEOVER  URE
ORE  CAL  BEAN  RECLAD
LETME  ADLER  ASNOT
   ARM  REP  PRE  REBA
ENVY  ITIS  BAR  ADREM
SUI  RSVP  MESA  WORSE
ETC  AHA  NASTYHABITS
   IAMA  MIRES  ARAT
GROSSPROFIT  BUD  OJS
ROUSE  ANTE  HUNS  RUE
ASSAY  BAY  PANT  BYTE
DECI  CID  ALL  SIR
   ILIAD  AGUST  OASES
BURSAR  ALUM  ROW  AGE
ORC  MEANTEMPERATURE
NIL  BERNE  EAVE  ITER
ASE  SNEER  TRIO  PETS
```

10

```
OFF  VOCE  LUCCI  SUMP
POI  USAC  ASIAN  ITEA
ACROSSTHEBOARD  ZANY
HISS  ACOW  OPINE
   TIP  HIED  EGO  AMI
ALDER  ACROSSTOWNBUS
GLORIA  WOO  SEUSS
HOW  MMS  UNTRIM  OTTO
AYN  APACHE  ALIAS
SDS  TEXASACROSS  DIP
   HERON  SCENEI  OVA
ANDI  ENACTS  ART  WAN
ROUGH  DIE  SWANNS
NOTHINGACROSS  ASSAY
ANY  FOR  SPAT  SKI
   MINOT  ECRU  EZIO
RIJO  COMEACROSSWITH
IRIS  OVALS  EDDY  NAN
GEMS  MENDS  DEAR  GTO
```

11

```
LAC  ARIL  GAITS  SSTS
ESA  VENI  INTHE  OTOE
CYR  EVAN  LOWERCOURT
OOPS ILES  NAB   AND
QUEENSLAND SEAR  EAR
     RYE  ROUT SILENCE
CARVE     ODOR  MARTHA
AGEE BAUD  PEGS  SPED
PUISSANT  DIAL  EER
SAG  THOMASCROWN  ISM
     NAY  DORM EVIDENCE
AMOS YESI  ADEN  NCAA
DEFILE  TAPS     STERN
DETAILS SOWS  OUI
STE  BLIP PALACECOUP
     RAE  COO  NEUT ELSE
CAROLEKING  ADES  DAR
AVON RENTE ZITI  AGO
BARE ANTON YOST  SEN
```

12

```
RAF  MEMO  LIP  CHAISE
ORO  ADAR  IRA  LANDED
YELLOWJACKET  ENNEAD
SOLARIA  RENEGADE
   ODIN RYNE RNS  BOA
DAWES MAP  DEE  CROP
RUSS  KEPTUNDERWRAPS
URU KENT PAST  REUSE
MAI OLD  APT  SAID
SETUPS  ISA  STONES
   MEOR MAL  ATE  ILO
ASPIC AUEL AXIS  GIN
CLOAKANDDAGGER  THAN
MARK TKO  RID  BETSY
EWE  OLE  REIN HUNS
   GRADUATE  MARTHAS
UNFAIR STUFFEDSHIRT
PARING AID  UNIT FIE
SPONGE FOE  NUTS TAP
```

13

```
LES  SHED  LAIN  LACES
ASP  PONE  URSA  INERT
STRAININGCAMP  NONES
TAINTED  HAY  OWENS
   NOES DON  ALIA USE
BATS TAOS SWELLBRED
ASSET NIT ENOL  REND
NTH  RAIN AGIN GIDDY
FRO  ACT  ABAN  PAM
FOP  SHAMBURGERS SOS
   SHY  OATS NOH  CUT
MISTY CRTS JAPE OTO
ONEA SHOE PUT  STREW
SCARELESS ALEC INRE
TAP  NAME ANY  LAMB
   ORIBI PSI ROBERTA
SHRUG SWITCHESBREWS
TOTEM TONI EPEE AIT
MISSA SEER NOSY DNA
```

14

```
FACT  WADER MISC  EBB
CLUE  INURE ODOR  LAO
CARNATIONS  DELIVERY
  TARTS  ISEE  TACKS
SHABBY ALDAS  HINT
WAILS BROUN SUCCORS
IDLE COOPERATE ERIE
GAS BLOWS EXUDE AVE
   ALAN GMEN  RATED
SADDEN AGOOD ORNERY
TWEEN AGRA  IRON
OAF DACHA LINER TWO
AREA SHAMROCKS CHIN
SENSATE MIDAS SHINE
   DONA LAPIN SPENDS
SLANG EURO  STALK
TANGENTS SUBMISSION
ACT LENT TRAIL  ENDO
YES SWAY ENATE  AGED
```

15

```
RABAT  GIPP  BBC  TOP
ALAMO ONOR SOIL  HIE
FORITISGOODTOBE INN
  TIDAL APPIAN RICKS
    ELLS  ERY  BILK
CPOS CHARLESDICKENS
LAB GRETA RUES  STEP
ONEWAY OVO PESO  STY
DIARY ONEAL MENO
CHILDRENSOMETIMES
   TEEN STOOD ONSET
AIM SRAS SKI SNITCH
BOAS ITEA ASSES ETA
ANDNEVERBETTER ERST
   RUDE LAD  AGHA
ALIBI TIBIAS EASES
LAG THANATCHRISTMAS
EVA HANG OREL TEMPE
CAL STS  REDS  ERASE
```

16

```
CASCA  ARA  NAURU  SGL
ONION  VAN  UNPEN  TEA
NINETEENNINETYONEIS
   VIA  CAT  MUS  URGE
PUPA  RIO  EMIR  ABNER
APALINDROMICNUMBER
TAR  SSE  USE    NEY
  AWL  AMT  SWISS  BAG
RADIAN  ORT  RNA  NULL
IFITMATTERSANYTOYOU
GAGS  MAT  YAP  SOVIET
ARM  LAGOS  USC  NAN
   SOT  HIC  AST  GEE
  ANOTHERONEISCOMING
CLEFT  SEED  RAU  UNDO
RITE  OTT  USO  BAD
INTWOTHOUSANDANDTWO
MEL  WHELP  RIA  ELIAS
ESE  LORDS  ICY  WENDS
```

17

```
SHADES  PILATE  INFRA
DIVEST  PRIZED  LOUIS
SPARSE  SECONDFIDDLE
  REEK  SIR  YAK  DEA
RAMI  PAC  TEA  BELY
IRON  BUS  STIR  ADAR
GANG  BURMA  ARI  DUDE
GRADUAL  ARC  ACTEDON
  ONS  ASSOON  ANDRE
MAD  DEADHEADING  YEW
ALAMO  ODENSE  OUR
MANAGER  SIT  DESERTS
BIDS  ATE  OATES  DIAL
ONES  RASP  LAB  OGLE
  LEAN  ELF  DIS  USED
ERI  LED  EER  THIN
RHODODENDRON  INDIAN
GENIE  NEGATE  NEEDLE
OASES  STELLA  SEDATE
```

18

```
SAD  GALA  ADDS  TASSO
ONA  EBAN  LIEU  EUTAW
STRETCHDRIVES  ATALL
OAKS  SORE  EMPEROR
  HST  REBS  SEW  STOW
EGO  USE  UAW  CEN  IRA
MORENO  FRONTRUNNER
OUSTERS  FADES  RIGGS
TREE  RUR  HEX  AST
EDS  BONET  NUDGE  WAD
  RAW  MAE  SEE  TINY
PRIES  MAMBA  LOZENGE
HANDICAPPER  LIMBER
ENS  SOL  ARC  UDO  YRS
WITS  PAS  THAN  NOA
  ACCEPTS  ERRS  ANTI
ADLER  RUNTRUETOFORM
MILNE  OPAH  BAUD  SIP
PASTE  PAGE  ALDA  EMS
```

19

```
PRO  BAUM  BAKER  FISH
LUV  ANNI  ALIVE  INTO
ATE  WINS  DELIGHTFUL
THRILLERS  SONNY  ODD
  JOS  REEF  CAPE
SCOW  EVANESCE  ELOPE
HOYA  MED  RHO  CRAVEN
AVENUE  ALSO  NERO
WED  GRAS  BROWNE  NIL
  HIGHSPIRITS
PAW  STARTS  SMUT  PAD
IBIS  ULAE  SHELVE
TULIPS  NRA  ARE  NEIN
STYLE  SKEWERED  NAVY
  TREK  ERAS  BUS
AME  INAPT  EBULLIENT
JUBILATION  IRAE  NOW
ANON  TENSE  AGRA  CRI
XING  ERASE  NEAT  EAT
```

20

```
EGG  SERIF  PURA  FRED
BOY  EVITA  AMID  LIME
BAROMETER  SAFETYPIN
STOA  LAMIAS  FLOWERS
  STAY  INDIA  ASH
MACHINE  ADORE  SEIZE
OHO  RSVP  INANE  EDER
COPY  ELAN  LINOLEUM
STEAM  LARGO  DON  ASA
  KEG  NAMES  LUG
OKA  NUB  RANUP  SUPER
PENDULUM  COME  TAXI
ANTI  FLESH  ORBS  RID
LOESS  LAPIS  ULULATE
  CIA  DINED  ERIC
STERNUM  DENOTE  AHOY
VIDEOGAME  SLIDERULE
ERNE  UXOR  ELLEN  TIL
NEAT  RIBS  DYERS  ENL
```

21

```
WAS  STEP  AWOL  GREEN
INC  URSA  THAI  ROUTE
SCARLETTOHARA  EDGAR
POROUS  ORAL  MAT  ETO
SNAG  SABINES  BEEN
 ABED  PROD  OMALLEYS
  REGAIN  INES  DOMO
FOR  FIRE  SLIDES  NAP
ENAMEL  NOTICE  CEE
REDEALS  LAU  AMERICA
 ANT  ENIGMA  ANALOG
FUR  SATINY  NAST  LOO
ANOA  BAGS  LINKED
YARMOUTH  PITT  DELS
 EATS  TRAVAIL  MEAT
SCI  HES  AGIO  OTOOLE
PULSE  SINEADOCONNOR
ABLER  TBAR  ADAM  IMP
REYES  SOTS  YALE  DES
```

22

```
HAYLEY  BIB  CAP  HUSH
AROUSE  ONE  URU  ORCA
STUNTS  RIDEEMCOWBOY
 RAE  REMISS  CREATE
ORE  ERE  IZE  TIN  NOD
REAP  ALICE  DANA
EDGE  WEWANTAHIT  KID
LOONS  NOL  ONO  ELENI
 ONSET  RUDER  AERO
OLDIES  CHARY  HARPER
SOME  SLOOP  BONGO
IWASA  IMP  SEE  DENSE
PEN  GIVEEMHELL  STOW
 HAIR  OAKIE  TRUE
ACT  AMA  POL  EGG  UPS
PRIEST  CARLOS  UNC
HOLDTHATLINE  WICKED
INEE  ANN  NON  ELAINE
DERN  TYS  GTO  STANDS
```

23

```
ADAPT  NESTS  SIT  YAP
PORER  INTRO  EBO  AGE
SUEDAMADEUS  DEVALUE
ORAL  ACUTE  MAX  MEEK
  AESIR  SEAT  CAR
STARR  NEW  FRESHSERF
PERSIA  DEPOT  LESLIE
ARE  ETH  BAR  TOW  ATE
RISE  LOPES  LOVELYAS
  DRAWERSREWARD
RESOUNDS  KUBEK  SALT
UTA  ATO  ZEB  RIB  QUO
SOLARI  SAYER  AUTUMN
SNACKCANS  SEC  SHAPE
 DES  MAUI  MOOSE
AFAR  PUP  FROMA  ORGY
BULBOUS  SEEREFEREES
UJA  IRE  MENSA  DENTE
TIS  LED  ALOES  SMEAR
```

24

```
CRANK  HIS  ASSE  ELF
RANIN  SETH  RAUL  LIE
ADOBE  OXBOWINCIDENT
VIM  EEL  EWES  CARPET
ASIA  ROW  OBESE  SHUL
THESEAWOLF  REEF  APE
 TNT  RAFT  ADDON
ATRIA  SKY  OAT  ANTED
BEARCAT  GUMMO  AWRY
APB  THEDEERPARK  ANA
BIBI  SWILL  TRILLIN
ADITS  BEL  AWE  NUKES
 TOSCA  ASTI  EEN
NBA  HALL  CATSCRADLE
OATH  PLUTO  TWO  REIN
STRAWS  GIRD  INS  ANT
THEYOUNGLIONS  HARTE
RES  ELIE  NEPS  ALTER
ART  SEND  GRR  DAHLS
```

25

```
MACH  PARK  JAVA  MAC
ISLE  ALEE  HOLES  AMO
STORMSOFPROTEST  ARM
SOU  OHO  IAN  TAHITI
 DOMANI  NCAA  AMEN
SABRES  LIGHTNINGBUG
UTURN  LLD  OUTRE  ARS
PER  TRAILS  BETSY
RASP  ASNEAT  TOFU
ASTI  WHIRLWIND  DONT
 ESCE  STOLES  AGRA
 OGLER  SALUTE  GEN
ACH  AIRED  NUT  ASYET
THUNDERBIRDS  STABLE
LANE  SAGE  ENCINO
ERGOTS  EME  ERN  THE
ATA  GALESOFLAUGHTER
SER  IDIOT  TERM  BORG
TRY  FATS  SASS  OMOO
```

26

```
DEFINE  SPOKE  BRENDA
ARECAS  TRAIN  EASTER
LATENT  OUTLANDISHLY
ETC CHANNEL  AONE
  HEY BEER KIN  OFT
SMIT SLY  BALEFULLY
TENANCY RIOTS ASIAN
ANGLER RANGY PLUNGE
ISL WAGONS  FALA
DAYS PATIENTLY LEDA
  TAPS  CORALS NON
HOMILY ARTSY ORIGIN
AVILA AROSE PAISANO
HALTINGLY BID  EGGY
ALL UNO AGES DEI
  OGRE AVERAGE NBA
EXPRESSIVELY IMAGES
TISANE MOREL MULLET
ASIDES ANTES PREYTO
```

27

```
RESIST INEPT PLACES
ERASER ROSIE REDONE
FIGURESKATER ENSUED
  PAVE ERSATZ NRA
ACE ONICE EXT ATON
NUMBERSGAME LYNCH
DRILL EER DIE AHEAD
ATRISK TACIT ISEASY
  SAUL ANOINT DIN
MESS DATABANKS ASSE
ALT MODULE ETON
ABACUS TERMS SITOUT
METAL EUR ULU SINGE
  ISLET TOTALRECALL
GASH LAP NEWTO NYE
EFT WILLIE RUDE
ELICIT ESTIMATEDTAX
SECURE ATWAR ELAINE
EASTER DOOMS DIMMED
```

28

```
MOP REAPED SAMP WAS
APR ATRACE PLEA ARC
HEADFORTHEHILLS IRE
ARIES OHO ANAT SLAP
LARA TWO PLOT TAINT
  IDEA SEAOF CRINGE
OCEANIC CLIFFHANGER
DAVID RILES LIST
EMIR LAMAS RICH MBA
OPE BIZET CARLY OOH
NOW OMIT TRITE CURE
  BRIE MAINE CONGA
DESERTSTORM DILUTED
INTROS WRAPS TUNA
SCREW SERS ACE SIAM
TOIT THAI INA SENSE
IMP PEAKSANDVALLEYS
LIE ORNE DERIDE EON
LAD PIED SEALED RUE
```

29

```
PESETA ASH DIGS ALA
ANKLES RUE OLEO GAS
PAULAS VEINGLORIOUS
  LAB INTRO LENORE
ALL ARR SIRS RESET
HOD GURUS SELL EELS
ARUT MUSCLEBOUND
BEGOT PERI AGRI SEC
  GOA TRIN SIC KEA
THEKID SPECS DEPICT
OUR PAL SOWS TEN
WHY ENID UNIT YEARS
  TISSUEPAPER KNOW
SEMI ELSA NEWER DNA
TROLL ETTE EVE BAG
AGREES EDGED TAO
MARROWMINDED DINNER
ETO NAIF IAN INTENT
NEW ETAS ERA RAISES
```

30

```
MALICE TASTE RANDOM
ISOBAR ALAIN ELAYNE
APAIROFPANTS TANNER
  SODA DELUDE CARE
ASK MESH SERE GYM
PANS TEST ELLE IPS
TWOTIMERS ASIAN CAN
  STOLEN HUM BEADLE
  ROLES POOR TRUER
ASTI TRAVERSES DODD
POWER SPAN ASYOU
PRISON IDS INROAD
LEN YEMEN ODDCOUPLE
ENC ATOM SONE SAVE
  ILL PERP ANTS TIN
SATI SENORA COPA
PRIMAL DOUBLEDECKER
ALEPPO EMCEE ONTIME
TOSSUP DYERS STATUS
```

31

```
SAC   ELON  IDES  WATER
OPA   SALE  NOME  ABIDE
HOMESWEETHOME   ROMEO
OREGANO  RARA    LIE
STORY  STUBS  ISOLATE
    ESE  UNI  AVEC  FOG
RAPT  BACKTOBACK  TUG
ORO  DARK  RANT  PETS
AMUSING  CARR  SPAR
MANTA  OPALINE  LITHE
   DALE  ONES  CHARIOT
IFFY  BRUT   THAT  MAN
TOO  YOUFOOLYOU  SERA
ERR  ENES  NER   LAC
REPLAYS  ASTER  LAIRS
   OAR   JOIE  OVERDUE
SPURN  FORDMADOXFORD
HINGE  RITE  DELI  LAG
ENDED  ANAS  DOES  SLY
```

32

```
BELA  FLIC   ARID  DEBT
ALAN  LOCO   NOSE  OVER
LITTLEBYLITTLE   RARE
   ELIA   UTICA  DINES
PARED  DUMAS   GUESTS
OMAR  ARAB    GOATS
LIN  FLYROBINFLY  ADO
ODD  ALE  SILONE  SNOW
  LOVERS  KEMO  SUEDE
KLAXON  ASIDE  CANYON
OATER  JUAN   SPARSE
OVEN  HECTIC  RUG  FIN
KER  ROSEISAROSE  ODE
   GISTS   LOPE  PROW
REDACT   CREWS  DEALT
AMOLE  GROAN   JOAN
JIMA  CREMEDELACREME
ALEX  RIME  AVID  LYON
HEDY  ODOR  RAZE  SEED
```

33

```
COD   POST  FLIC  OPINE
OCA   ANTA  AIDA  ORSON
MER   REAPSSPAREPEARS
MAEVE   SEETO  DASH
ANDI  LISA   DIS  ESTO
   DOVES  WAHINE  ATOP
  ORLON  MARINA  STAGE
STEALSTALETALES  ION
ETATS  SILAS   ATEN
TODO  PEN    ALT  STOA
   ARTE   PUTTY  STIRS
BID  STONENOTESTONES
ADDUP  VANITY  LANAS
TEEN   BERATE  REGIS
SARI  ARC   ANEW  ASKS
   TEST  MORON  SNAIL
SHEARHARESSHARE  TOO
IATRO  KEEL  IMAN  IWO
STAYS  ELKO  TENT  NAP
```

34

```
THUS  PITH  CHAP  FIRS
AUNT  ASWE  RASH  ITAL
UNCERTAIN  ALTO  ECCE
   HEISTS  UNFINISHED
SCALP   TANK  REGO
LUIS   TESS   SOLUTE
URN  UNWRITTEN  RENAL
RIM  SOO  FORCEPS  KIM
SAYSSO   PETER  ANNS
   HORNETS  TORONTO
TAEL  ACRES   PEEWEE
ANA  UNROLLS  IRE  NRA
LORIS  UNLIMITED  SOS
CATCHA   CONE   NODE
   EERO  REGT   AILED
UNABRIDGED  EARNED
TORO  SOAP  UNFAILING
ALMA  TRIO  ASAN  LEAD
HOST  ASTS  WERT  ORBS
```

35

```
SALT  USEUP   AGED  SRA
ERIE  NORMA   TORO  TAD
POSTSCRIPT   QUIZ  AVE
TUT  PORK   OURS  STEP
USE  IVY  ASKED  SAINT
MENAGE  KNEE   SALVO
   FORTNIGHT  VIENNA
INGOT  IOTA  SHIV  BUN
COAX  ANWAR  POSE  RAN
ERR  ESS    SIR   ENE
CUR  UTES  SCOTT  PACA
ALI  GALE  EAVE  BIKEL
PESTER   CAMPEDOUT
   OWNED  BIER  ATTIRE
ARNIE  AMISS  ITY  REV
FACT  KNIT  UMBO  EVE
ADA  JINX  BASERUNNER
TIP  ALEE  IGETA  BIRL
EOS  WORD  SEDAN  ACEY
```

36

```
RIG  GIAN  PATS  ROGER
ORO  POME  ASHE  ELITE
YELLOWBELLIED  DEGAS
ANDA  ALDOS  NACHO
LEFTS  ELL  SENSE  MAA
  IHAD  ELBOW  TAKING
RENEWED  LUSH  DONNA
ORGS  SENDUP  ETERNAL
OSE  GERE  TRADE
TERM  GRAYBEARD  ABLE
  ABNER  LEVI  RIA
DEVALUE  POKING  EONS
ANIMA  SOLO  GANGWAY
MENSCH  NUDES  SIGN
ASE  KAYES  APT  ANTIC
  HEMET  AVAIL  OHNO
ALLAY  SILVERTONGUES
GAUZE  EMEU  TARO  MET
EDGES  SETS  ANEW  BDS
```

37

```
WILMA  RASCAL  SWIFT
AROAR  ATTUNE  PINOAK
FASTFORWARDS  ASSUME
TEST  NEALS  ASHTRAY
  EST  REIVER  YAW
STEREOS  VISTA  RHUM
LOX  AUTORECEIVE  ERE
AMPS  RAMI  SEAN  EGG
TYROL  BETAS  RIDDLES
  ERIS  NESTS  LOUD
LASTLAP  SHELF  WARES
OPS  AHEM  RIOT  LIVE
RID  CLEARMEMORY  VIE
DEEP  SLATE  DANIELS
  FED  EMERGE  DEN
DIRTIED  CEASE  HUBS
AROUND  COUNTERRESET
MISLED  DARIEN  ARENA
  STARY  TRYERS  TEDDY
```

38

```
LEMMAS  DODGE  LAMAZE
ELAINE  ORIEL  OREGON
WILLIAMWESTMORELAND
SALT  BON  SPIN  RES
  OREL  AAH  ESAU
CLINTEASTWOOD  SMALL
HORSE  RECALL  ARIA
EDO  SELL  IWAS  ASS
FINALE  OLIVERNORTH
  VISITS  NESTER
REBECCAWEST  SECRET
ORA  KENO  TEAM  OAR
WILD  THRACE  JESSE
SALEM  ROBERTSOUTHEY
  WACO  OPS  MUTE
ASH  NOTS  LET  RICE
CNORTHCOTEPARKINSON
TAMARA  TOPAZ  ICANDO
APEMAN  SEAMY  DELTAS
```

39

```
RIO  THIS  CAP  MOHAWK
ETH  WASP  EWE  IBERIA
GUSTAVMAHLER  NICETY
OPUS  RETOLD  RITT
  SERE  IRA  TIC  IMAS
ERATO  FARRAHFAWCETT
MENSA  ELI  SELMA  NEO
MINERAL  DOTHE  CLUMP
ANA  SIL  SRA  WOE
  SHE  MAHARAJAH  IFA
  PES  ARI  ZIA  ODA
BEFIT  ALECS  UMPIRED
ACE  ANTIC  AHS  ANGLE
THEBLUEDAHLIA  IDEAS
HOLE  MAE  IAD  ALIA
  THEM  ISMAEL  AHOT
ORATOR  AHWILDERNESS
CAMERA  BAA  GERE  ALA
SPIRAL  EDY  ONTO  DOR
```

40

```
PAINTS  CLERC  STOKE
IGNORE  HOSEA  TONED
TASSEL  HASTYPUDDING
  THELMA  SEEP  ANYA
GOA  SEATOF  SLD  TEAR
NUNC  RICHES  LIME
ASTHE  SHORTCAKE  FLO
RECANT  MAE  ETALIA
  OMENS  NITRE  ABAFT
BUFO  TARA  EFTS  ASES
UNFIT  DIVAN  STASH
TIESON  FAD  ACHING
STE  BEEFJERKY  TENOR
  SEEN  OPINES  STLO
DADA  DLS  TOOTED  HOW
EVIL  LIED  TIRADE
MINUTESTEAKS  INAPET
OSAKA  TULSA  ASTARE
NOHIT  SPAIN  LEANED
```

41

```
PAD   CUBE  SHAH  SHADY
ORO   ARUN  TONI  PUREE
LOG   BIRDSANDTHEBEES
AMASS LOIRE SANS
RANT  FAWN  WILT  SOB
      DROOPS BERG  HOUR
GAPING      CATANDMOUSE
ANODE EARTHY ROLLED
ZONE  EXCITE RELY
ANY   FLEET ROUSE HAH
      EELS  IDEALS MALE
STPETE EQUATE JEWEL
COCKANDBULL    BALKED
ANTS  ABEL  HAIRDO
RES   BARS  NEWT  ERSE
      SOAK  ASTRE ADDAX
SPIDERANDTHEFLY  ORC
SONAR NEIL  TULE  VIE
HICKS DOMO  OLDS  ENL
```

42

```
APHIS      BASRA  TREBLE
COASTS UNCAP     UNREEL
EXCLAMATION      LASSOS
   KEFIR     TIMES    INA
DAS  FLAIRS      ELATED
EROS  EBRO  AND   ERECT
WOFAT LATENT     MAITAI
OFNORETURN  POR   HIP
   DYE  ENE  COS   CERO
LA E  SOLD  CODA  A OF
ALAR  ICY   NOL   ILL
REF   TNT   INFLECTION
KNIVES WOEFUL    SPREE
SENEX EEN   EDAM  HAIR
   GETUPS KEEPAT  TNS
CHE   PATRI      STEPI
HARASS     EDQUESTIONS
INAPIE ENDUP     URANUS
PATENT REYES     ASSTS
```

43

```
MOBBED     SCAPE  ALMOST
AXILLA COLOR     LOATHE
REBELS RAILROADTIES
ENLAI BATE  SAT   TSPS
   ETE   OPINE   TECH
LABS  SPES  DOM   OASES
AGE   LIED  LIBELSUITS
VOLPONE OUTLAST  ROT
ANTIC PROM  ALT   FENS
   COB   AMBIT   SRA
MESA  LSD   EVER  AIKEN
ALE   TOPIARY   ASCRIBE
SUGARCOATS  DRAY  DRU
CLOSE OLE   DEEP  IGOT
   SEAN  SHIVS   ELL
AGRI  BIO   EMIT  ELOPE
BLASTINGCAPS    OLIVER
BUTTED LILLE     VENETO
ATASTE EASED     ARISES
```

44

```
BANE  WAIF  FEAR  ACTA
IRED  ALDA  IAGO  SHIV
GREGARIOUSGREG   SERA
MIDAS ANNUL DENIROS
AVERTS TAMED RESULT
NED   IRA   AAAS  OTB
   FRANTICFRAN    SICS
TOGO  SKIN  KNOB  COP
APECK ALLEN GNOCCHI
MINUIT LATER ONAHOT
ANESTOF WAGON OBESE
LER   ERIC  EPEE  ORTS
EROS  EVASIVEEVAS
   UPA  EVER   RIG  DEN
INSULT EVADE LOCALE
DEGREES EQUUS RAMPS
IGET  PATRIARCHALPAT
ORNE  IDEA  LOUT  LESE
TIED  DEAL  SSTS  ANOD
```

45

```
ACHE       SASHA  STREAM
FEELS SCREEN     TROMPE
BRAINSTORMED    EASIER
SOD   AMATI DAMAGES
   SCRUB VEE   AMI  SCI
CUTLET TAXDEDUCTION
APRES MALT  LAP   WORK
STOA  FIG   STS   JONES
TON   ILK   SOLO  BUS
ENG   DEEPTHINKER  LES
   SEX  LAMP  NAY  ERA
FACTS JAY   SOU   SNAP
ALOE  BUY   SCAB  LEGTO
MAXWELLSMART    VICTOR
ENS   LEE   IDA   TENTH
   WHISPER WEARE  WAG
PLAIDS BRILLIANTINE
SOIREE BEFELL    SUSAN
TUNERS SNIDE     BETA
```

46

```
P R E F A B   ■ M A L E S ■   ■ C O B
B A N A C E K ■ A E R I E S ■ S A R A
S T A R T L E ■ C R A C K E D C R A B
■ ■ M I L E ■ A M B I ■ ■ E A R L Y
S G T ■ O N I C E ■ ■ T O M A T O ■ ■
C L A M S C A S I N O ■ B A R ■ T V A
A U D I T ■ N R A ■ R A I L ■ S C A B
M E S C A L ■ S L O B ■ I M P A L E
■ A R O M A ■ E N O S ■ O A K I E
S E C ■ C O R N C H O W D E R ■ E D T
E N O C H ■ S T O A ■ L I B O R ■ ■
A L L O Y S ■ I N R E ■ O N A G E R
M A D E ■ L O C I ■ N A P ■ I M E T A
S I C ■ G I N ■ C O T T O N C A N D Y
■ E X U D E S ■ B E E N E ■ ■ E S S
S E R R A ■ ■ C H E R ■ D A U B ■ ■
C R E A M C H E E S E ■ E R R A T I C
I M A Y ■ T E N S E D ■ R E G I O N S
S A L ■ ■ S W E A R ■ ■ R E L E N T
```

47

```
H A H A ■ H O M E ■ ■ T N T ■ A S T O
O N U S ■ I T A L ■ T H O U ■ S T E T
S T R A I G H T S T R E E T ■ C O A T
S I T ■ R H E A ■ R A I L ■ Z O R R O
■ ■ H O V E R ■ C A I N ■ I A T E ■
S E E F I T ■ R U I N ■ E S S ■ S P A
A G A I N ■ D E B T O R D O U B T E R
D A R T ■ N I S I ■ F A I L ■ L I N T
A N T ■ P U R E S T ■ S E A H O R S E
■ ■ C I T ■ E T H I C ■ T A B ■ ■
D E C L A R E D ■ O S A G E S ■ W P A
O A H U ■ I C E R ■ O L E S ■ C R E W
T R E B L E T R O U B L E ■ F L O O R
E N A ■ O N O ■ O S A Y ■ C R A N N Y
■ ■ P I N T ■ A M E R ■ S L A N G ■
C A C T I ■ A T T U ■ D E A N ■ R I O
O T H E ■ S C R A P P E D S C R I P T
L O O M ■ I L E X ■ A M E S ■ I N S O
A M P S ■ D U E ■ W I R Y ■ A G E E
```

48

```
G A L A H A D ■ E N C O D E ■ A W L S
E Y E S O R E ■ L E A N E R ■ S H O O
T R A I N E R ■ F O S T E R C H I L D
■ ■ S E T ■ ■ U A R ■ I O T A S
A G T ■ S H E ■ S C A P ■ E T T E
C R Y S T A L B A L L ■ D I E ■ S A P
T A L L Y ■ E R M A ■ S U N D A N C E
U V E A ■ A V A ■ S W E D E ■ N O T E
P E R V A D E ■ O S I P ■ A T W A R
■ ■ L O N G W I N T E R S ■ ■
D I C T A ■ N E C K ■ N O S T R U M
R O L E ■ G H A N A ■ O C T ■ H O P E
I N O N E E A R ■ L A R A ■ B A L S A
P A S ■ V E T ■ B L A C K M A I L E R
■ E R I S ■ S O Y A ■ E A R ■ S T S
A P N E A ■ M E W ■ ■ I C E ■
G R E E N F I E L D S ■ O D O R O U S
R O S S ■ E N T E R S ■ R E D O N D O
A P S E ■ E X O D U S ■ O N E S T O P
```

49

```
B O W ■ D A W E S ■ H A S P ■ A F R O
A S I ■ A L O R S ■ A N N E ■ V O I D
H O L L Y B U S H ■ B O A R ■ A X L E
■ L A T E N T ■ K I N G F I S H E R
R I P C O R D ■ P I T ■ E T T U ■
A M O U N T ■ A I D ■ O R C A ■ N I P
D A W N ■ S A G E ■ S W A T ■ S T O A
I D E A S ■ V E R D A N T ■ M E E T S
O E R ■ P O I ■ U T E ■ B E R R A S
■ S I L V E R S E R V I C E ■
A B S U R D ■ E E K ■ I N C ■ T A G
C U T I E ■ P L A Y F U L ■ A S U R E
T R E T ■ O R E L ■ A N E W ■ U N E S
E Y E ■ E V E R ■ Q U O ■ A S P E N S
■ L O V E ■ D E N ■ A S H E S T O
H A M M E R H E A D ■ A S T O R M ■
E R I N ■ D E M I ■ S H O R E B I R D
L I L I ■ I R I S ■ A S N E R ■ T O O
L A L A ■ D O R Y ■ N O E L S ■ H E N
```

50

```
A G O ■ A D A M ■ S P R Y ■ S C O W
L A V A ■ D I R E ■ T R E E ■ M I M I
T R A P E Z O I D ■ L O N G ■ A R A L
■ P L O Y ■ S P I T ■ T O G O ■ C R Y
■ O D E A ■ A C E R O ■ P A L ■ ■
A L F ■ F E R T I L E C R E S C E N T
D I F F U S E ■ A M O O N ■ R O U E
A R I E L ■ P O I ■ L E G L I F T S
M A C E ■ P L U S E S ■ A I D ■ ■
S S E ■ F L Y I N G W E D G E ■ S O T
■ ■ F R A ■ T O A T E E ■ A Q U A
O P T I O N A L ■ G A L ■ B R U T S
C A H N ■ T W E A K ■ E A R M A R K
T H E I R O N T R I A N G L E ■ R E S
■ G S A ■ S E L M A ■ A W E E ■
B A L ■ G R I D ■ N I T A ■ E S S E
A G O N ■ I D O L ■ C U B E R O O T S
C U B A ■ N E W S ■ U R I S ■ P F U I
K E E P ■ K A N T ■ S E T S ■ F I N
```

51

```
GIRLS HUSH ALAR SIT
ELIOT ANKA VARY USE
LEAVE SHIRLEYTEMPLE
  ERATO MONEY BEAM
HOPS CORP SUR BAR
ONAHOT SAC ESPY STS
RECAP CELLI RESTOW
ADECREE SUNDAY IONE
  KATYA BRAM INRED
OAF HOLDTHEFORT ERE
AWOLS OTHO TRASH
SARI ENSOUL ASTORIA
TREVOR USUAL OSAGE
SEC WARP ELM COPIER
  ALL ORE UNTO INTO
ALSO ABETS ERGOT
COTTAGECHEESE LANAI
HAL TERI ANTE LLOYD
YNE ARTS MAYS ASTRO
```

52

```
GAME WARES SWAP BAY
ALEX INERT IAMA RNA
SITTINGPRETTYINPINK
  ONES LEES AAMES
PARC TOILE ACC
THETHIRDMANONTHERUN
EERS CODA ROME EMU
TWO TOMS CHIVE ABIT
  LOM PROBE IDEAS
SHYPEOPLEWILLTALK
MAAMS REUPS AIM
EYRE BOAST ESTS COW
ASP SANK ELKE AUTO
LOOKWHOSTALKINGSROW
  EOS ALLOT AIDE
STENO SARI TART
WHATSUPDOCHOLLYWOOD
IOS IRED EASEL AURA
GUT ENDS SISSY STEM
```

53

```
AFFAIR BLANC SIMILE
SLANTS ROMEO TRADER
POCKETFULOFMIRACLES
  ELM ONLY PTA EKE
LIFE RIC RECTOR
URU WISHFULTHINKING
NIL HOT ONDE COMER
ASSAI SARDS PRE BOA
  CLU FIR MOO DENY
THEGRATEFULDEAD
MARY LOT SAN EST
AMI BYE ASLIP KEDGE
LATHE HIED ILE ROD
THEARTFULDODGER END
  STORMS OED CAGY
UDO TAI OSLO PAD
SOMEKINDOFWONDERFUL
ONEMAN ONAIR AROUSE
STRUNG RENTS BULLET
```

54

```
HAW CAMEL MELO WAS
OSHA ALONE IVAN ALL
WHIRLWINDS NEVERYOU
DETAIL DEE INA EWER
  ELL CAD FOE JOE
FEW AHOY WINDSOFWAR
PRANCED CAT INFEST
OISE LEMAT KIT ERIE
SCHOOL ODEONA AREAS
  WONDERWOMAN
DAWES OUTBET GNAWAT
RNAS STS UNSER MILO
ANDTWO ARS RESIDUE
WISHYWASHY DIET EMS
  WEE SEA SEN RAW
PLOT ITA ATA PATOIS
AIREDOUT WORDSWORTH
SET ANTE LIMAS PLEA
SSH DEED SCENT DAM
```

55

```
ERIS CARS SCAM NIBS
BENT ALIT TRIO AFAT
OFFENSIVEGUARD MORE
  EVOKE LEMS EMERGE
MARIN ELAPSE ELMER
UNNECESSARY VANYA
STA OSIER BART TAP
HAL MTNS ACADIA INS
  OSE ACASE LOONS
CUFF ROUGHNESS ANAT
ARRAS BLUES MOT
AGE POLAND ADIN FIB
NEE IRON UNITE IOU
  SETON PUNTRETURNS
DIANE GRANTS ITEAS
INFEST AGUA LIMOS
CUER INCOMPLETEPASS
ESTO NEED EASE ILIA
DAYS SODA DYER AERO
```

56

```
HOPPED  BEACH  GOODAT
AREOLA  ALCOA  UNSAFE
MORNINGGLORY   NOTYET
    ITEA   RESTS  IDEE
ESTEE  SLANDER  CAR
THUS   URS  EURO  EAR
TIN  SIEGE  ADDUP  ATO
EVENINGGOWN  GRAMMAR
   AMIGA  HOSE   EELY
 ADMIT  GIANT  SCARE
ALAE  SENT  ALEAN
LOWRANK  MIDNIGHTOIL
ANN  PRICE  ODEON  MAE
NEP  SADA  CRI   GAGA
  ASE  ORLEANS  AARON
HATH  COLOR   ACES
ARRIVE  TWILIGHTTIME
STOLEN  OLSEN  ANODES
PELLET  NYETS  PANELS
```

57

```
HERD  CARPS  CPAS  CUB
ECHO  IMEAN  ORNE  UNO
ROUE  TIARA  PINE  RIA
  BRAY  REFRIGERATOR
WPA  UDOS  FOES   BAND
AIR  DEN  SLUR  BALI
TABLESTAKES  PARENTS
   ANKARA  TIETO  COE
FACT  SPITS  RATS  ATA
ASHES   SEATO  EFLAT
STA  ABIT  DINAH  ILLS
TRI  LANAI  TISONS
SORBETS  COUCHPOTATO
 PUSH  PIUS  EER  QUO
STEM  AINT  ORCS  UGH
CARPETBAGGER  HERA
RMS  MOAN  RAISE  ARNA
APO  METO  ESNES  ZION
MAN  ADES  WEGET  EARN
```

58

```
SAFE  WANT   JAM  QUIT
TROT  ODIUM  IRE  UNTO
AIRCAVALRY  MCS  OSSA
BAT  REM  NOG  HASTE
   MET  SEENAS   TEASE
KICK   FRENCHPASTRY
INHERENT  GREAT  SSE
DDE  PRISED  ERNIE
MIN  MIS  NAME  CRESS
AGRA  CITIZENRY  ALTO
NOYES  EDER  EEE  MAL
  SALEM  DERMAL  END
OPS  TIPPY  AIRFORCE
DOTHELAUNDRY   AGER
EERIE   SERIES  BRA
  ANNEX  SOP  TOY  NAT
BOND  SIT  PLEASANTRY
URGE  ANA  SERIO  ERIN
DEER  UGO  YENS  PYLE
```

59

```
RICA  OPTS  DIAL  HASP
ODOR  ADAM  UGLY  ALAI
ALUM  SQUIRRELEPHANT
REGENT   TOAT  EARTH
 ADO  ALEUT  ASP  MAY
JAR  ROSE  NIECE
AIM  MASTODONKEY  GAB
GRAB  RATA  NEEDS  UNA
 DAR  YETI  REELING
OPINED  RHODA  DRONES
MULCHED  URIS  EVE
ELL  AMIES  ADMS  EASY
NEO  BUMBLEBEELS  PIE
   REBID  DAYI  INN
GAS  PES  PIPER  PUG
ASPER   ASTO  ASSUME
RHINOCEROSPREY  HAIR
BEND  ATTU  IONE  ENTO
ONES  MAST  NOGS  RATS
```

60

```
ENTAIL  BAKED  BANDIT
MARILU  EMILY  AROUSE
IWILLBENODIETSINNER
TSP  BLESS  RID  KEN
  ASOF   SAUCER
BIONIC  REPAST  ABAS
ONTURKEYDAYTHISFALL
OMIT  DEALER  LATELY
TYS  CVI  MORA  ITERS
   TREES   LAKER
OTHER  TORS  XED  JAM
PLEATS  EVINCE  AUTO
FIXMEASPECIALDINNER
COTE  CANOPY  INTENT
   SABOTS   AGAS
SDI  DRU  PLACE  AMP
WITHZEROCHOLESTEROL
ANCIEN  NAIVE  TIMETO
BEHEST  ARLES  SASSED
```

61

```
DAN  BASED ARCH  TSAR
EXO  ALTAI HIHO  RENO
FIFTYFIVESAVESLIVES
ALAI ARETE ASTI  ENE
CLIME    STS  TENANTS
EAR  BEAT TIS  DEBT
    FORTYWINKS  NOYES
 STA OAKEN ALA  USNA
FAWNED EEG TEND  ITS
ALE  RIO    DDE  XIS
TIN  ANDI SUB  ORNERY
ANTA GAR CLEAR  ORE
LAYUP SIXHUNDRED
 TREK SEE TOAD  HAJ
SAHARAN DRJ   SWORE
ISR  DRUB ZAIRE  AGAR
THESUMMEROFFORTYTWO
TEEM ABLE FIBRE  IAM
ANSA SSTS ATEST  EKE
```

62

```
TAPAS  LUNCH PLEASES
ALICE  ENERO EARNEST
ULTRAVIOLET  AGITATE
  ETC  DESK   HASP
TAP  TRA SILO  WREN
AURAL XOUT DREAMERS
GRAPEVINE ODIST  MEA
SAMP ESE TRENT  LOAF
 RAN STRING  PONCE
REWINDS REO SWIVETS
ABASE TRUANT AGE
COLE FAULT OUR  TWAS
ELL  JIFFY UPSYDAISY
RIFFRAFF IPSO  YPRES
 LIST LINA SUN  EAT
UPON   TENT   MAT
DOWAGER COMPASSROSE
ONELIFE UNION  TURIN
STREETS READY  YEARS
```

63

```
DISH  RITZ SLED  ATLI
ATTU  AGEE HALO  RHOS
BOYSFROMBRAZIL  EERO
 HEAR ROMY  LAWMEN
DICED HAW  CANEA
ROAD AGE SAVORY  NEB
AWL  CLERC REPS  GILA
MAIDOFORLEANS  SINGS
 FERAL ONCUE  IOTAS
SHOATS DOTHE  ANTHRA
HORDE LINEN  CRETE
ANNEX AMERICANWOMAN
DOIN GREY DAVIS  ONE
ERA  DRESSY SEE  VOTE
 GLUES OAT  MINED
SAILON SAYS  SLAV
OKRA ASHROPSHIRELAD
FILM DUET EPOS  CODE
ANSA ANDY NAPA  AWAY
```

64

```
SHARP  CAMP  ACHESON
PAPER  ACERB CHORINE
INAPEARTREE  HELIPAD
TAR  CUTS ABT  ELS
 TWINE AMOROSO  BRA
MARIST HAPPYNEWYEAR
ENID SHAHS TIS  ALIT
ADDER EMS HOT  TRADE
DIG  INA KID  DUN
SEE  TURTLEDOVES FLA
 EAT ROY INK  ROT
PLOTS MEG BUD  SMEAR
IOWA IAM PUPIL  ANTE
CALLINGBIRDS  AMECHE
ADS  STILTED SMASH
 OSE EES SEER  HRS
STATURE REDANDGREEN
PATIENT SNOBS  IONIA
AMASSES TRUE  NESTS
```

65

```
ASTO  RAISIN ABALONE
CAHN  ARCANA NINEVEH
TWICETTALES  IMITATE
ISSUES RES AMI  LSU
 HER MUM GLANCE
LAO  IOUS WILLIAMHEN
ABUSERS WAVY  RIATA
BESURE BANE  WRITING
SEEN ARID WHEN  LAS
 GENGATEBRIDGE
ITA  FEED REAM  ACID
TARIFFS ASAP  THRACE
CRANE AVID BOOSTER
HARSTASSEN FLAB  CDS
 TEMPER ALT  NTH
HAS  BEA ERA  TOHERE
ARTICLE IFIMAYBESOB
LEASHED STABLE  TATE
FARMERS ASSESS  ACAN
```

66

D O S A G E S		M I L A N		C A R T S
E N C L O S E		A M O R E		O V E R T
S E A L A N E		P A R K A A V E N U E
	R O D E		G I S		L E N D E R
S I F T S		P A R I S		L O N G	
A R F S		T E X A N		R A F		E P I C
D O A		F R E E Z E P O R T S		U D O
I N C		O U T R E		O U R		H U M A N
E Y E S O R E			P U N Y		E R A S E
	A T O		B E A R D		L A G
C O R G I		G R A Y		F O R E S T S
A L I E N		L A S		S I E V E		L E E
N I N		G L O V E L E T T E R		E N A
T O G S		I R E		A R E A S		T E E M
	P O N Y		A R A R S		C A T T Y
A D R O I T		A M O		C L U B
B O O T L E G G I N G		I H O P E T O
L O O T		L U A N D A		D E V E L O P
E M M Y		S T R E E T		O R E S T E S

67

R A F T		O K D		M A C		P O N D E R
A R A R		P E A		E L L		O R I O L E
J U L I E T P R O W S E		S C O N E S
A B S		V E T		F L O O D		A B O V E
H A T R E D		M G S		P O R		E V A N
	A Y N		S E A		S A M O S		A T T
L I F E		T H E B O T T O M L I N E S
A R F		P O E T		B R R		P Y M
S A I P A N S		C L E A		A C A T
S T A R R Y		H I S		L E G A T E
O E N O		P U G S		C A R E E R S
	B I G		U N O		S A G E		S I T
R A C E T R A C K R O M E O		S A P S
E V A		S U L K Y		F U N		C U R
F A M A		B E E		A U G		P O I S E D
U R I C H		C R I B S		E S S		A M A
T I L T O N		S L E E P Y H A M L E T
A C L O S E		U S A		O R A		B A N E
L E E R E D		P E R		P E W		A D D S

68

B I A S		R U S T Y		C R A B		I C E
I N C A		E L I O T		P A P A		F R A
D O U B T F U L S T A R T E R		S O S
E N T E R		S T I R S		E X T R A C T
S E E R E D		R I T A S		E O N
	S K I D S		U R S		G R U D G E
D R U		S A I N T M A Y B E		T S A R
E E N S		L E A R		E A T S		O R G
B A S T E		T R E A D		T O P A R
T R U I S M		L A M A S		N U M B E D
	R E N A L		T O R A H		R O U T E
A P E		E R I A		E N E S		S T A N
H I F I		I N Q U E S T I O N		S L Y
S P O N G E		U N A		A R O O M
	O S E		P A T R I		S T R E A M S
A N T O N I O		A L L A		I N L A W
D A I		I N D U B I O U S B A T T L E
A N N		U R I S		E V E N A		H A T E
R A G		S E A N		R E L A Y		E R A T

69

H A M		O S S A		N U B		A B J U R E
O R O		P O U F		A S I		S L A T E R
R O T T E N R A T T A N		T A M A L E
S W O R N		F R A U		R A N
	R A S P S		F R A M E		D R E A M
C A M P U S		S T A S I S		B O R N E
A L E		P A T E		L U N A R L O N E R
P I T T		L A T E		K L E E		E W E
E V E R		M O O R E D		E O N S
S E R I F		N I L E S		D O D G E
	P R I M		C O L L I E		L U L L
S A M		E M I T		L I M A		E T A T
P R I M E P R O M O		M A R V		C R O
A C T E D		A L E R T S		L I C H E N
S H E L F		G A R B O		S Y N O D
	R A E		I O N A		T W I N E
A E N E A S		P O S T A L P A S T E L
S T A T U E		E X O		S T A G		C A M
P A G O D A		A Y N		T Y N E		H R S

70

A S W E		S P A C E		B E T		D A M
S T E R E		K E M A L		E R I		A D O
T U E S D A Y W E L D		A R S E N A L
A S K A N C E		L E E R		S N A R L
	E T A T		S C O R N		K U D U
L E N Z		G O O F		J A D E		G A S
O L D		A P R I L F O O L S		F U N T
A S A		G A I L		G Y M		C A S T E
D E T R O I T		H A R E S		A T T A R
	E O N		C I T E D		B R A
B A S I S		D I N E S		B E L L J A R
I R E N E		R E D		M U T I		O U I
T I P S		J A N U A R Y M A N		E N D
S A T		V O T E		C A T S		E F T S
	E X I T		G A R T H		I B A R
J A M E S		B A B Y		S O R R I E R
U M B R A G E		B L A C K S U N D A Y
T E E		G I N		A I L E Y		T E A S E
S S R		E A T		S C A N S		D Y E S

71

```
NURSE   FAIRS   SALAMI
ATALL   GOTOUT  OBERON
BOGUSJOURNEY   WENTIN
OPIE  ABLY   LOIS   IRE
BIN  INA   GLENS   AFAR
SAGER   CURIO   CHELI
  MOCKTURTLE   LUCAN
REFINE   ADDTO   BEMINE
ARAT   ACHES   SLAM  AGA
INK  ASA     ANI   LOT
NEE  WETS   SHOWN   ALLA
ISHTAR   PRIOR   EASYAS
STARR   FAUXPEARLS
  NUDGE   STILL   MEDAL
CODE   HASTY   LIS   ITE
APO  ROTO     ASOF  AVAS
RIFLES   FALSEWITNESS
ENFANT   AVAILS   WASTE
YESSES   REGAL   OTTER
```

72

```
SIB   LEOS   THEIR   MAL
EWE   NOTRE   HORNE   UTA
EARTHSHATTERING   DOS
GNARLS   TOMAN   ISSUE
ETTA   SOLVE   BOILER
RTE   PAINE   DAVINCI
SODBUSTERS   SITS   NAH
  OTHER   NAPES   AGIO
  USURER   GALES   CRIME
STALIN   WAGON   DAMNED
LINED   LANGE   MENAGE
OLDS   JUDGE   AUBON
WEB   CANE   DIGSUPDIRT
  LEEWARD   NUTTY   SER
STAIRS   RATES   ETTE
MESNE   PIANO   UMBRIA
EAT   BREAKSNEWGROUND
ASE   RANGE   EVILS   TUE
RED   AUTOS   DENY   HER
```

73

```
LADS   OFF   LSD   DIAPER
ARIA   PAL   OCA   INNATE
BOVINEYOUTHS   LAIROF
OMANI   ESSE   CLIME
RAN   XER   EARTH   RUNTS
  ODIC   ZEAL   STOP
PAS   NIGHTHORSES   OUR
EVIL   EERIE   MEAT   FRY
ROBES   LILAC   DROOP
INLAWS   SERAC   SAGELY
  IDEAS   SKILL   TRAIN
ANN   ETTU   ERIES   ERSE
LAG   PERSONOFWAR   LTS
ARCS   SEEN   TINA
SCALP   AREAS   SAY   UTA
  REARM   UPTO   OASIS
MORALE   SPOUSEOFBATH
PRIZED   AOK   SAP   AGUE
STEEDS   ONE   OUT   TESS
```

74

```
MEG   PUCK   FEW   RASCAL
AVI   ISLE   AVA   ENCODE
MANSLAUGHTER   AVALON
ANGEL   SOAR   SPIRE
  EXACT   BLEST   LASTS
CAR   RUHR   TWOS   BLOC
AMSO   BEANSTALKS   AMA
RINK   SAMOA   BEET   WET
ONAIR   SORTS   SEAN
BOPEEP   NAILS   TIEDUP
  SHEA   DAUNT   DRONE
NIB   ANNI   TRAIT   OWLS
ICU   BATTLESCAR   SNIT
PACS   LIEU   KRIS   STS
ANKLE   CARPS   ASNEW
  SENDS   CLUE   AGILE
MAKEDO   CHERRYSTONES
OLIVER   PEA   MARC   GAP
WINERY   ADD   AMAH   SKY
```

75

```
LANOSE   THEIR   GRAPES
AMORAL   HALVE   LAVABO
PARADISELOSTHORIZON
STA   TIRE   ROWED
  ADELA   STERE   BAR
WINDSOFWARANDPEACE
CENTS   AXED   RATTY
OILS   RAMI   SLOSHES
SRA   PURIST   ONINE
IDYLLSOFTHEKINGLEAR
  EYEOF   ETAPES   LYE
ATAVISM   HYER   SIRE
RAVEN   SATI   ETHEL
THEEGGANDICLAUDIUS
SAC   ABODE   ABNER
  IDLER   ERAT   DEI
SEAGULLIVERSTRAVELS
IMPOSE   NOTME   UNISON
SPOTTY   GLEAN   ENCINO
```

76

```
CATS  VIAL  CLOD  AGRA
OCHO  ATTA  HERO  LEAD
PRETENSES  ATOM  OTTO
YES  DIM  HAI  AHAB
EAGLES  GREENSFEES
CHERYL  KIT  TWIT  TVA
HOYT  AMIS  BEE  ATAT
OBEYS  ALLAY  RAGGEDY
WES  PAUL  RMS  BEARER
BELLESLETTRES
ALBINO  TOE  ROAN  TAB
LAERTES  OSIER  ALENE
OMER  INN  DANK  ONTO
OAK  OOZE  AOK  IRONER
FREESPEECH  SALOME
ERAT  USE  BLT  SSS
KEPI  IBAR  THEJETSET
ALEC  NEWS  CIAO  HERA
NORA  GLEE  HEDY  YEAR
```

77

```
TATA  RIO  LISA  TUBAS
OFIT  ANN  ATOP  AGENT
GREENSKEEPERS  SHADE
GARNI  BATS  RISK  NIP
LIE  TRUTH  COST  ICES
EDD  WAS  SOW  ASTO
WITHRELISH  USUAL
AFATE  OVAL  ORLANDO
GIRLS  DUET  TREK  TRI
ARUT  LETS  SOSO  BEON
TOI  JUNE  JAPE  SARIS
OUTPACE  MUNI  FIRST
STEAK  BREADCRUMB
DYES  OWN  AMP  EPS
POPS  PASS  HAVEL  URI
AWL  WANT  AIDE  EDDIE
DEARE  DRESSINGROOMS
UNION  RULE  ONE  TRET
ASNOT  EMMA  SAM  SARA
```

78

```
LAP  PSST  AHEMS  ANDI
AMI  UHUH  MARAT  PEAT
BEN  BABE  BARKENTINE
ALAR  MURALS  EEE  GEM
MITER  ROVE  MULLAH
BAABAABAA  SOP  SISIS
ASSESS  DICTA  FORALL
CHAP  LOU  BAN  YOU
CST  EGOS  GNARL  END
HAH  ROARINGCAMP  RAG
AVE  OCALA  EVOE  SSE
ROC  ASH  ITS  AUER
GRANDE  SKEWS  TROCHE
ESTER  GEE  INTHEMOOD
SEEFIT  ALEE  DELTA
IAM  NOB  INLAND  SOLS
THEHOWLING  KNEE  RIN
OMOO  LEVEE  BIKE  ENE
NEWT  STEER  YSER  DER
```

79

```
AARON  BLASTS  CLARET
CREDO  ROSCOE  HELENA
REPERCUSSION  ENAMOR
EAR  MITT  TSAR  REST
EVADE  BASEL  GUM
COSINE  AYN  ALEMBIC
AXEL  RETRACTION  EGO
RENEW  FLOPPY  CARROT
ANT  ALLIN  ASTA  OSTE
ARIA  ETON
CORP  STOP  PANEL  ROE
ONEBIT  REMISS  EBERT
OOH  RESEARCHES  APAT
PRECEDE  EKE  PARADE
ARS  REEDY  BAMBI
BARE  LEAN  IATE  RIG
ONSALE  RECOLLECTION
ODESSA  TRIFLE  HENNA
RISEUP  HOTTER  EDGAR
```

80

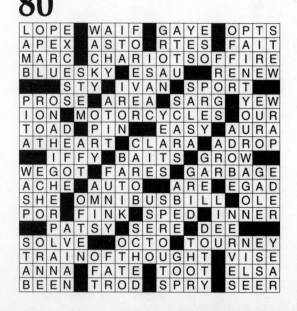

```
LOPE  WAIF  GAYE  OPTS
APEX  ASTO  RTES  FAIT
MARC  CHARIOTSOFFIRE
BLUESKY  ESAU  RENEW
STY  IVAN  SPORT
PROSE  AREA  SARG  YEW
ION  MOTORCYCLES  OUR
TOAD  PIN  EASY  AURA
ATHEART  CLARA  ADROP
IFFY  BAITS  GROW
WEGOT  FARES  GARBAGE
ACHE  AUTO  ARE  EGAD
SHE  OMNIBUSBILL  OLE
POR  FINK  SPED  INNER
PATSY  SERE  DEE
SOLVE  OCTO  TOURNEY
TRAINOFTHOUGHT  VISE
ANNA  FATE  TOOT  ELSA
BEEN  TROD  SPRY  SEER
```

81

```
SIGHS CUR  SEAS  VOLT
AVAIL USA  WACO  IDEA
MOTTO REDROSESORDER
PRETEST INRE ONE
     MESA SCAN  TOWER
CHAR LALA  PESO  AVA
HEN  PUPILSLIPUP RIG
IRS  ITUP TALON ISLE
CANTEEN PACES CRASS
   ARTS WALES FLAW
YEMAY HATED SLINGER
PREY FAIRS TEAM AGE
ROT BURSITISRUB GAP
ESA UNIT  OPEN  OWNS
SEGER CANS  TARA
   ARA OHIO ASSISTS
PARTONSNOTRAP TORAH
ALIA NICK TRE ALAMO
DEBT EPEE HEX REWED
```

82

```
SOFAR MISTER SWATHE
TRACE ONTIME ARCHER
RAINBOWTROUT VICUNA
ACLEAR RAS IMET NRS
ILED ESOP DNA EDDIE
TED UGO  SAUCE  RES
   SNOWGOOSE AGAR
BECKON OUCH GRABBER
IDLY PARK SELL IRA
DUO WELLS STAYS ROT
ECU HAUS PEAR ADSO
REDRESS HULL ARISEN
  BONE SUNFLOWER
BEA DICEY FAX PAS
SERRA LAY ALAN MICE
LAR ROLL ABC USANCE
EDISON LIGHTNINGBUG
PLEASE OFROME ANOSE
TESTER PAIRED PAYER
```

83

```
DIP HEADER  BBB MEN
ECU ANGELO MOIL APE
MONTICELLO ONTO RIM
INCA ANI MOUNTKISCO
   TRUST ASRS EER
AMI VESTS ASAN OVAL
RELIES HOLLER ANITA
ERICA TELAS BARSTOW
ALOE AHMAD SOIL AMS
   CHIAROSCURO
SRA ASSN NEARS MAID
CAMELOT SILLS TERSE
ATOLL LOCALE ARAMIS
MAKE PERU TRADE ASK
   NEO ELMO CAKED
PIRANDELLO SAM LIED
IDA TINS PECCADILLO
GEM RUDE ELAINE LAG
SAP EMS DONATE ONS
```

84

```
BORGS GALA  STE  TOAD
ISERE IBIS HAJ ARNO
GLEAN SOAP ERE KANE
*OFFORTUNE RECLINER
   SRO ANTI TEN
SAMP LEGS OFA AGHAS
TRUE ELL *OFJUSTICE
ATSEA MODE SSR HEAT
YET STEWERS GUESTS
  *HORSE WATER*
PHASER PROWESS BED
SORA SEA EBAN AMAZE
SPINNING*S ROB ACRE
TILDE DAI MERL CHAD
   DEW PESO OLA
NOSEDIVE TURNCART*S
ATTA LIT OLIO BOWIE
ITAL ECU NICE ONINE
LOGS YES ENOL RINGS
```

85

```
CLOTH STEPPE HORACE
HENRY ROARED AVENUE
ASSIDUOUSASS LETTER
SLATER REM  SERAI
MILE GAIL SOUR IPSO
SEE EELS EARN ALOOP
   DOGMATICDOG DOE
EYE INA BOL IRELAND
GAMUT DEN HANDEL
OPUS RAID KALE NAPA
   LEVELS FEY PANIC
SEASIDE BEE ANA TET
ART COWARDLYCOW
SMITE IRIS ULUS MUS
SAVE OFME SLUG DUPE
   ENTRE SHE AGENDA
ACETIC CATALYTICCAT
CAMERA ALANON BOITE
ELUDES MIRAGE BREED
```

86

```
MAJA  SHOE  ULAN  BERG
ISUP  POUT  LANE  AREA
LIMP  ANTHONYHOPKINS
ASPERSED  PASO  AESOP
      STEM  ISEE  NAPS
APHID ODOR  SEME  OAT
BRITONS  WARMSPRINGS
LIFE  OAR   TOUTS BEEP
EXT   ANGI  END   BIRDS
      SLEEPS  AGREED
FLAWS    OOH  EELY  RED
AURA  HASTO SAL   HERO
SKIPPEDTOWN  RAREBIT
TED   AARE  MOBS  ALONE
      ANDI  PURO  LULU
OMANI    ERIC  BOILINGS
BOUNCINGCHECKS  ODEA
IDEA  ANTA  PART  NETS
TELL  NESS  ITAS  SRAS
```

87

```
SEAM  TAB   STJOE CHEW
WACO  RIO   NOONE HORA
ACCUSERS  AUTOCRATIC
PHONES  WHITS    ARLES
      UTE  FEELS  SWIM
BINS  PALS  SEAL  TRA
AMT   WELLSUITED  AHEM
BAA   HAS   ENCORE RENO
EMBRACES  LENS  ESKER
      IATE  TRADE AVON
TELLS  BRAD  SEMINOLE
AXIL  DRIVEN  VIC  CIT
PITY  REFINEMENT  KEA
STY   BITE  WAND  GODS
      KEPT  SHEDS ERN
SHONE    ACARE  GROWLS
PAPERTIGER  OVERTOOK
OREL  AMEND  FIN  TONI
TENT  PARTY  FAT  ODIN
```

88

```
HAFT  DEARS EDO   RAGS
IGLU  APRIL MOM   AXIS
GRITTYCITY  INNOCENT
HAG   AFOOT  PRAISE
      HELOTS MEAT SPLAY
TATLER  ELECTED LADE
ARSENAL ELKE  AWARDS
POINT  IMA   SNACKS
ESTA  SLAVE  ANNIE
DEE   ELITESTREET  SRS
      FAITH  SITAR SHOE
      SEARCH  ASK  SHOVE
PICKLE  BOER  SCOURED
ONCE  ROADMAP ORNERY
PEELS  BRIE   ABORTS
      AUSTEN  ITALO TEA
STAKEOUT  HOODSWOODS
URGE  IST   INIGO  WRIT
BYES  LEA   ESSEN  LETS
```

89

```
FOGS  ERIC  EMIT  LARA
ISAT  GARO  DODO  OPAL
THROUGHTHEGRAPEVINE
SADDLES  OVEN  IRENIC
      EGAD  IRES  ACE
LINEN NATO  EVA   SUBS
OWED  HEM   FAMILYTREE
WAR   SAGAN LBS   EAGLE
ESS   CHE   ARLO  BAGELS
      LEAVESOFGRASS
ROBINS  ASTO  ART  BAD
ONINE AMA   RUNNY USE
WEEDINGOUT  PGS  OSTE
SARA  URN   HATE  UNHIP
      ORA   ARNO  ANEW
STROVE  FLOG  SLUSHES
THEMAYFLOWERCOMPACT
IONE  ELAN  LOAN  OCTA
RUER  VOTE  SONG  TKOS
```

90

```
SADE  PALL  PESO  PFCS
OBOL  ASIA  ATOP  ALAI
BEWITCHED  REFERRALS
ELDER    SLAV  ACERB
REY   EDD   ELEC  DOBBS
      AREO  SNOOP TERI
ATT   DUMBFOUNDED  RIN
HOHO  BOIL  EDNA  GOG
EXULT  STABS  SALSA
MONGOL  SMELT  LEASED
      DATUM  ELIOT SITAR
ALE   ERIE  NUIT  LESE
FOR   MINDBOGGLES  DEW
ERST  ENDOR  HEAP
WITHA  YNES  SRI  BAH
      RAISA  ELAN  TIARA
FLUMMOXED  BEDAZZLED
RICE  YEAR  LAUD  ESSE
ASKS  ARTY  ERNE  RATS
```

91

BABAR · ROUGH · · BELDAM
AMULE · ENTAIL · EROICA
DYNAMICSELFSTARTERS
· · MOT · · LITA · · STET
TRIO · ERATO · PLEA · ·
HANDYMANSPECIAL · CCS
ATSEA · INK · LORDS · RAT
WET · WADI · MAUS · EMERY
· CEDE · BANG · · IDOL
TALLDARKANDHANDSOME
ABOU · · · ARTS · SCUT · ·
CAVES · EURO · SLOB · ORE
ITE · TELAE · ETA · ASHOT
TED · INMINTCONDITION
· DREI · · AMATI · ROMA
AREA · RASH · · SMA
HIGHTRAFFICLOCATION
AMALIE · BATOUT · YUCCA
SENSED · XINGS · IMEAN

92

SANTA · MARIA · AMB · ILK
ACORN · OSAGE · LEO · SUE
CHRISTOPHER · LAG · ALY
KIM · WISEST · COLUMBUS
SPACEMEN · PAW · SEE
· ARE · SCHEMED · GLAD
SCARE · HUR · DEA · LIE
HAL · DIG · ITCH · STOATS
ILED · RATES · ASPER
VICEROYOF · THEINDIES
· MINER · LISAS · OTTO
FACILE · TRET · REM · TOY
USA · ERS · OCA · ILONA
NINA · STJOHNS · DSO
APE · IAM · TRADUCES
CARAVELS · ABRADE · AMP
UNI · ART · THEOCEANSEA
JOE · DIE · ASONE · LACES
ONS · END · GONGS · SWARM

93

CAMPUS · DECAL · MAMMON
AROUSE · AWARE · ALOUSE
STOREWATERCOLDANDUP
HERR · CERO · · ASIT
· SPAT · BOSC · NABOB
UDO · ALIEN · ULAE · NOLO
TIREMANDOORANDPAGES
ANON · EGANS · BASE · SOS
HANOI · MESS · DON
SHOWBETSWIPEANDWAYS
· IRA · SCOA · · SALOP
NCO · ZAPS · LOTSA · SAKI
CANVASPAPERANDCAMEL
ALTA · EIRE · STEER · ORT
ALOUD · NAST · ASIA
· LONG · RISK · · SHEA
BEATWASHLASHANDHAND
BAREST · AUDIO · ONEIDA
STEREO · SCENE · PARLOR

94

DIPL · SONOF · AIM · DEWY
OTOE · ORALE · BOA · EPEE
NOWVOYAGER · INHABITS
SNEERED · ACT · AMA
· REAR · JILL · FLOSSED
RIBS · REF · USO · LEPER
ERR · GOESINSTYLE · URE
POE · HUNT · ETATS · BRIG
ONADARE · EVER · THROES
· KIN · WAVERED · OAF
NOFEAR · FIRS · ARISTAS
ETAS · ASIDO · DUOS · HIP
GAS · CURRENTUNIT · ENA
ENTER · TEN · ANT · SMUT
VISTULA · CANE · ITTO
· CCI · RED · ASSUMES
FASHIONS · HOTPEPPERS
ELIE · NOV · OSIER · ONIT
WIND · SAP · COPSE · RTES

95

JONES · GAFFE · · SERAPE
ACALL · ATOLLS · STADIA
MERLE · STRAITJACKETS
BAR · ALPS · TRU · HELOT
SNOOZES · THEOLD · DANE
· WHYS · PRO · BEER · SSR
SIMI · SQUEEZEPLAY
ADIOS · ULTRA · TAPAS
DEN · TAIL · SNA · NIKITA
IAD · ESTER · ECLAT · NHL
STERNE · DEW · COPE · COO
MEDOC · · AREED · SCHMO
· TIGHTLIPPED · OPEN
ELM · LEAH · NET · UELE
RIOS · MIRAGE · MELANGE
ELROD · KEG · BUTI · NOV
CLOSEQUARTERS · ZAIRE
TISANE · TEASET · ADEER
SEEDED · ENTRY · SASSY

96

```
GEM   TABOO   RAIL    ASTA
AVE   OWERS   ESTE    STEW
LEDAANDTHESWAN        FORE
SNITS     SALT    DOORIS
  SCOTER      OUCH    ARM
    PELICANBRIEF      YOU
HOP   RILER   SEAL    APAT
IVES  ALLEN   ETA     VERA
DANTES    LOAD    UNFIT
ELGAR   HOLDUPS   MARCO
  UNITE   AIRA    ESTEEM
CHIC   OLD   RIGOR   ELLE
LONE  NOON   NENES    STN
UNI   SITTINGDUCKS
  SPA   SECA     STEAMS
SOLUTE    ENDS     TSAIS
OMAR  WILDGOOSECHASE
ANNE  ELIA   EDITH    MAX
RIDE  RELY   SANDY    SLY
```

97

```
OWLS    GIST    RAKE    AJS
SEAT   SENTA    ERRS    RAM
SPRUCINGUP   QUAT    IZE
OTC   AARON   JUNK    GAZE
    HARMED   DOE     OFA
SIMILES    PUSSYWILLOW
AMOROS   PRESTO   NEALE
RANI    ECHO     UPLANDS
ANTED   HONE   BREA    DST
    RIDINGTHEPINE
CPA   NOME    SERA    DEBTS
REVENGE      ELLS    LEAR
OLIVE   REVILE    TUPELO
CEDARRAPIDS    RELOCKS
    DSO    INA    DEARTH
FLOE   DOSE   BIDRI    WAD
LAX   UNDO   OLDHICKORY
AVE   SEED   TENON    ROME
WAN   EYRE    BUTT    ADAR
```

98

```
BOWS   AKA   TATUM    ALPS
AREA   LED   AMORE    ZEAL
HELLOOLDFRIEND        UGLY
   CUTUP    LAND    IER
SCOTTS   JANE    LUBEJOB
CAMEO   SUIT   AIME    AWE
OPED   HELLOAGAIN     MIA
ORS   QUAY    FIRS    BANC
PITBULL   VEILS    WEIGH
   RAIL   SIGNE    DISC
SHARP   DODGE   FANTASY
CONK   TONE   EATS    FEE
ORG   SAYGOODBYE     DANA
USE   EKES   RABE   COROT
TERRAIN   AILS    BALERS
   INN    IDEA    BELOW
AVID   GOODNIGHTIRENE
WING   INLET   OAT    ELEE
LAKE   NEARS   ATE    SLOG
```

99

```
ADAM   SPEC   RAPT    FOOL
BALI   HILO   ABLY    RARE
BRANDENBURGCONCERTO
EERIE    SEGO     DELI
   ONT    ALAI    AGREE
THENEWWORLDSYMPHONY
RAM   BOOM   ANOA    TIDE
AIDE   SKATE   TUNA    LOS
SKEGS     HEAT     UNTO
HUNGARIANRHAPSODIES
   SRAS    SLEW    MARNE
ASI   ADIN   YEARN    SIDE
NADA   ONCE   ROOF    AER
THESONGOFTHEISLANDS
ELAND     STOA     HEM
   IOTA    GUAM    ABNER
THEGRANDCANYONSUITE
OATH   XOUT   TARO    SCAN
PLAT   INNS   SHED    HELD
```

100

```
TAHITI   HINTED   SODAS
ORISON   IDEATE   CRAMP
TIGERS   GLOBETROTTER
ASHE   ASHEN   EAT    IRE
LES   ONUS   CURT    ONCE
   TAPER   ETAL   IMAGES
AMERE    FORERUNNER
DEPICT   CALM   AGE    PRE
EXPO   ABA   LEVI    TALUS
LIES   PELT   LOVE    BASS
ACRES   LAIR   TET    ACTA
SOS   EBO   LANE   CUTELY
   JAYWALKERS     POKES
BACALL   HEED    MAORI
ERRS   IHAD   BURN    CMS
AMI   INA   SWIGS    OKIE
NATIVEDANCER    OLDEST
EDILE   ERRAND   NEERDO
RACKS   STARTS   SEASON
```

101

```
GRIT  STOPS  TAPS  MPG
IOWA  UHURU  WHIP  IRA
STONEMASON  IONE  LOB
   GRANT  FOXY  CELLO
PUBLIC  TILT  STEWER
ARIES  LOOSE  EMEER
LAND  BONDHOLDER  IAM
OLD  CAGED  ODE  OGRE
   MANY  LUSTY  LAHTI
RIBALD  TENTS  SORTER
ARAIL  THROE  OTIS
GALL  LOU  RERAN  AMA
EEL  BIRDHUNTER  CRAM
   PARSE  USUAL  AHIKE
PILEUP  STEM  AMAZON
AVAST  MESA  LINER
COY  ILEX  BLACKSMITH
ERE  SOLE  LEVEL  ERIE
SYR  HATS  EVADE  DENY
```

102

```
PAIN  CABLE  WATT  AGS
ANNO  ONEAL  ALIE  TET
UNCHAINEDMELODY  ANY
LAR  UNI  DONKEY  FLUX
   ESTEEM  DOS  ORA
INDOOR  OUTOF  PRINCE
LOINS  UNLAWFULENTRY
ITBE  SPEAR  SPA  GAYE
ATL  WASTES  GIBE
DEE  ANTS  ORNE  IFS
   ANDA  STRATA  NRA
FOIL  BRR  COEDS  ADES
INDEFATIGABLE  BLISS
BEEPER  GENES  TRASHY
OPE  THE  ECHOIC
HALO  SATRAP  ARA  RDS
AGO  IMPOSSIBLEDREAM
RUG  REEF  OCALA  MENU
PAY  SERF  SALAD  STAG
```

103

```
JOB  SMEAR  WERT  TESS
EVA  IATRO  ARIA  ALTO
TIN  PRESSINGPROBLEM
DEEPIS  ARISE  LLAMA
   GEL  ORAN  NILE
LONGRUNNINGDEBATE
AMIS  ILO  IRES  XED
DOC  WAVY  AREST  JAVA
DOE  ORE  INIT  FAMED
   BURNINGISSUES
QUIRK  DERS  ARA  QED
ULNA  APLEY  AUNT  UDO
AUK  ACRE  END  SIGN
   SIMMERINGDISPUTES
MAES  NAGY  AAR
UBOAT  ASTHE  ACCEPT
NAGGINGHEADACHE  LYE
DIRE  BEEN  OTTER  UPA
OLES  ASST  NESTS  MET
```

104

```
ALB  MILAN  SISAL  WEB
SOL  ADARE  CANIO  IRA
SCARLETTANAGERS  NIT
NICE  SHY  ALOE  EDGES
   KNUTE  ETD  ZERO
PAGAN  SATI  GET  UPON
ANOMIE  LAVENDERBLUE
VOLE  ASI  EAU  UTURN
ENDS  RECAST  MLI  SSE
   STEEL  UNION
CAM  EHS  ASPECT  AMBS
USUAL  SIC  VAT  ROIL
PINKLEMONADE  EDISTO
STIR  PIN  MARC  ASSET
   OTIS  SPY  LAMER
FAUNA  CLUE  MIL  ROMA
ORG  BLUEGRAYCLASSIC
AIL  LIESA  ITHAD  ELI
LAY  ELDER  THETA  SOD
```

105

```
BEEF  CARS  CPA  BABEL
URDU  ASIT  AIM  ALICE
MASTERSDEGREE  RIGHT
   IDLE  PRO  XER  SOS
AZALEAS  EMS  SOUP
WOMEN  QUASH  TONER
ALA  SEUSS  EGOMANIA
RANSOMNOTES  OPS  DAY
   ADULT  DEANS  GENA
GIMME  IAM  EWE  EARTH
ANAP  ASSAM  EBERT
FER  BLT  JOYFULNOYES
FEVERISH  LOUTS  OLE
DEVON  AFOUL  WAGON
LAME  YET  BLATANT
BAL  ISA  ROB  LUSH
ALOAD  SERVICECHARGE
JOULE  AXE  TANK  NOON
APSES  POT  EDDY  DYAD
```

106

```
EMMAS  ■ CURDS  ■ HAMSTER
TOUCH  ■ OBOES  ■ ABILENE
TARTARSAUCE   ■ ISLANDS
ATM ■ REINER ■ SLOOP ■
■ UPPING ■ YOKER ■ PRE
RARA ■ MEIN ■ BARBARIAN
OLIVES ■ EDITS ■ LINGO
BONES ■ ALGAE ■ MANTEL
ENG ■ SAVORY ■ ISAID
DESI ■ BOBOLINKS ■ SCAB
■ SCENE ■ INGEST ■ IRE
KANSAS ■ SLEEP ■ RANGE
AFOUL ■ POLYP ■ RANCOR
REREMOUSE ■ TACO ■ TINY
LEA ■ BREWS ■ RADIAN
■ BASIS ■ CRISES ■ NAE
FEMALES ■ SHOSHONEANS
EVEREST ■ PESTO ■ OUTON
WETNESS ■ ADEAR ■ TRINE
```

107

```
MASUR ■ SLOUGH ■ BURIED
AWARE ■ MAITRE ■ IRONER
SAINTBERNARD ■ TIMELY
SYN ■ RANK ■ GUTSY ■
■ TIBER ■ REESE ■ USC
TAMARA ■ SANFRANCISCO
ABATED ■ PLATS ■ ARSON
SOYER ■ AIL ■ ASTARTE
TUB ■ SABRES ■ CROON
ETES ■ SAINTJOAN ■ ISAT
■ ALOFT ■ SOMBER ■ ATA
MORDANT ■ KEY ■ ARNAS
IDEAL ■ DAMES ■ STATUS
SANTABARBARA ■ TOMATO
TSE ■ OREAD ■ SONIC ■
■ QUITS ■ ICAN ■ LOG
UNFURL ■ SANTAFETRAIL
MIRAGE ■ ENABLE ■ HOUSE
PLAYER ■ REBELS ■ EBSEN
```

108

```
LISA ■ MUTE ■ TOPER ■ NIP
ENTS ■ ALOT ■ OPERA ■ ANE
ALEC ■ CUBA ■ PINSTRIPE
DIVERS ■ AGAINST ■ ELUL
ONINE ■ AGENCE ■ SEPTS
NEEDLEWORK ■ SAYSSO ■
■ SERA ■ EAT ■ MERELY
LAC ■ NAY ■ ADAMS ■ ICH
ORANT ■ OBLATE ■ ISLE
VICE ■ PENCILSIN ■ RHEA
ESTE ■ OGRADY ■ CREPT
STU ■ MURAL ■ BOO ■ STS
■ ASHORE ■ AIT ■ AULD
■ FEASTS ■ BRISTLEDAT
CALLS ■ IDIOMS ■ ABODE
OMOO ■ LINEDUP ■ DRONES
HAWTHORNE ■ NUDE ■ NAST
IRE ■ ICIER ■ CREW ■ ETTE
TAR ■ TODDS ■ EELY ■ DEED
```

109

```
AMPS ■ MAIL ■ BABS ■ PIMA
LORE ■ ANNE ■ EXIT ■ ADEN
FAIRBANKS ■ FINEPRINT
■ MIAMI ■ SAIL ■ LEAGUE
CLEFT ■ COST ■ CLAP ■
ROT ■ SAXONY ■ TRA ■ EZRA
ISIN ■ TOPSECRET ■ TOIL
SEMI ■ BUS ■ RESET ■ OVA
PRECOAT ■ GLOAT ■ AMMAN
■ HOT ■ POINT ■ SPA ■
QUEEN ■ SANDY ■ STENGEL
URN ■ ASTRE ■ COE ■ ORDO
IGOR ■ POORHOUSE ■ REUP
PELE ■ AWL ■ ENROLL ■ ACE
■ CANE ■ GAEL ■ OPTED
EGRESS ■ JOLT ■ BOOED ■
GOODHUMOR ■ WORSTCASE
GAVE ■ LAID ■ OPAL ■ ANOA
SLED ■ EDNA ■ SEGO ■ NEXT
```

110

```
DOWE ■ MAWS ■ SERAC ■ BOB
AMAT ■ ABIT ■ PLATO ■ RUE
LASTPICTURESHOW ■ ORE
ENNUI ■ SCONE ■ BOAST
SIT ■ ESS ■ KID ■ ABEND ■
■ LIST ■ OPALOCKA
ART ■ VIDEORENTAL ■ AIM
CUE ■ OVER ■ EXCEL ■ ESPY
ASLICE ■ FACIES ■ ANT
THEFARM ■ DRS ■ TORONTO
■ VAL ■ ELIOTS ■ RISERS
EMIT ■ ALAMO ■ ABLE ■ WET
LAS ■ ATTHEMOVIES ■ SEE
SPINSTER ■ PETS ■
■ OREAD ■ GAP ■ ESP ■ MUS
ASNAP ■ KILOS ■ AGENT
DOS ■ TRANSISTORRADIO
ARE ■ INSET ■ EASE ■ GOON
MET ■ CAPES ■ DYED ■ ACNE
```

111

```
REAP ALES TRAP FORD
ITSA MORE HADA IRAE
OAHU PURPLEMOUNTAIN
  ASI SAAR PLAINLY
CAMERAS LIMIT ENG
USE ALEF RACERS ETS
REDSQUARE LEDA OGRE
  TIM ARA SOARER
DOGS KNISH APPROVE
OUR BLACKFOREST VON
STEARIN SOLES PERE
ARENAS RUE HAT
GANN ZOLA BLUEBAYOU
ENS STRING SPRY EUR
THE DIGIN ABSTAIN
ACREAGE ERIS SIR
THEEMERALDCITY ANIL
TIED NENE KNEE REDO
ANTS ADDS SENT ADAM
```

112

```
GARS FEED ASPS WASP
NCAA ARLO SCUT ACTI
ARIVERRUNSTHROUGHIT
TENOR ALOE EELS ERA
DRAIN TRIM LED
TAR SATE VOICE EBBS
UNOPEN DROWNINGPOOL
NOPES ODA AGT ROONE
ANSA SUITE FITTED
STREAMLINED
HABITS SONAR ESSE
AGORA ACU ONS DREAD
VERONICALAKE FERVID
ADEN SERAI SAIN ELY
SAM NERO DROWN
AWL DEMI EACH VISTA
IHAVELOVEDTHEEOCEAN
DICE LIAR EARL KARA
APEX ALLI STEM SSTS
```

113

```
GUARD CRABBE SWIVEL
ANNIE BEVIES CHOICE
RATTLESNAKES RANCHO
EELY DIET HAT EON
TWAS DWELL GAP
OAT LIAR ANTELOPES
PREMIER ACLUE APART
STRUM MIGHT FASTONE
SEA NRA HUSH LIE
WIGS TARANTULA PIED
UDO COTE NOR PRE
RAMPANT TENTH ARESO
SHEET EVILS ANGULAR
TORTOISES SUES ELY
STE TEETH APEX
TAG ELS NOVA ROSH
EUROPA WATERBUFFALO
ARISEN EVINCE NINER
LAPSED SEETHE OTTER
```

114

```
QUIT COMB EPHS SPOT
URDU AREA FRAT CERO
ASON SLOW FORA ORAD
ALASHOWDREARYWOULD
SIC SAN ISAT
ARS ZONE IDES LEDGE
BETHEWORLDIF RERUNS
ASYOU MOE TOES BUS
SALOPS DEMI ABAS
EYED THEREWERE KISS
SPEE SLAV CRIMEA
ASA EMMA SEE ELEGY
RICHES NOSANTACLAUS
CREED NAPA TAPA NEO
REPO ORE ALF
THEREISASANTACLAUS
WADI CALS JOSH XRAY
OVEN ALOU OBIE EGAN
SANG SEEM YENS SERE
```

115

```
COIN CHORUS MERITS
ANNAS EUROPE AVENUE
STARTINGOVER DAMONE
TOURIST ENES DINER
GALA WORD TOES
BRUTE VOW ARE SOFT
LURE LAUNCHPADS NEO
ADA SINK LORI TATTY
BELDAMS BENET ASHES
BUFO SAMOS OBOE
DIANA INTER STAFFED
IDLER NEON WAIT IRE
GEL INVENTIONS CRIB
SASH EAR COD VASES
EKED SCUD AINT
HEMAN ECHO AKETTLE
OLIVIA HAPPYNEWYEAR
DURESS ANOINT SOAMI
SLOSHY RANGES UMPS
```

116

POPEOF RINSE KISSER
ATONAL ONEAL ANKARA
THETROUBLEWITHHARRY
SOTO NEED ANAT
MBAS ALIBI LETGO
TOBEPERFECTLYFRANK
HOP ASEA CUBA STAR
AYES ENNIS SAHL ETA
DONOR CROW COOS
JUSTINTHENICKOFTIME
SCOW DOLL TENON
MAB OTIS FLASH PYRE
ALAI RSVP SHOO OAS
ROBSPETERTOPAYPAUL
STELE ANEAR STAB
ICAN KILT ICES
JACKANDTHEBEANSTALK
APPEND LETIT BROLLY
MORASS CROSS COFFEE

117

ASS SHIP MICA LICKS
CAN EASE ATOM INONE
THECRYINGGAME UNFIT
SLEEVES RELENT EFTS
RAES TINY HERE
CHESS SILT ACRE EBO
AIDE THELAUGHINGMAN
SEA POOR SNAP OUSE
ASTARTE TRUER LUGES
NEO CHURL SER
LOFTY SHARP CHEDDAR
AGRI APIN JEER RBI
CROCODILETEARS AGED
KEW WEND ELKO IVIES
NONE SNEE ANAG
SHUN MOMISM ASSIGNS
LAPIS WEEPINGWILLOW
ALOOP LENO ROAD ERA
PENNY STAT ANNE SAG

118

GIRL SCAM AROW LUIS
PLEA ALLI BABA ETRE
OLDMEDALS AMEX ATON
CANDY SISSY EDENS
CORRAL NICHE AVERSE
AMO ECOLE SALONS V
HOSTWRITERS RIK NEA
NOSIR NAS OFT EPICS
RYAN ALA ADAPTS
AGRA RACENOTES MEON
DIADEM OWN VILE
ELVES JOE SHE ALFIE
SLY THE ROWINGPAINS
TRAITS KELSO NIT
STRUTS MOREL ROGETS
CHASE HADAT DINES
ERIS FOCI SPYLASSES
NENE INKS ORAL SEAT
TEST BEST PENA OSTE

119

RIB TRAIN LEG FOLKS
ODE RONDO AAA OMANI
ALLBUTTONEDUP NADIR
RETILES SLY ESTHETE
TOYS STELE TEA
HAIL BOOM XRAY NAP
ENG HAIRPINTURN EGO
ASH OLGA URNS SCUD
PATINA SEURAT DUKES
EVENS PAS SWEET
MONEY TROWEL ENSIGN
AVIS TOAD IFAT ENE
KEN GARTERSNAKE PAL
ERG RIME OWED BAWL
BEN SUSAN TOUR
TABLETS PET HEARTIS
EQUAL ONASHOESTRING
CURSE FAN EDITH EST
HASTY TED SARAS SOS

120

JAMB BRAM JAG EMIT
ALAR YOGIS EVE VISE
WAKEUPCALL TIN ELLE
SIENNA ROIL DEGREES
DITS GUM VIE
WEATHERFORECASTING
FOX SEEL KEA TRUE
ROALD SPEC TRAS ADE
ADMIRE AARE LINSEED
MEANDMYSHADOW
COLOSSI SOSO ARABIA
ABE TEXT FATS EMEND
DIVA OOP YOKE AID
STICKINGITSNECKOUT
QED OAR WHIR
ATTUNES FAST INAFOG
MAUI AUK SPRINGTIME
BUNT LEE HAIKU ORAN
ITAS STY TOES RENT

121

```
DECENT  TSP  ZED   IBIS
ORATOR  OOH  IOI   LONE
GOESTO  PLATONICLOVE
EDS  ALLS  EIN    ASKED
SEATTLE  MDS  PAL  IRE
    RAE  AFAR  WHIM  ETD
GASP  TROJANHORSE
ELA  RING   EATS  ALAR
NELSONS  TIETO  AGAVE
EXALTS  MUNDI  ARETES
VIDAL  SONNY  CITRINE
ASSN  MUNI   DAMS  NUN
    GREEKCHORUS  DQED
ABE  ENDS  OPUS  RAU
LIL  CEE  OUT  ACETATE
GRATA   IFS  PLAT  RAM
OLYMPICGAMES  GIOTTO
RENE  QUO  AMS  ENDEAR
EDEN   SET  NUT  STARRY
```

122

```
SADA  ASTIR  ALEC  DAB
ETUI  FORGE  LOGO  ALA
RONDARLING  PUGS  VIN
INKED  PINGS   TRICK
ACE  SGL  TAR  PRAISES
LEDA  ROBE  AEROSOL
    BEAUBRIDGES  TOMA
PEDANTIC  NURSE  VON
AROSEIS   SAES   FEUD
NOLESS  ATILT  STAIRS
GILD  GRAD   LEONINE
ACY  BLAKE  EULOGIST
SAMS  ROGERANGELL
    ARRIVES  SEEN  EDAM
BEDTIME  TRA  SEA  RNA
ILIAD  MOOLA   CLOGS
PAS  DRAY  VALENTINES
ETO  LIFT  ERICA  DELE
DEN  EACH  SKATE  OSAS
```

123

```
DEJECT  BELOW  SPEEDS
AMALIE  ARISE  HALLEY
DEMITS  JANETJACKSON
SUET  TEASE   INTO
    SEVER  SMELTS  LAS
HAJ  ARRET  ALLY  WELL
ADONIS  LIANA  PIETA
LOYAL  JUMPINGFORJOY
LUCY  RETIE   EASY
STE  BOWED  MATTE  JAB
    CUBE   GALES  SERE
JELLYSLASTJAM  TETRA
ADIOS  BLOOM  TRAJAN
DENY  DIEU  ROMEO  OSS
END  CENTER   MEDIC
    ALES   EDAMS  SKIP
JIMMYJOHNSON  HELENA
INEEDA  AREED  OBEYED
MERSEY  PATSY  TOSSES
```

124

```
CASH  REAR  HARP  ITCH
ASTA  ELLE  AGHA  DELI
RHUM  HILL  LEONLEMON
IBN  BAH  AXE  SAO  PUT
BUTTEBUTTER   CREEDS
OREAD   RED  BEHEST
UNDO  DEED  FAYE  TEAM
    SEATS  ELSE  LEMMA
EMS  DNA  IBAR  PIEPAN
LOP  WALESSWALES  LLD
GOALIE  ALES  ACT  ELY
ASIAN  OMEN   CHASE
RENT  DIET  TORN  VOWS
    SEPALS  JON  TEXAN
SCARRY   MAINEMARINE
TOP  OLE  AWL  MAX  DDE
OMANWOMAN  EDER  TIER
OBIE  NINE  RORY  EZRA
DONT   GRIT  SAYS  NEST
```

125

```
PIPAL  BASEST  PLATTE
ATRIA  ORNATE  REPAIR
COUNTRYMUSIC  AVALON
AUNTIE   GEM   STICK
STE  NESS  DUCAT  HOLD
    ILETA  LON  DEFOE
ABA  CITYSLICKER  TVA
COLD  NULLA  OILY  HEN
HOTAS  PEENS   NURSE
    METAL  SETTS  LOATH
    RAVES  PERCS  TROOP
ICE  ANAG  REATA  AWRY
OLD  NATIONALISM  NAM
WASNT   ORB   MENSA
ANTA  TULSA  STIR  SLD
    ADMIT  CDS  SIFTER
OPTION  QUIETVILLAGE
VIENNA  TROCHE  YETIS
INSETS  SESTET  NESTS
```

126

```
MARIOS  WCTU  PLATES
ATONCE  SHARP  RIDERS
YOUCANTMAKEANOMELET
ANT  SHAME  ETNA
 SPEAR  PAUSE  TALI
DEBAR  ITTAKESATHIEF
ERASES  ANILINE  DEF
LAYS  EPIC  NEE  TEARY
ATO  HARRIS  PCT
YOUVEGOTTOHAVEHEART
 ALA  BARFLY  WOE
SWARM  ABA  NEWT  JAVA
ROB  EAGERTO  SOURER
TOCATCHATHIEF  DRESS
ASSN  CAUSE  RODDY
 TARS  TRICE  OOP
WITHOUTBREAKINGEGGS
ATHENE  BOSSA  TORRES
SEEMED  BETH  STREET
```

127

```
MOB  PLUS  PALS  LONGS
ADO  AINT  ARIL  ABOUT
TEX  DATA  CANOFWORMS
HALO  ROTH  REPOSE
 UNO  LOOM  DER  SAWS
ASNEW  DREAM  SAD  PHI
PECANS  GAS  EOSIN
ATHLETE  BUCKETSHOPS
RAE  DRAMAS  AMAIN
TEST  IGET  ATEN  OBES
 RACER  SHEENS  AAH
BAGOFTRICKS  RIPOSTE
ANITA  TOE  CONKED
INS  RAT  GIVEN  TEENS
LETS  GOO  NONE  SAT
 AMOUSE  XRAY  TBAR
JUSTINCASE  AREA  AGO
AGAIN  AGTS  GLAD  LEA
BOONE  NEAT  EYRE  LED
```

128

```
BASH  CHAR  JARS  DOGS
BITE  ROSE  URIS  EBRO
CREAMEDSPINACH  ATAN
 WRAPS  ANKLE  BRUTA
ADESTE  TINE  EATSIN
CODAS  SHREDDEDWHEAT
ESPY  CHESS  OVALS
DER  AHEM  ITEMS  MIX
 URGE  EASTON  DADE
RUNNETH  PEA  SCISSOR
ITEA  IDEALS  ARCH
GAS  ANNEX  POLK  EME
 GLIDE  FORUM  SDAK
APPLETURNOVER  COPSE
BARONS  ALEE  SPOOKS
AROSE  TOSIR  SCOTT
TINS  CHOCOLATESHAKE
ESTE  LIZA  ADIN  ETAL
SHOD  USER  YORE  DONS
```

129

```
HERBAL  SEWER  BAWLS
OTELLO  MAILED  ASHOT
WHATSYOURNAME  THEME
 SOAR  SPITES  RAE
SOL  SLOTS  STAN  SEND
SHOE  NAIVE  IDAHO
HOWDOYOUDO  GLOWERED
 ERE  EWER  NEWLY
DOWNCAST  SNEAK  THIN
ISH  ASIAN  DEGAS  ETE
ATOE  TRIAL  DEPLANES
LISLE  NYET  PAS
SATIRIST  WHYBABYWHY
 HORDE  ADEER  EPEE
MEET  LENS  MOUES  AMP
ORB  DEPOSE  SPAT
NOONE  EVERYWHICHWAY
ESSEN  DANGER  CREATE
TESTY  STONY  SENNET
```

130

```
SECS  GUAM  PTAS  OHNO
ULAE  ANNO  ROBE  TOOK
MITT  LITTLEPITCHERS
PACTS  TITO  LEASE
 HEEL  CORGI  TARGET
CHEERED  NAGS  SEMI
LAR  FEELSATHOME  TOR
ANIL  SLOE  TAIL  STE
MANOF  LOTSA  KNITTED
 TRAP  MUSTS  TORO
COHERES  PETAL  TUFTS
ONE  ARAB  IRED  EIRE
AIR  DUGOUTCANOE  REA
TOYS  SARI  ADVISER
SNEAKS  SEPAL  DIRT
 LEAST  OLES  LOBED
OUTINLEFTFIELD  NAVE
AMEN  AGUE  CRUE  ESAU
FATE  DOLE  ESES  DENS
```

131

S	H	O	T		S	H	Y		G	A	M	I	N		B	R	O	W
A	I	D	A		P	E	A		A	D	A	N	O		A	U	R	A
D	E	E	R	P	A	R	K		R	O	C	K	R	I	B	B	E	D
		A	I	R	S		A	L	G	A			S	A	B	L	E	
S	C	E	N	T	S		E	P	I		W	R	A	S	S	E		
L	E	A	T	H	E	R	N	E	C	K		I	D	O		R	A	S
U	N	T	O			A	C	T		E	B	B	S		W	A	T	T
R	T	E		S	A	B	E		R	E	O	S		M	O	R	T	E
S	I	N	A	T	R	A		T	I	P	S		W	A	R	M	U	P
			B	U	T	T	E	R	F	I	N	G	E	R	S			
S	K	I	N	N	Y		V	O	L	T		U	P	S	T	A	R	T
W	A	R	E	S		P	I	P	E		M	A	T	H		L	A	O
A	M	O	R		B	A	L	I		P	A	R		T	I	N	A	
P	A	N		W	E	S		C	H	O	W	D	E	R	H	E	A	D
	H	E	A	L	T	H		A	S	S		G	I	A	N	T	S	
S	P	A	N	S		E	A	C	H		S	O	O	N				
C	A	N	V	A	S	B	A	C	K		W	H	I	S	K	E	R	S
A	L	D	O		L	O	R	R	E		E	O	S		E	C	H	O
N	O	S	Y		D	A	T	E	D		T	E	M		D	U	O	S

132

I	F	F	Y		F	E	A	T		H	E	A	P		A	B	E	D
N	O	L	A		R	A	S	H		A	C	R	E		P	O	P	E
F	L	O	P	H	O	U	S	E		R	O	A	N		A	M	E	N
U	D	A	S	I		T	R	O	T		B	U	Y		B	E	T	
S	E	T		N	S	A		E	A	S	T		M	O	U	S	S	E
E	D	S		D	E	S	P	O	T		A	M	B	U	S	H		
		B	U	S	T	O	F	H	O	M	E	R		S	E	T	H	
L	U	P	E		T	I	P		M	A	L	A	R		L	E	A	
O	N	O	R	D	E	R		K	N	E	L	L		N	O	T	E	S
A	S	W	E	E	T		B	R	I	N	E		S	A	F	E	S	T
D	U	E	T	S		S	E	A	L	S		I	T	S	T	R	U	E
E	R	R		K	A	U	A	I		A	R	A		A	S	P	S	
D	E	F	T		B	I	T	T	E	R	L	E	M	O	N			
	A	E	R	A	T	E		L	E	A	N	E	D		M	A	L	
M	A	I	D	E	N		R	O	B	S		E	N	D		A	C	E
I	L	L		A	D	D		G	E	T	S		L	A	T	I	N	
S	C	U	P		O	R	A	L		F	A	N	C	Y	D	U	D	S
T	A	R	A		N	O	D	E		U	V	E	A		E	R	I	E
Y	N	E	Z		S	P	A	R		L	E	W	D		S	E	C	S

133

C	L	A	M	O	R		O	M	A	R		A	N	G	L	E	R
R	E	M	A	K	E		G	E	N	O	A		S	O	R	A	R	E
O	F	O	R	A	H	O	R	S	E	W	I	T	H	W	I	N	G	S
P	T	S		A	G	E	S		L	A	R		P	E	S	T		
		O	I	S	E			C	O	M	B	A	T					
F	R	O	M	T	H	E	H	O	R	S	E	S	M	O	U	T	H	
L	I	V	E	S		O	N	I	O	N		S	O	S	O	O	N	
A	L	A	N		L	O	V	E		S	T	S		I	N	R	E	
G	E	L		H	A	V	E	A	T		O	P	E	N	I	N	G	
			N	E	V	E	R	L	A	S	T	L	O	N	G			
P	A	L	O	M	A	R		P	A	R	A	D	E		T	I	E	
A	H	O	T		T	A	R		F	U	R		S	I	N	S		
C	A	N	A	P	E		S	E	D	E	R		A	T	H	E	N	S
	B	E	T	O	N	T	H	E	W	R	O	N	G	H	O	R	S	E
	I	D	Y	L	L	S			O	R	E	O						
A	R	E	A		O	R	A		R	A	N	I		A	D	O		
D	I	F	F	E	R	E	N	C	E	O	F	O	P	I	N	I	O	N
A	C	O	R	N	S		D	E	L	T	A		P	O	O	D	L	E
M	O	R	O	S	E			O	M	E	R		A	N	G	E	L	A

134

R	I	N	K		W	I	S	H		I	P	S	O		F	L	I	P
A	N	O	A		O	N	C	E		O	A	K	S		L	A	N	E
F	A	W	N	S	O	V	E	R		U	N	I	S		A	M	P	S
	R	H	E	A		A	N	D	A		E	L	O	N		B	U	T
H	U	E		L	O	D	E		G	U	L	L		O	D	E	T	S
I	S	R		T	R	E		V	E	R	S	E		T	E	T		
T	H	E	Y	E	A	R	L	I	N	G		T	E	A	C	H	E	R
	E	R	N		A	S	T	E	R		D	R	O	W	S	E		
V	I	J	A	Y		S	P	A	S		O	R	G	Y		A	T	A
E	C	U	S		K	I	S	S		C	L	O	Y		B	L	E	D
G	A	S		J	I	B	E		A	U	L	D		P	O	K	E	Y
A	R	T	H	U	R		S	A	B	R	E		S	R	A			
S	E	K	A	N	I	S		C	U	B	R	E	P	O	R	T	E	R
	I	N	G		A	M	I	S	S		L	A	S		I	N	A	
V	I	D	A	L		T	I	D	E		A	L	T	O		E	L	M
E	N	D		E	L	I	S		R	A	M	I		D	I	D	I	
E	D	I	T		O	A	S	T		P	U	P	P	Y	L	O	V	E
P	I	N	E		U	T	A	H		E	S	S	E		E	N	E	S
S	A	G	E		D	E	L	E		D	E	E	P		D	E	N	T

135

V	I	D	A		L	O	I	S		C	U	L	T		P	E	L	F
I	T	A	L		A	U	N	T		U	T	A	H		E	R	I	E
M	O	N	T	E	V	I	D	E	O	T	A	P	E		N	I	N	E
	Z	A	N	E		O	N	U	S		S	M	A	C	K	E	D	
W	E	I	R	D		S	O	O	T	H	E		E	L	I			
O	R	G	S		J	A	R		L	O	L	L		I	L	S	A	S
V	I	Z		I	O	N		N	O	R	F	O	L	K	S	O	N	G
E	C	A	R	T	E		B	O	O	T		W	O	E		A	N	T
N	A	G	A	S		T	U	S	K		S	K	I		S	R	A	S
			F	A	I	R	L	Y		S	E	E	N	T	O			
C	O	L	T		C	O	B		C	L	A	Y		H	U	M	A	N
O	L	E		L	O	U		F	A	I	L		C	A	R	O	L	E
B	E	I	J	I	N	G	O	I	S	M		W	O	W		S	I	R
B	O	S	O	M		H	U	G	H		M	I	X		O	C	T	O
	U	P	S		T	H	I	S	I	S		M	A	O				
F	R	I	S	S	O	N		T	E	A	M		G	E	T	W	E	T
L	O	O	T		L	I	V	E	R	P	O	O	L	S	H	A	R	K
A	B	L	E		I	T	O	R		I	S	L	A	S		R	I	O
W	E	A	R		D	A	N	S		D	A	D	D	Y		D	A	S

136

```
BOLE  SOSO  NEON  ALLI
EVEN  SNUG  ECTO  TOUR
GINS  HOLLYWOODCHUCK
ANITA  KEEL  EEEE
TENABLE  SMEW  DENZEL
GREASE  EARP  SURE
HER  LISBONFIRES  RIA
ELAM  REST  TOVARICH
MIDAS  SETUP  MAGIC
PAUSED  NEGUS  NETHER
AUGER  ROLLA  SEATO
RETRACES  SARA  SNUB
ELI  RIYADHESIVE  DIE
ALOP  SIRE  HEATOF
DANIEL  LARK  SLOVAKS
NAIL  PEEP  NEMAT
MONTREALESTATE  RORY
EPEE  TIER  CRAB  DUAL
GEAR  ODAY  HERB  OSTE
```

137

```
MASUR  REACH  STOMATA
ASONE  UNCLE  HERETIC
CHAINLETTER  ENTREAT
KEPT  IDIOT  BAD  ESS
BEAN  CREDO  SUM
GOODTIME  ENS  HORSE
LOX  ANA  GROUNDFLOOR
IZES  GLARE  SUI  ATLI
BESTS  LIENS  BRUSHES
ERA  REDID  EMS
SPRAINS  DELOS  PESTS
ATOM  EAT  LOCAL  STUN
WATERWHEELS  BAY  ANI
SHORE  LAW  AUTOCRAT
SOP  RELAX  KNOB
SAO  AMY  ELISE  ROSE
ABSENCE  TABLESCRAPS
DISLIKE  ADULT  BERET
AGAINST  MAMAS  SADES
```

138

```
RAKE  SIR  TORT  KUDOS
ARIA  APE  EWER  ENATE
BUTTONED  ANNIEPOTTS
ENC  RECAP  START  EOS
HAD  ATOP  ADO
WHERE  CESAR  SIC  UTA
IONIAN  SITES  CAUSES
SHELLAC  THEPLATTERS
HORS  IRA  SLOE  EERIE
BLURT  SUGAR
PHOTO  MEAL  TAX  ERGS
HOWARDBAKER  LEFTOUT
EVENER  SETUP  DOUBLE
WED  DUB  SUBIC  IDIOM
DIS  SENA  LEN
APA  AGREE  SCREE  CSA
MAGGIEDISH  HOLDDOWN
OTHER  INTO  ELS  MOAN
SEAMY  NEED  SEA  SKYE
```

139

```
COPA  CRAB  WARD  RUB
ARAS  ERICA  AQUI  ERE
JOSSSTICKS  PUIG  TAD
UNSAID  HESSIAN  RUNE
NOSIR  RIOT  IONIC
ELECTS  SWISSSTEAK
TANS  HOIST  QUIZ
HST  JUMBO  BAUDS  CAD
OPENER  ARAMIS  ERLE
MINOT  CAROTID  VIOLA
ARCH  CLIENT  DANSON
SEE  BEARD  LEARN  SUN
PEEN  SERRA  ASTA
GRASSSKIRT  ASTARE
REMIT  SOAP  MACHE
IWAS  ARSENAL  RECTOS
PAZ  FRAU  DRESSSHIRT
PRE  ROTE  BENET  NONE
EDD  OWED  YEAR  ONES
```

140

```
TAPAS  RAFTER  COHERE
AROSE  ACUATE  ANORAK
CANST  PERMANENTWAVE
TRYOUTS  MALTS  ATES
TOPE  CAL  STEER
AMAN  ATONED  SADDLE
XII  ISEE  DISCS  REA
ENLACED  FRENCHTWIST
LISLE  SHOO  LIE  APTS
OSS  EXUDE  WAR
SOTO  AES  NOTA  RECAP
THEFLIPSIDE  CENSURE
AIR  ALIEN  ANNE  RIO
TOMATO  CHOSEN  PLAN
VERSA  ANI  UGLI
ALTO  TSARS  PIRANHA
NOWWEMUSTPART  ANGER
APIECE  AMELIA  STURM
TENDON  MODEMS  SEPOY
```

141

```
REDS  DIPL  SIRS  KIDD
EXIT  RARA  IVAN  AQUA
NICELYNICELYJOHNSON
ELEMI   OED      ROT
WED  TOUR  DRAWER  ERG
    HAPPILYEVERAFTER
ATTUNER  ASYET    IONA
THEBY   OOP    PUTNEY
MORO  MOTOR  ACAD
 UNFAITHFULLYYOURS
      ELSE  BETAS  SALE
BRAISE      VAN  MURAL
AHSO    CHIVE   IMARETS
JOHNNYCOMELATELY
ASE  EOLIAN  LENI  AST
   LOU      ASS  BELIE
FINANCIALLYTROUBLED
ARIZ  ACRE  NOOK  BOND
RELY  NEED  ENDS  STAY
```

142

```
SNOW  VERA  NOEL  SHUT
WINO  IVES  ORNO  LINA
AMERICATHEBEAUTIFUL
THATBE  SELL     ADIME
     HERO   LEI  STE
JUT  GODBLESSAMERICA
ONIT  YORE  TELE  SOON
STEEL  RAMA  ELLS  WRY
HOAXER  GANG  ALA  ANA
    THELANDOFHOPE
ARM  ALE  SOTO  FIXATE
SUI  RATS  RYES  DIVOT
ISME  PEAS  OHIO  TINT
THISISMYCOUNTRY  DYE
     TOE  SOU   EDAM
ASPEN    OCTO  ELIOTS
PHILADELPHIAFREEDOM
SILL  ETEE  PHIL  NERO
EPEE  WAND  SUNY  SANG
```

143

```
ADS  ARC  QUAFF  SALAD
BET  MAP  ENTER  ASONE
ALABAMA  DIRTYTRICKS
STILLS     TYE  WINKLE
HANOI  WHOS  MOS  OER
    EWE  AOK  FLEA  INST
HODS  MYNAMEISMUD
ENG  AONE  ORCA  NIGER
ALL  VOE  TURKS  BORNE
DIALED  MANIS  COMETS
UNSER  LILTS  VOL  ART
PESTS  IDEE  KILT  SEE
   HEATANDDUST  EYED
PACE  GUST  IDA  CDS
ASA  LIP   ONUS  REPEL
SCREEN  TOP   LENORE
TAMMYGRIMES  EYESORE
ALEUT  ALERT  POP  NOD
SENSE  STRAY  ANY  SRS
```

144

```
TAGS  HELP  ALIT  CREW
IDLE  ARIL  WIFE  LENO
BLACKTIEAFFAIR  ODOR
BASTE    SCOUR  MOUSSE
SIS  ASH  ALL  HINDU
    CACTI  CONE    SKY
RAY  WHITECOLLAR  PIE
ORE  HERS  PEEL  BENT
BELLAMY  FLEAS  JAN
SALUTE  SLANT  WONDER
   ORA  CHOPS  SINCERE
ASWE  CROW  ANNE  RIB
RAJ  GREENBERETS  SEA
FDA  RETS  ESKER
   CHIDE  SAP  RYE  CPA
BIKINI  STROP  SCRIP
EDEN  BLUESUEDESHOES
LETT  LUMP  SAID  ANTE
LASS  EGOS  ERGO  REYS
```

145

```
QUASH  BOATER  BORER
UNDUE  INSIDE  ALCOVE
ADMIX  TAKEITWITHYOU
DOI   BEN  BEAN  OAKS
   ROSE  NIL  LTS  LEE
CHEATANHONESTMAN
BARRE  AAHS  LEEBOARD
SIS  PAUL  FIR  LUNAR
    ISR  FLOG  TENURE
ASPS  HURRYLOVE  STEW
CHANCY  HEED  EAR
KOREA  DOT  ONLY  SHY
STRANDED  SILO  AIMEE
   KEEPAGOODMANDOWN
WEB  ALL  UPS  ISAT
ULAN  LOUD  FIT  HIM
RUNAWAYFROMIT  CREPE
STAIRS  OUTONA  HORSE
TELLY  SNOPES  INSET
```

146

AFT BRAC PIAF COSMO
DOI RUSH ACME HOTEL
ALG OGLE THELEOPARD
REEKS ELBE CLASSY
KYRA ESE THESE WAG
WPA PEA HEDY SINE
AROUSE ANTI AETNA
QUOTING PINKPANTHER
UND TARPON NIMES
ASSE BEET LOLA ATTA
NOLTE REBOZO HAW
LIONHEARTED TEMPERA
ALPES EDGE DEEJAY
USES FETA EVA NRA
DAR PIXEL RAG EGGS
ATONCE ESSE USUAL
INTHEKITTY INST ALI
SCOUT TEAR ODIA REM
LORDS ERNE NASH SAY

147

DAMAGE APSES VANDAL
ERASER GETAT ATEASE
MOTHERNATURE LEAVEN
INEE EVEN PLENTY
SHAVER SPAT JOT
HAI EWE KEEN AGONY
OLDMANRIVER DAVINCI
STEAD REPEL LATEEN
TOSS COATI OILS SAG
SCALDS MONETS
TAJ HIDE DUSTY EDEN
ORATOR SAUCE GRAVE
VICEROY JOHNQPUBLIC
ASKED ALAS URN ILK
HEF FLAX CLIENT
ROLLED SUET RIFF
SCOTIA YANKEEDOODLE
UPSHOT ONEOR APULIA
PATENT FIERY DETECT

148

CUP SPAT GORSE CLAW
APO PLIE ARULE RAVE
ROW RARE LABORCASES
ONEWAY MULLET OVENS
MARINAS PASS EMERGE
ORG ASIN IAM SEX
CLUE CLINTONSCAT
HAT BEAM RUTH ABAS
ODA OLD CHATS STRUT
PIGOUT WRENS CHEESE
INERT FAINT BOA ASA
NOSE ALLS FOND TIM
LEGALPAPERS WHEY
TWO NOW WANE SHE
RIBBON SPAR RIPOSTE
ANSEL FLARED GOSHEN
GOESAROUND UGLI ANE
INST IRENE POOL ROM
CASS BASED EGOS DRY

149

ANTIS FRESH BASTION
NEWTO OUNCE EXPENSE
CLIFFHANGER TEAPOTS
NEARLY NOAH INES
UPPERS OMENS BAD
REEL UNA TOUR TUB
ITA PCS DEVILSTOWER
ARK REAP GORDY FILE
HOSTEL GOGI AFTER
ISL AROCK ACE
SMITS ONEA THRUST
NORA CLAN NOTE PAR
UPONTHEROOF WAS PLO
BEN WIDE PEAL BELL
GOP ASHES DARRYL
HIVE ALAE TOOBAD
EVENING CLOUDCOVERS
RETINUE KINTE RECUT
ASSENTS SATES TSKED

150

JOBS SHARIF JAWBONE
AIRE PATINA ADHERES
BLOCKSLOCKS WOOLENS
OCA LAITHS AGEE
IMMORTAL EPA ASI
TAR AEF TRIBESTRIES
ORO TARSI NICHE ONE
LION REALM TOA UNIT
DAMON STEER MOPEDS
BOTHERSOTHERS
BOLERO SASHA BESOT
EMIL WAC STAGE TACO
ANA DACHA ERGOT BEA
TIMBERTIMER LAR LAS
AND CAR PENITENT
GYMS BONNIE ERS
REISSUE DEBARSDEARS
ATLEAST ASACAT KLEE
FIESTAS STREWN SEAM

151

```
PECOS   RAPT   WEED   MAT
INUSE   AGER   ARNO   ORE
ASTIR   GREATDICTATOR
    TRAP   ARCHIE    DOOR
CHOICES    STU   DHARMA
HUTS   REA   MEDIUM
UGH   OUTNUMBERED   CDS
BEERS   AINU   KIT   ALOE
   QUA   SLIDE   PENDANT
LOUNGE   SODAS   ROASTS
OPINERS   NIGER   MPS
RACY   ROD   EERO   ATSEA
ELK   POWERDRIVEN   TVS
    PERSIA    FEW   TRES
ARGOTS    JAG   RECOUNT
SHIN    ASABAT   SONG
HOLDINGTHEBAG   AGGER
END   ARIA   ALGA   SULFA
SEA   MANY   MESS   TEETH
```

152

```
PRUNES   RAMBO   STOGIE
AURORA   OLEAN   ERRORS
WISHINGWELLS   EAGLET
SNA   EDWARD   HERD   DDS
      WENT   JOE   ELM
BET   SIN   JERKS   OILS
ECHOIC   SHUTE   TORNUP
TRENCHCOATS   MAGNETO
HUNT   ANTE   HONE   SET
    ORANGE   JUDGES
HAD   ADOS   NAME   WAGS
EDITION   PANAMACANAL
RATING   MAVEN   NETTLE
ORCS   STUDY   ATE   SEW
    HAP   IRS   ABRI
HEM   OWED   STREET   SRI
EPOQUE   ORCHESTRAPIT
RESULT   CHAOS   AUBADE
BESOTS   HORST   MEANER
```

153

```
RASCALS    STEP   SABLE
AROUSES   SWIMS   AIRES
PAYMENT   CATBIRDSEAT
    SAD   MAMIE   OLLAS
RASH   STUMP   RESEED
ATTAR   ASP   ASTIR   FLA
FLOWERCHILD   UNSTRAP
TIP   BUOY   IRIDS   AUTO
    SETS   STORE   SLICK
IMPALA   TOTIE   SEETHE
DIALS   MOULT   PITS
ACRE   BOONE   ARGO   BTU
HARPERS   DRAGONFLIES
OHO   VIEWS   DAN   FALSE
   TREBLE   CARES   GETS
   AFORE   SHOPS   HAG
SPIDERPLANT   GALAHAD
RESET   TERNS   INARAGE
ASHOT   AYES   NEEDLES
```

154

```
BOLD   SORE   LADS   CRIB
AHOY   UNIT   ASIA   HOME
SAVE   NINE   PICKMEUPS
IRE   ERODED   TEE   TOE
CAMERON   INCA   GUEST
   ERGO   AVIATE   PRES
ACTI   FORGETMENOT
WRECK   POORAS   ALOHA
FAN   ALAINS   ACE   ENC
UND   RALLY   MALTA   LAO
LEE   ITS   SAFEST   PBS
   DRONE   SPIREA   EMMET
   HANDMEDOWNS   EELS
BRAN   TEETER   CHER
LETON   EWER   HEATHER
OCT   OOP   SILENT   OWE
COUNTMEIN   DOLT   SNIP
KINE   INTO   OGEE   EDNA
SLED   TSAR   LEND   CAGY
```

155

```
UMPS   SHIED   CROW   OAS
PILE   MANSE   REGO   URN
FLEAMARKET   IDLE   TRA
OLA   ARMY   RINSE   BRAC
ROBUST    LARGO   CRANK
    APT   STOCKEXCHANGE
MARS    CRATE    OINKED
ANGEL   IAN   DEMAND
HIATUS   MET   DIX   SLOW
AMI   COMPROMISED   ITA
NANA   DEL   RAF   DRAGON
    BADGES   LIP   SCHED
SPLICE    ALICE    ITSA
TRADINGPLACES    TNS
RAGED   IRATE   WIGWAM
ENOS   SNIDE   ALIT   ILO
ECO   PAGE   NEGOTIATOR
TEN   AGES   TROUT   ACHE
SRS   PERT   SANDY   AHAS
```

156

```
FAVOR ■ ABCS ■ LID ■ TILE
AGILE ■ CAHN ■ ONE ■ OZON
CALIFORNIA ■ DELAWARE
TREVINO ■ CRAZE ■ LEANS
■■ ITA ■ GAEL ■■ BERKE
EMMA ■■ PEG ■ AZTECS ■
LEI ■ FORNOW ■ OENO ■ ARC
MACKEREL ■ HORNES ■ REA
■ HAZE ■■ LIMBO ■ TOKEN
EVIL ■ LOUISIANA ■ DAFT
TIGER ■ UNAPT ■■ REIN ■
ATA ■ ATTIRE ■ DECLASSE
LAN ■ VETO ■ ROUGHS ■ AIM
■■ WINONA ■ ING ■■ TSPS
■ APRON ■ MILK ■ CPA ■■
AVAIL ■ KEBOB ■ CHINOOK
VIRGINIA ■ WASHINGTON
ESTH ■ ALS ■ ATTU ■ ELOPE
COST ■ PLY ■ SHAM ■ REESE
```

157

```
ABRI ■ POD ■ THEA ■ AFRO
LEAN ■ FILE ■ AILS ■ LEIS
BACKHANDCOMPLIMENTS
ANKLETS ■ ALPS ■■ APNEA
■■ EELS ■ UNI ■■ PICO ■■
MAT ■ POINTOFNORETURN
ONEIS ■ BUS ■ OOPS ■ PIE
ATEN ■ RIM ■■ ERTE ■ GEODE
BERLIOZ ■ ALAI ■ GUNNER
■ ITSALLMYFAULT ■
SHAKES ■ EVES ■ LAPROBE
HIVER ■ EVER ■ NOM ■ EFOR
ELI ■ OLEO ■ DAM ■ TESTA
LOVEISALLWEHAVE ■ EHS
■ MOON ■ UMA ■ ENGR ■
EBSEN ■ ASHE ■ ANDOVER
SUPREMECOURTJUSTICE
TRIG ■ OAHU ■ IRAE ■ ICON
SYNE ■ BUYS ■ TAX ■ TENT
```

158

```
BASES ■ LADD ■ BOTTLER
ETHNO ■ CAMEO ■ AUREATE
GOODLOOKING ■ STEEPED
■ OSAKA ■ SILT ■ LAM ■
EST ■ CITE ■ REREAD ■ ASK
MCPHEE ■ BOOGIEWOOGIE
MOORS ■ WED ■ SMN ■ NURSE
ENOS ■ PERIL ■ TYS ■ SEAL
TEL ■ IRA ■ SADA ■ HOTELS
■ COOKSTHEBOOKS ■
SCARUM ■ ESTA ■ VUS ■ BET
HORA ■ OCA ■ INLET ■ ALAR
ALGID ■ ALF ■ NAN ■ WROTE
MOOGOOGAIPAN ■ AIROUT
ERN ■ PRYNNE ■ EARN ■ DPS
■ APE ■ TENT ■ NADIR ■
ACHILLE ■ SCHOOLROOMS
LOUDEST ■ SIENA ■ OTOES
SOBERED ■ ELMS ■ WATTS
```

159

```
APT ■ TUTU ■ QUID ■ WHALE
CAR ■ EARP ■ ULAE ■ AUTOS
TREATWILLIAMS ■ XRAYS
UKASE ■ VAST ■ ICY ■ BOA
PATH ■ FIND ■ WIRE ■ ALLY
■ MYRIAD ■ MAVEN ■ TEAS
ABE ■ ELL ■ JIVE ■ TWO ■
PARCEL ■ LOSE ■ BEANPOT
ALOUD ■ BOLT ■ AIRY ■ ARA
CLUB ■ HATTRICKS ■ ATIT
HOG ■ EELS ■ ERIE ■ COROT
ETHICAL ■ MAID ■ TOKILL
■ ROD ■ WITS ■ GAR ■ CEE
MILK ■ STARS ■ DIKDIK ■
AMES ■ URGE ■ ZONE ■ TERI
OPT ■ APA ■ SUNG ■ IOWAN
RUSES ■ DOINGTHETRICK
IRONS ■ ECRU ■ BALE ■ NEE
SENSE ■ STAG ■ EMMA ■ GRR
```

160

```
LAHORE ■ RILLS ■ SWEAT
ELUDED ■ ADIEU ■ TANGO
TIRADE ■ FENDERBENDER
SAL ■ AND ■ ADA ■ HOPE ■
■ YIN ■ ELLA ■ CUBS ■ DIS
LOBOS ■ SOS ■ COMB ■ MATT
ACUT ■ MIA ■ NAMBYPAMBY
PARADIGM ■ UVEA ■ ANNEX
ILL ■ INN ■ GRID ■ ARE ■
SAYEST ■ TASTY ■ GOTFAR
■ AMY ■ IVEY ■ COL ■ UMA
OHARA ■ STER ■ TOREADOR
WILLYNILLY ■ RNA ■ IDLE
EDDY ■ AMES ■ RUT ■ DRYER
NEA ■ ADOS ■ BIER ■ OED ■
■ AGIO ■ OOP ■ ARR ■ USC
HUGGERMUGGER ■ AMADOU
UTURN ■ REUSE ■ MEDDLE
GETAT ■ NESTS ■ PREYED
```

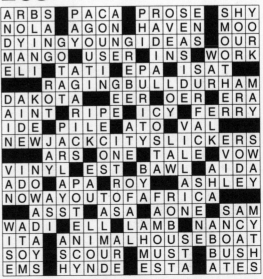

161

```
C P R   E N O L   I M P S   L I T H E
L A E   N O R A   N O L O   E T H E R
A L L E G H E N Y M O O N   S T E R N
S T I L L   L I E U   T E A S   H O I
P R E F I T     O F I T   R E F I N E
S Y S   S R A S   T R E   C R A M
    H I G H S I E R R A   T A G S
A T A N   P A R A   S I D E   L E A
R O L E O   R U L E R   P E A   A N N
M Y P A P A   G E N U S   S T A Y E D
A S I   A C H   M E N U S   S L A V E
D I N   L E E J   I L L S   A S A D
A N E W   T H E R O C K I E S
  S O R A   N I L   S P E C   A T T
M A K E I T   N O D S   M I L L I E
U R I   D E B I   L I M O   E B S E N
S E I Z E   O F K I L I M A N J A R O
I N N E R   R E I N   T A L C   C E N
C A G E S   E R N E   T R E E   E D S
```

162

```
B A D   M A I D   P O O H   I T S U P
E G O   A R G O   I N C A   R A I S E
T O M O R R O W W E C A N P O N D E R
A G E S   O R N A T E   D E N S E
    S A W   W H Y   T O R Y   L E W
C H A O S   T I O   R O U T   K I W I
R A G   H O W T O G E T T H I N N E R
U N I   H A H   A V E S   L E E R Y
M O N   D A S   D R U M   R I A
B I G S U R   T O N E S   H U D S O N
    T E E   H U E S   J I M   O W E
O R B I T   C E N T   I O N   F E E
F O R N O W L E T S E N J O Y   I N D
M O O T   R E N O   L A O   A M A S S
E M U   H E A D   L E S   A W E
  G R O A N   D E M E A N   A U R A
A T H A N K S G I V I N G D I N N E R
L E A V E   E A V E   S E R A   I A M
F A M E D   S T A R   E D E N   T R Y
```

163

```
P R O   G O B I   S C A T   M A C E S
E A R   I S A N   I A G O   T R U R O
T H E P A T H F I N D E R   V I T A L
    G E N E   U N G E R     O T T O
R O A S T   I S L E T   P A S S I O N
A I N T   A S I A   S E A L I O N
F L O O R S H O W S   N U L L   G O B
    I T O N   A M E S S   L A N A
N E W P O R T   G N O M E   C U R E D
O D E T T A   S A D L Y   C A N U T E
S I L A S   C H I D E   P A R A G O N
I T C H   A R E N A   P U R E
R H O   S L O E   B O A R D W A L K S
  M O T I O N S   U T E S   G A E L
B R E N D A N   A T T H E   D I N G Y
R O M A   S C O R E   C E N T
I D A H O   C A R P E T B A G G E R S
T E T O N   A G E S   I O T A   R I P
H O S T S   L A D Y   C O O S   N A Y
```

164

```
F A T A L E   S C H I S M   B L A S E
A S H L E Y   C R A D L E   R O V E S
T W E L V E   R O M E O & J U L I E T
    L I E     M A W   O B L A T E
J A M   E B B   G E L   E K E   N O R
O R A   S U L F U R   A L E C
A T & T   L O I S & C L A R K   D A M
D E L I   L A T H   L E N S   R A R E
  O N S E T   B A R D   R E P E L
C A U G H T   J O I N T   P A T H O S
E M I L Y   F O N T   D E M O N
R I S E   C L U E   M R E D   R I G A
O S E   P A U L & P A U L A   T S A R
  O K I E   O R M O N D   & G O
C A D   T E D   P R Y   S T E   C A N
A D O P T S   J E T     A S H
B O G I E & B A C A L L   E D I L E S
O R M E R   A D A G I O   A L L O U T
T E A R Y   G E N E V A   T Y L E R S
```

165

```
A R B S   P A C A   P R O S E   S H Y
N O L A   A G O N   H A V E N   M O O
D Y I N G Y O U N G I D E A S   O U R
M A N G O   U S E R   I N S   W O R K
E L I   T A T I   E P A   I S A T
    R A G I N G B U L L D U R H A M
D A K O T A   E E R   O E R   E R A
A I N T   R I P E   I C Y   F E R R Y
I D E   P I L E   A T O   V A L
N E W J A C K C I T Y S L I C K E R S
    A R S   O N E   T A L E   V O W
V I N Y L   E S T   B A W L   A I D A
A D O   A P A   R O Y   A S H L E Y
N O W A Y O U T O F A F R I C A
  A S S T   A S A   A O N E   S A M
W A D I   E L L   L A M B   N A N C Y
I T A   A N I M A L H O U S E B O A T
S O Y   S C O U R   M U S T   B U S H
E M S   H Y N D E   E S T A   A T E S
```

166

```
LAPP  FERRET  ASS  SIR
ABRI  ENABLE  THE  ENE
POINSETTIAS   OIL  TSP
ONCEA      STU  MANTUA
FEEBLE  ONTAPE  HOLLY
     OER  KAI  HAG  LETS
JERUSALEMCHERRIES
IBEG  TEM  ALLOTS
NOAHS  TORRID  VISITS
GNR  CAT  OAT  PES  MOP
SYMBOL  URSINE  AMATI
    EUGENE  OAR  IGET
CHRISTMASBLOSSOMS
ACRE  DOI  SUI  OTT
LOESS  PEAKED  FALDOS
ANDTHE  SRA  REEVE
UNI  IVY  INAPEARTREE
GIT  ROE  ACTIVE  OMNI
HES  KEN  SETTER  EAST
```

167

```
HORNET  SCARF  ENGAGE
ARABLE  ARIEL  TOUSLE
ISHALLSTARTANEWYEAR
LOS  LIEN  AGAR   ADO
   ODOR  KAI  SNAP
MOTIF  FLU  APOLLO
WITHAFIRMRESOLUTION
ATHOL  MOE  REV  SALVE
RTE  ELAINE  DES  STER
   BRIG  OTB  RUTH
ECHO  VIZ  HOTAIR  TAP
POEMS  NEA  SOL  AGILE
ILLBEPERFECTLYCLEAR
CAMERA  OFT  EKERS
   DANE  LEA  ESSE
PIA  ALAI  DALI   AGO
ANDNOCIRCUMLOCUTION
STARCH  ITSAT  ATONAL
TODATE  ASONE  NEATLY
```

168

```
OAKS  PIER  BATS  BASH
RANK  ALAI  ERAT  ACTA
THEINNERCIRCLE  TROY
   WRENS  HORACE  HIVE
METTLE  DENY  RHODES
ETHEL  SISI  ALIAS
RUED  ONATANGENT  GAR
VIA  IDOL  AGOG  BEBE
   NOHOW  GAMES  DATED
BEGGAR  BRIER  BURSTS
IDLED  SLEDS  GECKO
KNEE  SHOE  BOLT  USC
HAS  SQUAREDEAL  PTAH
   HAUNT  NEAT  QUOTA
PAPAYA  ADAR  SURFER
ARAL  BRACED  SPILL
LOUT  BESIDETHEPOINT
ESSE  LAID  NOON  INEE
DEER  ERAS  DEPT  NEWT
```

169

```
WARBLER  AGOOD  SMALL
AVERAGE  RICHE  POLIO
DOSINGS  TRANSPARENT
SNIDE  TAIL  OIL  AXES
  SESS  ISO   OWL
LETS  PILAF  SOYA  ALE
ETE  MAVEN  EPA  VALID
FUR  ACEY  SMOTHERING
TISSUES  RAMOSE  DENY
   AIM  AIKEN  RIO
SCUM  EAGLET  ENTRUST
CARBUNCLES  CRAB  NOR
ORGAN  TED  THINE  DUE
WEE  COST  CREED  SALE
   UHF  HIE  OAHU
AMEN  FRO  AGRA  GUNGA
JETTISONING  CHATTER
AMAIN  LUNGE  RIVIERA
ROSES  ESKER  EMENDER
```

170

```
PALOMAR  RANGE  CAJUN
EMIRATE  AVOID  OSAGE
DIGITAL  DAYFORNIGHT
   HOT  SPINET  OCA
TITLES  OATS  AGENDUM
OTHE  MAST  SLUR  ERE
WOE  BITTERSWEET  AGO
AVA  ELMS  APEX  KNEW
REVERIE  ANIL  STE
DRYDEN  ANGEL  TOPICA
   GAG  RIOS  SALINAS
COPY  MEMO  IATE  SST
HAL  OPENANDSHUT  AIR
ATE  FALA  ILLE  ANNA
WHATNOT  GAVE  STODGY
   HEL  DEVOTO  ORO
HOMEVISITOR  RAPTURE
ERASE  ANTIC  CREATOR
WADER  MOORE  ARRESTS
```

171

COLD	ARCH	PROF	HARM

```
COLD  ARCH  PROF  HARM
ORAN  VEER  AONE  ODEA
CANADIANSUNSET    AJAX
OLD  RAPT  LAY  LAX
    SNITE  ATM  OOP  MRS
RECOVER  GRANDCANYON
ABASES  BRA  EEK  ERMA
POPES  ORE  PAR  TRAPP
ILEX  ADESTE  OED
DIS  OVERTHEHILL  BBB
    MIA  AEROBE  GLEE
PERIL  MEL  GUN  ROUSE
ARES  CAL  CYR  DOTEON
LOSTHORIZON  SEXISTS
EST  EVE  OAT  PLANK
    EWE  ART  RAIN  YMA
QUIZ  REDRIVERVALLEY
USSR  URSA  ANTE  SANE
OSHA  PROS  LEAR  TWOS
```

172

```
CLEAN  DANUBE  DOCKS
HENRI  IRONER  URBANE
INSECURITIES  NAILON
    TEST  TRE  DWELLS
REVERE  GREY  DEN  OLE
ERI  SOLID  BOREUP
MACAO  ROC  AES  ANTIC
    JUNKBONDS  BRUISE
CAPSTONE  OZONE  MOSS
UDO  STE  ATE  OAF  NUT
ODOR  EYERS  STRESSES
MOLARS  STOCKEDUP
ONETO  OPS  AIR  DYLAN
    DEARLY  DRESS  IRE
ATF  SEA  TEES  ASPECT
FRUITS  AHA  ALTO
LINNET  CURRENTASSET
ENDERS  ALMOST  LEAVE
ASSES  DEEDEE  EDGED
```

173

```
GAFF  UNDER  SAGS  JIM
LULL  NOOSE  TENT  ETA
ARAYOFHOPE  IRAE  EER
DAS  HAIRY  GLOWWORMS
    HABIT  BIT  SEX
DEBTOR  SCENES  DITCH
ALARY  RARE  DUB  DORY
RICE  EBO  POWERED
TAKES  MICA  SPRY  EWE
    TWINKLETOES
SIS  ORNE  SKYS  EMMAS
NOTEPAD  EME  ROBE
ATAD  PEG  GRID  AMOLE
PARIS  REVISE  CLONED
    THE  RIG  MAIMS
ONTHEBEAM  SHARE  HAP
TEE  LOLL  BEACONHILL
TAX  LAUD  ATHOL  UNTO
ORT  STLO  THANE  MEOW
```

174

```
STA  REBEL  BOARD  MOD
TAD  EDINA  ENNUI  ICE
AMONTHOFSUNDAYS  DEN
BARRIS  CREES  MENAT
ALEAN  BRANT  MARINE
TED  USUAL  ONALOG
  NEWYEARSDAY  SHEL
USA  AMS  ACETAL  TVA
ANIMATE  SMOTE  ACHIP
MIXERS  THANS  HURONS
ASTRE  IRADE  LADOUCE
TOY  SEDAKA  IAN  ARE
INMY  SECONDSIGHT
  IMPOSE  RINSE  PHS
LANAIS  PROSE  APLOT
ABUSE  ALLOW  STREGA
MET  REMAINSOFTHEDAY
ALE  REEVE  EDILE  GNU
RES  ERNES  SAXON  ESP
```

175

```
MICAH  MITER  CRUMBS
OCALA  AWARE  REPEATS
CATSPAJAMAS  INSTALL
KNAT  ROSA  TOBAT  BOY
  MOLAR  REAL  TAMA
CRANE  SANTABARBARA
LAR  GAGA  DENY  TABOR
OVAL  MAXI  DRS  SALT
GENERAL  REL  DIP  ALS
  WIZ  ACE  MOE
HUB  GEL  QUE  KILLJOY
ITAL  DEA  JOEL  FADE
PALOS  ILSA  AYES  COW
SHARPASATACK  ADAMS
  KNEE  REAR  COWER
NFL  CRAMP  ICON  RAMA
COASTAL  PANAMACANAL
ORVIETO  EAGLE  DIDNT
  MACREE  SHEET  SLAYS
```

176

A	N	G	S	T	S		B	E	A	S	T		S	L	A	C	K	S
T	E	R	E	S	A		O	M	N	I	A		R	E	C	O	I	L
W	R	E	C	K	I	N	G	B	A	L	L		A	N	T	O	N	Y
A	V	E	R	S		I	S	R		L	E	D		I	S	L		
R	E	N	E		H	A	D	A		Y	S	E	R		U	R	G	E
			T	A	U		O	C	T			P	A	U	P	E	R	S
P	U	P		B	R	E	W	E	R	S	H	O	P	S		C	A	T
E	M	U		E	L	A	N		I	O	U	S		E	L	E	V	E
D	A	B	B	L	E	R		L	U	N	G	E	S		A	P	E	S
		L	E	E	R		N	A	M	E	S		O	A	S	T		
C	A	I	N		S	T	A	M	P	S		P	U	T	T	I	N	G
A	R	C	E	D		O	P	A	H		P	I	P	S		O	U	I
R	I	A		S	Q	U	A	R	E	D	A	N	C	E		N	I	L
L	E	F	T	O	U	T			D	E	L		O	A	T			
A	L	F	A		E	E	K	S		T	M	A	N		O	H	O	S
		A	R	T		D	N	A		O	T	C		S	H	I	F	T
A	S	I	G	H	T		I	N	J	U	R	E	D	P	A	R	T	Y
C	A	R	E	E	R		S	T	A	R	E		R	E	V	E	A	L
T	O	S	T	A	Y		H	A	W	S	E		S	T	E	R	N	E

177

T	Y	P	E		S	T	A	I	R		F	A	R		I	S	M	Y
E	P	I	C		C	I	N	D	Y		U	T	E		M	O	R	E
A	R	C	H	R	I	V	A	L	S		S	O	U	R	P	U	S	S
M	E	T	O	O		O	S	E		Y	I	P	P	I	E			
O	S	S		T	E	L		C	O	O			T	R	I	A	L	
			S	O	L	I	D	F	O	U	N	D	A	T	I	O	N	S
C	A	N	A	R	D		O	L	D		S	A	W		L	U	N	T
O	B	E	Y	S		S	T	A			B	A	D			S	O	S
R	O	S	S		S	H	I	V	E	R	S		R	I	A			
P	U	T	S	T	H	E	M	O	N	A	P	E	D	E	S	T	A	L
			O	R	A		E	R	A	S	E	R	S		S	A	L	E
R	O	W		A	K	A				H	N	D		R	U	N	I	N
A	L	E	C		E	G	O		S	E	C		P	A	C	K	E	T
P	I	L	L	A	R	O	F	S	T	R	E	N	G	T	H			
T	O	T	A	L			F	L	Y			E	A	T		N	I	B
			P	A	R	L	E	Y		J	O	B		A	L	O	N	E
K	N	I	T	W	E	A	R		C	O	L	U	M	N	I	S	T	S
D	O	D	O		A	V	E		A	V	I	L	A		F	I	R	E
S	W	A	N		L	A	D		P	E	N	A	L		T	R	O	T

178

W	A	D	I		B	O	A		P	A	W	N			G	B	S	
A	I	R	S		R	U	S	H		O	L	I	O		Q	U	A	T
T	R	E	A	S	U	R	E	I	S	L	A	N	D		U	R	S	A
T	O	N	Y	A	S		A	N	T	E		D	E	L	I	G	H	T
L	U	C		C	H	E		D	U	N	K			P	E	L	E	E
E	T	H	I	C		B	O	U	N	T	Y	H	U	N	T	E	R	S
			N	O	M	A	N			A	R	O	N					
E	M	M	A		E	N	O	L	A		A	N	T	S		A	B	T
R	E	E	L	I	N		F	O	R	A		O	I	L		R	O	E
W	E	A	L	T	H	O	F	I	N	F	O	R	M	A	T	I	O	N
I	S	T		T	A	N		S	E	R	F		E	G	R	E	S	S
N	E	Y		O	D	E	S		L	O	Y	A	L		O	S	T	E
			E	N	O	L		O	N	Y	O	U						
R	I	C	H	A	N	D	F	A	M	O	U	S		U	T	T	E	R
A	S	H	O	W		A	M	E	R		A	C	T		A	S	E	
B	R	A	N	S	O	N		O	N	A	N		O	T	I	O	S	E
B	A	R	E		F	O	R	T	U	N	E	C	O	O	K	I	E	S
L	E	T	S		O	M	I	T		T	E	A	K		E	S	N	E
E	L	S			R	E	B	A		D	Y	S			A	M	E	S

179

M	A	D	E	I	R	A		J	A	C	K	S		C	A	B	L	E
S	P	O	N	G	E	S		A	B	O	N	E		A	L	L	O	T
S	T	U	D	E	N	T		M	A	D	E	A	S	P	L	A	S	H
		B	E	T	E			F	E	W		A	S	A	B	E	E	
H	U	L	A		S	P	O	U	T	S		F	I	T		S	S	R
E	V	E	R	S		R	A	P			S	A	L	A	D			
L	E	D		H	A	I	R	S	P	R	A	Y		N	E	W	T	S
P	A	R		O	D	D	S		A	I	M	E	R		S	A	R	I
		I	R	A	D	E		I	T	S	A		E	D	I	S	O	N
A	B	E	L	L		E	S	T	E	S		P	U	S	H	Y		
O	N	B	A	S	E		A	N	E	S		P	A	R	T	I		
W	I	L	D		D	E	T	E	R		P	L	I	E		N	A	P
S	L	E	E	P		D	O	W	N	P	O	U	R	S		G	N	U
			R	O	B	I	N			R	U	M		S	I	T	O	N
G	I	S		W	O	E		Q	U	O	T	E	S		D	O	N	T
A	M	U	S	E	D		S	U	N				P	E	E	N		
S	P	I	L	L	E	D	M	I	L	K		M	A	L	A	I	S	E
P	E	T	A	L		R	E	T	I	A		A	C	E	T	A	T	E
S	L	E	W	S		T	E	S	T	Y		R	E	V	E	N	U	E

180

R	O	T		O	H	N	O		A	Q	U	A		W	A	R	E	S
A	V	E		P	O	O	R		L	U	N	G		O	C	A	L	A
D	E	A	L	E	R	S	C	H	O	I	C	E		K	E	V	I	N
I	N	C	E	N	S	E		O	U	T		P	E	R	I			
O	S	H	A		T	E	A	R	S		M	O	E		B	O	Z	O
			E	D	S		U	N	A		C	A	U	S	E		L	E	W
O	S	R	I	C		M	E	C	H	A	N	I	C	S	L	I	E	N
B	O	S	N	I	A		S	E	E	R	S			I	T	E		
I	M	P		E	X	I	T		N	E	E	D		R	E	D	D	Y
E	M	E		N	E	W		P	R	Y		E	T	A		R	U	E
S	E	T	A	T		O	S	A	Y		H	O	R	N		I	R	A
			R	I	O		T	R	I	B	E		A	G	A	V	E	S
C	H	E	F	S	S	P	E	C	I	A	L	S		E	B	E	R	T
P	A	L		T	O	O	T	H		M	O	O		D	O	R		
A	J	A	R		L	I	S		T	A	T	U	M		A	S	T	A
		P	A	V	E		A	O	K		P	O	U	R	S	O	N	
B	A	S	I	E		D	O	C	T	O	R	S	O	R	D	E	R	S
O	B	E	S	E		A	U	R	A		B	U	N	G		A	S	E
W	A	D	E	R		B	R	E	L		I	P	S	E		T	O	R

181

```
CROWES STAMPS PESTS
HONORE PURDUE OLLIE
IBERIA ONETRACKMIND
DOWN SIRES INRE VEE
ETA BOAT ITSY BEAR
YOUNG LAMA PARRS
METIN ONEFINEDAY
ORINGS IVAN PERSONA
TACK PAGER RINK NOL
TSK ORDER COCOA EMS
LEE PIER JOUST SHOT
ESTHETE SIDE ELTORO
ONEMANBAND LOREN
APRES WOES OLDAS
FLED SCAB AMAS ETC
LAC DUAL NOBOY ITOR
ONETRICKPONY UNDONE
ATSEA HOUSES PEEWIT
TESTY ENTERS STANCE
```

182

```
PSST MAX BASSO ONES
IOTA ILE ETHAN FETA
ENOL DIN HOUSEOFWAX
CANCUN ODE THANKS
ERE BIO ISMS SEMIS
TOUGH ATHOME YALE
CHEN HALLSOFIVY NOW
HEMS TROT FLEET
ALPHA ABOLT ENLISTS
SOLONG SNOOP SPRAIN
ETERNAL EXULT SANTA
EAMON CEES NDAK
COD SUGARSHACK ACNE
HEEL TOREUP HYENA
IDLED RAGA SLD SRS
MARINO ANN ASHTON
IVORYTOWER AIR ILSA
FERN CLETE INK DEER
AXES HIRED LAS ESSE
```

183

```
CHAIR PLIED CRAVAT
SAYNO BRASSY OBLATE
THEHOLLOWMEN NIACIN
EMAILS ASK APT
ODER SSE APSO AWN
RESENTS SCATS PITAS
LEONA PARRY TELLME
EMPTYNESTER PURLOIN
SASH SOLAR ITES
RSVP PTAS TOTE ESSE
HOAR LEWIS OREO
ENCASES MISSINGLINK
TAUNTS WORSE RAREE
TRUCE JANET CREWMAN
MER ARES MAE RAPT
PCT AMP MIRAGE
LAUREN ABSENTMINDED
UNBEND TREADS SCUBA
STEADY HOTLY TENOR
```

184

```
RAMOSE QUEASY MICRO
ARCHER UNTRUE OREAD
GRINDSTOAHALT SOAVE
OATH ORK SENSES
SHOWN RHOS JULIE
LOU STEEP AMES COZY
OUT WASTESAWAY POE
ORO FEDS PARENT ENA
PIFFLES SIBYL TARES
CUED MESAS ARNA
BRONX PIVOT PRINTER
ROM ELATED LAMA IRE
ELM DEGENERATE ONA
WEIR GARS BRETT NIT
SUDAN LIAR ATSEA
MUSSEL ROO NASA
ANITA RUNOUTOFSPACE
ATOLL ODETTA REESES
MONET WESSEX OLDIES
```

185

```
BEST ITEM SPED SHAW
ELLE MESA ARCA LOLA
AKIN PETROLEUMJELLY
MODULATE NAS ODEON
ERICH FEDERAL STE
INFEST ALA NOLL
LEAST PHOTOCOPY FIB
KOS SOME PET GLADE
TACKLE RES VOICED
NELLIE ION PEORIA
PONIES PRY SANDRA
IGETA GOO HURT LBS
NOR NYLONTAPE TITUS
SOUL INS VANISH
ATM OUTSOLD CENTS
UHURU IVE LARGESSE
GELATINDESSERT NUIT
UGLY NEER INRE SENT
ROSE NEST STYX ESSE
```

186

```
T O R M E ■ M A I N E ■ ■ S A D I S M
A S I A N ■ A R G A L I ■ T R I S H A
C H A T T A N O O G A C H O O C H O O
T A L C ■ S C O T ■ ■ E E R I E ■ ■ ■
■ ■ ■ H A S H ■ O S T I A L ■ L O W
C H E E C H A N D C H O N G ■ J A V A
L A N D R Y ■ E O S I N ■ E L U D E D
U N D U E ■ P W R ■ P G A ■ A N D R E
C O U P ■ O L E I C ■ ■ B A S K ■ ■
K I P ■ C H U R C H B E N C H ■ C A P
■ ■ Z O O M ■ E R L E S ■ L I S A ■
S P E E D ■ P E A ■ A E R ■ L O G O S
C A D R E S ■ P R I S M ■ S A V A N T
A R G O ■ C H I M C H I M C H E R E E
R E Y ■ D O O L E Y ■ ■ O A R S ■ ■
■ ■ B U R R O ■ N A T L ■ O D I A ■
C H A N G I N G T H E C H A N N E L S
R E M A I N ■ S O O T H E ■ O G L E S
T Y P I N G ■ M I S E R ■ A S I D E
```

187

```
T O T A L ■ C O H I T ■ F R E S H E N
O N I C E ■ O R O N O ■ O U T W O R E
W A S H I N G T O N □ ■ R E C A L L S
■ ■ ■ E G O I S T S ■ L T D ■ I L E S
O W L ■ H O T ■ ■ B A D ■ A N Y ■ ■
A H A B ■ N A S ■ G O D O W N ■ W C S
T Y P E A ■ T H E R E ■ D R Y ■ O O P
■ ■ □ S H O O T E R ■ G I A C O M O
A F T ■ P U R D U E ■ S E T ■ I D E O
B E H E S T ■ D I N G O ■ T H E □ O F
B A R N ■ T O Y ■ C R I M E A ■ S N S
E R E C T O R ■ F A I R A N D □ ■ ■
Y N E ■ A N A ■ A R M E D ■ A U D I T
S O □ ■ I S L A N D ■ E E R ■ P U M A
■ ■ M A L ■ D R S ■ ■ M I D ■ O P T
R E E D ■ A I M ■ ■ S A V E S U P ■
I N A M E S S ■ I N B E R K E L E Y □
P O L I T I C ■ T I B E R ■ L A B E L
E L S T O N S ■ S T A R Y ■ S T O N Y
```

188

```
B O S N I A ■ O B T E S T ■ T H A I S
A S T E R N ■ T R A L E E ■ H I L D A
W H O W A S T H A T M A S K E D M A N
L A W ■ A R E N A ■ S T A D E ■ ■ ■
■ ■ K I T E ■ ■ M A I ■ N O O S E S
■ T H E D E V I L I N D I S G U I S E
T H A N E ■ I L E ■ D E N ■ ■ T A T E
W A R N E D ■ I O N ■ S U R A ■ M A D
A N T E ■ A D O N I S ■ R I F F ■ ■
S K E L E T O N I N T H E C L O S E T
■ ■ S T E M ■ D E R I D E ■ R O L E
W A G ■ A D I M ■ S A T ■ R E S U L T
A G E S ■ N E A ■ T U B ■ M A C E S
T U R N E D I N T O A P U M P K I N ■
T A M A L E ■ H O P ■ R U S E ■ ■ ■
■ ■ P I E T A ■ O A S I S ■ A T T
G H O S T R I D E R S I N T H E S K Y
I S S U E ■ N E S T O R ■ E A S T O N
S T E P S ■ A N T O N S ■ R E P O S E
```

189

```
P U P I L ■ S T E L L A ■ C A N C E L
A G E N A ■ A R N E S S ■ I S O L D E
C H I C K E N E D O U T ■ N E V A D A
■ ■ H E F ■ V A N ■ S A C ■ A M A D
A P E ■ O P I N E D ■ C H A S M ■ ■
B A D G E R I N G ■ R I T E S ■ I A M
R A G E D ■ P O E T I C ■ S P O N G E
I R E N I C ■ R I V E R ■ S I G N S
■ A T R I A ■ R E B A ■ D U E S ■ ■
C I D ■ H O R S E A R O U N D ■ P L Y
O N U S ■ I H A D ■ X S O U T ■ ■
M A C H O ■ D O T E D ■ A M O E B A
I N K E R S ■ R E S O L E ■ B A L E R
C E E ■ L O N E R ■ P A R R O T I N G
■ D E E R E ■ S H A B B Y ■ E D O ■
A D D S ■ R Y E ■ A M O ■ N A G ■ ■
B O O T I E ■ S Q U I R R E L A W A Y
A S W E L L ■ T U N N E L ■ O Z O N E
G E N R E S ■ H A T E R S ■ P A W N S
```

190

```
N E G A T E ■ A R M O R ■ V E S S E L
A M E L I A ■ S U A V E ■ I N C O D E
G O O B E R ■ I N D I A N A J O N E S
■ ■ R E I N S ■ I N D O ■ O W E N S
F A G I N ■ T H O S E ■ M A I L ■ ■
A T I T ■ B R A V O ■ W A R N ■ V I M
I S A ■ J O E M O N T A N A ■ I O O
N E O ■ A N E S ■ E V I L ■ D R N O
T A K E N U P ■ F A X E S ■ S E G E R
■ ■ E R I S ■ P I C A S ■ F O C I ■
O N E I S ■ A R L E N ■ M A R I N E S
R I F E ■ A L O T ■ A A R E ■ I L L
E L F ■ W A S H I N G T O N ■ A D E
L E E ■ B A B Y ■ S E I Z E ■ S M E E
■ S O Y A ■ H O W T O ■ A P A R T ■
O S C A R ■ M E A L ■ ■ H I R E D ■
F L O R I D A E V A N S ■ S E E S A W
F A L A N A ■ L O T U S ■ U N D E R A
S P O N G Y ■ S C E N T ■ P A Y N E S
```

191

```
COME  NAPE  HEFT  AGEE
AMES  EMIT  ATEE  COAX
FEASTWITHUSANDSHARE
ENTERS SISAL  SHELLS
    NAYS  CIT  SHAD
 ALII  LOAN  BEAR  SPA
JOYANDALLGOODWISHES
ANON  ONE  SIGN  MOSE
YEN  ART  ELATE  QUOTA
   WRY  QUAKE  JUG
CREAK  SUTRA  CAM  FOG
PEAS  SHEA  POP  SABU
ANDAFTERWEHAVEEATEN
SOS  ORLY  DAZE  XRAY
   UNAS  RIB  TWIG
TRENDY  GOTIT  ATASTE
HELPUSWASHTHEDISHES
ALLIE  ERI  UELE  SOAP
RYANS  BYE  ENDS  OWLY
```

192

```
SOPHS  ALEAN  BOSSA
ATREE  DIABLO  PICKUP
THERETURNOFTHENAIVE
EOS  PROF  AYAS  TAX
  SISI  AIM  ONTOP
WOUK  OURMUTUALFIEND
HIRES  PEASE  ENLACE
ESE  AWL  END  OLDAS
WED  BAAL  STEEP  OSAS
   TURNOFTHECREW
ECTO  EDGES  DOOR  SAW
LAHTI  SYR  RAG  UTE
SLEETS  ASYOU  OWNER
AFAREWELLTOAMS  ANNE
  SMITE  YUK  EASY
OTB  TCBS  LSTS  SAT
THEITCHESOFEASTWICK
HURRAH  ATPLAY  RODEO
EDGAR  USEOF  ONERS
```

193

```
LAD  SOBS  RAPT  CANOE
UMA  AURA  ECRU  ALOSS
CANADIANBACON  BASIC
ANITA  ZEAL  MESS  ARA
NASD  PERT  FIRE  BLIP
  HELEN  SWISSCHEESE
SUPPER  IRE  TOT
ERATO  SPUN  RATED
RASH  GLANDS  UPS  UGO
INT  AMERICANPIE  RON
AIR  SAD  THREAT  OKIE
LAYUP  IDES  ANISE
   RIC  PAM  CHESTS
FRENCHFRIES  BRASH
LENS  ELAL  ALLY  ETAS
ONT  AWAY  AREA  PLACE
REINS  BELGIANWAFFLE
AGREE  BREA  SCOW  FUN
LEEZA  YSER  THEN  YEA
```

194

```
BATE  ETAL  WICK  RITA
USAC  LACE  HOLE  ENES
STLO  THROWAWAYLINES
YAK  1000  IRAN  ENATE
ARIADNE  ELF  STATES
SENSES  SAL  ETTU  ERS
  GYM  SCRAPHEAPS
MATE  JOAN  RENT  IAMB
ORR  JOLT  LOUD  ANWAR
DEADEYE  SEW  ENDGAME
UNSET  NANA  ARIZ  SIN
SAHL  IONA  APEX  STET
   INDISPOSED  QUE
ADS  AIDA  GIG  FURORE
METHOD  ALF  GRIFFON
IBEAM  IDLE  SAID  TUG
DOWNINTHEDUMPS  ZITI
ONES  ABOU  GEEK  AMEN
LEDA  NEWT  HEDY  PERE
```

195

```
RAT  FLOW  PLATO  IPSO
ABE  IOWA  LEMUR  MOOD
DEXTRALS  ADOBEABODE
ALAI  SPRIG  SLUR
RESTON  IDEST  MESSY
  TIPOFFS  ARES  ITO
SPA  STALETALES  DDAY
TAXI  ERA  OKAYS  REGO
OPENS  OKAPI  SABO
PASTEL  EDITS  YAWNER
  UTAS  ACALL  ASIDO
LIMN  UPONA  OOP  EGGS
IDEE  REGALLAGER  HEY
POD  LATE  UNSPENT
SLICE  SELLS  EXETER
  ERIE  OATES  WHEE
WIVESVIEWS  DEARSIRS
ALAS  INLET  DEMO  NIA
DOLT  LAIRS  YNEZ  GET
```

196

```
OCTAVE  ARARAT  HAWSE
MARGOT  MOTILE  USHER
BLUECHRISTMAS   TWINS
  LENA  EDS   MTS  ETTE
   CLUB  IAGO   KALE
WHEY  NEA   PAD  ISLAND
RIV  SILVERBELLS   SYR
ALEPOT  ELIS  ELECTRA
PORES  IDOL  WES  AHOY
  GOO   MON   JAR  HUE
BARN  IAN   DENY  ESSAY
OBEYING  BOAT  GLENDA
OBE  THEREDNOSED   OUR
SANTEE  UNG   NON  GWEN
  TEAR   STEW   REMO
FARM  EOS   ATE   ODIO
INEPT  FIVEGOLDRINGS
FIELD  FAIRER  REVIEW
ESSES   SNEERS  SLATES
```

197

```
MARS   STL   MOBY   GAS
ALOU  ACHES  ANOA  RUT
JOYINTHENEWYEAR   ARE
ONA  OREY   EIDER  SNAP
REL  NIL   STRAY   COD
   IFALLTHEYEARWERE
FORMAL  ORES  MINUET
ADOPT  BRA   REM   RAH
RAMA  CLENCH  ENES
   PLAYINGHOLIDAYS
   AMPS  EDWINS  NOEL
BOB  AHS   EVA   LOIRE
AVIATE  ROLE  BEDLAM
TOSPORTWOULDBEAS
   CAL  HALTS  LAN  SAP
BOUT  VEXER  PAST  TRI
ALI  TEDIOUSASTOWORK
NIT  ANON  NEWTS  ALOE
KOS  RIGG   ASS   YEWS
```

198

```
PSAT  PRAM  JONI   AQUA
ALGA  LULU  AVON  RUMP
NELL  ASIF  NEON  EAST
TWELFTHAFTERNOON
OSTIA   LOTS   NABOB
   ETO  MER  HAST  ABA
MIDAFTERNOONCOWBOY
MEG  LARA   LEAR  RYES
VALLI  ONTHE   ETE
BLUESINTHEAFTERNOON
   ATM   INNER  ASTRO
OURS  ARNE  AUDI  TAG
THEEDGEOFAFTERNOON
ION  OOPS  CUS   YIP
SHELF   TERR   NICHE
   AFTERNOONINGALES
ASIN  ARUN  RARE  TENT
RITZ  MIMI  ENOW  ERNE
FLEA  PASS  SANS  SKYS
```

199

```
JAG  EWAS  RARE  LACES
ORR  NORS  EGIS  UBOAT
GOESTOTHEDOGS  PIQUE
SOBERLY  DRUG   RITA
 MELEE  FIAT  CON  USA
DANCESWITHWOLVES
GODOT  ATON  WIS  AIMS
IDEM  STAN  ZIP  ANNIE
LEN  TOO   PAS   PIA
LAYDOWNWITHTHELIONS
   IBN  IVAN  IRS  REE
GRAVY  ITAS  GNU  MARX
IONE  DOC   BID  GIDDY
RUNSWITHTHEBULLS
LEE  ORA   HARE  EUROS
 XOUT  BEDE  FACADES
ALIGN  PLAYTHEPONIES
DINED  GARO  ATES  UTE
EDGES  ATTU  GERE  MOS
```

200

```
HURLED  FRANCE  AGHAS
ONEISA  RESEAT  PEALE
HOMESWEETHOME  ANNEX
   DANNER   ESS  EDGY
NEV  YET  YSER  PARI
ERIE  DIP  CRO  AMANDA
AMOLE  REMAINS  ETHOS
TALKTHETALK  ANNEALS
   SUA  END  PRO  SNEE
RAF  IVORY  DEATH  DST
ABAT  ERS   JOE   COT
MACHINE  WALKTHEWALK
USERS  SHANTER  DIVAN
SETONS  ECU  DUB  TIDE
   OTTO  MOSS  AIM  DEW
LOFT  NIL   TENSES
IFALL  TIMEAFTERTIME
EMCEE  INABIT  CRATER
NEEDS  SENORS  TYRONE
```

201

```
TAFT   CALLA   TAGS   SAW
ABOO   ALIAS   EBRO   AVA
TURNEDBACK   ASIS   FEN
ASKED   IRE   APOD   RANT
REE   UFO   SAVOR   FORGE
   DOCENT   POTBELLIED
SETTER   AMEN   SAUL
KNOTS   IVE   STASH
ITNO   TREED   KITE   TEM
DOG   SHORTHANDED   RAE
SMU   PENN   STAIR   LARA
   BELOW   EVE   RAITT
   OOHS   JANE   WEIGHS
FLATFOOTED   SWATCH
LOCUS   REEVE   ASU   TVA
ONUS   STAR   TEL   REFER
REM   BOOS   THELONGARM
ALE   BLUE   AARON   ACNE
LYN   COTS   SNOWS   DEED
```

202

```
QUOTED   FOAL   ATEASE
UNABLE   ALLAH   LORAIN
ITSASMALLSMALLWORLD
POT   INKA   BROWNS
   APSE   GEESE   EFTS
LITTLEWOMEN   STY   AIM
ANITAS   FOOT   ETUDE
REMIT   AFT   PAWNEE
EPIC   TREES   CAIRO
STD   SHORTSHORTS   MTS
   SPINS   HEMET   BOIL
SEQUIN   LEA   GOTTA
HAUNT   SPED   HOMELY
ASI   EMS   TINYBUBBLES
WEDS   ALERT   ERIE
   AURORA   STAR   LAW
ITSYBITSYTEENYWEENY
LOOSEN   TEARS   URANUS
EEYORE   DRAT   PYRITE
```

203

```
BETTES   LATER   BACON
OTOOLE   FIGARO   ICARE
MARJORIEMORNINGSTAR
BLOOP   CEBU   LAN   ADD
   YEARS   TIE   VAMP
ASK   SRI   MINNIEMOUSE
QUIZ   GENA   NIX   ENLAI
UPTON   DART   DIG   ATTN
ASSOON   STOA   OUT   SEE
   MARILYNMONROE
LUC   HAD   RIAL   UNCORK
OSHA   SIT   CZAR   ERNIE
ADAPT   OWL   OVAL   UCLA
MARSHAMASON   NIN   EEN
   TOIL   SUB   ASTIR
AWE   NIB   EBRO   METER
MARYMARGARETMCBRIDE
EDEMA   AARONS   PLUNGE
SEDAN   SPENT   SENSED
```

204

```
BABEL   MAHRES   PHASES
ITALO   AVOIDS   REPTIE
GLASSSLIPPER   ELAINE
   AES   EEN   SPELLED
AHA   SHAEF   IMPANEL
NISEI   BTU   CURIA   LAH
GROWTOOOLD   RED   SILO
LANE   FUN   ERIE   JIFFY
EME   ITT   CLUE   OUTEAT
   HAWAIIISLANDS
LUGANO   LASH   LEE   IQS
IPASS   CLOT   FLO   AGUA
MOTH   TRI   STIFFFINES
ANT   SHINS   ADO   ALIAS
   TOTEMIC   BORER   SKY
PLACATE   ALL   ETC
SALAMI   FREEEXCHANGE
ANKLED   LAMARE   EVANS
TISANE   ABSURD   REBUS
```

205

```
CHEST   BASS   JAM   STUB
AORTA   ABOW   AMI   AINU
GROUNDRULE   VANILLIN
ESOP   EAT   LOA   ICAL
DESIGN   ALP   AVIDEST
   DETAIL   IAMAN   DEA
GEL   MUDSLINGING   TAN
IVES   ROM   NILES   CHUG
LEFTIES   FOES   CUE
ANTICS   SCENT   TOSSUP
   INE   BIRR   FOXHOLE
SONG   DOGIN   MOM   YINS
PUT   DOWNTOEARTH   LAO
ACH   OWLET   BATHES
THEGUNS   ELO   UNITED
   DABS   URI   AIM   NOVA
EXULTING   SANDBAGGED
VISE   DEL   ZINA   BLAND
ESTS   ELY   TRES   TESTY
```

206

```
MAP  PTA  LITHE  MERIT
AMI  OWN  AGAIN  ARENA
DICTION   PETPROJECTS
ANKA  OAST  PARA  KIT
TOUCHTYPE  VEGA  TOME
  POURER  WORE  JONES
JET  MUD  PAT  DOUG
UNRIPE  COVET  PROPEL
STUNS  COME  HUEY  IMA
TICK  CLAPBOARD  SNOB
IRK  PLUS  APIN  HECTO
NESTLE  TONIS  BATHER
  HOOD  DDE  CRI  HRS
SETUP  ERIS  MAITAI
AVID  AMAN  APPOINTED
DEP  ERIQ  ASHE  ETRE
INTHECLUTCH  CONSENT
SEOUL  LEONE  ONE  RIO
TREES  ELVES  DAW  SEX
```

207

```
HAJJI  SIT  DOLL  NAVY
EQUUS  INK  EPEE  ALEE
RUNNINGCOMMENTARIES
SAGE  ANA  EEN  SIR
  SNIP  MAR    DOWSE
ARK  BLOWININTHEWIND
BAHIA  SIS  TORI  SMEE
ODAS  STEPS  BUTT  PEN
MAKEIT  SAYS  SCOT
BRINGOUTINTOTHEOPEN
  DEPP  DOES  ESTATE
COY  TOSS  DRAMS  ACHE
OVAL  NEER  IKE  BLEED
DELEGATEATLARGE  DRY
ARENA   RUE  COGS
  IFS  ZIP  OHO  ELSE
FREEFLOATINGANXIETY
EARN  ARNA  URN  ENSUE
WHET  BEEN  BET  DEEDS
```

208

```
PAROL  PARADE  FESTER
ANIMA  ARAMIS  LATHES
PICABOSTREET  ORIENT
ATHROB  SIR  BENCH
SAE  REE  NICHE  SKITS
  ERMA  CAULK  YGUN
PAR  ROADWARRIOR  HBO
ABUT  NIDI  TELE  WEB
DOERS  LENYA  SALSA
SOMUCH  REARM  SEEYOU
  CERES  STEAM  TAMES
PAC  UNCH  CRAG  LANE
OIL  BROADWAYJOE  NOD
ERAS  INDIA  SOFA
TENTH  CARVE  RRR  MAR
  AROSE  EDO  ELAINE
ATHOME  KIRSTIEALLEY
AWAKEN  INLETS  PULSE
HONEST  TAYLOR  SMITS
```

209

```
JADED  COILED  HASTEN
ALIVE  ASTONE  ASPIRE
RECAP  MEANDMYSHADOW
SEE  RAE  GOON  REST
  DEGREED  SEIZE
ECHOCHAMBER  ZOO  CUB
THALIA  BONUS  UNDONE
TELLA  MEN  MTS  EERIE
AWE  TOAD  PERIL  ANTS
  BESIDEONESELF
APSO  SNIPE  ASSE  UGO
CRISP  ENS  SKY  NAVAL
RANCID  GOSEE  ATTEND
EYE  CAR  MIRRORIMAGE
  GAMUT  CASUALS
OSSO  DESK  TBS  SPA
TWOFACESHAVEI  OUTER
TOLEDO  TENPIN  UNITE
OBERON  ADDING  PARES
```

210

```
STA  CAGE  BLOB  QUIT
TRAP  OVEN  AERO  UNTO
RARE  XING  BAABAABAA
AGORA  DIALED  FLOSS
WINING  EGO  ASTI  WIT
  NONOS  EMS  ERG  STY
ABED  OOHSANDAAHS
CIV  IDLE  OOM  TETRA
CLIFFS  SPARTAN  THEN
ELLISON  APT  NASTASE
SILL  NOBLEST  SOONER
SEEMS  NET  KISS  KEV
  YUMAARIZONA  HYDE
PRE  BUM  YMA  JULIO
REX  USES  PCS  SALUTE
ETHER   WISHED  RAMOS
SAARBASIN  APIG  RAMS
SILO  TUFT  RILE  YABA
ENES  ONTO  YALE  MAY
```

211

```
LILA   PSST   DITKA    TRA
AMAS   UTAH   ESKER    HEM
UPWHEREWEBELONG     EGO
REM LEE OLDAS    APRIL
ADEAL  PARIS    ELOISE
SENSES FEN  ASKING
    INTHEMIDDLE   SHOO
SAM   UAW   RAISA   TUN
CRYBABY  SLURP   NOTTE
ORBITS  STARK   RIFIFI
RIATA  SPICY   TELAMON
EBB  TITAN   OOP   ERA
DAYS  CENTERSTAGE
   LOWERS  GUT  DISCUS
THEROD  AGNES   MOUNT
REFER  SATAN  IAM  POI
EAT  DONTBRINGMEDOWN
ADM  ENOLA  NEMO  ALEG
DYE  DEBIT  GOAS  WADS
```

212

```
LISTS   ORANT   TANNER
ENTRE  ANOMIE  OTIOSE
AGUYWEVEMETNAMEDMAX
PANS  TETES   LAMIA
   TRURO   WAIT   TEE
DOESHISOWNINCOMETAX
EFT OSE HORDE   CREST
ATHOS  NAVY   SMART
THIN PAOLI  EVIL
HECOULDGETANADVISER
   NODS  ITONE  LAVA
TACIT   CASS   LEMAT
CACHE BRUTE  BSA  ODE
WHOISQUITEABITWISER
MAL  URGE   ELAND
  YOHOS  AEROS  EASE
BUTNOTTHISMAXHEACTS
ONETOA  AGOUTI  STEEP
BESOTS  MORSE   TESTY
```

213

```
SAPOR  DELLAS  BAREST
ABOUT  EQUATE  AGORAS
WARRENBURGER  GRUNGE
ASK  ARIES   PAGAN
   BAGMAN   DENY  DEMI
AMALIE  EATAND  SEDAN
MIRANDA  RIBTICKLING
MARIA  PALLS   HIATUS
AMEN  KAREL  STONY
NIL  PARIS  MARIS  KAN
   HERTZ  TAKER  CERO
OTIOSE  TOTEA  MAVIS
MUTTONCHOPS  THERISE
ENIDS  LAYSUP  ATONED
NANO  BUNS   APLOMB
   GREED  FACIE   ASI
DANGER  FLANKERBACKS
ONEEAR  EARNER  ABOIL
STARRY  DREADS  DANTE
```

214

```
CHANT   BASTE   BRITON
LABOR   OMAHA   VERDURE
ULTRAVIOLET  ENSILES
   EVILS   MERE   OILS
BALSAM   MANE   JUMP
AMATI  PAIN  LEON  BEG
AMY  LILYLIVERED  UMA
LOSS  BAR  EASY  SLIT
   MAIN  TERSE  AMBLE
CUPIDS  GORSE  ARISES
AMOLE  JUDGE   EXIT
RIPE  COMA  BYE  SAMP
PAP  DAISYWHEELS  CEO
SKY  OKEH  OATS  TSARS
   SAGE  OPRY   LITTLE
TIER  WEAK   AWARE
AVERAGE  COMPASSROSE
RADOMES  KUBEK  UNDID
ANSWER   STADE  PEEPS
```

215

```
CRAWLS   ABLE   RAINED
ATREAT  ALIEN  ENTREE
PEASOUPSIDEDOWNCAKE
SILT   OFT   IRISH
   BASSO  LEVAR   MIL
WESTERNOMELETTUCE
SPANKY   EYES   RULES
HANDS  PAR   SNIPERS
IND  NAIVE  SIENA
VEALPARMESANDWICHES
   EAVES  TRIES   ALE
AWINNER   ITS   ISSUE
RADII   OFME   BACALL
FRENCHFRIESCARGOT
SEA  ELDER   ALOOF
   PAREE  ASU   FIDS
STRAWBERRYJAMBALAYA
TAIPEI  LAMAS  ATAMAN
ARCADE  YEAR   ROWANS
```

216

217

218

219

220

221

B	A	S	S		A	M	I	S		B	E	R	G		A	B	A	S
O	T	T	O		N	O	T	A		I	D	O	L		J	A	N	E
W	O	O	D	S	T	O	C	K		L	I	V	E		S	Y	N	E
S	M	O	O	T	H		H	E	L	L	B	E	N	T		O	A	K
		D	I	R	E	L	Y		A	I	L	S		O	O	F		
A	L	F		E	R	A		M	I	N	E		D	U	F	F	Y	S
T	O	O	F	A	S	T		O	R	G		B	E	C	A	U	S	E
M	A	R	E	K		E	M	U		S	I	E	N	A		N	E	W
		A	S	S		U	S	A		L	A	I	N		D	R	E	
S	P	O	T		M	O	N	E	Y	M	O	R	E		E	Y	E	R
E	A	U		B	I	R	D		E	O	S		S	P	A			
N	U	T		A	T	T	I	C		I	T	S		A	S	S	A	Y
S	L	E	U	T	H	S		O	K	S		U	T	R	E	C	H	T
E	A	R	T	H	Y		O	M	I	T		C	I	V		O	S	S
		B	E	E		E	S	M	E		T	H	R	E	A	T		
Q	U	A		R	E	L	I	E	V	E	R		A	N	G	L	I	A
U	R	N	S		C	A	R	R		B	O	N	D	U	R	A	N	T
A	S	K	S		O	T	I	C		O	P	I	E		E	N	C	E
D	A	S	H		L	E	S	E		N	E	T	S		E	D	A	M

222

H	A	T		J	O	L	T		F	A	L	L			M	A	S
U	P	A		E	P	E	E		E	L	I	E		P	I	N	T
S	P	I	N	E	T	I	N	G	L	I	N	G		B	I	N	G	O
T	E	N	O	R	S		A	L	V	A		D	A	N	D	E	R
L	A	T	H		B	E	L	I	E		F	R	I	A	B	L	E
E	L	S		L	A	U	R	E	N		R	I	A	L	T	O	
		H	A	I	R	R	A	I	S	I	N	G		A	G	R	I
C	H	O	R	D	S		I	T	I	S	A		G	E	T		
C	H	E	N		E	T	C		O	N	U	S		M	A	L	T	A
H	E	A	D	E	D		L	A	N	K	A		S	O	C	I	A	L
R	E	R	A	N		W	I	S	E		L	O	P		I	N	K	Y
I	S	T		S	C	A	M	S			G	R	A	N	G	E	
S	E	R	F		R	I	B	T	I	C	K	L	I	N	G		
		E	A	S	E	L	S		M	O	I	E	T	Y		S	T	G
P	O	N	C	H	O	S		S	P	A	N	S		A	Q	U	A
R	A	D	I	A	N		S	P	E	C		S	P	R	U	N	G
I	S	I	N	G		M	O	U	T	H	W	A	T	E	R	I	N	G
S	I	N	G		U	R	D	U		E	P	I	C		N	E	L
M	S	G			M	E	S	S		B	A	R	K		T	Y	E

223

L	A	U	R	A		S	C	A	B	S		P	A	D	D	E	D
E	L	V	E	R		T	A	X	I	S		O	L	E	A	T	E
S	E	E	S	T	H	E	L	I	G	H	T		L	I	N	D	E	N
S	E	A	T		I	W	I	S	H		U	N	I	T	Y		
		O	W	N	S		E	A	T	A	T		S	O	U		
D	O	R	R	I	T		H	E	A	R	T	H	E	B	E	L	L	S
A	L	I	E	N		T	O	L	D	M	E		A	R	I	D	E
F	I	N		G	O	R	M	E		G	L	I	N	T	E	D	
T	O	G	A		V	O	I	C	E		G	R	A	Z	E	S	
		S	M	E	L	L	T	H	E	R	O	S	E	S		
	F	L	A	T	L	Y		S	L	O	T	S		T	A	L	L
F	A	L	A	N	A	S		L	U	T	E	S		D	E	I
E	V	A	N	S		L	O	V	E	S	O		A	G	A	V	E
T	A	S	T	E	T	H	E	W	I	N	E		A	R	A	M	I	S
E	L	K		E	D	G	E	S		M	U	I	R			
		Q	U	A	S	I		T	A	C	I	T		D	I	S	H
S	E	T	U	P	S		T	O	U	C	H	S	O	M	E	O	N	E
A	V	I	A	T	E		F	L	E	E	T		A	N	W	A	R
C	A	N	D	O	R		T	A	S	T	Y		O	S	A	G	E

224

L	A	S	T	S		H	A	I	F	A		A	S	F	O	R
A	L	L	O	W	S		A	I	D	A	N		I	B	E	R	I	A
P	L	Y	M	O	U	T	H	R	O	C	K		M	O	T	E	L	S
		E	B	R	O		S	A	L	Z	A		H	E	E	P	
R	U	B		S	E	R	U	M		D	E	E	R	E		C	R	Y
O	P	A	H		E	R	A	S	E		S	E	R	I	O		
W	A	T	E	R	M	U	S	I	C		A	T	T	I	T	U	D	E
	L	E	A	P		M	O	T	I	F		A	S	N	E	R	
D	A	M	P	E	R		W	A	D	U	P		A	T	N	O	
E	R	I		L	E	I	G	H		B	E	L	I	E		R	I	D
G	O	N	E		S	N	A	I	L		P	L	A	Y	M	E	
A	M	U	L	E		S	P	E	E	D		S	A	I	L	
S	A	T	U	R	A	T	E		S	I	M	P	L	E	F	O	L	K
	E	L	I	D	E		L	E	M	M	A		A	W	A	Y	
S	O	W		K	H	A	K	I		S	E	R	V	E		E	N	D
A	R	A	B		E	D	I	N	A		T	A	S	K		
M	I	L	L	E	R		N	E	O	C	L	A	S	S	I	C	A	L
O	B	T	U	S	E		D	A	N	A	E		T	A	T	A	M	I
S	I	Z	E	S		S	L	E	P	T		Y	E	T	I	S

225

B	U	T	S		R	A	G	E	S		E	C	H	O		J	I	G
A	L	O	T		A	M	I	T	Y		L	A	I	C		O	D	E
S	U	P	E	R	V	I	S	O	R		L	I	K	E		A	L	L
		B	R	I	E	S	T		F	I	N	E	L	I	N	E	S
B	R	A		C	N	S		S	O	L	O		R	O	D		
L	O	N	D	O	N		S	T	O	A	T		S	T	A	N	C	E
A	G	A	R		A	T	T	E	M	P	T	S		H	O	U	R
S	U	N	U	P		H	R	E			A	D	S	O	R	B	S
T	E	A		I	D	E	A	L	S		A	L	O	U		M	A	T
			P	E	R	F	E	C	T	F	O	R	M				
B	E	D		A	L	O	E		L	A	R	O	S	A		G	A	S
I	D	Y	L	L	I	C		L	A	N		C	A	R	G	O	
A	G	E	E		K	I	S	S	K	I	S	S		R	E	A	R
S	Y	S	T	E	M		S	P	E	E	D		L	O	C	A	T	E
		E	V	A		N	E	E	D		D	E	S		T	E	N
P	R	I	M	E	R	A	T	E			R	U	N	O	F	F	
A	I	R		N	I	B	S		G	R	A	N	D	S	L	A	M	S
N	B	A		U	N	C	H		N	O	N	C	E		O	L	I	O
E	S	Q		P	O	S	E		U	T	T	E	R		E	L	L	S

226

```
L S D S ■ P A Z ■ L A M B ■ S A F E S
I O W A ■ U N I ■ A L O E ■ C R A N E
E L E V A T I N G T O O L ■ H A S T E
■ ■ L E S T ■ C R E O N ■ T E T H E R
E E L ■ P Y M ■ A L F ■ H A M ■ I R S
S T E M ■ E N V Y ■ H E R E T O ■ ■
T H R O W A W A Y ■ B O L ■ R A N C H
■ ■ R A L L Y ■ S I N E ■ S P A R E
E M P I R E ■ W I N O N A ■ A B E L
L I L ■ S C H O O L G R A D E ■ L E O
G L A D ■ S U N D A E ■ A T B E S T
A N I O N ■ D I E S ■ S E P A L ■ ■
R E N T A ■ S O N ■ L I T T L E C U T
■ S E R M O N ■ P E R C ■ W A G E
S H P ■ R A N ■ W E T ■ H A J ■ L O X
T O O H O T ■ P I Q U E ■ B U Z Z ■
A S K E W ■ I L L U S T R A T I O N S
S T E A L ■ L I M O ■ O A T ■ O N U S
H A N D Y ■ L E A D ■ N Y E ■ N E T S
```

227

```
G A R I S H ■ O S A K A ■ N E A T E R
E L I S H A ■ A C R I D ■ A S C A L E
L A G O O N ■ T H E L E F T S T U F F
S S H ■ W A D ■ O I L ■ L I E S ■
■ T R E ■ E B O N ■ D I O N ■ D A M
A M O U R ■ M A N ■ S I G N ■ A R N E
C A V E ■ B O N E F I S H ■ A V A N T
T H E D I E T ■ R I G H T Y G O M E Z
O R R ■ T H I S ■ T H E ■ U R N ■
R E S ■ C A C T I ■ T R O P E ■ A D M
■ S O L ■ E N S ■ S U P E ■ L E A
B I L L O F L E F T S ■ R I D D L E R
U S U A L ■ A P O S T A T E ■ A L M A
S L I M ■ E V E R ■ E G O ■ I D E S T
H E S ■ A M I D ■ S P E W ■ N E F ■
■ E R I S ■ E C O ■ N A G ■ T I O
T H E R I G H T B A N K ■ L E A N O N
A I R I E R ■ A R N I E ■ I S D O N E
R E G A L E ■ D O T T Y ■ S T O W E D
```

228

```
G L U M ■ L O D G E ■ O X E N ■ A C C
R E N E ■ A I R E D ■ L A V A ■ B A R
U N T A N G L I N G ■ E N I D ■ S U E
N O O N E ■ V E E S ■ A L A M O S A
T R U ■ G A Z E S ■ A I D ■ E R A S
S E C ■ A X E L ■ U N S U I T A B L E
■ H A T E D ■ I N T O ■ D A N ■
S P A D E ■ A M M O ■ L E T T U C E
C A B S ■ A T S E A ■ S E A T ■ N O D
A L L ■ U N W I T T I N G L Y ■ V P I
L E E ■ S O O N ■ C R A S S ■ M A S T
P O S S U M S ■ W H I P ■ S O N E S
■ T R I ■ S H E S ■ L E C O Q ■
U N R E P E N T E D ■ P I T A ■ U S S
S E E M ■ U S A ■ D R E A M ■ I T A
A B A S H E D ■ T R U E ■ P O S E D
G U S ■ U R G E ■ U N F I N I S H E D
E L O ■ L I E N ■ S C E N E ■ S E L E
S A N ■ A N D S ■ H E R K Y ■ O D E R
```

229

```
B A B S ■ W A L K ■ W A D E ■ A Q U A
O P A H ■ O L I N ■ A T A D ■ F U S S
W I N A P R I Z E ■ L I V E S T O C K
E N D L E S S ■ S I L L Y ■ E E R
■ C L O T ■ A S C O T ■ S T R U C K
■ M O O N ■ U S E U P ■ A H S ■ M A E
R A N T ■ S N I T ■ M B A ■ I S M Y
E T C ■ R I D S ■ P R E A M P S ■
C U E ■ I R E ■ B O O S T ■ O R C A S
A R R ■ F E R R I S W H E E L ■ O F A
P E T A L ■ W A N E S ■ M A L ■ T I N
■ D E F E N D S ■ C E R O ■ T E D
B A S E ■ I N K ■ R U N S ■ R O L Y
I M Y ■ E A T ■ C H E S T ■ B E N D
D Y N A S T ■ C O U P S ■ R O T C
■ A I M ■ L L A M A ■ H O O R A Y S
A P P L E P I E S ■ S H O W R I N G S
M U S E ■ H E A T ■ T I R E ■ A D U E
O B E Y ■ I N N S ■ S E A L ■ L Y N S
```

230

```
M O L D ■ F O R A ■ G R U F F ■ G B S
I T E A ■ L A I C ■ A S P E R ■ E E E
S T A T E O F T H E S T A T E ■ L A R
S E V E N ■ T E X T ■ A G N A T E
A R E ■ O L D ■ D A R E D ■ O A T E N
■ S P L E E N ■ M I N E I S M I N E
R I L L ■ I C E R ■ C O N N I E ■
A D E E M ■ O W E D ■ S I S ■ S C A B
S E A B A G ■ E P I C ■ R O B ■ A R A
C A V ■ R O L L O N A R O L L ■ S I T
A T E ■ C L U ■ S A D E ■ E A S T O F
L E S T ■ D A I ■ H I N D ■ B A S S O
■ U P E N D S ■ Z E R O ■ S T E R
D O W N O N D O W N ■ W A B A S H ■
A R I E S ■ A L O E S ■ M I D ■ E V E
M I N D T O ■ O A T S ■ I N C A S
A S K ■ M E A N S T O T H E M E A N S
T O A ■ E N N U I ■ M A I L ■ E S N E
O N T ■ N O O N E ■ P R E Y ■ S T A N
```

231

```
JAB  CIAO TAPS SACS
ERR  AVID OMOO ABLE
ARES DIRECTORSCHAIR
NEWT DEY  HARP ALTER
STEROID MEL OLD ENA
   RAMS MAC PIE ISTS
MISTY TINKERSDAM
ANYA WAX ERIE VAPOR
STE WIM PROD DEMOTE
SUA IDEAL SEVER TIP
INSOLE BARE ART TOE
FETID ABIE CNN MESA
  SEAMANSEYE MOREL
ATME DPS PAD DADS
DEI NOH AIR FREEWAY
ELSIE OAST ARY SHOE
PLUMBERSHELPER TERM
TISA TAKE ASTO ETE
STEN ASSN POST LAN
```

232

```
CAPPED ABRA SHAPES
OPIATE AREAS COVERT
SIGNAL BUFFALOWINGS
AGE HOSNI IRED
 OSRIC TREVI BUY
SANTE HORSEFEATHERS
ESTEE OFA ITS RANGE
RHONDA SIFTS BUTTER
VEE SPLINE RAKE
ENDS HENSTEETH DOGS
 UPIN OWLETS LAP
BOOMED AERIE STUDIO
ATTAR OLD NVA OCCUR
CHICKENFINGER ILOST
HOC MEATY MACAW
 AMBI MYCAR HAT
THEBEESKNEES BEWARE
ISWEAR AETNA URANIA
STEELS NESS SANDAL
```

233

```
AMI RANG TECH SSRS
MERL ALOU OAHU NEAT
NAVE CARMENSANDIEGO
ORIOLES SATYR IDIOM
TANNER AHSO EVENUP
 GEE FLOE OONA GTS
ROB JULIELONDON
ODEA NET BIAS AMPS
MERMAID LIENS SMART
ASLANT POSSE DEBTOR
ISING ALGAE RETITLE
CANS BNAI SIN THEE
 JUDYCHICAGO EST
CDS ELIA ONUS NEW
RECALL PUNT SCAPES
AMALL SOUSA PEERAGE
MOREYAMSTERDAM TRAP
ITER SULU DELI HINT
NEST STOP SEES SSS
```

234

```
HEAROF THOLE PHASES
ARMADA HEMEN REPAVE
TRAGICHEROES OMELET
 STEREO ULU ANA
CAM TUNAS CRADLED
OMAR ARI SUED UNDUE
MAYOCLINICS AVIATE
IRANI RAPPER DYAN
CANARD FIN IBIS SHY
 SCOURS PUBLIC
CPO EURO MUS SNORES
OOHS BEMOAN EVADE
ROBERT FLYINGWEDGE
ALAMO ABAT NOR SIAM
 LINEMEN ATTAR ORS
HMO MIL SPEEDO
OENONE UNKINDESTCUT
LIEDER GUILD RIALTO
ANYDAY ANTES SEGUED
```

235

```
POPPED CHASE OBERON
ENRAGE ROCKY NOLINE
GEORGEMICHAELBOLTON
 ASPOT TRIO ARE
ABUD LISA MATT
JANETJACKSONBROWNE
OSU EER IAGO DRAINS
BEMINE RNA SCOT
 SERAC REESES ELY
 ETTAJAMESTAYLOR
ERN STAMIN SPEAR
BURT XER ONEWAY
BLOUSE STAR AFT ALE
 ELTONJOHNSEBASTIAN
 UNDO ATTY ITIS
STK UNAS USAGE
KEITHRICHARDSTARKEY
ENTREE HORAE AGOOSE
ONHAND YEATS DADOES
```

236

```
ALIMB  DEEPEN  THEROD
SONAR  APLATE  EUNICE
HUNTERWAITERANDACHE
ETO  VON  ISON  MOOD
    VAIL  ION  SOME
QUARTERSBANDANDLINE
TATTY  III  OATES  BOB
SEE  MCS  TIRES  EERS
   OPAH  PEST  ADAME
LIGHTWEARRESTANDMAN
ADAMS  GEMS  AWAY
ILLS  ARILS  INN  TIA
REE  ADANA  ANY  OREST
DRAGGINGWORKANDBALL
   RENO  CAY  ODIC
ANDI  URGE  ALL  APA
FAULTSTOOLANDLOCKER
AMELIA  DRONED  TREAT
RELENT  SETTOS  SISSY
```

237

```
ETHOS  VISOR  OWL  WAN
SHANT  INTRO  FEE  EGO
PEYTONPLACE  MATTERS
  MOPE  ANA  MEL  OKAY
TRAP  RAND  MARTHA
HUR  FIND  BARCHESTER
ANKARAN  TALKY  ATRIA
NEEDY  ARRAS  TRYING
ASTA  SOBIG  TAT  MEA
   YOKNAPATAWPHA
PAC  LIE  IONIA  TSPS
ASLEEP  TINES  HOHUM
DIANA  ERRED  CAMPARI
STMARYMEAD  SUMO  NET
  BYEBYE  OKRA  AGES
AXIL  MAS  SCI  HERR
FOREVER  EMERALDCITY
AUK  ENG  FEATS  GELEE
RTS  TIO  TENSE  EDAMS
```

238

```
AQUA  NIDI  RIB  TAIL
DUNS  ASIS  EATA  ORDO
DOGINTHEMANGER  TILT
UTE  EHEU  STEM  FAZES
PAR  GAL  SIT  ALL
   BULLINACHINASHOP
ITWASI  NAME  SOX  UNI
ORAN  ESSO  STAR  MEG
LIVES  PIMA  ORAL
AMY  APIGINAPOKE  JAR
   MINH  YAMS  AMOLE
RAW  RATS  ROES  ELAN
AIR  SAC  COOS  TSETSE
FLYINTHEOINTMENT
   CUE  ATL  ANA  ARA
CELEB  ISEE  SICK  WAN
ARAB  ABIRDINTHEHAND
TACO  MELS  TORE  URGE
STYX  STY  OWES  BEES
```

239

```
SAW  LEDGE  PHIL  HADA
AXE  ATALL  ROSE  OBIE
LIS  CHRISTOPHERWREN
VOLT  NIB  OBE  ROTATE
EMERSON  TWIST  LOVEA
  YIPS  TRET  USE  EDS
ESPY  SHERYLCROW
ANNE  ALIA  OKS  EFTS
SCI  PRINCESS  MARIN
TOPSTEP  LAP  CARNAGE
IDEAS  TERRIERS  SEA
REST  RNA  ANDA  DIRK
   ETHANHAWKE  PIES
IRA  WOG  ALLY  TEAR
NERIA  SAILS  CHANCEL
ACACIA  CRO  FOR  ERGO
ROBINGOODFELLOW  ARA
MAIL  EBRO  LEONE  NET
STAY  DINS  FARED  ETH
```

240

```
UHS  BAA  CAR  GAFFE
NOA  OURS  NAPE  AREEL
OFCHOCOLATES  REEVE
ITEASY  NOI  XED  ALEC
NITRO  TITLE  TIC  IRT
GEO  MIA  SRI  GRIN
   SPAN  ANN  ORG
OUT  ASI  VOICE  ES
SPELL  ORAN  ENC  DEMI
EAR  POSTOFFICE  DID
AURA  HAI  RAGE  ELITE
SLEDDOGS  ASH  WREN
  BAY  EAT  JEST
EYES  NUT  BOB  DSO
AWL  SOY  TRULY  POILU
MILA  BAS  ISA  COSSET
ALIBI  HITBACKTOTHE
SLOAN  OGRE  KARL  EVE
SAND  ONUS  ES  RED
```

241

```
A I R S   J A D E   U T I C A   B U D
B L A H   U S E R   N O R A S   E V A
B E N E A T H C O N T E M P T   S E W
E X T R A   O D O R   A R A B I A N
    R A I L   E M U S   I R E D
B A B Y   C O W   T E E   E L E C T
A C E   B E F O R E H A N D   A T L I
E T H E L   T R A Y S   D I M   H E E
Z A I R E   E V E   B O N E H E A D
    N I A   J O E B L O W   S U P
A N D E R S O N   R O N   S L O T H
R O T   Y O N   R O A D S   E L I H U
O T H E   B E L O W D E C K S   N E E
W E E P S   S O U   D U E   S T A Y
    T I T O   G N A T   M A M A
C H I C A N E   D R I P   E L E M I
R O M   B E T W E E N T H E L I N E S
A P E   A T T A R   T A O S   V O L E
W E S   T O U R S   S H E S   A L O E
```

242

```
L A C E S   D E L P H I   A B J E C T
O N I C E   E L A T E R   M O O R E R
O N T U R K E Y D A Y A S I D I N E I
K E Y   V I P S   D E N T O N
    C O D   A M A   I A N   K I M
M A Y A S S E S S M Y A T T I T U D E
A S E A   D O S E   L E E   E D I T
S T A N   F I X E   A D S   E X U D E
O R S   J O T   O W E   I D A
N O T T O W H I M P E R A N D S I G H
    B A L   N A S   S K Y   S R A
J A P A N   T L C   S I C S   A L I T
A G A R   E R E   A U T O   L I L T
B U T S O M E T I M E S T O A P P L Y
S E E   D A M   N O D   U G O
    T E N O R S   A P S E   D I E
A M E A S U R E O F G R A T I T U D E
C O A R S E   P L A I N S   S W E L L
C A U S A L   S E T S A T   M O S E S
```

243

```
B A H   O F F   R U S T S   S U R E R
O N O   A R E   E M A I L   P L E B E
A N D I R O N   G A L L I M A U F R Y
S I G N S   C H I   A T T I C   I O S
T E E N   S E A S I D E   S E E N
    P E S O   I T S   D I D   L I E D
C H O R T L E   E M U   V A N E S S A
H A D   A T W A R   P A S T I C H E S
E I G H T I E S   J O N   E X T
F R E E   S P R I N G S   O M A R
    L O B   E B B   L I C O R I C E
P O T P O U R R I   C E L L S   S H E
U N I F O R M   S P A   L A T C H E D
G E N U   Y S L   E R G   R E A M
    C L A Y   I S A G A M E   B A S K
A P T   N O I S E   O P E   C O S T A
S L U M G U L L I O N   L E A T H E R
P U R E E   S E N S E   O R G   E V E
S M E A R   A S E A T   N A Y   S E N
```

244

```
E L S E   G R E G   A T O M   B A R E
G O I N   R I M A   L I V E   U F O S
G O L D W A T E R   B E E R G L A S S
    K E E P E R   P U R R   A G R E E
R E W A S H   G R I M   R I V E
I T O R   H E E L   A I D E   S P A
L O O S E L Y   C O R N P L A S T E R
E N D   L I E N   T A N E Y   Q U A Y
    P I A N O   S T E   U R S A
P I T H   R A F S   E X A M   A M E N
I D E A   A I M   E L A N D
T A N S   P A U L A   D O L E   A L E
C H E E S E C L O T H   F L A C C I D
H O T   T O R T   H A R T   H I D E
    R E N O   M I M I   T I E D O N
E L S I E   P L U S   C L E V E R
S A N D P A P E R   S T O N E S O U P
P L I E   D E S K   C U B S   E C R U
Y A P S   A R T Y   I S E E   S K I N
```

245

```
V E N A L   H A S A T   F U S S E R S
A B U S E   I G O T A   E N T E B B E
T O S S A N D T U R N   A C E R B I C
    A D A   S L I G H T   R E A
H U M I D O R   S A L A   T E N N I S
I V Y   O M I T   E S T A   E D G E
T E M   G I V E A N D T A K E   F U N
S A Y A   E L L E   O R E L   L A S
    P R O   L A W N   O S E   O N E
J O B B E R S   I L O   T I M E W A S
U R U   H A H   N A H A   N I X
D I M   A T E M   N O R M   T O O L
G O P   B O B A N D W E A V E   O P E
E L A N   R A R E   S T E M   Z U G
S E N O R S   C U R D   A G E L E S S
    D O E   S O T H I S   A N A
C O R D A G E   R O C K A N D R O L L
B O U L D E R   A N T E S   E G R E T
S O N E S T A   L E A D S   D E G A S
```

246

```
MITT AHA  AMID SPUR
OGRE RUSH ZERO LINE
PAIR TREASURETROVES
EVEREST WERE  ABOVE
SEDAN SOAVE WHY  TEN
  ACES PIE CRI  ISNT
SANE TRAINTRACKS
HRD DEAL  ROT  INTHE
ART IRE SLASH BERET
MERMAN SLEWS COWISH
USUAL EQUAL BAS  CTA
STERE LUG  BATH  KEN
  TRAVISTRITT  LORE
OBEY DID  HER  YEAR
DEN ADS HINDU GETNO
EATAT IONA STORROW
TRIMMEDTHETREE TERN
TERI AINU AIRS EASE
ARES ROOM  ASS  STEN
```

247

```
EBBS BALA HARSH GPA
LYRE ABED ACUTE ORG
AMERRYCHRISTMAS DON
MEARA AYN  BRAMBLE
 DAMPER FALLS  ALES
IDA PAL PUREE  TIE
SANTACLAUSIS RANSOM
MYDOG SIRE EVANESCE
 REP MISS ILK  UTA
OILY ROSS PEAL ISON
UGO OOP TARA  YEN
REVERSES MARA MIMES
STEADY COMINGTOTOWN
AGO RANON  HOT  NEA
ACNE DEMON  LARIAT
BEDROOM IAO  OVATE
HAJ TOALLAGOODNIGHT
OSO INDIA ESPY LEAN
REY SEEDY SETS ASTA
```

248

```
MIL RBI SELES IDEAL
AGE HUT SLIDE NONCE
COFFERS HINGPATTERN
 TEAM  CEE  VEERED
FOOL ATTAIN TEN OSS
ABUTS HART AWNS
LOT ADEPT BEIGE SER
LEI SEGA FORCE ADZE
 NOSEE CANOE STORM
PATTERN RIN TOLLWAY
APHID STYLE TWAIN
GOES STEPS MALT TLC
ETC START PULSE HOI
 YETI JUTE  SPENT
ABS NEE CUTEST ORGY
REPEAL BAL  HOLI
GRUMPYMENII RECOVER
ORRIS ABOUT AMA ERI
SANTE DENSE YES RAM
```

249

```
PITH ALB REACT CHIN
ACHE AIR ACTOR LALO
PEER ALI HURRICANES
 POP ASP SIN RUDDY
BBL RECKON  PEPYS
ORATES ELEE ARP PEI
DIGEST TIARA OTHERS
ENURE CRASHCOURSE
SKEINS DES KEY BITE
 TEPID  DEMOS
OILY LON SOW NONFAT
FLOODLIGHTS  NOIRE
ALLURE YEAST ANDRES
NEA ERG WHIR RESEAT
 INSET LEERAT FLY
FRANC RRS RAE  SIL
EARTHQUAKE SUB FISH
TIER UNDID OSE FETE
ALSO ADEPT NET YSER
```

250

```
AMAN MAP  ALOT  QUA
DONO ARAB STORE URN
DOGSANDDOGWOODS IAN
ORIENT SLOE POTABLE
NEE ILE SWAY  EBB
 ELEPHANTSANDELMS
APER SEA SEGO  TEAL
BOXER EDAM RAHS SOY
CRANES ERIE NOAH
 MOLARSANDMAPLES
WALE GOGI  EVADED
BAD YETI SEXT ERATO
ALEC MINI UMA TKOS
TABLESANDTUPELOS
TEN SLAP NEV  AGO
BUFFALO EREI WEASEL
ERR BANKSANDBIRCHES
AGE LIMIT DEAF TONE
DEE EDEN  AYE  SWAN
```

251

ATHENS		SHEBA		MODEST
COOKIE		EATEN		ALOTTA
INTENT		SWEETANDSOUR
DEA	SSTS		FIDGET
NET	LEES	GOD		GAL
HIDESOUT		POUR		ARAGE
ACCLAIM		DAYANDNIGHT
SHOERS		JOSE		AIMSAT
TOLD		CALM	DELOS
ORD	BLAKE		TOXIN	HST
ELATE		DOSO		PILE
QUOTED		AONE	MEAGER
UPSANDDOWNS		FURTHER
ITOLD		OVEN	COGITATE
DOS	EYE		EARL	SIN
SAVERS		LADS		DAG
THICKANDTHIN		APULIA
DETAIN		ILOVE	RESORT
SWANNS		DOTES		DROWSE

252

DATA		STRUTS		FREAKS
ODOR		ARENOT		CRISPER
CAPCAPACITY		RIOTERS
TOW	CUTE		GEESE
ADO	ARES	MILAN		FAR
DAP	KOREA		DAMDAMAGE
UNITED		REEDY		GELID
LACE	SCHEMES		IHADNO
TESTS		AONE		ANALOG
WARWARNINGS
VANITY		GATO		TAHOE
NATIVE		THEROAD	BOND
ELITE		GRADE		ELATED
ALLALLIES		SHAME		HAI
PIT	OATHS		ERIC	OLE
FAWNS	PARC		OFT
SHERBET		BANBANQUETS
AUTEURS		OCTANE		SLOP
GREETS		SEALED		ESPY

253

ALICE		SHAG		QUM		AGRA
PAROL		PUMA		UNE		DOOM
BLANKFORMS		ANECDOTE
SANS	AUTO		SKATE		SEX
EMIT		THEM		ESE
LOANER		COHERE		WERE
EMPTYSPACES		DAMAGED
FOSSE		ASTRAY		PINGED
TOO	REDEEM		OARS	SLY
CURT		HUGO
FEZ	FLAN		CATONA	SIM
AGENDA		SEALER		NOTRE
LARIATS		NULLANDVOID
ANON		WEASEL		OREADS
IOS	ESTE		BAER
ANN	ARETE		CHEN	RATA
REGULATE		BLACKHOLES
TRIP	MER		RANK	ADORE
SONS		INS		AWAY	GEENA

254

MEMOS		RBI		MATS		PAL
AMATI		HELD		ACHE		ILE
BUSHLEAGUE		ICECREAM
COLDWAR		STEM		IRMA
LEA	DAR		ARNA		SCOT
EERIE	IDS		YET		VIE
GRANTWISHES		SLANDER
NOR		EROS		ANGELA
MOPE	EMBER		LIME	AIM
EFOR	SOAP		CURB	PROP
AWL	STAR		PARSE	ASTS
TOKILL		BARI		NAG
SEAWEED		FORDSTLREAS
DAW	ROT		OOH	ASCOT
AVON	PINE		RIP	COY
LETT	OVER		IMMENSE
INTAGLIO		ADAMSAPPLE
SUE	AINU		TONY	PUTON
TED	SSGT		ALT	ENSUE

255

CHIC		BAD		HATED		DEFT
OATH		OWE		AMORE		ELLA
ELSA		RAF		ROTARYCLUB
DEMI		GRIDDLE		EASES
YRS	ELITE		PLAY
BATMAN		ETO		SEAR	ODA
AQUATIC		SPINCONTROL
BURN	CLAY		OAKS		HAZE
YIN	SHUT		ALPS		JUNES
TIE	RECAP		BAG
LEMON		LIST		ELON	RAF
IRON	GAGA		PRIX	WEGO
SOCIALWHIRL		DELIVER
ASK	BUNT		OAF		RESORT
JAMS		DOZES		ATL
IDIOT		TISANES		EVER
DOTHETWIST		NEW		RIDE
OLIN		VINCE		ETA		INGA
LESS		ASTOR		LOY		AGES

256

M	E	T	A	L	■	O	R	N	A	T	E	■	J	U	D	A	S
O	V	A	T	E	■	R	O	U	G	E	D	■	C	O	R	O	N	A
T	E	X	A	N	■	G	O	T	H	E	W	R	O	N	G	W	A	Y
E	R	R	■	D	N	A	■	■	A	D	I	E	U	■	E	N	T	S
■	■	■	E	S	S	E	N	C	E	■	N	A	R	E	S	■	■	■
L	I	T	E	■	B	I	R	D	I	N	■	P	I	G	■	V	A	T
U	S	U	A	L	■	C	A	N	T	I	T	■	E	A	S	I	L	Y
C	O	R	N	E	A	■	B	A	C	K	W	A	R	D	L	O	O	K
I	N	N	■	E	G	G	■	S	H	E	A	R	■	A	L	E	E
■	■	■	D	R	E	A	D	■	■	S	A	L	E	M	■	■	■
M	A	U	I	■	R	E	C	T	A	■	B	O	X	■	F	R	A
U	P	F	R	O	M	B	E	H	I	N	D	■	G	I	B	L	E	T
G	I	O	T	T	O	■	M	I	N	T	E	D	■	T	R	I	P	E
U	N	S	■	T	N	T	■	S	O	O	N	A	S	■	E	P	O	S
■	■	■	M	O	S	E	S	■	■	N	E	W	L	E	A	F	■
A	N	D	A	■	T	A	T	A	R	■	■	B	O	A	■	L	I	V
D	O	U	B	L	E	R	E	V	E	R	S	E	■	R	H	O	D	E
A	P	P	E	A	R	■	L	I	N	E	A	R	■	T	O	P	E	R
R	E	E	L	S	■	■	A	D	D	O	N	S	■	H	I	S	S	Y

257

B	E	T	T	E	■	A	B	A	S	E	■	E	N	D	O	W	E	D
I	C	H	O	R	■	R	U	M	O	R	■	P	E	O	N	A	G	E
T	H	E	M	A	G	I	C	B	U	S	■	S	E	N	E	G	A	L
T	I	M	E	T	O	■	O	I	L	E	R	■	D	E	M	O	D	E
E	D	E	N	■	F	E	L	T	■	E	A	S	T	O	N	■
R	N	A	■	L	O	C	I	■	A	I	M	S	■	O	R	T	H	O
S	A	N	■	T	R	U	C	K	S	T	O	P	S	■	E	R	I	N
■	■	P	S	I	■	E	I	O	■	E	P	I	■	A	N	T
A	B	C	S	■	T	E	R	M	S	■	B	R	A	T	■	I	D	I
P	L	O	T	S	■	N	A	P	■	G	A	S	■	A	N	N	U	M
P	O	N	■	E	D	G	Y	■	Z	O	N	E	S	■	A	S	S	E
L	U	V	■	A	I	R	■	P	O	T	■	W	A	Y	■
E	S	E	S	■	V	A	N	J	O	H	N	S	O	N	■	C	A	P
S	E	R	A	I	■	V	E	S	T	■	E	L	O	N	■	H	U	I
■	■	T	I	N	S	E	L	■	■	T	A	D	S	■	G	A	G	A
I	M	I	N	T	O	■	L	I	F	E	R	■	I	C	A	R	U	S
D	E	B	T	O	R	S	■	T	A	X	I	D	E	R	M	I	S	T
A	R	L	E	N	E	S	■	O	M	A	N	I	■	E	M	O	T	E
S	E	E	D	E	R	S	■	R	A	N	G	E	■	W	A	T	E	R

258

G	I	F	T	S	■	S	I	A	M	■	B	A	L	D	■	S	I	T
A	G	R	E	E	■	A	L	A	I	■	O	N	O	R	■	I	S	H
S	N	E	E	R	■	C	L	A	S	S	S	T	R	U	G	G	L	E
P	I	E	M	A	N	■	■	D	I	C	E	D	■	A	N	I	S
A	T	E	S	■	B	E	S	E	E	C	H	■	D	R	A	K	E
R	E	X	■	C	A	N	O	L	A	■	■	B	E	A	T	L	E	S
■	■	C	P	O	■	F	U	L	L	L	E	N	G	T	H	■
■	C	H	A	M	O	I	S	■	I	M	A	G	E	■	P	H	I
T	R	A	D	E	I	N	■	M	I	A	M	I	■	S	E	E	S
R	A	N	D	A	L	■	W	E	A	R	Y	■	P	U	T	N	A	M
E	G	G	Y	■	■	C	A	L	M	S	■	A	S	S	E	N	T	S
E	S	E	■	C	L	O	S	E	■	■	I	N	T	E	R	N	S
■	■	Z	O	O	O	P	E	N	I	N	G	■	R	N	A	■
R	I	L	E	D	U	P	■	E	M	E	E	R	S	■	T	I	S
A	M	E	N	S	■	■	C	O	O	P	E	R	S	■	S	I	N	K
S	P	E	D	■	F	R	O	W	N	■	■	T	A	C	O	M	A
H	A	W	A	I	I	I	S	L	A	N	D	S	■	N	O	N	O	T
A	L	A	■	A	L	O	T	■	T	O	U	T	■	E	R	A	S	E
D	A	Y	■	N	E	T	S	■	E	D	G	Y	■	W	E	L	T	S

259

M	O	N	I	C	A	■	R	E	C	O	I	L	■	C	H	A	I	R
A	W	O	M	A	N	■	O	R	A	N	G	E	■	H	E	N	C	E
S	E	N	A	T	E	■	D	I	S	C	O	N	C	E	R	T	E	D
T	S	P	■	S	A	T	E	■	H	U	T	■	O	R	E	■
■	■	L	A	U	R	A	■	T	E	E	■	C	U	R	S	O	R	S
A	L	U	M	P	■	B	R	O	W	■	M	A	R	Y	■	N	U	T
R	A	S	P	■	C	L	I	P	■	I	O	N	A	■	A	I	N	U
D	R	S	■	A	R	E	A	S	■	D	I	S	G	U	S	T	E	D
O	V	E	R	D	I	D	■	■	P	O	R	T	E	N	T	■
R	A	D	A	R	■	■	O	C	A	L	A	■	C	R	U	E	L
■	■	N	A	T	I	V	E	S	■	■	M	E	L	A	N	G	E
D	E	L	I	G	H	T	E	D	■	G	R	O	V	E	■	D	A	D
R	U	I	N	■	R	E	N	E	■	L	O	R	E	■	W	E	N	G
O	R	A	■	M	O	M	S	■	T	U	B	A	■	P	A	R	S	E
P	O	M	P	O	U	S	■	Q	U	M	■	S	T	U	R	M	■
■	■	E	R	G	■	S	U	M	■	T	S	A	R	■	I	T	O
U	N	F	A	T	H	O	M	A	B	L	E	■	P	I	A	N	O	S
S	E	R	R	A	■	F	O	I	L	E	D	■	E	S	K	E	R	S
S	T	A	L	L	■	A	G	L	E	T	S	■	S	T	A	D	I	A

260

S	A	B	O	■	L	A	P	P	■	R	O	A	M	S	■	T	O	M
A	R	U	N	■	A	V	E	R	■	E	N	N	U	I	■	A	P	E
M	E	R	L	■	G	O	D	O	W	N	I	N	F	L	A	M	E	S
B	E	N	I	S	O	N	■	L	I	D	O	■	F	L	I	E	R	S
A	L	I	N	E	S	■	H	I	S	■	N	I	L	■	T	R	A	Y
■	■	N	E	A	■	F	I	F	E	S	■	L	E	A	S	■	■
A	R	G	■	T	H	E	F	I	R	E	B	I	R	D	■	G	I	T
U	A	D	■	E	R	I	C	■	V	I	A	■	A	L	O	N	E
D	I	E	■	A	W	N	■	M	E	N	D	■	G	E	E	S	E
I	N	S	I	P	S	■	S	H	A	R	D	■	F	I	T	S	I	N
B	O	I	S	E	■	P	O	E	T	■	L	A	O	■	U	D	A
L	U	R	E	R	■	L	A	R	■	C	H	I	T	■	P	E	G
E	T	E	■	C	H	A	R	B	R	O	I	L	E	D	■	I	R	E
■	■	Q	U	A	Y	■	S	O	R	R	Y	■	U	R	N	■	■
Z	A	S	U	■	V	A	L	■	U	R	E	■	B	O	O	S	T	S
E	N	T	I	R	E	■	A	N	N	I	■	P	O	S	T	M	A	N
B	L	A	Z	I	N	G	S	A	D	D	L	E	S	■	T	O	R	O
R	O	T	■	B	O	O	T	S	■	O	O	P	S	■	E	K	E	R
A	C	E	■	S	T	A	S	H	■	R	O	S	Y	■	N	E	S	T

261

```
OOH   POPE   TRIP   SPLAT
AVA   ILEX   HONE   LUISA
HEIRSAPPARENT    UTTER
UNRIG   POMES   TAMO
    SPA  YUMA  GYM  NATO
HOHOHO   NOTSO   STAMEN
ASIN   CAD   ITA   HIETO
SIR   CEL   ACT   NAIRNE
TET   HAILTO   STIRS
ORS   ANGELCHOIRS   DOR
   FLING   OUTWIT   ODA
 APIECE  JAG  ANY  WIN
INERT   DNA   ERG   SNUG
ODESSA   IMBED   SHESMY
SALT   WAX   OPUS   IRT
   BEER   ERICA   GRATE
IOWAN   MUSICALCHAIRS
QUASI   EGAN   TEAL   RIP
SIDED   DOUG   EMMY   SOY
```

262

```
DIADEM   BETTER   HOHUM
ENTIRE   ATHENA   ABASE
ATLOGGERHEADS    MIRED
FOOD   BRASSO   SPED
   NEWER  NEE  THE  WOE
JUG   INON   ATTHEREADY
UPLIFT   AFT   RED   ERIE
SPARE   MTA   BYA   TREND
TEST   JACKAL   TONS
ART   ATTHEMOMENT   ASH
   PSST   REWIRE   OTHO
PIQUE   EDS   UNS   BEHAN
SOUL   URE   APE   FURORE
ATALLCOSTS   SPIT   MID
TAN   ELF   AAC   ABIDE
   DANA   INBRED   IWAS
BLAND   ATYOURSERVICE
BORNE   LEANER   SOOTHE
LAYER   ASSETS   TETHER
```

263

```
LOT   BASIC   MPG   TALL
AVA   ASIDO   WEAR   ALII
MEL   DHLAWRENCEBLOCK
BRIDGET   LOAD   ARCHIE
   SUE   BINS   PTA   ATA
JAMESJOYCEKILMER
ORAL   ITAKE   DEE   ALEC
YEN   IVAN   ELAN   CITY
   HOER   HIVE   AHEAD
   HENRYJAMESJONES
STYLE   ULAN   ETAL
PIPE   UNDO   SSTS   MAD
AMEN   PIG   LEASE   PARE
   ALICEWALKERPERCY
MAI   ONE   RILE   ESQ
ATTICA   TONI   SOTOUGH
JOHNIRVINGSTONE   ELI
ONAN   MING   ORDER   SUN
REDS   SPY   NEARS   SET
```

264

```
CABLE   POSED   PARSLEY
ACRES   INTER   ADAMITE
CHEESEQUAKE   LAYOVER
HEAR   DUST   WHO   STE
EDD   PIE   IDIOMS   ERMA
   LAIT   CORNCAKE   POI
BOOST   BONY   INDOOR
ALAI   CAMS   TSP   ANOSE
DEFT   HUE   JOEL   TALES
   LOBSTERLAKE
BEEFY   LINT   FIE   USED
EDGAR   ENT   BING   POLE
SIGNET   CAST   JODIE
ETH   SANDWICH   KONA
THAT   BEDECK   BIT   VCR
   RHS   ASH   SALE   SIRE
ARBITER   APPLEVALLEY
NEOCENE   VEILS   PULSE
DARKRED   ENNIS   FRETS
```

265

```
CCC   TELE   DENS   DIJON
HAH   ONIT   ALOT   ELUTE
IFIHADAHAMMER   SOLTI
PESO   URALS   LAOS   YON
   EWER   NEER   PLEA
DELETES   CLIPPERSHIP
AXE   ASHE   SORE   THANA
MIR   OPE   ODE   ORGY
ETS   AGRIPPA   VARIES
   WRENCHINGTIME
NETHER   SPIRALS   ABC
ARIA   EWE   LIP   QUA
YIELD   ALOG   MESA   URN
SCREWDRIVER   RAMPANT
   SIAM   ONAN   HELP
ISM   NYET   TIARA   ILSA
SHEED   DRILLSERGEANT
PEARL   UELE   ALAI   NUN
YALIE   PEER   LYNN   EGO
```

266

```
QBS  OSSO  GALBA  CODE
UNO  UTAH  EDILE  APIG
IAN  TIPOFTHEICEBERG
DISOWNS  OWENS  MINTY
    RIG  KLEM  TREND
FIRSTOFALL  BEAU  OAK
ADIOS  AMYL  ORG  BORE
ZION  BRA  DAS  LARGE
EDT  MOE  OFUS  PARSON
    HEADOFLETTUCE
UNJUST  SMUT  WRY  PGA
LOUTS  PAY  HOE  DION
ARMS  JAG  CHAT  IWENT
NAP  CAME  RAZORSEDGE
    STUMP  SURE  ALL
AFTER  LEAST  KNITTED
LEADEROFTHEPACK  WAY
BARD  UNTIE  ALIE  ASA
ARTY  BASED  LEDA  SYN
```

267

```
BOCA  GAPE  BAEZ  FLAT
UFOS  ERIA  ISLE  RATA
FLIPFLOPS  OPAL  IDEM
FALSE  MAYS  HILO  YAM
ETE  VEAL  ETON  SASSY
REDNESS  GARDENHOSE
    ERS  MRLEE  EARL
TASS  ETUI  SLAV  TIER
HUNTS  ILLS  RELAPSE
ETO  IDLELOAFERS  PTA
COWERED  ODIN  TWEED
ASSN  LENS  IRAQ  ERRS
    HASH  ALIVE  UTA
SOCKITTOME  MIRRORS
POETA  ATTU  LIZA  HIE
HRH  TIME  STEN  SUDAN
ADAM  SPRY  HIGHHEELS
SIRE  NEED  UGLI  LATE
EDEN  ODDS  SHED  EROS
```

268

```
CALF  STOAT  PATELLA
ALOES  AWARE  ADONAIS
SUNDANCEKID  MERCURY
AMI  RICES  IDEST  RAE
    MACON  FOOL  SBA
HORACE  MAUMAU  AMOK
APACE  ALOUSE  NATALE
DAPHENMOON  SUCCORER
ALTO  RUGRAT  POURSON
    POSSE  ITSUP
EBBTIDE  STREET  SHES
NEARMISS  EARTHAKITT
OBRIAN  CADDIS  LORRE
LETT  GRANDE  PLATER
    SET  ANDY  GHOUL
ACT  RANTO  SOUND  SAD
BOATING  VENUSDEMILO
ARRANGE  EVERS  DOZEN
TERRIER  REEDY  WEST
```

269

```
CABANA  DOTAL  MAPLE
ARABIA  ECOLE  DEGREE
LACUNA  CHEEKTOCHEEK
IRKS  BLESS  INCAS
    TEMPLAR  STOA  EAR
ADO  ASTI  ASTIR  ANSA
KABUKI  MITER  ITCHY
INANEST  SEEEYETOEYE
TACO  ICON  EATEN
ASK  SIMON  ETHER  HUM
    SPAIN  ALSO  LANE
NECKANDNECK  OFFENDS
ALLIN  ORMER  ERODES
MAUD  SPREE  ETTE  TRY
ENT  BTUS  HORATIO
    CLEAT  WHERE  SHAM
GOHEADTOHEAD  BANANA
AVENUE  LEAVE  EDENIC
BASIS  DETER  DAWDLE
```

270

```
WETS  SKEW  HACK  VEND
ERIK  PITA  ACRE  OMOO
LIFEWITHFATHER  XING
DEFLATE  FREED  SPREE
    ESE  SLAT  IDEO
SMITH  THEBOSTONPOPS
POLO  PEAS  HOT  UVEA
QUANDARY  LIAR  SLEEP
REY  ETS  TASK  SMAIRS
    WHERESPOPPA
PISCES  ARTY  LAC  WHO
ALLAY  GYMS  TACKSHOP
ISIN  COO  GONE  TILT
DADDYLONGLEGS  SIZES
    YOUD  OENO  PET
JUMPS  LEONE  ORACLES
OLEO  OURFOREFATHERS
SNAP  ACNE  ALAN  EDIT
HATS  SKED  LINK  SANS
```

271

A	D	D	S		K	A	T	E		C	S	A		G	A	R	B	S
B	O	R	E		I	S	I	S		H	U	M		U	R	I	A	H
C	L	O	C	K	S	Y	M	P	H	O	N	Y		R	E	D	D	Y
S	E	P	T	I	M	E	S		A	S	S		Z	U	N	I		
			W	E	T		F	R	E	E	Z	E		O	C	T	O	
S	P	I	R	I	T		T	U	R	N	T	U	R	N	T	U	R	N
H	A	T	E	S		C	A	R	Y		L	O	A		L	E	E	
R	O	S	S		B	O	N	Y		E	C	U		D	R	E	S	S
E	L	I		A	L	O	G		A	L	A		H	I	E			
W	I	N	D	M	I	L	L	S	O	F	Y	O	U	R	M	I	N	D
	N	A	P		E	E	K		E	R	G	S		L	E	O		
M	E	T	A	L		R	S	T		I	N	C	H		D	I	R	T
I	C	E		F	I	E		U	L	N	A		S	U	A	V	E	
T	H	E	R	I	N	G	C	Y	C	L	E		B	I	N	D	E	R
T	O	T	O		S	T	O	O	L	S		D	O	N				
	E	U	R	O		O	K	A		P	A	L	E	T	T	E	S	
N	U	R	S	E		S	P	I	N	N	I	N	G	W	H	E	E	L
A	R	E	E	L		P	E	N		O	N	C	E		A	R	L	O
G	I	D	D	Y		A	R	G		D	E	E	R		W	I	S	P

272

S	A	P	S		B	O	A		A	B	E	A	M		M	A	C	
T	R	E	T		E	A	R	P		R	O	D	E	O		E	X	O
A	N	C	I	E	N	T	M	A	R	I	N	E	R	S		T	I	P
R	I	A	N	T		H	O	R	I	Z	O	N		U	K	A	S	E
T	E	N	T	H	S		R	E	P	O			S	L	I	M		
			S	I	T	E		O	N	E	U	P		N	O	M	O	
C	A	R		C	A	R	D	I	N	A	L	S	I	N		R	I	B
A	L	O	T		R	I	O	T		M	E	N	O		P	R	O	
L	A	Y	U	P		S	T	E	E	P		R	E	D	S	H	O	E
	A	P	A	R		S	M	A	R	T		S	U	M	O			
U	N	L	I	N	E	D		S	T	A	I	N		S	U	S	I	E
N	E	W		I	F	A	T		D	E	E	R		G	I	L	L	
I	V	E		C	U	B	R	E	P	O	R	T	E	R		S	K	Y
T	E	L	L		S	A	Y	S	O			S	E	E	P			
			C	O	L	E		T	I	T	O		D	R	E	A	M	S
P	H	O	T	O		S	E	E	S	A	W	S		A	R	R	E	T
R	U	M		Y	A	N	K	E	E	I	N	G	E	N	U	I	T	Y
A	G	E		A	D	E	E	M		L	E	T	S		S	E	A	L
Y	E	S		L	E	E	D	S		D	S	T		E	L	L	E	

273

I	M	P	A	L	E		A	G	H	A	S		S	P	O	O	K
L	O	U	V	E	R		I	R	A	D	E	S		H	A	O	L	E
E	C	L	A	I	R		R	A	Z	Z	L	E	D	A	Z	Z	L	E
		I	N	F	O	R		N	E	E		C	U	D		E	I	N
B	U	T	T		R	E	D	O		S	E	T	S		I	D	E	S
A	N	Z	I	O		I	O	L	A		V	O	T	E	D			
S	T	E		Z	I	G	Z	A	G	G	E	R		V	A	L	I	D
S	O	R	B	O	N	N	E		A	E	R	A	T	E		A	D	A
			P	E	N	D	S		S	M	E	L	L	A		I	Z	E	R
S	E	R	G	E	I		B	E	R	R	Y		B	A	N	Y	A	N
U	R	I	S		T	O	A	R	M	S		C	R	U	S	H		
L	I	Z		M	E	D	I	A	N		F	A	I	R	O	A	K	S
K	E	E	N	E		E	Z	I	O	P	I	N	Z	A		Z	O	E
			A	G	A	T	E		N	A	R	C		S	T	Y	L	E
D	I	R	T		R	O	S	A		T	E	E	M		I	C	A	N
O	N	A		H	I	J		C	A	T		L	A	G	E	R		
F	U	Z	Z	Y	Z	O	E	L	L	E	R		M	A	D	A	M	A
F	R	E	U	D		Y	O	U	A	R	E		E	L	I	Z	A	S
S	E	D	G	E			S	E	I	N	E		T	A	N	Y	A	S

274

R	E	B	I	D		S	P	O	T	S		D	A	L	L	A	S	
A	R	O	A	R		Y	O	K	E	S		E	L	O	I	S	E	
Y	O	U	M	U	S	T	S	E	E	T	H	I	S	M	O	V	I	E
S	S	T		C	A	T	T	Y			S	I	A	M				
			E	E	R	I	E		A	F	A	R			B	L	T	
T	H	I	S	F	I	L	M	W	I	L	L	K	E	E	P	Y	O	U
H	A	N	S	O	N		A	N	T	I	S		R	O	A	S	T	
E	D	G	E	R		B	A	S	K	E	T		P	R	U	N	E	S
G	O	O		M	O	U	T	H		B	L	O	T					
O	N	T	H	E	E	D	G	E	O	F	Y	O	U	R	S	E	A	T
			U	L	A	E		L	E	E	D	S			T	R	E	
A	D	O	N	I	S		D	E	L	R	A	Y		A	S	H	E	N
L	O	A	T	H		S	O	P	O	R		E	L	A	I	N	E	
I	T	S	S	U	R	E	T	O	W	I	N	A	N	O	S	C	A	R
T	O	T		A	R	E	S		O	B	O	E	S					
			A	C	T	I		I	O	N	I	C		P	I	E		
I	T	S	T	H	E	F	I	L	M	O	F	T	H	E	Y	E	A	R
R	E	P	A	I	R		D	I	A	N	A		N	O	R	M	S	
S	L	A	N	T	S		S	E	N	A	T		D	U	C	A	T	

275

D	I	M		M	A	L	O	N	E		A	G	O		B	U	M	P
A	V	A		A	N	O	R	A	K		S	O	U		E	N	O	L
M	A	R	V	I	N	G	A	Y	E		P	E	T		S	H	O	O
A	N	T	I		I	T	S		D	I	S	C		T	I	N	T	
	H	O	R	A	C	E		E	R	R		O	D	I	N			
H	E	A	L	E	R	S		J	A	Y	E	P	M	O	R	G	A	N
A	R	R	E	S	T		W	O	R	D		H	E	Y		E	C	O
I	R	A	T	E		S	H	Y		O	R	O		L	A	D	E	N
T	O	Y		T	A	T	I		S	C	O	N	C	E	S			
I	R	E	D		D	A	N	N	Y	K	A	Y	E		P	I	P	S
			P	R	O	T	E	A	N		M	A	L	E		S	E	A
R	E	N	T	A		I	S	M		P	E	S		A	G	A	R	S
A	R	A		N	C	O		E	G	A	D		S	T	O	A	T	S
F	A	Y	E	D	U	N	A	W	A	Y		S	K	E	T	C	H	Y
	S	A	Y	S		B	A	G		F	L	I	N	C	H			
A	H	A	S		T	A	O	S		B	O	A		H	A	Z	E	
M	A	Y	I		A	N	D		G	A	R	Y	P	L	A	Y	E	R
O	R	E	L		R	Y	E		A	N	G	E	R	S		E	R	I
S	P	R	Y		D	A	S		P	E	E	R	E	D		S	O	S

276

```
TRUANT  ABETS   VISIT
NASSER  MADEUP  INANE
THECRYINGGAME   CAUSE
   ADIPOSE  MAT  PLOD
CHOP  NET   GETAJOB
RID AGC EDER  BAKERS
ORIEL ADVERSE  MELEE
WEALLSCREAM  AVE  LED
   BYA URN OSOS   OSE
BABE  BEMY  GREW  EWER
ARA  PEPS  ARM  EBB
MOB ERI CHEERLEADER
BOYLE  CHIMERA  ENATE
AMBERS  ATEN  GMS  VAL
  OFSTYLE  AMI  EELY
ALOT  DEL  AIMEDAT
SAMOA  TWISTANDSHOUT
ONEUP  SADIES  LIOTTA
FORTE   YEARS   ENSTAR
```

277

```
ASHE  MAMBA  CRAB  TGT
GAUL  OCEAN  HERA  ORR
HURLYBURLY  AWED  SOU
ADDIE  ILK  GRAS  BTUS
  YEAST  SOLAR  ORANT
BEG  REYS  FUDDYDUDDY
AQUILA  CASTE  ADIOS
CURRY  KAN   SKINS
HADA  BANDS  BEETS
SLY  NITTYGRITTY  WAS
  BOGEY  TODAY  DONT
  RUTTY  PET  DOONE
  JUMBO  SEVER  COLLIE
NAMBYPAMBY  SOOT  YEP
AVILA  REBEL  REHAB
GENE  BRAS  OPE  ARUBA
ALA  LAIR  WILLYNILLY
NIN  LIVE  ERASE  SLUR
ONT  BLED  BENET  EYRE
```

278

```
MOTT  PSAT  AMAS  RASH
RUHR  RULA  WORK  ETTA
STEALINGBEAUTY  GRID
  HISSY  LAKES  FAINT
PAINTS  COTES  VIRAGO
INGE  YALIE  SEND
MAHRE  KIDNAPPED  TAR
ASW  TRIP  NEAR  HOLE
  ASHEN  CIDER  WECAN
HEYDAY  PANEL  ERRANT
OFMAN  SOCKS  OPART
SOAK  SHOT  SNIT  CPA
ERN  THEPIRATE  HOHUM
  QUID  ANAIS  RAMA
RETURN  PUDGY  CAFTAN
ALIEN  ARNIE  JONAH
TORE  THEKILLERELITE
OPEN  ISEE  EBAN  SEED
NEDS  PONY  SONS  EFTS
```

279

```
ACHAT   LAMAR   SATIE
REESES  IRATE  EIGHTS
PLAYTHEFIELD  CLORIS
  RESEAT   DART  OSE
OFT  ATTA  PERU  SWAN
DATES  MAR  ANT  PTA
DROPTHEBALL  SLEEPIN
  IRE  BOLE  INVADE
ETH  INSULT  VAL  IRER
CRISP  ATE  HID  GETNO
LITE  FLA  FOLDER  YTS
ANSATE  HART  PAD
TITTERS  CATCHABREAK
  HEX  TEA  URU  SUSIE
ACED  SEXT  BOAR  TRY
BAR  OUSE  ONEATA
AROUND  MAKINGAPITCH
SLATES  PRICE  MELEES
HADES   TAMER  RESEN
```

280

```
PIER  HATS  AWOL  ODDS
ANNI  ATOM  SORA  RAIN
SNAPDRAGONIONS  RIGA
CAB  ADDSTO  DOSI  SUR
ATLAST  EBB  TINTYPE
LEER  OCT  ERA  ERIC
  MAPLETTUCE  ENACT
CROSS  EAR  TAPS  AMOR
HER  HEALED  DINA  ORE
OPA  OWN  KOS  GAS  RON
PIN  TESS  SCARPS  END
INGA  RULA  ATA  ESSAY
NEEDY  POTATOMATO
  RAIL  BEL  PSU  ORES
SWAMPED  ELD  GENEVA
HEN  STIR  WISEUP  VAL
EDIT  SOYBEANDROMEDA
AGUE  ODAY  LINE  IRED
REMY  NENE  SPAR  REDS
```

281

```
NOSH  SARAH  IFS   FALA
ETTE  PIECE  RAH   ALEX
WOODCARVER   ALLOCATE
SENOR   ERES   LONE
  ENIGMAS  APACE   BET
MIMI  EEL  BLACKSMITH
AMASSED  RUSTY  HORAE
TASTY   SELAH   LORDLY
EGO  SAMUEL   TOTS
DONA  FIELDHAND  ERAS
   COAX   OUSTER   OWE
GUITAR  SIZES   EMCEE
ASFOR   JANES  SLEEKER
PEARLDIVER  FRA  ASKS
EST  OUTER  TRIPOLI
   SCAN  TERI   ETNAS
WRINKLED  MILLWRIGHT
AINU  LYE  MELEE  MESA
GONG  YSL  ASSET  EROS
```

282

```
SIT  CAGED  LOCAL  RCA
OOH  ABOVE  ENATE  EHS
SWEPTAWAY  MARIO  MIS
SABO  RIN   SUM   TONE
  RIANT  GLOSSEDOVER
BRUNT  HORATIO  ROAST
LESTER  HIGHS  WELLES
ASHE  ELAPSE  AHAS
MOOD  GERE  RABID  POT
ELF  PUMA  SEPS  ONE
DEF  ALOSS  APAS  ALBA
  GMAN  TACOMA  BIAS
STORER  SETTO  WRASSE
PAROL  STATURE  USHER
ALLWASHEDUP  LETHE
TEEN  TEL   PIE  EDNA
USA  PAILS  IRONEDOUT
LEN  ALLAY  MOTIF  FDA
ASS  LEARN  ASSET  FEN
```

283

```
PAGER  STREAM  SCARAB
EARTO  LEONIA  TODATE
THINTHINKING  ANVILS
  MASADA  DUNKS  INAT
BOG  MEND  SAO  BLINI
EERIE  BTUS  TONI  ETA
GRIZZLY  LATELATERAL
  MERE  MYTH   PEW
AHA  AWRY  EAST  SEMIS
PACA  DANG  WHIM  RIDE
EJECT  WAIL  UNAS  LAN
  MAD   SALT   MIND
PALEPALETTE  RADOMES
IVE  EYES  HOWE  EXILE
LIARS  ATM  SAGA  LIT
LADE  BREAM  FUSSED
ATEASE  FLATFLATTERY
GORDON  ATTILA  ATWAR
ERSATZ  NASSER  BUSTS
```

284

```
PILAF  PRAISE   MARAT
AGIRL  EASTON  AEROBE
PERCENTSHORTANDTEEN
ATA  EES  AVE  BTUS
  OCA  AME  SOIS  ERA
TEMPEROVERANDCARBON
ALOT  RID  RUES  IOTA
MIT  ARID  TAGS  JANET
POT  NAE  SORI  BET
STOCKBLOCKANDORANGE
  ALE  COIT  ILK  ORA
PARSE  AERO  ONLY  MAG
EPIC  ALAI  ARG  NAVE
ASSASSINANDCONSIDER
LEE  EPOS  EOS  AIX
  EXIT  REN  ANE  SEA
FRONTCOVERANDORPHAN
RONDOS  EDDIED  ROUST
ODEON   GOOSES  APNEA
```

285

```
JAMB  BRIDAL  PEA  BOO
OLIO  LONELY  EXT  ORB
TINYBUBBLES  ROMANCE
  ISEE  EVE  ACT  ROSY
ASS  ABODE  BLAISE
BIKINIS  SMALLCHANGE
ENID  REA  ABIE  AWARE
AGREED  LARS  AMATOL
METAL  TIDY  ALL  YEWS
  OOHBABYBABY
MEAD  PEI  AMOY  AFLEA
ATLAST  OKAY  SWAINS
SCORE  SINE  SIT  STOP
THEWEEHOURS  SEATTLE
  INLETS  PILAF  LAR
EVEN  ALA  VON  MERE
SETSAIL  LITTLEWOMEN
PRO  ONE  ESTHER  CERO
YON  KEY  SAYERS  KNEW
```

286

```
COSH  CADGE  AVE  TBAR
OGLE  APRIL  MEX  ALLY
BREATHLESS  INTIMATE
BEELINES  AINT  AIM
   PEN  ASE  DOUBTLESS
DELRAY  ERGO  RUE  LEE
EYES  ARRAU  KEY  MEND
ARS  AWES  IVES  PASSE
NESTING  ALAN  TENSER
    ADE  SMELT  IAN
MAPPED  POLE  STRAFES
ALOES  SAKE  ATES  AAH
DAWS  IQS  SANER  PURE
ATE  PLU  ASIT  SPELLS
MERCILESS  RIG  OTT
   LAN  ELIA  GRANULAR
ENERGIZE  GROUNDLESS
LIST  RED  HONEY  ISAT
MASS  ESS  ADELA  ASPS
```

287

```
MALAGA  RECAPS  HATLO
TRIBES  IRONIC  ICHOR
SEVENYEARITCH  STEVE
    TRET  LAKERS  BEA
ASK  ETHAN  UDO  BIRD
IONA  ICECAP  THUG
THEBIGCHILL  LAUGHER
OWEGO  LOOSE  ELUDE
   LETIT  DUETS  ERIA
LES  TULIP  DEMON  TED
ODOR  PITHS  MELEE
TIRED  KIOWA  VESPA
STEPONE  TICKLEDPINK
  LANE  DOTTIE  YETI
CLOY  AGE  SPATS  RID
IOS  DRAMAS  SATS
GRETA  TURNUPTHEHEAT
ARROW  ORNATE  ORELSE
RESTS  REAPER  ENLIST
```

288

```
IRED  DAB  SHOW  PIPPA
FIXE  RHO  NAPA  ONEOF
ICECREAMSUITS  ISALL
THROES  BAG  ITS  AJOY
   CRASHED  SMETANA
MAI  DYE  BOA  AMECHE
ESSAY  WAVERLY  ARKIN
THECORNBELT  SAT  ERI
    TRE  BAL  DETESTED
APU  TAEL  PERT  USS
PROPERLY  LOG  IDS
EER  POO  SUGARCOATED
ANKLE  TEAROSE  UNITE
RAPIER  VYE  ARB  RAW
  INSIDES  COLETTE
ALEE  BIN  SUR  PEEDEE
COHAN  COCKTAILDRESS
IMAGE  TUPI  NEA  ISNO
DATED  ATAN  TRY  STEP
```

289

```
CLIFF  CLASSA  AMICUS
OUTER  HOLMES  LENORE
SCARETACTICS  DATSUN
TANNER  HOT  DONOT
AND  DUN  STATE  SNUBS
   OMOO  ERICS  EMIT
ALB  MASKINGTAPE  ERA
HOOD  NEAR  OMAR  DRY
AMBER  SPORE  PRICE
BASKET  INANE  KELSEY
  FEARI  SMALL  SEIZE
BOO  LANA  TEES  AGRA
OUR  MISCHIEVOUS  NAS
ASAP  TITAN  ENCE
TEPID  DEISM  AKA  CDS
  PRIME  PAS  ETALIA
MILANO  TRICKORTREAT
ARETES  HEROIC  LIANA
LASERS  EMENDS  EATEN
```

290

```
WAR  SMACK  EDAM  LADD
IDA  AARON  FINE  ALAE
NOMANATMONTANA  WARM
GRADE  ETO  DOTH  SKA
SERA  AID  TOE  OAKEN
   MADLYRANMARYLAND
CRI  TRE  ABA  BYTE
RESHOE  LIL  GOA  SHED
IMEANMAINE  LUNA  OSO
MANIC  MAY  CAT  TEASE
PIT  EVEN  TEXASTAXES
SNAP  ALA  ILO  PATENT
   IONI  ARE  PAC  DEO
BASKNEARNEBRASKA
ARIEL  END  ELM  DAMP
DIN  YEAS  ORG  CAGER
BOND  ALIDFORFLORIDA
ASEA  RAGE  WEAIM  LAN
DORM  NINE  STYNE  ELK
```